Cisco IOS 12.0 Network Security

Cisco Systems, Inc.

Cisco Press

Cisco Press
201 West 103rd Street
Indianapolis, IN 46290 USA

Cisco IOS 12.0 Network Security

Cisco Systems, Inc.

Copyright© 1999 Cisco Systems, Inc.

Published by:
Cisco Press
201 West 103rd Street
Indianapolis, IN 46290 USA

Printed in the United States of America 3 4 5 6 7 8 9 0

Third Printing   August 2001

Library of Congress Cataloging-in-Publication Number 96-61685

ISBN: 1-57870-160 0

Warning and Disclaimer

This book is designed to provide information about *Cisco IOS 12.0 Network Security*. Every effort has been made to make this book as complete and as accurate as possible, but no warranty or fitness is implied.

The information is provided on an "as is" basis. The author, Cisco Press, and Cisco Systems, Inc., shall have neither liability nor responsibility to any person or entity with respect to any loss or damages arising from the information contained in this book or from the use of the discs or programs that may accompany it.

The opinions expressed in this book belong to the author and are not necessarily those of Cisco Systems, Inc.

Trademark Acknowledgments

All terms mentioned in this book that are known to be trademarks or service marks have been appropriately capitalized. Cisco Press or Cisco Systems, Inc., cannot attest to the accuracy of this information. Use of a term in this book should not be regarded as affecting the validity of any trademark or service mark.

Feedback Information

At Cisco Press, our goal is to create in-depth technical books of the highest quality and value. Each book is crafted with care and precision, undergoing rigorous development that involves the unique expertise of members from the professional technical community.

Readers' feedback is a natural continuation of this process. If you have any comments regarding how we could improve the quality of this book, or otherwise alter it to better suit your needs, you can contact us through e-mail at feedback@ciscopress.com. Please make sure to include the book title and ISBN in your message.

We greatly appreciate your assistance.

Publisher	John Wait
Editor-in-Chief	John Kane
Executive Editor	Alicia Buckley
Cisco Systems Management	Michael Hakkert
	Tom Geitner
	William Warren
Managing Editor	Patrick Kanouse
Acquisitions Editor	Tracy Hughes
Copy Editor	Kitty Jarrett
Team Coordinator	Amy Lewis
Book Designer	Scott Cook
Cover Designer	Karen Ruggles
Layout Technician	Jeannette McKay
Indexers	Cheryl Jackson
	Chris Wilcox
Proofreader	Elise Walter

CISCO SYSTEMS

Corporate Headquarters
Cisco Systems, Inc.
170 West Tasman Drive
San Jose, CA 95134-1706
USA
http://www.cisco.com
Tel: 408 526-4000
 800 553-NETS (6387)
Fax: 408 526-4100

European Headquarters
Cisco Systems Europe
11 Rue Camille Desmoulins
92782 Issy-les-Moulineaux
Cedex 9
France
http://www-europe.cisco.com
Tel: 33 1 58 04 60 00
Fax: 33 1 58 04 61 00

Americas Headquarters
Cisco Systems, Inc.
170 West Tasman Drive
San Jose, CA 95134-1706
USA
http://www.cisco.com
Tel: 408 526-7660
Fax: 408 527-0883

Asia Pacific Headquarters
Cisco Systems Australia,
Pty., Ltd
Level 17, 99 Walker Street
North Sydney
NSW 2059 Australia
http://www.cisco.com
Tel: +61 2 8448 7100
Fax: +61 2 9957 4350

Cisco Systems has more than 200 offices in the following countries. Addresses, phone numbers, and fax numbers are listed on the Cisco Web site at www.cisco.com/go/offices

Argentina • Australia • Austria • Belgium • Brazil • Bulgaria • Canada • Chile • China • Colombia • Costa Rica • Croatia • Czech Republic • Denmark • Dubai, UAE • Finland • France • Germany • Greece • Hong Kong • Hungary • India • Indonesia • Ireland Israel • Italy • Japan • Korea • Luxembourg • Malaysia • Mexico • The Netherlands • New Zealand • Norway • Peru • Philippines Poland • Portugal • Puerto Rico • Romania • Russia • Saudi Arabia • Scotland • Singapore • Slovakia • Slovenia • South Africa • Spain Sweden • Switzerland • Taiwan • Thailand • Turkey • Ukraine • United Kingdom • United States • Venezuela • Vietnam • Zimbabwe

Acknowledgments

The Cisco IOS Reference Library is the result of collaborative efforts of many Cisco technical writers and editors over the years. This bookset represents the continuing development and integration of user documentation for the ever-increasing set of Cisco IOS networking features and functionality.

The current team of Cisco IOS technical writers and editors includes Katherine Anderson, Hugh Bussell, Melanie Cheng, Christy Choate, Sue Cross, Meredith Fisher, Tina Fox, Sheryl Kelly, Marsha Kinnear, Doug MacBeth, Lavanya Mandavilli, Mary Mangone, Andy Mann, Bob Marburg, Greg McMillan, Madhu Mitra, Vicki Payne, Jeremy Pollock, Patricia Rohrs, Teresa Oliver Schick, Wink Schuetz, Grace Tai, Brian Taylor, Jamianne Von-Prudelle, and Amanda Worthington.

The writing team wants to acknowledge the many engineering, customer support, and marketing subject-matter experts for their participation in reviewing draft documents and, in many cases, providing source material from which this bookset is developed.

Contents at a Glance

Table of Contents

Security Overview

This chapter contains the following sections:

- About This Book—Preview the topics in this guide.

- Creating Effective Security Policies—Learn tips and hints for creating a security policy for your organization. A security policy should be finalized and up-to-date *before* you configure any security features.

- Identifying Security Risks and Cisco IOS Solutions—Identify common security risks that might be present in your network, and find the right Cisco IOS security feature to prevent security break-ins.

About This Book

This book describes how to configure Cisco IOS security features for your Cisco networking devices. These security features can protect your network against degradation or failure, and data loss or compromise, resulting from intentional attacks or from unintended but damaging mistakes by well-meaning network users.

This guide is divided into five parts:

- Authentication, Authorization, and Accounting (AAA)

- Security Server Protocols

- Traffic Filtering and Firewalls

- IP Security and Encryption

- Other Security Features

Each of these parts is briefly described next.

Authentication, Authorization, and Accounting (AAA)

This part describes how to configure Cisco's authentication, authorization, and accounting (AAA) paradigm. AAA is an architectural framework for configuring a set of three independent security functions in a consistent, modular manner.

- Authentication—Provides the method of identifying users, including login and password dialog, challenge and response, messaging support, and, depending on the security protocol you select, encryption. Authentication is the way a user is identified prior to being allowed access to the network and network services. You configure AAA authentication by defining a named list of authentication methods, and then applying that list to various interfaces.

- Authorization—Provides the method for remote access control, including one-time authorization or authorization for each service, per-user account list and profile, user group support, and support of IP, IPX, ARA, and Telnet.

  Remote security servers, such as RADIUS and TACACS+, authorize users for specific rights by associating attribute-value (AV) pairs, which define those rights, with the appropriate user. AAA authorization works by assembling a set of attributes that describe what the user is authorized to perform. These attributes are compared to the information contained in a database for a given user, and the result is returned to AAA to determine the user's actual capabilities and restrictions.

- Accounting—Provides the method for collecting and sending security server information used for billing, auditing, and reporting, such as user identities, start and stop times, executed commands (such as PPP), number of packets, and number of bytes. Accounting enables you to track the services users are accessing as well as the amount of network resources they are consuming.

NOTE   You can configure authentication outside AAA. However, you must configure AAA if you want to use RADIUS, Kerberos, or TACACS+, or if you want to configure a backup authentication method.

Security Server Protocols

In many circumstances, AAA uses security protocols to administer its security functions. If your router or access server is acting as a network access server, AAA is the means through which you establish communication between your network access server and your RADIUS, TACACS+, or Kerberos security server.

The chapters in this part describe how to configure the following security server protocols:

- RADIUS—A distributed client/server system implemented through AAA that secures networks against unauthorized access. In the Cisco implementation, RADIUS clients run on Cisco routers and send authentication requests to a central RADIUS server that contains all user authentication and network service access information.

- Kerberos—A secret-key network authentication protocol implemented through AAA that uses the Data Encryption Standard (DES) cryptographic algorithm for encryption and authentication. Kerberos was designed to authenticate requests for network resources. Kerberos is based on the concept of a trusted third party that performs secure verification of users and services. The primary use of Kerberos is to verify that users and the network services they use are really who and what they claim to be. To accomplish this, a trusted Kerberos server issues tickets to users. These tickets, which have a limited lifespan, are stored in a user's credential cache and can be used in place of the standard username-and-password authentication mechanism.

- TACACS+—A security application implemented through AAA that provides centralized validation of users attempting to gain access to a router or network access server. TACACS+ services are maintained in a database on a TACACS+ daemon running, typically, on a UNIX or Windows NT workstation. TACACS+ provides for separate and modular AAA facilities.

- TACACS and extended TACACS—TACACS is an older access protocol, which is incompatible with the newer TACACS+ protocol. TACACS provides password checking and authentication, and notification of user actions for security and accounting purposes. Extended TACACS is an extension to the older TACACS protocol, supplying additional functionality to TACACS.

Traffic Filtering and Firewalls

This part describes how to configure your networking devices to filter traffic or to function as a firewall:

- Cisco implements traffic filters with access control lists (also called *access lists*). Access lists determine what traffic is blocked and what traffic is forwarded at router interfaces. Cisco provides both basic and advanced access list capabilities.

    — Basic access lists—An overview of basic access lists is in Chapter 15, "Access Control Lists: Overview and Guidelines." This chapter describes tips, cautions, considerations, recommendations, and general guidelines for configuring access lists for the various network protocols. You should configure basic access lists for all network protocols that will be routed through your networking device, such as IP, IPX, AppleTalk, and so forth.

    — Advanced access lists—The advanced access list capabilities and configuration are described in the remaining chapters in Part 3, "Traffic Filtering and Firewalls." The advanced access lists provide sophisticated and dynamic traffic-filtering capabilities for stronger, more flexible network security.

- Cisco IOS software provides an extensive set of security features, allowing you to configure a simple or elaborate firewall, according to your particular requirements. Firewalls are discussed in Chapter 16, "Cisco IOS Firewall Overview" and Chapter 24, "Context-Based Access Control Commands."

IP Security and Encryption

This part describes how to configure IP security and encryption in the following chapters:

- Chapter 26, "Configuring Cisco Encryption Technology"—This chapter describes how to configure Cisco Encryption Technology (CET). CET provides network data encryption that is used to prevent routed traffic from being examined or tampered with while it travels across a network. This feature allows IP packets to be encrypted at a Cisco router, routed across a network as encrypted information, and decrypted at the destination Cisco router.

- Chapter 28, "Configuring IPSec Network Security"—This chapter describes how to configure IP Security (IPSec). IPSec provides security for transmission of sensitive information over unprotected networks such as the Internet and provides a more robust security solution than CET. IPSec also provides data authentication and anti-replay services in addition to data confidentiality services, whereas CET provides only data confidentiality services.

- Chapter 30, "Configuring Certification Authority Interoperability"—This chapter describes how to configure Certification Authority (CA) Interoperability. CA Interoperability permits Cisco IOS devices and CAs to communicate so that your Cisco IOS device can obtain and use digital certificates from the CA.

- Chapter 32, "Configuring Internet Key Exchange Security Protocol"—This chapter describes how to configure Internet Key Exchange (IKE). IKE is a key management protocol standard that is used in conjunction with the IPSec standard. IPSec can be configured without IKE, but IKE enhances IPSec by providing additional features, flexibility, and ease of configuration for the IPSec standard.

Other Security Features

This part describes three important security features in the following chapters:

- Chapter 34, "Configuring Passwords and Privileges"—This chapter describes how to configure static passwords stored on your networking device. These passwords are used to control access to the device's command-line prompt to view or change the device configuration.

  This chapter also describes how to assign privilege levels to the passwords. You can configure up to 16 different privilege levels, and assign each level to a password. For each privilege level you define a subset of Cisco IOS commands that can be executed. You can use these different levels to allow some users the capability to execute all Cisco IOS commands, and to restrict other users to a defined subset of commands.

  This chapter also describes how to recover lost passwords.

- Chapter 36, "Neighbor Router Authentication: Overview and Guidelines"—This chapter describes the security benefits and operation of neighbor router authentication.

  When neighbor authentication is configured on a router, the router authenticates its neighbor router before accepting any route updates from that neighbor. This ensures that a router always receives reliable routing update information from a trusted source.

- Chapter 37, "Configuring IP Security Options"—This chapter describes how to configure IP Security Options (IPSO), as described in RFC 1108. IPSO is generally used to comply with the U.S. Government's Department of Defense security policy.

Creating Effective Security Policies

An effective security policy works to ensure that your organization's network assets are protected from sabotage and from inappropriate access—both intentional and accidental.

All network security features should be configured in compliance with your organization's security policy. If you do not have a security policy, or if your policy is out-of-date, you should ensure that the policy is created or updated before you decide how to configure security on your Cisco device.

The following sections provide guidelines to help you create an effective security policy:

- The Nature of Security Policies
- Two Levels of Security Policies
- Tips for Developing an Effective Security Policy

The Nature of Security Policies

You should recognize these aspects of security policies:

- Security policies represent trade-offs. With all security policies, there is some trade-off between user productivity and security measures, which can be restrictive and time-consuming. The goal of any security design is to provide maximum security with minimum impact on user access and productivity. Some security measures, such as network data encryption, do not restrict access and productivity. On the other hand, cumbersome or unnecessarily redundant verification and authorization systems can frustrate users and even prevent access to critical network resources.

- Security policies should be determined by business needs. Business needs should dictate the security policy; a security policy should not determine how a business operates.

- Security policies are living documents. Because organizations are constantly subject to change, security policies must be systematically updated to reflect new business directions, technological changes, and resource allocations.

Two Levels of Security Policies

You can think of a security policy as having two levels:

- Requirements level—At the requirements level, a policy defines the degree to which your network assets must be protected against intrusion or destruction and also estimates the cost (consequences) of a security breach. For example, the policy could state that only human resources personnel should be able to access human resources records, or that only IS personnel should be able to configure the backbone routers. The policy could also address the consequences of a network outage (due to sabotage), or the consequences of sensitive information inadvertently being made public.

- Implementation level—At the implementation level, a policy defines guidelines to implement the requirements-level policy, using specific technology in a predefined way. For example, the implementation-level policy could require access lists to be configured so that only traffic from human resources host computers can access the server containing human resources records.

When creating a policy, define security requirements before defining security implementations so that you do not end up merely justifying particular technical solutions that might not actually be required.

Tips for Developing an Effective Security Policy

To develop an effective security policy, consider the recommendations in the following sections:

- Identifying Your Network Assets to Protect
- Determining Points of Risk
- Limiting the Scope of Access
- Identifying Assumptions
- Determining the Cost of Security Measures
- Considering Human Factors
- Keeping a Limited Number of Secrets
- Implementing Pervasive and Scalable Security
- Understanding Typical Network Functions
- Remembering Physical Security

Identifying Your Network Assets to Protect

The first step to developing a security policy is to understand and identify your organization's network assets. Network assets include the following:

- Networked hosts (such as PCs; includes the hosts' operating systems, applications, and data)
- Networking devices (such as routers)
- Network data (data that travels across the network)

You must both identify your network's assets and determine the degree to which each of these assets must be protected. For example, one subnetwork of hosts might contain extremely sensitive data that should be protected at all costs, and a different subnetwork of hosts might require only modest protection against security risks because there is less cost involved if the subnetwork is compromised.

Determining Points of Risk

You must understand how potential intruders can enter your organization's network or sabotage network operation. Special areas of consideration are network connections, dial-up access points, and misconfigured hosts. Misconfigured hosts, frequently overlooked as points of network entry, can be systems with unprotected login accounts (guest accounts), employ extensive trust in remote commands (such as **rlogin** and **rsh**), have illegal modems attached to them, and use easy-to-break passwords.

Limiting the Scope of Access

Organizations can create multiple barriers within networks, so that unlawful entry to one part of the system does not automatically grant entry to the entire infrastructure. Although maintaining a high level of security for the entire network can be prohibitively expensive (in terms of systems and equipment as well as productivity), you can often provide higher levels of security to the more sensitive areas of your network.

Identifying Assumptions

Every security system has underlying assumptions. For example, an organization might assume that its network is not tapped, that intruders are not very knowledgeable, that intruders are using standard software, or that a locked room is safe. It is important to identify, examine, and justify your assumptions: Any hidden assumption is a potential security hole.

Determining the Cost of Security Measures

In general, providing security comes at a cost. This cost can be measured in terms of increased connection times or inconveniences to legitimate users accessing the assets, or in terms of increased network management requirements, and sometimes in terms of actual dollars spent on equipment or software upgrades.

Some security measures inevitably inconvenience some sophisticated users. Security can delay work, create expensive administrative and educational overhead, use significant computing resources, and require dedicated hardware.

When you decide which security measures to implement, you must understand their costs and weigh them against potential benefits. If the security costs are out of proportion to the actual dangers, it is a disservice to the organization to implement them.

Considering Human Factors

If security measures interfere with essential uses of the system, users resist these measures and sometimes even circumvent them. Many security procedures fail because their designers do not take this fact into account. For example, because automatically generated "nonsense" passwords can be difficult to remember, users often write them on the undersides of keyboards. A "secure" door that leads to a system's only tape drive is sometimes propped open. For convenience, unauthorized modems are often connected to a network to avoid cumbersome dialin security procedures. To ensure compliance with your security measures, users must be able to get their work done as well as understand and accept the need for security.

Any user can compromise system security to some degree. For example, an intruder can often learn passwords by simply calling legitimate users on the telephone, claiming to be a system administrator and asking for the passwords. If users understand security issues and understand the reasons for them, they are far less likely to compromise security in this way.

Defining such human factors and any corresponding policies needs to be included as a formal part of your complete security policy.

At a minimum, users must be taught never to release passwords or other secrets over unsecured telephone lines (especially through cordless or cellular telephones) or electronic mail. They should be wary of questions asked by people who call them on the telephone. Some companies have implemented formalized network security training for their employees in which employees are not allowed access to the network until they have completed a formal training program.

Keeping a Limited Number of Secrets

Most security is based on secrets; for example, passwords and encryption keys are secrets. But the more secrets there are, the harder it is to keep them all. It is prudent, therefore, to design a security policy that relies on a limited number of secrets. Ultimately, the most important secret an organization has is the information that can help someone circumvent its security.

Implementing Pervasive and Scalable Security

Use a systematic approach to security that includes multiple, overlapping security methods.

Almost any change that is made to a system can affect security. This is especially true when new services are created. System administrators, programmers, and users need to consider the security implications of every change they make. Understanding the security implications of a change takes practice; it requires lateral thinking and a willingness to explore every way that a service could potentially be manipulated. The goal of any security policy is to create an environment that is not susceptible to every minor change.

Understanding Typical Network Functions

Understand how your network system normally functions, know what is expected and unexpected behavior, and be familiar with how devices are usually used. This kind of awareness helps the organization detect security problems. Noticing unusual events can help catch intruders before they can damage the system. Software auditing tools can help detect, log, and track unusual events. In addition, an organization should know exactly what software it relies on to provide auditing trails, and a security system should not operate on the assumption that all software is bug free.

Remembering Physical Security

The physical security of your network devices and hosts cannot be neglected. For example, many facilities implement physical security by using security guards, closed-circuit television, card-key entry systems, or other means to control physical access to network devices and hosts. Physical access to a computer or router usually gives a sophisticated user complete control over that device. Physical access to a network link usually allows a person to tap into that link, jam it, or inject traffic into it. Software security measures can often be circumvented when access to the hardware is not controlled.

Identifying Security Risks and Cisco IOS Solutions

Cisco IOS software provides a comprehensive set of security features to guard against specific security risks.

This section describes a few common security risks that might be present in your network, and describes how to use Cisco IOS software to protect against each of these risks:

- Preventing Unauthorized Access into Networking Devices
- Preventing Unauthorized Access into Networks
- Preventing Network Data Interception
- Preventing Fraudulent Route Updates

Preventing Unauthorized Access into Networking Devices

If someone were to gain console or terminal access into a networking device, such as a router, switch, or network access server, that person could do significant damage to your network—perhaps by reconfiguring the device, or even by simply viewing the device's configuration information.

Typically, you want administrators to have access to your networking device; you do not want other users on your local-area network or those dialing in to the network to have access to the router.

Users can access Cisco networking devices by dialing in from outside the network through an asynchronous port, connecting from outside the network through a serial port, or connecting via a terminal or workstation from within the local network.

To prevent unauthorized access into a networking device, you should configure one or more of these security features:

- At a minimum, you should configure passwords and privileges at each networking device for all device lines and ports, as described in Chapter 34, "Configuring Passwords and Privileges." These passwords are stored on the networking device. When users attempt to access the device through a particular line or port, they must enter the password applied to the line or port before they can access the device.
- For an additional layer of security, you can also configure username/password pairs, stored in a database on the networking device, as described in Chapter 34, "Configuring Passwords and Privileges." These pairs are assigned to lines or interfaces and authenticate each user before that user can access the device. If you have defined privilege levels, you can also assign a specific privilege level (with associated rights and privileges) to each username/password pair.

- If you want to use username/password pairs, but you want to store them centrally instead of locally on each individual networking device, you can store them in a database on a security server. Multiple networking devices can then use the same database to obtain user authentication (and, if necessary, authorization) information. Cisco supports a variety of security server protocols, such as RADIUS, TACACS+, and Kerberos. If you decide to use the database on a security server to store login username/password pairs, you must configure your router or access server to support the applicable protocol; in addition, because most supported security protocols must be administered through the AAA security services, you will probably need to enable AAA. For more information about security protocols and AAA, refer to the chapters in Part I, "Authentication, Authorization, and Accounting (AAA)."

NOTE Cisco recommends that, whenever possible, AAA be used to implement authentication.

- If you want to authorize individual users for specific rights and privileges, you can implement AAA's authorization feature, using a security protocol such as TACACS+ or RADIUS. For more information about security protocol features and AAA, refer to the chapters in Part I, "Authentication, Authorization, and Accounting (AAA)."

- If you want to have a backup authentication method, you must configure AAA. AAA allows you to specify the primary method for authenticating users (for example, a username/password database stored on a TACACS+ server) and then specify backup methods (for example, a locally stored username/password database.) The backup method is used if the primary method's database cannot be accessed by the networking device. To configure AAA, refer to the chapters in Part I, "Authentication, Authorization, and Accounting (AAA)." You can configure up to four sequential backup methods.

NOTE If you do not have backup methods configured, you will be denied access to the device if the username/password database cannot be accessed for any reason.

- If you want to keep an audit trail of user access, configure AAA accounting as described in Chapter 6, "Configuring Accounting."

Preventing Unauthorized Access into Networks

If someone were to gain unauthorized access to your organization's internal network, that person could cause damage in many ways, perhaps by accessing sensitive files from a host, by planting a virus, or by hindering network performance by flooding your network with illegitimate packets.

This risk can also apply to a person within your network attempting to access another internal network such as a research and development subnetwork with sensitive and critical data. That person could intentionally or inadvertently cause damage; for example, that person might access confidential files or tie up a time-critical printer.

To prevent unauthorized access through a networking device into a network, you should configure one or more of these security features:

- Traffic filtering—Cisco uses access lists to filter traffic at networking devices. Basic access lists allow only specified traffic through the device; other traffic is simply dropped. You can specify individual hosts or subnets that should be allowed into the network, and you can specify what type of traffic should be allowed into the network. Basic access lists generally filter traffic based on source and destination addresses, and protocol type of each packet.

  Advanced traffic filtering is also available, providing additional filtering capabilities; for example, the Lock-and-Key Security feature requires each user to be authenticated via a username/password before that user's traffic is allowed onto the network.

  All the Cisco IOS traffic filtering capabilities are described in the chapters in Part III, "Traffic Filtering and Firewalls."

- Authentication—You can require users to be authenticated before they gain access to a network. When users attempt to access a service or host (such as a Web site or file server) within the protected network, they must first enter certain data such as a username and password, and possibly additional information such as their date of birth or mother's maiden name. After successful authentication (depending on the method of authentication), users will be assigned specific privileges, allowing them to access specific network assets. In most cases, this type of authentication would be facilitated by using CHAP or PAP over a serial PPP connection in conjunction with a specific security protocol, such as TACACS+ or RADIUS.

  Just as in preventing unauthorized access to specific network devices, you need to decide whether you want the authentication database to reside locally or on a separate security server. In this case, a local security database is useful if you have very few routers providing network access. A local security database does not require a separate (and costly) security server. A remote, centralized security database is convenient when you have a large number of routers providing network access because it prevents you from having to update each router with new or changed username authentication and authorization information for potentially hundreds of thousands of dial-in users. A centralized security database also helps establish consistent remote access policies throughout a corporation.

  Cisco IOS software supports a variety of authentication methods. Although AAA is the primary (and recommended) method for access control, Cisco IOS software provides additional features for simple access control that are outside the scope of AAA. For more information, refer to Chapter 2, "Configuring Authentication."

Preventing Network Data Interception

When packets travel across a network, they are susceptible to being read, altered, or "hijacked." (Hijacking occurs when a hostile party intercepts a network traffic session and poses as one of the session endpoints.)

If the data is traveling across an unsecured network such as the Internet, the data is exposed to a fairly significant risk. Sensitive or confidential data could be exposed, critical data could be modified, and communications could be interrupted if data is altered.

To protect data as it travels across a network, configure network data encryption, as described in Chapter 26, "Configuring Cisco Encryption Technology."

CET prevents routed traffic from being examined or tampered with while it travels across a network. This feature causes IP packets to be encrypted at a Cisco router, routed across a network as encrypted information, and decrypted at the destination Cisco router. Between the two routers, the packets are in encrypted form and therefore the packets' contents cannot be read or altered. You define what traffic should be encrypted between the two routers, according to what data is most sensitive or critical.

If you want to protect traffic for protocols other than IP, you can encapsulate those other protocols into IP packets by using GRE encapsulation, and then encrypt the IP packets.

Typically, you do not use CET for traffic that is routed through networks that you consider secure. Consider using CET for traffic that is routed across unsecured networks, such as the Internet, if your organization could be damaged if the traffic is examined or tampered with by unauthorized individuals.

Preventing Fraudulent Route Updates

All routing devices determine where to route individual packets by using information stored in route tables. This route table information is created by using route updates obtained from neighboring routers.

If a router receives a fraudulent update, the router could be tricked into forwarding traffic to the wrong destination. This could cause sensitive data to be exposed, or could cause network communications to be interrupted.

To ensure that route updates are received only from known, trusted neighbor routers, configure neighbor router authentication as described in Chapter 36, "Neighbor Router Authentication: Overview and Guidelines."

About the Cisco IOS 12.0 Reference Library

The Cisco IOS 12.0 Reference Library books are Cisco documentation that describe the tasks and commands necessary to configure and maintain your Cisco IOS network.

The Cisco IOS software bookset is intended primarily for users who configure and maintain access servers and routers, but are not necessarily familiar with the tasks, the relationship between tasks, or the commands necessary to perform particular tasks.

Cisco IOS Reference Library Organization

The Cisco IOS 12.0 Reference Library consists of 11 books. Each book contains technology-specific configuration chapters with corresponding command reference chapters. Each configuration chapter describes Cisco's implementation of protocols and technologies, related configuration tasks, and contains comprehensive configuration examples. Each command reference chapter complements the organization of its corresponding configuration chapter and provides complete command syntax information.

Books Available in the Cisco IOS 12.0 Reference Library

- *Cisco IOS 12.0 Solutions for Network Protocols*, Volume I: IP, 1-57870-154-6

  This book is a comprehensive guide detailing available IP and IP routing alternatives. It describes how to implement IP addressing and IP services and how to configure support for a wide range of IP routing protocols including BGP for ISP networks and basic and advanced IP Multicast functionality.

- *Cisco IOS 12.0 Configuration Fundamentals*, 1-57870-155-4

  This comprehensive guide details Cisco IOS software configuration basics. It offers thorough coverage of router and access server configuration and maintenance techniques. In addition to hands-on implementation and task instruction, this book also presents the complete syntax for router and access server commands, and individual examples for each command.

- *Cisco IOS 12.0 Interface Configuration*, 1-57870-156-2

  This book is a comprehensive guide detailing how to configure physical and virtual interfaces–the two types of interfaces supported on Cisco routers. It provides readers with the most current router task and commands information for their network environments and teaches how to effectively implement these techniques and commands on their networks.

- *Cisco IOS 12.0 Wide Area Networking Solutions*, 1-57870-158-9

  This book offers thorough, comprehensive coverage of internetworking technologies, particularly ATM, Frame Relay, SMDS, LAPB, and X.25, teaching the reader how to configure the technologies in a LAN/WAN environment.

- *Cisco IOS 12.0 Switching Services*, 1-57870-157-0

  This book is a comprehensive guide detailing available Cisco IOS switching alternatives. Cisco's switching services range from fast switching and Netflow switching to LAN Emulation. This book describes how to configure routing between virtual LANs (VLANs) and teaches how to effectively configure and implement VLANs on switches.

- *Cisco IOS 12.0 Multiservice Applications*, 1-57870-159-7

  This book shows you how to configure your router or access server to support voice, video, and broadband transmission. Cisco's voice and video support are implemented using voice packet technology. In voice packet technology, voice signals are packetized and transported in compliance with ITU-T specification H.323, which is the ITU-T specification for transmitting multimedia (voice, video, and data) across a local-area network (LAN).

- *Cisco IOS 12.0 Network Security*, 1-57870-160-0

  This book documents security configuration from a remote site and for a central enterprise or service provider network. It describes AAA, Radius, TACACS+, and Kerberos network security features. It also explains how to encrypt data across enterprise networks. The book includes many illustrations that show configurations and functionality, along with a discussion of network security policy choices and some decision-making guidelines.

- *Cisco IOS 12.0 Quality of Service*, 1-57870-161-9

  Cisco IOS 12.0 Quality of Service Solutions is a comprehensive guide detailing available Cisco IOS quality of service (QoS) features. This book suggests benefits you can gain from implementing Cisco IOS QoS features, and describes how to effectively configure and implement the various QoS features. Some of the features described in this book include Committed Access Rate (CAR), Weighted Fair Queuing (WFQ), and Weighted Random Early Detection (WRED), as well as many other features.

- *Cisco IOS 12.0 Solutions for Network Protocols*, Volume II: IPX, AppleTalk, and More, 1-57870-164-3

  This book is a comprehensive guide detailing available network protocol alternatives. It describes how to implement various protocols in your network. This book includes documentation of the latest functionality for the IPX and AppleTalk desktop protocols as well as the following network protocols: Apollo Domain, Banyan VINES, DECnet, ISO CLNS, and XNS.

- *Cisco IOS 12.0 Bridging and IBM Networking Solutions*, 1-57870-162-7

  This book describes Cisco's support for networks in IBM and bridging environments. Support includes transparent and source-route transparent bridging, source-route bridging (SRB), remote source-route bridging (RSRB), data link switching plus (DLS+), serial tunnel and block serial tunnel, SDLC and LLC2 parameter, IBM network media translation, downstream physical unit and SNA service point, SNA Frame Relay access support, Advanced Peer-to-Peer Networking, and native client interface architecture (NCIA).

- *Cisco IOS 12.0 Dial Solutions*, 1-57870-163-5

  This book provides readers with real-world solutions and how to implement them on a network. Customers interested in implementing dial solutions across their network environment include remote sites dialing in to a central office, Internet service providers (ISPs), ISP customers at home offices, and enterprise WAN system administrators implementing dial-on-demand routing (DDR).

Book Conventions

The Cisco IOS documentation set uses the following conventions:

Convention	Description
^ or Ctrl	Represents the Control key. For example, when you read ^D or *Ctrl-D*, you should hold down the Control key while you press the D key. Keys are indicated in capital letters but are not case sensitive.

Convention	Description
string	A string is defined as a nonquoted set of characters. For example, when setting an SNMP community string to public, do not use quotation marks around the string; otherwise, the string will include the quotation marks.

Examples use the following conventions:

Convention	Description
screen	Shows an example of information displayed on the screen.
boldface screen	Shows an example of information that you must enter.
< >	Nonprinting characters, such as passwords, appear in angled brackets.
!	Exclamation points at the beginning of a line indicate a comment line. They are also displayed by the Cisco IOS software for certain processes.
[ ]	Default responses to system prompts appear in square brackets.

The following conventions are used to attract the reader's attention:

CAUTION Means *reader be careful*. In this situation, you might do something that could result in equipment damage or loss of data.

NOTE Means *reader take note*. Notes contain helpful suggestions or references to materials not contained in this manual.

TIMESAVER Means the *described action saves time*. You can save time by performing the action described in the paragraph.

Within the Cisco IOS 12.0 Reference Library, the term *router* is used to refer to both access servers and routers. When a feature is supported on the access server only, the term *access server* is used.

Within examples, routers and access servers are alternately shown. These products are used only for example purposes; that is, an example that shows one product does not indicate that the other product is not supported.

Command Syntax Conventions

Command descriptions use the following conventions:

Convention	Description
boldface	Indicates commands and keywords that are entered literally as shown.
italics	Indicates arguments for which you supply values; in contexts that do not allow italics, arguments are enclosed in angle brackets (< >).
[**x**]	Keywords or arguments that appear within square brackets are optional.
{**x** | **y** | **z**}	A choice of required keywords (represented by **x**, **y**, and **z**) appears in braces separated by vertical bars. You must select one.
[**x** {**y** | **z**}]	Braces and vertical bars within square brackets indicate a required choice within an optional element. You do not need to select one. If you do, you have some required choices.

Cisco Connection Online

Cisco Connection Online (CCO) is Cisco Systems' primary, real-time support channel. Maintenance customers and partners can self-register on CCO to obtain additional information and services.

Available 24 hours a day, 7 days a week, CCO provides a wealth of standard and value-added services to Cisco's customers and business partners. CCO services include product information, product documentation, software updates, release notes, technical tips, the Bug Navigator, configuration notes, brochures, descriptions of service offerings, and download access to public and authorized files.

CCO serves a wide variety of users through two interfaces that are updated and enhanced simultaneously: a character-based version and a multimedia version that resides on the World Wide Web (WWW). The character-based CCO supports Zmodem, Kermit, Xmodem, FTP, and Internet e-mail, and it is excellent for quick access to information over lower bandwidths. The WWW version of CCO provides richly formatted documents with photographs, figures, graphics, and video, as well as hyperlinks to related information.

You can access CCO in the following ways:

- WWW: http://www.cisco.com
- WWW: http://www-europe.cisco.com
- WWW: http://www-china.cisco.com
- Telnet: cco.cisco.com
- Modem: From North America, 408-526-8070; from Europe, 33 1 64 46 40 82. Use the following terminal settings: VT100 emulation; databits: 8; parity: none; stop bits: 1; and connection rates up to 28.8 kbps.

Using Cisco IOS Software

This section provides helpful tips for understanding and configuring Cisco IOS software using the command-line interface (CLI).

Getting Help

Entering a question mark (**?**) at the system prompt displays a list of commands available for each command mode. You can also get a list of any command's associated keywords and arguments with the context-sensitive help feature.

To get help specific to a command mode, a command, a keyword, or an argument, use one of the following commands:

Command	Purpose
help	Obtains a brief description of the help system in any command mode.
*abbreviated-command-entry***?**	Obtains a list of commands that begin with a particular character string. (No space between command and question mark.)
abbreviated-command-entry<**Tab**>	Completes a partial command name.
?	Lists all commands available for a particular command mode.
command **?**	Lists a command's associated keywords. (Space between command and question mark.)
command keyword **?**	Lists a keyword's associated arguments. (Space between the keyword and question mark.)

Example: How to Find Command Options

This section provides an example of how to display syntax for a command. The syntax can consist of optional or required keywords. To display keywords for a command, enter a question mark (**?**) at the configuration prompt, or after entering part of a command followed by a space. The Cisco IOS software displays a list of keywords available along with a brief description of the keywords. For example, if you were in global configuration mode, typed the command **arap**, and wanted to see all the keywords for that command, you would type **arap ?**.

Table I-1 shows examples of how you can use the question mark (**?**) to assist you in entering commands. It steps you through entering the following commands:

- **controller t1 1**
- **cas-group 1 timeslots 1-24 type e&m-fgb dtmf**

Table I-1 *How to Find Command Options*

Command	Comment

`Router> `**`enable`**
`Password: <password>`
`Router#`
	Enter the **enable** command and password to access privileged EXEC commands.
	
	You have entered privileged EXEC mode when the prompt changes to `Router#`.

`Router# `**`config terminal`**
`Enter configuration commands, one per line. End with`
`Ctrl-Z.`
`Router(config)#`
	Enter global configuration mode.
	
	You have entered global configuration mode when the prompt changes to `Router(config)#`.

`Router(config)# `**`controller t1 ?`**
`  <0-3>  Controller unit number`
`Router(config)# `**`controller t1 1`**
`Router(config-controller)#`
	Enter controller configuration mode by specifying the T1 controller that you want to configure using the **controller t1** global configuration command.
	
	Enter a **?** to display what you must enter next on the command line. In this example, you must enter a controller unit number from 0 to 3.
	
	You have entered controller configuration mode when the prompt changes to `Router(config-controller)#`.

`Router(config-controller)# `**`?`**
`Controller configuration commands:`
`  cablelength    Specify the cable length for a DS1 link`
`  cas-group      Configure the specified timeslots for CAS`
`                 (Channel Associate Signals)`
`  channel-group  Specify the timeslots to channel-group`
`                 mapping for an interface`
`  clock          Specify the clock source for a DS1 link`
`  default        Set a command to its defaults`
`  description    Controller specific description`
`  ds0            ds0 commands`
`  exit           Exit from controller configuration mode`
`  fdl            Specify the FDL standard for a DS1 data`
`                 link`
`  framing        Specify the type of Framing on a DS1 link`
`  help           Description of the interactive help`
`                 system`
`  linecode       Specify the line encoding method for a`
`                 DS1 link`
`  loopback       Put the entire T1 line into loopback`
`  no             Negate a command or set its defaults`
`  pri-group      Configure the specified timeslots for PRI`
`  shutdown       Shut down a DS1 link (send Blue Alarm)`
`Router(config-controller)#`
	Enter a **?** to display a list of all the controller configuration commands available for the T1 controller.

Table I-1 *How to Find Command Options (Continued)*

Command	Comment

`Router(config-controller)# `**`cas-group `**`?`
  `<0-23>`   `Channel number`
`Router(config-controller)# cas-group`
	Enter the command that you want to configure for the controller. In this example, the **cas-group** command is used.

	Enter a **?** to display what you must enter next on the command line. In this example, you must enter a channel number from 0 to 23.
	Because a <cr> is not displayed, it indicates that you must enter more keywords to complete the command.

`Router(config-controller)# `**`cas-group 1 `**`?`
  `timeslots`   `List of timeslots in the cas-group`
`Router(config-controller)# cas-group 1`
	After you enter the channel number, enter a **?** to display what you must enter next on the command line. In this example, you must enter the **timeslots** keyword.

	Because a <cr> is not displayed, it indicates that you must enter more keywords to complete the command.

`Router(config-controller)# `**`cas-group 1 timeslots `**`?`
  `<1-24>`   `List of timeslots which comprise the`
                `cas-group`
`Router(config-controller)# cas-group 1 timeslots`
	After you enter the **timeslots** keyword, enter a **?** to display what you must enter next on the command line. In this example, you must enter a list of timeslots from 1 to 24.

	You can specify timeslot ranges (for example, 1-24), individual timeslots separated by commas (for example 1, 3, 5), or a combination of the two (for example 1-3, 8, 17-24). The 16th time slot is not specified in the command line, because it is reserved for transmitting the channel signaling.
	Because a <cr> is not displayed, it indicates that you must enter more keywords to complete the command.

Continues

Table I-1 *How to Find Command Options (Continued)*

Command	Comment

`Router(config-controller)# ` **`cas-group 1 timeslots 1-24 ?`**
`  service        Specify the type of service`
`  type           Specify the type of signaling`
`Router(config-controller)# cas-group 1 timeslots 1-24`
	After you enter the timeslot ranges, enter a **?** to display what you must enter next on the command line. In this example, you must enter the **service** or **type** keyword.
	
	Because a \<cr\> is not displayed, it indicates that you must enter more keywords to complete the command.

`Router(config-controller)# ` **`cas-group 1 timeslots 1-24`**
`type ?`
`  e&m-fgb           E & M Type II FGB`
`  e&m-fgd           E & M Type IIFGD`
`  e&m-immediate-start   E & M Immediate Start`
`  fxs-ground-start      FXS Ground Start`
`  fxs-loop-start        FXS Loop Start`
`  sas-ground-start      SAS Ground Start`
`  sas-loop-start        SAS Loop Start`
`Router(config-controller)# cas-group 1 timeslots 1-24 type`
	In this example, the **type** keyword is entered. After you enter the **type** keyword, enter a **?** to display what you must enter next on the command line. In this example, you must enter one of the signaling types.
	
	Because a \<cr\> is not displayed, it indicates that you must enter more keywords to complete the command.

`Router(config-controller)# ` **`cas-group 1 timeslots 1-24 type`**
`e&m-fgb ?`
`  dtmf        DTMF tone signaling`
`  mf          MF tone signaling`
`  service     Specify the type of service`
`  <cr>`
`Router(config-controller)# cas-group 1 timeslots 1-24 type`
`e&m-fgb`
	In this example, the **e&m-fgb** keyword is entered. After you enter the **e&m-fgb** keyword, enter a **?** to display what you must enter next on the command line. In this example, you can enter the **dtmf**, **mf**, or **service** keyword to indicate the type of channel-associated signaling available for the **e&m-fgb** signaling type.
	
	Because a \<cr\> is displayed, it indicates that you can enter more keywords or press **\<cr\>** to complete the command.

`Router(config-controller)# ` **`cas-group 1 timeslots 1-24 type`**
`e&m-fgb dtmf ?`
`  dnis        DNIS addr info provisioned`
`  service     Specify the type of service`
`  <cr>`
`Router(config-controller)# cas-group 1 timeslots 1-24 type`
`e&m-fgb dtmf`
	In this example, the **dtmf** keyword is entered. After you enter the **dtmf** keyword, enter a **?** to display what you must enter next on the command line. In this example, you can enter the **dnis** or **service** keyword to indicate the options available for **dtmf** tone signaling.
	
	Because a \<cr\> is displayed, it indicates that you can enter more keywords or press **\<cr\>** to complete the command.

Table I-1 *How to Find Command Options (Continued)*

Command	Comment

`Router(config-controller)# cas-group 1 timeslots 1-24 type`
`e&m-fgb dtmf`
`Router(config-controller)#`
	In this example, enter a **<cr>** to complete the command.

Understanding Command Modes

The Cisco IOS user interface is divided into many different modes. The commands available to you at any given time depend on which mode you are currently in. Entering a question mark (**?**) at the system prompt allows you to obtain a list of commands available for each command mode.

When you start a session on the router, you begin in user mode, often called EXEC mode. Only a limited subset of the commands are available in EXEC mode. In order to have access to all commands, you must enter privileged EXEC mode. Normally, you must enter a password to enter privileged EXEC mode. From privileged mode, you can enter any EXEC command or enter global configuration mode. Most of the EXEC commands are one-time commands, such as **show** commands, which show the current status of something, and **clear** commands, which clear counters or interfaces. The EXEC commands are not saved across reboots of the router.

The configuration modes allow you to make changes to the running configuration. If you later save the configuration, these commands are stored across router reboots. In order to get to the various configuration modes, you must start at global configuration mode. From global configuration mode, you can enter interface configuration mode, subinterface configuration mode, and a variety of protocol-specific modes.

ROM Monitor mode is a separate mode used when the router cannot boot properly. If your router or access server does not find a valid system image when it is booting, or if its configuration file is corrupted at startup, the system might enter read-only memory (ROM) monitor mode.

Summary of Main Command Modes

Table I-2 summarizes the main command modes of the Cisco IOS software.

Table I-2 *Summary of Main Command Modes*

Command Mode	Access Method	Prompt	Exit Method
User EXEC	Log in.	`Router>`	Use the **logout** command.
Privileged EXEC	From user EXEC mode, use the **enable** EXEC command.	`Router#`	To exit back to user EXEC mode, use the **disable** command. To enter global configuration mode, use the **configure terminal** privileged EXEC command.

Continues

Table I-2 *Summary of Main Command Modes (Continued)*

Command Mode	Access Method	Prompt	Exit Method
Global configuration	From privileged EXEC mode, use the **configure terminal** privileged EXEC command.	`Router(config)#`	To exit to privileged EXEC mode, use the **exit** or **end** command or press **Ctrl-Z**. To enter interface configuration mode, enter an **interface** configuration command.
Interface configuration	From global configuration mode, enter by specifying an interface with an **interface** command.	`Router(config-if)#`	To exit to global configuration mode, use the **exit** command. To exit to privileged EXEC mode, use the **exit** command or press **Ctrl-Z**. To enter subinterface configuration mode, specify a subinterface with the **interface** command.
Subinterface configuration	From interface configuration mode, specify a subinterface with an **interface** command.	`Router(config-subif)#`	To exit to global configuration mode, use the **exit** command. To enter privileged EXEC mode, use the **end** command or press **Ctrl-Z**.
ROM Monitor	From privileged EXEC mode, use the **reload** EXEC command. Press the Break key during the first 60 seconds while the system is booting.	`>`	To exit to user EXEC mode, type **continue**.

Using the No and Default Forms of Commands

Almost every configuration command also has a **no** form. In general, use the **no** form to disable a function. Use the command without the keyword **no** to re-enable a disabled function or to enable a function that is disabled by default. For example, IP routing is enabled by default. To disable IP routing, specify the **no ip routing** command and specify **ip routing** to re-enable it. The Cisco IOS software command reference*s* provide the complete syntax for the configuration commands and describes what the **no** form of a command does.

Configuration commands can also have a **default** form. The **default** form of a command returns the command setting to its default. Most commands are disabled by default, so the **default** form is the same as the **no** form. However, some commands are enabled by default and have variables set to certain default values. In these cases, the **default** command enables the command and sets variables to their default values. The Cisco IOS software command reference*s* describe what the **default** form of a command does if the command is not the same as the **no** form.

Saving Configuration Changes

Enter the **copy system:running-config nvram:startup-config** command to save your configuration changes to your startup configuration so that they will not be lost if there is a system reload or power outage. For example:

```
Router# copy system:running-config nvram:startup-config
Building configuration...
```

It might take a minute or two to save the configuration. After the configuration has been saved, the following output appears:

```
[OK]
Router#
```

On most platforms, this step saves the configuration to nonvolatile random-access memory (NVRAM). On the Class A Flash file system platforms, this step saves the configuration to the location specified by the CONFIG_FILE environment variable. The CONFIG_FILE variable defaults to NVRAM.

Authentication, Authorization, and Accounting (AAA)

## CHAPTER 1

AAA Overview

Access control is the way you control who is allowed access to the network server and what services they are allowed to use once they have access. Authentication, authorization, and accounting (AAA) network security services provide the primary framework through which you set up access control on your router or access server.

AAA Security Services

AAA is an architectural framework for configuring a set of three independent security functions in a consistent manner. AAA provides a modular way of performing the following services:

- Authentication—Provides the method of identifying users, including login and password dialog, challenge and response, messaging support, and, depending on the security protocol you select, encryption.

  Authentication is the way a user is identified prior to being allowed access to the network and network services. You configure AAA authentication by defining a named list of authentication methods, and then applying that list to various interfaces. The method list defines the types of authentication to be performed and the sequence in which they will be performed; it must be applied to a specific interface before any of the defined authentication methods will be performed. The only exception is the default method list (which is named *default*). The default method list is automatically applied to all interfaces if no other method list is defined. A defined method list overrides the default method list.

  All authentication methods, except for local, line password, and enable authentication, must be defined through AAA. For information about configuring all authentication methods, including those implemented outside of the AAA security services, refer to Chapter 2, "Configuring Authentication."

- Authorization—Provides the method for remote access control, including one-time authorization or authorization for each service, per-user account list and profile, user group support, and support of IP, IPX, ARA, and Telnet.

  AAA authorization works by assembling a set of attributes that describe what the user is authorized to perform. These attributes are compared to the information contained in a database for a given user and the result is returned to AAA to determine the user's actual capabilities and restrictions. The database can be located locally on the access server or router or it can be hosted remotely on a RADIUS or TACACS+ security server. Remote security servers, such as RADIUS and TACACS+, authorize users for specific rights by associating attribute-value (AV) pairs, which define those rights, with the appropriate user. All authorization methods must be defined through AAA.

As with authentication, you configure AAA authorization by defining a named list of authorization methods, and then applying that list to various interfaces. For information about configuring authorization using AAA, refer to Chapter 4, "Configuring Authorization."

● Accounting—Provides the method for collecting and sending security server information used for billing, auditing, and reporting, such as user identities, start and stop times, executed commands (such as PPP), number of packets, and number of bytes.

Accounting enables you to track the services users are accessing as well as the amount of network resources they are consuming. When AAA accounting is activated, the network access server reports user activity to the TACACS+ or RADIUS security server (depending on which security method you have implemented) in the form of accounting records. Each accounting record is comprised of accounting AV pairs and is stored on the access control server. This data can then be analyzed for network management, client billing, and/or auditing. All accounting methods must be defined through AAA. As with authentication and authorization, you configure AAA accounting by defining a named list of accounting methods, and then applying that list to various interfaces. For information about configuring accounting using AAA, refer to Chapter 6, "Configuring Accounting."

In many circumstances, AAA uses protocols such as RADIUS, TACACS+, and Kerberos to administer its security functions. If your router or access server is acting as a network access server, AAA is the means through which you establish communication between your network access server and your RADIUS, TACACS+, or Kerberos security server.

Although AAA is the primary (and recommended) method for access control, Cisco IOS software provides additional features for simple access control that are outside the scope of AAA, such as local username authentication, line password authentication, and enable password authentication. However, these features do not provide the same degree of access control that is possible by using AAA.

Benefits of Using AAA

AAA provides the following benefits:

● Increased flexibility and control

● Scalability

● Standardized authentication methods, such as RADIUS, TACACS+, and Kerberos

● Multiple backup systems

NOTE   The deprecated protocols, TACACS and extended TACACS, are not compatible with AAA; if you select these security protocols, you will not be able to take advantage of the AAA security services.

The AAA Philosophy

AAA is designed to enable you to dynamically configure the type of authentication and authorization you want on a per-line (per-user) or per-service (for example, IP, IPX, or VPDN) basis. You define the type of authentication and authorization you want by creating method lists and then applying those method lists to specific services or interfaces.

Method Lists

A *method list* is a list defining the authentication methods to be used, in sequence, to authenticate a user. Method lists enable you to designate one or more security protocols to be used for authentication, thus ensuring a backup system for authentication in case the initial method fails. Cisco IOS software uses the first method listed to authenticate users; if that method does not respond, the Cisco IOS software selects the next authentication method that appears in the method list. This process continues until there is successful communication with a listed authentication method or the authentication method list is exhausted, in which case authentication fails.

NOTE	The Cisco IOS software attempts authentication with the next listed authentication method only when there is no response from the previous method. If authentication fails at any point in this cycle—meaning that the security server or local username database responds by denying the user access—the authentication process stops and no other authentication methods are attempted.

Where to Begin

You must first decide what kind of security solution you want to implement. You need to assess the security risks in your particular network and decide on the appropriate means to prevent unauthorized entry and attack. Cisco recommends that you use AAA, no matter how minor your security needs might be.

Overview of the AAA Configuration Process

Configuring AAA is relatively simple when you understand the basic process involved. To configure security on a Cisco router or access server using AAA, follow this process:

1   Enable AAA by using the **aaa new-model** global configuration command.

2   If you decide to use a separate security server, configure security protocol parameters, such as RADIUS, TACACS+, or Kerberos.

3   Define the method lists for authentication by using the **aaa authentication** command.

4 Apply the method lists to a particular interface or line, if required.

5 (Optional) Configure authorization by using the **aaa authorization** command.

6 (Optional) Configure accounting by using the **aaa accounting** command.

For a complete description of the commands used in this chapter, refer to Chapter 3, "Authentication Commands." To locate documentation of other commands that appear in this chapter, you can search online at www.cisco.com.

Enabling AAA

Before you can use any of the services AAA network security services provide, you need to enable AAA.

To enable AAA, use the following command in global configuration mode:

Command	Purpose
aaa new-model	Enables AAA.

NOTE When you enable AAA, you can no longer access the commands to configure the older deprecated protocols, TACACS or extended TACACS. If you decided to use TACACS or extended TACACS in your security solution, do not enable AAA.

Disabling AAA

You can disable AAA functionality with a single command if, for some reason, you decide that your security needs cannot be met by AAA but can be met by using TACACS, extended TACACS, or a line security method that can be implemented without AAA.

To disable AAA, use the following command in global configuration mode:

Command	Purpose
no aaa new-model	Disables AAA.

What To Do Next

After you have enabled AAA, you are ready to configure the other elements relating to your selected security solution. Table 1-1 describes AAA configuration tasks and where to find more information.

Table 1-1 *AAA Access Control Security Solutions Methods*

Task	Further Information
Configure local login authentication.	Chapter 2, "Configuring Authentication"
Control login using security server authentication.	Chapter 2, "Configuring Authentication"
Define method lists for authentication.	Chapter 2, "Configuring Authentication"
Apply method lists to a particular interface or line.	Chapter 2, "Configuring Authentication"
Configure RADIUS security protocol parameters.	Chapter 8, "Configuring RADIUS"
Configure TACACS+ security protocol parameters.	Chapter 10, "Configuring TACACS+"
Configure Kerberos security protocol parameters.	Chapter 13, "Configuring Kerberos"
Enable TACACS+ authorization.	Chapter 4, "Configuring Authorization"
Enable RADIUS authorization.	Chapter 4, "Configuring Authorization"
View supported IETF RADIUS attributes.	Appendix A, "RADIUS Attributes"
View supported vendor-specific RADIUS attributes.	Appendix A, "RADIUS Attributes"
View supported TACACS+ AV pairs.	Appendix B, "TACACS+ Attribute-Value Pairs"
Enable accounting.	Chapter 6, "Configuring Accounting"

Table 1-2 describes non-AAA configuration tasks and where to find more information.

Table 1-2 *Non-AAA Access Control Security Solutions Methods*

Task	Further Information
Configure login authentication.	Chapter 2, "Configuring Authentication"
Configure TACACS.	Chapter 11, "Configuring TACACS and Extended TACACS"
Configure extended TACACS.	Chapter 11, "Configuring TACACS and Extended TACACS"

Configuring Authentication

Authentication identifies users before they are allowed access to the network and network services. Basically, the Cisco IOS software implementation of authentication is divided into two main categories:

- AAA Authentication Methods
- Non-AAA Authentication Methods

Authentication, for the most part, is implemented through the AAA security services. Cisco recommends that, whenever possible, AAA be used to implement authentication.

This chapter describes both AAA and non-AAA authentication methods. For configuration examples, refer to the "Authentication Examples" section at the end of this chapter. For a complete description of the AAA commands used in this chapter, refer to the rest of the chapters in Part I, "Authentication, Authorization, and Accounting (AAA)." To locate documentation of other commands that appear in this chapter, you can search online at www.cisco.com.

AAA Authentication Method Lists

To configure AAA authentication, first define a named list of authentication methods, and then apply that list to various interfaces. The method list defines the types of authentication to be performed and the sequence in which they will be performed; it must be applied to a specific interface before any of the defined authentication methods will be performed. The only exception is the default method list (which is named *default*). The default method list is automatically applied to all interfaces except those that have a named method list explicitly defined. A defined method list overrides the default method list.

A method list is a list describing the authentication methods to be queried, in sequence, to authenticate a user. Method lists enable you to designate one or more security protocols to be used for authentication, thus ensuring a backup system for authentication in case the initial method fails. Cisco IOS software uses the first method listed to authenticate users; if that method fails to respond, the Cisco IOS software selects the next authentication method listed in the method list. This process continues until there is successful communication with a listed authentication method, or all methods defined are exhausted.

It is important to note that the Cisco IOS software attempts authentication with the next listed authentication method only when there is no response from the previous method. If authentication fails at any point in this cycle—meaning that the security server or local username database responds by denying the user access—the authentication process stops and no other authentication methods are attempted.

Method List Examples

Figure 2-1 shows a typical AAA network configuration that includes four security servers: R1 and R2 are RADIUS servers, and T1 and T2 are TACACS+ servers. Suppose that the system administrator has decided on a security solution in which all interfaces will use the same authentication methods to authenticate Point-to-Point Protocol (PPP) connections: R1 is contacted first for authentication information; then, if there is no response, R2 is contacted. If R2 does not respond, T1 is contacted; if T1 does not respond, T2 is contacted. If all designated servers fail to respond, authentication falls over to the local username database on the access server itself. To implement this, the system administrator would create a default method list by entering the following command:

```
aaa authentication ppp default radius tacacs+ local
```

In this example, *default* is the name of the method list. The protocols included in this method list are listed after the name in the order in which they are to be queried. The default list is automatically applied to all interfaces.

Figure 2-1   *Typical AAA Network Configuration*

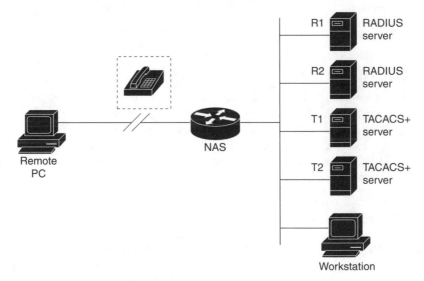

When a remote user attempts to dial in to the network, the network access server first queries R1 for authentication information. If R1 authenticates the user, it issues a PASS response to the network access server and the user is allowed to access the network. If R1 returns a FAIL response, the user is denied access and the session is terminated. If R1 does not respond, then the network access server processes that as an error and queries R2 for authentication information. This pattern would continue through the remaining designated methods until the user is either authenticated or rejected, or the session terminated.

It is important to remember that a FAIL response is significantly different from an error. A FAIL means that the user has not met the criteria contained in the applicable authentication database to be successfully authenticated. Authentication ends with a FAIL response. An error means that the security server has not responded to an authentication query. Because of this, no authentication has been attempted. Only when an error is detected does AAA select the next authentication method defined in the authentication method list.

Suppose that the system administrator wanted to apply a method list only to a particular interface or set of interfaces. In this case, the system administrator would create a named method list and then apply this named list to the applicable interfaces. The following example shows how the system administrator would implement an authentication method that will be applied only to interface 3:

```
aaa authentication ppp default radius tacacs+ local
aaa authentication ppp apple radius tacacs+ local none
 interface async 3
 ppp authentication chap apple
```

In this example, *apple* is the name of the method list, and the protocols included in this method list are listed after the name in the order in which they are to be performed. After the method list has been created, it is applied to the appropriate interface. Note that the method list name in both the **aaa authentication** command and the **ppp authentication** commands must match.

AAA Authentication General Configuration Procedure

To configure AAA authentication, you need to perform the following tasks:

1   Enable AAA by using the **aaa new-model** global configuration command. For more information about configuring AAA, refer to Chapter 1, "AAA Overview."

2   Configure security protocol parameters, such as RADIUS, TACACS+, or Kerberos, if you are using a security server. For more information about RADIUS, refer to Chapter 8, "Configuring RADIUS." For more information about TACACS+, refer to Chapter 10, "Configuring TACACS+." For more information about Kerberos, refer to Chapter 13, "Configuring Kerberos."

3   Define the method lists for authentication by using the **aaa authentication** command.

4   Apply the method lists to a particular interface or line, if required.

AAA Authentication Methods

This section discusses the following AAA authentication methods:

● Configuring Login Authentication Using AAA

● Configuring PPP Authentication Using AAA

● Configuring AAA Scalability for PPP Requests

● Configuring ARA Authentication Using AAA

● Configuring NASI Authentication Using AAA

● Specifying the Amount of Time for Login Input

- Enabling Password Protection at the Privileged Level

- Enabling an Authentication Override

- Changing the Text Displayed at the Password Prompt

- Configuring Message Banners for AAA Authentication

- Enabling Double Authentication

- Enabling Automated Double Authentication

NOTE   AAA features are not available for use until you enable AAA globally by issuing
the **aaa new-model** command. For more information about enabling AAA, refer
to Chapter 1, "AAA Overview."

Configuring Login Authentication Using AAA

The AAA security services facilitate a variety of login authentication methods. Use the **aaa
authentication login** command to enable AAA authentication no matter which of the supported login
authentication methods you decide to use. With the **aaa authentication login** command, you create one
or more lists of authentication methods that are tried at login. These lists are applied using the **login
authentication** line configuration command.

To configure login authentication by using AAA, use the following commands, beginning in global
configuration mode:

Step	Command	Purpose
1	**aaa new-model**	Enables AAA globally.
2	**aaa authentication login** {**default**	*list-name*}*method1* [*method2...*]	Creates a local authentication list.
3	**line** [**aux**	**console**	**tty**	**vty**] *line-number* [*ending-line-number*]	Enters line configuration mode for the lines to which you want to apply the authentication list.
4	**login authentication** {**default**	*list-name*}	Applies the authentication list to a line or set of lines.

The keyword *list-name* is a character string used to name the list you are creating. The keyword *method*
refers to the actual method the authentication algorithm tries. The additional methods of authentication
are used only if the previous method returns an error, not if it fails. To specify that the authentication
should succeed even if all methods return an error, specify *none* as the final method in the command
line.

For example, to specify that authentication should succeed even if (in this example) the TACACS+ server returns an error, enter the following:

```
aaa authentication login default tacacs+ none
```

NOTE	Because the *none* keyword enables *any* user logging in to successfully authenticate, it should be used only as a backup method of authentication.

To create a default list that is used when a named list is *not* specified in the **login authentication** command, use the *default* argument followed by the methods you want used in default situations. The default method list is automatically applied to all interfaces.

For example, to specify RADIUS as the default method for user authentication during login, enter the following:

```
aaa authentication login default radius
```

Table 2-1 lists the supported login authentication methods.

Table 2-1   *AAA Authentication Login Methods*

Keyword	Description
enable	Uses the enable password for authentication.
krb5	Uses Kerberos 5 for authentication.
krb5-telnet	Uses Kerberos 5 Telnet authentication protocol when using Telnet to connect to the router. If selected, this keyword must be listed as the first method in the method list.
line	Uses the line password for authentication.
local	Uses the local username database for authentication.
none	Uses no authentication.
radius	Uses RADIUS authentication.
tacacs+	Uses TACACS+ authentication.

NOTE	The **login** command changes only username and privilege level, but it does not execute a shell; therefore, autocommands will not be executed. To execute autocommands under this circumstance, you need to establish a Telnet session back into the router (loopback). Make sure that the router has been configured for secure Telnet sessions if you choose to implement autocommands this way.

Login Authentication Using an Enable Password

Use the **aaa authentication login** command with the **enable** *method* keyword to specify the enable password as the login authentication method. For example, to specify the enable password as the method of user authentication at login when no other method list has been defined, enter the following:

```
aaa authentication login default enable
```

Before you can use the enable password as the login authentication method, you need to define the enable password. For more information about defining enable passwords, refer to Chapter 34, "Configuring Passwords and Privileges."

Login Authentication Using Kerberos

Authentication via Kerberos is different from most other authentication methods: The user's password is never sent to the remote access server. Remote users logging in to the network are prompted for a username. If the key distribution center (KDC) has an entry for that user, it creates an encrypted ticket granting ticket (TGT) with the password for that user and sends it back to the router. The user is then prompted for a password, and the router attempts to decrypt the TGT with that password. If it succeeds, the user is authenticated and the TGT is stored in the user's credential cache on the router.

A user does not need to run the KINIT program to get a TGT to authenticate to the router. This is because KINIT has been integrated into the login procedure in the Cisco IOS implementation of Kerberos.

Use the **aaa authentication login** command with the **krb5** *method* keyword to specify Kerberos as the login authentication method. For example, to specify Kerberos as the method of user authentication at login when no other method list has been defined, enter the following:

```
aaa authentication login default krb5
```

Before you can use Kerberos as the login authentication method, you need to enable communication with the Kerberos security server. For more information about establishing communication with a Kerberos server, refer to Chapter 13, "Configuring Kerberos."

Login Authentication Using a Line Password

Use the **aaa authentication login** command with the **line** *method* keyword to specify the line password as the login authentication method. For example, to specify the line password as the method of user authentication at login when no other method list has been defined, enter the following:

```
aaa authentication login default line
```

Before you can use a line password as the login authentication method, you need to define a line password. For more information about defining line passwords, refer to the "Configuring Line Password Protection" section in this chapter.

Login Authentication Using a Local Password

Use the **aaa authentication login** command with the **local** *method* keyword to specify that the Cisco router or access server will use the local username database for authentication. For example, to specify the local username database as the method of user authentication at login when no other method list has been defined, enter the following:

```
aaa authentication login default local
```

For information about adding users into the local username database, refer to the "Establishing Username Authentication" section in this chapter.

Login Authentication Using RADIUS

Use the **aaa authentication login** command with the **radius** *method* keyword to specify RADIUS as the login authentication method. For example, to specify RADIUS as the method of user authentication at login when no other method list has been defined, enter the following:

```
aaa authentication login default radius
```

Before you can use RADIUS as the login authentication method, you need to enable communication with the RADIUS security server. For more information about establishing communication with a RADIUS server, refer to Chapter 8, "Configuring RADIUS."

Login Authentication Using TACACS+

Use the **aaa authentication login** command with the **tacacs+** *method* keyword to specify TACACS+ as the login authentication method. For example, to specify TACACS+ as the method of user authentication at login when no other method list has been defined, enter the following:

```
aaa authentication login default tacacs+
```

Before you can use TACACS+ as the login authentication method, you need to enable communication with the TACACS+ security server. For more information about establishing communication with a TACACS+ server, refer to Chapter 10, "Configuring TACACS+."

Configuring PPP Authentication Using AAA

Many users access network access servers through dialup via async or ISDN. Dialup via async or ISDN bypasses the command-line interface (CLI) completely; a network protocol (such as PPP or ARA) starts as soon as the connection is established.

The AAA security services facilitate a variety of authentication methods for use on serial interfaces running PPP. Use the **aaa authentication ppp** command to enable AAA authentication no matter which of the supported PPP authentication methods you decide to use.

To configure AAA authentication methods for serial lines using PPP, use the following commands in global configuration mode:

Step	Command	Purpose
1	**aaa new-model**	Enables AAA globally.
2	**aaa authentication ppp** {**default** | *list-name*} *method1* [*method2...*]	Creates a local authentication list.
3	**interface** *interface-type interface-number*	Enters interface configuration mode for the interface to which you want to apply the authentication list.
4	**ppp authentication** {**chap** | **pap** | **chap pap** | **pap chap**} [**if-needed**] {**default** | *list-name*} [**callin**]	Applies the authentication list to a line or set of lines.

With the **aaa authentication ppp** command, you create one or more lists of authentication methods that are tried when a user tries to authenticate via PPP. These lists are applied using the **ppp authentication** line configuration command.

To create a default list that is used when a named list is *not* specified in the **ppp authentication** command, use the *default* argument, followed by the methods you want used in default situations.

For example, to specify the local username database as the default method for user authentication, enter the following:

```
aaa authentication ppp default local
```

The keyword *list-name* is any character string used to name the list you are creating. The keyword *method* refers to the actual method the authentication algorithm tries. The additional methods of authentication are used only if the previous method returns an error, not if it fails. To specify that the authentication should succeed even if all methods return an error, specify *none* as the final method in the command line.

For example, to specify that authentication should succeed even if (in this example) the TACACS+ server returns an error, enter the following:

```
aaa authentication ppp default tacacs+ none
```

NOTE Because *none* allows all users logging in to authenticate successfully, it should be used as a backup method of authentication.

Table 2-2 lists the supported login authentication methods.

Table 2-2 *AAA Authentication PPP Methods*

Keyword	Description
if-needed	Does not authenticate if user has already been authenticated on a TTY line.
krb5	Uses Kerberos 5 for authentication (can only be used for PAP authentication).
local	Uses the local username database for authentication.
none	Uses no authentication.
radius	Uses RADIUS authentication.
tacacs+	Uses TACACS+ authentication.

PPP Authentication Using Kerberos

Use the **aaa authentication ppp** command with the **krb5** *method* keyword to specify Kerberos as the authentication method for use on interfaces running PPP. For example, to specify Kerberos as the method of user authentication when no other method list has been defined, enter the following:

```
aaa authentication ppp default krb5
```

Before you can use Kerberos as the login authentication method, you need to enable communication with the Kerberos security server. For more information about establishing communication with a Kerberos server, refer to Chapter 13, "Configuring Kerberos."

NOTE   Kerberos login authentication works only with PPP PAP authentication.

PPP Authentication Using a Local Password

Use the **aaa authentication ppp** command with the *method* keyword **local** to specify that the Cisco router or access server will use the local username database for authentication. For example, to specify the local username database as the method of authentication for use on lines running PPP when no other method list has been defined, enter the following:

```
aaa authentication ppp default local
```

For information about adding users into the local username database, refer to the "Establishing Username Authentication" section in this chapter.

PPP Authentication Using RADIUS

Use the **aaa authentication ppp** command with the **radius** *method* keyword to specify RADIUS as the authentication method for use on interfaces running PPP. For example, to specify RADIUS as the method of user authentication when no other method list has been defined, enter the following:

```
aaa authentication ppp default radius
```

Before you can use RADIUS as the authentication method, you need to enable communication with the RADIUS security server. For more information about establishing communication with a RADIUS server, refer to Chapter 8, "Configuring RADIUS."

PPP Authentication Using TACACS+

Use the **aaa authentication ppp** command with the **tacacs+** *method* keyword to specify TACACS+ as the authentication method for use on interfaces running PPP. For example, to specify TACACS+ as the method of user authentication when no other method list has been defined, enter the following:

```
aaa authentication ppp default tacacs+
```

Before you can use TACACS+ as the authentication method, you need to enable communication with the TACACS+ security server. For more information about establishing communication with a TACACS+ server, refer to Chapter 10, "Configuring TACACS+."

Configuring AAA Scalability for PPP Requests

You can configure and monitor the number of background processes allocated by the PPP manager in the network access server (NAS) to deal with AAA authentication and authorization requests. In previous Cisco IOS releases, only one background process was allocated to handle all AAA requests for PPP. This meant that parallelism in AAA servers could not be fully exploited. The AAA Scalability feature enables you to configure the number of processes used to handle AAA requests for PPP, thus increasing the number of users that can be simultaneously authenticated or authorized.

To allocate a specific number of background processes to handle AAA requests for PPP, use the following command in global configuration mode:

Command	Purpose
aaa processes *number*	Allocates a specific number of background processes to handle AAA authentication and authorization requests for PPP.

The argument *number* defines the number of background processes earmarked to process AAA authentication and authorization requests for PPP and can be configured for any value from 1 to 2,147,483,647. Because of the way the PPP manager handles requests for PPP, this argument also defines the number of new users that can be simultaneously authenticated. This argument can be increased or decreased at any time.

NOTE	Allocating additional background processes can be expensive. You should configure the minimum number of background processes capable of handling the AAA requests for PPP.

Configuring ARA Authentication Using AAA

With the **aaa authentication arap** command, you create one or more lists of authentication methods that are tried when AppleTalk Remote Access (ARA) users attempt to log in to the router. These lists are used with the **arap authentication** line configuration command.

Use at least the first of the following commands starting in global configuration mode:

Step	Command	Purpose
1	**aaa new-model**	Enables AAA globally.
2	**aaa authentication arap** {**default** | *list-name*} *method1* [*method2*...]	Enables authentication for ARA users.
3	**line** *number*	(Optional) Changes to line configuration mode.
4	**autoselect arap**	(Optional) Enables autoselection of ARA.
5	**autoselect during-login**	(Optional) Starts the ARA session automatically at user login.
6	**arap authentication** *list-name*	(Optional—not needed if **default** is used in the **aaa authentication arap** command) Enables TACACS+ authentication for ARA on a line.

list-name is any character string used to name the list you are creating. *method* refers to the actual list of methods the authentication algorithm tries, in the sequence entered.

To create a default list that is used when a named list is *not* specified in the **arap authentication** command, use the *default* argument, followed by the methods you want to be used in default situations.

The additional methods of authentication are used only if the previous method returns an error, not if it fails. To specify that the authentication should succeed even if all methods return an error, specify *none* as the final method in the command line.

NOTE	Because *none* allows all users logging in to authenticate successfully, it should be used as a backup method of authentication.

Table 2-3 lists the supported login authentication methods.

Table 2-3 *AAA Authentication ARAP Methods*

Keyword	Description
auth-guest	Allows guest logins only if the user has already logged into EXEC.
guest	Allows guest logins.
line	Uses the line password for authentication.
local	Uses the local username database for authentication.
radius	Uses RADIUS authentication.
tacacs+	Uses TACACS+ authentication.

For example, to create a default AAA authentication method list used with the ARA protocol, enter the following:

```
aaa authentication arap default if-needed none
```

To create the same authentication method list for the ARA protocol but name the list *MIS-access,* enter the following:

```
aaa authentication arap MIS-access if-needed none
```

ARA Authentication Allowing Authorized Guest Logins

Use the **aaa authentication arap** command with the **auth-guest** keyword to allow guest logins only if the user has already successfully logged in to the EXEC. This method must be the first listed in the ARA authentication method list, but it can be followed by other methods if it does not succeed. For example, to allow all authorized guest logins—meaning logins by users who have already successfully logged in to the EXEC—as the default method of authentication, using RADIUS only if that method fails, enter the following:

```
aaa authentication arap default auth-guest radius
```

NOTE   By default, guest logins through ARA are disabled when you initialize AAA. To allow guest logins, you must use the **aaa authentication arap** command with either the **guest** or **auth-guest** keyword.

ARA Authentication Allowing Guest Logins

Use the **aaa authentication arap** command with the *guest* keyword to allow guest logins. This method must be the first listed in the ARA authentication method list but it can be followed by other methods if it does not succeed. For example, to allow all guest logins as the default method of authentication, using RADIUS only if that method fails, enter the following:

```
aaa authentication arap default guest radius
```

ARA Authentication Using a Line Password

Use the **aaa authentication arap** command with the *method* keyword **line** to specify the line password as the authentication method. For example, to specify the line password as the method of ARA user authentication when no other method list has been defined, enter the following:

```
aaa authentication arap default line
```

Before you can use a line password as the ARA authentication method, you need to define a line password. For more information about defining line passwords, refer to the "Configuring Line Password Protection" section in this chapter.

ARA Authentication Using a Local Password

Use the **aaa authentication arap** command with the *method* keyword **local** to specify that the Cisco router or access server will use the local username database for authentication. For example, to specify the local username database as the method of ARA user authentication when no other method list has been defined, enter the following:

```
aaa authentication arap default local
```

For information about adding users to the local username database, refer to the "Establishing Username Authentication" section in this chapter.

ARA Authentication Using RADIUS

Use the **aaa authentication arap** command with the **radius** *method* keyword to specify RADIUS as the ARA authentication method. For example, to specify RADIUS as the method of ARA user authentication when no other method list has been defined, enter the following:

```
aaa authentication arap default radius
```

Before you can use RADIUS as the ARA authentication method, you need to enable communication with the RADIUS security server. For more information about establishing communication with a RADIUS server, refer to Chapter 8, "Configuring RADIUS."

ARA Authentication Using TACACS+

Use the **aaa authentication arap** command with the **tacacs+** *method* keyword to specify TACACS+ as the ARA authentication method. For example, to specify TACACS+ as the method of ARA user authentication when no other method list has been defined, enter the following:

```
aaa authentication arap default tacacs+
```

Before you can use TACACS+ as the ARA authentication method, you need to enable communication with the TACACS+ security server. For more information about establishing communication with a TACACS+ server, refer to Chapter 10, "Configuring TACACS+."

Configuring NASI Authentication Using AAA

With the **aaa authentication nasi** command, you create one or more lists of authentication methods that are tried when NetWare Asynchronous Services Interface (NASI) users attempt to log in to the router. These lists are used with the **nasi authentication** line configuration command.

Use at least the first of the following commands, starting in global configuration mode:

Step	Command	Purpose
1	**aaa new-model**	Enables AAA globally.
2	**aaa authentication nasi** {**default**	*list-name*} *method1* [*method2*...]	Enables authentication for NASI users.
3	**line** *number*	(Optional—not needed if **default** is used in the **aaa authentication nasi** command.) Changes to line configuration mode.
4	**nasi authentication** *list-name*	(Optional—not needed if **default** is used in the **aaa authentication nasi** command) Enables authentication for NASI on a line.

list-name is any character string used to name the list you are creating. *method* refers to the actual list of methods the authentication algorithm tries, in the sequence entered.

To create a default list that is used when a named list is *not* specified in the **aaa authentication nasi** command, use the *default* argument, followed by the methods you want to be used in default situations.

The additional methods of authentication are used only if the previous method returns an error, not if it fails. To specify that the authentication should succeed even if all methods return an error, specify *none* as the final method in the command line.

NOTE	Because *none* allows all users logging in to authenticate successfully, it should be used as a backup method of authentication.

Table 2-4 lists the supported login authentication methods.

Table 2-4 *AAA Authentication NASI Methods*

Keyword	Description
enable	Uses the enable password for authentication.
line	Uses the line password for authentication.
local	Uses the local username database for authentication.
none	Uses no authentication.
tacacs+	Uses TACACS+ authentication.

NASI Authentication Using an Enable Password

Use the **aaa authentication nasi** command with the argument **enable** to specify the enable password as the authentication method. For example, to specify the enable password as the method of NASI user authentication when no other method list has been defined, enter the following:

```
aaa authentication nasi default enable
```

Before you can use the enable password as the authentication method, you need to define the enable password. For more information about defining enable passwords, refer to Chapter 34, "Configuring Passwords and Privileges."

NASI Authentication Using a Line Password

Use the **aaa authentication nasi** command with the *method* keyword **line** to specify the line password as the authentication method. For example, to specify the line password as the method of NASI user authentication when no other method list has been defined, enter the following:

```
aaa authentication nasi default line
```

Before you can use a line password as the NASI authentication method, you need to define a line password. For more information about defining line passwords, refer to the "Configuring Line Password Protection" section in this chapter.

NASI Authentication Using a Local Password

Use the **aaa authentication nasi** command with the *method* keyword **local** to specify that the Cisco router or access server will use the local username database for authentication information. For example, to specify the local username database as the method of NASI user authentication when no other method list has been defined, enter the following:

```
aaa authentication nasi default local
```

For information about adding users to the local username database, refer to the "Establishing Username Authentication" section in this chapter.

NASI Authentication Using TACACS+

Use the **aaa authentication nasi** command with the **tacacs+** *method* keyword to specify TACACS+ as the NASI authentication method. For example, to specify TACACS+ as the method of NASI user authentication when no other method list has been defined, enter the following:

```
aaa authentication nasi default tacacs+
```

Before you can use TACACS+ as the authentication method, you need to enable communication with the TACACS+ security server. For more information about establishing communication with a TACACS+ server, refer to Chapter 10, "Configuring TACACS+."

Specifying the Amount of Time for Login Input

The **timeout login response** command allows you to specify how long the system will wait for login input (such as username and password) before timing out. The default login value is 30 seconds; with the **timeout login response** command, you can specify a timeout value from 1 to 300 seconds. Use the following command in global configuration mode to change the login timeout value from the default of 30 seconds:

Command	Purpose
timeout login response *seconds*	Specifies how long the system will wait for login information before timing out.

Enabling Password Protection at the Privileged Level

Use the **aaa authentication enable default** command to create a series of authentication methods that determine whether a user can access the privileged EXEC command level. You can specify up to four authentication methods. The additional methods of authentication are used only if the previous method returns an error, not if it fails. To specify that the authentication succeed even if all methods return an error, specify *none* as the final method in the command line.

Use the following command in global configuration mode:

Command	Purpose
aaa authentication enable default *method1* [*method2...*]	Enables user ID and password checking for users requesting privileged EXEC level.

method refers to the actual list of methods the authentication algorithm tries, in the sequence entered. Table 2-5 lists the supported login authentication methods.

Table 2-5 *AAA Authentication Enable Default Methods*

Keyword	Description
enable	Uses the enable password for authentication.
line	Uses the line password for authentication.
none	Uses no authentication.
radius	Uses RADIUS authentication.
tacacs+	Uses TACACS+ authentication.

Enabling an Authentication Override

To configure the Cisco IOS software to check the local user database for authentication before attempting another form of authentication, use the **aaa authentication local-override** command. This command is useful when you want to configure an override to the normal authentication process for certain personnel (such as system administrators).

Use the following command in global configuration mode:

Command	Purpose
aaa authentication local-override	Creates an override for authentication.

Changing the Text Displayed at the Password Prompt

Use the **aaa authentication password-prompt** command to change the default text that the Cisco IOS software displays when prompting a user to enter a password. This command changes the password prompt for the enable password as well as for login passwords that are not supplied by remote security servers. The **no** form of this command returns the password prompt to the following default value:

`Password:`

The **aaa authentication password-prompt** command does not change any dialog that is supplied by a remote TACACS+ or RADIUS server.

Use the following command in global configuration mode:

Command	Purpose
aaa authentication password-prompt *text-string*	Changes the default text displayed when a user is prompted to enter a password.

Configuring Message Banners for AAA Authentication

AAA supports the use of configurable, personalized login and failed-login banners. You can configure message banners that will be displayed when a user logs in to the system to be authenticated using AAA and when authentication, for whatever reason, fails.

Configuring a Login Banner

To create a login banner, you need to configure a delimiting character, which notifies the system that the following text string is to be displayed as the banner, and then the text string itself. The delimiting character is repeated at the end of the text string to signify the end of the banner. The delimiting character can be any single character in the extended ASCII character set, but once defined as the delimiter, that character cannot be used in the text string making up the banner.

To configure a banner that will be displayed whenever a user logs in (replacing the default message for login), use the following commands in global configuration mode:

Step	Command	Purpose
1	**aaa new-model**	Enables AAA.
2	**aaa authentication banner** *delimiter string delimiter*	Creates a personalized login banner.

The maximum number of characters that can be displayed in the login banner is 2996.

Configuring a Failed-Login Banner

To create a failed-login banner, you need to configure a delimiting character, which notifies the system that the following text string is to be displayed as the banner, and then the text string itself. The delimiting character is repeated at the end of the text string to signify the end of the failed-login banner. The delimiting character can be any single character in the extended ASCII character set, but once defined as the delimiter, that character cannot be used in the text string making up the banner.

To configure a message that will be displayed whenever a user fails login (replacing the default message for failed login), use the following commands in global configuration mode:

Step	Command	Purpose
1	**aaa new-model**	Enables AAA.
2	**aaa authentication fail-message** *delimiter string delimiter*	Creates a message to be displayed when a user fails login.

The maximum number of characters that can be displayed in the failed-login banner is 2996.

Enabling Double Authentication

Double authentication provides additional authentication for PPP sessions. Previously, PPP sessions could be authenticated only by using a single authentication method: either Password Authentication Protocol (PAP) or Challenge Handshake Authentication Protocol (CHAP). Double authentication requires remote users to pass a second stage of authentication—after CHAP or PAP authentication—before gaining network access.

This second ("double") authentication requires a password that is known to the user but *not* stored on the user's remote host. Therefore, the second authentication is specific to a user, not to a host. This provides an additional level of security that will be effective even if information from the remote host is stolen. In addition, this also provides greater flexibility by allowing customized network privileges for each user.

The second-stage authentication can use one-time passwords such as token card passwords, which are not supported by CHAP. If one-time passwords are used, a stolen user password is of no use to the perpetrator.

How Double Authentication Works

With double authentication, there are two authentication/authorization stages. These two stages occur after a remote user dials in and a PPP session is initiated.

In the first stage, the user logs in using the remote host name; CHAP (or PAP) authenticates the remote host, and then PPP negotiates with AAA to authorize the remote host. In this process, the network access privileges associated with the remote host are assigned to the user.

NOTE	Cisco suggests that the network administrator restrict authorization at this first stage to allow only Telnet connections to the local host.

In the second stage, the remote user must Telnet to the network access server to be authenticated. When the remote user logs in, the user must be authenticated with AAA login authentication. The user then must enter the **access-profile** command to be reauthorized using AAA. When this authorization is complete, the user has been double authenticated, and can access the network according to per-user network privileges.

The system administrator determines what network privileges remote users will have after each stage of authentication by configuring appropriate parameters on a security server. To use double authentication, the user must activate it by issuing the **access-profile** command.

CAUTION   Double authentication can cause certain undesirable events if multiple hosts share a PPP connection to a network access server, as shown in Figure 2-2.

First, if a user, Bob, initiates a PPP session and activates double authentication at the network access server (per Figure 2-2), any other user will automatically have the same network privileges as Bob until Bob's PPP session expires. This happens because Bob's authorization profile is applied to the network access server's interface during the PPP session, and any PPP traffic from other users will use the PPP session Bob established.

Second, if Bob initiates a PPP session and activates double authentication, and then—before Bob's PPP session has expired—another user, Jane, executes the **access-profile** command (or, if she Telnets to the network access server and **autocommand access-profile** is executed), a reauthorization will occur and Jane's authorization profile will be applied to the interface—replacing Bob's profile. This can disrupt or halt Bob's PPP traffic, or grant Bob additional authorization privileges he should not have.

Figure 2-2   *Possibly Risky Topology: Multiple Hosts Share a PPP Connection to a Network Access Server*

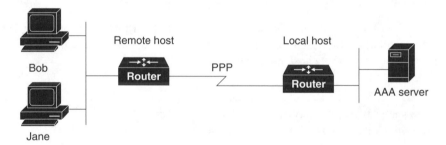

Configuring Double Authentication

To configure double authentication, you must complete the following steps:

1   Enable AAA by using the **aaa-new model** global configuration command. For more information about enabling AAA, refer to Chapter 1, "AAA Overview."

2   Use the **aaa authentication** command to configure your network access server to use login and PPP authentication method lists, and then apply those method lists to the appropriate lines or interfaces.

3   Use the **aaa authorization** command to configure AAA network authorization at login. For more information about configuring network authorization, refer to Chapter 4, "Configuring Authorization."

4 Configure security protocol parameters (for example, RADIUS or TACACS+). For more information about RADIUS, refer to Chapter 8, "Configuring RADIUS." For more information about TACACS+, refer to Chapter 10, "Configuring TACACS+."

5 Use access control list (ACL) AV pairs on the security server that the user can use to connect to the local host only by establishing a Telnet connection.

6 (Optional) Configure the **access-profile** command as an autocommand. If you configure the autocommand, remote users will not have to manually enter the **access-profile** command to access authorized rights associated with their personal user profile.

NOTE   If the **access-profile** command is configured as an autocommand, users will still have to Telnet to the local host and log in to complete double authentication.

Follow these rules, which relate to the default behavior of the **access-profile** command, when creating the user-specific authorization statements:

● Use valid AV pairs when configuring ACL AV pairs on the security server. For a list of valid AV pairs, refer to Chapter 3, "Authentication Commands."

● If you want remote users to use the interface's existing authorization (that which existed prior to the second-stage authentication/authorization), but you want them to have different ACLs, you should specify *only* ACL AV pairs in the user-specific authorization definition. This might be desirable if you set up a default authorization profile to apply to the remote host, but want to apply specific ACLs to specific users.

● When these user-specific authorization statements are later applied to the interface, they can either be *added to* the existing interface configuration, or *replace* the existing interface configuration— depending on which form of the **access-profile** command is used to authorize the user. You should understand how the **access-profile** command works before configuring the authorization statements.

● If you will be using ISDN or Multilink PPP, you must also configure virtual templates at the local host.

To troubleshoot double authentication, use the **debug aaa per-user** debug command.

Accessing a User Profile After Double Authentication

In double authentication, when a remote user establishes a PPP link to the local host using the local host name, the remote host is CHAP (or PAP) authenticated. After CHAP (or PAP) authentication, PPP negotiates with AAA to assign network access privileges associated with the remote host to the user. (Cisco suggests that privileges at this stage be restricted to allow the user to connect to the local host only by establishing a Telnet connection.)

When the user needs to initiate the second phase of double authentication, establishing a Telnet connection to the local host, the user enters a personal username and password (different from the CHAP or PAP username and password). This action causes AAA reauthentication to occur according to the personal username/password. The initial rights associated with the local host, though, are still in place. By using the **access-profile** command, the rights associated with the local host are replaced by or merged with those defined for the user in the user's profile.

Use the following command in EXEC configuration mode:

Command	Purpose
access-profile [**merge**	**replace**	**ignore-sanity-checks**]	Accesses the rights associated with the user after double authentication.

If you configured the **access-profile** command to be executed as an autocommand, it will be executed automatically after the remote user logs in.

Enabling Automated Double Authentication

You can make the double authentication process easier for users by implementing automated double authentication. Automated double authentication provides all the security benefits of double authentication, but offers a simpler, more user-friendly interface for remote users. With double authentication, a second level of user authentication is achieved when the user Telnets to the network access server or router and enters a username and password. With automated double authentication, the user does not have to Telnet to the network access server; instead, the user responds to a dialog box that requests a username and password or personal identification number (PIN). To use the automated double authentication feature, the remote user hosts must be running a companion client application. As of Cisco IOS Release 12.0, the only client application software available is the Glacier Bay application server software for PCs.

NOTE	Automated double authentication, like the existing double authentication feature, is for Multilink PPP ISDN connections only. Automated double authentication cannot be used with other protocols such as X.25 or SLIP.

Configuring Double Authentication

Automated double authentication is an enhancement to the existing double authentication feature. To configure automated double authentication, you must first configure double authentication by completing the following steps:

1 Enable AAA by using the **aaa-new model** global configuration command. For more information about enabling AAA, refer to Chapter 1, "AAA Overview."

2 Use the **aaa authentication** command to configure your network access server to use login and PPP authentication method lists, and then apply those method lists to the appropriate lines or interfaces.

3 Use the **aaa authorization** command to configure AAA network authorization at login. For more information about configuring network authorization, refer to Chapter 4, "Configuring Authorization."

4 Configure security protocol parameters (for example, RADIUS or TACACS+). For more information about RADIUS, refer to Chapter 8, "Configuring RADIUS." For more information about TACACS+, refer to Chapter 10, "Configuring TACACS+."

5 Use ACL AV pairs on the security server that the user can use to connect to the local host only by establishing a Telnet connection.

6 (Optional) Configure the **access-profile** command as an autocommand. If you configure the autocommand, remote users will not have to manually enter the **access-profile** command to access authorized rights associated with their personal user profile.

NOTE   If the **access-profile** command is configured as an autocommand, users will still have to Telnet to the local host and log in to complete double authentication.

Follow these rules, which relate to the default behavior of the **access-profile** command, when creating the user-specific authorization statements:

● Use valid AV pairs when configuring ACL AV pairs on the security server. For a list of valid AV pairs, refer to Chapter 3, "Authentication Commands."

● If you want remote users to use the interface's existing authorization (that which existed prior to the second stage authentication/authorization), but you want them to have different ACLs, you should specify *only* ACL AV pairs in the user-specific authorization definition. This might be desirable if you set up a default authorization profile to apply to the remote host, but want to apply specific ACLs to specific users.

● When these user-specific authorization statements are later applied to the interface, they can either be *added to* the existing interface configuration, or *replace* the existing interface configuration—depending on which form of the **access-profile** command is used to authorize the user. You should understand how the **access-profile** command works before configuring the authorization statements.

● If you will be using ISDN or Multilink PPP, you must also configure virtual templates at the local host.

To troubleshoot double authentication, use the **debug aaa per-user** debug command.

After you have configured double authentication, you are ready to configure the automation enhancement.

To configure automated double authentication, use the following commands, starting in global configuration mode:

Step	Command	Purpose
1	**ip trigger-authentication** [**timeout** *seconds*] [**port** *number*]	Enables automation of double authentication.
2	**interface bri** *number* or **interface serial** *number***:23**	Selects an ISDN BRI or ISDN PRI interface and enters the interface configuration mode.
3	**ip trigger-authentication**	Applies automated double authentication to the interface.

To troubleshoot automated double authentication, use the following commands in privileged EXEC mode:

Step	Command	Purpose
1	**show ip trigger-authentication**	Views the list of remote hosts for which automated double authentication has been attempted (successfully or unsuccessfully).
2	**clear ip trigger-authentication**	Clears the list of remote hosts for which automated double authentication has been attempted. (This clears the table displayed by the **show ip trigger-authentication** command.)
3	**debug ip trigger-authentication**	Views **debug** output related to automated double authentication.

Non-AAA Authentication Methods

This section discusses the following non-AAA authentication tasks:

- Configuring Line Password Protection
- Establishing Username Authentication
- Enabling CHAP or PAP Authentication
- Using MS-CHAP
- Configuring TACACS and Extended TACACS Password Protection

Configuring Line Password Protection

You can provide access control on a terminal line by entering the password and establishing password checking. To do so, use the following commands in line configuration mode:

Step	Command	Purpose
1	**password** *password*	Assigns a password to a terminal or other device on a line.
2	**login**	Enables password checking at login.

The password checker is case sensitive and can include spaces; for example, the password *Secret* is different from the password *secret*, and *two words* is an acceptable password.

You can disable line password verification by disabling password checking. To do so, use the following command in line configuration mode:

Command	Purpose
no login	Disables password checking or allows access to a line without password verification.

If you configure line password protection and then configure TACACS or extended TACACS, the TACACS username and password take precedence over line passwords. If you have not yet implemented a security policy, Cisco recommends that you use AAA.

NOTE	The **login** command changes only username and privilege level, but it does not execute a shell; therefore, autocommands will not be executed. To execute autocommands under this circumstance, you need to establish a Telnet session back into the router (loopback). Make sure that the router has been configured for secure Telnet sessions if you choose to implement autocommands this way.

Establishing Username Authentication

You can create a username-based authentication system, which is useful in the following situations:

- To provide a TACACS-like username and encrypted password-authentication system for networks that cannot support TACACS

- To provide special-case logins; for example, access list verification, no password verification, autocommand execution at login, and "no escape" situations

To establish username authentication, use the following commands in global configuration mode as needed for your system configuration:

Step	Command	Purpose
1	**username** *name* [**nopassword** | **password** *encryption-type* **password**]	Establishes username authentication with encrypted passwords.
		or
	username *name* [**access-class** *number*]	(Optional) Establishes username authentication by access list.
2	**username** *name* **privilege** *level*	(Optional) Sets the privilege level for the user.
3	**username** *name* [**autocommand** *command*]	(Optional) Specifies a command to automatically execute.
4	**username** *name* [**noescape**] [**nohangup**]	(Optional) Sets a "no escape" login environment.

The keyword **noescape** prevents users from using escape characters on the hosts to which they are connected. The **nohangup** feature does not disconnect after using the autocommand.

CAUTION   Passwords will be displayed in clear text in your configuration unless you enable the **service password-encryption** command. For more information about the **service password-encryption** command, refer to Chapter 35, "Passwords and Privileges Commands."

Enabling CHAP or PAP Authentication

One of the most common transport protocols used in Internet service providers' (ISPs') dial solutions is PPP. Traditionally, remote users dial in to an access server to initiate a PPP session. After PPP has been negotiated, remote users are connected to the ISP network and to the Internet.

Because ISPs want only customers to connect to their access servers, remote users are required to authenticate to the access server before they can start up a PPP session. Normally, a remote user authenticates by typing in a username and password when prompted by the access server. Although this is a workable solution, it is difficult to administer and awkward for the remote user.

A better solution is to use the authentication protocols built into PPP. In this case, the remote user dials in to the access server and starts up a minimal subset of PPP with the access server. This does not give the remote user access to the ISP's network—it merely allows the access server to talk to the remote device.

PPP currently supports two authentication protocols: PAP and CHAP. Both are specified in RFC 1334 and are supported on synchronous and asynchronous interfaces. Authentication via PAP or CHAP is equivalent to typing in a username and password when prompted by the server. CHAP is considered to be more secure because the remote user's password is never sent across the connection.

PPP (with or without PAP or CHAP authentication) is also supported in dialout solutions. An access server utilizes a dialout feature when it initiates a call to a remote device and attempts to start up a transport protocol such as PPP.

NOTE   To use CHAP or PAP, you must be running PPP encapsulation.

When CHAP is enabled on an interface and a remote device attempts to connect to it, the access server sends a CHAP packet to the remote device. The CHAP packet requests or "challenges" the remote device to respond. The challenge packet consists of an ID, a random number, and the host name of the local router.

When the remote device receives the challenge packet, it concatenates the ID, the remote device's password, and the random number, and then encrypts all of it using the remote device's password. The remote device sends the results back to the access server, along with the name associated with the password used in the encryption process.

When the access server receives the response, it uses the name it received to retrieve a password stored in its user database. The retrieved password should be the same password the remote device used in its encryption process. The access server then encrypts the concatenated information with the newly retrieved password; if the result matches the result sent in the response packet, authentication succeeds.

The benefit of using CHAP authentication is that the remote device's password is never transmitted in clear text. This prevents other devices from stealing it and gaining illegal access to the ISP's network.

CHAP transactions occur only at the time a link is established. The access server does not request a password during the rest of the call. (The local device can, however, respond to such requests from other devices during a call.)

When PAP is enabled, the remote router attempting to connect to the access server is required to send an authentication request. If the username and password specified in the authentication request are accepted, the Cisco IOS software sends an authentication acknowledgment.

After you have enabled CHAP or PAP, the access server will require authentication from remote devices dialing in to the access server. If the remote device does not support the enabled protocol, the call will be dropped.

To use CHAP or PAP, you must perform the following tasks:

1   Enable PPP encapsulation.

2   Enable CHAP or PAP on the interface.

3   For CHAP, configure host name authentication and the secret or password for each remote system with which authentication is required.

Enabling PPP Encapsulation

To enable PPP encapsulation, use the following command in interface configuration mode:

Command	Purpose
encapsulation ppp	Enables PPP on an interface.

Enabling PAP or CHAP Authentication

To enable CHAP or PAP authentication on an interface configured for PPP encapsulation, use the following command in interface configuration mode:

Command	Purpose
ppp authentication {**chap** | **chap pap** | **pap chap** | **pap**} [**if-needed**] [*list-name* | **default**] [**callin**] [**one-time**]	Defines the authentication methods supported and the order in which they are used.

If you configure **ppp authentication chap** on an interface, all incoming calls on that interface that initiate a PPP connection will have to be authenticated using CHAP; likewise, if you configure **ppp authentication pap**, all incoming calls that start a PPP connection will have to be authenticated via PAP. If you configure **ppp authentication chap pap**, the access server will attempt to authenticate all incoming calls that start a PPP session with CHAP. If the remote device does not support CHAP, the access server will try to authenticate the call using PAP. If the remote device doesn't support either CHAP or PAP, authentication will fail and the call will be dropped. If you configure **ppp authentication pap chap**, the access server will attempt to authenticate all incoming calls that start a PPP session with PAP. If the remote device does not support PAP, the access server will try to authenticate the call using CHAP. If the remote device doesn't support either protocol, authentication will fail and the call will be dropped. If you configure the **ppp authentication** command with the **callin** keyword, the access server will authenticate the remote device only if the remote device initiated the call.

Authentication method lists and the **one-time** keyword are available only if you have enabled AAA—they will not be available if you are using TACACS or extended TACACS. If you specify the name of an authentication method list with the **ppp authentication** command, PPP will attempt to authenticate the connection using the methods defined in the specified method list. If AAA is enabled and no method list is defined by name, PPP will attempt to authenticate the connection using the methods defined as the default. The **ppp authentication** command with the **one-time** keyword enables support for one-time passwords during authentication.

The **if-needed** keyword is available only if you are using TACACS or extended TACACS. The **ppp authentication** command with the **if-needed** keyword means that PPP will authenticate the remote device via PAP or CHAP only if they have not yet authenticated during the life of the current call. If the remote device authenticated via a standard login procedure and initiated PPP from the EXEC prompt, PPP will not authenticate via CHAP if **ppp authentication chap if-needed** is configured on the interface.

CAUTION	If you use a *list-name* that has not been configured with the **aaa authentication ppp** command, you disable PPP on the line.

For information about adding a **username** entry for each remote system from which the local router or access server requires authentication, see the "Establishing Username Authentication" section.

Inbound and Outbound Authentication

PPP supports two-way authentication. Normally, when a remote device dials in to an access server, the access server requests that the remote device prove that it is allowed access. This is known as *inbound authentication*. At the same time, the remote device can also request that the access server prove that it is who it says it is. This is known as *outbound authentication*. An access server also does outbound authentication when it initiates a call to a remote device.

Enabling Outbound PAP Authentication

To enable outbound PAP authentication, use the following command in interface configuration mode:

Command	Purpose
ppp pap sent-username *username* **password** *password*	Enables outbound PAP authentication.

The access server uses the username and password specified by the **ppp pap sent-username** command to authenticate itself whenever it initiates a call to a remote device or when it has to respond to a remote device's request for outbound authentication.

Creating a Common CHAP Password

For remote CHAP authentication only, you can configure your router to create a common CHAP secret password to use in response to challenges from an unknown peer; for example, if your router calls a rotary of routers (either from another vendor, or running an older version of the Cisco IOS software) to which a new (that is, unknown) router has been added. The **ppp chap password** command allows you to replace several username and password configuration commands with a single copy of this command on any dialer interface or asynchronous group interface.

To enable a router calling a collection of routers to configure a common CHAP secret password, use the following command in interface configuration mode:

Command	Purpose
ppp chap password *secret*	Enables a router calling a collection of routers to configure a common CHAP secret password.

Refusing CHAP Authentication Requests

To refuse CHAP authentication from peers requesting it, meaning that CHAP authentication is disabled for all calls, use the following command in interface configuration mode:

Command	Purpose
ppp chap refuse [**callin**]	Refuses CHAP authentication from peers requesting CHAP authentication.

If the **callin** keyword is used, the router will refuse to answer CHAP authentication challenges received from the peer, but will still require the peer to answer any CHAP challenges the router sends.

If outbound PAP has been enabled (using the **ppp pap sent-username** command), PAP will be suggested as the authentication method in the refusal packet.

Delaying CHAP Authentication Until the Peer Authenticates

To specify that the router will not authenticate to a peer requesting CHAP authentication until after the peer has authenticated itself to the router, use the following command in interface configuration mode:

Command	Purpose
ppp chap wait *secret*	Configures the router to delay CHAP authentication until after the peer has authenticated itself to the router.

This command (which is the default) specifies that the router will not authenticate to a peer requesting CHAP authentication until the peer has authenticated itself to the router. The **no ppp chap wait** command specifies that the router will respond immediately to an authentication challenge.

Using MS-CHAP

Microsoft CHAP (MS-CHAP) is the Microsoft version of CHAP and is an extension to RFC 1994. Like the standard version of CHAP, MS-CHAP is used for PPP authentication; in this case, authentication occurs between a PC using Microsoft Windows NT or Microsoft Windows 95 and a Cisco router or access server acting as a network access server.

MS-CHAP differs from the standard CHAP as follows:

- MS-CHAP is enabled by negotiating CHAP Algorithm 0x80 in LCP option 3, Authentication Protocol.

- The MS-CHAP Response packet is in a format designed to be compatible with Microsoft Windows NT 3.5 and 3.51, Microsoft Windows 95, and Microsoft LAN Manager 2.*x*. This format does not require the authenticator to store a clear or reversibly encrypted password.

- MS-CHAP provides an authenticator-controlled authentication retry mechanism.

- MS-CHAP provides an authenticator-controlled change password mechanism.

- MS-CHAP defines a set of reason-for failure codes returned in the Failure packet message field.

Depending on the security protocols you have implemented, PPP authentication using MS-CHAP can be used with or without AAA security services. If you have enabled AAA, PPP authentication using MS-CHAP can be used in conjunction with both TACACS+ and RADIUS. Two new vendor-specific RADIUS attributes (IETF Attribute 26) were added to enable RADIUS to support MS-CHAP. These new attributes are listed in Table 2-6.

Table 2-6 *Vendor-Specific RADIUS Attributes for MS-CHAP*

Vendor-ID Number	Vendor-Type Number	Vendor-Proprietary Attribute	Description
311	11	MSCHAP-Challenge	Contains the challenge sent by a network access server to an MS-CHAP user. It can be used in both Access-Request and Access-Challenge packets.
311	1	MSCHAP-Response	Contains the response value provided by a PPP MS-CHAP user in response to the challenge. It is used only in Access-Request packets. This attribute is identical to the PPP CHAP Identifier.

Use the following commands in interface configuration mode:

Step	Command	Purpose
1	**encapsulation ppp**	Enables PPP encapsulation.
2	**ppp authentication ms-chap** [**if-needed**] [*list-name* | **default**] [**callin**] [**one-time**]	Defines PPP authentication using MS-CHAP.

If you configure **ppp authentication ms-chap** on an interface, all incoming calls on that interface that initiate a PPP connection will have to be authenticated using MS-CHAP. If you configure the **ppp authentication** command with the **callin** keyword, the access server will authenticate the remote device only if the remote device initiated the call.

Authentication method lists and the **one-time** keyword are available only if you have enabled AAA— they will not be available if you are using TACACS or extended TACACS. If you specify the name of an authentication method list with the **ppp authentication** command, PPP will attempt to authenticate the connection using the methods defined in the specified method list. If AAA is enabled and no method list is defined by name, PPP will attempt to authenticate the connection using the methods defined as the default. The **ppp authentication** command with the **one-time** keyword enables support for one-time passwords during authentication.

The **if-needed** keyword is available only if you are using TACACS or extended TACACS. The **ppp authentication** command with the **if-needed** keyword means that PPP will authenticate the remote device via MS-CHAP only if that device has not yet authenticated during the life of the current call. If the remote device authenticated through a standard login procedure and initiated PPP from the EXEC prompt, PPP will not authenticate through MS-CHAP if **ppp authentication chap if-needed** is configured.

NOTE   If PPP authentication using MS-CHAP is used with username authentication, you must include the MS-CHAP secret in the local username/password database. For more information about username authentication, refer to the "Establishing Username Authentication" section in this chapter.

Configuring TACACS and Extended TACACS Password Protection

You can use TACACS or extended TACACS to control login access to the router. Perform the tasks in the following sections:

- Setting TACACS Password Protection at the User Level
- Disabling Password Checking at the User Level

Before performing these tasks, you must have enabled communication with a TACACS host on the network. For more information, refer to Chapter 11, "Configuring TACACS and Extended TACACS."

Setting TACACS Password Protection at the User Level

You can enable TACACS password checking at login by using the following command in line configuration mode:

Command	Purpose
login tacacs	Sets the TACACS-style user ID and password-checking mechanism.

Disabling Password Checking at the User Level

If a TACACS server does not respond to a login request, the Cisco IOS software denies the request by default. However, you can prevent login failure in two ways:

- Allow a user to access privileged EXEC mode if that user enters the password set by the **enable** command.

- Ensure a successful login by allowing the user to access the privileged EXEC mode without further question.

To specify one of these features, use either of the following commands in global configuration mode:

Command	Purpose
tacacs-server last-resort password or **tacacs-server last-resort succeed**	Allows a user to access privileged EXEC mode, or sets last resort options for logins.

Authentication Examples

This section contains the following authentication configuration examples:

- RADIUS Authentication Examples

- TACACS+ Authentication Examples

- TACACS and Extended TACACS Authentication Examples

- Kerberos Authentication Examples

- AAA Scalability Example

- Login and Failed Banner Configuration Examples

- Double Authentication Configuration Examples

- Automated Double Authentication Configuration Example

- MS-CHAP Configuration Example

RADIUS Authentication Examples

This section provides two sample configurations using RADIUS.

The following example shows how to configure the router to authenticate and authorize using RADIUS:

```
aaa authentication login radius-login RADIUS local
aaa authentication ppp radius-ppp if-needed radius
aaa authorization exec radius if-authenticated
aaa authorization network radius
line 3
login authentication radius-login
interface serial 0
ppp authentication radius-ppp
```

The lines in this sample RADIUS authentication and authorization configuration are defined as follows:

- The **aaa authentication login radius-login RADIUS local** command configures the router to use RADIUS for authentication at the login prompt. If RADIUS returns an error, the user is authenticated using the local database.

- The **aaa authentication ppp radius-ppp if-needed radius** command configures the Cisco IOS software to use PPP authentication using CHAP or PAP if the user has not already logged in. If the EXEC facility has authenticated the user, PPP authentication is not performed.

- The **aaa authorization exec radius if-authenticated** command queries the RADIUS database for information that is used during EXEC authorization, such as autocommands and privilege levels, but provides authorization only if the user has successfully authenticated.

- The **aaa authorization network radius** command queries RADIUS for network authorization, address assignment, and other access lists.

- The **login authentication radius-login** command enables the use-radius method list for line 3.

- The **ppp authentication radius-ppp** command enables the user-radius method list for serial interface 0.

The following example shows how to configure the router to prompt for and verify a username and password, authorize the user's EXEC level, and specify it as the method of authorization for privilege level 2. In this example, if a local username is entered at the username prompt, that username is used for authentication.

If the user is authenticated using the local database, EXEC authorization using RADIUS will fail because no data is saved from the RADIUS authentication. The method list also uses the local database to find an autocommand. If there is no autocommand, the user becomes the EXEC user. If the user then attempts to issue commands that are set at privilege level 2, TACACS+ is used to attempt to authorize the command.

```
aaa authentication local-override
aaa authentication login default radius local
aaa authorization exec radius local
aaa authorization command 2 tacacs+ if-authenticated
```

The lines in this sample RADIUS authentication and authorization configuration are defined as follows:

- The **aaa authentication local-override** command specifies that the username prompt appear before authentication starts and that the authentication always use the local database if the user has a local account.

- The **aaa authentication login default radius local** command specifies that the username and password be verified by RADIUS or, if RADIUS is not responding, by the router's local user database.

- The **aaa authorization exec radius local** command specifies that RADIUS authentication information be used to set the user's EXEC level if the user authenticates with RADIUS. If no RADIUS information is used, this command specifies that the local user database be used for EXEC authorization.

- The **aaa authorization command 2 tacacs+ if-authenticated** command specifies TACACS+ authorization for commands set at privilege level 2, if the user has already successfully authenticated.

TACACS+ Authentication Examples

The following example configures TACACS+ as the security protocol to be used for PPP authentication:

```
aaa new-model
aaa authentication ppp test tacacs+ local
interface serial 0
ppp authentication chap pap test
tacacs-server host 10.1.2.3
tacacs-server key goaway
```

The lines in this sample TACACS+ authentication configuration are defined as follows:

- The **aaa new-model** command enables the AAA security services.

- The **aaa authentication** command defines a method list, *test*, to be used on serial interfaces running PPP. The keyword **tacacs+** means that authentication will be done through TACACS+. If TACACS+ returns an error of some sort during authentication, the keyword **local** indicates that authentication will be attempted using the local database on the network access server.

- The **interface** command selects the line.

- The **ppp authentication** command applies the test method list to this line.

- The **tacacs-server host** command identifies the TACACS+ daemon as having an IP address of 10.1.2.3.

- The **tacacs-server key** command defines the shared encryption key to be *goaway*.

The following example configures AAA authentication for PPP:

```
aaa authentication ppp default if-needed tacacs+ local
```

In this example, the keyword **default** means that PPP authentication is applied by default to all interfaces. The **if-needed** keyword means that if the user has already authenticated by going through the ASCII login procedure, then PPP is not necessary and can be skipped. If authentication is needed, the keyword **tacacs+** means that authentication will be done through TACACS+. If TACACS+ returns an error of some sort during authentication, the keyword **local** indicates that authentication will be attempted using the local database on the network access server.

The following example creates the same authentication algorithm for PAP but calls the method list *MIS-access* instead of *default*:

```
aaa authentication pap MIS-access if-needed tacacs+ local
interface serial 0
ppp authentication MIS-access
```

In this example, because the list does not apply to any interfaces (unlike the default list, which applies automatically to all interfaces), the administrator must select interfaces to which this authentication scheme should apply by using the **interface** command. The administrator must then apply this method list to those interfaces by using the **ppp authentication** command.

TACACS and Extended TACACS Authentication Examples

The following example shows TACACS enabled for PPP authentication:

```
int async 1
 ppp authentication chap
 ppp use-tacacs
```

The following example shows TACACS enabled for ARAP authentication:

```
line 3
 arap use-tacacs
```

Kerberos Authentication Examples

To specify Kerberos as the authentication method, use the following command:

```
aaa authentication login default krb5
```

Use the following command to specify Kerberos authentication for PPP:

```
aaa authentication ppp default krb5
```

AAA Scalability Example

The following example shows a general security configuration using AAA with RADIUS as the security protocol. In this example, the network access server is configured to allocate 16 background processes to handle AAA requests for PPP:

```
aaa new-model
radius-server host alcatraz
radius-server key myRaDiUSpassWoRd
radius-server configure-nas
username root password ALongPassword
aaa authentication ppp dialins radius local
aaa authentication login admins local
aaa authorization network radius local
aaa accounting network start-stop radius
aaa processes 16
line 1 16
 autoselect ppp
 autoselect during-login
 login authentication admins
 modem dialin
interface group-async 1
 group-range 1 16
 encapsulation ppp
 ppp authentication pap dialins
```

The lines in this sample RADIUS AAA configuration are defined as follows:

- The **aaa new-model** command enables AAA network security services.

- The **radius-server host** command defines the name of the RADIUS server host.

- The **radius-server key** command defines the shared secret text string between the network access server and the RADIUS server host.

- The **radius-server configure-nas** command defines that the Cisco router or acccss server will query the RADIUS server for static routes and IP pool definitions when the device first starts up.

- The **username** command defines the username and password to be used for the PPP PAP caller identification.

- The **aaa authentication ppp dialins radius local** command defines the authentication method list **dialins**, which specifies that RADIUS authentication, then (if the RADIUS server does not respond) local authentication will be used on serial lines using PPP.

- The **aaa authentication login admins local** command defines another method list, *admins*, for login authentication.

- The **aaa authorization network radius local** command is used to assign an address and other network parameters to the RADIUS user.

- The **aaa accounting network start-stop radius** command tracks PPP usage.

- The **aaa processes** command allocates 16 background processes to handle AAA requests for PPP.

- The **line** command switches the configuration mode from global configuration to line configuration and identifies the specific lines being configured.

- The **autoselect ppp** command configures the Cisco IOS software to allow a PPP session to start up automatically on these selected lines.

- The **autoselect during-login** command is used to display the username and password prompt without pressing the Return key. After the user logs in, the autoselect function (in this case, PPP) begins.

- The **login authentication admins** command applies the *admins* method list for login authentication.

- The **modem dialin** command configures modems attached to the selected lines to accept only incoming calls.

- The **interface group-async** command selects and defines an asynchronous interface group.

- The **group-range** command defines the member asynchronous interfaces in the interface group.

- The **encapsulation ppp** command sets PPP as the encapsulation method used on the specified interfaces.

- The **ppp authentication pap dialins** command applies the *dialins* method list to the specified interfaces.

Login and Failed Banner Configuration Examples

The following example configures a login banner (in this case, the phrase "Unauthorized Access Prohibited") that will be displayed when a user logs in to the system. The asterisk (*) is used as the delimiting character. (RADIUS is specified as the default login authentication method.)

```
aaa new-model
aaa authentication banner *Unauthorized Access Prohibited*
aaa authentication login default radius
```

This configuration produces the following login banner:

```
Unauthorized Access Prohibited
Username:
```

The following example additionally configures a login-fail banner (in this case, the phrase "Failed login. Try again.") that will be displayed when a user tries to log in to the system and fails. The asterisk (*) is used as the delimiting character. (RADIUS is specified as the default login authentication method.)

```
aaa new-model
aaa authentication banner *Unauthorized Access Prohibited*
aaa authentication fail-message *Failed login. Try again.*
aaa authentication login default radius
```

This configuration produces the following login and failed login banner:

```
Unauthorized Access Prohibited
Username:
Password:
Failed login. Try again.
```

Double Authentication Configuration Examples

The examples in this section illustrate possible configurations to be used with double authentication. Your configurations could differ significantly, depending on your network and security requirements.

These examples are included:

● Configuring the Local Host for AAA with Double Authentication Examples

● Configuring the AAA Server for First-Stage (PPP) Authentication/Authorization Example

● Configuring the AAA Server for Second-Stage (Per-User) Authentication/Authorization Examples

● Complete Sample Configuration with TACACS+

NOTE   These configuration examples include specific IP addresses and other specific information. This information is for illustrative purposes only: Your configuration will use different IP addresses, different usernames and passwords, and different authorization statements.

Configuring the Local Host for AAA with Double Authentication Examples

These two examples configure a local host to use AAA for PPP and login authentication, and for network and EXEC authorization. One example is shown for RADIUS and one example for TACACS+.

In both examples, the first three lines configure AAA, with a specific server as the AAA server. The next two lines configure AAA for PPP and login authentication, and the last two lines configure network and EXEC authorization. The last line is necessary only if the **access-profile** command will be executed as an autocommand.

Router Configuration with a RADIUS AAA Example

```
aaa new-model
radius-server host secureserver
radius-server key myradiuskey
aaa authentication ppp default radius
aaa authentication login default radius
aaa authorization network radius
aaa authorization exec radius
```

Router Configuration with a TACACS+ Server Example

```
aaa new-model
tacacs-server host security
tacacs-server key mytacacskey
aaa authentication ppp default tacacs+
aaa authentication login default tacacs+
aaa authorization network tacacs+
aaa authorization exec tacacs+
```

Configuring the AAA Server for First-Stage (PPP) Authentication/Authorization Example

This example shows a configuration on the AAA server. A partial sample AAA configuration is shown for RADIUS.

TACACS+ servers can be configured similarly. (See the "Complete Sample Configuration with TACACS+" section later in this chapter.)

This example defines authentication/authorization for a remote host named *hostx* that will be authenticated by CHAP in the first stage of double authentication. Note that the ACL AV pair limits the remote host to Telnet connections to the local host. The local host has the IP address 10.0.0.2.

RADIUS AAA Server Configuration Example

```
hostx    Password = "welcome"
         User-Service-Type = Framed-User,
         Framed-Protocol = PPP,
         cisco-avpair = "lcp:interface-config=ip unnumbered ethernet 0",
         cisco-avpair = "ip:inacl#3=permit tcp any 172.21.114.0 0.0.0.255 eq telnet",
         cisco-avpair = "ip:inacl#4=deny icmp any any",
         cisco-avpair = "ip:route#5=55.0.0.0 255.0.0.0",
         cisco-avpair = "ip:route#6=66.0.0.0 255.0.0.0",
         cisco-avpair = "ipx:inacl#3=deny any"
```

Configuring the AAA Server for Second-Stage (Per-User) Authentication/Authorization Examples

This section contains partial sample AAA configurations on a RADIUS server. These configurations define authentication/authorization for a user (Bob) with the username *bobuser*, who will be user-authenticated in the second stage of double authentication.

TACACS+ servers can be configured similarly. (See the "Complete Sample Configuration with TACACS+" section later in this chapter.)

RADIUS AAA Server Configuration Examples

Three examples show sample RADIUS AAA configurations that could be used with each of the three forms of the **access-profile** command.

The first example shows a partial sample AAA configuration that works with the default form (no keywords) of the **access-profile** command. Note that only ACL AV pairs are defined. This example also sets up the **access-profile** command as an autocommand:

```
bobuser          Password = "welcome"
       User-Service-Type = Shell-User,
       cisco-avpair = "shell:autocmd=access-profile"
       User-Service-Type = Framed-User,
       Framed-Protocol = PPP,
       cisco-avpair = "ip:inacl#3=permit tcp any host 10.0.0.2 eq telnet",
       cisco-avpair = "ip:inacl#4=deny icmp any any"
```

The second example shows a partial sample AAA configuration that works with the **access-profile merge** form of the **access-profile** command. This example also sets up the **access-profile merge** command as an autocommand:

```
bobuser          Password = "welcome"
       User-Service-Type = Shell-User,
       cisco-avpair = "shell:autocmd=access-profile merge"
       User-Service-Type = Framed-User,
       Framed-Protocol = PPP,
       cisco-avpair = "ip:inacl#3=permit tcp any any"
       cisco-avpair = "ip:route=10.0.0.0 255.255.0.0",
       cisco-avpair = "ip:route=10.1.0.0 255.255.0.0",
       cisco-avpair = "ip:route=10.2.0.0 255.255.0.0"
```

The third example shows a partial sample AAA configuration that works with the **access-profile replace** form of the **access-profile** command. This example also sets up the **access-profile replace** command as an autocommand:

```
bobuser          Password = "welcome"
       User-Service-Type = Shell-User,
       cisco-avpair = "shell:autocmd=access-profile replace"
       User-Service-Type = Framed-User,
       Framed-Protocol = PPP,
       cisco-avpair = "ip:inacl#3=permit tcp any any",
       cisco-avpair = "ip:inacl#4=permit icmp any any",
       cisco-avpair = "ip:route=10.10.0.0 255.255.0.0",
       cisco-avpair = "ip:route=10.11.0.0 255.255.0.0",
       cisco-avpair = "ip:route=10.12.0.0 255.255.0.0"
```

Complete Sample Configuration with TACACS+

This example shows TACACS+ authorization profile configurations both for the remote host (used in the first stage of double authentication) and for specific users (used in the second stage of double authentication). This TACACS+ example contains approximately the same configuration information as shown in the previous RADIUS examples.

This sample configuration shows authentication/authorization profiles on the TACACS+ server for the remote host *hostx* and for three users, with the usernames *bob_default*, *bob_merge*, and *bob_replace*. The configurations for these three usernames illustrate different configurations that correspond to the three different forms of the **access-profile** command. The three user configurations also illustrate setting up the autocommand for each form of the **access-profile** command.

Figure 2-3 shows the topology. The example following the figure shows a TACACS+ configuration file.

Figure 2-3 *Example Topology for Double Authentication*

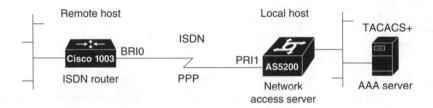

TACACS+ Configuration File

This sample configuration shows authentication/authorization profiles on the TACACS+ server for the remote host *hostx* and for three users, with the usernames *bob_default*, *bob_merge*, and *bob_replace*:

```
key = "mytacacskey"

default authorization = permit


#---------------------------Remote Host (BRI)------------------------
#
# This allows the remote host to be authenticated by the local host
# during first-stage authentication, and provides the remote host
# authorization profile.
#
#-------------------------------------------------------------------

user = hostx
{
    login = cleartext "welcome"
    chap = cleartext "welcome"


    service = ppp protocol = lcp {
                interface-config="ip unnumbered ethernet 0"
    }

    service = ppp protocol = ip {
            # It is important to have the hash sign and some string after
            # it. This indicates to the NAS that you have a per-user
            # config.
```

```
                inacl#3="permit tcp any 172.21.114.0 0.0.0.255 eq telnet"
                inacl#4="deny icmp any any"

                route#5="55.0.0.0 255.0.0.0"
                route#6="66.0.0.0 255.0.0.0"
        }

    service = ppp protocol = ipx {
                # see previous comment about the hash sign and string, in protocol = ip
                inacl#3="deny any"
        }


}


#------------------ "access-profile" default user "only acls" ---------------
#
# - Without arguments, access-profile removes any access-lists it can find
#   in the old configuration (both per-user and per-interface), and makes sure
#   that the new profile contains ONLY access-list definitions.
#
#------------------------------------------------------------------------------

user = bob_default
{
        login = cleartext "welcome"
        chap = cleartext "welcome"

        service = exec

        {
                # this is the autocommand that executes when bob_default logs in
                autocmd = "access-profile"
        }

        service = ppp protocol = ip {
                # Put whatever access-lists, static routes, whatever
                # here.
                # If you leave this blank, the user will have NO IP
                # access-lists (not even the ones installed prior to
                # this)!

                inacl#3="permit tcp any host 10.0.0.2 eq telnet"
                inacl#4="deny icmp any any"
        }


        service = ppp protocol = ipx {
                # Put whatever access-lists, static routes, whatever
                # here.
                # If you leave this blank, the user will have NO IPX
                # access-lists (not even the ones installed prior to
                # this)!
```

```
        }


}


#-------------------- "access-profile merge" user  --------------------
#
# With the 'merge' option, first all old access-lists are removed (as before),
#  but then (almost) all AV pairs are uploaded and installed. This
#  will allow for uploading any custom static routes, sap-filters, and so on,
#  that the user may need in his or her profile. This needs to be used with
#  care, as it leaves open the possibility of conflicting configurations.
#
#-----------------------------------------------------------------------------

user = bob_merge
{
        login = cleartext "welcome"
        chap = cleartext "welcome"


        service = exec
        {
                # this is the autocommand that executes when bob_merge logs in
                autocmd = "access-profile merge"
        }

        service = ppp protocol = ip
        {
                # Put whatever access-lists, static routes, whatever
                # here.
                # If you leave this blank, the user will have NO IP
                # access-lists (not even the ones installed prior to
                # this)!

                inacl#3="permit tcp any any"
                route#2="10.0.0.0 255.255.0.0"
                route#3="10.1.0.0 255.255.0.0"
                route#4="10.2.0.0 255.255.0.0"


        }

        service = ppp protocol = ipx
        {
                # Put whatever access-lists, static routes, whatever
                # here.
                # If you leave this blank, the user will have NO IPX
                # access-lists (not even the ones installed prior to
                # this)!


        }


}
```

```
#-------------------- "access-profile replace" user  ----------------------
#
#- With the 'replace' option,
#  ALL old configuration is removed and ALL new configuration is installed.
#
# One caveat: access-profile checks the new configuration for address-pool and
# address AV pairs. As addresses cannot be renegotiated at this point, the
# command will fail (and complain) when it encounters such an AV pair.
# Such AV pairs are considered to be "invalid" for this context.
#---------------------------------------------------------------------------


user = bob_replace
{
        login = cleartext "welcome"
        chap = cleartext "welcome"


        service = exec
        {
                # this is the autocommand that executes when bob_replace logs in
                autocmd = "access-profile replace"
        }

        service = ppp protocol = ip
        {
                # Put whatever access-lists, static routes, whatever
                # here.
                # If you leave this blank, the user will have NO IP
                # access-lists (not even the ones installed prior to
                # this)!

                inacl#3="permit tcp any any"
                inacl#4="permit icmp any any"


                route#2="10.10.0.0 255.255.0.0"
                route#3="10.11.0.0 255.255.0.0"
                route#4="10.12.0.0 255.255.0.0"
        }

        service = ppp protocol = ipx
        {
                # put whatever access-lists, static routes, whatever
                # here.
                # If you leave this blank, the user will have NO IPX
                # access-lists (not even the ones installed prior to
                # this)!
        }

}
```

Automated Double Authentication Configuration Example

This example shows a complete configuration file for a Cisco 2509 router with automated double authentication configured. The configuration commands that apply to automated double authentication are preceded by descriptions with a double asterisk (**):

```
Current configuration:
!
version 11.3
no service password-encryption
!
hostname myrouter
!
!
! **The following AAA commands are used to configure double authentication:
!
! **The following command enables AAA:
aaa new-model
! **The following command enables user authentication via the TACACS+ AAA server:
aaa authentication login default tacacs+
aaa authentication login console none
! **The following command enables device authentication via the TACACS+ AAA server:
aaa authentication ppp default tacacs+
! **The following command causes the remote user's authorization profile
!        to be downloaded from the AAA server to the Cisco 2509 router when required:
aaa authorization exec tacacs+
! **The following command causes the remote device's authorization profile
!        to be downloaded from the AAA server to the Cisco 2509 router when required:
aaa authorization network tacacs+
enable password mypassword
!
ip host blue 172.21.127.226
ip host green 172.21.127.218
ip host red 172.21.127.114
ip domain-name mycompany.com
ip name-server 171.69.2.75
! **The following command globally enables automated double authentication:
ip trigger-authentication timeout 60 port 7500
isdn switch-type basic-5ess
!
!
interface Ethernet0
 ip address 172.21.127.186 255.255.255.248
 no ip route-cache
 no ip mroute-cache
 no keepalive
 ntp disable
 no cdp enable
!
interface Virtual-Template1
 ip unnumbered Ethernet0
 no ip route-cache
 no ip mroute-cache
!
```

```
interface Serial0
 ip address 172.21.127.105 255.255.255.248
 encapsulation ppp
 no ip mroute-cache
 no keepalive
 shutdown
 clockrate 2000000
 no cdp enable
!
interface Serial1
 no ip address
 no ip route-cache
 no ip mroute-cache
 shutdown
 no cdp enable
!
! **Automated double authentication occurs via the ISDN BRI interface BRI0:
interface BRI0
 ip unnumbered Ethernet0
! **The following command turns on automated double authentication at this interface:
 ip trigger-authentication
! **PPP encapsulation is required:
 encapsulation ppp
 no ip route-cache
 no ip mroute-cache
 dialer idle-timeout 500
 dialer map ip 172.21.127.113 name myrouter 60074
 dialer-group 1
 no cdp enable
! **The following command specifies that device authentication occur via PPP CHAP:
 ppp authentication chap
!
router eigrp 109
 network 172.21.0.0
 no auto-summary
!
ip default-gateway 172.21.127.185
no ip classless
ip route 172.21.127.114 255.255.255.255 172.21.127.113
! **Virtual profiles are required for double authentication to work:
virtual-profile virtual-template 1
dialer-list 1 protocol ip permit
no cdp run
! **The following command defines where the TACACS+ AAA server is:
tacacs-server host 171.69.57.35 port 1049
tacacs-server timeout 90
! **The following command defines the key to use with TACACS+ traffic (required):
tacacs-server key mytacacskey
snmp-server community public RO
!
line con 0
 exec-timeout 0 0
 login authentication console
line aux 0
 transport input all
```

```
line vty 0 4
 exec-timeout 0 0
 password lab
!
end
```

MS-CHAP Configuration Example

The following example configures a Cisco AS5200 (enabled for AAA and communication with a RADIUS security server) for PPP authentication using MS-CHAP:

```
aaa new-model
aaa authentication login admins local
aaa authentication ppp dialins radius local
aaa authorization network radius local
aaa accounting network start-stop radius

username root password ALongPassword

radius-server host alcatraz
radius-server key myRaDiUSpassWoRd

interface group-async 1
 group-range 1 16
 encapsulation ppp
 ppp authentication ms-chap dialins

line 1 16
 autoselect ppp
 autoselect during-login
 login authentication admins
 modem dialin
```

The lines in this sample RADIUS AAA configuration are defined as follows:

- The **aaa new-model** command enables AAA network security services.

- The **aaa authentication login admins local** command defines another method list, *admins*, for login authentication.

- The **aaa authentication ppp dialins radius local** command defines the authentication method list *dialins*, which specifies that RADIUS authentication then (if the RADIUS server does not respond) local authentication will be used on serial lines using PPP.

- The **aaa authorization network radius local** command is used to assign an address and other network parameters to the RADIUS user.

- The **aaa accounting network start-stop radius** command tracks PPP usage.

- The **username** command defines the username and password to be used for the PPP PAP caller identification.

- The **radius-server host** command defines the name of the RADIUS server host.

- The **radius-server key** command defines the shared secret text string between the network access server and the RADIUS server host.

- The **interface group-async** command selects and defines an asynchronous interface group.

- The **group-range** command defines the member asynchronous interfaces in the interface group.

- The **encapsulation ppp** command sets PPP as the encapsulation method used on the specified interfaces.

- The **ppp authentication ms-chap dialins** command selects MS-CHAP as the method of PPP authentication and applies the *dialins* method list to the specified interfaces.

- The **line** command switches the configuration mode from global configuration to line configuration and identifies the specific lines being configured.

- The **autoselect ppp** command configures the Cisco IOS software to allow a PPP session to start up automatically on these selected lines.

- The **autoselect during-login** command is used to display the username and password prompt without pressing the Return key. After the user logs in, the autoselect function (in this case, PPP) begins.

- The **login authentication admins** command applies the *admins* method list for login authentication.

- The **modem dialin** command configures modems attached to the selected lines to accept only incoming calls.

## CHAPTER 3

Authentication Commands

This chapter describes the commands used to configure both AAA and non-AAA authentication methods. Authentication identifies users before they are allowed access to the network and network services. Basically, the Cisco IOS software implementation of authentication is divided into two main categories:

- AAA authentication methods
- Non-AAA authentication methods

Authentication, for the most part, is implemented through the AAA security services. Cisco recommends that, whenever possible, AAA be used to implement authentication.

For information on how to configure authentication using either AAA or non-AAA methods, refer to Chapter 2, "Configuring Authentication." For configuration examples using the commands in this chapter, refer to the "Authentication Examples" section located at the end of Chapter 2, "Configuring Authentication."

aaa authentication arap

To enable an AAA authentication method for AppleTalk Remote Access (ARA) using RADIUS or TACACS+, use the **aaa authentication arap** global configuration command. Use the **no** form of this command to disable this authentication.

> **aaa authentication arap** {**default** | *list-name*} *method1* [*method2...*]
> **no aaa authentication arap** {**default** | *list-name*} *method1* [*method2...*]

Syntax	Description
default	Uses the listed methods that follow this argument as the default list of methods when a user logs in.
list-name	Character string used to name the following list of authentication methods tried when a user logs in.
method	One of the keywords described in Table 3-1.

Default

If the **default** list is not set, only the local user database is checked. This has the same effect as the following command:

```
aaa authentication arap default local
```

Command Mode

Global configuration

Usage Guidelines

This command first appeared in Cisco IOS Release 10.3.

The list names and default that you set with the **aaa authentication arap** command are also used with the **arap authentication** command. Note that ARAP guest logins are disabled by default when you enable AAA. To allow guest logins, you must use either the **guest** or **auth-guest** method listed in Table 3-1. You can only use one of these methods; they are mutually exclusive.

Create a list by entering the **aaa authentication arap** *list-name method* command, where *list-name* is any character string used to name this list (such as *MIS-access*.) The *method* argument identifies the list of methods the authentication algorithm tries in the given sequence. See Table 3-1 for descriptions of method keywords.

To create a default list that is used if no list is specified in the **arap authentication** command, use the **default** keyword followed by the methods you want to be used in default situations.

The additional methods of authentication are used only if the previous method returns an error, not if it fails.

Use the **more system:running-config** command to view currently configured lists of authentication methods.

Table 3-1 *AAA Authentication ARAP Methods*

Keyword	Description
guest	Allows guest logins. This method must be the first method listed, but it can be followed by other methods if it does not succeed.
auth-guest	Allows guest logins only if the user has already logged in to EXEC. This method must be the first method listed, but can be followed by other methods if it does not succeed.
line	Uses the line password for authentication.
local	Uses the local username database for authentication.
tacacs+	Uses TACACS+ authentication.
radius	Uses RADIUS authentication.

NOTE   This command cannot be used with TACACS or extended TACACS.

Examples

The following example creates a list called *MIS-access*, which first tries TACACS+ authentication and then none:

```
aaa authentication arap MIS-access tacacs+ none
```

The following example creates the same list, but sets it as the default list that is used for all ARA protocol authentications if no other list is specified:

```
aaa authentication arap default tacacs+ none
```

Related Commands

You can search online at www.cisco.com to find documentation of related commands.

aaa authentication local-override
aaa new-model

aaa authentication banner

To configure a personalized banner that will be displayed at user login, use the **aaa authentication banner** global configuration command. Use the **no** form of this command to remove the banner.

> **aaa authentication banner** *dstringd*
> **no aaa authentication banner**

Syntax	Description
d	The delimiting character at the beginning and end of the *string* that notifies the system that the *string* is to be displayed as the banner. The delimiting character can be any character in the extended ASCII character set, but once defined as the delimiter, that character cannot be used in the text string making up the banner.
string	Any group of characters, excluding the one used as the delimiter. The maximum number of characters that you can display is 2996.

Default

Not enabled

Command Mode

Global configuration

Usage Guidelines

This command first appeared in Cisco IOS Release 11.3(4) T.

Use the **aaa authentication banner** command to create a personalized message that appears when a user logs in to the system. This message or banner will replace the default message for user login.

To create a login banner, you need to configure a delimiting character, which notifies the system that the following text string is to be displayed as the banner, and then the text string itself. The delimiting character is repeated at the end of the text string to signify the end of the banner. The delimiting character can be any character in the extended ASCII character set, but once defined as the delimiter, that character cannot be used in the text string making up the banner.

Examples

The following example shows the default login message if **aaa authentication banner** is not configured. (RADIUS is specified as the default login authentication method.)

```
aaa new-model
aaa authentication login default radius
```

This configuration produces the following standard output:

```
User Verification Access
Username:
Password:
```

The following example configures a login banner (in this case, the phrase "Unauthorized use is prohibited.") that will be displayed when a user logs in to the system. In this case, the asterisk (*) symbol is used as the delimiter. (RADIUS is specified as the default login authentication method.)

```
aaa new-model
aaa authentication banner *Unauthorized use is prohibited.*
aaa authentication login default radius
```

This configuration produces the following login banner:

```
Unauthorized use is prohibited.
Username:
```

Related Commands

You can search online at www.cisco.com to find documentation of related commands.

aaa authentication fail-message

aaa authentication enable default

To enable AAA authentication to determine if a user can access the privileged command level, use the **aaa authentication enable default** global configuration command. Use the **no** form of this command to disable this authorization method.

> **aaa authentication enable default** *method1* [*method2...*]
> **no aaa authentication enable default** *method1* [*method2...*]

Syntax   Description

method   At least one of the keywords described in Table 3-2.

Default

If the **default** list is not set, only the enable password is checked. This has the same effect as the following command:

```
aaa authentication enable default enable
```

On the console, the enable password is used if it exists. If no password is set, the process will succeed anyway.

Command Mode

Global configuration

Usage Guidelines

This command first appeared in Cisco IOS Release 10.3.

Use the **aaa authentication enable default** command to create a series of authentication methods that are used to determine whether a user can access the privileged command level. Method keywords are described in Table 3-2. The additional methods of authentication are used only if the previous method returns an error, not if it fails. To specify that the authentication should succeed even if all methods return an error, specify **none** as the final method in the command line.

If a default authentication routine is not set for a function, the default is **none** and no authentication is performed. Use the **more system:running-config** command to view currently configured lists of authentication methods.

Table 3-2 *AAA Authentication Enable Default Methods*

Keyword	Description
enable	Uses the enable password for authentication.
line	Uses the line password for authentication.

Continues

Table 3-2 *AAA Authentication Enable Default Methods (Continued)*

Keyword	Description
none	Uses no authentication.
tacacs+	Uses TACACS+ authentication.
radius	Uses RADIUS authentication.

NOTE   This command cannot be used with TACACS or extended TACACS.

Example

The following example creates an authentication list that first tries to contact a TACACS+ server. If no server can be found, AAA tries to use the enable password. If this attempt also returns an error (because no enable password is configured on the server), the user is allowed access with no authentication.

```
aaa authentication enable default tacacs+ enable none
```

Related Commands

You can search online at www.cisco.com to find documentation of related commands.

aaa authentication local-override
aaa authorization
aaa new-model
enable password

aaa authentication fail-message

To configure a personalized banner that will be displayed when a user fails login, use the **aaa authentication fail-message** global configuration command. Use the **no** form of this command to remove the failed login message.

> **aaa authentication fail-message** *dstringd*
> **no aaa authentication fail-message**

Syntax   Description

d	The delimiting character at the beginning and end of the *string* that notifies the system that the *string* is to be displayed as the banner. The delimiting character can be any character in the extended ASCII character set, but once defined as the delimiter, that character cannot be used in the text string making up the banner.
string	Any group of characters, excluding the one used as the delimiter. The maximum number of characters that you can display is 2996.

Default

Not enabled

Command Mode

Global configuration

Usage Guidelines

This command first appeared in Cisco IOS Release 11.3(4) T.

Use the **aaa authentication fail-message** command to create a personalized message that appears when a user login fails. This message will replace the default message for failed login.

To create a failed-login banner, you need to configure a delimiting character, which notifies the system that the following text string is to be displayed as the banner, and then the text string itself. The delimiting character is repeated at the end of the text string to signify the end of the banner. The delimiting character can be any character in the extended ASCII character set, but once defined as the delimiter, that character cannot be used in the text string making up the banner.

Examples

The following example shows the default login message and failed login message that is displayed if **aaa authentication banner** and **aaa authentication fail-message** are not configured. (RADIUS is specified as the default login authentication method.)

```
aaa new-model
aaa authentication login default radius
```

This configuration produces the following standard output:

```
User Verification Access
Username:
Password:

% Authentication failed.
```

The following example configures both a login banner ("Unauthorized use is prohibited.") and a login-fail message ("Failed login. Try again."). The login message will be displayed when a user logs in to the system. The failed-login message will be displayed when a user tries to log in to the system and fails. (RADIUS is specified as the default login authentication method.) In this example, the asterisk (*) is used as the delimiting character.

```
aaa new-model
aaa authentication banner *Unauthorized use is prohibited.*
aaa authentication fail-message *Failed login. Try again.*
aaa authentication login default radius
```

This configuration produces the following login and failed login banner:

```
Unauthorized use is prohibited.
Username:
Password:
Failed login. Try again.
```

Related Commands

You can search online at www.cisco.com to find documentation of related commands.

aaa authentication banner

aaa authentication local-override

To configure the Cisco IOS software to check the local user database for authentication before attempting another form of authentication, use the **aaa authentication local-override** global configuration command. Use the **no** form of this command to disable the override.

> **aaa authentication local-override**
> **no aaa authentication local-override**

Syntax Description

This command has no arguments or keywords.

Default

Override is disabled.

Command Mode

Global configuration

Usage Guidelines

This command first appeared in Cisco IOS Release 10.3.

This command is useful when you want to configure an override to the normal authentication process for certain personnel such as system administrators.

When this override is set, the user is always prompted for the username. The system then checks to see if the entered username corresponds to a local account. If the username is not found in the local database, login proceeds with the methods configured with other **aaa** commands (such as **aaa authentication login**). Note that when you're using this command, the Username: prompt is fixed as the first prompt.

Example

The following example enables AAA authentication override:

```
aaa authentication local-override
```

Related Commands

You can search online at www.cisco.com to find documentation of related commands.

aaa authentication arap
aaa authentication enable default
aaa authentication login
aaa authentication ppp
aaa new-model

aaa authentication login

To set AAA authentication at login, use the **aaa authentication login** global configuration command. Use the **no** form of this command to disable AAA authentication.

> **aaa authentication login** {**default** | *list-name*} *method1* [*method2...*]
> **no aaa authentication login** {**default** | *list-name*} *method1* [*method2...*]

Syntax	Description
default	Uses the listed authentication methods that follow this argument as the default list of methods when a user logs in.
list-name	Character string used to name the list of authentication methods activated when a user logs in.
method	At least one of the keywords described in Table 3-3.

Default

If the **default** list is not set, only the local user database is checked. This has the same effect as the following command:

```
aaa authentication login default local
```

| NOTE | On the console, login will succeed without any authentication checks if **default** is not set. |

Command Mode

Global configuration

Usage Guidelines

This command first appeared in Cisco IOS Release 10.3.

The default and optional list names that you create with the **aaa authentication login** command are used with the **login authentication** command.

Create a list by entering the **aaa authentication** *list-name method* command for a particular protocol, where *list-name* is any character string used to name this list (such as *MIS-access*). The *method* argument identifies the list of methods that the authentication algorithm tries in the given sequence. Method keywords are described in Table 3-3.

To create a default list that is used if no list is assigned to a line, use the **login authentication** command with the default argument followed by the methods you want to use in default situations.

The additional methods of authentication are used only if the previous method returns an error, not if it fails. To ensure that the authentication succeeds even if all methods return an error, specify **none** as the final method in the command line.

If authentication is not specifically set for a line, the default is to deny access and no authentication is performed. Use the **more system:running-config** command to display currently configured lists of authentication methods.

Table 3-3 *AAA Authentication Login Methods*

Keyword	Description
enable	Uses the enable password for authentication.
krb5	Uses Kerberos 5 for authentication.
line	Uses the line password for authentication.
local	Uses the local username database for authentication.

Table 3-3 *AAA Authentication Login Methods (Continued)*

Keyword	Description
none	Uses no authentication.
radius	Uses RADIUS authentication.
tacacs+	Uses TACACS+ authentication.
krb5-telnet	Uses Kerberos 5 Telnet authentication protocol when using Telnet to connect to the router.

NOTE   This command cannot be used with TACACS or extended TACACS.

Examples

The following example creates an AAA authentication list called *MIS-access*. This authentication first tries to contact a TACACS+ server. If no server is found, TACACS+ returns an error and AAA tries to use the enable password. If this attempt also returns an error (because no enable password is configured on the server), the user is allowed access with no authentication.

```
aaa authentication login MIS-access tacacs+ enable none
```

The following example creates the same list, but it sets it as the default list that is used for all login authentications if no other list is specified:

```
aaa authentication login default tacacs+ enable none
```

The following example sets authentication at login to use the Kerberos 5 Telnet authentication protocol when using Telnet to connect to the router:

```
aaa authentication login default KRB5-TELNET krb5
```

Related Commands

You can search online at www.cisco.com to find documentation of related commands.

aaa authentication local-override
aaa new-model
login authentication

aaa authentication nasi

To specify AAA authentication for Netware Asynchronous Services Interface (NASI) clients connecting through the access server, use the **aaa authentication nasi** global configuration command. Use the **no** form of this command to disable authentication for NASI clients.

aaa authentication nasi {**default** | *list-name*} *method1* [*method2...*]
no aaa authentication nasi {**default** | *list-name*} *method1* [*method2...*]

Syntax	Description
default	Makes the listed authentication methods that follow this argument the default list of methods used when a user logs in.
list-name	Character string used to name the list of authentication methods activated when a user logs in.
method1 [*method2...*]	At least one of the methods described in Table 3-4.

Default

If the **default** list is not set, only the local user database is selected. This has the same effect as the following command:

```
aaa authentication nasi default local
```

Command Mode

Global configuration

Usage Guidelines

This command first appeared in Cisco IOS Release 11.1.

The default and optional list names that you create with the **aaa authentication nasi** command are used with the **nasi authentication** command.

Create a list by entering the **aaa authentication nasi** command, where *list-name* is any character string that names the list (such as *MIS-access*). The *method* argument identifies the list of methods the authentication algorithm tries in the given sequence. Method keywords are described in Table 3-4.

To create a default list that is used if no list is assigned to a line with the **nasi authentication** command, use the default argument followed by the methods that you want to use in default situations.

The remaining methods of authentication are used only if the previous method returns an error, not if it fails. To ensure that the authentication succeeds even if all methods return an error, specify **none** as the final method in the command line.

If authentication is not specifically set for a line, the default is to deny access and no authentication is performed. Use the **more system:running-config** command to display currently configured lists of authentication methods.

Table 3-4 *AAA Authentication NASI Methods*

Keyword	Description
enable	Uses the enable password for authentication.
line	Uses the line password for authentication.
local	Uses the local username database for authentication.
none	Uses no authentication.
tacacs+	Uses TACACS+ authentication.

NOTE   This command cannot be used with TACACS or extended TACACS.

Examples

The following example creates an AAA authentication list called *list1*. This authentication first tries to contact a TACACS+ server. If no server is found, TACACS+ returns an error and AAA tries to use the enable password. If this attempt also returns an error (because no enable password is configured on the server), the user is allowed access with no authentication.

```
aaa authentication nasi list1 tacacs+ enable none
```

The following example creates the same list, but sets it as the default list that is used for all login authentications if no other list is specified:

```
aaa authentication nasi default tacacs+ enable none
```

Related Commands

You can search online at www.cisco.com to find documentation of related commands.

ipx nasi-server enable
ip trigger-authentication (global configuration)
nasi authentication
show ipx nasi connections
show ipx spx-protocol

aaa authentication password-prompt

To change the text displayed when users are prompted for a password, use the **aaa authentication password-prompt** global configuration command. Use the **no** form of this command to return to the default password prompt text.

> **aaa authentication password-prompt** *text-string*
> **no aaa authentication password-prompt** *text-string*

Syntax	Description
text-string	String of text that will be displayed when the user is prompted to enter a password. If this text-string contains spaces or unusual characters, it must be enclosed in double-quotes (for example, "Enter your password:").

Default

There is no user-defined *text-string*, and the password prompt appears as "Password."

Command Mode

Global configuration

Usage Guidelines

This command first appeared in Cisco IOS Release 11.0.

Use the **aaa authentication password-prompt** command to change the default text that the Cisco IOS software displays when prompting a user to enter a password. This command changes the password prompt for the enable password as well as for login passwords that are not supplied by remote security servers. The **no** form of this command returns the password prompt to the default value:

```
Password:
```

The **aaa authentication password-prompt** command does not change any dialog that is supplied by a remote TACACS+ or RADIUS server.

Example

The following example changes the text for the password prompt:

```
aaa authentication password-prompt "Enter your password now:"
```

Related Commands

You can search online at www.cisco.com to find documentation of related commands.

aaa authentication username-prompt
aaa new-model
enable password

aaa authentication ppp

To specify one or more AAA authentication methods for use on serial interfaces running PPP, use the **aaa authentication ppp** global configuration command. Use the **no** form of this command to disable authentication.

> **aaa authentication ppp** {**default** | *list-name*} *method1* [*method2...*]
> **no aaa authentication ppp** {**default** | *list-name*} *method1* [*method2...*]

Syntax	Description
default	Uses the listed authentication methods that follow this argument as the default list of methods when a user logs in.
list-name	Character string used to name the list of authentication methods tried when a user logs in.
method1 [*method2...*]	At least one of the keywords described in Table 3-5.

Default

If the **default** list is not set, only the local user database is checked. This has the same effect as the following command:

```
aaa authentication ppp default local
```

Command Mode

Global configuration

Usage Guidelines

This command first appeared in Cisco IOS Release 10.3.

The lists that you create with the **aaa authentication ppp** command are used with the **ppp authentication** command. These lists contain up to four authentication methods that are used when a user tries to log in to the serial interface.

Create a list by entering the **aaa authentication ppp** *list-name method* command, where *list-name* is any character string used to name this list (such as *MIS-access*). The *method* argument identifies the list of methods that the authentication algorithm tries in the given sequence. You can enter up to four methods. Method keywords are described in Table 3-5.

The additional methods of authentication are only used if the previous method returns an error, not if it fails. Specify **none** as the final method in the command line to have authentication succeed even if all methods return an error.

If authentication is not specifically set for a function, the default is **none** and no authentication is performed. Use the **more system:running-config** command to display currently configured lists of authentication methods.

Table 3-5   *AAA Authentication PPP Methods*

Keyword	Description
if-needed	Does not authenticate if user has already been authenticated on a TTY line.
krb5	Uses Kerberos 5 for authentication (can only be used for PAP authentication).
local	Uses the local username database for authentication.
none	Uses no authentication.
radius	Uses RADIUS authentication.
tacacs+	Uses TACACS+ authentication.

NOTE   This command cannot be used with TACACS or extended TACACS.

Example

The following example creates an AAA authentication list called *MIS-access* for serial lines that use PPP. This authentication first tries to contact a TACACS+ server. If this action returns an error, the user is allowed access with no authentication.

```
aaa authentication ppp MIS-access tacacs+ none
```

Related Commands

You can search online at www.cisco.com to find documentation of related commands.

aaa authentication local-override
aaa new-model
ppp authentication

aaa authentication username-prompt

To change the text displayed when users are prompted to enter a username, use the **aaa authentication username-prompt** global configuration command. Use the **no** form of this command to return to the default username prompt text.

> **aaa authentication username-prompt** *text-string*
> **no aaa authentication username-prompt** *text-string*

Syntax	Description
text-string	String of text that will be displayed when the user is prompted to enter a username. If this text-string contains spaces or unusual characters, it must be enclosed in double-quotes (for example, "Enter your name:").

Default

There is no user-defined *text-string*, and the username prompt appears as "Username."

Command Mode

Global configuration

Usage Guidelines

This command first appeared in Cisco IOS Release 11.0.

Use the **aaa authentication username-prompt** command to change the default text that the Cisco IOS software displays when prompting a user to enter a username. The **no** form of this command returns the username prompt to the default value:

```
Username:
```

Some protocols (for example, TACACS+) have the ability to override the use of local username prompt information. Using the **aaa authentication username-prompt** command will not change the username prompt text in these instances.

NOTE   The **aaa authentication username-prompt** command does not change any dialog that is supplied by a remote TACACS+ server.

Example

The following example changes the text for the username prompt:

```
aaa authentication username-prompt "Enter your name here:"
```

Related Commands

You can search online at www.cisco.com to find documentation of related commands.

aaa authentication password-prompt
aaa new-model
enable password

aaa new-model

To enable the AAA access control model, issue the **aaa new-model** global configuration command. Use the **no** form of this command to disable the AAA access control model.

> **aaa new-model**
> **no aaa new-model**

Syntax Description

This command has no arguments or keywords.

Default

AAA is not enabled.

Command Mode

Global configuration

Usage Guidelines

This command first appeared in Cisco IOS Release 10.0.

This command enables the AAA access control system. After you have enabled AAA, TACACS and extended TACACS commands are no longer available. If you initialize AAA functionality and later decide to use TACACS or extended TACACS, issue the **no** form of this command, and then enable the version of TACACS that you want to use.

Example

The following example initializes AAA:

```
aaa new-model
```

Related Commands

You can search online at www.cisco.com to find documentation of related commands.

aaa accounting
aaa authentication arap
aaa authentication enable default
aaa authentication local-override
aaa authentication login

aaa authentication ppp
aaa authorization
tacacs-server key

aaa processes

To allocate a specific number of background processes to be used to process AAA authentication and authorization requests for PPP, use the **aaa processes** global configuration command. Use the **no** form of this command to restore the default value for this command.

> **aaa processes** *number*
> **no aaa processes** *number*

Syntax   Description

number   Specifies the number of background processes allocated for AAA requests for PPP.
                  Valid entries are 1 to 2,147,483,647.

Default

The default for this command is one allocated background process.

Command Mode

Global configuration

Usage Guidelines

This command first appeared in Cisco IOS Release 11.3(2)AA.

Use the **aaa processes** command to allocate a specific number of background processes to simultaneously handle multiple AAA authentication and authorization requests for PPP. Previously, only one background process handled all AAA requests for PPP, so only one new user could be authenticated or authorized at a time. This command configures the number of processes used to handle AAA requests for PPP, increasing the number of users that can be simultaneously authenticated or authorized.

The argument *number* defines the number of background processes earmarked to process AAA authentication and authorization requests for PPP. This argument also defines the number of new users that can be simultaneously authenticated and can be increased or decreased at any time.

Example

This example shows the **aaa processes** command within a standard AAA configuration. The authentication method list *dialins* specifies RADIUS as the method of authentication, then (if the RADIUS server does not respond) local authentication will be used on serial lines using PPP. Ten background processes have been allocated to handle AAA requests for PPP.

```
configure terminal
 aaa new-model
 aaa authentication ppp dialins radius local
 aaa processes 10
interface 10
 encap ppp
 ppp authentication pap dialins
```

Related Commands

You can search online at www.cisco.com to find documentation of related commands.

show ppp queues

access-profile

To apply your per-user authorization attributes to an interface during a PPP session, use the **access-profile** EXEC command. Use the default form of the command (no keywords) to cause existing access control lists (ACLs) to be removed, and ACLs defined in your per-user configuration to be installed.

> **access-profile** [**merge** | **replace**] [**ignore-sanity-checks**]

Syntax	Description
merge	(Optional) Like the default form of the command, this option removes existing ACLs while retaining other existing authorization attributes for the interface.
	However, using this option also installs per-user authorization attributes in addition to the existing attributes. (The default form of the command installs only new ACLs.) The per-user authorization attributes come from all attribute-value (AV) pairs defined in the AAA per-user configuration (the user's authorization profile).
	The interface's resulting authorization attributes are a combination of the previous and new configurations.

Syntax	Description
replace	(Optional) This option removes existing ACLs *and* all other existing authorization attributes for the interface.
	A complete new authorization configuration is then installed, using all AV pairs defined in the AAA per-user configuration.
	This option is not normally recommended because it initially deletes *all* existing configuration, including static routes. This could be detrimental if the new user profile does not reinstall appropriate static routes and other critical information.
ignore-sanity-checks	(Optional) Enables you to use any AV pairs, whether or not they are valid.

Command Mode

User EXEC

Usage Guidelines

This command first appeared in Cisco IOS Release 11.2 F.

Remote users can use this command to activate double authentication for a PPP session. Double authentication must be correctly configured for this command to have the desired effect.

You should use this command when remote users establish a PPP link to gain local network access.

After you have been authenticated with CHAP (or PAP), you will have limited authorization. To activate double authentication and gain your appropriate user network authorization, you must Telnet to the network access server and execute the **access-profile** command. (This command could also be set up as an autocommand, which would eliminate the need to manually enter the command.)

This command causes all subsequent network authorizations to be made in *your* username, instead of in the remote *host's* username.

Any changes to the interface caused by this command will stay in effect for as long as the interface stays up. These changes will be removed when the interface goes down. This command does not affect the normal operation of the router or the interface.

The default form of the command, **access-profile**, causes existing ACLs to be unconfigured (removed) and new ACLs to be installed. The new ACLs come from your per-user configuration on an AAA server (such as a TACACS+ server). The ACL replacement constitutes a reauthorization of your network privileges.

The default form of the command can fail if your per-user configuration contains statements other than ACL AV pairs. Any protocols with non-ACL statements will be deconfigured, and no traffic for that protocol can pass over the PPP link.

The **access-profile merge** form of the command causes existing ACLs to be unconfigured (removed) and new authorization information (including new ACLs) to be added to the interface. This new authorization information consists of your complete per-user configuration on an AAA server. If any of the new authorization statements conflict with existing statements, the new statements could "override" the old statements or be ignored, depending on the statement and applicable parser rules. The resulting interface configuration is a combination of the original configuration and the newly installed per-user configuration.

CAUTION   The new user authorization profile (per-user configuration) must *not* contain any invalid mandatory AV pairs, otherwise the command will fail and the PPP protocol (containing the invalid pair) will be dropped. If invalid AV pairs are included as *optional* in the user profile, the command will succeed, but the invalid AV pair will be ignored. Invalid AV pair types are listed later in this section.

The **access-profile replace** form of the command causes the entire existing authorization configuration to be removed from the interface, and the complete per-user authorization configuration to be added. This per-user authorization consists of your complete per-user configuration on an AAA server.

CAUTION   Use extreme caution when using the **access-profile replace** form of the command. It might have detrimental and unexpected results, because this option deletes *all* authorization configuration information (including static routes) before reinstalling the new authorization configuration.

Invalid AV pair types:

- addr
- addr-pool
- zonelist
- tunnel-id
- ip-addresses
- x25-addresses
- frame-relay
- source-ip

NOTE	These AV pair types are only invalid when used with double authentication; in the user-specific authorization profile, they cause the **access-profile** command to fail. However, these AV pair types can be appropriate when used in other contexts.

Example

This example activates double authentication for a remote user. This example assumes that the **access-profile** command was *not* configured as an autocommand.

The remote user connects to the corporate headquarters network per Figure 3-1.

Figure 3-1   *Network Topology for Activating Double Authentication (Example)*

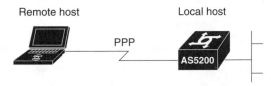

The remote user runs a terminal emulation application to Telnet to the corporate network access server, an AS5200 local host named *hqnas*. The remote user, named Bob, has the username *bobuser*.

This example replaces ACLs on the local host PPP interface. The ACLs previously applied to the interface during PPP authorization are replaced with ACLs defined in the per-user configuration AV pairs.

The remote user Telnets to the local host and logs in:

```
login: bobuser
Password: <welcome>
hqnas> access-profile
```

Bob is reauthenticated when he logs in to hqnas, because hqnas is configured for login AAA authentication using the corporate RADIUS server. When Bob enters the **access-profile** command, he is reauthorized with his per-user configuration privileges. This causes the access lists and filters in his per-user configuration to be applied to the network access server interface.

After the reauthorization is complete, Bob is automatically logged out of the AS5200 local host.

Related Commands

You can search online at www.cisco.com to find documentation of related commands.

connect
telnet

arap authentication

To enable AAA authentication for ARA on a line, use the **arap authentication** line configuration command. Use the **no** form of the command to disable authentication for an ARA line.

> **arap authentication** {**default** | *list-name*} [**one-time**]
> **no arap authentication** {**default** | *list-name*}

CAUTION   If you use a *list-name* value that was not configured with the **aaa authentication arap** command, ARA protocol will be disabled on this line.

Syntax	Description
default	Default list created with the **aaa authentication arap** command.
list-name	Indicated list created with the **aaa authentication arap** command.
one-time	(Optional) Accepts the username and password in the username field.

Default

ARA protocol authentication uses the default set with **aaa authentication arap** command. If no default is set, the local user database is checked.

Command Mode

Line configuration

Usage Guidelines

This command first appeared in Cisco IOS Release 11.0.

This command is a per-line command that specifies the name of a list of AAA authentication methods to try at login. If no list is specified, the default list is used (whether or not it is specified in the command line). You create defaults and lists with the **aaa authentication arap** command. Entering the **no** form of **arap authentication** has the same effect as entering the command with the **default** argument.

Before issuing this command, create a list of authentication processes by using the **aaa authentication arap** global configuration command.

Example

The following example specifies that the TACACS+ authentication list called *MIS-access* is used on ARA line 7:

```
line 7
 arap authentication MIS-access
```

Related Commands

You can search online at www.cisco.com to find documentation of related commands.

aaa authentication arap

clear ip trigger-authentication

To clear the list of remote hosts for which automated double authentication has been attempted, use the **clear ip trigger-authentication** privileged EXEC configuration command.

> **clear ip trigger-authentication**

Syntax Description

This command has no arguments or keywords.

Default

Table entries are cleared after a timeout if you do not clear them manually with this command.

Command Mode

Privileged EXEC

Usage Guidelines

This command first appeared in Cisco IOS Release 11.3 T.

Use this command when troubleshooting automated double authentication. This command clears the entries in the list of remote hosts displayed by the **show ip trigger-authentication** command.

Example

The following example clears the remote host table:

```
router# show ip trigger-authentication
Trigger-authentication Host Table:
Remote Host        Time Stamp
172.21.127.114       2940514234
router# clear ip trigger-authentication
router# show ip trigger-authentication
router#
```

Related Commands

You can search online at www.cisco.com to find documentation of related commands.

show ip trigger-authentication

ip trigger-authentication (global configuration)

To enable the automated part of double authentication at a device, use the **ip trigger-authentication** global configuration command. Use the **no** form of this command to disable the automated part of double authentication.

> **ip trigger-authentication** [**timeout** *seconds*] [**port** *number*]
> **no ip trigger-authentication**

Syntax	Description
timeout *seconds*	(Optional) Specifies how frequently the local device sends a UDP packet to the remote host to request the user's username and password (or PIN). The default is 90 seconds. See "The Timeout Keyword" below for details.
port *number*	(Optional) Specifies the UDP port to which the local router should send the UPD packet requesting the user's username and password (or PIN). The default is port 7500. See "The Port Keyword" below for details.

Default

The default timeout is 90 seconds, and the default port number is 7500.

Command Mode

Global configuration

Usage Guidelines

This command first appeared in Cisco IOS Release 11.3 T.

Configure this command on the local device (router or network access server) that remote users dial in to. Use this command only if the local device has already been configured to provide double authentication; this command enables automation of the second authentication of double authentication.

The Timeout Keyword

During the second authentication stage of double authentication—when the remote user is authenticated—the remote user must send a username and password (or PIN) to the local device. With automated double authentication, the local device sends a UDP packet to the remote user's host during the second user-authentication stage. This UDP packet triggers the remote host to launch a dialog box requesting a username and password (or PIN).

If the local device does not receive a valid response to the UDP packet within a timeout period, the local device will send another UDP packet. The device will continue to send UDP packets at the timeout intervals until it receives a response and can authenticate the user.

By default, the UDP packet timeout interval is 90 seconds. Use the **timeout** keyword to specify a different interval.

(This timeout also applies to how long entries will remain in the remote host table; see the **show ip trigger-authentication** command for details.)

The Port Keyword

As described in the previous section, the local device sends a UDP packet to the remote user's host to request the user's username and password (or PIN). This UDP packet is sent to UDP port 7500 by default. (The remote host client software listens to UDP port 7500 by default.) If you need to change the port number because port 7500 is used by another application, you should change the port number using the **port** keyword. If you change the port number, you need to change it in both places—both on the local device and in the remote host client software.

Example

The following example globally enables automated double authentication and sets the timeout to 120 seconds:

```
ip trigger-authentication timeout 120
```

Related Commands

You can search online at www.cisco.com to find documentation of related commands.

ip trigger-authentication (interface configuration)
show ip trigger-authentication

ip trigger-authentication (interface configuration)

To specify automated double authentication at an interface, use the **ip trigger-authentication** interface configuration command. Use the **no** form of this command to turn off automated double authentication at an interface.

> **ip trigger-authentication**
> **no ip trigger-authentication**

Syntax Description

This command has no arguments or keywords.

Default

Automated double authentication is not enabled for specific interfaces.

Command Mode

Interface configuration

Usage Guidelines

This command first appeared in Cisco IOS Release 11.3 T.

Configure this command on the local router or network access server that remote users dial in to. Use this command only if the local device has already been configured to provide double authentication and if automated double authentication has been enabled with the **ip trigger-authentication (global configuration)** command.

This command causes double authentication to occur automatically when users dial into the interface.

Example

The following example turns on automated double authentication at the ISDN Basic Rate Interface (BRI) interface BRI0:

```
interface BRI0
 ip trigger-authentication
 encapsulation ppp
 ppp authentication chap
```

Related Commands

You can search online at www.cisco.com to find documentation of related commands.

ip trigger-authentication (global configuration)

login authentication

To enable AAA authentication for logins, use the **login authentication** line configuration command. Use the **no** form of this command to either disable TACACS+ authentication for logins or to return to the default.

> **login authentication** {**default** | *list-name*}
> **no login authentication** {**default** | *list-name*}

Syntax	Description
default	Uses the default list created with the **aaa authentication login** command.
list-name	Uses the indicated list created with the **aaa authentication login** command.

Default

Uses the default set with **aaa authentication login**.

Command Mode

Line configuration

Usage Guidelines

This command first appeared in Cisco IOS Release 10.3.

This command is a per-line command used with AAA that specifies the name of a list of AAA authentication methods to try at login. If no list is specified, the default list is used (whether or not it is specified in the command line).

CAUTION If you use a *list-name* value that was not configured with the **aaa authentication login** command, you will disable login on this line.

Entering the **no** form of **login authentication** has the same effect as entering the command with the **default** argument.

Before issuing this command, create a list of authentication processes by using the global configuration **aaa authentication login** command.

Examples

The following example specifies that the default AAA authentication is to be used on line 4:

```
line 4
 login authentication default
```

The following example specifies that the AAA authentication list called *list1* is to be used on line 7:

```
line 7
 login authentication list1
```

Related Commands

You can search online at www.cisco.com to find documentation of related commands.

aaa authentication login

login tacacs

To configure your router to use TACACS user authentication, use the **login tacacs** line configuration command. Use the **no** form of this command to disable TACACS user authentication for a line.

> **login tacacs**
> **no login tacacs**

Syntax Description

This command has no arguments or keywords.

Default

Disabled

Command Mode

Line configuration

Usage Guidelines

This command first appeared in Cisco IOS Release 10.0.

You can use TACACS security if you have configured a TACACS server and you have a command control language (CCL) script that allows you to use TACACS security.

NOTE   This command cannot be used with AAA. Use the **login authentication** command instead.

Example

In the following example, lines 1 through 16 are configured for TACACS user authentication:

```
line 1 16
 login tacacs
```

nasi authentication

To enable AAA authentication for NASI clients connecting to a router, use the **nasi authentication** line configuration command. Use the **no** form of the command to return to the default, as specified by the **aaa authentication nasi** command.

> **nasi authentication** {**default** | *list-name*}
> **no login authentication** {**default** | *list-name*}

Syntax	Description
default	Uses the default list created with the **aaa authentication nasi** command.
list-name	Uses the list created with the **aaa authentication nasi** command.

Default

Uses the default set with the **aaa authentication nasi** command.

Command Mode

Line configuration

Usage Guidelines

This command first appeared in Cisco IOS Release 11.1.

This command is a per-line command used with AAA authentication that specifies the name of a list of authentication methods to try at login. If no list is specified, the default list is used, even if it is not specified in the command line. (You create defaults and lists with the **aaa authentication nasi** command.) Entering the **no** form of this command has the same effect as entering the command with the **default** argument.

CAUTION	If you use a *list-name* value that was not configured with the **aaa authentication nasi** command, you will disable login on this line.

Before issuing this command, create a list of authentication processes by using the **aaa authentication nasi** global configuration command.

Examples

The following example specifies that the default AAA authentication be used on line 4:

```
line 4
 nasi authentication default
```

The following example specifies that the AAA authentication list called *list1* be used on line 7:

```
line 7
 nasi authentication list1
```

Related Commands

You can search online at www.cisco.com to find documentation of related commands.

aaa authentication nasi
ipx nasi-server enable
show ipx nasi connections
show ipx spx-protocol

ppp authentication

To enable CHAP or PAP (or both) and to specify the order in which CHAP and PAP authentication are selected on the interface, use the **ppp authentication** interface configuration command. Use the **no** form of this command to disable this authentication.

ppp authentication {**chap** | **chap pap** | **pap chap** | **pap**} [**if-needed**]
[*list-name* | **default**] [**callin**] [**one-time**]
no ppp authentication

Syntax   Description

chap   Enables CHAP on a serial interface.

pap   Enables PAP on a serial interface.

chap pap   Enables both CHAP and PAP, and performs CHAP authentication before PAP.

pap chap   Enables both CHAP and PAP, and performs PAP authentication before CHAP.

ms-chap   Enables Microsoft's version of CHAP (MS-CHAP) on a serial interface.

if-needed   (Optional) Used with TACACS and extended TACACS. Does not perform CHAP or PAP authentication if the user has already provided authentication. This option is available only on asynchronous interfaces.

list-name   (Optional) Used with AAA. Specifies the name of a list of methods of authentication to use. If no list name is specified, the system uses the default. The list is created with the **aaa authentication ppp** command.

default   (Optional) The name of the method list is created with the **aaa authentication ppp** command.

callin   (Optional) Specifies authentication on incoming (received) calls only.

one-time   (Optional) Accepts the username and password in the username field.

CAUTION   If you use a *list-name* value that was not configured with the **aaa authentication ppp** command, you will disable PPP on this interface.

Default
PPP authentication is not enabled.

Command Mode
Interface configuration

Usage Guidelines
This command first appeared in Cisco IOS Release 10.0.

When you enable CHAP or PAP authentication (or both), the local router requires the remote device to prove its identity before allowing data traffic to flow. PAP authentication requires the remote device to send a name and a password, which is checked against a matching entry in the local username database or in the remote security server database. CHAP authentication sends a challenge to the remote device. The remote device encrypts the challenge value with a shared secret and returns the encrypted value and its name to the local router in a response message. The local router attempts to match the remote device's name with an associated secret stored in the local username or remote security server database; it uses the stored secret to encrypt the original challenge and verify that the encrypted values match.

You can enable PAP or CHAP (or both) in either order. If you enable both methods, the first method specified is requested during link negotiation. If the peer suggests using the second method, or refuses the first method, the second method is tried. Some remote devices support only CHAP and some support only PAP. Base the order in which you specify methods on the remote device's ability to correctly negotiate the appropriate method, and on the level of data line security you require. PAP usernames and passwords are sent as clear text strings, which can be intercepted and reused. CHAP has eliminated most of the known security holes.

Enabling or disabling PPP authentication does not affect the local router's ability to authenticate itself to the remote device.

If you are using autoselect on a TTY line, you can use the **ppp authentication** command to turn on PPP authentication for the corresponding interface.

MS-CHAP is the Microsoft version of CHAP. Like the standard version of CHAP, MS-CHAP is used for PPP authentication; in this case, authentication occurs between a PC using Microsoft Windows NT or Microsoft Windows 95 and a Cisco router or access server acting as a network access server.

Enabling or disabling PPP authentication does not affect the local router's willingness to authenticate itself to the remote device.

If you are using autoselect on a TTY line, you probably want to use the **ppp authentication** command to turn on PPP authentication for the corresponding interface.

Example

The following example enables CHAP on asynchronous interface 4 and uses the authentication list **MIS-access**:

```
interface async 4
 encapsulation ppp
 ppp authentication chap MIS-access
```

Related Commands

You can search online at www.cisco.com to find documentation of related commands.

aaa authentication ppp
aaa new-model
autoselect
encapsulation ppp
ppp-use-tacacs
username

ppp chap hostname

To create a pool of dialup routers that all appear to be the same host when authenticating with CHAP, use the **ppp chap hostname** interface configuration command. To disable this function, use the **no** form of the command.

> **ppp chap hostname** *hostname*
> **no ppp chap hostname** *hostname*

Syntax   Description

hostname   The name sent in the CHAP challenge.

Default

Disabled. The router name is sent in any CHAP challenges.

Command Mode

Interface configuration

Usage Guidelines

This command first appeared in Cisco IOS Release 11.2.

Currently, a router dialing a pool of access routers requires a username entry for each possible router in the pool because each router challenges with its hostname. If a router is added to the dialup rotary pool, all connecting routers must be updated. The **ppp chap hostname** command allows you to specify a common alias for all routers in a rotary group to use so that only one username must be configured on the dialing routers.

This command is normally used with local CHAP authentication (when the router authenticates to the peer), but it can also be used for remote CHAP authentication.

Example

The commands in the following example identify dialer interface 0 as the dialer rotary group leader and specifies ppp as the encapsulation method used by all member interfaces. This example shows that CHAP authentication is used on received calls only and the username *ISPCorp* will be sent in all CHAP challenges and responses:

```
interface dialer 0
 encapsulation ppp
 ppp authentication chap callin
 ppp chap hostname ISPCorp
```

Related Commands

You can search online at www.cisco.com to find documentation of related commands.

aaa authentication ppp
ppp authentication
ppp chap password
ppp chap refuse
ppp chap wait

ppp chap password

To enable a router calling a collection of routers that do not support this command (such as routers running older Cisco IOS software images) to configure a common CHAP secret password to use in response to challenges from an unknown peer, use the **ppp chap password** interface configuration command. Use the **no** form of this command to disable the PPP CHAP password.

> **ppp chap password** *secret*
> **no ppp chap password** *secret*

Syntax   Description

secret   The secret used to compute the response value for any CHAP challenge from an unknown peer.

Default

Disabled

Command Mode

Interface configuration

Usage Guidelines

This command first appeared in Cisco IOS Release 11.2.

This command allows you to replace several username and password configuration commands with a single copy of this command on any dialer interface or asynchronous group interface.

This command is used for remote CHAP authentication only (when routers authenticate to the peer) and does not affect local CHAP authentication.

Example

The commands in the following example specify ISDN BRI number 0. The method of encapsulation on the interface is PPP. If a CHAP challenge is received from a peer whose name is not found in the global list of usernames, the encrypted secret 7 1234567891 is decrypted and used to create a CHAP response value.

```
interface bri 0
 encapsulation ppp
 ppp chap password 7 1234567891
```

Related Commands

You can search online at www.cisco.com to find documentation of related commands.

aaa authentication ppp
ppp authentication
ppp chap hostname
ppp chap refuse
ppp chap wait

ppp chap refuse

To refuse CHAP authentication from peers requesting it, use the **ppp chap refuse** interface configuration command. Use the **no** form of this command to allow CHAP authentication.

> **ppp chap refuse** [**callin**]
> **no ppp chap refuse** [**callin**]

Syntax   Description

callin   (Optional) This keyword specifies that the router will refuse to answer CHAP authentication challenges received from the peer, but will still require the peer to answer any CHAP challenges the router sends.

Default

Disabled

Command Mode

Interface configuration

Usage Guidelines

This command first appeared in Cisco IOS Release 10.3.

This command specifies that CHAP authentication is disabled for all calls, meaning that all attempts by the peer to force the user to authenticate using CHAP will be refused. If the **callin** keyword is used, CHAP authentication is disabled for incoming calls from the peer, but will still be performed on outgoing calls to the peer.

If outbound PAP has been enabled (using the **ppp pap sent-username** command), PAP will be suggested as the authentication method in the refusal packet.

Example

The commands in the following example specify ISDN BRI number 0. The method of encapsulation on the interface is PPP. This example disables CHAP authentication from occurring if a peer calls in requesting CHAP authentication:

```
interface bri 0
 encapsulation ppp
 ppp chap refuse
```

Related Commands

You can search online at www.cisco.com to find documentation of related commands.

aaa authentication ppp
ppp authentication
ppp chap hostname
ppp chap password
ppp chap wait

ppp chap wait

To specify that the router will not authenticate to a peer requesting CHAP authentication until after the peer has authenticated itself to the router, use the **ppp chap wait** interface configuration command. Use the **no** form of this command to allow the router to respond immediately to an authentication challenge.

> **ppp chap wait** *secret*
> **no ppp chap wait** *secret*

Syntax	Description
secret	The secret used to compute the response value for any CHAP challenge from an unknown peer.

Default

Enabled

Command Mode

Interface configuration

Usage Guidelines

This command first appeared in Cisco IOS Release 10.3.

This command (which is the default) specifies that the router will not authenticate to a peer requesting CHAP authentication until the peer has authenticated itself to the router. The **no** form of this command specifies that the router will respond immediately to an authentication challenge.

Example

The commands in the following example specify ISDN BRI number 0. The method of encapsulation on the interface is PPP. This example disables the default, meaning that users do not have to wait for peers to complete CHAP authentication before authenticating themselves:

```
interface bri 0
 encapsulation ppp
 no ppp chap wait
```

Related Commands

You can search online at www.cisco.com to find documentation of related commands.

aaa authentication ppp
ppp authentication
ppp chap hostname
ppp chap password
ppp chap refuse

ppp pap sent-username

To re-enable remote PAP support for an interface and use the **sent-username** and **password** in the PAP authentication request packet to the peer, use the **ppp pap sent-username** interface configuration command. Use the **no** form of this command to disable remote PAP support.

> **ppp pap sent-username** *username* **password** *password*
> **no ppp pap sent-username**

Syntax	Description
username	Username sent in the PAP authentication request.
password	Password sent in the PAP authentication request.
password	Must contain from 1 to 25 uppercase and lowercase alphanumeric characters.

Default

Remote PAP support disabled.

Command Mode

Interface configuration

Usage Guidelines

This command first appeared in Cisco IOS Release 11.2.

Use this command to re-enable remote PAP support (for example, to respond to the peer's request to authenticate with PAP) and to specify the parameters to be used when sending the PAP Authentication Request.

This is a per-interface command. You must configure this command for each interface.

Example

The commands in the following example identify dialer interface 0 as the dialer rotary group leader and specify PPP as the method of encapsulation used by the interface. Authentication is by CHAP or PAP on received calls only. *ISPCorp* is the username sent to the peer if the peer requires the router to authenticate with PAP.

```
interface dialer0
 encapsulation ppp
 ppp authentication chap pap callin
 ppp chap hostname ISPCorp
 ppp pap sent username ISPCorp password 7 fjhfeu
 ppp pap sent-username ISPCorp password 7 1123659238
```

Related Commands

You can search online at www.cisco.com to find documentation of related commands.

aaa authentication ppp
ppp authentication
ppp chap hostname
ppp chap password
ppp use-tacacs

ppp use-tacacs

To enable TACACS for PPP authentication, use the **ppp use-tacacs** interface configuration command. Use the **no** form of the command to disable TACACS for PPP authentication.

> **ppp use-tacacs** [**single-line**]
> **no ppp use-tacacs**

NOTE   This command is not used in TACACS+. It has been replaced with the **aaa authentication ppp** command.

Syntax	Description
single-line	(Optional) Accept the username and password in the username field. This option applies only when using CHAP authentication.

Default

TACACS is not used for PPP authentication.

Command Mode

Interface configuration

Usage Guidelines

This command first appeared in Cisco IOS Release 10.3.

This is a per-interface command. Use this command only when you have set up an extended TACACS server.

When CHAP authentication is being used, the **ppp use-tacacs** command with the **single-line** option specifies that if a username and password are specified in the username, separated by an asterisk (*), a standard TACACS login query is performed using that username and password. If the username does not contain an asterisk, then normal CHAP authentication is performed.

This feature is useful when integrating TACACS with other authentication systems that require a clear text version of the user's password. Such systems include one-time password systems, token card systems, and Kerberos.

CAUTION   Normal CHAP authentications prevent the clear text password from being transmitted over the link. When you use the single-line option, passwords cross the link as clear text.

If the username and password are contained in the CHAP password, the CHAP secret is not used by the Cisco IOS software. Because most PPP clients require that a secret be specified, you can use any arbitrary string, and the Cisco IOS software ignores it.

Examples

The following example configures asynchronous interface 1 to use TACACS for CHAP authentication:

```
interface async 1
 ppp authentication chap
 ppp use-tacacs
```

The following example configures asynchronous interface 1 to use TACACS for PAP authentication:

```
interface async 1
 ppp authentication pap
 ppp use-tacacs
```

Related Commands

You can search online at www.cisco.com to find documentation of related commands.

ppp authentication
tacacs-server extended
tacacs-server host

show ip trigger-authentication

To view the list of remote hosts for which automated double authentication has been attempted, use the **show ip trigger-authentication** privileged EXEC command.

show ip trigger-authentication

Syntax Description

This command has no arguments or keywords.

Command Mode

Privileged EXEC

Usage Guidelines

This command first appeared in Cisco IOS Release 11.3 T.

Whenever a remote user needs to be user-authenticated in the second stage of automated double authentication, the local device sends a UDP packet to the remote user's host. When the UDP packet is sent, the user's host IP address is added to a table. If additional UDP packets are sent to the same remote host, a new table entry is not created; instead, the existing entry is updated with a new time stamp. This remote host table contains a cumulative list of host entries; entries are deleted after a timeout period or after you manually clear the table using the **clear ip trigger-authentication** command. You can change the timeout period with the **ip trigger-authentication (global configuration)** command.

Use this command to view the list of remote hosts for which automated double authentication has been attempted.

Sample Display

The following is sample output from the **show ip trigger-authentication** command:

```
myfirewall# show ip trigger-authentication
Trigger-authentication Host Table:
Remote Host        Time Stamp
172.21.127.114     2940514234
```

This output shows that automated double authentication was attempted for a remote user; the remote user's host has the IP address 172.21.127.114. The attempt to automatically double authenticate occurred when the local host (myfirewall) sent the remote host (172.21.127.114) a packet to UDP port 7500. (The default port was not changed in this example.)

Related Commands

You can search online at www.cisco.com to find documentation of related commands.

clear ip trigger-authentication

show ppp queues

To monitor the number of requests processed by each AAA background process, use the **show ppp queues** privileged EXEC command.

> **show ppp queues**

Syntax Description

This command has no arguments or keywords.

Command Mode

Privileged EXEC

Usage Guidelines

This command first appeared in Cisco IOS Release 11.3(2)AA.

Use the **show ppp queues** command to display the number of requests handled by each AAA background process, the average amount of time it takes to complete each request, and the requests still pending in the work queue. This information can help you balance the data load between the network access server and the AAA server.

This command displays information about the background processes configured by the **aaa processes** global configuration command. Each line in the display contains information about one of the background processes. If there are AAA requests in the queue when you enter this command, the requests will be printed as well as the background process data.

Sample Display

The following is sample output from the **show ppp queues** command:

```
router# show ppp queues
Proc #0   pid=73   authens=59    avg. rtt=118s. authors=160  avg. rtt=94s.
Proc #1   pid=74   authens=52    avg. rtt=119s. authors=127  avg. rtt=115s.
Proc #2   pid=75   authens=69    avg. rtt=130s. authors=80   avg. rtt=122s.
Proc #3   pid=76   authens=44    avg. rtt=114s. authors=55   avg. rtt=106s.
Proc #4   pid=77   authens=70    avg. rtt=141s. authors=76   avg. rtt=118s.
Proc #5   pid=78   authens=64    avg. rtt=131s. authors=97   avg. rtt=113s.
Proc #6   pid=79   authens=56    avg. rtt=121s. authors=57   avg. rtt=117s.
Proc #7   pid=80   authens=43    avg. rtt=126s. authors=54   avg. rtt=105s.
Proc #8   pid=81   authens=139   avg. rtt=141s. authors=120  avg. rtt=122s.
Proc #9   pid=82   authens=63    avg. rtt=128s. authors=199  avg. rtt=80s.
queue len=0 max len=499
```

Table 3-6 describes the fields shown in the sample display.

Table 3-6   *show ppp queues Command Field Descriptions*

Field	Description
Proc #	Identifies the background process allocated by the **aaa processes** command to handle AAA requests for PPP. All of the data in this row relates to this process.
pid=	Identification number of the background process.
authens=	Number of authentication requests the process has performed.
avg. rtt=	Average delay (in seconds) until the authentication request was completed.
authors=	Number of authorization requests the process has performed.
avg. rtt=	Average delay (in seconds) until the authorization request was completed.
queue len=	Current queue length.
max len=	Maximum length the queue ever reached.

Related Commands

You can search online at www.cisco.com to find documentation of related commands.

aaa processes
debug ppp

timeout login response

To specify how long the system will wait for login input (such as username and password) before timing out, use the **timeout login response** line configuration command. Use the **no** form of this command to set the timeout value to 0 seconds.

> **timeout login response** *seconds*
> **no timeout login response** *seconds*

Syntax   Description

seconds   Integer that determines the number of seconds the system will wait for login input before timing out. Available settings are from 1 to 300 seconds.

Default

The default login timeout value is 30 seconds.

Command Mode

Line configuration

Usage Guidelines

This command first appeared in Cisco IOS Release 11.3.

Example

The following example changes the login timeout value to 60 seconds:

```
line 10
 timeout login response 60
```

## CHAPTER 4

Configuring Authorization

AAA authorization enables you to limit the services available to a user. When AAA authorization is enabled, the network access server uses information retrieved from the user's profile, which is located either in the local user database or on the security server, to configure the user's session. After this is done, the user will be granted access to a requested service only if the information in the user profile allows it.

This chapter describes the following topics and tasks:

- AAA Authorization Types
- Named Method Lists for Authorization
- AAA Authorization Methods
- AAA Authorization Prerequisites
- AAA Authorization Configuration
- Configuring Authorization
- Configuring AAA Authorization Using Named Method Lists
- Disabling Authorization for Global Configuration Commands
- Authorization for Reverse Telnet
- Authorization Attribute-Value Pairs
- Authorization Configuration Examples

For a complete description of the authorization commands used in this chapter, refer to Chapter 5, "Authorization Commands." To locate documentation of other commands that appear in this chapter, you can search online at www.cisco.com.

AAA Authorization Types

Cisco IOS software supports three different types of authorization:

- EXEC—Applies to the attributes associated with a user EXEC terminal session.
- Command—Applies to the EXEC mode commands a user issues. Command authorization attempts authorization for all EXEC mode commands, including global configuration commands, associated with a specific privilege level.
- Network—Applies to network connections, including PPP, SLIP, or ARAP connections.

Named Method Lists for Authorization

Method lists for authorization define the ways authorization will be performed and the sequence in which these methods will be performed. A method list is a named list describing the authorization methods to be queried (such as RADIUS or TACACS+) in sequence. Method lists enable you to designate one or more security protocols to be used for authorization, thus ensuring a backup system in case the initial method fails. Cisco IOS software uses the first method listed to authorize users for specific network services; if that method fails to respond, the Cisco IOS software selects the next method listed in the method list. This process continues until there is successful communication with a listed authorization method or all methods defined are exhausted.

NOTE   The Cisco IOS software attempts authorization with the next listed method only when there is no response from the previous method. If authorization fails at any point in this cycle—meaning that the security server or local username database responds by denying the user services—the authorization process stops and no other authorization methods are attempted.

Cisco IOS software supports the following six methods for authorization:

- TACACS+—The network access server exchanges authorization information with the TACACS+ security daemon. TACACS+ authorization defines specific rights for users by associating attribute-value (AV) pairs, which are stored in a database on the TACACS+ security server, with the appropriate user.

- If-Authenticated—The user is allowed to access the requested function, provided that the user has been authenticated successfully.

- None—The network access server does not request authorization information; authorization is not performed over this line/interface.

- Local—The router or access server consults its local database, as defined by the **username** command, to authorize specific rights for users. Only a limited set of functions can be controlled via the local database.

- RADIUS—The network access server requests authorization information from the RADIUS security server. RADIUS authorization defines specific rights for users by associating attributes, which are stored in a database on the RADIUS server, with the appropriate user.

- Kerberos Instance Map—The network access server uses the instance defined by the **kerberos instance map** command for authorization.

Method lists are specific to the type of authorization being requested. AAA supports four different types of authorization:

- Network—Applies to network connections, including PPP, SLIP, or ARAP connections.

- EXEC—Applies to the attributes associated with a user EXEC terminal session.

- Commands—Applies to the EXEC mode commands a user issues. Command authorization attempts authorization for all EXEC mode commands, including global configuration commands, associated with a specific privilege level.

- Reverse Access—Applies to reverse Telnet sessions.

When you create a named method list, you are defining a particular list of authorization methods for the indicated authorization type.

Once defined, method lists must be applied to specific lines or interfaces before any of the defined methods will be performed. The only exception is the default method list (which is named *default*). If the **aaa authorization** command for a particular authorization type is issued without a named method list specified, the default method list is automatically applied to all interfaces or lines except those that have a named method list explicitly defined. (A defined method list overrides the default method list.) If no default method list is defined, then no authorization takes place.

AAA Authorization Methods

AAA supports five different methods of authorization:

- TACACS+—The network access server exchanges authorization information with the TACACS+ security daemon. TACACS+ authorization defines specific rights for users by associating attribute-value pairs, which are stored in a database on the TACACS+ security server, with the appropriate user.

- If-Authenticated—The user is allowed to access the requested function provided the user has been authenticated successfully.

- Local—The router or access server consults its local database, as defined by the **username** command, to authorize specific rights for users. Only a limited set of functions can be controlled via the local database.

- RADIUS—The network access server requests authorization information from the RADIUS security server. RADIUS authorization defines specific rights for users by associating attributes, which are stored in a database on the RADIUS server, with the appropriate user.

- Kerberos Instance Map—The network access server uses the instance defined by the **kerberos instance map** command for authorization.

AAA Authorization Prerequisites

Before configuring authorization using named method lists, you must first perform the following tasks:

- Enable AAA on your network access server. For more information about enabling AAA on your Cisco router or access server, refer to Chapter 1, "AAA Overview."

- Configure AAA authentication. Authorization generally takes place after authentication and relies on authentication to work properly. For more information about AAA authentication, refer to Chapter 2, "Configuring Authentication."

- Define the characteristics of your RADIUS or TACACS+ security server if you are issuing RADIUS or TACACS+ authorization. For more information about configuring your Cisco network access server to communicate with your RADIUS security server, refer to Chapter 8, "Configuring RADIUS." For more information about configuring your Cisco network access server to communicate with your TACACS+ security server, refer to Chapter 10, "Configuring TACACS+."

- Define the rights associated with specific users by using the **username** command if you are issuing local authorization.

- Create the administrative instances of users in the Kerberos key distribution center by issuing the **kerberos instance map** command if you are using Kerberos. For more information about Kerberos, refer to Chapter 13, "Configuring Kerberos."

AAA Authorization Configuration

This section describes the following:

- Configuring Authorization

- Configuring AAA Authorization Using Named Method Lists

- Disabling Authorization for Global Configuration Commands

- Authorization for Reverse Telnet

- Authorization Attribute-Value Pairs

For authorization configuration examples using the commands in this chapter, refer to the "TACACS+ Configuration Examples" section located at the end of the this chapter.

Configuring Authorization

The **aaa authorization** command allows you to set parameters that restrict a user's network access. To enable AAA authorization, use the following command in global configuration mode:

Command	Purpose
aaa authorization {**network** I **exec** I **command** *level*} {**tacacs+** I **if-authenticated** I **none** I **local** I **radius** I **krb5-instance**}	Sets parameters that restrict a user's network access.

NOTE	Authorization is bypassed for authenticated users who log in using the console line, even if authorization has been configured.

To enable authorization for all network-related service requests (including SLIP, PPP, PPP NCPs, and ARA protocols), use the **network** keyword. To enable authorization to determine whether a user is allowed to run an EXEC shell, use the **exec** keyword.

To enable authorization for specific, individual EXEC commands associated with a specific privilege level, use the **command** keyword. This allows you to authorize all commands associated with a specified command level from 0 to 15.

TACACS+ Authorization

To have the network access server request authorization information via a TACACS+ security server, use the **aaa authorization** command with the **tacacs+** *method* keyword. For more specific information about configuring authorization using a TACACS+ security server, refer to Chapter 10, "Configuring TACACS+." For an example of how to enable a TACACS+ server to authorize the use of network services, including PPP and ARA, see the "TACACS+ Authorization Example" section at the end of this chapter.

If-Authenticated Authorization

To allow users to have access to the functions they request as long as they have been authenticated, use the **aaa authorization** command with the **if-authenticated** *method* keyword. If you select this method, all requested functions are automatically granted to authenticated users.

None Authorization

To perform no authorization for the actions associated with a particular type of authentication, use the **aaa authorization** command with the **none** *method* keyword. If you select this method, authorization is disabled for all actions.

Local Authorization

To select local authorization, which means that the router or access server consults its local user database to determine the functions a user is permitted, use the **aaa authorization** command with the **local** *method* keyword. The functions associated with local authorization are defined by using the **username** global configuration command. For a list of permitted functions, refer to Chapter 2, "Configuring Authentication."

RADIUS Authorization

To have the network access server request authorization via a RADIUS security server, use the **aaa authorization** command with the **radius** *method* keyword. For more specific information about configuring authorization using a RADIUS security server, refer to Chapter 8, "Configuring RADIUS." For an example of how to enable a RADIUS server to authorize services, see the "RADIUS Authorization Example" section at the end of this chapter.

Kerberos Authorization

To run authorization to determine whether a user is allowed to run an EXEC shell at a specific privilege level based on a mapped Kerberos instance, use the **krb5-instance** *method* keyword. For more information, refer to the "Enabling Kerberos Instance Mapping" section of Chapter 13, "Configuring Kerberos." For an example of how to enable Kerberos instance mapping, see the "Kerberos Instance Mapping Examples" section at the end of this chapter.

Configuring AAA Authorization Using Named Method Lists

To configure AAA authorization using named method lists, use the following commands, beginning in global configuration mode:

Step	Command	Purpose
1	**aaa authorization** {**network** | **exec** | **commands** *level* | **reverse-access**} {**default** | *list-name*} [*method1* [*method2...*]]	Creates an authorization method list for a particular authorization type and enables authorization.

Step	Command	Purpose
2	**line** [**aux** I **console** I **tty** I **vty**] *line-number* [*ending-line-number*]	Enters the line configuration mode for the lines to which you want to apply the authorization method list.
		or
	interface *interface-type interface-number*	Enters the interface configuration mode for the interfaces to which you want to apply the authorization method list.
3	**authorization** {**arap** I **commands** *level* I **exec** I **reverse-access**} {**default** I *list-name*}	Applies the authorization list to a line or set of lines.
		or
	ppp authorization {**default** I *list-name*}	Applies the authorization list to an interface or set of interfaces.

Authorization Types

Named authorization method lists are specific to the indicated type of authorization. To create a method list to enable authorization for all network-related service requests (including SLIP, PPP, PPP NCPs, and ARA protocols), use the **network** keyword.

To create a method list to enable authorization to determine if a user is allowed to run an EXEC shell, use the **exec** keyword.

To create a method list to enable authorization for specific, individual EXEC commands associated with a specific privilege level, use the **commands** keyword. (This allows you to authorize all commands associated with a specified command level from 0 to 15.)

To create a method list to enable authorization for reverse Telnet functions, use the **reverse-access** keyword.

For information about the types of authorization supported by the Cisco IOS software, refer to the "AAA Authorization Types" section in this chapter.

Authorization Methods

To have the network access server request authorization information via a TACACS+ security server, use the **aaa authorization** command with the **tacacs+** *method* keyword. For more specific information about configuring authorization using a TACACS+ security server, refer to Chapter 10, "Configuring TACACS+."

To allow users to have access to the functions they request as long as they have been authenticated, use the **aaa authorization {type}** command with the **if-authenticated** *method* keyword. If you select this method, all requested functions are automatically granted to authenticated users.

There may be times when you do not want to run authorization from a particular interface or line. To stop authorization activities on designated lines or interfaces, use the **none** *method* keyword.

To select local authorization, which means that the router or access server consults its local user database to determine the functions a user is permitted, use the **local** *method* keyword. The functions associated with local authorization are defined by using the **username** global configuration command. For a list of permitted functions, refer to Chapter 2, "Configuring Authentication."

To have the network access server request authorization via a RADIUS security server, use the **radius** *method* keyword. For more specific information about configuring authorization using a RADIUS security server, refer to Chapter 8, "Configuring RADIUS."

To run authorization to determine whether a user is allowed to run an EXEC shell at a specific privilege level based on a mapped Kerberos instance, use the **krb5-instance** *method* keyword. For more information, refer to the "Enabling Kerberos Instance Mapping" section of Chapter 13, "Configuring Kerberos."

NOTE   Authorization method lists for SLIP follow whatever is configured for PPP on the relevant interface. If no lists are defined and applied to a particular interface (or no PPP settings are configured), the default setting for authorization applies.

Disabling Authorization for Global Configuration Commands

The **aaa authorization** command with the keyword **command** attempts authorization for all EXEC mode commands, including global configuration commands, associated with a specific privilege level. Because there are configuration commands that are identical to some EXEC-level commands, there can be some confusion in the authorization process. Using **no aaa authorization config-commands** stops the network access server not from attempting configuration command authorization. To disable AAA authorization for all global configuration commands, use the following command in global configuration mode:

Command	Purpose
no aaa authorization config-command	Disables authorization for all global configuration commands.

Authorization for Reverse Telnet

Telnet is a standard terminal emulation protocol used for remote terminal connection. Normally, you log in to a network access server (typically through a dialup connection) and then use Telnet to access other network devices from that network access server. There are times, however, when it is necessary to establish a reverse Telnet session. In reverse Telnet sessions, the Telnet connection is established in the opposite direction—from inside a network to a network access server on the network periphery to gain access to modems or other devices connected to that network access server. Reverse Telnet is used to provide users with dialout capability by allowing them to Telnet to modem ports attached to a network access server.

It is important to control access to ports accessible through reverse Telnet. Failure to do so could, for example, allow unauthorized users free access to modems where they can trap and divert incoming calls or make outgoing calls to unauthorized destinations.

Authentication during reverse Telnet is performed through the standard AAA login procedure for Telnet. Typically, the user has to provide a username and password to establish either a Telnet or reverse Telnet session. Reverse Telnet authorization provides an additional (optional) level of security by requiring authorization in addition to authentication. When enabled, reverse Telnet authorization can use RADIUS or TACACS+ to authorize whether or not this user is allowed reverse Telnet access to specific asynchronous ports, after the user successfully authenticates through the standard Telnet login procedure.

Reverse Telnet authorization offers the following benefits:

● An additional level of protection by ensuring that users engaged in reverse Telnet activities are indeed authorized to access a specific asynchronous port using reverse Telnet.

● An alternative method (other than access lists) to manage reverse Telnet authorization.

To configure a network access server to request authorization information from a TACACS+ or RADIUS server before allowing a user to establish a reverse Telnet session, use the following command in global configuration mode:

Command	Purpose
aaa authorization reverse-access {**radius**	**tacacs+**}	Configures the network access server to request authorization information before allowing a user to establish a reverse Telnet session.

This feature enables the network access server to request reverse Telnet authorization information from the security server, whether RADIUS or TACACS+. You must configure the specific reverse Telnet privileges for the user on the security server itself.

Authorization Attribute-Value Pairs

RADIUS and TACACS+ authorization both define specific rights for users by processing attributes, which are stored in a database on the security server. For both RADIUS and TACACS+, attributes are defined on the security server, associated with the user, and sent to the network access server where they are applied to the user's connection.

For a list of supported RADIUS attributes, refer to the "RADIUS Attributes" appendix. For a list of supported TACACS+ AV pairs, refer to Appendix B, "TACACS+ Attribute-Value Pairs."

Authorization Configuration Examples

This section contains the following configuration examples:

● Named Method List Configuration Example

● TACACS+ Authorization Examples

● RADIUS Authorization Example

● Kerberos Instance Mapping Examples

● Reverse Telnet Authorization Examples

Named Method List Configuration Example

The following example configures a Cisco AS5200 (enabled for AAA and communication with a RADIUS security server) for AAA services to be provided by the RADIUS server. If the RADIUS server fails to respond, then the local database will be queried for authentication and authorization information, and accounting services will be handled by a TACACS+ server.

```
aaa new-model
aaa authentication login admins local
aaa authentication ppp dialins radius local
aaa authorization network scoobee radius local
aaa accounting network charley start-stop radius

username root password ALongPassword

radius-server host alcatraz
radius-server key myRaDiUSpassWoRd

interface group-async 1
 group-range 1 16
 encapsulation ppp
 ppp authentication chap dialins
 ppp authorization scoobee
 ppp accounting charley

line 1 16
 autoselect ppp
 autoselect during-login
 login authentication admins
 modem dialin
```

The lines in this sample RADIUS AAA configuration are defined as follows:

- The **aaa new-model** command enables AAA network security services.

- The **aaa authentication login admins local** command defines a method list, *admins*, for login authentication.

- The **aaa authentication ppp dialins radius local** command defines the authentication method list *dialins*, which specifies that RADIUS authentication, and then (if the RADIUS server does not respond) local authentication will be used on serial lines using PPP.

- The **aaa authorization network scoobee radius local** command defines the network authorization method list named *scoobee*, which specifies that RADIUS authorization will be used on serial lines using PPP. If the RADIUS server fails to respond, then local network authorization will be performed.

- The **aaa accounting network charley start-stop radius** command defines the network accounting method list named charley, which specifies that RADIUS accounting services (in this case, start and stop records for specific events) will be used on serial lines using PPP.

- The **username** command defines the username and password to be used for the PPP Password Authentication Protocol (PAP) caller identification.

- The **radius-server host** command defines the name of the RADIUS server host.

- The **radius-server key** command defines the shared secret text string between the network access server and the RADIUS server host.

- The **interface group-async** command selects and defines an asynchronous interface group.

- The **group-range** command defines the member asynchronous interfaces in the interface group.

- The **encapsulation ppp** command sets PPP as the encapsulation method used on the specified interfaces.

- The **ppp authentication chap dialins** command selects Challenge Handshake Authentication Protocol (CHAP) as the method of PPP authentication and applies the *dialins* method list to the specified interfaces.

- The **ppp authorization scoobee** command applies the scoobee network authorization method list to the specified interfaces.

- The **ppp accounting charley** command applies the charley network accounting method list to the specified interfaces.

- The **line** command switches the configuration mode from global configuration to line configuration and identifies the specific lines being configured.

- The **autoselect ppp** command configures the Cisco IOS software to allow a PPP session to start up automatically on these selected lines.

- The **autoselect during-login** command is used to display the username and password prompt without pressing the Return key. After the user logs in, the autoselect function (in this case, PPP) begins.

- The **login authentication admins** command applies the *admins* method list for login authentication.

- The **modem dialin** command configures modems attached to the selected lines to only accept incoming calls.

TACACS+ Authorization Examples

The following example uses a TACACS+ server to authorize the use of network services, including PPP and ARA. If the TACACS+ server is not available or an error occurs during the authorization process, the fallback method (none) is to grant all authorization requests:

```
aaa authorization network tacacs+ none
```

The following example allows network authorization using TACACS+:

```
aaa authorization network tacacs+
```

The following example provides the same authorization, but also creates address pools called *mci* and *att*:

```
aaa authorization network tacacs+
ip address-pool local
ip local-pool mci 172.16.0.1 172.16.0.255
ip local-pool att 172.17.0.1 172.17.0.255
```

These address pools can then be selected by the TACACS daemon. A sample configuration of the daemon follows:

```
        user = mci_customer1 {
            login = cleartext "some password"
            service = ppp protocol = ip {
                addr-pool=mci
            }
        }

        user = att_customer1 {
            login = cleartext "some other password"
            service = ppp protocol = ip {
                addr-pool=att
            }
```

RADIUS Authorization Example

The following example shows how to configure the router to authorize using RADIUS:

```
aaa authorization exec radius if-authenticated
aaa authorization network radius
```

The lines in this sample RADIUS authorization configuration are defined as follows:

● The **aaa authorization exec radius if-authenticated** command configures the network access server to contact the RADIUS server to determine whether users are permitted to start an EXEC shell when they log in. If an error occurs when the network access server contacts the RADIUS server, the fallback method is to permit the CLI to start, provided that the user has been properly authenticated.

The RADIUS information returned may be used to specify an autocommand or a connection access list be applied to this connection.

● The **aaa authorization network radius** command configures network authorization via RADIUS. This can be used to govern address assignment, the application of access lists, and various other per-user quantities.

NOTE   Because no fallback method is specified in this example, authorization will fail if, for any reason, there is no response from the RADIUS server.

Kerberos Instance Mapping Examples

The following global configuration example maps the Kerberos instance, *admin*, to enable mode:

```
kerberos instance map admin 15
```

The following example configures the router to check users' Kerberos instances and set appropriate privilege levels:

```
aaa authorization exec krb5-instance
```

For more information about configuring Kerberos, refer to Chapter 13, "Configuring Kerberos."

Reverse Telnet Authorization Examples

The following example causes the network access server to request authorization information from a TACACS+ security server before allowing a user to establish a reverse Telnet session:

```
aaa new-model
aaa authentication login default tacacs+
aaa authorization reverse-access tacacs+
!
tacacs-server host 172.31.255.0
tacacs-server timeout 90
tacacs-server key goaway
```

The lines in this sample TACACS+ reverse Telnet authorization configuration are defined as follows:

- The **aaa new-model** command enables AAA.

- The **aaa authentication login default tacacs+** command specifies TACACS+ as the default method for user authentication during login.

- The **aaa authorization reverse-access tacacs+** specifies TACACS+ as the method for user authorization when trying to establish a reverse Telnet session.

- The **tacacs-server host** command identifies the TACACS+ server.

- The **tacacs-server timeout** command sets the interval of time that the network access server waits for the TACACS+ server to reply.

- The **tacacs-server key** command defines the encryption key used for all TACACS+ communications between the network access server and the TACACS+ daemon.

The following example configures a generic TACACS+ server to grant a user, *jim*, reverse Telnet access to port tty2 on the network access server named *godzilla* and to port tty5 on the network access server named *gamera*:

```
user = jim
  login = cleartext lab
  service = raccess {
    port#1 = godzilla/tty2
    port#2 = gamera/tty5
```

NOTE   In this example, *godzilla* and *gamera* are the configured host names of network access servers, not DNS names or alias.

The following example configures the TACACS+ server (CiscoSecure) to grant a user named *jim* reverse Telnet access:

```
user = jim
profile_id = 90
profile_cycle = 1
member = Tacacs_Users
service=shell {
default cmd=permit
}
service=raccess {
allow "c2511e0" "tty1" ".*"
refuse ".*" ".*" ".*"
password = clear "goaway"
```

<table>
<tr><td>**NOTE**</td><td>CiscoSecure only supports reverse Telnet using the command line interface in versions 2.1(*x*) through version 2.2(1).</td></tr>
</table>

An empty *service=raccess {}* clause permits a user to have unconditional access to network access server ports for reverse Telnet. If no *service=raccess* clause exists, the user is denied access to any port for reverse Telnet.

For more information about configuring TACACS+, refer to Chapter 10, "Configuring TACACS+."

The following example causes the network access server to request authorization from a RADIUS security server before allowing a user to establish a reverse Telnet session:

```
aaa new-model
aaa authentication login default radius
aaa authorization reverse-access radius
!
radius-server host 172.31.255.0
radius-server key go away
```

The lines in this sample RADIUS reverse Telnet authorization configuration are defined as follows:

- The **aaa new-model** command enables AAA.

- The **aaa authentication login default radius** command specifies RADIUS as the default method for user authentication during login.

- The **aaa authorization reverse-access radius** specifies RADIUS as the method for user authorization when trying to establish a reverse Telnet session.

- The **radius-server host** command identifies the RADIUS server.

- The **radius-server key** command defines the encryption key used for all RADIUS communications between the network access server and the RADIUS daemon.

The following example configures the RADIUS server to grant a user named *jim* reverse Telnet access at port tty2 on the network access server named *godzilla*:

```
Password = "goaway"
User-Service-Type = Shell-User
cisco-avpair = "raccess:port#1=godzilla/tty2"
```

An empty *raccess:port#1=nasname1/tty2* clause permits a user to have unconditional access to network access server ports for reverse Telnet. If no *raccess:port#1=nasname1/tty2* clause exists, the user is denied access to any port for reverse Telnet.

For more information about configuring RADIUS, refer to Chapter 8, "Configuring RADIUS."

## CHAPTER 5

Authorization Commands

This chapter describes the commands used to configure authentication, authorization, and accounting (AAA) authorization. AAA authorization enables you to limit the services available to a user. When AAA authorization is enabled, the network access server uses information retrieved from the user's profile, which is located either in the local user database or on the security server, to configure the user's session. When this is done, the user will be granted access to a requested service only if the information in the user profile allows it.

For information on how to configure authorization using AAA, refer to Chapter 4, "Configuring Authorization." For configuration examples using the commands in this chapter, refer to the "Authorization Configuration Examples" section located at the end of Chapter 4.

aaa authorization

Use the **aaa authorization** global configuration command to set parameters that restrict a user's network access. Use the **no** form of this command to disable authorization for a function.

> **aaa authorization** {**network** | **exec** | **commands** *level* | **reverse-access**} {**default** | *list-name*} [*method1* [*method2...*]]
>
> **no aaa authorization** {**network** | **exec** | **commands** *level* | **reverse-access**}

Syntax	Description
network	Runs authorization for all network-related service requests, including SLIP, PPP, PPP NCPs, and ARA.
exec	Runs authorization to determine whether the user is allowed to run an EXEC shell. This facility might return user profile information such as **autocommand** information.
commands	Runs authorization for all commands at the specified privilege level.
level	Specific command level that should be authorized. Valid entries are 0 through 15.
reverse-access	Runs authorization for reverse access connections, such as reverse Telnet.
default	Uses the listed authorization methods that follow this argument as the default list of methods for authorization.
list-name	Character string used to name the list of authorization methods.
method1 [*method2...*]	One of the keywords listed in Table 5-1.

Default

Authorization is disabled for all actions (equivalent to the method keyword **none**). If the **aaa authorization** command for a particular authorization type is issued without a named method list specified, the default method list is automatically applied to all interfaces or lines (where this authorization type applies) except those that have a named method list explicitly defined. (A defined method list overrides the default method list.) If no default method list is defined, then no authorization takes place.

Command Mode

Global configuration

Usage Guidelines

This command first appeared in Cisco IOS Release 10.0.

NOTE	This command cannot be used with TACACS or extended TACACS.

Use the **aaa authorization** command to enable authorization and to create named methods lists, defining authorization methods that can be used when a user accesses the specified function. Method lists for authorization define the ways authorization will be performed and the sequence in which these methods will be performed. A method list is simply a named list describing the authorization methods to be queried (such as RADIUS or TACACS+), in sequence. Method lists enable you to designate one or more security protocols to be used for authorization, thus ensuring a backup system in case the initial method fails. Cisco IOS software uses the first method listed to authorize users for specific network services; if that method fails to respond, the Cisco IOS software selects the next method listed in the method list. This process continues until there is successful communication with a listed authorization method, or all methods defined are exhausted.

NOTE	The Cisco IOS software attempts authorization with the next listed method only when there is no response from the previous method. If authorization fails at any point in this cycle—meaning that the security server or local username database responds by denying the user services—the authorization process stops and no other authorization methods are attempted.

Use the **aaa authorization** command to create a list by entering *list-name* and *method*, where *list-name* is any character string used to name this list (excluding all method names) and *method* identifies the list of authorization method(s) tried in the given sequence.

Method keywords are described in Table 5-1.

Table 5-1 *AAA Authorization Keywords*

Keyword	Description
tacacs+	Requests authorization information from the TACACS+ server.
if-authenticated	Allows the user to access the requested function if the user is authenticated.
none	No authorization is performed.
local	Uses the local database for authorization.
radius	Uses RADIUS to get authorization information.
krb5-instance	Uses the instance defined by the **kerberos instance map** command.

Cisco IOS software supports the following six methods for authorization:

- TACACS+—The network access server exchanges authorization information with the TACACS+ security daemon. TACACS+ authorization defines specific rights for users by associating attribute-value (AV) pairs, which are stored in a database on the TACACS+ security server, with the appropriate user.

- If-Authenticated—The user is allowed to access the requested function provided the user has been authenticated successfully.

- None—The network access server does not request authorization information; authorization is not performed over this line/interface.

- Local—The router or access server consults its local database, as defined by the **username** command, to authorize specific rights for users. Only a limited set of functions can be controlled via the local database.

- RADIUS—The network access server requests authorization information from the RADIUS security server. RADIUS authorization defines specific rights for users by associating attributes, which are stored in a database on the RADIUS server, with the appropriate user.

- Kerberos Instance Map—The network access server uses the instance defined by the **kerberos instance map** command for authorization.

Method lists are specific to the type of authorization being requested. AAA supports four different types of authorization:

- Network—Applies to network connections, including PPP, SLIP, or ARA connections.

- EXEC—Applies to the attributes associated with a user EXEC terminal session.

- Commands—Applies to the EXEC mode commands a user issues. Command authorization attempts authorization for all EXEC mode commands, including global configuration commands, associated with a specific privilege level.

- Reverse Access—Applies to reverse Telnet sessions.

When you create a named method list, you are defining a particular list of authorization methods for the indicated authorization type.

Once defined, method lists must be applied to specific lines or interfaces before any of the defined methods will be performed.

The authorization command causes a request packet containing a series of AV pairs to be sent to the RADIUS or TACACS daemon as part of the authorization process. The daemon can do one of the following:

- Accept the request as is

- Make changes to the request

- Refuse the request and refuse authorization

For a list of supported RADIUS attributes, refer to Appendix A, "RADIUS Attributes." For a list of supported TACACS+ AV pairs, refer to Appendix B, "TACACS+ Attribute-Value Pairs."

NOTE   There are five commands associated with privilege level 0: **disable**, **enable**, **exit**, **help**, and **logout**. If you configure AAA authorization for a privilege level greater than 0, these five commands will not be included in the privilege level command set.

Example

The following example defines the network authorization method list named *scoobee*, which specifies that RADIUS authorization will be used on serial lines using PPP. If the RADIUS server fails to respond, then local network authorization will be performed.

```
aaa authorization network scoobee radius local
```

Related Commands

You search online at www.cisco.com to find documentation of related commands.

aaa accounting
aaa new-model

aaa authorization config-commands

To disable AAA configuration command authorization in the EXEC mode, use the **no** form of the **aaa authorization config-commands** global configuration command. Use the standard form of this command to re-establish the default created when the **aaa authorization commands** *level method1* command was issued.

> **aaa authorization config-commands**
> **no aaa authorization config-commands**

Syntax Description

This command has no arguments or keywords.

Default

After the **aaa authorization** *command level method* has been issued, this command is enabled by default—meaning that all configuration commands in the EXEC mode will be authorized.

Command Mode

Global configuration

Usage Guidelines

This command first appeared in Cisco IOS Release 11.2.

If **aaa authorization** *command level method* is enabled, all commands, including configuration commands, are authorized by AAA using the method specified. Because there are configuration commands that are identical to some EXEC-level commands, there can be some confusion in the authorization process. Using **no aaa authorization config-commands** stops the network access server from attempting configuration command authorization.

After the **no** form of this command has been entered, AAA authorization of configuration commands is completely disabled. Care should be taken before entering the **no** form of this command because it potentially reduces the amount of administrative control on configuration commands.

Use the **aaa authorization config-commands command** if, after using the no form of this command, you need to re-establish the default set by the **aaa authorization** *command level method* command.

Example

The following example specifies that TACACS+ authorization is run for level 15 commands and that AAA authorization of configuration commands is disabled:

```
aaa new-model
aaa authorization command 15 tacacs+ none
no aaa authorization config-commands
```

Related Commands

You search online at www.cisco.com to find documentation of related commands.

aaa authorization

aaa authorization reverse-access

To configure a network access server to request authorization information from a security server before allowing a user to establish a reverse Telnet session, use the **aaa authorization reverse-access** global configuration command. Use the **no** form of this command to restore the default value for this command.

> **aaa authorization reverse-access** {**radius** | **tacacs+**}
> **no aaa authorization reverse-access** {**radius** | **tacacs+**}

Syntax	Description
radius	Specifies that the network access server will request authorization from a RADIUS security server before allowing a user to establish a reverse Telnet session.
tacacs+	Specifies that the network access server will request authorization from a TACACS+ security server before allowing a user to establish a reverse Telnet session.

Default

The default for this command is disabled, meaning that authorization for reverse Telnet is not requested.

Command Mode

Global configuration

Usage Guidelines

This command first appeared in Cisco IOS Release 11.3.

Telnet is a standard terminal emulation protocol used for remote terminal connection. Normally, you log in to a network access server (typically through a dialup connection) and then use Telnet to access other network devices from that network access server. There are times, however, when it is necessary to establish a reverse Telnet session. In reverse Telnet sessions, the Telnet connection is established in the opposite direction—from inside a network to a network access server on the network periphery to gain access to modems or other devices connected to that network access server. Reverse Telnet is used to provide users with dialout capability by allowing them to Telnet to modem ports attached to a network access server.

It is important to control access to ports accessible through reverse Telnet. Failure to do so could, for example, allow unauthorized users free access to modems where they can trap and divert incoming calls or make outgoing calls to unauthorized destinations.

Authentication during reverse Telnet is performed through the standard AAA login procedure for Telnet. Typically the user has to provide a username and password to establish either a Telnet or reverse Telnet session. This command provides an additional (optional) level of security by requiring authorization in addition to authentication. When this command is enabled, reverse Telnet authorization can use RADIUS or TACACS+ to authorize whether or not this user is allowed reverse Telnet access to specific asynchronous ports, after the user successfully authenticates through the standard Telnet login procedure.

Examples

The following example causes the network access server to request authorization information from a TACACS+ security server before allowing a user to establish a reverse Telnet session:

```
aaa new-model
aaa authentication login default tacacs+
aaa authorization reverse-access tacacs+
!
tacacs-server host 172.31.255.0
tacacs-server timeout 90
tacacs-server key goaway
```

The lines in this sample TACACS+ reverse Telnet authorization configuration are defined as follows:

● The **aaa new-model** command enables AAA.

● The **aaa authentication login default tacacs+** command specifies TACACS+ as the default method for user authentication during login.

● The **aaa authorization reverse-access tacacs+** specifies TACACS+ as the method for user authorization when trying to establish a reverse Telnet session.

● The **tacacs-server host** command identifies the TACACS+ server.

- The **tacacs-server timeout** command sets the interval of time that the network access server waits for the TACACS+ server to reply.

- The **tacacs-server key** command defines the encryption key used for all TACACS+ communications between the network access server and the TACACS+ daemon.

The following example configures a generic TACACS+ server to grant a user, *jim*, reverse Telnet access to port tty2 on the network access server named *godzilla* and to port tty5 on the network access server named *gamera*:

```
user = jim
  login = cleartext lab
  service = raccess {
    port#1 = godzilla/tty2
    port#2 = gamera/tty5
```

NOTE   In this example, *godzilla* and *gamera* are the configured host names of network access servers, not DNS names or alias.

The following example configures the TACACS+ server (CiscoSecure) to authorize a user named *jim* for reverse Telnet:

```
user = jim
profile_id = 90
profile_cycle = 1
member = Tacacs_Users
service=shell {
default cmd=permit
}
service=raccess {
allow "c2511e0" "tty1" ".*"
refuse ".*" ".*" ".*"
password = clear "goaway"
```

NOTE   CiscoSecure only supports reverse Telnet using the command line interface in versions 2.1(*x*) through version 2.2(1).

An empty *service=raccess {}* clause permits a user to have unconditional access to network access server ports for reverse Telnet. If no *service=raccess* clause exists, the user is denied access to any port for reverse Telnet.

For more information about configuring TACACS+, refer to Chapter 10, "Configuring TACACS+."

The following example causes the network access server to request authorization from a RADIUS security server before allowing a user to establish a reverse Telnet session:

```
aaa new-model
aaa authentication login default radius
aaa authorization reverse-access radius
!
radius-server host 172.31.255.0
radius-server key go away
```

The lines in this sample RADIUS reverse Telnet authorization configuration are defined as follows:

- The **aaa new-model** command enables AAA.

- The **aaa authentication login default radius** command specifies RADIUS as the default method for user authentication during login.

- The **aaa authorization reverse-access radius** specifies RADIUS as the method for user authorization when trying to establish a reverse Telnet session.

- The **radius-server host** command identifies the RADIUS server.

- The **radius-server key** command defines the encryption key used for all RADIUS communications between the network access server and the RADIUS daemon.

The following example configures the RADIUS server to grant a user named *jim* reverse Telnet access at port tty2 on network access server *godzilla*:

```
Password = "goaway"
User-Service-Type = Shell-User
cisco-avpair = "raccess:port#1=godzilla/tty2"
```

An empty *raccess:port#1=nasname1/tty2* clause permits a user to have unconditional access to network access server ports for reverse Telnet. If no *raccess:port#1=nasname1/tty2* clause exists, the user is denied access to any port for reverse Telnet.

For more information about configuring RADIUS, refer to Chapter 8, "Configuring RADIUS."

Related Commands

You search online at www.cisco.com to find documentation of related commands.

aaa authorization

aaa new-model

To enable the AAA access control model, use the **aaa new-model** global configuration command. Use the **no** form of this command to disable the AAA access control model.

> **aaa new-model**
> **no aaa new-model**

Syntax Description

This command has no arguments or keywords.

Default

AAA is not enabled.

Command Mode

Global configuration

Usage Guidelines

This command first appeared in Cisco IOS Release 10.0.

This command enables the AAA access control system. After you have enabled AAA, TACACS and extended TACACS commands are no longer available. If you initialize AAA functionality and later decide to use TACACS or extended TACACS, issue the **no** version of this command then enable the version of TACACS that you want to use.

Example

The following example initializes AAA:

```
aaa new-model
```

Related Commands

You search online at www.cisco.com to find documentation of related commands.

aaa accounting
aaa authentication arap
aaa authentication enable default
aaa authentication local-override
aaa authentication login
aaa authentication ppp
aaa authorization
tacacs-server key

authorization

To enable AAA authorization for a specific line or group of lines, use the **authorization** line configuration command. Use the **no** form of this command to disable authorization.

authorization {**arap** | **commands** *level* | **exec** | **reverse-access**} [**default** | *list-name*]
no authorization {**arap** | **commands** *level* | **exec** | **reverse-access**} [**default** |
list-name]

Syntax	Description
arap	Enables authorization for line(s) configured for AppleTalk Remote Access (ARA) protocol.
commands	Enables authorization on the selected line(s) for all commands at the specified privilege level.
level	Specific command level to be authorized. Valid entries are 0 through 15.
exec	Enables authorization to determine if the user is allowed to run an EXEC shell on the selected line(s).
reverse-access	Enables authorization to determine if the user is allowed reverse access privileges.
default	(Optional) The name of the default method list, created with the **aaa authorization** command.
list-name	(Optional) Specifies the name of a list of authorization methods to use. If no list name is specified, the system uses the default. The list is created with the **aaa authorization** command.

Default

Authorization is not enabled.

Command Mode

Line configuration

Usage Guidelines

This command first appeared in Cisco IOS Release 11.3T.

After you enable the **aaa authorization** command and define a named authorization method list (or use the default method list) for a particular type of authorization, you must apply the defined lists to the appropriate lines for authorization to take place. Use the **authorization** command to apply the specified method lists (or if none is specified, the default method list) to the selected line or group of lines.

Example

The following example enables command authorization (for level 15), using the method list named *charlie* on line 10:

```
line 10
 authorization commands 15 charlie
```

Related Commands

You search online at www.cisco.com to find documentation of related commands.

aaa accounting
aaa authentication arap
login authentication
nasi authentication

ppp authorization

To enable AAA authorization on the selected interface, use the **ppp authorization** interface configuration command. Use the **no** form of this command to disable authorization.

> **ppp authorization** [**default** | *list-name*]
> **no ppp authorization**

Syntax   Description

default   (Optional) The name of the method list is created with the **aaa authorization** command.

list-name   (Optional) Specifies the name of a list of authorization methods to use. If no list name is specified, the system uses the default. The list is created with the **aaa authorization** command.

Default

Authorization is disabled.

Command Mode

Interface configuration

Usage Guidelines

This command first appeared in Cisco IOS Release 11.3T.

After you enable the **aaa authorization** command and define a named authorization method list (or use the default method list), you must apply the defined lists to the appropriate interfaces for authorization to take place. Use the **ppp authorization** command to apply the specified method lists (or if none is specified, the default method list) to the selected interface.

Example

The following example enables authorization on asynchronous interface 4 and uses the method list named *charlie*:

```
interface async 4
 encapsulation ppp
 ppp authorization charlie
```

Related Commands

You search online at www.cisco.com to find documentation of related commands.

aaa authorization

## CHAPTER 6

Configuring Accounting

The AAA accounting feature enables you to track the services users are accessing as well as the amount of network resources they are consuming. When **aaa accounting** is enabled, the network access server reports user activity to the TACACS+ or RADIUS security server (depending on which security method you have implemented) in the form of accounting records. Each accounting record contains accounting attribute-value (AV) pairs and is stored on the security server. This data can then be analyzed for network management, client billing, and/or auditing.

This chapter describes the following topics and tasks:

- Named Method Lists for Accounting
- AAA Accounting Types
- AAA Accounting Prerequisites
- AAA Accounting Configuration Task List
- Configuring AAA Accounting Using Named Method Lists
- Enabling Accounting
- Monitoring Accounting
- Accounting Attribute-Value Pairs
- Accounting Configuration Example

For a complete description of the accounting commands used in this chapter, refer to Chapter 7, "Accounting Commands." To locate documentation of other commands that appear in this chapter, you can search online at www.cisco.com.

Named Method Lists for Accounting

Like authentication and authorization method lists, method lists for accounting define the way accounting will be performed. Named accounting method lists enable you to designate a particular security protocol to be used on specific lines or interfaces for accounting services.

Cisco IOS software supports the following two methods for accounting:

- TACACS+—The network access server reports user activity to the TACACS+ security server in the form of accounting records. Each accounting record contains accounting AV pairs and is stored on the security server.

- RADIUS—The network access server reports user activity to the RADIUS security server in the form of accounting records. Each accounting record contains accounting AV pairs and is stored on the security server.

Accounting method lists are specific to the type of accounting being requested. AAA supports five types of accounting:

- Network—Provides information for all PPP, SLIP, or ARAP sessions, including packet and byte counts.

- EXEC—Provides information about user EXEC terminal sessions of the network access server.

- Commands—Applies to the EXEC mode commands a user issues. Command authorization attempts authorization for all EXEC mode commands, including global configuration commands, associated with a specific privilege level.

- Connection—Provides information about all outbound connections made from the network access server, such as Telnet, local-area transport (LAT), TN3270, packet assembler/disassembler (PAD), and rlogin.

- System—Provides information about system-level events.

NOTE   System accounting does not use named accounting lists; you can only define the default list for system accounting.

Once again, when you create a named method list, you are defining a particular list of accounting methods for the indicated accounting type.

Accounting method lists must be applied to specific lines or interfaces before any of the defined methods will be performed. The only exception is the default method list (which is named *default*). If the **aaa accounting** command for a particular accounting type is issued without a named method list specified, the default method list is automatically applied to all interfaces or lines except those that have a named method list explicitly defined. (A defined method list overrides the default method list.) If no default method list is defined, then no accounting takes place.

AAA Accounting Types

Cisco IOS software supports five kinds of accounting:

- Network Accounting
- Connection Accounting

- EXEC Accounting

- System Accounting

- Command Accounting

Network Accounting

Network accounting provides information for all PPP, SLIP, or ARAP sessions, including packet and byte counts.

The following example shows the information contained in a RADIUS network accounting record for a PPP user who comes in through an EXEC session:

```
Wed Jun 25 04:44:45 1997
        NAS-IP-Address = "172.16.25.15"
        NAS-Port = 5
        User-Name = "fgeorge"
        Client-Port-DNIS = "4327528"
        Caller-ID = "562"
        Acct-Status-Type = Start
        Acct-Authentic = RADIUS
        Service-Type = Exec-User
        Acct-Session-Id = "0000000D"
        Acct-Delay-Time = 0
        User-Id = "fgeorge"
        NAS-Identifier = "172.16.25.15"

Wed Jun 25 04:45:00 1997
        NAS-IP-Address = "172.16.25.15"
        NAS-Port = 5
        User-Name = "fgeorge"
        Client-Port-DNIS = "4327528"
        Caller-ID = "562"
        Acct-Status-Type = Start
        Acct-Authentic = RADIUS
        Service-Type = Framed
        Acct-Session-Id = "0000000E"
        Framed-IP-Address = "10.1.1.2"
        Framed-Protocol = PPP
        Acct-Delay-Time = 0
        User-Id = "fgeorge"
        NAS-Identifier = "172.16.25.15"

Wed Jun 25 04:47:46 1997
        NAS-IP-Address = "172.16.25.15"
        NAS-Port = 5
        User-Name = "fgeorge"
        Client-Port-DNIS = "4327528"
        Caller-ID = "562"
        Acct-Status-Type = Stop
        Acct-Authentic = RADIUS
        Service-Type = Framed
```

```
        Acct-Session-Id = "0000000E"
        Framed-IP-Address = "10.1.1.2"
        Framed-Protocol = PPP
        Acct-Input-Octets = 3075
        Acct-Output-Octets = 167
        Acct-Input-Packets = 39
        Acct-Output-Packets = 9
        Acct-Session-Time = 171
        Acct-Delay-Time = 0
        User-Id = "fgeorge"
        NAS-Identifier = "172.16.25.15"

Wed Jun 25 04:48:45 1997
        NAS-IP-Address = "172.16.25.15"
        NAS-Port = 5
        User-Name = "fgeorge"
        Client-Port-DNIS = "4327528"
        Caller-ID = "408"
        Acct-Status-Type = Stop
        Acct-Authentic = RADIUS
        Service-Type = Exec-User
        Acct-Session-Id = "0000000D"
        Acct-Delay-Time = 0
        User-Id = "fgeorge"
        NAS-Identifier = "172.16.25.15"
```

The following example shows the information contained in a TACACS+ network accounting record for a PPP user who first started an EXEC session:

```
Wed Jun 25 04:00:35 1997        172.16.25.15    fgeorge    tty4        562/4327528
starttask_id=28       service=shell
Wed Jun 25 04:00:46 1997        172.16.25.15    fgeorge    tty4        562/4327528
starttask_id=30       addr=10.1.1.1    service=ppp
Wed Jun 25 04:00:49 1997        172.16.25.15    fgeorge    tty4        408/4327528
update        task_id=30       addr=10.1.1.1    service=ppp      protocol=ip      addr=10.1.1.1
Wed Jun 25 04:01:31 1997        172.16.25.15    fgeorge    tty4        562/4327528
stoptask_id=30        addr=10.1.1.1    service=ppp      protocol=ip      addr=10.1.1.1
bytes_in=2844         bytes_out=1682   paks_in=36       paks_out=24     elapsed_time=51
Wed Jun 25 04:01:32 1996        172.16.25.15    fgeorge    tty4        562/4327528
stoptask_id=28        service=shell    elapsed_time=57
```

NOTE   The precise format of accounting packets records may vary, depending on your particular security server daemon.

The following example shows the information contained in a RADIUS network accounting record for a PPP user who comes in through autoselect:

```
Wed Jun 25 04:30:52 1997
        NAS-IP-Address = "172.16.25.15"
        NAS-Port = 3
        User-Name = "fgeorge"
        Client-Port-DNIS = "4327528"
        Caller-ID = "562"
        Acct-Status-Type = Start
        Acct-Authentic = RADIUS
        Service-Type = Framed
        Acct-Session-Id = "0000000B"
        Framed-Protocol = PPP
        Acct-Delay-Time = 0
        User-Id = "fgeorge"
        NAS-Identifier = "172.16.25.15"

Wed Jun 25 04:36:49 1997
        NAS-IP-Address = "172.16.25.15"
        NAS-Port = 3
        User-Name = "fgeorge"
        Client-Port-DNIS = "4327528"
        Caller-ID = "562"
        Acct-Status-Type = Stop
        Acct-Authentic = RADIUS
        Service-Type = Framed
        Acct-Session-Id = "0000000B"
        Framed-Protocol = PPP
        Framed-IP-Address = "10.1.1.1"
        Acct-Input-Octets = 8630
        Acct-Output-Octets = 5722
        Acct-Input-Packets = 94
        Acct-Output-Packets = 64
        Acct-Session-Time = 357
        Acct-Delay-Time = 0
        User-Id = "fgeorge"
        NAS-Identifier = "172.16.25.15"
```

The following example shows the information contained in a TACACS+ network accounting record for a PPP user who comes in through autoselect:

```
Wed Jun 25 04:02:19 1997        172.16.25.15        fgeorge        Async5   562/4327528
starttask_id=35         service=ppp
Wed Jun 25 04:02:25 1997        172.16.25.15        fgeorge        Async5   562/4327528
update          task_id=35      service=ppp        protocol=ip        addr=10.1.1.2
Wed Jun 25 04:05:03 1997        172.16.25.15        fgeorge        Async5   562/4327528
stoptask_id=35          service=ppp     protocol=ip        addr=10.1.1.2   bytes_in=3366
bytes_out=2149          paks_in=42      paks_out=28        elapsed_time=164
```

Connection Accounting

Connection accounting provides information about all outbound connections made from the network access server, such as Telnet, LAT, TN3270, PAD, and rlogin.

The following example shows the information contained in a RADIUS connection accounting record for an outbound Telnet connection:

```
Wed Jun 25 04:28:00 1997
        NAS-IP-Address = "172.16.25.15"
        NAS-Port = 2
        User-Name = "fgeorge"
        Client-Port-DNIS = "4327528"
        Caller-ID = "5622329477"
        Acct-Status-Type = Start
        Acct-Authentic = RADIUS
        Service-Type = Login
        Acct-Session-Id = "00000008"
        Login-Service = Telnet
        Login-IP-Host = "171.68.202.158"
        Acct-Delay-Time = 0
        User-Id = "fgeorge"
        NAS-Identifier = "172.16.25.15"

Wed Jun 25 04:28:39 1997
        NAS-IP-Address = "172.16.25.15"
        NAS-Port = 2
        User-Name = "fgeorge"
        Client-Port-DNIS = "4327528"
        Caller-ID = "5622329477"
        Acct-Status-Type = Stop
        Acct-Authentic = RADIUS
        Service-Type = Login
        Acct-Session-Id = "00000008"
        Login-Service = Telnet
        Login-IP-Host = "171.68.202.158"
        Acct-Input-Octets = 10774
        Acct-Output-Octets = 112
        Acct-Input-Packets = 91
        Acct-Output-Packets = 99
        Acct-Session-Time = 39
        Acct-Delay-Time = 0
        User-Id = "fgeorge"
        NAS-Identifier = "172.16.25.15"
```

The following example shows the information contained in a TACACS+ connection accounting record for an outbound Telnet connection:

```
Wed Jun 25 03:47:43 1997        172.16.25.15       fgeorge   tty3  5622329430/4327528
start     task_id=10         service=connection     protocol=telnet addr=171.68.202.158
cmd=telnet fgeorge-sun
Wed Jun 25 03:48:38 1997        172.16.25.15       fgeorge   tty3  5622329430/4327528 stop
task_id=10                 service=connection      protocol=telnet addr=171.68.202.158
cmd=telnet fgeorge-sun        bytes_in=4467   bytes_out=96    paks_in=61      paks_out=72 e
lapsed_time=55
```

The following example shows the information contained in a RADIUS connection accounting record for an outbound rlogin connection:

```
Wed Jun 25 04:29:48 1997
        NAS-IP-Address = "172.16.25.15"
        NAS-Port = 2
        User-Name = "fgeorge"
        Client-Port-DNIS = "4327528"
        Caller-ID = "5622329477"
        Acct-Status-Type = Start
        Acct-Authentic = RADIUS
        Service-Type = Login
        Acct-Session-Id = "0000000A"
        Login-Service = Rlogin
        Login-IP-Host = "171.68.202.158"
        Acct-Delay-Time = 0
        User-Id = "fgeorge"
        NAS-Identifier = "172.16.25.15"

Wed Jun 25 04:30:09 1997
        NAS-IP-Address = "172.16.25.15"
        NAS-Port = 2
        User-Name = "fgeorge"
        Client-Port-DNIS = "4327528"
        Caller-ID = "5622329477"
        Acct-Status-Type = Stop
        Acct-Authentic = RADIUS
        Service-Type = Login
        Acct-Session-Id = "0000000A"
        Login-Service = Rlogin
        Login-IP-Host = "171.68.202.158"
        Acct-Input-Octets = 18686
        Acct-Output-Octets = 86
        Acct-Input-Packets = 90
        Acct-Output-Packets = 68
        Acct-Session-Time = 22
        Acct-Delay-Time = 0
        User-Id = "fgeorge"
        NAS-Identifier = "172.16.25.15"
```

The following example shows the information contained in a TACACS+ connection accounting record for an outbound rlogin connection:

```
Wed Jun 25 03:48:46 1997          172.16.25.15      fgeorge   tty3    5622329430/4327528
start     task_id=12       service=connection        protocol=rlogin addr=171.68.202.158
cmd=rlogin fgeorge-sun /user fgeorge
Wed Jun 25 03:51:37 1997          172.16.25.15      fgeorge   tty3    5622329430/4327528
stop      task_id=12       service=connection        protocol=rlogin addr=171.68.202.158
cmd=rlogin fgeorge-sun /user fgeorge bytes_in=659926 bytes_out=138   paks_in=2378
paks_
out=1251          elapsed_time=171
```

The following example shows the information contained in a TACACS+ connection accounting record for an outbound LAT connection:

```
Wed Jun 25 03:53:06 1997          172.16.25.15      fgeorge   tty3    5622329430/4327528
start     task_id=18       service=connection        protocol=lat      addr=VAX
cmd=lat VAX
Wed Jun 25 03:54:15 1997          172.16.25.15      fgeorge   tty3    5622329430/4327528
stop      task_id=18       service=connection        protocol=lat      addr=VAX
cmd=lat VAX  bytes_in=0       bytes_out=0      paks_in=0       paks_out=0
elapsed_time=6
```

EXEC Accounting

EXEC accounting provides information about user EXEC terminal sessions (user shells) on the network access server, including username, date, start and stop times, the access server IP address, and (for dialin users) the telephone number the call originated from.

The following example shows the information contained in a RADIUS EXEC accounting record for a dialin user:

```
Wed Jun 25 04:26:23 1997
          NAS-IP-Address = "172.16.25.15"
          NAS-Port = 1
          User-Name = "fgeorge"
          Client-Port-DNIS = "4327528"
          Caller-ID = "5622329483"
          Acct-Status-Type = Start
          Acct-Authentic = RADIUS
          Service-Type = Exec-User
          Acct-Session-Id = "00000006"
          Acct-Delay-Time = 0
          User-Id = "fgeorge"
          NAS-Identifier = "172.16.25.15"
```

```
Wed Jun 25 04:27:25 1997
        NAS-IP-Address = "172.16.25.15"
        NAS-Port = 1
        User-Name = "fgeorge"
        Client-Port-DNIS = "4327528"
        Caller-ID = "5622329483"
        Acct-Status-Type = Stop
        Acct-Authentic = RADIUS
        Service-Type = Exec-User
        Acct-Session-Id = "00000006"
        Acct-Session-Time = 62
        Acct-Delay-Time = 0
        User-Id = "fgeorge"
        NAS-Identifier = "172.16.25.15"
```

The following example shows the information contained in a TACACS+ EXEC accounting record for a dialin user:

```
Wed Jun 25 03:46:21 1997    172.16.25.15    fgeorge    tty3    5622329430/4327528
start    task_id=2    service=shell
Wed Jun 25 04:08:55 1997    172.16.25.15    fgeorge    tty3    5622329430/4327528
stop    task_id=2    service=shell    elapsed_time=1354
```

The following example shows the information contained in a RADIUS EXEC accounting record for a Telnet user:

```
Wed Jun 25 04:48:32 1997
        NAS-IP-Address = "172.16.25.15"
        NAS-Port = 26
        User-Name = "fgeorge"
        Caller-ID = "171.68.202.158"
        Acct-Status-Type = Start
        Acct-Authentic = RADIUS
        Service-Type = Exec-User
        Acct-Session-Id = "00000010"
        Acct-Delay-Time = 0
        User-Id = "fgeorge"
        NAS-Identifier = "172.16.25.15"

Wed Jun 25 04:48:46 1997
        NAS-IP-Address = "172.16.25.15"
        NAS-Port = 26
        User-Name = "fgeorge"
        Caller-ID = "171.68.202.158"
        Acct-Status-Type = Stop
        Acct-Authentic = RADIUS
        Service-Type = Exec-User
        Acct-Session-Id = "00000010"
        Acct-Session-Time = 14
        Acct-Delay-Time = 0
        User-Id = "fgeorge"
        NAS-Identifier = "172.16.25.15"
```

The following example shows the information contained in a TACACS+ EXEC accounting record for a Telnet user:

```
Wed Jun 25 04:06:53 1997    172.16.25.15    fgeorge        tty26        171.68.202.158
starttask_id=41      service=shell
Wed Jun 25 04:07:02 1997    172.16.25.15    fgeorge        tty26        171.68.202.158
stoptask_id=41       service=shell   elapsed_time=9
```

System Accounting

System accounting provides information about all system-level events (for example, when the system reboots or when accounting is turned on or off). The following accounting record is an example of a typical TACACS+ system accounting record server indicating that AAA accounting has been turned off:

```
Wed Jun 25 03:55:32 1997    172.16.25.15    unknown        unknown     unknown
start   task_id=25    service=system  event=sys_acct  reason=reconfigure
```

NOTE	The precise format of accounting packets records may vary, depending on your particular TACACS+ daemon.

The following accounting record is an example of a TACACS+ system accounting record indicating that AAA accounting has been turned on:

```
Wed Jun 25 03:55:22 1997            172.16.25.15    unknown unknown unknown stop
task_id=23   service=system   event=sys_acct   reason=reconfigure
```

NOTE	Cisco's implementation of RADIUS does not support system accounting.

Command Accounting

Command accounting provides information about the EXEC shell commands for a specified privilege level that are being executed on a network access server. Each command accounting record includes a list of the commands executed for that privilege level, as well as the date and time each command was executed, and the user who executed it.

The following example shows the information contained in a TACACS+ command accounting record for privilege level 1:

```
Wed Jun 25 03:46:47 1997    172.16.25.15    fgeorge    tty3    5622329430/4327528
stop    task_id=3    service=shell    priv-lvl=1    cmd=show version <cr>
Wed Jun 25 03:46:58 1997    172.16.25.15    fgeorge    tty3    5622329430/4327528
stop    task_id=4    service=shell    priv-lvl=1    cmd=show interfaces Ethernet 0 <cr>
Wed Jun 25 03:47:03 1997    172.16.25.15    fgeorge    tty3    5622329430/4327528
stop    task_id=5    service=shell    priv-lvl=1    cmd=show ip route <cr>
```

The following example shows the information contained in a TACACS+ command accounting record for privilege level 15:

```
Wed Jun 25 03:47:17 1997    172.16.25.15    fgeorge    tty3    5622329430/4327528
stop    task_id=6    service=shell    priv-lvl=15    cmd=configure terminal <cr>
Wed Jun 25 03:47:21 1997    172.16.25.15    fgeorge    tty3    5622329430/4327528
stop    task_id=7    service=shell    priv-lvl=15    cmd=interface Serial 0 <cr>
Wed Jun 25 03:47:29 1997    172.16.25.15    fgeorge    tty3    5622329430/4327528
stop    task_id=8    service=shell    priv-lvl=15    cmd=ip address 1.1.1.1
255.255.255.0 <cr>
```

NOTE   Cisco's implementation of RADIUS does not support command accounting.

AAA Accounting Prerequisites

Before configuring accounting using named method lists, you must first perform the following tasks:

- Enable AAA on your network access server. For more information about enabling AAA on your Cisco router or access server, refer to Chapter 1, "AAA Overview."

- Define the characteristics of your RADIUS or TACACS+ security server if you are issuing RADIUS or TACACS+ authorization. For more information about configuring your Cisco network access server to communicate with your RADIUS security server, refer to Chapter 8, "Configuring RADIUS." For more information about configuring your Cisco network access server to communicate with your TACACS+ security server, refer to Chapter 10, "Configuring TACACS+."

AAA Accounting Configuration Task List

This section describes the following tasks:

- Configuring AAA Accounting Using Named Method Lists

- Enabling Accounting

- Monitoring Accounting

For accounting configuration examples using the commands in this chapter, refer to the "Accounting Configuration Examples" section at the end of the this chapter.

Configuring AAA Accounting Using Named Method Lists

To configure AAA accounting using named method lists, use the following commands, beginning in global configuration mode:

Step	Command	Purpose
1	**aaa accounting** {**system** I **network** I **exec** I **connection** I **commands** *level*} {**default** I *list-name*} {**start-stop** I **wait-start** I **stop-only** I **none**} [*method1* [*method2...*]]	Creates an accounting method list and enables accounting.
2	**line** [**aux** I **console** I **tty** I **vty**] *line-number* [*ending-line-number*]	Enters the line configuration mode for the lines to which you want to apply the accounting method list.
	or	
	interface *interface-type interface-number*	Enters the interface configuration mode for the interfaces to which you want to apply the accounting method list.
3	**accounting** {**arap** I **exec** I **connection** I **commands** *level*} {**default** I *list-name*}	Applies the accounting method list to a line or set of lines.
	or	
	ppp accounting {**default** I *list-name*}	Applies the accounting method list to an interface or set of interfaces.

NOTE   System accounting does not use named method lists. For system accounting, you can only define the default method list.

Accounting Types

Named accounting method lists are specific to the indicated type of accounting. To create a method list to provide accounting information for ARAP (network) sessions, use the **arap** keyword. To create a method list to provide accounting records about user EXEC terminal sessions on the network access server, including username, date, start and stop times, use the **exec** keyword. To create a method list to provide accounting information about specific, individual EXEC commands associated with a specific privilege level, use the **commands** keyword. To create a method list to provide accounting information about all outbound connections made from the network access server, use the **connection** keyword.

System accounting does not support named method lists.

For minimal accounting, use the **stop-only** keyword, which instructs the specified method (RADIUS or TACACS+) to send a stop record accounting notice at the end of the requested user process. For more accounting information, use the **start-stop** keyword to send a start accounting notice at the beginning of the requested event and a stop accounting notice at the end of the event. You can further control access and accounting by using the **wait-start** keyword, which ensures that the RADIUS or TACACS+ security server acknowledges the start notice before granting the user's process request. To stop all accounting activities on this line or interface, use the **none** keyword.

Accounting Methods

To have the network access server send accounting information from a TACACS+ security server, use the **tacacs+** *method* keyword. For more specific information about configuring TACACS+ for accounting services, refer to Chapter 10, "Configuring TACACS+."

To have the network access server send accounting information from a RADIUS security server, use the **radius** *method* keyword. For more specific information about configuring RADIUS for accounting services, refer to Chapter 8, "Configuring RADIUS."

NOTE   Accounting method lists for SLIP follow whatever is configured for PPP on the relevant interface. If no lists are defined and applied to a particular interface (or no PPP settings are configured), the default setting for accounting applies.

Enabling Accounting

The **aaa accounting** command enables you to create a record for any or all of the accounting functions monitored. To enable AAA accounting, use the following command in global configuration mode:

Command	Purpose
aaa accounting {**system** | **network** | **connection** | **exec** | **command** *level*} {**start-stop** | **wait-start** | **stop-only**} {**tacacs+** | **radius**}	Enables accounting.

For minimal accounting, use the **stop-only** keyword, which instructs the specified authentication system (RADIUS or TACACS+) to send a stop record accounting notice at the end of the requested user process. For more accounting information, use the **start-stop** keyword to send a start accounting notice at the beginning of the requested event and a stop accounting notice at the end of the event. You can further control access and accounting by using the **wait-start** keyword, which ensures that the RADIUS or TACACS+ security server acknowledges the start notice before granting the user's process request.

Suppressing Generation of Accounting Records for Null Username Sessions

When **aaa accounting** is activated, the Cisco IOS software issues accounting records for all users on the system, including users whose username string, because of protocol translation, is NULL. An example of this is users who come in on lines where the **aaa authentication login** *method-list* **none** command is applied. To prevent accounting records from being generated for sessions that do not have usernames associated with them, use the following command in global configuration mode:

Command	Purpose
aaa accounting suppress null-username	Prevents accounting records from being generated for users whose username string is NULL.

Generating Interim Accounting Records

To enable periodic interim accounting records to be sent to the accounting server, use the following command in global configuration mode:

Command	Purpose
aaa accounting update {**newinfo** I **periodic** *number*}	Enables periodic interim accounting records to be sent to the accounting server.

When the **aaa accounting update** command is activated, the Cisco IOS software issues interim accounting records for all users on the system. If the keyword **newinfo** is used, interim accounting records will be sent to the accounting server every time there is new accounting information to report. An example of this would be when IPCP completes IP address negotiation with the remote peer. The interim accounting record will include the negotiated IP address used by the remote peer.

When used with the keyword **periodic**, interim accounting records are sent periodically as defined by the argument number. The interim accounting record contains all of the accounting information recorded for that user up to the time the interim accounting record is sent.

Both of these keywords are mutually exclusive, meaning that whichever keyword is configured last takes precedence over the previous configuration. For example, if you configure **aaa accounting update periodic**, and then configure **aaa accounting update newinfo**, all users currently logged in will continue to generate periodic interim accounting records. All new users will generate accounting records based on the **newinfo** algorithm.

CAUTION	Using the **aaa accounting update periodic** command can cause heavy congestion when many users are logged in to the network.

Monitoring Accounting

No specific **show** command exists for either RADIUS or TACACS+ accounting. To obtain accounting records displaying information about users currently logged in, use the following command in privileged EXEC mode:

Command	Purpose
show accounting	Steps through all active sessions and prints all the accounting records for the actively accounted functions.

Accounting Attribute-Value Pairs

The network access server monitors the accounting functions defined in either TACACS+ AV pairs or RADIUS attributes, depending on which security method you have implemented. For a list of supported RADIUS accounting attributes, refer to Appendix A, "RADIUS Attributes." For a list of supported TACACS+ accounting AV pairs, refer to Appendix B, "TACACS+ Attribute-Value Pairs."

Accounting Configuration Examples

This section contains the following configuration examples:

- Accounting Configuration Example

- Named Method List Configuration Example

Accounting Configuration Example

In the following sample configuration, RADIUS-style accounting is used to track all usage of EXEC commands and network services, such as SLIP, PPP, and ARAP:

```
aaa accounting exec start-stop radius
aaa accounting network start-stop radius
```

The **show accounting** command yields the following output for the above configuration:

```
Active Accounted actions on tty0, User georgef Priv 1
 Task ID 2, EXEC Accounting record, 00:02:13 Elapsed
 task_id=2 service=shell
 Task ID 3, Connection Accounting record, 00:02:07 Elapsed
 task_id=3 service=connection protocol=telnet address=172.21.14.90 cmd=synth

Active Accounted actions on tty1, User rubble Priv 1
 Task ID 5, Network Accounting record, 00:00:52 Elapsed
 task_id=5 service=ppp protocol=ip address=10.0.0.98

Active Accounted actions on tty10, User georgef Priv 1
 Task ID 4, EXEC Accounting record, 00:00:53 Elapsed
 task_id=4 service=shell
```

Table 6-1 describes the fields contained in this example.

Table 6-1   *show accounting Field Descriptions*

Field	Description
Active Accounted actions on	Terminal line or interface name user with which the user logged in.
User	User's ID
Priv	User's privilege level.
Task ID	Unique identifier for each accounting session.
Accounting Record	Type of accounting session.
Elapsed	Length of time (hh:mm:ss) for this session type.
attribute=value	AV pairs associated with this accounting session.

Named Method List Configuration Example

The following example configures a Cisco AS5200 (enabled for AAA and communication with a RADIUS security server) for AAA services to be provided by the RADIUS server. If the RADIUS server fails to respond, then the local database will be queried for authentication and authorization information, and accounting services will be handled by a TACACS+ server.

```
aaa new-model
aaa authentication login admins local
aaa authentication ppp dialins radius local
aaa authorization network scoobee radius local
aaa accounting network charlie start-stop radius

username root password ALongPassword

radius-server host alcatraz
radius-server key myRaDiUSpassWoRd

interface group-async 1
 group-range 1 16
 encapsulation ppp
 ppp authentication chap dialins
 ppp authorization scoobee
 ppp accounting charlie

line 1 16
 autoselect ppp
 autoselect during-login
 login authentication admins
 modem dialin
```

The lines in this sample RADIUS AAA configuration are defined as follows:

● The **aaa new-model** command enables AAA network security services.

● The **aaa authentication login admins local** command defines a method list, *admins*, for login authentication.

- The **aaa authentication ppp dialins radius local** command defines the authentication method list *dialins*, which specifies that RADIUS authentication, and then (if the RADIUS server does not respond) local authentication will be used on serial lines using PPP.

- The **aaa authorization network scoobee radius local** command defines the network authorization method list named *scoobee*, which specifies that RADIUS authorization will be used on serial lines using PPP. If the RADIUS server fails to respond, then local network authorization will be performed.

- The **aaa accounting network charlie start-stop radius** command defines the network accounting method list named *charlie*, which specifies that RADIUS accounting services (in this case, start and stop records for specific events) will be used on serial lines using PPP.

- The **username** command defines the username and password to be used for the PPP PAP caller identification.

- The **radius-server host** command defines the name of the RADIUS server host.

- The **radius-server key** command defines the shared secret text string between the network access server and the RADIUS server host.

- The **interface group-async** command selects and defines an asynchronous interface group.

- The **group-range** command defines the member asynchronous interfaces in the interface group.

- The **encapsulation ppp** command sets PPP as the encapsulation method used on the specified interfaces.

- The **ppp authentication chap dialins** command selects CHAP as the method of PPP authentication and applies the *dialins* method list to the specified interfaces.

- The **ppp authorization scoobee** command applies the *scoobee* network authorization method list to the specified interfaces.

- The **ppp accounting charlie** command applies the *charlie* network accounting method list to the specified interfaces.

- The **line** command switches the configuration mode from global configuration to line configuration and identifies the specific lines being configured.

- The **autoselect ppp** command configures the Cisco IOS software to allow a PPP session to start up automatically on these selected lines.

- The **autoselect during-login** command is used to display the username and password prompt without pressing the Return key. After the user logs in, the autoselect function (in this case, PPP) begins.

- The **login authentication admins** command applies the *admins* method list for login authentication.

- The **modem dialin** command configures modems attached to the selected lines to only accept incoming calls.

## CHAPTER 7

Accounting Commands

This chapter describes the commands used to manage accounting on the network. Accounting management allows you to track individual and group usage of network resources. The AAA accounting feature enables you to track the services users are accessing as well as the amount of network resources they are consuming. When **aaa accounting** is activated, the network access server reports user activity to the TACACS+ or RADIUS security server (depending on which security method you have implemented) in the form of accounting records. Each accounting record contains accounting attribute-value (AV) pairs and is stored on the security server. This data can then be analyzed for network management, client billing, and/or auditing.

For information on how to configure accounting using AAA, refer to Chapter 6, "Configuring Accounting." For configuration examples using the commands in this chapter, refer to the "Accounting Configuration Examples" section located at the end of Chapter 6, "Configuring Accounting."

aaa accounting

To enable AAA accounting of requested services for billing or security purposes when you use RADIUS or TACACS+, use the **aaa accounting** global configuration command. Use the **no** form of this command to disable accounting.

> **aaa accounting** {**system** | **network** | **exec** | **connection** | **commands** *level*} {**default** | *list-name*}{**start-stop** | **wait-start** | **stop-only** | **none**} [*method1* [*method2...*]]
> **no aaa accounting** {**system** | **network** | **exec** | **commands** *level*}

Syntax	Description
system	Performs accounting for all system-level events not associated with users, such as reloads.
network	Runs accounting for all network-related service requests, including SLIP, PPP, PPP NCPs, and ARA.
exec	Runs accounting for EXEC session (user shells). This keyword might return user profile information such as **autocommand** information.
connection	Provides information about all outbound connections made from the network access server, such as Telnet, local-area transport (LAT), TN3270, packet assembler/disassembler (PAD), and rlogin.
commands	Runs accounting for all commands at the specified privilege level.
level	Specific command level to track for accounting. Valid entries are 0 through 15.

Syntax	Description
default	Uses the listed accounting methods that follow this argument as the default list of methods for accounting services.
list-name	Character string used to name the list of accounting methods.
start-stop	Sends a start accounting notice at the beginning of a process and a stop accounting notice at the end of a process. The start accounting record is sent in the background. The requested user process begins regardless of whether or not the start accounting notice was received by the accounting server.
wait-start	As in **start-stop**, sends both a start and a stop accounting notice to the accounting server. However, if you use the **wait-start** keyword, the requested user service does not begin until the start accounting notice is acknowledged. A stop accounting notice is also sent.
stop-only	Sends a stop accounting notice at the end of the requested user process.
none	Disables accounting services on this line or interface.
method1 [*method2...*]	At least one of the keywords described in Table 7-1.

Default

AAA accounting is disabled. If the **aaa accounting** command for a particular accounting type is issued without a named method list specified, the default method list is automatically applied to all interfaces or lines (where this accounting type applies) except those that have a named method list explicitly defined. (A defined method list overrides the default method list.) If no default method list is defined, then no accounting takes place.

Command Mode

Global configuration

Usage Guidelines

This command first appeared in Cisco IOS Release 10.3.

Use the **aaa accounting** command to enable accounting and to create named method lists defining specific accounting methods on a per-line or per-interface basis. Method keywords are described in Table 7-1.

Table 7-1 *AAA Accounting Keywords*

Keyword	Description
radius	Uses RADIUS to provide accounting service.
tacacs+	Uses TACACS+ to provide accounting services.

Cisco IOS software supports the following two methods for accounting:

● TACACS+—The network access server reports user activity to the TACACS+ security server in the form of accounting records. Each accounting record contains AV pairs and is stored on the security server.

● RADIUS—The network access server reports user activity to the RADIUS security server in the form of accounting records. Each accounting record contains AV pairs and is stored on the security server.

Method lists for accounting define the way accounting will be performed. Named accounting method lists enable you to designate a particular security protocol to be used on specific lines or interfaces for particular types of accounting services. You create a list by entering *list-name* and *method*, where *list-name* is any character string used to name this list (excluding the names of methods, such as radius or tacacs+) and *method* identifies the method(s) tried in the given sequence.

Named accounting method lists are specific to the indicated type of accounting. To create a method list to provide accounting information for ARA (network) sessions, use the **arap** keyword. To create a method list to provide accounting records about user EXEC terminal sessions on the network access server, including username, date, and start and stop times, use the **exec** keyword. To create a method list to provide accounting information about specific, individual EXEC commands associated with a specific privilege level, use the **commands** keyword. To create a method list to provide accounting information about all outbound connections made from the network access server, use the **connection** keyword.

NOTE	System accounting does not use named accounting lists; you can only define the default list for system accounting.

For minimal accounting, include the **stop-only** keyword to send a stop record accounting notice at the end of the requested user process. For more accounting, you can include the **start-stop** keyword, so that RADIUS or TACACS+ sends a start accounting notice at the beginning of the requested process and a stop accounting notice at the end of the process. For even more accounting control, you can include the **wait-start** keyword, which ensures that the start notice is received by the RADIUS or TACACS+ server before granting the user's process request. Accounting is stored only on the RADIUS or TACACS+ server. The **none** keyword disables accounting services for the specified line or interface.

When **aaa accounting** is activated, the network access server monitors either RADIUS accounting attributes or TACACS+ AV pairs pertinent to the connection, depending on the security method you have implemented. The network access server reports these attributes as accounting records, which are then stored in an accounting log on the security server. For a list of supported RADIUS accounting attributes, refer to Appendix A, "RADIUS Attributes." For a list of supported TACACS+ accounting AV pairs, refer to Appendix B, "TACACS+ Attribute-Value Pairs."

NOTE   This command cannot be used with TACACS or extended TACACS.

Example

The following example defines a default commands accounting method list, where commands accounting services are provided by a TACACS+ security server, set for privilege level 15 commands with a stop-only restriction.

```
aaa accounting commands 15 default stop-only tacacs+
```

Related Commands

You can search online at www.cisco.com to find documentation of related commands.

aaa authentication
aaa authorization
aaa new-model

aaa accounting suppress null-username

To prevent the Cisco IOS software from sending accounting records for users whose username string is NULL, use the **aaa accounting suppress null-username** global configuration command. Use the **no** form of this command to allow sending records for users with a NULL username.

> **aaa accounting suppress null-username**
> **no aaa accounting suppress null-username**

Syntax Description

This command has no arguments or keywords.

Default

Disabled

Command Mode

Global configuration

Usage Guidelines

This command first appeared in Cisco IOS Release 11.2.

When **aaa accounting** is activated, the Cisco IOS software issues accounting records for all users on the system, including users whose username string, because of protocol translation, is NULL. This command prevents accounting records from being generated for those users who do not have usernames associated with them.

Example

The following example suppresses accounting records for users who do not have usernames associated with them:

```
aaa accounting suppress null-username
```

Related Commands

You can search online at www.cisco.com to find documentation of related commands.

aaa accounting

aaa accounting update

To enable periodic interim accounting records to be sent to the accounting server, use the **aaa accounting update** global configuration command. Use the **no** form of this command to disable interim accounting updates.

> **aaa accounting update** {**newinfo** | **periodic** *number*}
> **no aaa accounting update**

Syntax	Description
newinfo	Causes an interim accounting record to be sent to the accounting server whenever there is new accounting information to report relating to the user in question.
periodic	Causes an interim accounting record to be sent to the accounting server periodically, as defined by the argument *number*.
number	Integer specifying number of minutes.

Default

Disabled

Command Mode

Global configuration

Usage Guidelines

This command first appeared in Cisco IOS Release 11.3.

When **aaa accounting update** is activated, the Cisco IOS software issues interim accounting records for all users on the system. If the keyword **newinfo** is used, interim accounting records will be sent to the accounting server every time there is new accounting information to report. An example of this would be when IPCP completes IP address negotiation with the remote peer. The interim accounting record will include the negotiated IP address used by the remote peer.

When used with the keyword **periodic**, interim accounting records are sent periodically as defined by the argument number. The interim accounting record contains all of the accounting information recorded for that user up to the time the accounting record is sent.

Both of these keywords are mutually exclusive, meaning that whichever keyword is configured last takes precedence over the previous configuration. For example, if you configure **aaa accounting update periodic** and then configure **aaa accounting update newinfo**, all users currently logged in will continue to generate periodic interim accounting records. All new users will generate accounting records based on the **newinfo** algorithm.

CAUTION Using the **aaa accounting update periodic** command can cause heavy congestion when many users are logged in to the network.

Example

The following example sends PPP accounting records to a remote RADIUS server and, when IPCP completes negotiation, sends an interim accounting record to the RADIUS server that includes the negotiated IP address for this user:

```
aaa accounting network start-stop radius
aaa accounting update newinfo
```

Related Commands

You can search online at www.cisco.com to find documentation of related commands.

aaa accounting exec
aaa accounting network

accounting

To enable AAA accounting services to a specific line or group of lines, use the **accounting** line configuration command. Use the **no** form of this command to disable AAA accounting services.

accounting {**arap** | **commands** *level* | **connection** | **exec**} [**default** | *list-name*]
no accounting {**arap** | **commands** *level* | **connection** | **exec**} [**default** | *list-name*]

Syntax	Description
arap	Enables accounting on line(s) configured for AppleTalk Remote Access (ARA) protocol.
commands	Enables accounting on the selected line(s) for all commands at the specified privilege level.
level	Specifies the command level to track for accounting. Valid entries are 0 through 15.
connection	Enables both CHAP and PAP, and performs PAP authentication before CHAP.
exec	Enables accounting for all system-level events not associated with users, such as reloads on the selected line(s).
default	(Optional) The name of the default method list, created with the **aaa accounting** command.
list-name	(Optional) Specifies the name of a list of accounting methods to use. If no list name is specified, the system uses the default. The list is created with the **aaa accounting** command.

Default

Accounting is disabled.

Command Mode

Line configuration

Usage Guidelines

This command first appeared in Cisco IOS Release 11.3 T.

After you enable the **aaa accounting** command and define a named accounting method list (or use the default method list) for a particular type of accounting, you must apply the defined lists to the appropriate lines for accounting services to take place. Use the **accounting** command to apply the specified method lists (or if none is specified, the default method list) to the selected line or group of lines.

Example

The following example enables command accounting services (for level 15) using the accounting method list named *charlie* on line 10:

```
line 10
 accounting commands 15 charlie
```

Related Commands

You can search online at www.cisco.com to find documentation of related commands.

arap authentication
authorization
login authentication
nasi authentication

ppp accounting

To enable AAA accounting services on the selected interface, use the **ppp accounting** interface configuration command. Use the **no** form of this command to disable AAA accounting services.

> **ppp accounting** [**default** | *list-name*]
> **no ppp accounting**

Syntax	Description
default	(Optional) The name of the method list is created with the **aaa accounting** command.
list-name	(Optional) Specifies the name of a list of accounting methods to use. If no list name is specified, the system uses the default. The list is created with the **aaa accounting** command.

Default
Accounting is disabled.

Command Mode
Interface configuration

Usage Guidelines
This command first appeared in Cisco IOS Release 11.3 T.

After you enable the **aaa accounting** command and define a named accounting method list (or use the default method list), you must apply the defined lists to the appropriate interfaces for accounting services to take place. Use the **ppp accounting** command to apply the specified method lists (or if none is specified, the default method list) to the selected interface.

Example
The following example enables accounting on asynchronous interface 4 and uses the accounting method list named *charlie*:

```
interface async 4
 encapsulation ppp
 ppp accounting charlie
```

Related Commands
You can search online at www.cisco.com to find documentation of related commands.

aaa accounting

show accounting

Use the **show accounting** EXEC command to step through all active sessions and to print all the accounting records for actively accounted functions. Use the **no** form of this command to disable viewing and printing accounting records.

> **show accounting** {**system** | **network** | **exec** | **command** *level*} {**start-stop** | **wait-start** | **stop-only**} **tacacs+**
> **no show accounting** {**system** | **network** | **exec** | **command** *level*}

Syntax	Description
system	Displays accounting for all system-level events not associated with users, such as reloads.
network	Displays accounting for all network-related service requests, including SLIP, PPP, PPP NCPs, and ARA.
exec	Displays accounting for EXEC session (user shells). This keyword might return user profile information such as **autocommand** information.
command	Displays accounting for all commands at the specified privilege level.
level	Specifies the command level to display. Valid entries are 0 through 15.
start-stop	Displays a start record accounting notice at the beginning of a process and a stop record at the end of a process. The start accounting record is sent in the background. The requested user process begins regardless of whether or not the start accounting record was received by the accounting server.
wait-start	Displays both a start and a stop accounting notice to the accounting server.
stop-only	Displays a stop record accounting notice at the end of the requested user process.
tacacs+	Displays the TACACS-style accounting.

Default
Disabled

Command Mode
EXEC

Usage Guidelines
This command first appeared in Cisco IOS Release 11.1.

The **show accounting** command allows you to display the active accountable events on the network. It provides system administrators with a quick look at what is going on, and it also can help collect information in the event of a data loss on the accounting server.

The **show accounting** command displays additional data on the internal state of AAA if **debug aaa accounting** is activated.

Sample Displays

The following is sample output from the **show accounting** command, showing accounting records for an EXEC login and an outgoing Telnet session:

```
router# show accounting

Active Accounted actions on tty0, User (not logged in) Priv 1
 Task ID 1, EXEC Accounting record, 00:22:14 Elapsed
 task_id=1 service=shell
 Task ID 10, Connection Accounting record, 00:00:03 Elapsed
 task_id=10 service=connection protocol=telnet addr=172.16.57.11 cmd=connect tom-ss20

Active Accounted actions on tty66, User tom Priv 1
 Task ID 9, EXEC Accounting record, 00:02:14 Elapsed
 task_id=9 service=shell
```

The following is sample output from the **show accounting** command, showing accounting records for a network connection:

```
router# show accounting

Active Accounted actions on tty33, User tom Priv 1
 Task ID 13, Network Accounting record, 00:00:10 Elapsed
 task_id=13 service=ppp protocol=ip addr=10.0.0.1
```

The following is sample output from the **show accounting** command, showing accounting records for a PPP session started from an EXEC prompt:

```
router# show accounting

Active Accounted actions on tty0, User (not logged in) Priv 1
 Task ID 1, EXEC Accounting record, 00:35:16 Elapsed
 task_id=1 service=shell

Active Accounted actions on tty33, User ellie Priv 1
 Task ID 16, EXEC Accounting record, 00:00:17 Elapsed
 task_id=16 service=shell

Active Accounted actions on Interface Async33, User tom Priv 1
 Task ID 17, Network Accounting record, 00:00:13 Elapsed
 task_id=17 service=ppp protocol=ip addr=10.0.0.1
```

Table 7-2 describes the fields contained in this example.

Table 7-2 *show accounting Field Descriptions*

Field	Description
Active Accounted actions on	Terminal line or interface name user with which the user logged in.
User	User's ID.
Priv	User's privilege level.
Task ID	Unique identifier for each accounting session.

Continues

Table 7-2 *show accounting* Field Descriptions *(Continued)*

Field	Description
Accounting Record	Type of accounting session.
Elapsed	Length of time (hh:mm:ss) for this session type.
attribute=value	AV pairs associated with this accounting session.

Related Commands

You can search online at www.cisco.com to find documentation of related commands.

debug aaa accounting
show line
show users

Security Server Protocols

## CHAPTER 8

Configuring RADIUS

This chapter describes the Remote Authentication Dial-In User Service (RADIUS) security system, defines its operation, and identifies appropriate and inappropriate network environments for using RADIUS technology. The "RADIUS Configuration Task List" section describes how to configure RADIUS with the authentication, authorization, and accounting (AAA) command set. The "RADIUS Authentication and Authorization Example" section at the end of this chapter offers two possible implementation scenarios.

This chapter covers the following topics:

- RADIUS Overview

- RADIUS Operation

- RADIUS Configuration Task List

For a complete description of the radius commands used in this chapter, refer to Chapter 9, "RADIUS Commands." To locate documentation of other commands that appear in this chapter, you can search online at www.cisco.com.

RADIUS Overview

RADIUS is a distributed client/server system that secures networks against unauthorized access. In the Cisco implementation, RADIUS clients run on Cisco routers and send authentication requests to a central RADIUS server that contains all user authentication and network service access information.

RADIUS is a fully open protocol, distributed in source code format, that can be modified to work with any security system currently available on the market.

Cisco supports RADIUS under its AAA security paradigm. RADIUS can be used with other AAA security protocols, such as TACACS+, Kerberos, or local username lookup. RADIUS is supported on all Cisco platforms.

RADIUS has been implemented in a variety of network environments that require high levels of security while maintaining network access for remote users.

Use RADIUS in the following network environments that require access security:

- Networks with multiple-vendor access servers, each supporting RADIUS. For example, access servers from several vendors use a single RADIUS server-based security database. In an IP-based network with multiple vendors' access servers, dialin users are authenticated through a RADIUS server that has been customized to work with the Kerberos security system.

- Turnkey network security environments in which applications support the RADIUS protocol, such as in an access environment that uses a smart card access control system. In one case, RADIUS has been used with Enigma's security cards to validate users and grant access to network resources.

- Networks already using RADIUS. You can add a Cisco router with RADIUS to the network. This might be the first step when you make the transition to the Terminal Access Controller Access Control System (TACACS+) server.

- Networks in which a user must only access a single service. Using RADIUS, you can control user access to a single host, to a single utility such as Telnet, or to a single protocol such as Point-to-Point Protocol (PPP). For example, when a user logs in, RADIUS identifies this user as having authorization to run PPP using IP address 10.2.3.4 and the defined access list is started.

- Networks that require resource accounting. You can use RADIUS accounting independent of RADIUS authentication or authorization. The RADIUS accounting functions allow data to be sent at the start and end of services, indicating the amount of resources (such as time, packets, bytes, and so on) used during the session. An Internet service provider (ISP) might use a freeware-based version of RADIUS access control and accounting software to meet special security and billing needs.

RADIUS is not suitable in the following network security situations:

- Multiprotocol access environments. RADIUS does not support the following protocols:

    — AppleTalk Remote Access (ARA) Protocol

    — NetBIOS Frame Control Protocol (NBFCP)

    — NetWare Asynchronous Services Interface (NASI)

    — X.25 PAD connections

- Router-to-router situations. RADIUS does not provide two-way authentication. RADIUS can be used to authenticate from one router to a non-Cisco router if the non-Cisco router requires RADIUS authentication.

- Networks using a variety of services. RADIUS generally binds a user to one service model.

RADIUS Operation

When a user attempts to log in and authenticate to an access server using RADIUS, the following steps occur:

1   The user is prompted for and enters a username and password.

2   The username and encrypted password are sent over the network to the RADIUS server.

3 The user receives one of the following responses from the RADIUS server:

(a) ACCEPT—The user is authenticated.

(b) REJECT—The user is not authenticated and is prompted to reenter the username and password, or access is denied.

(c) CHALLENGE—A challenge is issued by the RADIUS server. The challenge collects additional data from the user.

(d) CHANGE PASSWORD—A request is issued by the RADIUS server, asking the user to select a new password.

The ACCEPT or REJECT response is bundled with additional data that is used for EXEC or network authorization. You must first complete RADIUS authentication before using RADIUS authorization. The additional data included with the ACCEPT or REJECT packets consists of the following:

● Services that the user can access, including Telnet, rlogin, or local-area transport (LAT) connections, and PPP, Serial Line Internet Protocol (SLIP), or EXEC services.

● Connection parameters, including the host or client IP address, access list, and user timeouts.

RADIUS Configuration Task List

To configure RADIUS on your Cisco router or access server, you must perform the following tasks:

● Use the **aaa new-model** global configuration command to enable AAA. AAA must be configured if you plan to use RADIUS. For more information about using the **aaa new-model** command, refer to Chapter 1, "AAA Overview."

● Use the **aaa authentication** global configuration command to define method lists for RADIUS authentication. For more information about using the **aaa authentication** command, refer to Chapter 2, "Configuring Authentication."

● Use **line** and **interface** commands to enable the defined method lists to be used. For more information, refer to Chapter 2, "Configuring Authentication."

The following configuration tasks are optional:

● If needed, use the **aaa authorization** global command to authorize specific user functions. For more information about using the **aaa authorization** command, refer to Chapter 4, "Configuring Authorization."

● If needed, use the **aaa accounting** command to enable accounting for RADIUS connections. For more information about using the **aaa accounting** command, refer to Chapter 6, "Configuring Accounting."

This chapter describes how to set up RADIUS for authentication, authorization, and accounting on your network, and includes the following sections:

- Configuring the Router for RADIUS Server Communication

- Configuring the Router to Use Vendor-Specific RADIUS Attributes

- Configuring the Router for Vendor-Proprietary RADIUS Server Communication

- Configuring the Router to Query the RADIUS Server for Static Routes and IP Addresses

- Configuring the Router to Expand Network Access Server Port Information

- Specifying RADIUS Authentication

- Specifying RADIUS Authorization

- Specifying RADIUS Accounting

- RADIUS Attributes

- RADIUS Configuration Examples

Configuring the Router for RADIUS Server Communication

The RADIUS host is normally a multiuser system running RADIUS server software from Livingston, Merit, Microsoft, or another software provider. A RADIUS server and a Cisco router use a shared secret text string to encrypt passwords and exchange responses.

To configure RADIUS to use the AAA security commands, you must specify the host running the RADIUS server daemon and a secret text string that it shares with the router. Use the **radius-server** commands to specify the RADIUS server host and a secret text string.

To specify a RADIUS server host and shared secret text string, use the following commands in global configuration mode:

Step	Command	Purpose
1	**radius-server host** {*hostname*	*ip-address*} [**auth-port** *port-number*] [**acct-port** *port-number*]	Specifies the IP address or host name of the remote RADIUS server host and assigns authentication and accounting destination port numbers.
2	**radius-server key** *string*	Specifies the shared secret text string used between the router and the RADIUS server.

To customize communication between the router and the RADIUS server, use the following optional **radius-server** global configuration commands:

Step	Command	Purpose
1	**radius-server retransmit** *retries*	Specifies the number of times the router transmits each RADIUS request to the server before giving up (the default is three).
2	**radius-server timeout** *seconds*	Specifies the number of seconds a router waits for a reply to a RADIUS request before retransmitting the request.
3	**radius-server dead-time** *minutes*	Specifies the number of minutes a RADIUS server, which is not responding to authentication requests, is passed over by requests for RADIUS authentication.

Configuring the Router to Use Vendor-Specific RADIUS Attributes

The Internet Engineering Task Force (IETF) draft standard specifies a method for communicating vendor-specific information between the network access server and the RADIUS server by using the vendor-specific attribute (Attribute 26). Vendor-specific attributes (VSAs) allow vendors to support their own extended attributes not suitable for general use. The Cisco RADIUS implementation supports one vendor-specific option using the format recommended in the specification. Cisco's vendor ID is 9, and the supported option has vendor type 1, which is named *cisco-avpair*. The value is a string of the format:

```
protocol : attribute sep value *
```

protocol is a value of the Cisco *protocol* attribute for a particular type of authorization. *attribute* and *value* are an appropriate attribute/value (AV) pair defined in the Cisco TACACS+ specification, and *sep* is = for mandatory attributes and * for optional attributes. This allows the full set of features available for TACACS+ authorization to also be used for RADIUS.

For example, the following AV pair causes Cisco's multiple named ip address pools feature to be activated during IP authorization (during PPP's IPCP address assignment):

```
cisco-avpair= "ip:addr-pool=first"
```

The following example causes a user logging in from a network access server to have immediate access to EXEC commands.

```
cisco-avpair= "shell:priv-lvl=15"
```

Other vendors have their own unique vendor IDs, options, and associated VSAs. For more information about vendor IDs and VSAs, refer to RFC 2138, "Remote Authentication Dial-In User Service (RADIUS)."

To configure the network access server to recognize and use VSAs, use the following command in global configuration mode:

Command	Purpose
radius-server vsa send [**accounting**	**authentication**]	Enables the network access server to recognize and use VSAs as defined by RADIUS IETF Attribute 26.

For a complete list of RADIUS attributes or more information about vendor-specific Attribute 26, refer to Appendix A, "RADIUS Attributes."

Configuring the Router for Vendor-Proprietary RADIUS Server Communication

Although an IETF draft standard for RADIUS specifies a method for communicating vendor-proprietary information between the network access server and the RADIUS server, some vendors have extended the RADIUS attribute set in a unique way. Cisco IOS software supports a subset of vendor-proprietary RADIUS attributes.

As mentioned earlier, to configure RADIUS (whether vendor proprietary or IETF draft compliant), you must specify the host running the RADIUS server daemon and the secret text string it shares with the Cisco device. You specify the RADIUS host and secret text string by using the **radius-server** commands. To identify that the RADIUS server is using a vendor-proprietary implementation of RADIUS, use the **radius-server host non-standard** command. Vendor-proprietary attributes will not be supported unless you use the **radius-server host non-standard** command.

To specify a vendor-proprietary RADIUS server host and a shared secret text string, use the following commands in global configuration mode:

Step	Command	Purpose
1	**radius-server host** {*hostname*	*ip-address*} **non-standard**	Specifies the IP address or host name of the remote RADIUS server host and identifies that it is using a vendor-proprietary implementation of RADIUS.
2	**radius-server key** *string*	Specifies the shared secret text string used between the router and the vendor-proprietary RADIUS server. The router and the RADIUS server use this text string to encrypt passwords and exchange responses.

Configuring the Router to Query the RADIUS Server for Static Routes and IP Addresses

Some vendor-proprietary implementations of RADIUS let the user define static routes and IP pool definitions on the RADIUS server instead of on each individual network access server in the network. Each network access server then queries the RADIUS server for static route and IP pool information.

To have the Cisco router or access server query the RADIUS server for static routes and IP pool definitions when the device first starts up, use the following command in global configuration mode:

Command	Purpose
radius-server configure-nas	Tells the Cisco router or access server to query the RADIUS server for the static routes and IP pool definitions used throughout its domain.

NOTE   Because the **radius-server configure-nas** command is performed when the Cisco router starts up, it will not take effect until you issue a **copy system:running config nvram:startup-config** command.

Configuring the Router to Expand Network Access Server Port Information

There are some situations when PPP or login authentication occurs on an interface that is different from the interface on which the call itself comes in. For example, in a V.120 ISDN call, login or PPP authentication occurs on a virtual asynchronous interface ttt, but the call itself occurs on one of the channels of the ISDN interface.

The **radius-server attribute nas-port extended** command configures RADIUS to expand the size of the NAS-Port attribute (RADIUS IETF Attribute 5) field to 32 bits. The upper 16 bits of the NAS-Port attribute display the type and number of the controlling interface; the lower 16 bits indicate the interface undergoing authentication.

To display expanded interface information in the NAS-Port attribute field, use the following command in global configuration mode:

Command	Purpose
radius-server attribute nas-port extended	Expands the size of the NAS-Port attribute from 16 to 32 bits to display extended interface information.

NOTE	This command replaces the deprecated **radius-server extended-portnames** command.

On platforms with multiple interfaces (ports) per slot, the Cisco RADIUS implementation will not provide a unique NAS-Port attribute that permits distinguishing between the interfaces. For example, if a dual PRI interface is in slot 1, calls on both Serial1/0:1 and Serial1/1:1 will appear as NAS-Port = 20101.

Once again, this is because of the 16-bit field size limitation associated with RADIUS IETF NAS-port attribute. In this case, the solution is to replace the NAS-port attribute with a vendor-specific attribute (RADIUS IETF Attribute 26). Cisco's vendor ID is 9, and the Cisco-NAS-Port attribute is subtype 2. VSAs can be turned on by entering the **radius-server vsa send** command. The port information in this attribute is provided and configured using the **aaa nas port extended** command.

To replace the NAS-Port attribute with RADIUS IETF Attribute 26 and to display extended field information, use the following commands in global configuration mode:

Step	Command	Purpose
1	**radius-server vsa send** [**accounting** | **authentication**]	Enables the network access server to recognize and use VSAs as defined by RADIUS IETF Attribute 26.
2	**aaa nas-port extended**	Expands the size of the VSA NAS-Port field from 16 to 32 bits to display extended interface information.

The standard NAS-Port attribute (RADIUS IETF Attribute 5) will continue to be sent. If you do not want this information to be sent, you can suppress it by using the **no radius-server attribute nas-port** command. When this command is configured, the standard NAS-Port attribute will no longer be sent.

For a complete list of RADIUS attributes, refer to Appendix A, "RADIUS Attributes."

Specifying RADIUS Authentication

After you have identified the RADIUS server and defined the RADIUS authentication key, you need to define method lists for RADIUS authentication. Because RADIUS authentication is facilitated through AAA, you need to enter the **aaa authentication** command, specifying RADIUS as the authentication method. For more information, refer to Chapter 2, "Configuring Authentication."

Specifying RADIUS Authorization

AAA authorization lets you set parameters that restrict a user's network access. Authorization using RADIUS provides one method for remote access control, including one-time authorization or authorization for each service, per-user account list and profile, user group support, and support of IP, IPX, ARA, and Telnet. Because RADIUS authorization is facilitated through AAA, you need to issue the **aaa authorization** command, specifying RADIUS as the authorization method. For more information, refer to Chapter 4, "Configuring Authorization."

Specifying RADIUS Accounting

The AAA accounting feature enables you to track the services users are accessing as well as the amount of network resources they are consuming. Because RADIUS accounting is facilitated through AAA, you need to issue the **aaa accounting** command, specifying RADIUS as the accounting method. For more information, refer to Chapter 6, "Configuring Accounting."

RADIUS Attributes

The network access server monitors the RADIUS authorization and accounting functions defined by RADIUS attributes in each user-profile. For a list of supported RADIUS attributes, refer to Appendix A, "RADIUS Attributes."

Vendor-Proprietary RADIUS Attributes

An IETF draft standard for RADIUS specifies a method for communicating vendor-proprietary information between the network access server and the RADIUS server. Some vendors, nevertheless, have extended the RADIUS attribute set in a unique way. Cisco IOS software supports a subset of vendor-proprietary RADIUS attributes. For a list of supported vendor-proprietary RADIUS attributes, refer to Appendix A, "RADIUS Attributes."

RADIUS Configuration Examples

RADIUS configuration examples in this section include the following:

● RADIUS Authentication and Authorization Example

● RADIUS AAA Example

● Vendor-Proprietary RADIUS Configuration Example

RADIUS Authentication and Authorization Example

The following example shows how to configure the router to authenticate and authorize using RADIUS:

```
aaa authentication login use-radius radius local
aaa authentication ppp user-radius if-needed radius
aaa authorization exec radius
aaa authorization network radius
```

The lines in this sample RADIUS authentication and authorization configuration are defined as follows:

● The **aaa authentication login use-radius radius local** command configures the router to use RADIUS for authentication at the login prompt. If RADIUS returns an error, the user is authenticated using the local database. In this example, **use-radius** is the name of the method list, which specifies RADIUS and then local authentication.

● The **aaa authentication ppp user-radius if-needed radius** command configures the Cisco IOS software to use RADIUS authentication for lines using PPP with CHAP or PAP if the user has not already been authorized. If the EXEC facility has authenticated the user, RADIUS authentication is not performed. In this example, **user-radius** is the name of the method list defining RADIUS as the if-needed authentication method.

● The **aaa authorization exec radius** command sets the RADIUS information that is used for EXEC authorization, autocommands, and access lists.

● The **aaa authorization network radius** command sets RADIUS for network authorization, address assignment, and access lists.

RADIUS AAA Example

The following example is a general configuration using RADIUS with the AAA command set:

```
radius-server host 123.45.1.2
radius-server key myRaDiUSpassWoRd
username root password ALongPassword
aaa authentication ppp dialins radius local
aaa authorization network radius local
aaa accounting network start-stop radius
aaa authentication login admins local
aaa authorization exec local
line 1 16
 autoselect ppp
 autoselect during-login
 login authentication admins
 modem ri-is-cd
interface group-async 1
 encaps ppp
 ppp authentication pap dialins
```

The lines in this sample RADIUS AAA configuration are defined as follows:

● The **radius-server host** command defines the IP address of the RADIUS server host.

● The **radius-server key** command defines the shared secret text string between the network access server and the RADIUS server host.

- The **aaa authentication ppp dialins radius local** command defines the authentication method list *dialins*, which specifies that RADIUS authentication, and then (if the RADIUS server does not respond) local authentication will be used on serial lines using PPP.

- The **ppp authentication pap dialins** command applies the *dialins* method list to the lines specified.

- The **aaa authorization network radius local** command is used to assign an address and other network parameters to the RADIUS user.

- The **aaa accounting network start-stop radius** command tracks PPP usage.

- The **aaa authentication login admins local** command defines another method list, *admins*, for login authentication.

- The **login authentication admins** command applies the *admins* method list for login authentication.

Vendor-Proprietary RADIUS Configuration Example

The following example is a general configuration using vendor-proprietary RADIUS with the AAA command set:

```
radius-server host alcatraz non-standard
radius-server key myRaDiUSpassWoRd
radius-server configure-nas
username root password ALongPassword
aaa authentication ppp dialins radius local
aaa authorization network radius local
aaa accounting network start-stop radius
aaa authentication login admins local
aaa authorization exec local
line 1 16
autoselect ppp
autoselect during-login
login authentication admins
modem ri-is-cd
interface group-async 1
encaps ppp
ppp authentication pap dialins
```

The lines in this sample configuration using the vendor-proprietary RADIUS with the AAA command set are defined as follows:

- The **radius-server host non-standard** command defines the name of the RADIUS server host and identifies that this RADIUS host uses a vendor-proprietary version of RADIUS.

- The **radius-server key** command defines the shared secret text string between the network access server and the RADIUS server host.

- The **radius-server configure-nas** command defines that the Cisco router or access server will query the RADIUS server for static routes and IP pool definitions when the device first starts up.

- The **aaa authentication ppp dialins radius local** command defines the authentication method list *dialins*, which specifies that RADIUS authentication, and then (if the RADIUS server does not respond) local authentication will be used on serial lines using PPP.

- The **ppp authentication pap dialins** command applies the *dialins* method list to the lines specified.

- The **aaa authorization network radius local** command is used to assign an address and other network parameters to the RADIUS user.

- The **aaa accounting network start-stop radius** command tracks PPP usage.

- The **aaa authentication login admins local** command defines another method list, *admins*, for login authentication.

- The **login authentication admins** command applies the *admins* method list for login authentication.

## CHAPTER 9

RADIUS Commands

This chapter describes the commands used to configure RADIUS.

RADIUS is a distributed client/server system that secures networks against unauthorized access. In the Cisco implementation, RADIUS clients run on Cisco routers and send authentication requests to a central RADIUS server that contains all user authentication and network service access information. Cisco supports RADIUS under its authentication, authorization, and accounting (AAA) security paradigm.

For information on how to configure RADIUS, refer to Chapter 8, "Configuring RADIUS." For configuration examples using the commands in this chapter, refer to the "RADIUS Configuration Examples" section located at the end of Chapter 8, "Configuring RADIUS."

aaa nas-port extended

To replace the NAS-Port attribute with RADIUS Internet Engineering Task Force (IETF) Attribute 26 and to display extended field information, use the **aaa nas-port extended** global configuration command. Use the **no** form of this command to not display extended field information.

> **aaa nas-port extended**
> **no aaa nas-port extended**

Syntax Description

This command has no arguments or keywords.

Default

Disabled

Command Mode

Global configuration

Usage Guidelines

This command first appeared in Cisco IOS Release 11.3.

On platforms with multiple interfaces (ports) per slot, the Cisco RADIUS implementation will not provide a unique NAS-Port attribute that permits distinguishing between the interfaces. For example, if a dual PRI interface is in slot 1, calls on both Serial1/0:1 and Serial1/1:1 will appear as NAS-Port = 20101.

Once again, this is because of the 16-bit field size limitation associated with RADIUS IETF NAS-port attribute. In this case, the solution is to replace the NAS-Port attribute with a vendor-specific attribute (RADIUS IETF Attribute 26). Cisco's vendor ID is 9, and the cisco-nas-port attribute is subtype 2. Vendor-specific attributes (VSAs) can be turned on by entering the **radius-server vsa send** command. The port information in this attribute is provided and configured using the **aaa nas port extended** command.

The standard NAS-Port attribute (RADIUS IETF attribute 5) will continue to be sent. If you do not want this information to be sent, you can suppress it by using the **no radius-server attribute nas-port** command. When this command is configured, the standard NAS-Port attribute will no longer be sent.

Example

The following example specifies that RADIUS will display extended interface information:

```
radius-server vsa send
aaa nas-port extended
```

Related Commands

You can search online at www.cisco.com to find documentation of related commands.

radius-server attribute nas-port
radius-server vsa send

ip radius source-interface

To force RADIUS to use the IP address of a specified interface for all outgoing RADIUS packets, use the **ip radius source-interface** global configuration command.

> **ip radius source-interface** *subinterface-name*
> **no ip radius source-interface**

Syntax   Description

subinterface-name   Name of the interface that RADIUS uses for all its outgoing packets.

Default

This command has no factory-assigned default.

Command Mode

Global configuration

Usage Guidelines

This command first appeared in Cisco IOS Release 11.3.

Use this command to set a subinterface's IP address to be used as the source address for all outgoing RADIUS packets. This address is used as long as the interface is in the *up* state. In this way, the RADIUS server can use one IP address entry for every network access client instead of maintaining a list of IP addresses.

This command is especially useful in cases where the router has many interfaces and you want to ensure that all RADIUS packets from a particular router have the same IP address.

The specified interface must have an IP address associated with it. If the specified subinterface does not have a IP address or is in the *down* state, then RADIUS reverts to the default. To avoid this, add an IP address to the subinterface or bring the interface to the *up* state.

Example

The following example makes RADIUS use the IP address of subinterface s2 for all outgoing RADIUS packets:

```
ip radius source-interface s2
```

Related Commands

You can search online at www.cisco.com to find documentation of related commands.

ip tacacs source-interface
ip telnet source-interface
ip tftp source-interface

radius-server attribute nas-port extended

To display expanded interface information in the NAS-Port-Type attribute, use the **radius-server attribute nas-port extended** global configuration command. Use the **no** form of this command to not display expanded interface information.

> **radius-server attribute nas-port extended**
> **no radius-server attribute nas-port extended**

Syntax Description

This command has no arguments or keywords.

Part
II

Command Reference

Default
Disabled

Command Mode
Global configuration

Usage Guidelines
This command first appeared in Cisco IOS Release 11.3.

There are some situations when PPP or login authentication occurs on an interface that's different from the interface on which the call itself comes in. For example, in a V.120 ISDN call, login or PPP authentication occurs on a virtual asynchronous interface ttt, but the call itself occurs on one of the channels of the ISDN interface.

The **radius-server attribute nas-port extended** command configures RADIUS to expand the size of the NAS-Port attribute (RADIUS IETF Attribute 5) field to 32 bits. The upper 16 bits of the NAS-Port attribute display the type and number of the controlling interface; the lower 16 bits indicate the interface undergoing authentication.

NOTE	This command replaces the deprecated **radius-server extended-portnames** command.

Example
The following example specifies that RADIUS will display extended interface information:

```
radius-server attribute nas-port extended
```

Related Commands
You can search online at www.cisco.com to find documentation of related commands.

aaa nas-port extended

radius-server configure-nas

To have the Cisco router or access server query the vendor-proprietary RADIUS server for the static routes and IP pool definitions used throughout its domain when the device starts up, use the **radius-server configure-nas** global configuration command.

       radius-server configure-nas

Syntax Description

This command has no arguments or keywords.

Command Mode

Global configuration

Usage Guidelines

This command first appeared in Cisco IOS Release 11.3.

Use the **radius-server configure-nas** command to have the Cisco router query the vendor-proprietary RADIUS server for static routes and IP pool definitions when the router first starts up. Some vendor-proprietary implementations of RADIUS let the user define static routes and IP pool definitions on the RADIUS server instead of on each individual network access server in the network. As each network access server starts up, it queries the RADIUS server for static route and IP pool information. This command enables the Cisco router to obtain static routes and IP pool definition information from the RADIUS server.

NOTE	Because the **radius-server configure-nas** command is performed when the Cisco router starts up, it will not take effect until you issue a **copy system:running-config nvram:startup-config** command.

Example

The following example shows how to tell the Cisco router or access server to query the vendor-proprietary RADIUS server for already-defined static routes and IP pool definitions when the device first starts up:

```
radius-server configure-nas
```

Related Commands

You can search online at www.cisco.com to find documentation of related commands.

radius-server host non-standard

radius-server dead-time

To improve RADIUS response times when some servers might be unavailable, use the **radius-server dead-time** global configuration command to cause the unavailable servers to be skipped immediately. Use the **no** form of this command to set **dead-time** to 0.

> **radius-server dead-time** *minutes*
> **no radius-server dead-time**

Syntax

Syntax	Description
minutes	Length of time a RADIUS server is skipped over by transaction requests, up to a maximum of 1440 minutes (24 hours).

Default

Dead time is set to 0.

Command Mode

Global configuration

Usage Guidelines

Use this command to cause the Cisco IOS software to mark as "dead" any RADIUS servers that fail to respond to authentication requests, thus avoiding the wait for the request to time out before trying the next configured server. A RADIUS server marked as dead is skipped by additional requests for the duration of *minutes* or unless there are no servers not marked dead.

Example

The following example specifies 5 minutes dead-time for RADIUS servers that fail to respond to authentication requests:

```
radius-server dead-time 5
```

Related Commands

You can search online at www.cisco.com to find documentation of related commands.

radius-server host
radius-server retransmit
radius-server timeout

radius-server extended-portnames

To display expanded interface information in the NAS-Port-Type attribute, use the **radius-server extended-portnames** global configuration command. Use the **no** form of this command to not display expanded interface information.

> **radius-server extended-portnames**
> **no radius-server extended-portnames**

Syntax Description

This command has no arguments or keywords.

Default

Disabled

Command Mode

Global configuration

Usage Guidelines

NOTE   This command has been replaced by the **radius-server attribute nas-port** extended command.

Example

The following example specifies that RADIUS will display extended interface information:

```
radius-server extended-portnames
```

radius-server host

To specify a RADIUS server host, use the **radius-server host** global configuration command. Use the **no** form of this command to delete the specified RADIUS host.

> **radius-server host** {*hostname* | *ip-address*} [**auth-port** *port-number*]
> [**acct-port** *port-number*]
> **no radius-server host** {*hostname* | *ip-address*}

Syntax	Description
hostname	DNS name of the RADIUS server host.
ip-address	IP address of the RADIUS server host.
auth-port	(Optional) Specifies the UDP destination port for authentication requests.
port-number	(Optional) Port number for authentication requests; the host is not used for authentication if set to 0.
acct-port	(Optional) Specifies the UDP destination port for accounting requests.
port-number	(Optional) Port number for accounting requests; the host is not used for accounting if set to 0.

Default

No RADIUS host is specified.

Command Mode

Global configuration

Usage Guidelines

You can use multiple **radius-server host** commands to specify multiple hosts. The software searches for hosts in the order you specify them.

Examples

The following example specifies *host1* as the RADIUS server and uses default ports for both accounting and authentication:

```
radius-server host host1.domain.com
```

The following example specifies port 12 as the destination port for authentication requests and port 16 as the destination port for accounting requests on a RADIUS host named *host1*:

```
radius-server host host1.domain.com auth-port 12 acct-port 16
```

Because entering a line resets all the port numbers, you must specify a host and configure accounting and authentication ports on a single line.

To use separate servers for accounting and authentication, use the zero port value as appropriate. The following example specifies that RADIUS server *host1* be used for accounting but not for authentication, and that RADIUS server *host2* be used for authentication but not for accounting:

```
        radius-server host host1.domain.com auth-port 0
        radius-server host host2.domain.com acct-port 0
```

Related Commands

You can search online at www.cisco.com to find documentation of related commands.

aaa accounting
aaa authentication
aaa authorization
login authentication
login tacacs
ppp
ppp authentication
radius-server key
slip
tacacs-server
username

radius-server host non-standard

To identify that the security server is using a vendor-proprietary implementation of RADIUS, use the **radius-server host non-standard** global configuration command. This command tells the Cisco IOS software to support non-standard RADIUS attributes. Use the **no** form of this command to delete the specified vendor-proprietary RADIUS host.

> **radius-server host** {*hostname* | *ip-address*} **non-standard**
> **no radius-server host** {*hostname* | *ip-address*} **non-standard**

Syntax	Description
hostname	DNS name of the RADIUS server host.
ip-address	IP address of the RADIUS server host.

Default

No RADIUS host is specified.

Command Mode

Global configuration

Usage Guidelines

This command first appeared in Cisco IOS Release 11.3.

The **radius-server host non-standard** command enables you to identify that the RADIUS server is using a vendor-proprietary implementation of RADIUS. Although an IETF draft standard for RADIUS specifies a method for communicating information between the network access server and the RADIUS server, some vendors have extended the RADIUS attribute set in a unique way. This command enables the Cisco IOS software to support the most common vendor-proprietary RADIUS attributes. Vendor-proprietary attributes will not be supported unless you use the **radius-server host non-standard** command.

For a list of supported vendor-specific RADIUS attributes, refer to Appendix A, "RADIUS Attributes."

Example

The following example specifies a vendor-proprietary RADIUS server host named *alcatraz*:

```
radius-server host alcatraz non-standard
```

Related Commands

You can search online at www.cisco.com to find documentation of related commands.

radius-server host
radius-server configure-nas

radius-server optional passwords

To specify that the first RADIUS request to a RADIUS server be made *without* password verification, use the **radius-server optional-passwords** global configuration command. Use the **no** form of this command to restore the default.

> **radius-server optional-passwords**
> **no radius-server optional-passwords**

Syntax Description

This command has no arguments or keywords.

Default

Disabled

Command Mode

Global configuration

Usage Guidelines

This command first appeared in Cisco IOS Release 11.2.

When the user enters the login name, the login request is transmitted with the name and a zero-length password. If accepted, the login procedure completes. If the RADIUS server refuses this request, the server software prompts for a password and tries again when the user supplies a password. The RADIUS server must support authentication for users without passwords to make use of this feature.

Example

The following example configures the first login to not require RADIUS verification:

```
radius-server optional-passwords
```

radius-server key

To set the authentication and encryption key for all RADIUS communications between the router and the RADIUS daemon, use the **radius-server key** global configuration command. Use the **no** form of this command to disable the key.

> **radius-server key** {*string*}
> **no radius-server key**

Syntax   Description

string   The key used to set authentication and encryption. This key must match the encryption used on the RADIUS daemon.

Default

Disabled

Command Mode

Global configuration

Usage Guidelines

This command first appeared in Cisco IOS Release 11.1.

After enabling AAA authentication with the **aaa new-model** command, you must set the authentication and encryption key using the **radius-server key** command.

NOTE   Specify a RADIUS key after you issue the **aaa new-model** command.

The key entered must match the key used on the RADIUS daemon. All leading spaces are ignored, but spaces within and at the end of the key are used. If you use spaces in your key, do not enclose the key in quotation marks unless the quotation marks themselves are part of the key.

Example

The following example sets the authentication and encryption key to "dare to go":

```
radius-server key dare to go
```

Related Commands

You can search online at www.cisco.com to find documentation of related commands.

login authentication
login tacacs
ppp
ppp authentication
radius-server host
slip
tacacs-server
username

radius-server retransmit

To specify the number of times the Cisco IOS software searches the list of RADIUS server hosts before giving up, use the **radius-server retransmit** global configuration command. Use the **no** form of this command to disable retransmission.

> **radius-server retransmit** *retries*
> **no radius-server retransmit**

Syntax   Description

retries   Maximum number of retransmission attempts. The default is three attempts.

Default

Three retries

Command Mode

Global configuration

Usage Guidelines

This command first appeared in Cisco IOS Release 11.1.

The Cisco IOS software tries all servers, allowing each one to time out before increasing the retransmit count.

Example

The following example specifies a retransmit counter value of five times:

```
radius-server retransmit 5
```

radius-server timeout

To set the interval a router waits for a server host to reply, use the **radius-server timeout** global configuration command. Use the **no** form of this command to restore the default.

>**radius-server timeout** *seconds*
>**no radius-server timeout**

Syntax	Description
seconds	Number that specifies the timeout interval in seconds. The default is 5 seconds.

Default

5 seconds

Command Mode

Global configuration

Usage Guidelines

This command first appeared in Cisco IOS Release 11.1.

Example

The following example changes the interval timer to 10 seconds:

```
radius-server timeout 10
```

Related Commands

You can search online at www.cisco.com to find documentation of related commands.

login authentication
login tacacs
ppp
ppp authentication
slip
tacacs-server
username

radius-server vsa send

To configure the network access server to recognize and use VSAs, use the **radius-server vsa send** global configuration command. Use the **no** form of this command to restore the default.

radius-server vsa send [accounting | authentication]
no radius-server vsa send [accounting | authentication]

Syntax	Description
accounting	(Optional) Limits the set of recognized vendor-specific attributes to only accounting attributes.
authentication	(Optional) Limits the set of recognized vendor-specific attributes to only authentication attributes.

Default

Disabled

Command Mode

Global configuration

Usage Guidelines

This command first appeared in Cisco IOS Release 11.3 T.

The IETF draft standard specifies a method for communicating vendor-specific information between the network access server and the RADIUS server by using the vendor-specific attribute (Attribute 26). VSAs allow vendors to support their own extended attributes not suitable for general use. The **radius-server vsa send** command enables the network access server to recognize and use both accounting and authentication vendor-specific attributes. Use the **accounting** keyword with the **radius-server vsa send** command to limit the set of recognized vendor-specific attributes to just accounting attributes. Use the **authentication** keyword with the **radius-server vsa send** command to limit the set of recognized vendor-specific attributes to just authentication attributes.

The Cisco RADIUS implementation supports one vendor-specific option using the format recommended in the specification. Cisco's vendor-ID is 9, and the supported option has vendor type 1, which is named *cisco-avpair*. The value is a string with the following format:

```
protocol : attribute sep value *
```

protocol is a value of the Cisco *protocol* attribute for a particular type of authorization. *attribute* and *value* are an appropriate AV pair defined in the Cisco TACACS+ specification, and *sep* is = for mandatory attributes and * for optional attributes. This allows the full set of features available for TACACS+ authorization to also be used for RADIUS.

For example, the following AV pair causes Cisco's multiple named ip address pools feature to be activated during IP authorization (during PPP's IPCP address assignment):

```
cisco-avpair= "ip:addr-pool=first"
```

The following example causes a "NAS Prompt" user to have immediate access to EXEC commands.

```
cisco-avpair= "shell:priv-lvl=15"
```

Other vendors have their own unique vendor IDs, options, and associated VSAs. For more information about vendor IDs and VSAs, refer to RFC 2138, "Remote Authentication Dial-In User Service (RADIUS)."

Example

The following example configures the network access server to recognize and use vendor-specific accounting attributes:

```
radius-server vsa send accounting
```

Related Commands

You can search online at www.cisco.com to find documentation of related commands.

aaa nas-port extended

## CHAPTER 10

Configuring TACACS+

Cisco IOS software currently supports three versions of the Terminal Access Controller Access Control System (TACACS) security protocol, each one of which is a separate and unique protocol:

- TACACS+—A recent protocol providing detailed accounting information and flexible administrative control over authentication and authorization processes. TACACS+ is facilitated through AAA and can be enabled only through AAA commands.

- TACACS—An older access protocol, incompatible with the newer TACACS+ protocol, that is now deprecated by Cisco. It provides password checking and authentication, and notification of user actions for security and accounting purposes.

- Extended TACACS—An extension to the older TACACS protocol, supplying additional functionality to TACACS. Extended TACACS provides information about protocol translator and router use. This information is used in UNIX auditing trails and accounting files. Extended TACACS is incompatible with TACACS+ and is also deprecated.

This chapter discusses how to enable and configure TACACS+. For information about the deprecated protocols TACACS and extended TACACS, refer to Chapter 11, "Configuring TACACS and Extended TACACS." To locate documentation of other commands that appear in this chapter, you can search online at www.cisco.com.

TACACS+ Overview

TACACS+ is a security application that provides centralized validation of users attempting to gain access to a router or network access server. TACACS+ services are maintained in a database on a TACACS+ daemon that typically runs on a UNIX or Windows NT workstation. You must have access to and must configure a TACACS+ server before the configured TACACS+ features on your network access server are available.

TACACS+ provides for separate and modular authentication, authorization, and accounting facilities. TACACS+ allows for a single access control server (the TACACS+ daemon) to provide each service— authentication, authorization, and accounting—independently. Each service can be tied into its own database to take advantage of other services available on that server or on the network, depending on the capabilities of the daemon.

The goal of TACACS+ is to provide a methodology for managing multiple network access points from a single management service. The Cisco family of access servers and routers and the Cisco IOS user interface (for both routers and access servers) can be network access servers.

Network access points enable traditional "dumb" terminals, terminal emulators, workstations, personal computers (PCs), and routers in conjunction with suitable adapters (for example, modems or ISDN adapters) to communicate using protocols such as Point-to-Point Protocol (PPP), Serial Line Internet

Protocol (SLIP), Compressed SLIP (CSLIP), or AppleTalk Remote Access (ARA) Protocol. In other words, a network access server provides connections to a single user, to a network or subnetwork, and to interconnected networks. The entities connected to the network through a network access server are called *network access clients*; for example, a PC running PPP over a voice-grade circuit is a network access client. TACACS+, administered through the AAA security services, can provide the following services:

● Authentication—Provides complete control of authentication through login and password dialog, challenge and response, and messaging support.

  The authentication facility provides the ability to conduct an arbitrary dialog with the user (for example, after a login and password are provided, to challenge a user with a number of questions, such as home address, mother's maiden name, service type, and Social Security number). In addition, the TACACS+ authentication service supports sending messages to user screens. For example, a message could notify users that their passwords must be changed because of the company's password aging policy.

● Authorization—Provides fine-grained control over user capabilities for the duration of the user's session, including but not limited to setting autocommands, access control, session duration, or protocol support. You can also enforce restrictions on what commands a user may execute with the TACACS+ authorization feature.

● Accounting—Collects and sends information used for billing, auditing, and reporting to the TACACS+ daemon. Network managers can use the accounting facility to track user activity for a security audit or to provide information for user billing. Accounting records include user identities, start and stop times, executed commands (such as PPP), number of packets, and number of bytes.

The TACACS+ protocol provides authentication between the network access server and the TACACS+ daemon, and it ensures confidentiality, because all protocol exchanges between a network access server and a TACACS+ daemon are encrypted.

You need a system running TACACS+ daemon software to use the TACACS+ functionality on your network access server.

Cisco makes the TACACS+ protocol specification available as a draft RFC for those customers interested in developing their own TACACS+ software.

NOTE   TACACS+, in conjunction with AAA, is a separate and distinct protocol from the earlier TACACS or extended TACACS, which are now deprecated. After AAA has been enabled, many of the original TACACS and extended TACACS commands can no longer be configured. For more information about TACACS or extended TACACS, refer to Chapter 11, "Configuring TACACS and Extended TACACS."

TACACS+ Operation

When a user attempts a simple ASCII login by authenticating to a network access server using TACACS+, the following process typically occurs:

1 When the connection is established, the network access server contacts the TACACS+ daemon to obtain a username prompt, which is then displayed to the user. The user enters a username, and the network access server then contacts the TACACS+ daemon to obtain a password prompt. The network access server displays the password prompt to the user, the user enters a password, and the password is then sent to the TACACS+ daemon.

NOTE   TACACS+ allows an arbitrary conversation to be held between the daemon and the user until the daemon receives enough information to authenticate the user. This is usually done by prompting for a username and password combination, but may include other items, such as mother's maiden name, all under the control of the TACACS+ daemon.

---

2 The network access server eventually receives one of the following responses from the TACACS+ daemon:

(a) ACCEPT—The user is authenticated and service may begin. If the network access server is configured to requite authorization, authorization will begin at this time.

(b) REJECT—The user has failed to authenticate. The user may be denied further access, or will be prompted to retry the login sequence depending on the TACACS+ daemon.

(c) ERROR—An error occurred at some time during authentication. This can be either at the daemon or in the network connection between the daemon and the network access server. If an ERROR response is received, the network access server will typically try to use an alternative method for authenticating the user.

(d) CONTINUE—The user is prompted for additional authentication information.

3 A PAP login is similar to an ASCII login, except that the username and password arrive at the network access server in a PAP protocol packet instead of being typed in by the user, so the user is not prompted. PPP CHAP logins are also similar in principle.

Following authentication, the user will also be required to undergo an additional authorization phase, if authorization has been enabled on the network access server. Users must first successfully complete TACACS+ authentication before proceeding to TACACS+ authorization.

4 If TACACS+ authorization is required, the TACACS+ daemon is again contacted and it returns an ACCEPT or REJECT authorization response. If an ACCEPT response is returned, the response will contain data in the form of attributes that are used to direct the EXEC or NETWORK session for that user, determining services that the user can access. Services include the following:

(a) Telnet, rlogin, PPP, SLIP, or EXEC services

(b) Connection parameters, including the host or client IP address, access list, and user timeouts

TACACS+ Configuration Task List

To configure your router to support TACACS+, you must perform the following tasks:

- Use the **aaa new-model** global configuration command to enable AAA. AAA must be configured if you plan to use TACACS+. For more information about using the **aaa new-model** command, refer to Chapter 1, "AAA Overview."

- Use the **tacacs-server host** command to specify the IP address of one or more TACACS+ daemons. Use the **tacacs-server key** command to specify an encryption key that will be used to encrypt all exchanges between the network access server and the TACACS+ daemon. This same key must also be configured on the TACACS+ daemon.

- Use the **aaa authentication** global configuration command to define method lists that use TACACS+ for authentication. For more information about using the **aaa authentication** command, refer to Chapter 2, "Configuring Authentication."

- Use **line** and **interface** commands to apply the defined method lists to various interfaces. For more information, refer to Chapter 2, "Configuring Authentication."

- If needed, use the **aaa authorization** global command to configure authorization for the network access server. Unlike authentication, which can be configured per line or per interface, authorization is configured globally for the entire network access server. For more information about using the **aaa authorization** command, refer to Chapter 4, "Configuring Authorization."

- If needed, use the **aaa accounting** command to enable accounting for TACACS+ connections. For more information about using the **aaa accounting** command, refer to Chapter 6, "Configuring Accounting."

To configure TACACS+, you need to perform the tasks in the following sections:

- Identifying the TACACS+ Server Host

- Setting the TACACS+ Authentication Key

- Specifying TACACS+ Authentication

- Specifying TACACS+ Accounting

For TACACS+ configuration examples using the commands in this chapter, refer to the "TACACS+ Configuration Examples" section located at the end of the chapter.

Identifying the TACACS+ Server Host

The **tacacs-server host** command enables you to specify the names of the IP host or hosts maintaining a TACACS+ server. Because the TACACS+ software searches for the hosts in the order specified, this feature can be useful for setting up a list of preferred daemons.

To specify a TACACS+ host, use the following command in global configuration mode:

Command	Purpose
tacacs-server host *name* [**single-connection**] [**port** *integer*] [**timeout** *integer*] [**key** *string*]	Specifies a TACACS+ host.

Using the **tacacs-server host** command, you can also configure the following options:

- Use the **single-connection** keyword to specify single-connection (only valid with CiscoSecure Release 1.0.1 or later). Rather than have the router open and close a TCP connection to the daemon each time it must communicate, the single-connection option maintains a single open connection between the router and the daemon. This is more efficient, because it allows the daemon to handle a higher number of TACACS operations.

NOTE	The daemon must support single-connection mode for this to be effective; otherwise, the connection between the network access server and the daemon will lock up, or you will receive spurious errors.

- Use the **port** *integer* argument to specify the TCP port number to be used when making connections to the TACACS+ daemon. The default port number is 49.

- Use the **timeout** *integer* argument to specify the period of time (in seconds) the router will wait for a response from the daemon before it times out and declares an error.

NOTE	Specifying the timeout value with the **tacacs-server host** command overrides the default timeout value set with the **tacacs-server timeout** command for this server only.

- Use the **key** *string* argument to specify an encryption key for encrypting and decrypting all traffic between the network access server and the TACACS+ daemon.

NOTE	Specifying the encryption key with the **tacacs-server host** command overrides the default key set by the global configuration **tacacs-server key** command for this server only.

Because some of the parameters of the **tacacs-server host** command override global settings made by the **tacacs-server timeout** and **tacacs-server key** commands, you can use this command to enhance security on your network by uniquely configuring individual TACACS+ connections.

Setting the TACACS+ Authentication Key

To set the TACACS+ authentication key and encryption key, use the following command in global configuration mode:

Command	Purpose
tacacs-server key *key*	Sets the encryption key to match that used on the TACACS+ daemon.

NOTE	You must configure the same key on the TACACS+ daemon for encryption to be successful.

Specifying TACACS+ Authentication

After you have identified the TACACS+ daemon and defined an associated TACACS+ encryption key, you need to define method lists for TACACS+ authentication. Because TACACS+ authentication is operated via AAA, you need to issue the **aaa authentication** command, specifying TACACS+ as the authentication method. For more information, refer to Chapter 2, "Configuring Authentication."

Specifying TACACS+ Authorization

AAA authorization enables you to set parameters that restrict a user's network access. Authorization via TACACS+ may be applied to commands, network connections, and EXEC sessions. Because TACACS+ authorization is facilitated through AAA, you need to issue the **aaa authorization** command, specifying TACACS+ as the authorization method. For more information, refer to Chapter 4, "Configuring Authorization."

Specifying TACACS+ Accounting

AAA accounting enables you to track the services users are accessing as well as the amount of network resources they are consuming. Because TACACS+ accounting is facilitated through AAA, you need to issue the **aaa accounting** command, specifying TACACS+ as the accounting method. For more information, refer to Chapter 6, "Configuring Accounting."

TACACS+ AV Pairs

The network access server implements TACACS+ authorization and accounting functions by transmitting and receiving TACACS+ attribute-value (AV) pairs for each user session. For a list of supported TACACS+ AV pairs, refer to Appendix B, "TACACS+ Attribute-Value Pairs."

TACACS+ Configuration Examples

TACACS+ configuration examples in this section include the following:

- TACACS+ Authentication Examples

- TACACS+ Authorization Example

- TACACS+ Accounting Example

- TACACS+ Daemon Configuration Example

TACACS+ Authentication Examples

The following example configures TACACS+ as the security protocol to be used for PPP authentication.

```
aaa new-model
aaa authentication ppp test tacacs+ local
tacacs-server host 10.1.2.3
tacacs-server key goaway
interface serial 0
 ppp authentication chap pap test
```

In this example

- The **aaa new-model** command enables the AAA security services.

- The **aaa authentication** command defines a method list, *test*, to be used on serial interfaces running PPP. The keyword **tacacs+** means that authentication will be done through TACACS+. If TACACS+ returns an ERROR of some sort during authentication, the keyword **local** indicates that authentication will be attempted using the local database on the network access server.

- The **tacacs-server host** command identifies the TACACS+ daemon as having an IP address of 10.1.2.3. The **tacacs-server key** command defines the shared encryption key to be *goaway*.

- The **interface** command selects the line, and the **ppp authentication** command applies the test method list to this line.

The following example configures TACACS+ as the security protocol to be used for PPP authentication but instead of the method list *test*, the method list, *default*, is used:

```
aaa new-model
aaa authentication ppp default if-needed tacacs+ local
tacacs-server host 10.1.2.3
tacacs-server key goaway
interface serial 0
 ppp authentication default
```

In this example

- The **aaa new-model** command enables the AAA security services.

- The **aaa authentication** command defines a method list, *default*, to be used on serial interfaces running PPP. The keyword **default** means that PPP authentication is applied by default to all interfaces. The **if-needed** keyword means that if the user has already authenticated by going through the ASCII login procedure, then PPP authentication is not necessary and can be skipped. If authentication is needed, the keyword **tacacs+** means that authentication will be done through TACACS+. If TACACS+ returns an ERROR of some sort during authentication, the keyword **local** indicates that authentication will be attempted using the local database on the network access server.

- The **tacacs-server host** command identifies the TACACS+ daemon as having an IP address of 10.1.2.3. The **tacacs-server key** command defines the shared encryption key to be *goaway*.

- The **interface** command selects the line, and the **ppp authentication** command applies the default method list to this line.

The following example creates the same authentication algorithm for PAP but calls the method list *MIS-access* instead of *default*:

```
aaa new-model
aaa authentication pap MIS-access if-needed tacacs+ local
tacacs-server host 10.1.2.3
tacacs-server key goaway
interface serial 0
 ppp authentication pap MIS-access
```

In this example

- The **aaa new-model** command enables the AAA security services.

- The **aaa authentication** command defines a method list, *MIS-access*, to be used on serial interfaces running PPP. The method list, *MIS-access*, means that PPP authentication is applied to all interfaces. The **if-needed** keyword means that if the user has already authenticated by going through the ASCII login procedure, then PPP authentication is not necessary and can be skipped. If authentication is needed, the keyword **tacacs+** means that authentication will be done through TACACS+. If TACACS+ returns an ERROR of some sort during authentication, the keyword **local** indicates that authentication will be attempted using the local database on the network access server.

- The **tacacs-server host** command identifies the TACACS+ daemon as having an IP address of 10.1.2.3. The **tacacs-server key** command defines the shared encryption key to be *goaway*.

- The **interface** command selects the line, and the **ppp authentication** command applies the default method list to this line.

The following example shows the configuration for a TACACS+ daemon with an IP address of 10.2.3.4 and an encryption key of *apple*:

```
aaa new-model
aaa authentication login default tacacs+ local
tacacs-server host 10.2.3.4
tacacs-server key apple
```

In this example

- The **aaa new-model** command enables the AAA security services.

- The **aaa authentication** command defines the default method list. Incoming ASCII logins on all interfaces (by default) will use TACACS+ for authentication. If no TACACS+ server responds, then the network access server will use the information contained in the local username database for authentication.

- The **tacacs-server host** command identifies the TACACS+ daemon as having an IP address of 10.2.3.4. The **tacacs-server key** command defines the shared encryption key to be *apple*.

TACACS+ Authorization Example

The following example configures TACACS+ as the security protocol to be used for PPP authentication using the default method list, and configures network authorization via TACACS+:

```
aaa new-model
aaa authentication ppp default if-needed tacacs+ local
aaa authorization network tacacs+
tacacs-server host 10.1.2.3
tacacs-server key goaway
interface serial 0
 ppp authentication default
```

In this example

- The **aaa new-model** command enables the AAA security services.

- The **aaa authentication** command defines a method list, *default*, to be used on serial interfaces running PPP. The keyword **default** means that PPP authentication is applied by default to all interfaces. The **if-needed** keyword means that if the user has already authenticated by going through the ASCII login procedure, then PPP authentication is not necessary and can be skipped. If authentication is needed, the keyword **tacacs+** means that authentication will be done through TACACS+. If TACACS+ returns an ERROR of some sort during authentication, the keyword **local** indicates that authentication will be attempted using the local database on the network access server.

- The **aaa authorization** command configures network authorization via TACACS+. Unlike authentication lists, this authorization list always applies to all incoming network connections made to the network access server.

- The **tacacs-server host** command identifies the TACACS+ daemon as having an IP address of 10.1.2.3. The **tacacs-server key** command defines the shared encryption key to be *goaway*.

- The **interface** command selects the line, and the **ppp authentication** command applies the default method list to this line.

TACACS+ Accounting Example

The following example configures TACACS+ as the security protocol to be used for PPP authentication using the default method list, and configures accounting via TACACS+:

```
aaa new-model
aaa authentication ppp default if-needed tacacs+ local
aaa accounting network stop-only tacacs+
tacacs-server host 10.1.2.3
tacacs-server key goaway
interface serial 0
 ppp authentication default
```

In this example

- The **aaa new-model** command enables the AAA security services.

- The **aaa authentication** command defines a method list, *default*, to be used on serial interfaces running PPP. The keyword **default** means that PPP authentication is applied by default to all interfaces. The **if-needed** keyword means that if the user has already authenticated by going through the ASCII login procedure, then PPP authentication is not necessary and can be skipped. If authentication is needed, the keyword **tacacs+** means that authentication will be done through TACACS+. If TACACS+ returns an ERROR of some sort during authentication, the keyword **local** indicates that authentication will be attempted using the local database on the network access server.

- The **aaa accounting** command configures network accounting via TACACS+. In this example, accounting records describing the session that just terminated will be sent to the TACACS+ daemon whenever a network connection terminates.

- The **tacacs-server host** command identifies the TACACS+ daemon as having an IP address of 10.1.2.3. The **tacacs-server key** command defines the shared encryption key to be *goaway*.

- The **interface** command selects the line, and the **ppp authentication** command applies the default method list to this line.

TACACS+ Daemon Configuration Example

The following example shows a sample configuration of the TACACS+ daemon; the precise syntax used by your TACACS+ daemon may be different than that included in this example:

```
user = mci_customer1 {
    chap = cleartext "some chap password"
    service = ppp protocol = ip {
  inacl#1="permit ip any any precedence immediate"
  inacl#2="deny igrp 0.0.1.2 255.255.0.0 any"
}

}
```

## CHAPTER 11

Configuring TACACS and Extended TACACS

The Terminal Access Controller Access Control System (TACACS) provides a way to centrally validate users attempting to gain access to a router or access server. Basic Cisco TACACS support is modeled after the original Defense Data Network (DDN) application. TACACS services are maintained in a database on a TACACS server running, typically, on a UNIX workstation. You must have access to and must configure a TACACS server before configuring the TACACS features on your Cisco router.

Cisco implements TACACS in the Cisco IOS software to allow centralized control over access to routers and access servers. Authentication can also be provided for Cisco IOS administration tasks on the router and access server user interfaces. With TACACS enabled, the router or access server prompts for a username and password, then verifies the password with a TACACS server.

This chapter describes the TACACS and extended TACACS protocols and the various ways you can use them to secure access to your network.

NOTE   Both TACACS and extended TACACS are now deprecated by Cisco.

For a complete description of the TACACS and extended TACACS commands used in this chapter, refer to Chapter 12, "TACACS, Extended TACACS, and TACACS+ Commands." To locate documentation of other commands that appear in this chapter, you can search online at www.cisco.com.

TACACS Protocol Description

Cisco IOS software currently supports three versions of the Terminal Access Controller Access Control System (TACACS) security protocol, each of which is a separate and unique protocol:

- TACACS+—A recent protocol providing detailed accounting information and flexible administrative control over authentication and authorization processes. TACACS+ is facilitated through AAA and can be enabled only through AAA commands.

- TACACS—An older access protocol, incompatible with the newer TACACS+ protocol, that is now deprecated by Cisco. It provides password checking and authentication, and notification of user actions for security and accounting purposes.

- Extended TACACS—An extension to the older TACACS protocol, supplying additional functionality to TACACS. Extended TACACS provides information about protocol translator and router use. This information is used in UNIX auditing trails and accounting files. Extended TACACS is incompatible with TACACS+ and is also deprecated.

This chapter discusses how to enable and configure TACACS and extended TACACS. For information about TACACS+, refer to Chapter 10, "Configuring TACACS+."

Table 11-1 identifies Cisco IOS commands available to the different versions of TACACS.

Table 11-1 *TACACS Command Comparison*

Cisco IOS Command	TACACS	Extended TACACS	TACACS+
aaa accounting	–	–	Yes
aaa authentication arap	–	–	Yes
aaa authentication enable default	–	–	Yes
aaa authentication login	–	–	Yes
aaa authentication local override	–	–	Yes
aaa authentication ppp	–	–	Yes
aaa authorization	–	–	Yes
aaa new-model	–	–	Yes
arap authentication	–	–	Yes
arap use-tacacs	Yes	Yes	–
enable last-resort	Yes	Yes	–
enable use-tacacs	Yes	Yes	–
ip tacacs source-interface	Yes	Yes	Yes
login authentication	–	–	Yes
login tacacs	Yes	Yes	–
ppp authentication	Yes	Yes	Yes
ppp use-tacacs	Yes	Yes	Yes
tacacs-server attempts	Yes	–	–
tacacs-server authenticate	Yes	Yes	–
tacacs-server directed-request	Yes	Yes	Yes
tacacs-server extended	–	Yes	–
tacacs-server host	Yes	Yes	Yes

Table 11-1 *TACACS Command Comparison (Continued)*

Cisco IOS Command	TACACS	Extended TACACS	TACACS+
tacacs-server key	–	–	Yes
tacacs-server last-resort	Yes	Yes	–
tacacs-server notify	Yes	Yes	–
tacacs-server optional-passwords	Yes	Yes	–
tacacs-server retransmit	Yes	Yes	–
tacacs-server timeout	Yes	Yes	Yes

TACACS and Extended TACACS Configuration Task List

You can establish TACACS-style password protection on both user and privileged levels of the system EXEC.

NOTE   TACACS and extended TACACS commands cannot be used after you have initialized AAA. To identify which commands can be used with the three versions, refer to Table 11-1 earlier in this chapter.

The following sections describe the features available with TACACS and extended TACACS; the extended TACACS software is available using the File Transfer Protocol (FTP)—see the README file in the ftp-eng.cisco.com directory:

- Setting TACACS Password Protection at the User Level

- Disabling Password Checking at the User Level

- Setting Optional Password Verification

- Setting TACACS Password Protection at the Privileged Level

- Disabling Password Checking at the Privileged Level

- Setting Notification of User Actions

- Setting Authentication of User Actions

- Establishing the TACACS Server Host

- Setting Limits on Login Attempts

- Enabling the Extended TACACS Mode

- Enabling Extended TACACS for PPP Authentication

- Enabling Standard TACACS for ARA Authentication

- Enabling Extended TACACS for ARA Authentication

- Enabling TACACS to Use a Specific IP Address

For TACACS configuration examples, refer to the "TACACS Configuration Examples" section at the end of the this chapter.

Setting TACACS Password Protection at the User Level

To enable password checking at login, use the following command in line configuration mode:

Command	Purpose
login tacacs	Sets the TACACS-style user ID and password-checking mechanism.

NOTE When configuring TACACS, any usernames locally defined on the router will be used. The router will not go to the TACACS server for authentication.

Disabling Password Checking at the User Level

If a TACACS server does not respond to a login request, the Cisco IOS software denies the request by default. However, you can prevent that login failure in one of the following two ways:

- Allow a user to access privileged EXEC mode if that user enters the password set by the **enable** command.

- Allow the user to access the privileged EXEC mode without further question.

To specify one of these features, use either of the following commands in global configuration mode:

Command	Purpose
tacacs-server last-resort password	Allows a user to access privileged EXEC mode.
tacacs-server last-resort succeed	Sets last resort options for logins.

Setting Optional Password Verification

You can specify that the first TACACS request to a TACACS server is made without password verification. To do so, use the following command in global configuration mode:

Command	Purpose
tacacs-server optional-passwords	Sets TACACS password as optional.

When the user enters the login name, the login request is transmitted with the name and a zero-length password. If accepted, the login procedure is completed. If the TACACS server refuses this request, the terminal server prompts for a password and tries again when the user supplies a password. The TACACS server must support authentication for users without passwords to make use of this feature. This feature supports all TACACS requests such as login, SLIP, and enable.

Setting TACACS Password Protection at the Privileged Level

You can set the TACACS protocol to determine whether a user can access the privileged EXEC level. To do so, use the following command in global configuration mode:

Command	Purpose
enable use-tacacs	Sets the TACACS-style user ID and password-checking mechanism at the privileged EXEC level.

When you set TACACS password protection at the privileged EXEC level, the EXEC **enable** command will ask for both a new username and a password. This information is then passed to the TACACS server for authentication. If you are using the extended TACACS, it also passes any existing UNIX user identification code to the server.

CAUTION   If you use the **enable use-tacacs** command, you must also specify **tacacs-server authenticate enable**; otherwise, you will be locked out.

NOTE   When used without extended TACACS, this task allows anyone with a valid username and password to access the privileged command level, creating a potential security problem. This is because the TACACS query resulting from entering the **enable** command is indistinguishable from an attempt to log in without extended TACACS.

Disabling Password Checking at the Privileged Level

You can specify a last resort if the TACACS servers used by the **enable** command do not respond. To invoke this last-resort login feature, use either of the following commands in global configuration mode:

Command	Purpose
enable last-resort password	Allows user to enable by asking for the privileged EXEC-level password.
enable last-resort succeed	Allows user to enable without further questions.

Setting Notification of User Actions

The **tacacs-server notify** command allows you to configure the TACACS server to send a message when a user does the following:

- Makes a TCP connection

- Enters the **enable** command

- Logs out

To specify that the TACACS server send notification, use the following command in global configuration mode:

Command	Purpose
tacacs-server notify {**connection** [**always**] | **enable** | **logout** [**always**] | **slip** [**always**]}	Sets server notification of user actions.

The retransmission of the message is performed by a background process for up to 5 minutes. The terminal user, however, receives an immediate response, allowing access to the terminal.

The **tacacs-server notify** command is available only if you have set up an extended TACACS server using the latest Cisco extended TACACS server software, available via FTP. (See the README file in the ftp-eng.cisco.com directory.)

Setting Authentication of User Actions

For a SLIP or PPP session, you can specify that if a user tries to start a session, the TACACS software requires a response (either from the TACACS server host or the router) indicating whether the user can start the session. You can specify that the TACACS software perform authentication even when a user is not logged in; you can also request that the TACACS software install access lists.

If a user issues the **enable** command, the TACACS software must respond indicating whether the user can give the command. You can also specify authentication when a user enters the **enable** command.

To configure any of these scenarios, use the following command in global configuration mode:

Command	Purpose
tacacs-server authenticate {**connection**[**always**] **enable**	**slip** [**always**] [**access-lists**]}	Sets server authentication of user actions.

The **tacacs-server authenticate** command is available only when you have set up an extended TACACS server using the latest Cisco extended TACACS server software, which is available via FTP. (See the README file in the ftp.cisco.com directory).

Establishing the TACACS Server Host

The **tacacs-server host** command allows you to specify the names of the IP host or hosts maintaining a TACACS server. Because the TACACS software searches for the hosts in the order specified, this feature can be useful for setting up a list of preferred servers.

With TACACS and extended TACACS, the **tacacs-server retransmit** command allows you to modify the number of times the system software searches the list of TACACS servers (from the default of two times) and the interval it waits for a reply (from the default of 5 seconds).

To define the number of times the Cisco IOS software searches the list of servers, and how long the server waits for a reply, use the following commands as needed for your system configuration, in global configuration mode:

Step	Command	Purpose
1	**tacacs-server host** *name*	Specifies a TACACS host.
2	**tacacs-server retransmit** *retries*	Specifies the number of times the server will search the list of TACACS and extended TACACS server hosts before giving up.
3	**tacacs-server timeout** *seconds*	Sets the interval the server waits for a TACACS and extended TACACS server host to reply.

Setting Limits on Login Attempts

The **tacacs-server attempts** command allows you to specify the number of login attempts that can be made on a line set up for TACACS. Use the following command in global configuration mode to limit login attempts:

Command	Purpose
tacacs-server attempts *count*	Controls the number of login attempts that can be made on a line set for TACACS verification.

Enabling the Extended TACACS Mode

Whereas standard TACACS provides only username and password information, extended TACACS mode provides information about the terminal requests to help set up UNIX auditing trails and accounting files for tracking the use of protocol translators, access servers, and routers. The information includes responses from these network devices and validation of user requests.

An unsupported, extended TACACS server is available via FTP for UNIX users who want to create the auditing programs (see the README file in the ftp-eng.cisco.com directory).

To enable extended TACACS mode, use the following command in global configuration mode:

Command	Purpose
tacacs-server extended	Enables an extended TACACS mode.

NOTE	When configuring extended TACACS, any usernames locally defined on the router will be used. The router will not go to the TACACS server for authentication.

Enabling Extended TACACS for PPP Authentication

You can use extended TACACS for authentication within PPP sessions. To do so, use the following commands in interface configuration mode:

Step	Command	Purpose
1	**ppp authentication** {**chap** | **chap pap** | **pap chap** | **pap**} [**if-needed**] [*list-name* | **default**] [**callin**]	Enables CHAP or PAP.
2	**ppp use-tacacs** [**single-line**]	Enables extended TACACS under PPP.

For an example of enabling TACACS for PPP protocol authentication, see the "TACACS Configuration Examples" section at the end of this chapter.

Enabling Standard TACACS for ARA Authentication

You can use the standard TACACS protocol for authentication within AppleTalk Remote Access (ARA) protocol sessions. To do so, use the following commands, starting in line configuration mode:

Step	Command	Purpose
1	**arap use-tacacs single-line**	Enables standard TACACS under the ARA protocol.
2	**autoselect arap**	Enables autoselection of ARA.
3	**autoselect during-login**	(Optional) Has the ARA session start automatically at user login.

The **arap use-tacacs single-line** command is useful when integrating TACACS with other authentication systems that require a clear text version of the user's password. Such systems include one-time passwords, token card systems, and others.

By using the optional **during-login** argument with the **autoselect** command, you can display the username or password prompt without pressing the **Return** key. While the username or password name is displayed, you can choose to answer these prompts or to start sending packets from an autoselected protocol.

The remote user logs in through ARA as follows:

Step 1   When prompted for a username by the ARA application, the remote user enters *username*password* and presses **Return**.

Step 2   When prompted for password by the ARA application, the remote user enters **arap** and presses **Return**.

For examples of enabling TACACS for ARA protocol authentication, see the "TACACS Configuration Examples" section at the end of this chapter.

Enabling Extended TACACS for ARA Authentication

You can use extended TACACS for authentication within ARA protocol sessions. The extended TACACS server software is available via FTP (see the README file in the ftp.cisco.com directory).

NOTE   Before entering the commands listed in the following task table, you must edit the file called Makefile in the extended TACACS server software to use ARA. To do this, you must uncomment the lines that enable ARA support and recompile the file.

After installing an extended TACACS server with ARA support, use the following commands in line configuration mode on each line:

Step	Command	Purpose
1	**arap use-tacacs**	Enables extended TACACS under the ARA protocol on each line.
2	**autoselect arap**	(Optional) Enables autoselection of ARA.
3	**autoselect during-login**	(Optional) Has the ARA session start automatically at user login.

By using the optional **during-login** argument with the **autoselect** command, you can display the username or password prompt without pressing the Return key. While the Username or Password name is being presented, you can choose to answer these prompts or to start sending packets from an autoselected protocol.

Enabling TACACS to Use a Specific IP Address

You can designate a fixed source IP address for all outgoing TACACS packets. The feature enables TACACS to use the IP address of a specified interface for all outgoing TACACS packets. This is especially useful if the router has many interfaces, and you want to make sure that all TACACS packets from a particular router have the same IP address.

To enable TACACS to use the address of a specified interface for all outgoing TACACS packets, use the following command in configuration mode:

Command	Purpose
ip tacacs source-interface *subinterface-name*	Enables TACACS to use the IP address of a specified interface for all outgoing TACACS packets.

TACACS Configuration Examples

The following example shows TACACS enabled for PPP authentication:

```
int async 1
 ppp authentication chap
 ppp use-tacacs
```

The following example shows TACACS enabled for ARA authentication:

```
line 3
 arap use-tacacs
```

The following example shows a complete TACACS configuration for the Cisco AS5200 using Cisco IOS Release 11.1:

```
version 11.1
service udp-small-servers
service tcp-small-servers
!
hostname isdn-14
!
enable password ww
!
username cisco password lab
isdn switch-type primary-5ess
!
controller T1 1
 framing esf
 clock source line primary
 linecode b8zs
 pri-group timeslots 1-24
!
interface Loopback20
 no ip address
!
interface Ethernet0
 ip address 172.16.25.15 255.255.255.224
!
interface Serial0
 no ip address
 shutdown
!
interface Serial1
 no ip address
 shutdown
 no cdp enable
!
interface Serial1:23
 ip address 150.150.150.2 255.255.255.0
 no ip mroute-cache
 encapsulation ppp
 isdn incoming-voice modem
 no peer default ip address pool
 dialer idle-timeout 1
 dialer map ip 150.150.150.1 name isdn-5 broadcast 1234
 dialer-group 1
 no fair-queue
 ppp multilink
 ppp authentication pap
 ppp pap sent-username isdn-14 password 7 05080F1C2243
!
interface Group-Async1
 ip unnumbered Ethernet0
 encapsulation ppp
 async mode interactive
 peer default ip address pool default
```

```
 no cdp enable
 ppp authentication chap
 ppp use-tacacs
 group-range 1 24
!
ip local pool default 171.68.187.1 171.68.187.8
no ip classless
ip route 0.0.0.0 0.0.0.0 172.16.25.1
ip route 192.100.0.12 255.255.255.255 Serial1:23
tacacs-server host 171.68.186.35
tacacs-server last-resort succeed
tacacs-server extended
tacacs-server authenticate slip access-lists
tacacs-server notify connections always
tacacs-server notify logout always
tacacs-server notify slip always
!
dialer-list 1 protocol ip permit
!
line con 0
line 1 24
 session-timeout 30  output
 exec-timeout 1 0
 no activation-character
 autoselect during-login
 autoselect ppp
 no vacant-message
 modem InOut
 modem autoconfigure type microcom_hdms
 transport input all
 speed 115200
line aux 0
line vty 0 4
 password ww
 login
end
```

## CHAPTER 12

TACACS, Extended TACACS, and TACACS+ Commands

This chapter describes the commands used to configure TACACS, extended TACACS, and TACACS+.

TACACS Command Comparison

There are currently three versions of the TACACS security protocol, each a separate entity. The Cisco IOS software supports the following versions of TACACS:

- TACACS+—Provides detailed accounting information and flexible administrative control over authentication and authorization processes. TACACS+ is facilitated through AAA and can be enabled only through AAA commands.

- Extended TACACS—Provides information about protocol translator and router use. This information is used in UNIX auditing trails and accounting files.

- TACACS—Provides password checking and authentication, and notification of user actions for security and accounting purposes.

Although TACACS+ is enabled through AAA and uses commands specific to AAA, there are some commands that are common to TACACS, extended TACACS, and TACACS+. Table 11-1Table 11-1 in Chapter 11, "Configuring TACACS and Extended TACACS," identifies Cisco IOS commands available to the different versions of TACACS.

NOTE	Refer to Chapter 3, "Authentication Commands," Chapter 5, "Authorization Commands," and Chapter 7, "Accounting Commands," for information about commands specific to AAA.

For information on how to configure TACACS or extended TACACS, refer to Chapter 11, "Configuring TACACS and Extended TACACS." For configuration examples using the commands in this chapter, refer to the "TACACS Configuration Examples" section located at the end of Chapter 11, "Configuring TACACS and Extended TACACS."

For information on how to configure TACACS+, refer to Chapter 10, "Configuring TACACS+." For configuration examples using the commands in this chapter, refer to the "TACACS+ Configuration Examples" section located at the end of Chapter 10, "Configuring TACACS+."

arap use-tacacs

To enable TACACS for ARA authentication, use the **arap use-tacacs** line configuration command. Use the **no** form of this command to disable TACACS for ARA authentication.

> **arap use-tacacs [single-line]**
> **no arap use-tacacs**

Syntax	Description
single-line	(Optional) Accepts the username and password in the username field. If you are using an older version of TACACS (before extended TACACS), you must use this keyword.

Default

Disabled

Command Mode

Line configuration

Usage Guidelines

Use this command only when you have set up an extended TACACS server. This command requires the new extended TACACS server.

NOTE   This command cannot be used with TACACS+. Use the **arap authentication** command instead.

The command specifies that if a username and password are specified in the username, separated by an asterisk (*), then a standard TACACS login query is performed, using that username and password. If the username does not contain an asterisk, then normal ARA authentication is performed, using TACACS.

This feature is useful when integrating TACACS with other authentication systems that require a clear text version of the user's password. Such systems include one-time passwords, token card systems, and others.

CAUTION Normal ARA authentications prevent the clear-text password from being transmitted over the link. When you use the single-line keyword, passwords cross the link in the clear, exposing them to anyone looking for such information.

Because of the two-way nature of the ARA authentication, the ARA application requires that a password value be entered in the Password field in the ARA dialog box. This secondary password must be *arap*. First, enter the username and password in the form *username*password* in the Name field of the dialog box, then enter **arap** in the Password field.

Part
II

Command Reference

Example

The following example enables TACACS for ARA authentication:

```
line 3
 arap use-tacacs
```

Related Commands

You can search online at www.cisco.com to find documentation of related commands.

arap enable
arap noguest
autoselect
tacacs-server extended
tacacs-server host

enable last-resort

To specify what happens if the TACACS and extended TACACS servers used by the enable command do not respond, use the **enable last-resort** global configuration command. Use the **no** form of this command to restore the default.

> **enable last-resort** {**password** | **succeed**}
> **no enable last-resort** {**password** | **succeed**}

Syntax	Description
password	Allows you to enter enable mode by entering the privileged command level password. A password must contain from 1 to 25 uppercase and lowercase alphanumeric characters.
succeed	Allows you to enter enable mode without further question.

Default

Access to enable mode is denied.

Command Mode

Global configuration

Usage Guidelines

This secondary authentication is used only if the first attempt fails.

NOTE   This command is not used with TACACS+, which uses the **aaa authentication** suite of commands instead.

Example

In the following example, if the TACACS servers do not respond to the enable command, the user can enable by entering the privileged level password:

```
enable last-resort password
```

Related Commands

You can search online at www.cisco.com to find documentation of related commands.

enable

enable use-tacacs

To enable the use of TACACS to determine whether a user can access the privileged command level, use the **enable use-tacacs** global configuration command. Use the **no** form of this command to disable TACACS verification.

> **enable use-tacacs**
> **no enable use-tacacs**

CAUTION   If you use the **enable use-tacacs** command, you must also use the **tacacs-server authenticate enable** command or you will be locked out of the privileged command level.

Syntax Description

This command has no arguments or keywords.

Default

Disabled

Command Mode

Global configuration

Usage Guidelines

When you add this command to the configuration file, the EXEC enable command prompts for a new username and password pair. This pair is then passed to the TACACS server for authentication. If you are using extended TACACS, it also passes any existing UNIX user identification code to the server.

NOTE   This command initializes TACACS. Use the **tacacs server-extended** command to initialize extended TACACS or use the **aaa new-model** command to initialize AAA and TACACS+.

Example

The following example sets TACACS verification on the privileged EXEC-level login sequence:

```
enable use-tacacs
tacacs-server authenticate enable
```

Related Commands

You can search online at www.cisco.com to find documentation of related commands.

tacacs-server authenticate enable

ip tacacs source-interface

To use the IP address of a specified interface for all outgoing TACACS packets, use the **ip tacacs source-interface** global configuration command. Use the **no** form of this command to disable use of the specified interface IP address.

ip tacacs source-interface *subinterface-name*
no ip tacacs source-interface

Syntax	Description
subinterface-name	Name of the interface that TACACS uses for all of its outgoing packets.

Default

This command has no factory-assigned default.

Command Mode

Global configuration

Usage Guidelines

Use this command to set a subinterface's IP address for all outgoing TACACS packets. This address is used as long as the interface is in the *up* state. In this way, the TACACS server can use one IP address entry associated with the network access client instead of maintaining a list of all IP addresses.

This command is especially useful in cases where the router has many interfaces and you want to ensure that all TACACS packets from a particular router have the same IP address.

The specified interface must have an IP address associated with it. If the specified subinterface does not have an IP address or is in a *down* state, TACACS reverts to the default. To avoid this, add an IP address to the subinterface or bring the interface to the *up* state.

Example

The following example makes TACACS use the IP address of subinterface s2 for all outgoing TACACS (TACACS, extended TACACS, or TACACS+) packets:

```
ip tacacs source-interface s2
```

Related Commands

You can search online at www.cisco.com to find documentation of related commands.

ip radius source-interface
ip telnet source-interface
ip tftp source-interface

tacacs-server attempts

To control the number of login attempts that can be made on a line set up for TACACS verification, use the **tacacs-server attempts** global configuration command. Use the **no** form of this command to restore the default.

tacacs-server attempts *count*
no tacacs-server attempts

Syntax   Description

count   Integer that sets the number of attempts. The default is three attempts.

Default

Three attempts

Command Mode

Global configuration

Example

The following example allows only one login attempt:

```
tacacs-server attempts 1
```

tacacs-server authenticate

To configure the Cisco IOS software to indicate whether users can perform an attempted action under TACACS and extended TACACS, use the **tacacs-server authenticate** global configuration command. Use the **no** form of this command to remove authentication.

tacacs-server authenticate {**connection** [**always**] **enable** | **slip** [**always**] [**access-lists**]} **no tacacs-server authenticate**

Syntax   Description

connection   Configures a required response when a user makes a TCP connection.

always   (Optional) Performs authentication even when a user is not logged in.

enable   Configures a required response when a user enters the **enable** command.

slip   Configures a required response when a user starts a SLIP or PPP session.

access-lists   (Optional) Requests and installs access lists. This option only applies to the **slip** keyword.

Default
Disabled

Command Mode
Global configuration

Usage Guidelines
The **tacacs-server authenticate** [**connection** | **enable**] command first appeared in Cisco IOS Release 10.0. The **tacacs-server authenticate** {**connection** [**always**] **enable** | **slip** [**always**] [**access-lists**]} command first appeared in Cisco IOS Release 10.3.

Enter one of the keywords to specify the action (when a user enters enable mode, for example).

Before you use the **tacacs-server authenticate** command, you must enable the **tacacs-server extended** command.

NOTE	This command is not used in TACACS+. It has been replaced by the **aaa authorization** command.

Example
The following example configures TACACS logins that authenticate users to use Telnet or rlogin:

```
tacacs-server authenticate connect
```

Related Commands
You can search online at www.cisco.com to find documentation of related commands.

enable secret
enable use-tacacs

tacacs-server directed-request

To send only a username to a specified server when a direct request is issued, use the **tacacs-server directed-request** global configuration command. Use the **no** form of this command to send the entire string to the TACACS server.

> **tacacs-server directed-request**
> **no tacacs-server directed-request**

Syntax Description

This command has no arguments or keywords.

Default

Enabled

Command Mode

Global configuration

Usage Guidelines

This command first appeared in Cisco IOS Release 11.1.

This command sends only the portion of the username before the @ symbol to the host specified after the @ symbol. In other words, with the directed-request feature enabled, you can direct a request to any of the configured servers, and only the username is sent to the specified server.

Disabling **tacacs-server directed-request** causes the whole string, both before and after the @ symbol, to be sent to the default TACACS server. When the directed-request feature is disabled, the router queries the list of servers, starting with the first one in the list, sending the whole string, and accepting the first response that it gets from the server. The **tacacs-server directed-request** command is useful for sites that have developed their own TACACS server software that parses the whole string and makes decisions based on it.

With **tacacs-server directed-request** enabled, only configured TACACS servers can be specified by the user after the @ symbol. If the host name specified by the user does not match the IP address of a TACACS server configured by the administrator, the user input is rejected.

Use **no tacacs-server directed-request** to disable the ability of the user to choose between configured TACACS servers and to cause the entire string to be passed to the default server.

Example

The following example enables **tacacs-server directed-request** so that the entire user input is passed to the default TACACS server:

```
no tacacs-server directed-request
```

tacacs-server extended

To enable an extended TACACS mode, use the **tacacs-server extended** global configuration command. Use the **no** form of this command to disable the mode.

> **tacacs-server extended**
> **no tacacs-server extended**

Syntax Description

This command has no arguments or keywords.

Default

Disabled

Command Mode

Global configuration

Usage Guidelines

This command first appeared in Cisco IOS Release 10.0.

This command initializes extended TACACS.

Example

The following example enables extended TACACS mode:

```
tacacs-server extended
```

Related Commands

You can search online at www.cisco.com to find documentation of related commands.

aaa new-model

tacacs-server host

To specify a TACACS host, use the **tacacs-server host** global configuration command. Use the **no** form of this command to delete the specified name or address.

> **tacacs-server host** *hostname* [**single-connection**] [**port** *integer*] [**timeout** *integer*]
> [**key** *string*]
> **no tacacs-server host** *hostname*

Syntax	Description
hostname	Name or IP address of the host.
single-connection	(Optional) Specifies that the router maintain a single open connection for confirmation from a AAA/TACACS+ server (CiscoSecure Release 1.0.1 or later). This command contains no autodetect and fails if the specified host is not running a CiscoSecure daemon.
port	(Optional) Specifies a server port number. This option overrides the default, which is port 49.
integer	(Optional) Port number of the server. Valid port numbers range from 1 to 65,535.
timeout	(Optional) Specifies a timeout value. This overrides the global timeout value set with the **tacacs-server timeout** command for this server only.
integer	(Optional) Integer value, in seconds, of the timeout interval.
key	(Optional) Specifies an authentication and encryption key. This must match the key used by the TACACS+ daemon. Specifying this key overrides the key set by the global command **tacacs-server key** for this server only.
string	(Optional) Character string specifying authentication and encryption key.

Default

No TACACS host is specified.

Command Mode

Global configuration

Usage Guidelines

This command first appeared in Cisco IOS Release 10.0.

You can use multiple **tacacs-server host** commands to specify additional hosts. The Cisco IOS software searches for hosts in the order in which you specify them. Use the **single-connection**, **port**, **timeout**, and **key** options only when running an AAA/TACACS+ server.

Because some of the parameters of the **tacacs-server host** command override global settings made by the **tacacs-server timeout** and **tacacs-server key** commands, you can use this command to enhance security on your network by uniquely configuring individual routers.

Examples

The following example specifies a TACACS host named *Sea_Change*:

```
tacacs-server host Sea_Change
```

The following example specifies that, for AAA confirmation, the router consult the CiscoSecure TACACS+ host named *Sea_Cure* on port number 51. The timeout value for requests on this connection is three seconds; the encryption key is *a_secret*.

```
tacacs-server host Sea_Cure single-connection port 51 timeout 3 key a_secret
```

Related Commands

You can search online at www.cisco.com to find documentation of related commands.

login tacacs
ppp
slip
tacacs-server key
tacacs-server timeout

tacacs-server key

To set the authentication encryption key used for all TACACS+ communications between the access server and the TACACS+ daemon, use the **tacacs-server key** global configuration command. Use the **no** form of this command to disable the key.

> **tacacs-server key** *key*
> **no tacacs-server key** [*key*]

Syntax   Description

key   Key used to set authentication and encryption. This key must match the key used on the TACACS+ daemon.

Command Mode
Global configuration

Usage Guidelines

This command first appeared in Cisco IOS Release 11.1.

After enabling AAA with the **aaa new-model** command, you must set the authentication and encryption key using the **tacacs-server key** command.

The key entered must match the key used on the TACACS+ daemon. All leading spaces are ignored; spaces within and at the end of the key are not. If you use spaces in your key, do not enclose the key in quotation marks unless the quotation marks themselves are part of the key.

Example

The following example sets the authentication and encryption key to *dare to go*:

```
tacacs-server key dare to go
```

Related Commands

You can search online at www.cisco.com to find documentation of related commands.

aaa new-model
tacacs-server host

tacacs-server last-resort

To cause the network access server to request the privileged password as verification, or to allow successful login without further input from the user, use the **tacacs-server last-resort** global configuration command. Use the **no** form of this command to deny requests when the server does not respond.

> **tacacs-server last-resort** {**password** | **succeed**}
> **no tacacs-server last-resort** {**password** | **succeed**}

Syntax	Description
password	Allows the user to access the EXEC command mode by entering the password set by the **enable** command.
succeed	Allows the user to access the EXEC command mode without further question.

Default

If, when running the TACACS server, the TACACS server does not respond, the default action is to deny the request.

Command Mode

Global configuration

Usage Guidelines

This command first appeared in Cisco IOS Release 10.0.

Use the **tacacs-server last-resort** command to be sure that login can occur; for example, when a systems administrator needs to log in to troubleshoot TACACS servers that might be down.

NOTE   This command is not used in TACACS+.

Example

The following example forces successful login:

```
tacacs-server last-resort succeed
```

Related Commands

You can search online at www.cisco.com to find documentation of related commands.

enable password
login (EXEC)

tacacs-server login-timeout

The **timeout login response** command replaces this command. Refer to the description of the **timeout login response** command for more information.

tacacs-server notify

To cause a message to be transmitted to the TACACS server, with retransmission being performed by a background process for up to 5 minutes, use the **tacacs-server notify** global configuration command. Use the **no** form of this command to disable notification.

> **tacacs-server notify** {**connection** [**always**] | **enable** | **logout** [**always**] | **slip** [**always**]}
> **no tacacs-server notify**

Syntax	Description
connection	Specifies that a message be transmitted when a user makes a TCP connection.
always	(Optional) Sends a message even when a user is not logged in. This option applies only to SLIP or PPP sessions and can be used with the **logout** or **slip** keywords.
enable	Specifies that a message be transmitted when a user enters the **enable** command.
logout	Specifies that a message be transmitted when a user logs out.
slip	Specifies that a message be transmitted when a user starts a SLIP or PPP session.

Default

No message is transmitted to the TACACS server.

Command Mode

Global configuration

Usage Guidelines

This command first appeared in Cisco IOS Release 10.0. The **always** and **slip** commands first appeared in Cisco IOS Release 11.0.

The terminal user receives an immediate response, allowing access to the feature specified. Enter one of the keywords to specify notification of the TACACS server upon receipt of the corresponding action (when a user logs out, for example).

NOTE   This command is not used in TACACS+. It has been replaced by the **aaa accounting** suite of commands.

Example

The following example sets up notification of the TACACS server when a user logs out:

```
tacacs-server notify logout
```

tacacs-server optional-passwords

To specify that the first TACACS request to a TACACS server be made *without* password verification, use the **tacacs-server optional-passwords** global configuration command. Use the **no** form of this command to restore the default.

> **tacacs-server optional-passwords**
> **no tacacs-server optional-passwords**

Syntax Description

This command has no arguments or keywords.

Default

Disabled

Command Mode

Global configuration

Usage Guidelines

This command first appeared in Cisco IOS Release 10.0.

When the user enters the login name, the login request is transmitted with the name and a zero-length password. If accepted, the login procedure completes. If the TACACS server refuses this request, the server software prompts for a password and tries again when the user supplies a password. The TACACS server must support authentication for users without passwords to make use of this feature. This feature supports all TACACS requests, such as login, SLIP, and enable.

NOTE   This command is not used by TACACS+.

Example

The following example configures the first login to not require TACACS verification:

```
tacacs-server optional-passwords
```

tacacs-server retransmit

To specify the number of times the Cisco IOS software searches the list of TACACS server hosts before giving up, use the **tacacs-server retransmit** global configuration command. Use the **no** form of this command to disable retransmission.

> **tacacs-server retransmit** *retries*
> **no tacacs-server retransmit**

Syntax	Description
retries	Integer that specifies the retransmit count.

Default

Two retries

Command Mode

Global configuration

Usage Guidelines

This command first appeared in Cisco IOS Release 10.0.

The Cisco IOS software will try all servers, allowing each one to time out before increasing the retransmit count.

Example

The following example specifies a retransmit counter value of five times:

```
tacacs-server retransmit 5
```

tacacs-server timeout

To set the interval that the server waits for a server host to reply, use the **tacacs-server timeout** global configuration command. Use the **no** form of this command to restore the default.

> **tacacs-server timeout** *seconds*
> **no tacacs-server timeout**

Syntax	Description
seconds	Integer that specifies the timeout interval in seconds (between 1 and 300). The default is 5 seconds.

Default

5 seconds

Command Mode

Global configuration

Usage Guidelines

This command first appeared in Cisco IOS Release 10.0.

Example

The following example changes the interval timer to 10 seconds:

```
tacacs-server timeout 10
```

Related Commands

You can search online at www.cisco.com to find documentation of related commands.

tacacs-server host

## CHAPTER 13

Configuring Kerberos

This chapter describes the Kerberos security system and includes the following topics and tasks:

- Kerberos Overview
- Kerberos Client Support Operation
- Kerberos Configuration Task List

For a complete description of the Kerberos commands used in this chapter, refer to Chapter 14, "Kerberos Commands." To locate documentation of other commands that appear in this chapter, you can search online at www.cisco.com.

Kerberos Overview

Kerberos is a secret-key network authentication protocol, developed at Massachusetts Institute of Technology (MIT), that uses the Data Encryption Standard (DES) cryptographic algorithm for encryption and authentication. Kerberos was designed to authenticate requests for network resources. Kerberos, like other secret-key systems, is based on the concept of a trusted third party that performs secure verification of users and services. In the Kerberos protocol, this trusted third party is called the *key distribution center* (KDC).

The primary use of Kerberos is to verify that users and the network services they use are really who and what they claim to be. To accomplish this, a trusted Kerberos server issues tickets to users. These tickets, which have a limited life span, are stored in a user's credential cache and can be used in place of the standard username-and-password authentication mechanism.

The Kerberos credential scheme embodies a concept called *single logon*. This process requires authenticating a user once, and then allows secure authentication (without encrypting another password) wherever that user's credential is accepted.

Starting with Cisco IOS Release 11.2, Cisco IOS software includes Kerberos 5 support, which allows organizations already deploying Kerberos 5 to use the same Kerberos authentication database on their routers that they are already using on their other network hosts (such as UNIX servers and PCs).

The following network services are supported by the Kerberos authentication capabilities in Cisco IOS software:

- Telnet
- rlogin
- rsh
- rcp

NOTE	Cisco's implementation of Kerberos client support is based on code developed by CyberSafe that was derived from the MIT code. As a result, the Cisco Kerberos implementation has successfully undergone full compatibility testing with the CyberSafe Challenger commercial Kerberos server and MIT's server code, which is freely distributed.

Table 13-1 lists common Kerberos-related terms and their definitions.

Table 13-1 *Kerberos Terminology*

Term	Definition
Authentication	A process by which a user or service identifies itself to another service. For example, a client can authenticate to a router or a router can authenticate to another router.
Authorization	A means by which the router determines what privileges you have in a network or on the router and what actions you can perform.
Credential	A general term that refers to authentication tickets, such as TGTs and service credentials. Kerberos credentials verify the identity of a user or service. If a network service decides to trust the Kerberos server that issued a ticket, it can be used in place of retyping a username and password. Credentials have a default life span of eight hours.
Instance	An authorization level label for Kerberos principals. Most Kerberos principals are of the form *user@REALM* (for example, *smith@DOMAIN*.COM). A Kerberos principal with a Kerberos instance has the form *user/instance@REALM* (for example, *smith/ admin@DOMAIN*.COM). The Kerberos instance can be used to specify the authorization level for the user if authentication is successful. It is up to the server of each network service to implement and enforce the authorization mappings of Kerberos instances. Note that the Kerberos realm name must be in uppercase characters.
Kerberized	Applications and services that have been modified to support the Kerberos credential infrastructure.
Kerberos realm	A domain consisting of users, hosts, and network services that are registered to a Kerberos server. The Kerberos server is trusted to verify the identity of a user or network service to another user or network service. Kerberos realms must always be in uppercase characters.
Kerberos server	A daemon running on a network host. Users and network services register their identity with the Kerberos server. Network services query the Kerberos server to authenticate to other network services.
Key distribution center (KDC)	A Kerberos server and database program running on a network host.

Table 13-1   *Kerberos Terminology (Continued)*

Term	Definition
Principal	Also known as a *Kerberos identity*, this is who you are or what a service is according to the Kerberos server.
Service credential	A credential for a network service. When issued from the KDC, this credential is encrypted with the password shared by the network service and the KDC, and with the user's TGT.
SRVTAB	A password that a network service shares with the KDC. The network service authenticates an encrypted service credential by using the SRVTAB (also known as a KEYTAB) to decrypt it.
Ticket granting ticket (TGT)	A credential that the KDC issues to authenticated users. When users receive a TGT, they can authenticate to network services within the Kerberos realm represented by the KDC.

Kerberos Client Support Operation

This section describes how the Kerberos security system works with a Cisco router functioning as the security server. Although (for convenience or technical reasons) you can customize Kerberos in a number of ways, remote users attempting to access network services must pass through the following three layers of security before they can access network services:

● Authenticating to the Boundary Router

● Obtaining a TGT from a KDC

● Authenticating to Network Services

Authenticating to the Boundary Router

This section describes the first layer of security that remote users must pass through when they attempt to access a network. The first step in the Kerberos authentication process is for users to authenticate themselves to the boundary router. The following process describes how users authenticate to a boundary router:

1   The remote user opens a PPP connection to the corporate site router.

2   The router prompts the user for a username and password.

3   The router requests a TGT from the KDC for this particular user.

4   The KDC sends an encrypted TGT to the router that includes (among other things) the user's identity.

5   The router attempts to decrypt the TGT using the password the user entered. If the decryption is successful, the remote user is authenticated to the router.

A remote user who successfully initiates a PPP session and authenticates to the boundary router is inside the firewall but still must authenticate to the KDC directly before being allowed to access network services. This is because the TGT issued by the KDC is stored on the router and is not useful for additional authentication unless the user physically logs on to the router.

Obtaining a TGT from a KDC

This section describes how remote users who are authenticated to the boundary router authenticate themselves to a KDC.

When a remote user authenticates to a boundary router, that user technically becomes part of the network; that is, the network is extended to include the remote user and the user's machine or network. To gain access to network services, however, the remote user must obtain a TGT from the KDC. The following process describes how remote users authenticate to the KDC:

1   The remote user, at a workstation on a remote site, launches the KINIT program (part of the client software provided with the Kerberos protocol).

2   The KINIT program finds the user's identity and requests a TGT from the KDC.

3   The KDC creates a TGT, which contains the identity of the user, the identity of the KDC, and the TGT's expiration time.

4   Using the user's password as a key, the KDC encrypts the TGT and sends the TGT to the workstation.

5   When the KINIT program receives the encrypted TGT, it prompts the user for a password (this is the password that is defined for the user in the KDC).

6   If the KINIT program can decrypt the TGT with the password the user enters, the user is authenticated to the KDC, and the KINIT program stores the TGT in the user's credential cache.

At this point, the user has a TGT and can communicate securely with the KDC. In turn, the TGT allows the user to authenticate to other network services.

Authenticating to Network Services

The following process describes how a remote user with a TGT authenticates to network services within a given Kerberos realm. Assume that the user is on a remote workstation (Host A) and wants to log in to Host B.

1   The user on Host A initiates a Kerberized application (such as Telnet) to Host B.

2   The Kerberized application builds a service credential request and sends it to the KDC. The service credential request includes (among other things) the user's identity and the identity of the desired network service. The TGT is used to encrypt the service credential request.

3   The KDC tries to decrypt the service credential request with the TGT it issued to the user on Host A. If the KDC can decrypt the packet, it is assured that the authenticated user on Host A sent the request.

4   The KDC notes the network service identity in the service credential request.

5   The KDC builds a service credential for the appropriate network service on Host B on behalf of the user on Host A. The service credential contains the client's identity and the desired network service's identity.

6   The KDC then encrypts the service credential twice. It first encrypts the credential with the SRVTAB that it shares with the network service identified in the credential. It then encrypts the resulting packet with the TGT of the user (who, in this case, is on Host A).

7   The KDC sends the twice-encrypted credential to Host A.

8   Host A attempts to decrypt the service credential with the user's TGT. If Host A can decrypt the service credential, it is assured the credential came from the real KDC.

9   Host A sends the service credential to the desired network service. Note that the credential is still encrypted with the SRVTAB shared by the KDC and the network service.

10   The network service attempts to decrypt the service credential using its SRVTAB.

11   If the network service can decrypt the credential, it is assured the credential was in fact issued from the KDC. Note that the network service trusts anything it can decrypt from the KDC, even if it receives it indirectly from a user. This is because the user first authenticated with the KDC.

At this point, the user is authenticated to the network service on Host B. This process is repeated each time a user wants to access a network service in the Kerberos realm.

Kerberos Configuration Task List

In order for hosts and the KDC in your Kerberos realm to communicate and mutually authenticate, you must identify them to each other. To do this, you add entries for the hosts to the Kerberos database on the KDC and add SRVTAB files generated by the KDC to all hosts in the Kerberos realm. You also make entries for users in the KDC database.

This section describes how to set up a Kerberos-authenticated client/server system and contains the following topics:

● Configuring the KDC Using Kerberos Commands

● Configuring the Router to Use the Kerberos Protocol

This section assumes that you have installed the Kerberos administrative programs on a UNIX host, known as the KDC, initialized the database, and selected a Kerberos realm name and password. For instructions about completing these tasks, refer to documentation that came with your Kerberos software.

NOTE   Write down the host name or IP address of the KDC, the port number you want the KDC to monitor for queries, and the name of the Kerberos realm it will serve. You need this information to configure the router.

Configuring the KDC Using Kerberos Commands

After you set up a host to function as the KDC in your Kerberos realm, you must make entries to the KDC database for all principals in the realm. Principals can be network services on Cisco routers and hosts or they can be users.

To use Kerberos commands to add services to the KDC database (and to modify existing database information), complete the tasks in the following sections:

● Adding Users to the KDC Database

● Creating SRVTABs on the KDC

● Extracting SRVTABs

NOTE   All Kerberos command examples are based on Kerberos 5 Beta 5 of the original MIT implementation. Later versions use a slightly different interface.

Adding Users to the KDC Database

To add users to the KDC and create privileged instances of those users, use the **su** command to become root on the host running the KDC and use the kdb5_edit program to use the following commands:

Step	Command	Purpose
1	**ank** *username@REALM*	Uses the **ank** (add new key) command to add a user to the KDC. This command prompts for a password, which the user must enter to authenticate to the router.
2	**ank** *username/instance@REALM*	Uses the **ank** command to add a privileged instance of a user.

For example, to add user *loki* of Kerberos realm CISCO.COM, enter the following Kerberos command:

```
ank loki@CISCO.COM
```

NOTE	The Kerberos realm name must be in uppercase characters.

You might want to create privileged instances to allow network administrators to connect to the router at the enable level, for example, so that they need not enter a clear text password (and compromise security) to enter enable mode.

To add an instance of *loki* with additional privileges (in this case, *enable*, although it could be anything) enter the following Kerberos command:

```
ank loki/enable@CISCO.COM
```

In each of these examples, you are prompted to enter a password, which you must give to user *loki* to use at login.

The "Enabling Kerberos Instance Mapping" section describes how to map Kerberos instances to various Cisco IOS privilege levels.

Creating SRVTABs on the KDC

All routers that you want to authenticate to use the Kerberos protocol must have a SRVTAB. This section and the "Extracting SRVTABs" section describe how to create and extract SRVTABs for a router called *router1*. The section "Copying SRVTAB Files" describes how to copy SRVTAB files to the router.

To make SRVTAB entries on the KDC, use the following command:

Command	Purpose
ark *SERVICE/HOSTNAME@REALM*	Uses the **ark** (add random key) command to add a network service supported by a host or router to the KDC.

For example, to add a Kerberized authentication service for a Cisco router called *router1* to the Kerberos realm CISCO.COM, enter the following Kerberos command:

```
ark host/router1.cisco.com@CISCO.COM
```

Make entries for all network services on all Kerberized hosts that use this KDC for authentication.

Extracting SRVTABs

SRVTABs contain (among other things) the passwords or randomly generated keys for the service principals you entered into the KDC database. Service principal keys must be shared with the host running that service. To do this, you must save the SRVTAB entries to a file, then copy the file to the router and all hosts in the Kerberos realm. Saving SRVTAB entries to a file is called *extracting* SRVTABs. To extract SRVTABs, use the following command:

Command	Purpose
xst *router-name host*	Uses the kdb5_edit command **xst** to write a SRVTAB entry to a file.

For example, to write the host/router1.cisco.com@CISCO.COM SRVTAB to a file, enter the following Kerberos command:

```
xst router1.cisco.com@CISCO.COM host
```

Use the **quit** command to exit the kdb5_edit program.

Configuring the Router to Use the Kerberos Protocol

To configure a Cisco router to function as a network security server and authenticate users using the Kerberos protocol, complete the tasks in the following sections:

- Defining a Kerberos Realm
- Copying SRVTAB Files
- Specifying Kerberos Authentication
- Enabling Credentials Forwarding

- Telneting to the Router

- Establishing an Encrypted Kerberized Telnet Session

- Enabling Mandatory Kerberos Authentication

- Enabling Kerberos Instance Mapping

- Monitoring and Maintaining Kerberos

Defining a Kerberos Realm

For a router to authenticate a user defined in the Kerberos database, it must know the host name or IP address of the host running the KDC, the name of the Kerberos realm and, optionally, be able to map the host name or Domain Name System (DNS) domain to the Kerberos realm.

To configure the router to authenticate to a specified KDC in a specified Kerberos realm, use the following commands in global configuration mode. Note that DNS domain names must begin with a leading dot (.):

Step	Command	Purpose
1	**kerberos local-realm** *kerberos-realm*	Defines the default realm for the router.
2	**kerberos server** *kerberos-realm* {*hostname* | *ip-address*} [*port-number*]	Specifies to the router which KDC to use in a given Kerberos realm and, optionally, the port number the KDC is monitoring. (The default is 88.)
3	**kerberos realm** {*dns-domain* | *host*} *kerberos-realm*	Optionally, maps a host name or DNS domain to a Kerberos realm.

NOTE	Because the machine running the KDC and all Kerberized hosts must interact within a 5-minute window or authentication fails, all Kerberized machines, and especially the KDC, should be running the Network Time Protocol (NTP).

The **kerberos local-realm**, **kerberos realm**, and **kerberos server** commands are equivalent to the UNIX *krb.conf* file. Table 13-2 identifies mappings from the Cisco IOS configuration commands to a Kerberos 5 configuration file (krb5.conf).

Table 13-2 *Kerberos 5 Configuration File and Commands*

krb5.conf file	Cisco IOS Configuration Command
[libdefaults]	(in config mode)
default_realm = *DOMAIN.COM*	**kerberos local-realm** *DOMAIN.COM*

Continues

Table 13-2 *Kerberos 5 Configuration File and Commands (Continued)*

krb5.conf file	Cisco IOS Configuration Command
[domain_realm]	(in config mode)
.domain.com = *DOMAIN.COM*	**kerberos realm** *.domain.com DOMAIN.COM*
domain.com = *DOMAIN.COM*	**kerberos realm** *domain.com DOMAIN.COM*
[realms]	(in config mode)
kdc = *DOMAIN.PIL.COM:750*	**kerberos server** *DOMAIN.COM 172.65.44.2*
admin_server = *DOMAIN.PIL.COM*	(*172.65.44.2* is the example IP address for
default_domain = *DOMAIN.COM*	*DOMAIN.PIL.COM*)

For an example of defining a Kerberos realm, see the "Defining a Kerberos Realm Examples" section at the end of this chapter.

Copying SRVTAB Files

To make it possible for remote users to authenticate to the router using Kerberos credentials, the router must share a secret key with the KDC. To do this, you must give the router a copy of the SRVTAB you extracted on the KDC.

The most secure method to copy SRVTAB files to the hosts in your Kerberos realm is to copy them onto physical media and go to each host in turn and manually copy the files onto the system. To copy SRVTAB files to the router, which does not have a physical media drive, you must transfer them via the network using the Trivial File Transfer Protocol (TFTP).

To copy SRVTAB files to the router from the KDC remotely, use the following command in global configuration mode:

Command	Purpose
kerberos srvtab remote {*hostname*	*ip-address*} {*file name*}	Retrieves a SRVTAB file from the KDC.

When you copy the SRVTAB file from the router to the KDC, the **kerberos srvtab remote** command parses the information in this file and stores it in the router's running configuration in the **kerberos srvtab entry** format. To ensure that the SRVTAB is available (does not need to be acquired from the KDC) when you reboot the router, use the **write memory** configuration command to write your running configuration (which contains the parsed SRVTAB file) to NVRAM.

For an example of copying SRVTAB files, see the "Copying SRVTAB Files Example" section at the end of this chapter.

Specifying Kerberos Authentication

You have now configured Kerberos on your router. This makes it possible for the router to authenticate using Kerberos. The next step is to tell it to do so. Because Kerberos authentication is facilitated through AAA, you need to enter the **aaa authentication** command, specifying Kerberos as the authentication method. For more information, refer to Chapter 2, "Configuring Authentication."

Enabling Credentials Forwarding

With Kerberos configured thus far, a user authenticated to a Kerberized router has a TGT and can use it to authenticate to a host on the network. However, if the user tries to list credentials after authenticating to a host, the output will show no Kerberos credentials present.

You can optionally configure the router to forward users' TGTs with them as they authenticate from the router to Kerberized remote hosts on the network when using Kerberized Telnet, rcp, rsh, and rlogin (with the appropriate flags).

To force all clients to forward users' credentials as they connect to other hosts in the Kerberos realm, use the following command in global configuration mode:

Command	Purpose
kerberos credentials forward	Forces all clients to forward user credentials upon successful Kerberos authentication.

With credentials forwarding enabled, users' TGTs are automatically forwarded to the next host they authenticate to. In this way, users can connect to multiple hosts in the Kerberos realm without running the KINIT program each time to get a new TGT.

Telneting to the Router

To use Kerberos to authenticate users opening a Telnet session to the router from within the network, use the following command in global configuration mode:

Command	Purpose
aaa authentication login {**default**	*list-name*} **krb5_telnet**	Sets login authentication to use the Kerberos 5 Telnet authentication protocol when using Telnet to connect to the router.

Although Telnet sessions to the router are authenticated, users must still enter a clear text password if they want to enter enable mode. The **kerberos instance map** command allows them to authenticate to the router at a predefined privilege level.

Establishing an Encrypted Kerberized Telnet Session

Another way for users to open a secure Telnet session is to use Encrypted Kerberized Telnet. With Encrypted Kerberized Telnet, users are authenticated by their Kerberos credentials before a Telnet session is established. The Telnet session is encrypted using 56-bit DES encryption with 64-bit Cipher Feedback (CFB). Because data sent or received is encrypted, not clear text, the integrity of the dialed router or access server can be more easily controlled.

NOTE	This feature is available only if you have the 56-bit encryption image. The 56-bit DES encryption is subject to U.S. government export control regulations.

To establish an encrypted Kerberized Telnet session from a router to a remote host, use either of the following commands in EXEC command mode:

Command	Purpose
connect *host* [*port*] **/encrypt kerberos**	Establishes an encrypted Telnet session.
or	
telnet *host* [*port*] **/encrypt kerberos**	

When a user opens a Telnet session from a Cisco router to a remote host, the router and remote host negotiate to authenticate the user using Kerberos credentials. If this authentication is successful, the router and remote host then negotiate whether or not to use encryption. If this negotiation is successful, both inbound and outbound traffic is encrypted using 56-bit DES encryption with 64-bit CFB.

When a user dials in from a remote host to a Cisco router configured for Kerberos authentication, the host and router will attempt to negotiate whether or not to use encryption for the Telnet session. If this negotiation is successful, the router will encrypt all outbound data during the Telnet session.

If encryption is not successfully negotiated, the session will be terminated and the user will receive a message stating that the encrypted Telnet session was not successfully established.

For information about enabling bidirectional encryption from a remote host, refer to the documentation specific to the remote host device.

For an example of using encrypted Kerberized Telnet to open a secure Telnet session, see the "Specifying an Encrypted Telnet Session Example" section at the end of this chapter.

Enabling Mandatory Kerberos Authentication

As an added layer of security, you can optionally configure the router so that after remote users authenticate to it, these users can authenticate to other services on the network only with Kerberized

Telnet, rlogin, rsh, and rcp. If you do not make Kerberos authentication mandatory and Kerberos authentication fails, the application attempts to authenticate users using the default method of authentication for that network service; for example, Telnet and rlogin prompt for a password, and rsh attempts to authenticate using the local rhost file.

To make Kerberos authentication mandatory, use the following command in global configuration mode:

Command	Purpose
kerberos clients mandatory	Sets Telnet, rlogin, rsh, and rcp to fail if they cannot negotiate the Kerberos protocol with the remote server.

Enabling Kerberos Instance Mapping

As mentioned in the section "Creating SRVTABs on the KDC," you can create administrative instances of users in the KDC database. The **kerberos instance map** command allows you to map those instances to Cisco IOS privilege levels so that users can open secure Telnet sessions to the router at a predefined privilege level, obviating the need to enter a clear-text password to enter enable mode.

To map a Kerberos instance to a Cisco IOS privilege level, use the following command in global configuration mode:

Command	Purpose
kerberos instance map *instance privilege-level*	Maps a Kerberos instance to a Cisco IOS privilege level.

If there is a Kerberos instance for user *loki* in the KDC database (for example, *loki/admin*), user *loki* can now open a Telnet session to the router as loki/admin and authenticate automatically at privilege level 15, assuming instance *admin* is mapped to privilege level 15. (See the section "Adding Users to the KDC Database" earlier in this chapter.)

Cisco IOS commands can be set to various privilege levels using the **privilege level** command.

After you map a Kerberos instance to a Cisco IOS privilege level, you must configure the router to check for Kerberos instances each time a user logs in. To run authorization to determine if a user is allowed to run an EXEC shell based on a mapped Kerberos instance, use the **aaa authorization** command with the **krb5-instance** keyword. For more information, refer to Chapter 4, "Configuring Authorization."

Monitoring and Maintaining Kerberos

To display or remove a current user's credentials, use the following commands in EXEC mode:

Step	Command	Purpose
1	**show kerberos creds**	Lists the credentials in a current user's credentials cache.
2	**clear kerberos creds**	Destroys all credentials in a current user's credentials cache.

For an example of Kerberos configuration, see the "Non-Kerberos Configuration Examples" section at the end of this chapter.

Kerberos Configuration Examples

Configuration examples in this section include the following:

- Defining a Kerberos Realm Examples
- Copying SRVTAB Files Example
- Non-Kerberos Configuration Examples
- Specifying an Encrypted Telnet Session Example

Defining a Kerberos Realm Examples

To define CISCO.COM as the default Kerberos realm, use the following command:

```
kerberos local-realm CISCO.COM
```

To tell the router that the CISCO.COM KDC is running on host 10.2.3.4 at port number 170, use the following Kerberos command:

```
kerberos server CISCO.COM 10.2.3.4 170
```

To map the DNS domain cisco.com to the Kerberos realm CISCO.COM, use the following command:

```
kerberos realm .cisco.com CISCO.COM
```

Copying SRVTAB Files Example

To copy over the SRVTAB file on a host named host123.cisco.com for a router named router1.cisco.com, the command would look like this:

```
kerberos srvtab remote host123.cisco.com router1.cisco.com-new-srvtab
```

Non-Kerberos Configuration Examples

This section provides a typical non-Kerberos router configuration and shows output for this configuration from the **write term** command, and then builds on this configuration by adding optional Kerberos functionality. Output for each configuration is presented for comparison against the previous configuration.

This example shows how to use the kdb5_edit program to perform the following configuration tasks:

1 Add user chet to the Kerberos database.

2 Add a privileged Kerberos instance of user *chet* (*chet/admin*) to the Kerberos database.

3 Add a restricted instance of *chet* (*chet/restricted*) to the Kerberos database.

4 Add workstation chet-ss20.cisco.com.

5 Add router chet-2500.cisco.com to the Kerberos database.

6 Add workstation chet-ss20.cisco.com to the Kerberos database.

7 Extract SRVTABs for the router and workstations.

8 List the contents of the KDC database (with the **ldb** command).

Note that, in this sample configuration, host chet-ss20 is also the KDC:

```
chet-ss20# sbin/kdb5_edit
kdb5_edit:  ank chet
Enter password:
Re-enter password for verification:
kdb5_edit:  ank chet/admin
Enter password:
Re-enter password for verification:
kdb5_edit:  ank chet/restricted
Enter password:
Re-enter password for verification:
kdb5_edit:  ark host/chet-ss20.cisco.com
kdb5_edit:  ark host/chet-2500.cisco.com
kdb5_edit:  xst chet-ss20.cisco.com host
'host/chet-ss20.cisco.com@CISCO.COM' added to keytab
'WRFILE:chet-ss20.cisco.com-new-srvtab'
kdb5_edit:  xst chet-2500.cisco.com host
'host/chet-2500.cisco.com@CISCO.COM' added to keytab
'WRFILE:chet-2500.cisco.com-new-srvtab'
kdb5_edit:  ldb
entry: host/chet-2500.cisco.com@CISCO.COM
entry: chet/restricted@CISCO.COM
entry: chet@CISCO.COM
entry: K/M@CISCO.COM
entry: host/chet-ss20.cisco.com@CISCO.COM
entry: krbtgt/CISCO.COM@CISCO.COM
entry: chet/admin@CISCO.COM
kdb5_edit:  q
chet-ss20#
```

The following example shows output from a **write term** command, which displays the configuration of router chet-2500. This is a typical configuration with no Kerberos authentication.

```
chet-2500# write term
Building configuration...

Current configuration:
!
! Last configuration
change at 14:03:55 PDT Mon May 13 1996
!
version 11.2
service udp-small-servers
```

```
service tcp-small-servers
!
hostname chet-2500
!
clock timezone PST -8
clock summer-time PDT recurring
aaa new-model
aaa authentication login console none
aaa authentication ppp local local
enable password sMudgKin
!
username chet-2500 password 7 sMudgkin
username chet-3000 password 7 sMudgkin
username chetin password 7 sMudgkin
!
interface Ethernet0
 ip address 172.16.0.0 255.255.255.0
!
interface Serial0
 no ip address
 shutdown
 no fair-queue
!
interface Serial1
 no ip address
 shutdown
 no fair-queue
!
interface Async2
 ip unnumbered Ethernet0
 encapsulation ppp
 shutdown
 async dynamic routing
 async mode dedicated
 no cdp enable
 ppp authentication pap local
 no tarp propagate
!
interface Async3
 ip unnumbered Ethernet0
 encapsulation ppp
 shutdown
 async dynamic address
 async dynamic routing
 async mode dedicated
 no cdp enable
 ppp authentication pap local
 no tarp propagate
!
router eigrp 109
 network 172.17.0.0
 no auto-summary
!
ip default-gateway 172.30.55.64
ip domain-name cisco.com
```

```
ip name-server 192.168.0.0
ip classless
!
!
line con 0
 exec-timeout 0 0
 login authentication console
line 1 16
 transport input all
line aux 0
 transport input all
line vty 0 4
 password sMudgKin
!
ntp clock-period 17179703
ntp peer 172.19.10.0
ntp peer 172.19.0.0
end
```

The following example shows how to enable user authentication on the router via the Kerberos database. To enable user authentication via the Kerberos database, you would perform the following tasks:

1 Enter configuration mode.

2 Define the Kerberos local realm.

3 Identify the machine hosting the KDC.

4 Enable credentials forwarding.

5 Specify Kerberos as the method of authentication for login.

6 Exit configuration mode (CTRL-Z).

7 Write the new configuration to the terminal:

```
chet-2500# configure term
Enter configuration commands, one per line.  End with CTRL-Z.
chet-2500(config)# kerberos local-realm CISCO.COM
chet-2500(config)# kerberos server CISCO.COM chet-ss20
Translating "chet-ss20"...domain server (192.168.0.0) [OK]

chet-2500(config)# kerberos credentials forward
chet-2500(config)# aaa authentication login default krb5
chet-2500(config)#
chet-2500#
%SYS-5-CONFIG_I: Configured from console by console
chet-2500# write term
```

Compare the following configuration with the previous one. In particular, look at the lines beginning with the words *aaa*, *username*, and *kerberos* (lines 10 through 20) in this new configuration:

```
Building configuration...

Current configuration:
!
```

```
! Last configuration change at 14:05:54 PDT Mon May 13 1996
!
version 11.2
service udp-small-servers
service tcp-small-servers
!
hostname chet-2500
!
clock timezone PST -8
clock summer-time PDT recurring
aaa new-model
aaa authentication login default krb5
aaa authentication login console none
aaa authentication ppp local local
enable password sMudgKin
!
username chet-2500 password 7 sMudgkin
username chet-3000 password 7 sMudgkin
username chetin password 7 sMudgkin
kerberos local-realm CISCO.COM
kerberos server CISCO.COM 172.71.54.14
kerberos credentials forward
!
interface Ethernet0
 ip address 172.16.0.0 255.255.255.0
!
interface Serial0
 no ip address
 shutdown
 no fair-queue
!
interface Serial1
 no ip address
 shutdown
 no fair-queue
!
interface Async2
 ip unnumbered Ethernet0
 encapsulation ppp
 shutdown
 async dynamic routing
 async mode dedicated
 no cdp enable
 ppp authentication pap local
 no tarp propagate
!
interface Async3
 ip unnumbered Ethernet0
 encapsulation ppp
 shutdown
 async dynamic address
 async dynamic routing
 async mode dedicated
 no cdp enable
 ppp authentication pap local
```

```
 no tarp propagate
 !
 router eigrp 109
  network 172.17.0.0
  no auto-summary
 !
 ip default-gateway 172.30.55.64
 ip domain-name cisco.com
 ip name-server 192.168.0.0
 ip classless
 !
 !
 line con 0
  exec-timeout 0 0
  login authentication console
 line 1 16
  transport input all
 line aux 0
  transport input all
 line vty 0 4
  password sMudgKin
 !
 ntp clock-period 17179703
 ntp peer 172.19.10.0
 ntp peer 172.19.0.0
 end
```

With the router configured thus far, user *chet* can log in to the router with a username and password and automatically obtain a TGT, as illustrated in the next example. With possession of a credential, user chet successfully authenticates to host chet-ss20 without entering a username/password:

```
chet-ss20% telnet chet-2500
Trying 172.16.0.0 ...
Connected to chet-2500.cisco.com.
Escape character is '^]'.


User Access Verification

Username: chet
Password:

chet-2500> show kerberos creds
Default Principal:  chet@CISCO.COM
Valid Starting          Expires                 Service Principal
13-May-1996 14:05:39    13-May-1996 22:06:40    krbtgt/CISCO.COM@CISCO.COM

chet-2500> telnet chet-ss20
Trying chet-ss20.cisco.com (172.71.54.14)... Open
Kerberos:        Successfully forwarded credentials


SunOS UNIX (chet-ss20) (pts/7)

Last login: Mon May 13 13:47:35 from chet-ss20.cisco.c
```

```
Sun Microsystems Inc.    SunOS 5.4       Generic July 1994
unknown mode: new
chet-ss20%
```

The following example shows how to authenticate to the router using Kerberos credentials. To authenticate using Kerberos credentials, you would perform the following tasks:

● Enter configuration mode

● Remotely copy the SRVTAB file from the KDC

● Set authentication at login to use the Kerberos 5 Telnet authentication protocol when using Telnet to connect to the router

● Write the configuration to the terminal

Note that the new configuration contains a **kerberos srvtab entry** line. This line is created by the **kerberos srvtab remote** command:

```
chet-2500# configure term
Enter configuration commands, one per line.  End with CTRL-Z.
chet-2500(config)#kerberos srvtab remote earth chet/chet-2500.cisco.com-new-srvtab
Translating "earth"...domain server (192.168.0.0) [OK]

Loading chet/chet-2500.cisco.com-new-srvtab from 172.68.1.123 (via Ethernet0): !
[OK - 66/1000 bytes]

chet-2500(config)# aaa authentication login default krb5-telnet krb5
chet-2500(config)#
chet-2500#
%SYS-5-CONFIG_I: Configured from console by console
chet-2500# write term
Building configuration...

Current configuration:
!
! Last configuration change at 14:08:32 PDT Mon May 13 1996
!
version 11.2
service udp-small-servers
service tcp-small-servers
!
hostname chet-2500
!
clock timezone PST -8
clock summer-time PDT recurring
aaa new-model
aaa authentication login default krb5-telnet krb5
aaa authentication login console none
aaa authentication ppp local local
enable password sMudgKin
!
username chet-2500 password 7 sMudgkin
username chet-3000 password 7 sMudgkin
username chetin password 7 sMudgkin
```

```
kerberos local-realm CISCO.COM
kerberos srvtab entry host/chet-2500.cisco.com@CISCO.COM 0 832015393 1 1 8 7 sMudgkin
kerberos server CISCO.COM 172.71.54.14
kerberos credentials forward
!
interface Ethernet0
 ip address 172.16.0.0 255.255.255.0
!
interface Serial0
 no ip address
 shutdown
 no fair-queue
!

interface Serial1
 no ip address
 shutdown
 no fair-queue
!
interface Async2
 ip unnumbered Ethernet0
 encapsulation ppp
 shutdown
 async dynamic routing
 async mode dedicated
 no cdp enable
 ppp authentication pap local
 no tarp propagate
!
interface Async3
 ip unnumbered Ethernet0
 encapsulation ppp
 shutdown
 async dynamic address
 async dynamic routing
 async mode dedicated
 no cdp enable
 ppp authentication pap local
 no tarp propagate
!
router eigrp 109
 network 172.17.0.0
 no auto-summary
!
ip default-gateway 172.30.55.64
ip domain-name cisco.com
ip name-server 192.168.0.0
ip classless
!
!
line con 0
 exec-timeout 0 0
 login authentication console
line 1 16
 transport input all
```

```
line aux 0
 transport input all
line vty 0 4
 password sMudgKin
!
ntp clock-period 17179703
ntp peer 172.19.10.0
ntp peer 172.19.0.0
end
```

```
chet-2500#
```

With this configuration, the user can Telnet to the router using Kerberos credentials, as illustrated in the next example:

```
chet-ss20% bin/telnet -a -F chet-2500
Trying 172.16.0.0...
Connected to chet-2500.cisco.com.
Escape character is '^]'.
[ Kerberos V5 accepts you as "chet@CISCO.COM" ]


User Access Verification

chet-2500>[ Kerberos V5 accepted forwarded credentials ]

chet-2500> show kerberos creds
Default Principal:  chet@CISCO.COM
Valid Starting          Expires                 Service Principal
13-May-1996 15:06:25    14-May-1996 00:08:29    krbtgt/CISCO.COM@CISCO.COM

chet-2500>q
Connection closed by foreign host.
chet-ss20%
```

The following example shows how to map Kerberos instances to Cisco's privilege levels. To map Kerberos instances to privilege levels, you would perform the following tasks:

1 Enter configuration mode.

2 Map the Kerberos instance, *admin*, to privilege level 15.

3 Map the Kerberos instance, *restricted*, to privilege level 3.

4 Specify that the instance defined by the **Kerberos instance map** command be used for AAA authorization.

5 Write the configuration to the terminal:

```
chet-2500# configure term
Enter configuration commands, one per line.  End with CTRL-Z.
chet-2500(config)# kerberos instance map admin 15
chet-2500(config)# kerberos instance map restricted 3
chet-2500(config)# aaa authorization exec krb5-instance
```

```
chet-2500(config)#
chet-2500#
%SYS-5-CONFIG_I: Configured from console by console
chet-2500# write term
Building configuration...

Current configuration:
!
! Last configuration change at 14:59:05 PDT Mon May 13 1996
!
version 11.2
service udp-small-servers
service tcp-small-servers
!
hostname chet-2500
!
aaa new-model
aaa authentication login default krb5-telnet krb5
aaa authentication login console none
aaa authentication ppp default krb5 local
aaa authorization exec krb5-instance
enable password sMudgKin
!
username chet-2500 password 7 sMudgkin
username chet-3000 password 7 sMudgkin
username chetin password 7 sMudgkin
ip domain-name cisco.com
ip name-server 192.168.0.0
kerberos local-realm CISCO.COM
kerberos srvtab entry host/chet-2500.cisco.com@CISCO.COM 0 832015393 1 1 8 7 sMudgkin
kerberos server CISCO.COM 172.71.54.14
kerberos instance map admin 15
kerberos instance map restricted 3
kerberos credentials forward
clock timezone PST -8
clock summer-time PDT recurring
!
interface Ethernet0
 ip address 172.16.0.0 255.255.255.0
!
interface Serial0
 no ip address
 shutdown
 no fair-queue
!
interface Serial1
 no ip address
 shutdown
 no fair-queue
!
interface Async2
 ip unnumbered Ethernet0
 encapsulation ppp
 shutdown
 async dynamic routing
```

```
 async mode dedicated
 no cdp enable
 ppp authentication pap local
 no tarp propagate
!
interface Async3
 ip unnumbered Ethernet0
 encapsulation ppp
 shutdown
 async dynamic address
 async dynamic routing
 async mode dedicated
 no cdp enable
 ppp authentication pap local
 no tarp propagate
!
router eigrp 109
 network 172.17.0.0
no auto-summary
!
ip default-gateway 172.30.55.64
ip classless
!
!
line con 0
 exec-timeout 0 0
 login authentication console
line 1 16
 transport input all
line aux 0
 transport input all
line vty 0 4
 password sMudgKin
!
ntp clock-period 17179703
ntp peer 172.19.10.0
ntp peer 172.19.0.0
end

chet-2500#
```

The following example shows output from the three types of sessions now possible for user *chet* with Kerberos instances turned on:

```
chet-ss20% telnet chet-2500
Trying 172.16.0.0 ...
Connected to chet-2500.cisco.com.
Escape character is '^]'.

User Access Verification

Username: chet
Password:
```

```
chet-2500> show kerberos creds
Default Principal:  chet@CISCO.COM
Valid Starting          Expires               Service Principal
13-May-1996 14:58:28    13-May-1996 22:59:29  krbtgt/CISCO.COM@CISCO.COM

chet-2500> show privilege
Current privilege level is 1
chet-2500> q
Connection closed by foreign host.
chet-ss20% telnet chet-2500
Trying 172.16.0.0 ...
Connected to chet-2500.cisco.com.
Escape character is '^]'.


User Access Verification

Username: chet/admin
Password:

chet-2500# show kerberos creds
Default Principal:  chet/admin@CISCO.COM
Valid Starting          Expires               Service Principal
13-May-1996 14:59:44    13-May-1996 23:00:45  krbtgt/CISCO.COM@CISCO.COM

chet-2500# show privilege
Current privilege level is 15
chet-2500# q
Connection closed by foreign host.
chet-ss20% telnet chet-2500
Trying 172.16.0.0 ...
Connected to chet-2500.cisco.com.
Escape character is '^]'.

User Access Verification

Username: chet/restricted
Password:

chet-2500# show kerberos creds
Default Principal:  chet/restricted@CISCO.COM
Valid Starting          Expires               Service Principal
13-May-1996 15:00:32    13-May-1996 23:01:33  krbtgt/CISCO.COM@CISCO.COM

chet-2500# show privilege
Current privilege level is 3
chet-2500# q
Connection closed by foreign host.
chet-ss20%
```

Specifying an Encrypted Telnet Session Example

The following example establishes an encrypted Telnet session from a router to a remote host named
host1:

```
Router> telnet host1 /encrypt kerberos
```

## CHAPTER 14

Kerberos Commands

This chapter describes the commands used to configure Kerberos. Kerberos is a secret-key network authentication protocol, developed at Massachusetts Institute of Technology (MIT), that uses the Data Encryption Standard (DES) cryptographic algorithm for encryption and authentication. Kerberos was designed to authenticate requests for network resources. Kerberos, like other secret-key systems, is based on the concept of a trusted third party that performs secure verification of users and services. In the Kerberos protocol, this trusted third party is called the key distribution center (KDC).

For information on how to configure Kerberos, refer to Chapter 13, "Configuring Kerberos." For configuration examples using the commands in this chapter, refer to the "Kerberos Configuration Examples" section located at the end of Chapter 13, "Configuring Kerberos."

clear kerberos creds

To delete the contents of the credentials cache, use the **clear kerberos creds** EXEC command.

> **clear kerberos creds**

Syntax Description

This command has no keywords or arguments.

Command Mode

EXEC

Usage Guidelines

This command first appeared in Cisco IOS Release 11.1.

Credentials are cleared when the user logs out.

Cisco supports Kerberos 5.

Example

The following example illustrates the **clear kerberos creds** command:

```
cisco-2500> show kerberos creds
Default Principal: chet@cisco.com
Valid Starting          Expires                 Service Principal
18-Dec-1995 16:21:07    19-Dec-1995 00:22:24    krbtgt/CISCO.COM@CISCO.COM
```

```
cisco-2500> clear kerberos creds
cisco-2500> show kerberos creds
No Kerberos credentials.

cisco-2500>
```

Related Commands

You can search online at www.cisco.com to find documentation of related commands.

show kerberos creds

connect

To log in to a host that supports Telnet, rlogin, or LAT, use the **connect** EXEC command.

connect *host* [*port*] [*keyword*]

Syntax	Description
host	A host name or an IP address.
port	(Optional) A decimal TCP port number; the default is the Telnet router port (decimal 23) on the host.
keyword	(Optional) One of the options listed in Table 14-1.

Table 14-1 describes the options that can be used for the argument *keyword*.

Table 14-1 *Connection Options*

Option	Description
/debug	Enables Telnet debugging mode.
/encrypt kerberos	Enables an encrypted Telnet session. This keyword is available only if you have the Kerberized Telnet subsystem. If you authenticate using Kerberos credentials, the use of this keyword initiates an encryption negotiation with the remote server. If the encryption negotiation fails, the Telnet connection will be reset. If the encryption negotiation is successful, the Telnet connection will be established, and the Telnet session will continue in encrypted mode (all Telnet traffic for the session will be encrypted).
/line	Enables Telnet line mode. In this mode, the Cisco IOS software sends no data to the host until you press **Return**. You can edit the line using the standard Cisco IOS software command editing characters. The **/line** keyword is a local switch; the remote router is not notified of the mode change.

Table 14-1 *Connection Options (Continued)*

Option	Description
/noecho	Disables local echo.
/route *path*	Specifies loose source routing. The *path* argument is a list of host names or IP addresses that specify network nodes and ends with the final destination.
/source-interface	Specifies source interface.
/stream	Turns on *stream* processing, which enables a raw TCP stream with no Telnet control sequences. A stream connection does not process Telnet options and can be appropriate for connections to ports running UUCP and other non-Telnet protocols.
port-number	Port number.
bgp	Border Gateway Protocol.
chargen	Character generator.
cmd *rcmd*	Remote commands.
daytime	Daytime.
discard	Discard.
domain	Domain Name System.
echo	Echo.
exec	EXEC.
finger	Finger.
ftp	File Transfer Protocol.
ftp-data	FTP data connections (used infrequently).
gopher	Gopher.
hostname	Network Information Center (NIC) host name server.
ident	Ident Protocol.
irc	Internet Relay Chat.
klogin	Kerberos login.
kshell	Kerberos shell.
login	Login (rlogin).
lpd	Printer service.
nntp	Network News Transport Protocol.
node	Connect to a specific LAT node.
pop2	Post Office Protocol v2.
pop3	Post Office Protocol v3.

Continues

Table 14-1 *Connection Options (Continued)*

Option	Description
port	Destination LAT port name.
smtp	Simple Mail Transport Protocol.
sunrpc	Sun Remote Procedure Call.
syslog	Syslog.
tacacs	Specify TACACS security.
talk	Talk.
telnet	Telnet.
time	Time.
uucp	UNIX-to-UNIX Copy Program.
whois	Nickname.
www	World Wide Web (HTTP).

Command Mode

EXEC

Usage Guidelines

This command first appeared in a release prior to Cisco IOS Release 10.0.

With the Cisco IOS software implementation of TCP/IP, you are not required to enter the **connect**, **telnet**, **lat**, or **rlogin** commands to establish a terminal connection. You can just enter the learned host name—as long as the host name is different from a command word in the Cisco IOS software.

To display a list of the available hosts, enter the following command:

> **show hosts**

To display the status of all TCP connections, enter the following command:

> **show tcp**

The Cisco IOS software assigns a logical name to each connection, and several commands use these names to identify connections. The logical name is the same as the host name, unless that name is already in use, or you change the connection name with the EXEC command **name-connection**. If the name is already in use, the Cisco IOS software assigns a null name to the connection.

Examples

The following example establishes an encrypted Telnet session from a router to a remote host named *host1*:

```
Router> connect host1 /encrypt kerberos
```

The following example routes packets from the source system *host1* to kl.domain.com, then to 10.1.0.11, and finally back to *host1*:

```
Router> connect host1 /route:kl.domain.com 10.1.0.11 host1
```

The following example connects to a host with logical name *host1*:

```
Router> host1
```

Related Commands

You can search online at www.cisco.com to find documentation of related commands.

kerberos clients mandatory
lat

kerberos clients mandatory

To cause the **rsh**, **rcp**, **rlogin**, and **telnet** commands to fail if they cannot negotiate the Kerberos protocol with the remote server, use the **kerberos clients mandatory** global configuration command. Use the **no** form of this command to make Kerberos optional.

> **kerberos clients mandatory**
> **no kerberos clients mandatory**

Syntax Description

This command has no arguments or keywords.

Default

Disabled

Command Mode

Global configuration

User Guidelines

This command first appeared in Cisco IOS Release 11.2.

If this command is not configured and the user has Kerberos credentials stored locally, the **rsh**, **rcp**, **rlogin**, and **telnet** commands attempt to negotiate the Kerberos protocol with the remote server and will use the non-Kerberized protocols if unsuccessful.

If this command is not configured and the user has no Kerberos credentials, the standard protocols for **rcp** and **rsh** are used to negotiate the Kerberos protocol.

Example

The following example causes the **rsh**, **rcp**, **rlogin**, and **telnet** commands to fail if they cannot negotiate the Kerberos protocol with the remote server:

```
kerberos clients mandatory
```

Related Commands

You can search online at www.cisco.com to find documentation of related commands.

kerberos credentials forward
rlogin
rsh
telnet

kerberos credentials forward

To force all network application clients on the router to forward users' Kerberos credentials upon successful Kerberos authentication, use the **kerberos credentials forward** global configuration command. Use the **no** form of this command to turn off Kerberos credentials forwarding.

> **kerberos credentials forward**
> **no kerberos credentials forward**

Syntax Description

This command has no arguments or keywords.

Default

Disabled

Command Mode

Global configuration

Usage Guidelines

This command first appeared in Cisco IOS Release 11.2.

Enable credentials forwarding to have users' TGTs forwarded to the host on which they authenticate. In this way, users can connect to multiple hosts in the Kerberos realm without running the KINIT program each time they need to get a TGT.

Example

The following example forces all network application clients on the router to forward users' Kerberos credentials upon successful Kerberos authentication:

```
kerberos credentials forward
```

Related Commands

You can search online at www.cisco.com to find documentation of related commands.

copy rcp
rlogin
rsh
telnet

kerberos instance map

To map Kerberos instances to Cisco IOS privilege levels, use the **kerberos instance map** global configuration command. Use the **no** form of this command to remove a Kerberos instance map.

> **kerberos instance map** *instance privilege-level*
> **no kerberos instance map** *instance*

Syntax	Description
instance	Name of a Kerberos instance.
privilege-level	The privilege level at which a user is set if the user's Kerberos principal contains the matching Kerberos instance. You can specify up to 16 privilege levels, using numbers 0 through 15. Level 1 is normal EXEC-mode user privileges.

Default

Privilege level 1

Command Mode

Global configuration

Usage Guidelines

This command first appeared in Cisco IOS Release 11.2.

Use this command to create user instances with access to administrative commands.

Example

The following example sets the privilege level to 15 for authenticated Kerberos users with the *admin* instance in Kerberos realm:

```
kerberos instance map admin 15
```

Related Commands

You can search online at www.cisco.com to find documentation of related commands.

aaa authorization

kerberos local-realm

To specify the Kerberos realm in which the router is located, use the **kerberos local-realm** global configuration command. Use the **no** form of this command to remove the specified Kerberos realm from this router.

> **kerberos local-realm** *kerberos-realm*
> **no kerberos local-realm**

Syntax	Description
kerberos-realm	The name of the default Kerberos realm. A Kerberos realm consists of users, hosts, and network services that are registered to a Kerberos server. The Kerberos realm must be in uppercase characters.

Default
Disabled

Command Mode
Global configuration

Usage Guidelines
This command first appeared in Cisco IOS Release 11.1.

The router can be located in more than one realm at a time. However, there can only be one instance of Kerberos **local-realm**. The realm specified with this command is the default realm.

Example
The following example specifies the Kerberos realm in which the router is located as DOMAIN.COM:

```
kerberos local-realm DOMAIN.COM
```

Related Commands
You can search online at www.cisco.com to find documentation of related commands.

kerberos preauth
kerberos realm
kerberos server
kerberos srvtab entry
kerberos srvtab remote

kerberos preauth

To specify a preauthentication method to use to communicate with the KDC, use the **kerberos preauth** global configuration command. Use the **no** form of this command to disable Kerberos preauthentication.

> **kerberos preauth** [**encrypted-unix-timestamp** | **none**]
> **no kerberos preauth**

Syntax	Description
encrypted-unix-timestamp	(Optional) Uses an encrypted UNIX timestamp as a quick authentication method when communicating with the KDC.
none	(Optional) Do not use Kerberos preauthentication.

Default
Disabled

Command Mode
Global configuration

Usage Guidelines
This command first appeared in Cisco IOS Release 11.2.

It is more secure to use a preauthentication for communications with the KDC. However, communication with the KDC will fail if the KDC does not support this particular version of **kerberos preauth**. If that happens, turn off the preauthentication with the **none** option.

The **no** form of this command is equivalent to using the **none** keyword.

Examples
The following example enables Kerberos preauthentication:

```
kerberos preauth encrypted-unix-timestamp
```

The following example disables Kerberos preauthentication:

```
kerberos preauth none
```

Related Commands
You can search online at www.cisco.com to find documentation of related commands.

kerberos local-realm
kerberos server
kerberos srvtab entry
kerberos srvtab remote

kerberos realm

To map a host name or Domain Name System (DNS) domain to a Kerberos realm, use the **kerberos realm** global configuration command. Use the **no** form of this command to remove a Kerberos realm map.

> **kerberos realm** {*dns-domain* | *host*} *kerberos-realm*
> **no kerberos realm** {*dns-domain* | *host*} *kerberos-realm*

Syntax	Description
dns-domain	Name of a DNS domain or host.
host	Name of a DNS host.
kerberos-realm	Name of the Kerberos realm to which the specified domain or host belongs.

Default
Disabled

Command Mode
Global configuration

Usage Guidelines
This command first appeared in Cisco IOS Release 11.1.

DNS domains are specified with a leading dot (.) character; host names cannot begin with a dot (.) character. There can be multiple entries of this line.

A Kerberos realm consists of users, hosts, and network services that are registered to a Kerberos server. The Kerberos realm must be in uppercase characters. The router can be located in more than one realm at a time. Kerberos realm names must be in all uppercase characters.

Example
The following example maps the domain name, domain.com, to the Kerberos realm, DOMAIN.COM:

```
kerberos realm .domain.com DOMAIN.COM
```

Related Commands

You can search online at www.cisco.com to find documentation of related commands.

kerberos local-realm
kerberos server
kerberos srvtab entry
kerberos srvtab remote

kerberos server

To specify the location of the Kerberos server for a given Kerberos realm, use the **kerberos server** global configuration command. Use the **no** form of this command to remove a Kerberos server for a specified Kerberos realm.

> **kerberos server** *kerberos-realm* {*hostname* | *ip-address*} [*port-number*]
> **no kerberos server** *kerberos-realm* {*hostname* | *ip-address*}

Syntax	Description
kerberos-realm	Name of the Kerberos realm. A Kerberos realm consists of users, hosts, and network services that are registered to a Kerberos server. The Kerberos realm must be in uppercase letters.
hostname	Name of the host functioning as a Kerberos server for the specified Kerberos realm (translated into an IP address at the time of entry).
ip-address	IP address of the host functioning as a Kerberos server for the specified Kerberos realm.
port-number	(Optional) Port that the KDC/TGS monitors (defaults to 88).

Default

Disabled

Command Mode

Global configuration

Usage Guidelines

This command first appeared in Cisco IOS Release 11.1.

Example

The following example specifies 192.168.47.66 as the Kerberos server for the Kerberos realm DOMAIN.COM:

```
kerberos server DOMAIN.COM 192.168.47.66
```

Related Commands

You can search online at www.cisco.com to find documentation of related commands.

kerberos local-realm
kerberos realm
kerberos srvtab entry
kerberos srvtab remote

kerberos srvtab entry

To retrieve a SRVTAB file from a remote host and automatically generate a Kerberos SRVTAB entry configuration, use the **kerberos srvtab remote** global configuration command (not **kerberos srvtab entry**). (The Kerberos SRVTAB entry is the router's locally stored SRVTAB.) Use the **no** form of this command to remove a SRVTAB entry from the router's configuration.

kerberos srvtab entry *kerberos-principal principal-type timestamp key-version
number key-type key-length encrypted-keytab*
no kerberos srvtab entry *kerberos-principal principal-type*

Syntax	Description
kerberos-principal	A service on the router.
principal-type	Version of the Kerberos SRVTAB.
timestamp	Number representing the date and time the SRVTAB entry was created.
key-version number	Version of the encryption key format.
key-type	Type of encryption used.
key-length	Length, in bytes, of the encryption key.
encrypted-keytab	Secret key the router shares with the KDC. It is encrypted with the private DES key (if available) when you write out your configuration.

Command Mode

Global configuration

Usage Guidelines

This command first appeared in Cisco IOS Release 11.2.

When you use the **kerberos srvtab remote** command to copy the SRVTAB file from a remote host (generally the KDC), it parses the information in this file and stores it in the router's running configuration in the **kerberos srvtab entry** format. The key for each SRVTAB entry is encrypted with a private DES key if one is defined on the router. To ensure that the SRVTAB is available (that is, that it does not need to be acquired from the KDC) when you reboot the router, use the **write memory** router configuration command to write the router's running configuration to NVRAM.

If you reload a configuration with a SRVTAB encrypted with a private DES key onto a router that does not have a private DES key defined, the router displays a message informing you that the SRVTAB entry has been corrupted, and discards the entry.

If you change the private DES key and reload an old version of the router's configuration that contains SRVTAB entries encrypted with the old private DES keys, the router will restore your Kerberos SRVTAB entries, but the SRVTAB keys will be corrupted. In this case, you must delete your old Kerberos SRVTAB entries and reload your Kerberos SRVTABs on to the router using the **kerberos srvtab remote** command.

Although you can configure **kerberos srvtab entry** on the router manually, generally you should not do this because the keytab is encrypted automatically by the router when you copy the SRVTAB using the **kerberos srvtab remote** command.

Example

In the following example, host/new-router.domain.com@DOMAIN.COM is the host, 0 is the type, 817680774 is the timestamp, 1 is the version of the key, 1 indicates the DES is the encryption type, 8 is the number of bytes, and .cCN.YoU.okK is the encrypted key:

```
kerberos srvtab entry host/new-router.domain.com@DOMAIN.COM 0 817680774 1 1 8 .cCN.YoU.okK
```

Related Commands

You can search online at www.cisco.com to find documentation of related commands.

kerberos srvtab remote
key config-key

kerberos srvtab remote

To retrieve a krb5 SRVTAB file from the specified host, use the **kerberos srvtab remote** global configuration command.

> **kerberos srvtab remote** {*hostname* | *ip-address*} *filename*

Syntax	Description
hostname	Machine with the Kerberos SRVTAB file.
ip-address	IP address of the machine with the Kerberos SRVTAB file.
filename	Name of the SRVTAB file.

Command Mode

Global configuration

Usage Guidelines

This command first appeared in Cisco IOS Release 11.2.

When you use the **kerberos srvtab remote** command to copy the SRVTAB file from the remote host (generally the KDC), it parses the information in this file and stores it in the router's running configuration in the **kerberos srvtab entry** format. The key for each SRVTAB entry is encrypted with the private DES key if one is defined on the router. To ensure that the SRVTAB is available (that is, that it does not need to be acquired from the KDC) when you reboot the router, use the **write memory** configuration command to write the router's running configuration to NVRAM.

Example

The command in the following example copies the SRVTAB file residing on b1.domain.com to a router named s1.domain.com:

```
kerberos srvtab remote b1.domain.com s1.domain.com-new-srvtab
```

Related Commands

You can search online at www.cisco.com to find documentation of related commands.

kerberos srvtab entry
key config-key

key config-key

To define a private DES key for the router, use the **key config-key** global configuration command. Use the **no** form of this command to delete a private DES key for the router.

key config-key 1 *string*

Syntax	Description
string	Private DES key (can be up to eight alphanumeric characters).

Default

No DES key defined

Command Mode

Global configuration

Usage Guidelines

This command first appeared in Cisco IOS Release 11.2.

This command defines a private DES key for the router that will not show up in the router configuration. This private DES key can be used to DES-encrypt certain parts of the router's configuration.

CAUTION The private DES key is unrecoverable. If you encrypt part of your configuration with the private DES key and lose or forget the key, you will not be able to recover the encrypted data.

Example

The command in the following example sets *keyxx* as the private DES key on the router:

```
key config-key 1 keyxx
```

Related Commands

You can search online at www.cisco.com to find documentation of related commands.

kerberos srvtab entry
kerberos srvtab remote

show kerberos creds

To display the contents of your credentials cache, use the **show kerberos creds** EXEC command.

show kerberos creds

Syntax Description

This command has no keywords or arguments.

Command Mode

EXEC

Usage Guidelines

This command first appeared in Cisco IOS Release 11.1.

The **show kerberos creds** command is equivalent to the UNIX **klist** command.

When users authenticate themselves with Kerberos, they are issued an authentication ticket called a *credential*. The credential is stored in a credential cache.

Sample Displays

The following example displays entries in the credentials cache:

```
Router> show kerberos creds

 Default Principal: user@domain.com
 Valid Starting          Expires                 Service Principal
 18-Dec-1995 16:21:07    19-Dec-1995 00:22:24    krbtgt/DOMAIN.COM@DOMAIN.COM
```

The following example returns output that acknowledges that credentials do *not* exist in the credentials cache:

```
Router> show kerberos creds

 No Kerberos credentials
```

Related Commands

You can search online at www.cisco.com to find documentation of related commands.

clear kerberos creds

telnet

To log in to a host that supports Telnet, use the **telnet** EXEC command.

> **telnet** *host* [*port*] [*keyword*]

Syntax	Description
host	A host name or IP address.
port	(Optional) A decimal TCP port number; the default is the Telnet router port (decimal 23) on the host.
keyword	(Optional) One of the options listed in Table 14-2.

Table 14-2 describes the options that can be used for the argument *keyword*.

Table 14-2   *Telnet Connection Options*

Option	Description
/debug	Enables Telnet debugging mode.
/encrypt kerberos	Enables an encrypted Telnet session. This keyword is available only if you have the Kerberized Telnet subsystem. If you authenticate using Kerberos credentials, the use of this keyword initiates an encryption negotiation with the remote server. If the encryption negotiation fails, the Telnet connection will be reset. If the encryption negotiation is successful, the Telnet connection will be established, and the Telnet session will continue in encrypted mode (all Telnet traffic for the session will be encrypted).
/line	Enables Telnet line mode. In this mode, the Cisco IOS software sends no data to the host until you press **Return**. You can edit the line using the standard Cisco IOS software command-editing characters. The **/line** keyword is a local switch; the remote router is not notified of the mode change.
/noecho	Disables local echo.
/route *path*	Specifies loose source routing. The *path* argument is a list of host names or IP addresses that specify network nodes and ends with the final destination.
/source-interface	Specifies source interface.
/stream	Turns on *stream* processing, which enables a raw TCP stream with no Telnet control sequences. A stream connection does not process Telnet options and can be appropriate for connections to ports running UUCP and other non-Telnet protocols.
bgp	Border Gateway Protocol.
chargen	Character generator.
cmd *rcmd*	Remote commands.
daytime	Daytime.
discard	Discard.
domain	Domain Name System.
echo	Echo.

Table 14-2 *Telnet Connection Options (Continued)*

Option	Description
exec	EXEC.
finger	Finger.
ftp	File Transfer Protocol.
ftp-data	FTP data connections (used infrequently).
gopher	Gopher.
hostname	NIC hostname server.
ident	Ident Protocol.
irc	Internet Relay Chat.
klogin	Kerberos login.
kshell	Kerberos shell.
login	Login (rlogin).
lpd	Printer service.
nntp	Network News Transport Protocol.
node	Connect to a specific LAT node.
pop2	Post Office Protocol v2.
pop3	Post Office Protocol v3.
port	Destination LAT port name.
port-number	Port number.
smtp	Simple Mail Transport Protocol.
sunrpc	Sun Remote Procedure Call.
syslog	Syslog.
tacacs	Specify TACACS security.
talk	Talk.
telnet	Telnet.
time	Time.
uucp	UNIX-to-UNIX Copy Program.
whois	Nickname.
www	World Wide Web (HTTP).

Command Mode

EXEC

Usage Guidelines

This command first appeared in a release prior to Cisco IOS Release 10.0.

With the Cisco IOS implementation of TCP/IP, you are not required to enter the **connect** or **telnet** commands to establish a Telnet connection. You can just enter the learned host name—as long as the following conditions are met:

- The host name is different from a command word for the router

- The preferred transport protocol is set to Telnet

To display a list of the available hosts, use the **show hosts** command. To display the status of all TCP connections, use the **show tcp** command.

The Cisco IOS software assigns a logical name to each connection, and several commands use these names to identify connections. The logical name is the same as the host name, unless that name is already in use, or you change the connection name with the **name-connection** EXEC command. If the name is already in use, the Cisco IOS software assigns a null name to the connection.

The Telnet software supports special Telnet commands in the form of Telnet sequences that map generic terminal control functions to operating system-specific functions. To issue a special Telnet command, enter the escape sequence and then a command character. The default escape sequence is Ctrl-^ (press and hold the Control and Shift keys and the 6 key). You can enter the command character as you hold down Ctrl or with Ctrl released; you can use either uppercase or lowercase letters. Table 14-3 lists the special Telnet escape sequences.

Table 14-3 *Special Telnet Escape Sequences*

Task	Escape Sequence[1]
Break	**Ctrl-^ b**
Interrupt Process (IP)	**Ctrl-^ c**
Erase Character (EC)	**Ctrl-^ h**
Abort Output (AO)	**Ctrl-^ o**
Are You There? (AYT)	**Ctrl-^ t**
Erase Line (EL)	**Ctrl-^ u**

1. The caret (^) symbol refers to Shift-6 on your keyboard.

At any time during an active Telnet session, you can list the Telnet commands by pressing the escape sequence keys followed by a question mark at the system prompt:

Ctrl-^ ?

A sample of this list follows. In this sample output, the first caret (^) symbol represents the Control key, and the second caret represents Shift-6 on the keyboard:

```
Router> ^^?
[Special telnet escape help]
^^B  sends telnet BREAK
^^C  sends telnet IP
^^H  sends telnet EC
^^O  sends telnet AO
^^T  sends telnet AYT
^^U  sends telnet EL
```

You can have several concurrent Telnet sessions open and switch back and forth between them. To open a subsequent session, first suspend the current connection by pressing the escape sequence (**Ctrl-Shift-6** then **x** [**Ctrl^x**] by default) to return to the system command prompt. Then open a new connection with the **telnet** command.

To terminate an active Telnet session, issue any of the following commands at the prompt of the device to which you are connecting:

> **close**
> **disconnect**
> **exit**
> **logout**
> **quit**

Examples

The following example establishes an encrypted Telnet session from a router to a remote host named *host1*:

```
Router> telnet host1 /encrypt kerberos
```

The following example routes packets from the source system *host1* to kl.domain.com, then to 10.1.0.11, and finally back to *host1*:

```
Router> telnet host1 /route:kl.domain.com 10.1.0.11 host1
```

The following example connects to a host with logical name *host1*:

```
Router> host1
```

Related Commands

You can search online at www.cisco.com to find documentation of related commands.

connect
rlogin

PART III

Traffic Filtering and Firewalls

## CHAPTER 15

Access Control Lists: Overview and Guidelines

Cisco provides basic traffic filtering capabilities with access control lists (also referred to as *access lists*). Access lists can be configured for all routed network protocols (IP, AppleTalk, and so on) to filter those protocols' packets as the packets pass through a router.

You can configure access lists at your router to control access to a network: Access lists can prevent certain traffic from entering or exiting a network.

This chapter describes access lists as part of a security solution. This chapter includes tips, cautions, considerations, recommendations, and general guidelines for how to use access lists.

This chapter has the following sections:

- About Access Control Lists

- Overview of Access List Configuration

- Finding Complete Configuration and Command Information for Access Lists

About Access Control Lists

This section briefly describes what access lists do, why and when you should configure access lists, and basic versus advanced access lists.

What Access Lists Do

Access lists filter network traffic by controlling whether routed packets are forwarded or blocked at the router's interfaces. Your router examines each packet to determine whether to forward or drop the packet, based on the criteria you specified within the access lists.

Access list criteria could be the source address of the traffic, the destination address of the traffic, the upper-layer protocol, or other information. Note that sophisticated users can sometimes successfully evade or fool basic access lists because no authentication is required.

Why You Should Configure Access Lists

There are many reasons to configure access lists—for example, you can use access lists to restrict contents of routing updates or to provide traffic flow control. But one of the most important reasons to configure access lists is to provide security for your network; this is the reason on which this chapter focuses.

You should use access lists to provide a basic level of security for accessing your network. If you do not configure access lists on your router, all packets passing through the router could be allowed onto all parts of your network.

For example, access lists can allow one host to access a part of your network, and prevent another host from accessing the same area. In Figure 15-1, Host A is allowed to access the Human Resources network and Host B is prevented from accessing the Human Resources network.

Figure 15-1 *Using Traffic Filters to Prevent Traffic from Being Routed to a Network*

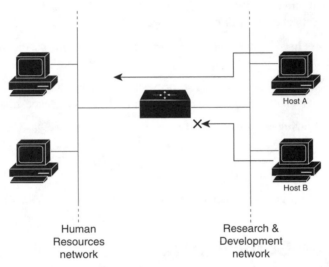

Human Resources network

Research & Development network

Host A

Host B

You can also use access lists to decide which types of traffic are forwarded or blocked at the router interfaces. For example, you can permit e-mail traffic to be routed, but at the same time block all Telnet traffic.

When to Configure Access Lists

Access lists should be used in *firewall routers*, which are often positioned between your internal network and an external network such as the Internet. You can also use access lists on a router positioned between two parts of your network to control traffic entering or exiting a specific part of your internal network.

To provide the security benefits of access lists, you should at a minimum configure access lists on border routers—routers situated at the edges of your networks. This provides a basic buffer from the outside network or from a less controlled area of your own network into a more sensitive area of your network.

On these routers, you should configure access lists for each network protocol configured on the router interfaces. You can configure access lists so that inbound traffic or outbound traffic or both are filtered on an interface.

Access lists must be defined on a per-protocol basis. In other words, you should define access lists for every protocol enabled on an interface if you want to control traffic flow for that protocol.

NOTE   Some protocols refer to access lists as *filters* and refer to the act of applying the access lists to interfaces as *filtering*.

Basic Versus Advanced Access Lists

This chapter describes how to use standard and static extended access lists, which are the basic types of access lists. Some type of basic access list should be used with each routed protocol that you have configured for router interfaces.

Besides the basic types of access lists described in this chapter, there are also more advanced access lists available, which provide additional security features and give you greater control over packet transmission. These advanced access lists and features are described in the other chapters within Part 3, "Traffic Filtering and Firewalls."

Overview of Access List Configuration

Although each protocol has its own set of specific tasks and rules required for you to provide traffic filtering, in general most protocols require at least two basic steps to be accomplished. The first step is to create an access list definition, and the second step is to apply the access list to an interface.

The two steps are described next in these sections:

- Creating Access Lists
- Applying Access Lists to Interfaces

Creating Access Lists

Create access lists for each protocol you wish to filter, per router interface. For some protocols, you create one access list to filter inbound traffic and one access list to filter outbound traffic.

To create an access list, you specify the protocol to filter, assign a unique name or number to the access list, and define packet-filtering criteria. A single access list can have multiple filtering criteria statements.

Cisco recommends that you create your access lists on a TFTP server and then download the access lists to your router. This can considerably simplify maintenance of your access lists. For details, see the section "Creating and Editing Access List Statements on a TFTP Server" later in this chapter.

The protocols for which you can configure access lists are identified in Table 15-1 and Table 15-2.

Assigning a Unique Name or Number to Each Access List

When configuring access lists on a router, you must identify each access list uniquely within a protocol by assigning either a name or a number to the protocol's access list.

NOTE	Access lists of some protocols must be identified by a name, and access lists of other protocols must be identified by a number. Some protocols can be identified by either a name or a number. When a number is used to identify an access list, the number must be within the specific range of numbers that is valid for the protocol.

You can specify access lists by names for the protocols listed in Table 15-1.

Table 15-1 *Protocols with Access Lists Specified by Names*

Protocol
Apollo Domain
IP
IPX
ISO CLNS
NetBIOS IPX
Source-route bridging NetBIOS

You can specify access lists by numbers for the protocols listed in Table 15-2. Table 15-2 also lists the range of access list numbers that is valid for each protocol.

Table 15-2 *Protocols with Access Lists Specified by Numbers*

Protocol	Range
IP	1 to 99
Extended IP	100 to 199
Ethernet type code	200 to 299
Ethernet address	700 to 799
Transparent bridging (protocol type)	200 to 299
Transparent bridging (vendor code)	700 to 799
Extended transparent bridging	1100 to 1199

Table 15-2 *Protocols with Access Lists Specified by Numbers (Continued)*

Protocol	Range
DECnet and extended DECnet	300 to 399
XNS	400 to 499
Extended XNS	500 to 599
AppleTalk	600 to 699
Source-route bridging (protocol type)	200 to 299
Source-route bridging (vendor code)	700 to 799
IPX	800 to 899
Extended IPX	900 to 999
IPX SAP	1000 to 1099
Standard VINES	1 to 100
Extended VINES	101 to 200
Simple VINES	201 to 300

Defining Criteria for Forwarding or Blocking Packets

When creating an access list, you define criteria that are applied to each packet that is processed by the router; the router decides whether to forward or block each packet based on whether the packet matches the criteria.

Typical criteria you define in access lists are packet source addresses, packet destination addresses, and upper-layer protocol of the packet. However, each protocol has its own specific set of criteria that can be defined.

For a single access list, you can define multiple criteria in multiple, separate access list statements. Each of these statements should reference the same identifying name or number, to tie the statements to the same access list. You can have as many criteria statements as you want, limited only by the available memory. Of course, the more statements you have, the more difficult it will be to comprehend and manage your access lists.

The Implied "Deny All Traffic" Criteria Statement

At the end of every access list is an implied "deny all traffic" criteria statement. Therefore, if a packet does not match any of your criteria statements, the packet will be blocked.

NOTE	For most protocols, if you define an inbound access list for traffic filtering, you should include explicit access list criteria statements to permit routing updates. If you do not, you might effectively lose communication from the interface when routing updates are blocked by the implicit "deny all traffic" statement at the end of the access list.

The Order in Which You Enter Criteria Statements

Note that each additional criteria statement that you enter is appended to the *end* of the access list statements. Also note that you cannot delete individual statements after they have been created. You can only delete an entire access list.

The order of access list statements is important! When the router is deciding whether to forward or block a packet, the Cisco IOS software tests the packet against each criteria statement in the order the statements were created. After a match is found, no more criteria statements are checked.

If you create a criteria statement that explicitly permits all traffic, no statements added later will ever be checked. If you need additional statements, you must delete the access list and retype it with the new entries.

Creating and Editing Access List Statements on a TFTP Server

Because the order of access list criteria statements is important, and because you cannot reorder or delete criteria statements on your router, Cisco recommends that you create all access list statements on a TFTP server, and then download the entire access list to your router.

To use a TFTP server, create the access list statements using any text editor, and save the access list in ASCII format to a TFTP server that is accessible by your router. Then, from your router, use the **copy tftp:***file_id* **system:running-config** command to copy the access list to your router. Finally, perform the **copy system:running-config nvram:startup-config** command to save the access list to your router's NVRAM.

Then, if you ever want to make changes to an access list, you can make them to the text file on the TFTP server, and copy the edited file to your router as before.

NOTE	The first command of an edited access list file should delete the previous access list (for example, type a **no access-list** command at the beginning of the file). If you do not first delete the previous version of the access list, when you copy the edited file to your router you will merely be appending additional criteria statements to the end of the existing access list.

Applying Access Lists to Interfaces

For some protocols, you can apply up to two access lists to an interface: one inbound access list and one outbound access list. With other protocols, you apply only one access list, which checks both inbound and outbound packets.

If the access list is inbound, when the router receives a packet, the Cisco IOS software checks the access list's criteria statements for a match. If the packet is permitted, the software continues to process the packet. If the packet is denied, the software discards the packet.

If the access list is outbound, after receiving and routing a packet to the outbound interface, the software checks the access list's criteria statements for a match. If the packet is permitted, the software transmits the packet. If the packet is denied, the software discards the packet.

Finding Complete Configuration and Command Information for Access Lists

The guidelines discussed in this chapter apply in general to all protocols. The specific instructions for creating access lists and applying them to interfaces vary from protocol to protocol, and this specific information is not included in this chapter.

## CHAPTER 16

Cisco IOS Firewall Overview

This chapter describes how you can configure your Cisco networking device to function as a firewall by using Cisco IOS security features.

This chapter has the following sections:

- Overview of Firewalls
- The Cisco IOS Firewall Solution
- Creating a Customized Firewall
- Other Guidelines for Configuring a Firewall

Overview of Firewalls

Firewalls are networking devices that control access to your organization's network assets. Firewalls are positioned at the entrance points into your network. If your network has multiple entrance points, you must position a firewall at each point to provide effective network access control.

Firewalls are often placed between the internal network and an external network such as the Internet. With a firewall between your network and the Internet, all traffic coming from the Internet must pass through the firewall before entering your network.

Firewalls can also be used to control access to a specific part of your network. For example, you can position firewalls at all the entry points into a research and development network to prevent unauthorized access to proprietary information.

The most basic function of a firewall is to monitor and filter traffic. Firewalls can be simple or elaborate, depending on your network requirements. Simple firewalls are usually easier to configure and manage. However, you might require the flexibility of a more elaborate firewall.

The Cisco IOS Firewall Solution

Cisco IOS software provides an extensive set of security features, allowing you to configure a simple or elaborate firewall, according to your particular requirements. You can configure a Cisco device as a firewall if the device is positioned appropriately at a network entry point. Security features that provide firewall functionality are listed in the "Creating a Customized Firewall" section.

In addition to the security features available in standard Cisco IOS feature sets, there is a Cisco IOS Firewall feature set that gives your router additional firewall capabilities.

The Cisco IOS Firewall Feature Set

The Cisco IOS Firewall feature set combines existing Cisco IOS firewall technology and the new context-based access control (CBAC) feature. When you configure the Cisco IOS Firewall feature set on your Cisco router, you turn your router into an effective, robust firewall.

The Cisco IOS Firewall feature set is designed to prevent unauthorized, external individuals from gaining access to your internal network and to block attacks on your network, while at the same time allowing authorized users to access network resources.

You can use the Cisco IOS Firewall feature set to configure your Cisco IOS router as

- An Internet firewall or part of an Internet firewall

- A firewall between groups in your internal network

- A firewall providing secure connections to or from branch offices

- A firewall between your company's network and your company's partners' networks

The Cisco IOS Firewall feature set provides the following benefits:

- Protects internal networks from intrusion

- Monitors traffic through network perimeters

- Enables network commerce via the World Wide Web

Creating a Customized Firewall

To create a firewall customized to fit your organization's security policy, you should determine which Cisco IOS security features are appropriate, and configure those features. At a minimum, you must configure basic traffic filtering to provide a basic firewall. You can configure your Cisco networking device to function as a firewall by using the following Cisco IOS security features:

- Standard access lists and static extended access lists

- Lock-and-key (dynamic access lists)

- Reflexive access lists

- TCP intercept

- Context-based access control

- Security server support

- Network address translation

- Cisco Encryption Technology

- IPSec network security

- Neighbor router authentication

- Event Logging

- User authentication and authorization

As well as configuring these features, you should follow the guidelines listed in the section "Other Guidelines for Configuring Your Firewall," which outlines important security practices to protect your firewall and network. Table 16-1 describes Cisco IOS security features.

Table 16-1 *Cisco IOS Features for a Robust Firewall*

Feature	Chapter	Comments
Standard access lists and static extended access lists	Chapter 15, "Access Control Lists: Overview and Guidelines"	Standard and static extended access lists provide basic traffic filtering capabilities. You configure criteria that describe which packets should be forwarded and which packets should be dropped at an interface, based on each packet's network layer information. For example, you can block all UDP packets from a specific source IP address or address range. Some extended access lists can also examine transport layer information to determine whether to block or forward packets.
		To configure a basic firewall, at a minimum you should configure basic traffic filtering. You should configure basic access lists for all network protocols that will be routed through your firewall, such as IP, IPX, AppleTalk, and so forth.
Lock-and-key (dynamic access lists)	Chapter 17, "Configuring Lock-and-Key Security (Dynamic Access Lists)"	Lock-and-key security provides traffic filtering with the ability to allow temporary access through the firewall for certain individuals. These individuals must first be authenticated (by a username/password mechanism) before the firewall allows their traffic through the firewall. Afterward, the firewall closes the temporary opening. This provides tighter control over traffic at the firewall than with standard or static extended access lists.
Reflexive access lists	Chapter 19, "Configuring IP Session Filtering (Reflexive Access Lists)"	Reflexive access lists filter IP traffic so that TCP or UDP session traffic is only permitted through the firewall if the session originated from within the internal network.
		You would only configure reflexive access lists when not using CBAC.

Continues

Table 16-1 *Cisco IOS Features for a Robust Firewall (Continued)*

Feature	Chapter	Comments
TCP intercept	Chapter 21, "Configuring TCP Intercept (Prevent Denial-of-Service Attacks)"	TCP Intercept protects TCP servers within your network from TCP SYN-flooding attacks, a type of denial-of-service attack. You would only configure TCP Intercept when not using CBAC.
Context-based access control	Chapter 23, "Configuring Context-Based Access Control"	CBAC examines not only network-layer and transport-layer information, but also examines the application-layer protocol information (such as FTP information) to learn about the state of TCP and UDP connections. CBAC maintains connection state information for individual connections. This state information is used to make intelligent decisions about whether packets should be permitted or denied and dynamically creates and deletes temporary openings in the firewall. CBAC is only available in the Cisco IOS Firewall feature set.
Security server support	Chapter 10, "Configuring TACACS+," Chapter 11, "Configuring TACACS and Extended TACACS," Chapter 8, "Configuring RADIUS," and Chapter 13, "Configuring Kerberos"	The Cisco IOS Firewall feature set can be configured as a client of the following supported security servers: • TACACS, TACACS+, and extended TACACS • RADIUS • Kerberos You can use any of these security servers to store a database of user profiles. To gain access into your firewall or to gain access through the firewall into another network, users must enter authentication information (such as a username and password), which is matched against the information on the security server. When users pass authentication, they are granted access according to their specified privileges.

Table 16-1 *Cisco IOS Features for a Robust Firewall (Continued)*

Feature	Chapter	Comments
Network address translation	Chapter 37, "Configuring IP Security Options"	You can use network address translation (NAT) to hide internal IP network addresses from the world outside the firewall.
		NAT was designed to provide IP address conservation and for internal IP networks that have unregistered (not globally unique) IP addresses: NAT translates these unregistered IP addresses into legal addresses at the firewall. NAT can also be configured to advertise only one address for the entire internal network to the outside world. This provides security by effectively hiding the entire internal network from the world.
		NAT gives you limited spoof protection because internal addresses are hidden. Additionally, NAT removes all your internal services from the external name space.
		NAT does not work with the application-layer protocols RPC, VDOLive, or SQL*Net "Redirected." (NAT does work with SQL*Net "Bequeathed.") Do not configure NAT with networks that will carry traffic for these incompatible protocols.
Cisco Encryption Technology	Chapter 26, "Configuring Cisco Encryption Technology"	Cisco Encryption Technology (CET) selectively encrypts IP packets that are transmitted across unprotected networks such as the Internet. You specify which traffic is considered sensitive and should be encrypted. This encryption prevents sensitive IP packets from being intercepted and read or tampered with.
IPSec network security	Chapter 28, "Configuring IPSec Network Security"	IPSec is a framework of open standards developed by the Internet Engineering Task Force (IETF) that provides security for transmission of sensitive information over unprotected networks such as the Internet. IPSec acts at the network layer, protecting and authenticating IP packets between participating IPSec devices (or *peers*) such as Cisco routers.
		IPSec services are similar to those provided by Cisco Encryption Technology, a proprietary security solution introduced in Cisco IOS Software Release 11.2. (The IPSec standard was not yet available at Release 11.2.) However, IPSec provides a more robust security solution and is standards based.

Continues

Table 16-1 *Cisco IOS Features for a Robust Firewall (Continued)*

Feature	Chapter	Comments
Neighbor router authentication	Chapter 36, "Neighbor Router Authentication: Overview and Guidelines"	Neighbor router authentication requires the firewall to authenticate all neighbor routers before accepting any route updates from that neighbor. This ensures that the firewall receives legitimate route updates from a trusted source.
User authentication and authorization	Chapter 2, "Configuring Authentication" and Chapter 4, "Configuring Authorization"	Authentication and authorization help protect your network from access by unauthorized users.

Other Guidelines for Configuring a Firewall

As with all networking devices, you should always protect access into the firewall by configuring passwords as described in Chapter 34, "Configuring Passwords and Privileges." You should also consider configuring user authentication, authorization, and accounting as described in the chapters in Part 1, "Authentication, Authorization, and Accounting (AAA)."

You should also consider the following recommendations:

● When setting passwords for privileged access to the firewall, use the **enable secret** command rather than the **enable password** command, which does not have as strong an encryption algorithm.

● Put a password on the console port. In AAA environments, use the same authentication for the console as for elsewhere. In non-AAA environments, at a minimum configure the **login** and **password** *password* commands.

● Think about access control *before* you connect a console port to the network in any way, including attaching a modem to the port. Be aware that a *break* on the console port might give total control of the firewall, even with access control configured.

● Apply access lists and password protection to all virtual terminal ports. Use access lists to limit who can Telnet into your router.

● Do not enable any local service (such as SNMP or NTP) that you do not use. Cisco Discovery Protocol (CDP) and Network Time Protocol (NTP) are on by default, and you should turn these off if you do not need them.

   To turn off CDP, enter the **no cdp run** global configuration command. To turn off NTP, enter the **ntp disable** interface configuration command on each interface not using NTP.

   If you must run NTP, configure NTP only on required interfaces, and configure NTP to listen only to certain peers.

Any enabled service could present a potential security risk. A determined, hostile party might be able to find creative ways to misuse the enabled services to access the firewall or the network.

For local services that are enabled, protect against misuse. Protect by configuring the services to communicate only with specific peers, and protect by configuring access lists to deny packets for the services at specific interfaces.

- Protect against spoofing: Protect the networks on both sides of the firewall from being spoofed from the other side. You could protect against spoofing by configuring input access lists at all interfaces to pass only traffic from expected source addresses and to deny all other traffic.

  You should also disable source routing. For IP, enter the **no ip source-route** global configuration command. Disabling source routing at *all* routers can also help prevent spoofing.

  You should also disable minor services. For IP, enter the **no service tcp-small-servers** and **no service udp-small-servers** global configuration commands.

- Prevent the firewall from being used as a relay by configuring access lists on any asynchronous Telnet ports.

- Normally, you should disable directed broadcasts for all applicable protocols on your firewall and on all your other routers. For IP, use the **no ip directed-broadcast** command. Rarely, some IP networks require directed broadcasts; if this is the case, do not disable directed broadcasts.

  Directed broadcasts can be misused to multiply the power of denial-of-service attacks because every denial-of-service packet sent is broadcast to every host on a subnet. Furthermore, some hosts have other intrinsic security risks present when handling broadcasts.

- Configure the **no proxy-arp** command to prevent internal addresses from being revealed. (This is important to do if you do not already have NAT configured to prevent internal addresses from being revealed.)

- Keep the firewall in a secured (locked) room.

## CHAPTER 17

Configuring Lock-and-Key Security (Dynamic Access Lists)

This chapter describes how to configure lock-and-key security at your router. Lock-and-key is a traffic filtering security feature available for the IP protocol.

For a complete description of lock-and-key commands, refer to Chapter 18, "Lock-and-Key Commands." To locate documentation of other commands that appear in this chapter, you can search online at www.cisco.com.

This chapter has the following sections:

- About Lock-and-Key
- Compatibility with Releases Prior to Cisco IOS Release 11.1
- Risk of Spoofing with Lock-and-Key
- Router Performance Impacts with Lock-and-Key
- Prerequisites to Configuring Lock-and-Key
- Configuring Lock-and-Key
- Verifying Lock-and-Key Configuration
- Lock-and-Key Maintenance
- Lock-and-Key Configuration Examples

About Lock-and-Key

Lock-and-key is a traffic filtering security feature that dynamically filters IP protocol traffic. Lock-and-key is configured using IP dynamic extended access lists. Lock-and-key can be used in conjunction with other standard access lists and static extended access lists.

When lock-and-key is configured, designated users whose IP traffic is normally blocked at a router can gain temporary access through the router. When triggered, lock-and-key reconfigures the interface's existing IP access list to permit designated users to reach their designated host(s). Afterward, lock-and-key reconfigures the interface back to its original state.

For a user to gain access to a host through a router with lock-and-key configured, the user must first Telnet to the router. When a user initiates a standard Telnet session to the router, lock-and-key automatically attempts to authenticate the user. If the user is authenticated, the user then gains temporary access through the router and can reach the destination host.

Benefits of Lock-and-Key

Lock-and-key provides the same benefits as standard and static extended access lists (these benefits are discussed in Chapter 15, "Access Control Lists: Overview and Guidelines"). However, lock-and-key also has the following security benefits over standard and static extended access lists:

- Lock-and-key uses a challenge mechanism to authenticate individual users.

- Lock-and-key provides simpler management in large internetworks.

- In many cases, lock-and-key reduces the amount of router processing required for access lists.

- Lock-and-key reduces the opportunity for network break-ins by network hackers.

With lock-and-key, you can specify which users are permitted access to which source/destination hosts. These users must pass a user authentication process before they are permitted access to their designated host(s). Lock-and-key creates dynamic user access through a firewall, without compromising other configured security restrictions.

When to Use Lock-and-Key

Two examples of when you might use lock-and-key are as follows:

- When you want a specific remote user (or group of remote users) to be able to access a host within your network, connecting from their remote host(s) via the Internet. Lock-and-key authenticates the user and then permits limited access through your firewall router for the individual's host or subnet for a finite period of time.

- When you want a subset of hosts on a local network to access a host on a remote network protected by a firewall. With lock-and-key, you can enable access to the remote host only for the desired set of local user's hosts. Lock-and-key requires the users to authenticate through a TACACS+ server, or other security server, before allowing their hosts to access the remote hosts.

How Lock-and-Key Works

The following process describes the lock-and-key access operation:

1 A user opens a Telnet session to a border (firewall) router configured for lock-and-key. The user connects via the virtual terminal port on the router.

2 The Cisco IOS software receives the Telnet packet, opens a Telnet session, prompts for a password, and performs a user authentication process. The user must pass authentication before access through the router is allowed. The authentication process can be done by the router or by a central access security server such as a TACACS+ or RADIUS server.

3 When the user passes authentication, he or she is logged out of the Telnet session, and the software creates a temporary entry in the dynamic access list. (Depending on the configuration, this temporary entry can limit the range of networks to which the user is given temporary access.)

4 The user exchanges data through the firewall.

5 The software deletes the temporary access list entry when a configured timeout is reached, or when the system administrator manually clears it. The configured timeout can either be an idle timeout or an absolute timeout.

NOTE   The temporary access list entry is not automatically deleted when the user terminates a session. The temporary access list entry remains until a configured timeout is reached or until it is cleared by the system administrator.

Compatibility with Releases Prior to Cisco IOS Release 11.1

Enhancements to the **access-list** command are used for lock-and-key. These enhancements are backward compatible—if you migrate from a release prior to Cisco IOS Release 11.1 to a newer release, your access lists will be automatically converted to reflect the enhancements. However, if you try to use lock-and-key with a release prior to Cisco IOS Release 11.1, you might encounter problems as described in the following caution paragraph.

CAUTION   Cisco IOS releases prior to Release 11.1 are not upwardly compatible with the lock-and-key access list enhancements. Therefore, if you save an access list with software older than Release 11.1, and then use this software, the resulting access list will not be interpreted correctly. *This could cause you severe security problems.* You must save your old configuration files with Cisco IOS Release 11.1 or later software before booting an image with these files.

Risk of Spoofing with Lock-and-Key

CAUTION   Lock-and-key access allows an external event (a Telnet session) to place an opening in the firewall. While this opening exists, the router is susceptible to source address spoofing.

When lock-and-key is triggered, it creates a dynamic opening in the firewall by temporarily reconfiguring an interface to allow user access. While this opening exists, another host might spoof the authenticated user's address to gain access behind the firewall. Lock-and-key does not cause the address spoofing problem; the problem is only identified here as a concern to the user. Spoofing is a problem inherent to all access lists, and lock-and-key does not specifically address this problem.

To prevent spoofing, you could configure network data encryption as described in Chapter 26, "Configuring Cisco Encryption Technology." Configure encryption so that traffic from the remote host is encrypted at a secured remote router and decrypted locally at the router interface providing lock-and-key. You want to ensure that all traffic using lock-and-key will be encrypted when entering the router; this way no hackers can spoof the source address, because they will be unable to duplicate the encryption or to be authenticated as required by the encryption setup process.

Router Performance Impacts with Lock-and-Key

When lock-and-key is configured, router performance can be affected in the following ways:

- When lock-and-key is triggered, the dynamic access list forces an access list rebuild on the silicon switching engine (SSE). This causes the SSE switching path to slow down momentarily.

- Dynamic access lists require the idle timeout facility (even if the timeout is left to default) and therefore cannot be SSE switched. These entries must be handled in the protocol fast-switching path.

- When remote users trigger lock-and-key at a border router, additional access list entries are created on the border router interface. The interface's access list grows and shrinks dynamically. Entries are dynamically removed from the list after either the idle-timeout or max-timeout period expires. Large access lists can degrade packet switching performance, so if you notice performance problems, you should look at the border router configuration to see if you should remove temporary access list entries generated by lock-and-key.

Prerequisites to Configuring Lock-and-Key

Lock-and-key uses IP extended access lists. You must have a solid understanding of how access lists are used to filter traffic before you attempt to configure lock-and-key. Access lists are described in Chapter 15, "Access Control Lists: Overview and Guidelines."

Lock-and-key employs user authentication and authorization as implemented in Cisco's authentication, authorization, and accounting (AAA) paradigm. You must understand how to configure AAA user authentication and authorization before you configure lock-and-key. User authentication and authorization is explained in Part I, "Authentication, Authorization, and Accounting (AAA)."

Lock-and-key uses the **autocommand** command, which you should understand.

Configuring Lock-and-Key

To configure lock-and-key, use the following commands beginning in global configuration mode. While completing these steps, be sure to follow the guidelines listed in the "Lock-and-Key Configuration Tips" section.

Step	Command	Purpose
1	**access-list** *access-list-number* [**dynamic** *dynamic-name* [**timeout** *minutes*]] {**deny**	**permit**} **telnet** *source source-wildcard destination destination-wildcard* [**precedence** *precedence*] [**tos** *tos*] [**established**] [**log**]	Configures a dynamic access list, which serves as a template and placeholder for temporary access list entries.
2	**interface** *type number*	Configures an interface.
3	**ip access-group** *access-list-number*	In interface configuration mode, applies the access list to the interface.
4	**line VTY** *line-number* [*ending-line-number*]	In global configuration mode, defines one or more virtual terminal (VTY) ports. If you specify multiple VTY ports, they must all be configured identically because the software hunts for available VTY ports on a round-robin basis. If you do not want to configure all your VTY ports for lock-and-key access, you can specify a group of VTY ports for lock-and-key support only.

Step	Command	Purpose
5	**login tacacs** or **username** *name* **password** *secret* or **password** *password* **login local**	Configures user authentication.
6	**autocommand access-enable** [**host**] [**timeout** *minutes*]	Enables the creation of temporary access list entries. If the **host** argument is *not* specified, all hosts on the entire network are allowed to set up a temporary access list entry. The dynamic access list contains the network mask to enable the new network connection.

For an example of a lock-and-key configuration, see the section "Lock-and-Key Configuration Examples" later in this chapter.

Lock-and-Key Configuration Tips

You should understand the tips in this section before you configure lock-and-key.

Dynamic Access Lists

Use the following tips for configuring dynamic access lists:

- Do *not* create more than one dynamic access list for any one access list. The software only refers to the first dynamic access list defined.

- Do *not* assign the same *dynamic-name* to another access list. Doing so instructs the software to reuse the existing list. All named entries must be globally unique within the configuration.

- Assign attributes to the dynamic access list in the same way you assign attributes for a static access list. The temporary access list entries inherit the attributes assigned to this list.

- Configure Telnet as the protocol, so that the user must Telnet into the router to be authenticated before he or she can gain access through the router.

- Either define an idle timeout now with the **timeout** keyword in the **access-list** command, or define an absolute timeout value later with the **access-enable** command in the **autocommand** command. You must define either an idle timeout or an absolute timeout—otherwise, the temporary access list entry remains configured indefinitely on the interface (even after the user has terminated their session) until the entry is removed manually by an administrator. (You could configure both idle and absolute timeouts.)

- If you configure an idle timeout, the idle timeout value should be equal to the WAN idle timeout value.

- If you configure both idle and absolute timeouts, the idle timeout value must be less than the absolute timeout value.

- The only values replaced in the temporary entry are the source or destination address, depending whether the access list was in the input access list or output access list. All other attributes, such as port, are inherited from the main dynamic access list.

- Each addition to the dynamic list is always put at the beginning of the dynamic list. You cannot specify the order of temporary access list entries.

- Temporary access list entries are never written to NVRAM.

- To manually clear or to display dynamic access lists, refer to the section "Lock-and-Key Maintenance" later in this chapter.

Lock-and-Key Authentication

There are three possible methods to configure an authentication query process. These three methods are described in this section.

NOTE   Cisco recommends that you use the TACACS+ server for your authentication query process. TACACS+ provides authentication, authorization, and accounting services. It also provides protocol support, protocol specification, and a centralized security database. Using a TACACS+ server is described in the next section, "Method 1—Configuring a Security Server."

Method 1—Configuring a Security Server

Use a network access security server such as TACACS+ server. This method requires additional configuration steps on the TACACS+ server but allows for stricter authentication queries and more sophisticated tracking capabilities.

```
Router# login tacacs
```

Method 2—Configuring the **username** Command

Use the **username** command. This method is more effective because authentication is determined on a user basis.

```
Router# username name password password
```

Method 3—Configuring the **password** and **login** Commands

Use the **password** and **login** commands. This method is less effective because the password is configured for the port, not for the user. Therefore, any user who knows the password can authenticate successfully.

```
Router# password password
Router# login local
```

The **autocommand** Command

Use the following tips for configuring the **autocommand** command:

- If you use a TACACS+ server to authenticate the user, you should configure the **autocommand** command on the TACACS+ server as a per-user autocommand. If you use local authentication, use the **autocommand** command on the line.

- Configure all VTY ports with the same **autocommand** command. Omitting an **autocommand** command on a VTY port allows a random host to gain EXEC mode access to the router and does not create a temporary access list entry in the dynamic access list.

- If you did not previously define an idle timeout with the **access-list** command, you must define an absolute timeout now with the **autocommand access-enable** command. You must define either an idle timeout or an absolute timeout—otherwise, the temporary access list entry remains configured indefinitely on the interface (even after the user has terminated their session) until the entry is removed manually by an administrator. (You could configure both idle and absolute timeouts.)

- If you configure both idle and absolute timeouts, the absolute timeout value must be greater than the idle timeout value.

Verifying Lock-and-Key Configuration

You can verify that lock-and-key is successfully configured on the router by asking a user to test the connection. The user should be at a host that is permitted in the dynamic access list, and the user should have AAA authentication and authorization configured.

To test the connection, the user should Telnet to the router, allow the Telnet session to close, and then attempt to access a host on the other side of the router. This host must be one that is permitted by the dynamic access list. The user should access the host with an application that uses IP.

The following sample display illustrates what end users might see if they are successfully authenticated. Notice that the Telnet connection is closed immediately after the password is entered and authenticated. The temporary access list entry is then created, and the host that initiated the Telnet session now has access inside the firewall.

```
Router% telnet corporate
Trying 172.21.52.1 ...
Connected to corporate.domain.com.
```

```
Escape character is '^]'.
User Access Verification
Password:Connection closed by foreign host.
```

You can then use the **show access-lists** command at the router to view the dynamic access lists, which should include an additional entry permitting the user access through the router.

Lock-and-Key Maintenance

When lock-and-key is in use, dynamic access lists dynamically grow and shrink as entries are added and deleted. You need to make sure that entries are being deleted in a timely way, because while entries exist, the risk of a spoofing attack is present. Also, the more entries there are, the bigger the router performance impact will be.

If you do not have an idle or absolute timeout configured, entries remain in the dynamic access list until you manually remove them. If this is the case, make sure that you are extremely vigilant about removing entries.

Displaying Dynamic Access List Entries

You can display temporary access list entries when they are in use. After a temporary access list entry is cleared by you or by the absolute or idle timeout parameter, it can no longer be displayed. The number of matches displayed indicates the number of times the access list entry was hit.

To view dynamic access lists and any temporary access list entries that are currently established, use the following command in privileged EXEC mode:

Command	Purpose
show access-lists [*access-list-number*]	Displays dynamic access lists and temporary access list entries.

Manually Deleting Dynamic Access List Entries

To manually delete a temporary access list entry, use the following command in privileged EXEC mode:

Command	Purpose
clear access-template [*access-list-number* | *name*] [*dynamic-name*] [*source*] [*destination*]	Deletes a dynamic access list.

Lock-and-Key Configuration Examples

There are two examples in this section:

- Example of Lock-and-Key with Local Authentication

- Example of Lock-and-Key with TACACS+ Authentication

Cisco recommends that you use a TACACS+ server for authentication, as shown in the second example.

Example of Lock-and-Key with Local Authentication

This example shows how to configure lock-and-key access with authentication occurring locally at the router. Lock-and-key is configured on the Ethernet 0 interface.

```
interface ethernet0
 ip address 172.18.23.9 255.255.255.0
 ip access-group 101 in

access-list 101 permit tcp any host 172.18.21.2 eq telnet
access-list 101 dynamic mytestlist timeout 120 permit ip any any

line vty 0
login local
autocommand access-enable timeout 5
```

The first access-list entry allows only Telnet into the router. The second access-list entry is always ignored until lock-and-key is triggered.

After a user Telnets into the router, the router attempts to authenticate the user. If authentication is successful, the **autocommand** executes and the Telnet session terminates. The **autocommand** creates a temporary inbound access list entry at the Ethernet 0 interface, based on the second access-list entry (mytestlist). This temporary entry expires after 5 minutes, as specified by the timeout.

Example of Lock-and-Key with TACACS+ Authentication

The following example shows how to configure lock-and-key access with authentication on a TACACS+ server. Lock-and-key access is configured on the BRI0 interface. Four VTY ports are defined with the password *cisco*.

```
aaa authentication login default tacacs+ enable
aaa accounting exec stop-only tacacs+
aaa accounting network stop-only tacacs+
enable password ciscotac
!
isdn switch-type basic-dms100
!
interface ethernet0
ip address 172.18.23.9 255.255.255.0
!!
```

```
interface BRI0
 ip address 172.18.21.1 255.255.255.0
 encapsulation ppp
 dialer idle-timeout 3600
 dialer wait-for-carrier-time 100
 dialer map ip 172.18.21.2 name diana
 dialer-group 1
 isdn spid1 2036333715291
 isdn spid2 2036339371566
 ppp authentication chap
 ip access-group 102 in
!
access-list 102 permit tcp any host 172.18.21.2 eq telnet
access-list 102 dynamic testlist timeout 5 permit ip any any
!
!
ip route 172.18.250.0 255.255.255.0 172.18.21.2
priority-list 1 interface BRI0 high
tacacs-server host 172.18.23.21
tacacs-server host 172.18.23.14
tacacs-server key test1
tftp-server rom alias all
!
dialer-list 1 protocol ip permit
!
line con 0
 password cisco
line aux 0
line VTY 0 4
autocommand access-enable timeout 5
password cisco
!
```

## CHAPTER 18

Lock-and-Key Commands

This chapter describes lock-and-key commands. Lock-and-key security is a traffic filtering security feature that uses dynamic access lists. Lock-and-key is available for IP traffic only.

You can search online at www.cisco.com to find complete descriptions of other commands used when configuring lock-and-key.

For lock-and-key configuration information, refer to Chapter 17, "Configuring Lock-and-Key Security (Dynamic Access Lists)."

access-enable

To enable the router to create a temporary access list entry in a dynamic access list, use the **access-enable** EXEC command.

> **access-enable** [**host**] [**timeout** *minutes*]

Syntax	Description
host	(Optional) Tells the software to enable access only for the host from which the Telnet session originated. If not specified, the software allows all hosts on the defined network to gain access. The dynamic access list contains the network mask to use for enabling the new network.
timeout *minutes*	(Optional) Specifies an idle timeout for the temporary access list entry. If the access list entry is not accessed within this period, it is automatically deleted and requires the user to authenticate again. The default is for the entries to remain permanently. Cisco recommends that this value equal the idle timeout set for the WAN connection.

Command Mode
EXEC

Usage Guidelines
This command first appeared in Cisco IOS Release 11.1.

This command enables the lock-and-key access feature.

You should always define either an idle timeout (with the **timeout** keyword in this command) or an absolute timeout (with the **timeout** keyword in the **access-list** command). Otherwise, the temporary access list entry will remain, even after the user terminates the session.

Use the **autocommand** command with the **access-enable** command to cause the **access-enable** command to execute when a user Telnets into the router.

Example

The following example causes the software to create a temporary access list entry and tells the software to enable access only for the host from which the Telnet session originated. If the access list entry is not accessed within 2 minutes, it is deleted.

```
autocommand access-enable host timeout 2
```

Related Commands

You can search online at www.cisco.com to find documentation of related commands.

access-list (extended)
autocommand

access-template

To manually place a temporary access list entry on a router to which you are connected, use the **access-template** EXEC command.

> **access-template** [*access-list-number* | *name*] [*dynamic-name*] [*source*] [*destination*] [**timeout** *minutes*]

Syntax	Description
access-list-number	(Optional) Number of the dynamic access list.
name	(Optional) Name of an IP access list. The name cannot contain a space or quotation mark, and must begin with an alphabetic character to avoid ambiguity with numbered access lists.
dynamic-name	(Optional) Name of a dynamic access list.
source	(Optional) Source address in a dynamic access list. The keywords **host** and **any** are allowed. All other attributes are inherited from the original access list entry.
destination	(Optional) Destination address in a dynamic access list. The keywords **host** and **any** are allowed. All other attributes are inherited from the original access list entry.

Syntax	Description
timeout *minutes*	(Optional) Specifies a maximum time limit for each entry within this dynamic list. This is an absolute time, from creation, that an entry can reside in the list. The default is an infinite time limit and allows an entry to remain permanently.

Command Mode

EXEC

Usage Guidelines

This command first appeared in Cisco IOS Release 11.1.

This command provides a way to enable the lock-and-key access feature.

You should always define either an idle timeout (with the **timeout** keyword in this command) or an absolute timeout (with the **timeout** keyword in the **access-list** command). Otherwise, the dynamic access list will remain, even after the user has terminated the session.

Example

In the following example, the software enables IP access on incoming packets in which the source address is 172.29.1.129 and the destination address is 192.168.52.12. All other source and destination pairs are discarded.

```
access-template 101 payroll host 172.29.1.129 host 192.168.52.12 timeout 2
```

Related Commands

You can search online at www.cisco.com to find documentation of related commands.

access-list (extended)
autocommand
clear access-template

clear access-template

To manually clear a temporary access list entry from a dynamic access list, use the **clear access-template** EXEC command.

> **clear access-template** [*access-list-number* | *name*] [*dynamic-name*] [*source*]
> [*destination*]

Syntax	Description
access-list-number	(Optional) Number of the dynamic access list from which the entry is to be deleted.
name	(Optional) Name of an IP access list from which the entry is to be deleted. The name cannot contain a space or quotation mark and must begin with an alphabetic character to avoid ambiguity with numbered access lists.
dynamic-name	(Optional) Name of the dynamic access list from which the entry is to be deleted.
source	(Optional) Source address in a temporary access list entry to be deleted.
destination	(Optional) Destination address in a temporary access list entry to be deleted.

Command Mode

EXEC

Usage Guidelines

This command first appeared in Cisco IOS Release 11.1.

This command is related to the lock-and-key access feature. It clears any temporary access list entries that match the parameters you define.

Example

The following example clears any temporary access list entries with a source of 172.20.1.12 from the dynamic access list named vendor:

```
clear access-template vendor 172.20.1.12
```

Related Commands

You can search online at www.cisco.com to find documentation of related commands.

access-list (extended)
access-template

show ip accounting

To display the active accounting or checkpointed database or to display access-list violations, use the **show ip accounting** privileged EXEC command.

> **show ip accounting** [**checkpoint**] [**output-packets** | **access-violations**]

Syntax	Description
checkpoint	(Optional) Indicates that the checkpointed database should be displayed.
output-packets	(Optional) Indicates that information pertaining to packets that passed access control and were successfully routed should be displayed. This is the default value if neither **output-packet**s nor **access-violations** is specified.
access-violations	(Optional) Indicates that information pertaining to packets that failed access lists and were not routed should be displayed.

Defaults

If neither the **output-packets** nor **access-violations** keyword is specified, **show ip accounting** displays information pertaining to packets that passed access control and were successfully routed.

Command Mode

Privileged EXEC

Usage Guidelines

This command first appeared in Cisco IOS Release 10.0.

To use this command, you must first enable IP accounting on a per-interface basis.

Sample Displays

Following is sample output from the **show ip accounting** command:

```
Router# show ip accounting

Source          Destination        Packets           Bytes
172.30.19.40    172.30.67.20             7             306
172.30.13.55    172.30.67.20            67            2749
172.30.2.50     172.30.33.51            17            1111
172.30.2.50     172.30.2.1               5             319
172.30.2.50     172.30.1.2             463           30991
172.30.19.40    172.30.2.1               4             262
172.30.19.40    172.30.1.2              28            2552
172.30.20.2     172.30.6.100            39            2184
172.30.13.55    172.30.1.2              35            3020
172.30.19.40    172.30.33.51          1986           95091
172.30.2.50     172.30.67.20           233           14908
172.30.13.28    172.30.67.53           390           24817
172.30.13.55    172.30.33.51        214669         9806659
```

```
172.30.13.111   172.30.6.23          27739        1126607
172.30.13.44    172.30.33.51         35412        1523980
172.30.7.21     172.30.1.2              11            824
172.30.13.28    172.30.33.2             21           1762
172.30.2.166    172.30.7.130           797         141054
172.30.3.11     172.30.67.53             4            246
172.30.7.21     172.30.33.51         15696         695635
172.30.7.24     172.30.67.20            21            916
172.30.13.111   172.30.10.1             16           1137
```

Table 18-1 describes fields shown in the display.

Table 18-1 *show ip accounting* *Field Descriptions*

Field	Description
Source	Source address of the packet.
Destination	Destination address of the packet.
Packets	Number of packets transmitted from the source address to the destination address.
Bytes	Number of bytes transmitted from the source address to the destination address.

Following is sample output from the **show ip accounting access-violations** command, which displays information pertaining to packets that failed access lists and were not routed:

```
Router# show ip accounting access-violations

  Source          Destination     Packets       Bytes        ACL
  172.30.19.40    172.30.67.20          7          306         77
  172.30.13.55    172.30.67.20         67         2749        185
  172.30.2.50     172.30.33.51         17         1111        140
  172.30.2.50     172.30.2.1            5          319        140
  172.30.19.40    172.30.2.1            4          262         77
Accounting data age is 41
```

Table 18-2 describes fields shown in the display.

Table 18-2 *show ip accounting access-violation* *Field Descriptions*

Field	Description
Source	Source address of the packet.
Destination	Destination address of the packet.
Packets	For **accounting** keyword, number of packets transmitted from the source address to the destination address. For **access-violations** keyword, number of packets transmitted from the source address to the destination address that violated the access control list.

Table 18-2 *show ip accounting access-violation* Field Descriptions (Continued)

Field	Description
Bytes	For **accounting** keyword, number of bytes transmitted from the source address to the destination address.
	For **access-violations** keyword, number of bytes transmitted from the source address to the destination address that violated the access control list.
ACL	Number of the access list of the last packet transmitted from the source to the destination that failed an access list.

Related Commands

You can search online at www.cisco.com to find documentation of related commands.

clear ip accounting
ip accounting
ip accounting-list
ip accounting-threshold
ip accounting-transits

## CHAPTER 19

Configuring IP Session Filtering (Reflexive Access Lists)

This chapter describes how to configure reflexive access lists on your router. Reflexive access lists provide the ability to filter network traffic at a router, based on IP upper-layer protocol session information.

For a complete description of reflexive access list commands, refer to Chapter 20, "Reflexive Access List Commands." To locate documentation of other commands that appear in this chapter, you can search online at www.cisco.com.

This chapter has the following sections:

- About Reflexive Access Lists

- Prework: Before You Configure Reflexive Access Lists

- Configuring Reflexive Access Lists

- Reflexive Access Lists Configuration Examples

About Reflexive Access Lists

Reflexive access lists allow IP packets to be filtered based on upper-layer session information. You can use reflexive access lists to permit IP traffic for sessions originating from within your network but to deny IP traffic for sessions originating from outside your network. This is accomplished by reflexive filtering, a kind of session filtering.

Reflexive access lists can be defined with extended named IP access lists only. You cannot define reflexive access lists with numbered or standard named IP access lists or with other protocol access lists.

You can use reflexive access lists in conjunction with other standard access lists and static extended access lists.

Benefits of Reflexive Access Lists

Reflexive access lists are an important part of securing your network against network hackers and can be included in a firewall defense. Reflexive access lists provide a level of security against spoofing and certain denial-of-service attacks. Reflexive access lists are simple to use, and compared to basic access lists, provide greater control over which packets enter your network.

What Is a Reflexive Access List?

Reflexive access lists are similar in many ways to other access lists. Reflexive access lists contain condition statements (entries) that define criteria for permitting IP packets. These entries are evaluated in order, and when a match occurs, no more entries are evaluated.

However, reflexive access lists have significant differences from other types of access lists. Reflexive access lists contain only temporary entries; these entries are automatically created when a new IP session begins (for example, with an outbound packet), and the entries are removed when the session ends. Reflexive access lists are not themselves applied directly to an interface, but are nested within an extended named IP access list that is applied to the interface. (For more information about this, see the section "Configuring Reflexive Access Lists" later in this chapter.) Also, reflexive access lists do not have the usual implicit "deny all traffic" statement at the end of the list because of the nesting.

How Reflexive Access Lists Implement Session Filtering

This section compares session filtering with basic access lists to session filtering with reflexive access lists.

Implementing Session Filtering with Basic Access Lists

With basic standard and static extended access lists, you can approximate session filtering by using the **established** keyword with the **permit** command. The **established** keyword filters TCP packets based on whether the ACK or RST bits are set. (Set ACK or RST bits indicate that the packet is not the first in the session, and therefore, that the packet belongs to an established session.) This filter criterion would be part of an access list applied permanently to an interface.

Implementing Session Filtering with Reflexive Access Lists

Reflexive access lists provide a truer form of session filtering, which is much harder to spoof because more filter criteria must be matched before a packet is permitted through. (For example, source and destination addresses and port numbers are checked, not just ACK and RST bits.) Also, session filtering uses temporary filters, which are removed when a session is over. This limits the hacker's attack opportunity to a smaller time window.

Moreover, the previous method of using the **established** keyword was available only for the TCP upper-layer protocol. So, for the other upper-layer protocols (such as UDP, ICMP, and so forth), you would have to either permit all incoming traffic or define all possible permissible source/destination host/port address pairs for each protocol. (Besides being an unmanageable task, this could exhaust NVRAM space.)

Where to Configure Reflexive Access Lists

Configure reflexive access lists on border routers—routers that pass traffic between an internal and external network. Often, these are firewall routers.

NOTE	In this chapter, the phrases *within your network* and *internal network* refer to a network that is controlled (secured), such as your organization's intranet, or to a part of your organization's internal network that has higher security requirements than another part. *Outside your network* and *external network* refer to a network that is uncontrolled (unsecured), such as the Internet, or to a part of your organization's network that is not as highly secured.

How Reflexive Access Lists Work

A reflexive access list is triggered when a new IP upper-layer session (such as TCP or UDP) is initiated from inside your network, with a packet traveling to the external network. When triggered, the reflexive access list generates a new, temporary entry. This entry will permit traffic to enter your network if the traffic is part of the session, but will not permit traffic to enter your network if the traffic is not part of the session.

For example, if an outbound TCP packet is forwarded to outside your network and this packet is the first packet of a TCP session, then a new, temporary reflexive access list entry will be created. This entry is added to the reflexive access list, which applies to inbound traffic. The temporary entry has the following characteristics:

- The entry is always a **permit** entry.

- The entry specifies the same protocol (TCP) as the original outbound TCP packet.

- The entry specifies the same source and destination addresses as the original outbound TCP packet, except the addresses are swapped.

- The entry specifies the same source and destination port numbers as the original outbound TCP packet, except the port numbers are swapped. (This entry characteristic applies only for TCP and UDP packets. Other protocols, such as ICMP and IGMP, do not have port numbers, and other criteria are specified. For example, for ICMP, type numbers are used instead.)

- Inbound TCP traffic will be evaluated against the entry until the entry expires. If an inbound TCP packet matches the entry, the inbound packet will be forwarded into your network.

- The entry will expire (be removed) after the last packet of the session passes through the interface.

- If no packets belonging to the session are detected for a configurable length of time (the timeout period), the entry will expire.

Temporary reflexive access list entries are removed at the end of the session. For TCP sessions, the entry is removed 5 seconds after two set FIN bits are detected or immediately after matching a TCP packet with the RST bit set. (Two set FIN bits in a session indicate that the session is about to end; the 5-second window allows the session to close gracefully. A set RST bit indicates an abrupt session close.) Or, the temporary entry is removed after no packets of the session have been detected for a configurable length of time (the timeout period).

For UDP and other protocols, the end of the session is determined differently than for TCP. Because other protocols are considered to be connectionless (sessionless) services, there is no session tracking information embedded in packets. Therefore, the end of a session is considered to be when no packets of the session have been detected for a configurable length of time (the timeout period).

Restrictions on Using Reflexive Access Lists

Reflexive access lists do not work with some applications that use port numbers that change during a session. For example, if the port numbers for a return packet are different from those for the originating packet, the return packet will be denied, even if the packet is actually part of the same session.

The TCP application of FTP is an example of an application with changing port numbers. With reflexive access lists, if you start an FTP request from within your network, the request will not complete. Instead, you must use passive FTP when originating requests from within your network.

Prework: Before You Configure Reflexive Access Lists

Before you configure reflexive access lists, you must decide whether to configure reflexive access lists on an internal or external interface, as described in the next section, "Choosing an Interface: Internal or External."

You should also be sure that you have a basic understanding of IP and of access lists; specifically, you should know how to configure extended named IP access lists.

Choosing an Interface: Internal or External

Reflexive access lists are most commonly used with one of two basic network topologies. Determining which of these topologies is most like your own can help you decide whether to use reflexive access lists with an internal interface or with an external interface (the interface connecting to an internal network, or the interface connecting to an external network).

The first topology is shown in Figure 19-1. In this simple topology, reflexive access lists are configured for the *external* interface Serial 1. This prevents IP traffic from entering the router and the internal network, unless the traffic is part of a session already established from within the internal network.

Figure 19-1 *Simple Topology—Reflexive Access Lists Configured at the External Interface*

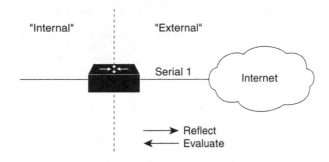

The second topology is shown in Figure 19-2. In this topology, reflexive access lists are configured for the *internal* interface Ethernet 0. This allows external traffic to access the services in the Demilitarized Zone (DMZ), such as DNS services, but prevents IP traffic from entering your internal network—unless the traffic is part of a session already established from within the internal network.

Figure 19-2 *DMZ Topology—Reflexive Access Lists Configured at the Internal Interface*

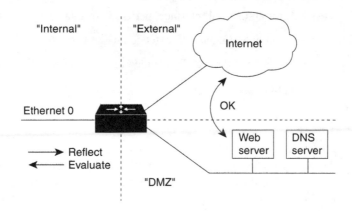

Use these two sample topologies to determine whether to configure reflexive access lists for an internal or external interface.

Configuring Reflexive Access Lists

In the previous section, "Prework: Before You Configure Reflexive Access Lists," you decided whether to configure reflexive access lists for an internal or external interface.

Now, complete the tasks in one of the following configuration task lists.

External Interface Configuration Task List

To configure reflexive access lists for an external interface, perform these tasks:

1 Define the reflexive access list(s) in an *outbound* IP extended named access list.

2 Nest the reflexive access list(s) in an *inbound* IP extended named access list.

3 Set a global timeout value (optional).

These tasks are described in the sections following the internal interface configuration task list.

NOTE   The defined (outbound) reflexive access list evaluates traffic traveling out of your network: If the defined reflexive access list is matched, temporary entries are created in the nested (inbound) reflexive access list. These temporary entries will then be applied to traffic traveling into your network.

Internal Interface Configuration Task List

To configure reflexive access lists for an internal interface, perform these tasks:

1 Define the reflexive access list(s) in an *inbound* IP extended named access list.

2 Nest the reflexive access list(s) in an *outbound* IP extended named access list.

3 Set a global timeout value (optional).

These tasks are described in the next sections.

NOTE   The defined (inbound) reflexive access list is used to evaluate traffic traveling out of your network: If the defined reflexive access list is matched, temporary entries are created in the nested (outbound) reflexive access list. These temporary entries will then be applied to traffic traveling into your network.

Defining the Reflexive Access List(s)

To define a reflexive access list, you use an entry in an extended named IP access list. This entry must use the **reflect** keyword:

● If you are configuring reflexive access lists for an external interface, the extended named IP access list should be one that is applied to outbound traffic.

● If you are configuring reflexive access lists for an internal interface, the extended named IP access list should be one that is applied to inbound traffic.

To define reflexive access lists, use the following commands, beginning in global configuration mode:

Step	Command	Purpose
1	**ip access-list extended** *name*	External interface: Specifies the outbound access list.
		or
		Internal interface: Specifies the inbound access list.
		(Using this command also causes you to enter the access-list configuration mode).
2	**permit** *protocol* **any any reflect** *name* [**timeout** *seconds*]	Defines the reflexive access list using the reflexive **permit** entry.
		Repeat this step for each IP upper-layer protocol; for example, you can define reflexive filtering for TCP sessions and also for UDP sessions. You can use the same *name* for multiple protocols.
		For additional guidelines for this task, see the following section, "Mixing Reflexive Access List Statements with Other Permit and Deny Entries."

If the extended named IP access list you just specified has never been applied to the interface, you must also apply the extended named IP access list to the interface.

To apply the extended named IP access list to the interface, use the following command in interface configuration mode:

Command	Purpose
ip access-group *name* **out**	External interface: Applies the extended access list to the interface's outbound traffic.
or	
ip access-group *name* **in**	Internal interface: Applies the extended access list to the interface's inbound traffic.

Mixing Reflexive Access List Statements with Other Permit and Deny Entries

The extended IP access list that contains the reflexive access list **permit** statement can also contain other normal **permit** and **deny** statements (entries). However, as with all access lists, the order of entries is important, as explained in the next few paragraphs.

If you configure reflexive access lists for an external interface, when an outbound IP packet reaches the interface, the packet will be evaluated sequentially by each entry in the outbound access list until a match occurs.

If the packet matches an entry prior to the reflexive **permit** entry, the packet will not be evaluated by the reflexive **permit** entry, and no temporary entry will be created for the reflexive access list (reflexive filtering will not be triggered).

The outbound packet will be evaluated by the reflexive **permit** entry only if no other match occurs first. Then, if the packet matches the protocol specified in the reflexive **permit** entry, the packet is forwarded out of the interface and a corresponding temporary entry is created in the inbound reflexive access list (unless the corresponding entry already exists, indicating the outbound packet belongs to a session in progress). The temporary entry specifies criteria that permits inbound traffic only for the same session.

Nesting the Reflexive Access List(s)

After you define a reflexive access list in one IP extended access list, you must nest the reflexive access list within a different extended named IP access list:

● If you are configuring reflexive access lists for an external interface, nest the reflexive access list within an extended named IP access list applied to inbound traffic.

● If you are configuring reflexive access lists for an internal interface, nest the reflexive access list within an extended named IP access list applied to outbound traffic.

After you nest a reflexive access list, packets heading into your internal network can be evaluated against any reflexive access list temporary entries, along with the other entries in the extended named IP access list.

To nest reflexive access lists, use the following commands, beginning in global configuration mode:

Step	Command	Purpose
1	**ip access-list extended** *name*	External interface: Specifies the inbound access list.
		or
		Internal interface: Specifies the outbound access list.
		(Using this command also causes you to enter the access-list configuration mode.)
2	**evaluate** *name*	Adds an entry that points to the reflexive access list. Adds an entry for each reflexive access list *name* previously defined.

Again, the order of entries is important. Normally, when a packet is evaluated against entries in an access list, the entries are evaluated in sequential order, and when a match occurs, no more entries are evaluated. With a reflexive access list nested in an extended access list, the extended access list entries are evaluated sequentially up to the nested entry, the reflexive access list entries are evaluated sequentially, and then the remaining entries in the extended access list are evaluated sequentially. As usual, after a packet matches *any* of these entries, no more entries will be evaluated.

If the extended named IP access list you just specified has never been applied to the interface, you must also apply the extended named IP access list to the interface.

To apply the extended named IP access list to the interface, use the following command in interface configuration mode:

Command	Purpose
ip access-group *name* **in**	External interface: applies the extended access list to the interface's inbound traffic.
or	
ip access-group *name* **out**	Internal interface: applies the extended access list to the interface's outbound traffic.

Setting a Global Timeout Value (Optional)

Reflexive access list entries expire after no packets in the session have been detected for a certain length of time (the *timeout period*). You can specify the timeout for a particular reflexive access list when you define the reflexive access list. If you do not specify the timeout for a given reflexive access list, the list will use the global timeout value instead.

The global timeout value is 300 seconds by default. However, you can change the global timeout to a different value at any time. To change the global timeout value, use the following command in global configuration mode:

Command	Purpose
ip reflexive-list timeout *seconds*	Changes the global timeout value for temporary reflexive access list entries.

Reflexive Access Lists Configuration Examples

There are two examples in this section:

- External Interface Configuration Example
- Internal Interface Configuration Example

External Interface Configuration Example

This example has reflexive access lists configured for an external interface, for a topology similar to the one in Figure 19-1.

This configuration example permits both inbound and outbound TCP traffic at interface Serial 1, but only if the first packet (in a given session) originated from inside your network. The interface Serial 1 connects to the Internet.

Define the interface where the session-filtering configuration is to be applied:

```
interface serial 1
 description Access to the Internet via this interface
```

Apply access lists to the interface for inbound traffic and for outbound traffic:

```
ip access-group inboundfilters in
ip access-group outboundfilters out
```

Define the outbound access list. This is the access list that evaluates all outbound traffic on interface Serial 1.

```
ip access-list extended outboundfilters
```

Define the reflexive access list *tcptraffic*. This entry permits all outbound TCP traffic and creates a new access list named *tcptraffic*. Also, when an outbound TCP packet is the first in a new session, a corresponding temporary entry will be automatically created in the reflexive access list *tcptraffic*.

```
permit tcp any any reflect tcptraffic
```

Define the inbound access list. This is the access list that evaluates all inbound traffic on interface Serial 1.

```
ip access-list extended inboundfilters
```

Define the inbound access list entries. This example shows BGP and Enhanced IGRP running on the interface. Also, no ICMP traffic is permitted. The last entry points to the reflexive access list. If a packet does not match the first three entries, the packet will be evaluated against all the entries in the reflexive access list *tcptraffic*.

```
permit bgp any any
permit eigrp any any
deny icmp any any
evaluate tcptraffic
```

Define the global idle timeout value for all reflexive access lists. In this example, when the reflexive access list *tcptraffic* was defined, no timeout was specified, so *tcptraffic* uses the global timeout. Therefore, if for 120 seconds there is no TCP traffic that is part of an established session, the corresponding reflexive access list entry will be removed.

```
ip reflexive-list timeout 120
```

This is what the sample configuration looks like:

```
interface Serial 1
 description Access to the Internet via this interface
 ip access-group inboundfilters in
 ip access-group outboundfilters out
!
ip reflexive-list timeout 120
!
```

```
ip access-list extended outboundfilters
 permit tcp any any reflect tcptraffic
!
ip access-list extended inboundfilters
 permit bgp any any
 permit eigrp any any
 deny icmp any any
 evaluate tcptraffic
!
```

With this configuration, before any TCP sessions have been initiated the **show access-list** EXEC command displays the following:

```
Extended IP access list inboundfilters
 permit bgp any any
 permit eigrp any any
 deny icmp any any
 evaluate tcptraffic
Extended IP access list outboundfilters
 permit tcp any any reflect tcptraffic
```

Notice that the reflexive access list does not appear in this output. This is because before any TCP sessions have been initiated, no traffic has triggered the reflexive access list, and the list is empty (has no entries). When empty, reflexive access lists do not show up in **show access-list** output.

After a Telnet connection is initiated from within your network to a destination outside of your network, the **show access-list** EXEC command displays the following:

```
Extended IP access list inboundfilters
 permit bgp any any (2 matches)
 permit eigrp any any
 deny icmp any any
 evaluate tcptraffic
Extended IP access list outboundfilters
 permit tcp any any reflect tcptraffic
Reflexive IP access list tcptraffic
 permit tcp host 172.19.99.67 eq telnet host 192.168.60.185 eq 11005 (5 matches)
 (time left 115 seconds)
```

Notice that the reflexive access list *tcptraffic* now appears and displays the temporary entry generated when the Telnet session initiated with an outbound packet.

Internal Interface Configuration Example

This is a sample configuration for reflexive access lists configured for an internal interface. This example has a topology similar to the one in Figure 19-2.

This example is similar to the previous example; the only difference between this example and the previous example is that the entries for the outbound and inbound access lists are swapped. Please refer to the previous example for more details and descriptions:

```
interface Ethernet 0
 description Access from the I-net to our Internal Network via this interface
```

```
 ip access-group inboundfilters in
 ip access-group outboundfilters out
!
ip reflexive-list timeout 120
!
ip access-list extended outboundfilters
 permit bgp any any
 permit eigrp any any
 deny icmp any any
 evaluate tcptraffic
!
ip access-list extended inboundfilters
 permit tcp any any reflect tcptraffic
!
```

## CHAPTER 20

Reflexive Access List Commands

This chapter describes reflexive access list commands, which are used to configure IP session filtering. IP session filtering provides the ability to filter IP packets based on upper-layer protocol session information.

You can search online at www.cisco.com to find complete descriptions of other commands used when configuring reflexive access lists.

For reflexive access list configuration information, refer to Chapter 19, "Configuring IP Session Filtering (Reflexive Access Lists)."

evaluate

To nest a reflexive access list within an access list, use the **evaluate** access list configuration command. Use the **no** form of this command to remove a nested reflexive access list from the access list.

> **evaluate** *name*
> **no evaluate** *name*

Syntax	Description
name	The name of the reflexive access list that you want evaluated for IP traffic entering your internal network. This is the name defined in the **permit (reflexive)** command.

Default

Reflexive access lists are not evaluated.

Command Mode

Access list configuration

Usage Guidelines

This command first appeared in Cisco IOS Release 11.3.

This command is used to achieve reflexive filtering, a form of session filtering.

Before this command will work, you must define the reflexive access list, using the **permit (reflexive)** command.

This command nests a reflexive access list within an extended named IP access list.

If you are configuring reflexive access lists for an external interface, the extended named IP access list should be one that is applied to inbound traffic. If you are configuring reflexive access lists for an internal interface, the extended named IP access list should be one which is applied to outbound traffic. (In other words, use the access list opposite of the one used to define the reflexive access list.)

This command allows IP traffic entering your internal network to be evaluated against the reflexive access list. Use this command as an entry (condition statement) in the IP access list; the entry points to the reflexive access list to be evaluated.

As with all access list entries, the order of entries is important. Normally, when a packet is evaluated against entries in an access list, the entries are evaluated in sequential order, and when a match occurs, no more entries are evaluated. With a reflexive access list nested in an extended access list, the extended access list entries are evaluated sequentially up to the nested entry, the reflexive access list entries are evaluated sequentially, and then the remaining entries in the extended access list are evaluated sequentially. As usual, after a packet matches *any* of these entries, no more entries will be evaluated.

Example

This example is for reflexive filtering at an external interface. This example defines an extended named IP access list *inboundfilters*, and applies it to inbound traffic at the interface. The access list definition permits all BGP and Enhanced IGRP traffic, denies all ICMP traffic, and causes all TCP traffic to be evaluated against the reflexive access list *tcptraffic*.

If the reflexive access list *tcptraffic* has an entry that matches an inbound packet, the packet will be permitted into the network. *tcptraffic* only has entries that permit inbound traffic for existing TCP sessions.

```
interface Serial 1
 description Access to the Internet via this interface
 ip access-group inboundfilters in
!
ip access-list extended inboundfilters
 permit bgp any any
 permit eigrp any any
 deny icmp any any
 evaluate tcptraffic
```

Related Commands

You can search online at www.cisco.com to find documentation of related commands.

ip access-list (extended)
ip reflexive-list timeout
permit (reflexive)

ip reflexive-list timeout

To specify the length of time that reflexive access list entries will continue to exist when no packets in the session are detected, use the **ip reflexive-list timeout** global configuration command. Use the **no** form to reset the timeout period to the default timeout. This command applies only to reflexive access lists that do not already have a specified timeout.

> **ip reflexive-list timeout** *seconds*
> **no ip reflexive-list timeout**

Syntax   Description

seconds   Specifies the number of seconds to wait (when no session traffic is being detected) before temporary access list entries expire. Use a positive integer from 0 to $2^{32}-1$.

Default

The reflexive access list entry is removed after no packets in the session are detected for 300 seconds.

Command Mode

Global configuration

Usage Guidelines

This command first appeared in Cisco IOS Release 11.3.

This command is used with reflexive filtering, a form of session filtering.

This command specifies when a reflexive access list entry will be removed after a period of no traffic for the session (the timeout period).

With reflexive filtering, when an IP upper-layer session begins from within your network, a temporary entry is created within the reflexive access list, and a timer is set. Whenever a packet belonging to this session is forwarded (inbound or outbound), the timer is reset. When this timer counts down to zero without being reset, the temporary reflexive access list entry is removed.

The timer is set to the *timeout period*. Individual timeout periods can be defined for specific reflexive access lists, but for reflexive access lists that do not have individually defined timeout periods, the global timeout period is used. The global timeout value is 300 seconds by default; however, you can change the global timeout to a different value at any time by using this command.

This command does not take effect for reflexive access list entries that were already created when the command is entered; this command only changes the timeout period for entries created after the command is entered.

Examples

This example sets the global timeout period for reflexive access list entries to 120 seconds:

```
ip reflexive-list timeout 120
```

This example returns the global timeout period to the default of 300 seconds:

```
no ip reflexive-list timeout
```

Related Commands

You can search online at www.cisco.com to find documentation of related commands.

evaluate
ip access-list (extended)
permit (reflexive)

permit (reflexive)

To create a reflexive access list and to enable its temporary entries to be automatically generated, use the **permit (reflexive)** access list configuration command. Use the **no** form of this command to delete the reflexive access list (if only one protocol was defined) or to delete protocol entries from the reflexive access list (if multiple protocols are defined).

> **permit** *protocol* **any any reflect** *name* [**timeout** *seconds*]
> **no permit** *protocol* **any any reflect** *name*

Syntax	Description
protocol	Name or number of an IP protocol. It can be one of the keywords **gre**, **icmp**, **ip**, **ipinip**, **nos**, **tcp**, or **udp**, or an integer in the range 0 to 255 representing an IP protocol number. To match any Internet protocol (including ICMP, TCP, and UDP), use the keyword **ip**.
name	Specifies the name of the reflexive access list. Names cannot contain a space or quotation mark and must begin with an alphabetic character to prevent ambiguity with numbered access lists. The name can be up to 64 characters long.
timeout *seconds*	(Optional) Specifies the number of seconds to wait (when no session traffic is being detected) before entries expire in this reflexive access list. Use a positive integer from 0 to $2^{32}-1$. If not specified, the number of seconds defaults to the global timeout value.

Default

If this command is not configured, no reflexive access lists will exist, and no session filtering will occur.

If this command is configured without specifying a **timeout** value, entries in this reflexive access list will expire after the global timeout period.

Command Mode

Access list configuration

Usage Guidelines

This command first appeared in Cisco IOS Release 11.3.

This command is used to achieve reflexive filtering, a form of session filtering.

For this command to work, you must also nest the reflexive access list using the **evaluate** command.

This command creates a reflexive access list and triggers the creation of entries in the same reflexive access list. This command must be an entry (condition statement) in an extended named IP access list.

If you are configuring reflexive access lists for an external interface, the extended named IP access list should be one that is applied to outbound traffic.

If you are configuring reflexive access lists for an internal interface, the extended named IP access list should be one which is applied to inbound traffic.

IP sessions that originate from within your network are initiated with a packet exiting your network. When such packet is evaluated against the statements in the extended named IP access list, the packet is also evaluated against this reflexive **permit** entry.

As with all access list entries, the order of entries is important because entries are evaluated in sequential order. When an IP packet reaches the interface, it will be evaluated sequentially by each entry in the access list until a match occurs.

If the packet matches an entry prior to the reflexive **permit** entry, the packet will not be evaluated by the reflexive **permit** entry, and no temporary entry will be created for the reflexive access list (session filtering will not be triggered).

The packet will be evaluated by the reflexive **permit** entry if no other match occurs first. Then, if the packet matches the protocol specified in the reflexive **permit** entry, the packet is forwarded and a corresponding temporary entry is created in the reflexive access list (unless the corresponding entry already exists, indicating the packet belongs to a session in progress). The temporary entry specifies criteria that permits traffic into your network only for the same session.

Characteristics of Reflexive Access List Entries

This command enables the creation of temporary entries in the same reflexive access list that was defined by this command. The temporary entries are created when a packet exiting your network matches the protocol specified in this command. (The packet triggers the creation of a temporary entry.) These entries have the following characteristics:

● The entry is a **permit** entry.

● The entry specifies the same IP upper-layer protocol as the original triggering packet.

● The entry specifies the same source and destination addresses as the original triggering packet, except that the addresses are swapped.

● If the original triggering packet is TCP or UDP, the entry specifies the same source and destination port numbers as the original packet, except the port numbers are swapped.

   If the original triggering packet is a protocol other than TCP or UDP, port numbers do not apply, and other criteria are specified. For ICMP, for example, type numbers are used. The temporary entry specifies the same type number as the original packet (with only one exception: if the original ICMP packet is type 8, the returning ICMP packet must be type 0 to be matched).

● The entry inherits all the values of the original triggering packet, with exceptions only as noted in the previous four bullets.

● IP traffic entering your internal network will be evaluated against the entry, until the entry expires. If an IP packet matches the entry, the packet will be forwarded into your network.

● The entry will expire (be removed) after the last packet of the session is matched.

● If no packets belonging to the session are detected for a configurable length of time (the timeout period), the entry will expire.

Example

This example defines a reflexive access list *tcptraffic* in an outbound access list that permits all BGP and Enhanced IGRP traffic and denies all ICMP traffic. This example is for an external interface (an interface connecting to an external network).

First, the interface is defined and the access list is applied to the interface for outbound traffic:

```
interface Serial 1
 description Access to the Internet via this interface
 ip access-group outboundfilters out
```

Next, the outbound access list is defined and the reflexive access list *tcptraffic* is created with a reflexive **permit** entry:

```
ip access-list extended outboundfilters
 permit tcp any any reflect tcptraffic
```

Related Commands

You can search online at www.cisco.com to find documentation of related commands.

evaluate
ip access-list (extended)
ip reflexive-list timeout

## CHAPTER 21

Configuring TCP Intercept (Prevent Denial-of-Service Attacks)

This chapter describes how to configure your router to protect TCP servers from TCP SYN-flooding attacks, a type of denial-of-service attack. This is accomplished by configuring the Cisco IOS feature known as *TCP intercept*.

For a complete description of TCP intercept commands, refer to Chapter 22, "TCP Intercept Commands." To locate documentation of other commands that appear in this chapter, you can search online at www.cisco.com.

This chapter has the following sections:

- About TCP Intercept
- TCP Intercept Configuration Task List
- TCP Intercept Configuration Example

About TCP Intercept

The TCP intercept feature implements software to protect TCP servers from TCP SYN-flooding attacks, which are a type of denial-of-service attack.

A SYN-flooding attack occurs when a hacker floods a server with a barrage of requests for connection. Because these messages have unreachable return addresses, the connections cannot be established. The resulting volume of unresolved open connections eventually overwhelms the server and can cause it to deny service to valid requests, thereby preventing legitimate users from connecting to a Web site, accessing e-mail, using FTP service, and so on.

The TCP intercept feature helps prevent SYN-flooding attacks by intercepting and validating TCP connection requests. In intercept mode, the TCP intercept software intercepts TCP synchronization (SYN) packets from clients to servers that match an extended access list. The software establishes a connection with the client on behalf of the destination server, and if successful, establishes the connection with the server on behalf of the client and knits the two half-connections together transparently. Thus, connection attempts from unreachable hosts will never reach the server. The software continues to intercept and forward packets throughout the duration of the connection.

In the case of illegitimate requests, the software's aggressive timeouts on half-open connections and its thresholds on TCP connection requests protect destination servers while still allowing valid requests.

When establishing your security policy using TCP intercept, you can choose to intercept all requests or only those coming from specific networks or destined for specific servers. You can also configure the connection rate and threshold of outstanding connections.

You can choose to operate TCP intercept in watch mode, as opposed to intercept mode. In watch mode, the software passively watches the connection requests flowing through the router. If a connection fails to get established in a configurable interval, the software intervenes and terminates the connection attempt.

TCP options that are negotiated on handshake (such as RFC 1323 on window scaling, for example) will not be negotiated because the TCP intercept software does not know what the server can do or will negotiate.

TCP Intercept Configuration Task List

Perform the following tasks to configure TCP intercept; the first task is required and the rest are optional:

- Enabling TCP Intercept
- Setting the TCP Intercept Mode
- Setting the TCP Intercept Drop Mode
- Changing the TCP Intercept Timers
- Changing the TCP Intercept Aggressive Thresholds
- Monitoring and Maintaining TCP Intercept

Enabling TCP Intercept

To enable TCP intercept, use the following commands in global configuration mode:

Step	Command	Purpose
1	**access-list** *access-list-number* {**deny** | **permit**} **tcp any** *destination destination-wildcard*	Defines an IP extended access list.
2	**ip tcp intercept list** *access-list-number*	Enables TCP intercept.

You can define an access list to intercept all requests or only those coming from specific networks or destined for specific servers. Typically the access list will define the source as **any** and define specific destination networks or servers. That is, you do not attempt to filter on the source addresses because you do not necessarily know who to intercept packets from. You identify the destination in order to protect destination servers.

If no access list match is found, the router allows the request to pass with no further action.

Setting the TCP Intercept Mode

The TCP intercept can operate in either active intercept mode or passive watch mode. The default is intercept mode.

In intercept mode, the software actively intercepts each incoming connection request (SYN) and responds on behalf of the server with an acknowledgement (ACK) and SYN, then waits for an ACK of the SYN from the client. When that ACK is received, the original SYN is set to the server and the software performs a three-way handshake with the server. When this is complete, the two half-connections are joined.

In watch mode, connection requests are allowed to pass through the router to the server but are watched until they become established. If they fail to become established within 30 seconds (configurable with the **ip tcp intercept watch-timeout** command), the software sends a Reset to the server to clear up its state.

To set the TCP intercept mode, use the following command in global configuration mode:

Command	Purpose
ip tcp intercept mode {**intercept** | **watch**}	Sets the TCP intercept mode.

Setting the TCP Intercept Drop Mode

When a server is under attack, the TCP intercept feature becomes more aggressive in its protective behavior. If the number of incomplete connections exceeds 1100 or the number of connections arriving in the last one minute exceeds 1100, each new arriving connection causes the oldest partial connection to be deleted. Also, the initial retransmission timeout is reduced by half to 0.5 seconds (so the total time trying to establish a connection is cut in half).

By default, the software drops the oldest partial connection. Alternatively, you can configure the software to drop a random connection. To set the drop mode, use the following command in global configuration mode:

Command	Purpose
ip tcp intercept drop-mode {**oldest** | **random**}	Sets the drop mode.

Changing the TCP Intercept Timers

By default, the software waits for 30 seconds for a watched connection to reach established state before sending a Reset to the server. To change this value, use the following command in global configuration mode:

Command	Purpose
ip tcp intercept watch-timeout *seconds*	Changes the time allowed to reach established state.

By default, the software waits for 5 seconds from receipt of a reset or FIN-exchange before it ceases to manage the connection. To change this value, use the following command in global configuration mode:

Command	Purpose
ip tcp intercept finrst-timeout *seconds*	Changes the time between receipt of a reset or FIN-exchange and dropping the connection.

By default, the software still manages a connection for 24 hours after no activity. To change this value, use the following command in global configuration mode:

Command	Purpose
ip tcp intercept connection-timeout *seconds*	Changes the time the software will manage a connection after no activity.

Changing the TCP Intercept Aggressive Thresholds

Two factors determine when aggressive behavior begins and ends: total incomplete connections and connection requests during the last one-minute sample period. Both thresholds have default values that can be redefined.

When a threshold is exceeded, the TCP intercept assumes that the server is under attack and goes into aggressive mode. When the TCP intercept is in aggressive mode, the following occurs:

● Each new arriving connection causes the oldest partial connection to be deleted. (You can change to a random drop mode.)

● The initial retransmission timeout is reduced by half, to 0.5 seconds, and so the total time trying to establish the connection is cut in half. (When the TCP intercept is not in aggressive mode, the code does exponential back-off on its retransmissions of SYN segments. The initial retransmission timeout is 1 second. The subsequent timeouts are 2 seconds, 4 seconds, 8 seconds, and 16 seconds. The code retransmits 4 times before giving up, so it gives up after 31 seconds of no acknowledgment.)

● If in watch mode, the watch timeout is reduced by half. (If the default is in place, the watch timeout becomes 15 seconds.)

The drop strategy can be changed from the oldest connection to a random connection with the **ip tcp intercept drop-mode** command.

NOTE   The two factors that determine aggressive behavior are related and work together. When *either* of the **high** values is exceeded, aggressive behavior begins. When *both* quantities fall below the **low** value, aggressive behavior ends.

You can change the threshold for triggering aggressive mode based on the total number of incomplete connections. The default values for **low** and **high** are 900 and 1100 incomplete connections, respectively. To change these values, use the following commands in global configuration mode:

Command	Purpose
ip tcp intercept max-incomplete low *number*	Sets the threshold for stopping aggressive mode.
ip tcp intercept max-incomplete high *number*	Sets the threshold for triggering aggressive mode.

You can also change the threshold for triggering aggressive mode based on the number of connection requests received in the last 1-minute sample period. The default values for **low** and **high** are 900 and 1100 connection requests, respectively. To change these values, use the following commands in global configuration mode:

Command	Purpose
ip tcp intercept one-minute low *number*	Sets the threshold for stopping aggressive mode.
ip tcp intercept one-minute high *number*	Sets the threshold for triggering aggressive mode.

Monitoring and Maintaining TCP Intercept

To display TCP intercept information, use either of the following commands in EXEC mode:

Command	Purpose
show tcp intercept connections	Displays incomplete connections and established connections.
show tcp intercept statistics	Displays TCP intercept statistics.

TCP Intercept Configuration Example

The following configuration defines extended IP access list 101, causing the software to intercept packets for all TCP servers on the 192.168.1.0/24 subnet:

```
ip tcp intercept list 101
!
access-list 101 permit tcp any 192.168.1.0 0.0.0.255
```

## CHAPTER 22

TCP Intercept Commands

This chapter describes TCP intercept commands. TCP intercept is a traffic-filtering security feature that protects TCP servers from TCP SYN-flooding attacks, which are a type of denial-of-service attack. TCP intercept is available for IP traffic only.

You can search online at www.cisco.com to find complete descriptions of other commands used when configuring TCP intercept.

For TCP intercept configuration information, refer to Chapter 21, "Configuring TCP Intercept (Prevent Denial-of-Service Attacks)."

ip tcp intercept connection-timeout

To change how long a TCP connection will be managed by the TCP intercept after no activity, use the **ip tcp intercept connection-timeout** global configuration command. Use the **no** form of this command to restore the default.

> **ip tcp intercept connection-timeout** *seconds*
> **no ip tcp intercept connection-timeout** [*seconds*]

Syntax	Description
seconds	Time (in seconds) that the software will still manage the connection after no activity. The minimum value is 1 second. The default is 86,400 seconds (24 hours).

Default
86,400 seconds (24 hours)

Command Mode
Global configuration

Usage Guidelines
This command first appeared in Cisco IOS Release 11.2 F.

Example

The following example sets the software to manage the connection for 12 hours (43,200 seconds) after no activity:

```
ip tcp intercept connection-timeout 43200
```

ip tcp intercept drop-mode

To set the TCP intercept drop mode, use the **ip tcp intercept drop-mode** global configuration command. Use the **no** form of this command to restore the default.

> **ip tcp intercept drop-mode** {**oldest** | **random**}
> **no ip tcp intercept drop-mode** [**oldest** | **random**]

Syntax	Description
oldest	Software drops the oldest partial connection. This is the default.
random	Software drops a randomly selected partial connection.

Default
oldest

Command Mode
Global configuration

Usage Guidelines
This command first appeared in Cisco IOS Release 11.2 F.

If the number of incomplete connections exceeds 1,100 or the number of connections arriving in the last 1 minute exceeds 1,100, the TCP intercept feature becomes more aggressive. When this happens, each new arriving connection causes the oldest partial connection to be deleted, and the initial retransmission timeout is reduced by half to 0.5 seconds (and so the total time trying to establish the connection will be cut in half).

Note that the 1,100 thresholds can be configured with the **ip tcp intercept max-incomplete high** and **ip tcp intercept one-minute high** commands.

Use the **ip tcp intercept drop-mode** command to change the dropping strategy from oldest to a random drop.

Example

The following example sets the drop mode to random:

```
ip tcp intercept drop-mode random
```

Related Commands

You can search online at www.cisco.com to find documentation of related commands.

ip tcp intercept max-incomplete high
ip tcp intercept max-incomplete low
ip tcp intercept one-minute high
ip tcp intercept one-minute low

ip tcp intercept finrst-timeout

To change how long after receipt of a reset or FIN exchange the software ceases to manage the connection, use the **ip tcp intercept finrst-timeout** global configuration command. Use the **no** form of this command to restore the default.

> **ip tcp intercept finrst-timeout** *seconds*
> **no ip tcp intercept finrst-timeout** [*seconds*]

Syntax

Description

seconds   Time (in seconds) after receiving a reset or FIN exchange that the software ceases to manage the connection. The minimum value is 1 second. The default is 5 seconds.

Default

5 seconds

Command Mode

Global configuration

Usage Guidelines

This command first appeared in Cisco IOS Release 11.2 F.

Even after the two ends of the connection are joined, the software intercepts packets being sent back and forth. Use this command if you need to adjust how soon after receiving a reset or FIN exchange the software stops intercepting packets.

Part
III

Command Reference

Example

The following example sets the software to wait for 10 seconds before it leaves intercept mode:

```
ip tcp intercept finrst-timeout 10
```

ip tcp intercept list

To enable TCP intercept, use the **ip tcp intercept list** global configuration command. Use the **no** form of this command to disable TCP intercept.

> **ip tcp intercept list** *access-list-number*
> **no ip tcp intercept list** *access-list-number*

Syntax   Description

access-list-number   Extended access list number in the range 100 to 199.

Default

Disabled

Command Mode

Global configuration

Usage Guidelines

This command first appeared in Cisco IOS Release 11.2 F.

The TCP intercept feature intercepts TCP connection attempts and shields servers from TCP SYN-flood attacks, also known as denial-of-service attacks.

TCP packets matching the access list are presented to the TCP intercept code for processing, as determined by the **ip tcp intercept mode** command. The TCP intercept code either intercepts or watches the connections.

To have all TCP connection attempts submitted to the TCP intercept code, have the access list match everything.

Example

The following configuration defines access list 101, causing the software to intercept packets for all TCP servers on the 192.168.1.0/24 subnet:

```
ip tcp intercept list 101
!
access-list 101 permit tcp any 192.168.1.0 0.0.0.255
```

Related Commands

You can search online at www.cisco.com to find documentation of related commands.

access-list (extended)
ip tcp intercept mode
show tcp intercept connections
show tcp intercept statistics

ip tcp intercept max-incomplete high

To define the maximum number of incomplete connections allowed before the software enters aggressive mode, use the **ip tcp intercept max-incomplete high** global configuration command. Use the **no** form of this command to restore the default.

> **ip tcp intercept max-incomplete high** *number*
> **no ip tcp intercept max-incomplete high** [*number*]

Syntax	Description
number	Defines the number of incomplete connections allowed, above which the software enters aggressive mode. The range is 1 to 2,147,483,647. The default is 1100.

Default

1100 incomplete connections

Command Mode

Global configuration

Usage Guidelines

This command first appeared in Cisco IOS Release 11.2 F.

If the number of incomplete connections exceeds the *number* configured, the TCP intercept feature becomes aggressive. These are the characteristics of aggressive mode:

● Each new arriving connection causes the oldest partial connection to be deleted.

● The initial retransmission timeout is reduced by half, to 0.5 seconds (and so the total time trying to establish the connection is cut in half).

● The watch-timeout is cut in half, to 15 seconds.

You can change the drop strategy from the oldest connection to a random connection with the **ip tcp intercept drop-mode** command.

NOTE   The two factors that determine aggressive mode (connection requests and incomplete connections) are related and work together. When the value of *either* **ip tcp intercept one-minute high** or **ip tcp intercept max-incomplete high** is exceeded, aggressive mode begins. When *both* connection requests and incomplete connections fall below the values of **ip tcp intercept one-minute low** and **ip tcp intercept max-incomplete low**, aggressive mode ends.

The software backs off from aggressive mode when the number of incomplete connections falls below the number specified by the **ip tcp intercept max-incomplete low** command.

Example

The following example allows 1500 incomplete connections before the software enters aggressive mode:

```
ip tcp intercept max-incomplete high 1500
```

Related Commands

You can search online at www.cisco.com to find documentation of related commands.

ip tcp intercept drop-mode
ip tcp intercept max-incomplete low
ip tcp intercept one-minute high
ip tcp intercept one-minute low

ip tcp intercept max-incomplete low

To define the number of incomplete connections below which the software leaves aggressive mode, use the **ip tcp intercept max-incomplete low** global configuration command. Use the **no** form of this command to restore the default.

> **ip tcp intercept max-incomplete low** *number*
> **no ip tcp intercept max-incomplete low** [*number*]

Syntax   Description

number   Defines the number of incomplete connections below which the software leaves aggressive mode. The range is 1 to 2,147,483,647. The default is 900.

Default

900 incomplete connections

Command Mode

Global configuration

Usage Guidelines

This command first appeared in Cisco IOS Release 11.2 F.

When *both* connection requests and incomplete connections fall below the values of **ip tcp intercept one-minute low** and **ip tcp intercept max-incomplete low**, the TCP intercept feature leaves aggressive mode.

NOTE   The two factors that determine aggressive mode (connection requests and incomplete connections) are related and work together. When the value of *either* **ip tcp intercept one-minute high** or **ip tcp intercept max-incomplete high** is exceeded, aggressive mode begins. When *both* connection requests and incomplete connections fall below the values of **ip tcp intercept one-minute low** and **ip tcp intercept max-incomplete low**, aggressive mode ends.

See the **ip tcp intercept max-incomplete high** command for a description of aggressive mode.

Example

The following example sets the software to leave aggressive mode when the number of incomplete connections falls below 1000:

```
ip tcp intercept max-incomplete low 1000
```

Related Commands

You can search online at www.cisco.com to find documentation of related commands.

ip tcp intercept drop-mode
ip tcp intercept max-incomplete high
ip tcp intercept one-minute high
ip tcp intercept one-minute low

ip tcp intercept mode

To change the TCP intercept mode, use the **ip tcp intercept mode** global configuration command. Use the **no** form of this command to restore the default.

> **ip tcp intercept mode** {**intercept** | **watch**}
> **no ip tcp intercept mode** [**intercept** | **watch**]

Syntax	Description
intercept	Active mode in which the TCP intercept software intercepts TCP packets from clients to servers that match the configured access list and performs intercept duties. This is the default.
watch	Monitoring mode in which the software allows connection attempts to pass through the router and watches them until they are established.

Default

intercept

Command Mode

Global configuration

Usage Guidelines

This command first appeared in Cisco IOS Release 11.2 F.

When TCP intercept is enabled, it operates in intercept mode by default. In intercept mode, the software actively intercepts TCP SYN packets from clients to servers that match the specified access list. For each SYN, the software responds on behalf of the server with an ACK and SYN, and waits for an ACK of the SYN from the client. When that ACK is received, the original SYN is sent to the server, and the code then performs a three-way handshake with the server. Then the two half-connections are joined.

In watch mode, the software allows connection attempts to pass through the router, but watches them until they become established. If they fail to become established in 30 seconds (or the value set by the **ip tcp intercept watch-timeout** command), a Reset is sent to the server to clear its state.

Example

The following example sets the mode to watch mode:

```
ip tcp intercept mode watch
```

Related Commands

You can search online at www.cisco.com to find documentation of related commands.

ip tcp intercept watch-timeout

Part III

Command Reference

ip tcp intercept one-minute high

To define the number of connection requests received in the last 1-minute sample period before the software enters aggressive mode, use the **ip tcp intercept one-minute high** global configuration command. Use the **no** form of this command to restore the default.

> **ip tcp intercept one-minute high** *number*
> **no ip tcp intercept one-minute high** [*number*]

Syntax   Description

Syntax	Description
number	Specifies the number of connection requests that can be received in the last one-minute sample period before the software enters aggressive mode. The range is 1 to 2,147,483,647. The default is 1100.

Default

1100 connection requests

Command Mode

Global configuration

Usage Guidelines

This command first appeared in Cisco IOS Release 11.2 F.

If the number of connection requests exceeds the *number* value configured, the TCP intercept feature becomes aggressive. These are the characteristics of aggressive mode:

● Each new arriving connection causes the oldest partial connection to be deleted.

● The initial retransmission timeout is reduced by half, to 0.5 seconds (and so the total time trying to establish the connection is cut in half).

● The watch-timeout is cut in half, to 15 seconds.

You can change the drop strategy from the oldest connection to a random connection with the **ip tcp intercept drop-mode** command.

NOTE   The two factors that determine aggressive mode (connection requests and incomplete connections) are related and work together. When the value of *either* **ip tcp intercept one-minute high** or **ip tcp intercept max-incomplete high** is exceeded, aggressive mode begins. When *both* connection requests and incomplete connections fall below the values of **ip tcp intercept one-minute low** and **ip tcp intercept max-incomplete low**, aggressive mode ends.

Example

The following example allows 1400 connection requests before the software enters aggressive mode:

```
ip tcp intercept one-minute high 1400
```

Related Commands

You can search online at www.cisco.com to find documentation of related commands.

ip tcp intercept drop-mode
ip tcp intercept max-incomplete high
ip tcp intercept max-incomplete low
ip tcp intercept one-minute low

ip tcp intercept one-minute low

To define the number of connection requests below which the software leaves aggressive mode, use the **ip tcp intercept one-minute low** global configuration command. Use the **no** form of this command to restore the default.

> **ip tcp intercept one-minute low** *number*
> **no ip tcp intercept one-minute low** [*number*]

Syntax

Syntax	Description
number	Defines the number of connection requests in the last 1-minute sample period below which the software leaves aggressive mode. The range is 1 to 2,147,483,647. The default is 900.

Default

900 connection requests

Command Mode

Global configuration

Usage Guidelines

This command first appeared in Cisco IOS Release 11.2 F.

When *both* connection requests and incomplete connections fall below the values of **ip tcp intercept one-minute low** and **ip tcp intercept max-incomplete low**, the TCP intercept feature leaves aggressive mode.

NOTE   The two factors that determine aggressive mode (connection requests and incomplete connections) are related and work together. When the value of *either* **ip tcp intercept one-minute high** or **ip tcp intercept max-incomplete high** is exceeded, aggressive mode begins. When *both* connection requests and incomplete connections fall below the values of **ip tcp intercept one-minute low** and **ip tcp intercept max-incomplete low**, aggressive mode ends.

See the **ip tcp intercept one-minute high** command for a description of aggressive mode.

Example

The following example sets the software to leave aggressive mode when the number of connection requests falls below 1000:

```
ip tcp intercept one-minute low 1000
```

Related Commands

You can search online at www.cisco.com to find documentation of related commands.

ip tcp intercept drop-mode
ip tcp intercept max-incomplete high
ip tcp intercept max-incomplete low
ip tcp intercept one-minute high

ip tcp intercept watch-timeout

To define how long the software will wait for a watched TCP intercept connection to reach established state before sending a Reset to the server, use the **ip tcp intercept watch-timeout** global configuration command. Use the **no** form of this command to restore the default.

> **ip tcp intercept watch-timeout** *seconds*
> **no ip tcp intercept watch-timeout** [*seconds*]

Syntax   Description

seconds   Time (in seconds) that the software waits for a watched connection to reach established state before sending a Reset to the server. The minimum value is 1 second. The default is 30 seconds.

Default

30 seconds

Command Mode

Global configuration

Usage Guidelines

This command first appeared in Cisco IOS Release 11.2 F.

Use this command if you have set the TCP intercept to passive watch mode and you want to change the default time the connection is watched. During aggressive mode, the watch timeout time is cut in half.

Example

The following example sets the software to wait 60 seconds for a watched connection to reach established state before sending a Reset to the server:

```
ip tcp intercept watch-timeout 60
```

Related Commands

You can search online at www.cisco.com to find documentation of related commands.

ip tcp intercept mode

show tcp intercept connections

To display TCP incomplete and established connections, use the **show tcp intercept connections** EXEC command.

> **show tcp intercept connections**

Syntax Description

This command has no arguments or keywords.

Command Mode

EXEC

Usage Guidelines

This command first appeared in Cisco IOS Release 11.2 F.

Sample Display

The following is sample output from the **show tcp intercept connections** command:

```
Router# show tcp intercept connections
Incomplete:
Client                   Server               State   Create    Timeout   Mode
172.19.160.17:58190      10.1.1.30:23         SYNRCVD 00:00:09 00:00:05 I
172.19.160.17:57934      10.1.1.30:23         SYNRCVD 00:00:09 00:00:05 I

Established:
Client                   Server               State   Create    Timeout   Mode
171.69.232.23:1045       10.1.1.30:23         ESTAB   00:00:08 23:59:54 I
```

Table 22-1 describes significant fields shown in the display.

Table 22-1   *show tcp intercept connections* *Field Descriptions*

Field	Description
Incomplete:	Rows of information under Incomplete indicate connections that are not yet established.
Client	IP address and port of the client.
Server	IP address and port of the server being protected by TCP intercept.
State	SYNRCVD—establishing with client.
	SYNSENT—establishing with server.
	ESTAB—established with both, passing data.
Create	Hours:minutes:seconds since the connection was created.
Timeout	Hours:minutes:seconds until the retransmission timeout.
Mode	I—intercept mode.
	W—watch mode.
Established:	Rows of information under Established indicate connections that are established. The fields are the same as those under Incomplete, except for the Timeout field, described below.
Timeout	Hours:minutes:seconds until the connection will timeout, unless the software sees a FIN exchange, in which case this indicates the hours:minutes:seconds until the FIN or RESET timeout.

Related Commands

You can search online at www.cisco.com to find documentation of related commands.

ip tcp intercept connection-timeout
ip tcp intercept finrst-timeout
ip tcp intercept list
show tcp intercept statistics

show tcp intercept statistics

To display TCP intercept statistics, use the **show tcp intercept statistics** EXEC command.

        show tcp intercept statistics

Syntax Description

This command has no arguments or keywords.

Command Mode

EXEC

Usage Guidelines

This command first appeared in Cisco IOS Release 11.2 F.

Sample Display

The following is sample output from the **show tcp intercept statistics** command:

```
Router# show tcp intercept statistics
intercepting new connections using access-list 101
2 incomplete, 1 established connections (total 3)
1 minute connection request rate 2 requests/sec
```

Related Commands

You can search online at www.cisco.com to find documentation of related commands.

ip tcp intercept connection-timeout
ip tcp intercept finrst-timeout
ip tcp intercept list
show tcp intercept connections

## CHAPTER 23

Configuring Context-Based Access Control

This chapter describes how to configure context-based access control (CBAC). CBAC provides advanced traffic filtering functionality and can be used as an integral part of your network's firewall.

For more information regarding firewalls, refer to Chapter 16, "Cisco IOS Firewall Overview."

For a complete description of the CBAC commands used in this chapter, refer to Chapter 24, "Context-Based Access Control Commands." To locate documentation of other commands that appear in this chapter, you can search online at www.cisco.com.

CBAC Overview

This section describes:

- What CBAC Does
- What CBAC Does Not Do
- How CBAC Works
- When and Where to Configure CBAC
- The CBAC Process
- Supported Protocols
- Restrictions
- Memory and Performance Impact

What CBAC Does

CBAC intelligently filters TCP and UDP packets based on application-layer protocol session information and can be used for intranets, extranets and the Internet. You can configure CBAC to permit specified TCP and UDP traffic through a firewall only when the connection is initiated from within the network you want to protect. (In other words, CBAC can inspect traffic for sessions that originate from the external network.) However, although this example discusses inspecting traffic for sessions that originate from the external network, CBAC can inspect traffic for sessions that originate from either side of the firewall.

Without CBAC, traffic filtering is limited to access list implementations that examine packets at the network layer, or at most, the transport layer. However, CBAC examines not only network-layer and transport-layer information, but also examines the application-layer protocol information (such as FTP connection information) to learn about the state of the TCP or UDP session. This allows support of protocols that involve multiple channels created as a result of negotiations in the control channel. Most of the multimedia protocols as well as some other protocols (such as FTP, RPC, and SQL*Net) involve multiple channels.

CBAC inspects traffic that travels through the firewall to discover and manage state information for TCP and UDP sessions. This state information is used to create temporary openings in the firewall's access lists to allow return traffic and additional data connections for permissible sessions (sessions that originated from within the protected internal network).

CBAC also provides the following benefits:

● Java blocking

● Denial-of-service prevention and detection

● Real-time alerts and audit trails

What CBAC Does Not Do

CBAC does not provide intelligent filtering for all protocols; it only works for the protocols that you specify. If you do not specify a certain protocol for CBAC, the existing access lists will determine how that protocol is filtered. No temporary openings will be created for protocols not specified for CBAC inspection.

CBAC does not protect against attacks originating from within the protected network. CBAC only detects and protects against attacks that travel through the firewall.

CBAC protects against certain attacks but should not be considered a perfect, impenetrable defense. Determined, skilled attackers might be able to launch effective attacks. While there is no such thing as a perfect defense, CBAC detects and prevents most of the popular attacks on your network.

How CBAC Works

You should understand the material in this section before you configure CBAC. If you do not understand how CBAC works, you might inadvertently introduce security risks by configuring CBAC inappropriately.

How CBAC Works—Overview

CBAC creates temporary openings in access lists at firewall interfaces. These openings are created when specified traffic exits your internal network through the firewall. The openings allow returning traffic (that would normally be blocked) and additional data channels to enter your internal network back through the firewall. The traffic is allowed back through the firewall only if it is part of the same session as the original traffic that triggered CBAC when exiting through the firewall.

In Figure 23-1, the inbound access lists at S0 and S1 are configured to block Telnet traffic, and there is no outbound access list configured at E0. When the connection request for John's Telnet session passes through the firewall, CBAC creates a temporary opening in the inbound access list at S0 to permit returning Telnet traffic for John's Telnet session. (If the same access list is applied to both S0 and S1, the same opening would appear at both interfaces.) If necessary, CBAC would also have created a similar opening in an outbound access list at E0 to permit return traffic.

Figure 23-1 *CBAC Opens Temporary Holes in Firewall Access Lists*

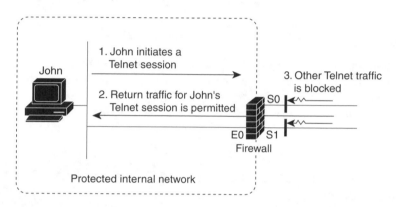

How CBAC Works—Details

This section describes how CBAC inspects packets and maintains state information about sessions to provide intelligent filtering.

Packets Are Inspected

With CBAC, you specify which protocols you want to be inspected, and you specify an interface and interface direction (in or out) where inspection originates. Only specified protocols will be inspected by CBAC. For these protocols, packets flowing through the firewall in any direction are inspected, as long as they flow through the interface where inspection is configured.

Packets entering the firewall are inspected by CBAC only if they first pass the inbound access list at the interface. If a packet is denied by the access list, the packet is simply dropped and not inspected by CBAC.

CBAC inspects and monitors only the control channels of connections; the data channels are not inspected. For example, during FTP sessions both the control and data channels (which are created when a data file is transferred) arc monitored for state changes, but only the control channel is inspected (that is, the CBAC software parses the FTP commands and responses).

CBAC inspection recognizes application-specific commands in the control channel, and detects and prevents certain application-level attacks.

A State Table Maintains Session State Information

Whenever a packet is inspected, a state table is updated to include information about the state of the packet's connection.

Return traffic is only permitted back through the firewall if the state table contains information indicating that the packet belongs to a permissible session. Inspection controls the traffic that belongs to a valid session and forwards the traffic it does not know. When return traffic is inspected, the state table information is updated as necessary.

UDP Sessions Are Approximated

With UDP—a connectionless service—there are no actual sessions, so the software approximates sessions by examining the information in the packet and determining whether the packet is similar to other UDP packets (for example, similar source/destination addresses and port numbers) and whether the packet was detected soon after another similar UDP packet. (*Soon* means within the configurable UDP idle timeout period.)

Access List Entries Are Dynamically Created and Deleted to Permit Return Traffic and Additional Data Connections

CBAC dynamically creates and deletes access list entries at the firewall interfaces, according to the information maintained in the state tables. These access list entries are applied to the interfaces to examine traffic flowing back into the internal network. These entries create temporary openings in the firewall to permit only traffic that is part of a permissible session.

The temporary access list entries are never saved to NVRAM.

When and Where to Configure CBAC

Configure CBAC at firewalls protecting internal networks. Such firewalls should be Cisco routers with the Cisco Firewall feature set configured, as described previously in the section "The Cisco IOS Firewall Feature Set."

Use CBAC when the firewall will be passing traffic such as

- Standard TCP and UDP Internet applications
- Multimedia applications
- Oracle support

Use CBAC for these applications if you want the application's traffic to be permitted through the firewall only when the traffic session is initiated from a particular side of the firewall (usually from the protected internal network).

In many cases, you will configure CBAC in one direction only at a single interface, which causes traffic to be permitted back into the internal network only if the traffic is part of a permissible (valid, existing) session.

In rare cases, you might want to configure CBAC in two directions at one or more interface, which is a more complex solution. CBAC is usually only configured in two directions when the networks on both sides of the firewall should be protected, such as with extranet or intranet configurations. For example, if the firewall is situated between two partner companies' networks, you might wish to restrict traffic in one direction for certain applications and restrict traffic in the other direction for other applications.

The CBAC Process

This section describes a sample sequence of events that occurs when CBAC is configured at an external interface that connects to an external network such as the Internet.

In this example, a TCP packet exits the internal network through the firewall's external interface. The TCP packet is the first packet of a Telnet session, and Telnet is configured for CBAC inspection.

1 The packet reaches the firewall's external interface.

2 The packet is evaluated against the interface's existing outbound access list, and the packet is permitted. (A denied packet would simply be dropped at this point.)

3 The packet is inspected by CBAC to determine and record information about the state of the packet's connection. This information is recorded in a new state table entry created for the new connection.

   (If the packet's application—Telnet—was not configured for CBAC inspection, the packet would simply be forwarded out the interface at this point without being inspected by CBAC. See the section "Defining an Inspection Rule" for configuring CBAC inspection information.)

4 Based on the obtained state information, CBAC creates a temporary access list entry, which is inserted at the beginning of the external interface's inbound extended access list. This temporary access list entry is designed to permit inbound packets that are part of the same connection as the outbound packet just inspected.

5 The outbound packet is forwarded out the interface.

6 Later, an inbound packet reaches the interface. This packet is part of the same Telnet connection previously established with the outbound packet. The inbound packet is evaluated against the inbound access list, and it is permitted because of the temporary access list entry previously created.

7 The permitted inbound packet is inspected by CBAC, and the connection's state table entry is updated as necessary. Based on the updated state information, the inbound extended access list temporary entries might be modified in order to permit only packets that are valid for the current state of the connection.

8 Any additional inbound or outbound packets that belong to the connection are inspected to update the state table entry and to modify the temporary inbound access list entries as required, and they are forwarded through the interface.

9 When the connection terminates or times out, the connection's state table entry is deleted, and the connection's temporary inbound access list entries are deleted.

In the sample process just described, the firewall access lists are configured as follows:

● An outbound IP access list (standard or extended) is applied to the external interface. This access list permits all packets that you want to allow to exit the network, including packets you want to be inspected by CBAC. In this case, Telnet packets are permitted.

● An inbound extended IP access list is applied to the external interface. This access list denies any traffic to be inspected by CBAC, including Telnet packets. When CBAC is triggered with an outbound packet, CBAC creates a temporary opening in the inbound access list to permit only traffic that is part of a valid, existing session.

    If the inbound access list had been configured to permit *all* traffic, CBAC would be creating pointless openings in the firewall for packets that would be permitted anyway.

Supported Protocols

You can configure CBAC to inspect the following types of sessions:

● All TCP sessions, regardless of the application-layer protocol (sometimes called *single-channel* or *generic* TCP inspection)

● All UDP sessions, regardless of the application-layer protocol (sometimes called *single-channel* or *generic* UDP inspection)

You can also configure CBAC to specifically inspect certain application-layer protocols. The following application-layer protocols can all be configured for CBAC:

● CU-SeeMe (only the White Pine version)

● FTP

● H.323 (such as NetMeeting, ProShare)

● Java

● UNIX r commands (such as rlogin, rexec, and rsh)

● RealAudio

● RPC (Sun RPC, not DCE RPC or Microsoft RPC)

● SMTP

● SQL*Net

- StreamWorks

- TFTP

- VDOLive

When a protocol is configured for CBAC, the protocol's traffic is inspected, state information is maintained, and in general, packets are allowed back through the firewall only if they belong to a permissible session.

Restrictions

CBAC is available only for IP protocol traffic. Only TCP and UDP packets are inspected. (Other IP traffic, such as ICMP, cannot be filtered with CBAC and should be filtered with basic access lists instead.)

You can use CBAC together with all the other firewall features mentioned in Chapter 16, "Cisco IOS Firewall Overview."

CBAC works with fast switching and process switching.

If you reconfigure your access lists when you configure CBAC, be aware that if your access lists block TFTP traffic into an interface, you will not be able to netboot over that interface. (This is not a CBAC-specific limitation, but is part of existing access list functionality.)

Packets with the firewall as the source or destination address are not inspected by CBAC or evaluated by access lists.

CBAC ignores ICMP Unreachable messages.

FTP Traffic and CBAC

With FTP, CBAC does not allow third-party connections (three-way FTP transfer).

When CBAC inspects FTP traffic, it only allows data channels with the destination port in the range of 1024 to 65,535.

CBAC will not open a data channel if the FTP client-server authentication fails.

Cisco Encryption Technology and CBAC Compatibility

If encrypted traffic is exchanged between two routers, and the firewall is in between the two routers, CBAC might not work as anticipated. This is because the packets' payloads are encrypted, so CBAC cannot accurately inspect the payloads.

Also, if both encryption and CBAC are configured at the same firewall, CBAC will not work for certain protocols. In this case, CBAC will work with single-channel TCP and UDP, except for Java and SMTP.

But CBAC will not work with multichannel protocols, except for StreamWorks and CU-SeeMe. So if you configure encryption at the firewall, you should configure CBAC for only the following protocols:

- Generic TCP
- Generic UDP
- CU-SeeMe
- StreamWorks

IPSec and CBAC Compatibility

When CBAC and IPSec are enabled on the same router, and the target router is an endpoint for IPSec for the particular flow, then IPSec is compatible with CBAC (that is, CBAC can do its normal inspection processing on the flow).

If the router is not an IPSec endpoint, but the packet is an IPSec packet, then CBAC will not inspect the packets because the protocol number in the IP header of the IPSec packet is not TCP or UDP. CBAC only inspects UDP and TCP packets.

Memory and Performance Impact

Using CBAC uses less than approximately 600 bytes of memory per connection. Because of the memory usage, you should use CBAC only when you need to. There is also a slight amount of additional processing that occurs whenever packets are inspected.

Sometimes CBAC must evaluate long access lists, which might have presented a negative impact to performance. However, this impact is avoided, because CBAC evaluates access lists using an accelerated method (CBAC hashes access lists and evaluates the hash).

CBAC Configuration Task List

To configure CBAC, complete the tasks described in the following sections:

- Picking an Interface: Internal or External
- Configuring IP Access Lists at the Interface
- Configuring Global Timeouts and Thresholds
- Defining an Inspection Rule
- Applying the Inspection Rule to an Interface

You can also perform the tasks described in the following sections; these tasks are optional:

- Defining an Inspection Rule

- Debugging Context-Based Access Control
- Interpreting Syslog and Console Messages Generated by Context-Based Access Control
- Turning Off CBAC

NOTE   If you try to configure CBAC but do not have a good understanding of how CBAC works, you might inadvertently introduce security risks to the firewall and to the protected network. You should be sure you understand what CBAC does before you configure CBAC.

For CBAC configuration examples, refer to the "CBAC Configuration Example" section at the end of this chapter.

Picking an Interface: Internal or External

You must decide whether to configure CBAC on an internal or external interface of your firewall. *Internal* refers to the side where sessions must originate for their traffic to be permitted through the firewall. *External* refers to the side where sessions cannot originate (sessions originating from the external side will be blocked).

If you will be configuring CBAC in two directions, you should configure CBAC in one direction first, using the appropriate internal and external interface designations. When you configure CBAC in the other direction, the interface designations will be swapped. (CBAC is rarely configured in two directions, and usually only when the firewall is between two networks that need protection from each other, such as with two partners' networks connected by the firewall.)

The firewall is most commonly used with one of two basic network topologies. Determining which of these topologies is most like your own can help you decide whether to configure CBAC on an internal interface or on an external interface.

The first topology is shown in Figure 23-2. In this simple topology, CBAC is configured for the *external* interface Serial 1. This prevents specified protocol traffic from entering the firewall and the internal network, unless the traffic is part of a session initiated from within the internal network.

Figure 23-2 *Simple Topology—CBAC Configured at the External Interface*

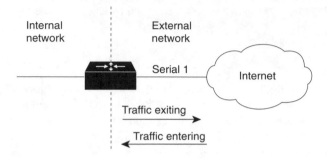

The second topology is shown in Figure 23-3. In this topology, CBAC is configured for the *internal* interface Ethernet 0. This allows external traffic to access the services in the Demilitarized Zone (DMZ), such as DNS services, but prevents specified protocol traffic from entering your internal network—unless the traffic is part of a session initiated from within the internal network.

Figure 23-3 *DMZ Topology—CBAC Configured at the Internal Interface*

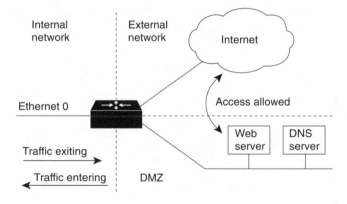

Using these two sample topologies, decide whether to configure CBAC on an internal or external interface.

Configuring IP Access Lists at the Interface

For CBAC to work properly, you need to make sure that you have IP access lists configured appropriately at the interface.

Follow these two general rules when evaluating your IP access lists at the firewall:

● Permit CBAC traffic leaving the network through the firewall. All access lists that evaluate traffic leaving the protected network should permit traffic that will be inspected by CBAC. For example, if Telnet will be inspected by CBAC, then Telnet traffic should be permitted on all access lists that apply to traffic leaving the network.

● Use extended access lists to deny CBAC return traffic entering the network through the firewall. For temporary openings to be created in an access list, the access list must be an extended access list. So wherever you have access lists that will be applied to returning traffic, you must use extended access lists. The access lists should deny CBAC return traffic because CBAC will open up temporary holes in the access lists. (You want traffic to be normally blocked when it enters your network.)

NOTE   If your firewall only has two connections (one to the internal network and one to the external network), using all inbound access lists works well because packets are stopped before they get a chance to affect the router itself.

External Interface

Here are some tips for your access lists when you will be configuring CBAC on an external interface:

● If you have an outbound IP access list at the external interface, the access list can be a standard or extended access list. This outbound access list should permit traffic that you want to be inspected by CBAC. If traffic is not permitted, it will not be inspected by CBAC, but will be simply dropped.

● The inbound IP access list at the external interface must be an extended access list. This inbound access list should deny traffic that you want to be inspected by CBAC. (CBAC will create temporary openings in this inbound access list as appropriate to permit only return traffic that is part of a valid, existing session.)

Internal Interface

Here are some tips for your access lists when you will be configuring CBAC on an internal interface:

● If you have an inbound IP access list at the internal interface or an outbound IP access list at external interface(s), these access lists can be either a standard or extended access list. These access lists should permit traffic that you want to be inspected by CBAC. If traffic is not permitted, it will not be inspected by CBAC, but will be simply dropped.

● The outbound IP access list at the internal interface and the inbound IP access list at the external interface must be extended access lists. These outbound access lists should deny traffic that you want to be inspected by CBAC. (CBAC will create temporary openings in these outbound access lists as appropriate to permit only return traffic that is part of a valid, existing session.) You do not necessarily need to configure an extended access list at both the outbound internal interface and the inbound external interface, but at least one is necessary to restrict traffic flowing through the firewall into the internal protected network.

Configuring Global Timeouts and Thresholds

CBAC uses timeouts and thresholds to determine how long to manage state information for a session and to determine when to drop sessions that do not become fully established. These timeouts and thresholds apply globally to all sessions.

You can use the default timeout and threshold values, or you can change to values more suitable to your security requirements. You should make any changes to the timeout and threshold values before you continue configuring CBAC. Note that if you want to enable the more aggressive TCP host-specific denial-of-service prevention that includes the blocking of connection initiation to a host, you must set the **block-time** specified in the **ip inspect tcp max-incomplete host** command (see the last row in the following table).

All the available CBAC timeouts and thresholds are listed in the following table, along with the corresponding command and default value.

To change a global timeout or threshold listed in the Timeout of Threshold Value to Change column, use the global configuration command in the Command column:

Timeout or Threshold Value to Change	Command	Default
The length of time the software waits for a TCP session to reach the established state before dropping the session.	**ip inspect tcp synwait-time** *seconds*	30 seconds
The length of time a TCP session will still be managed after the firewall detects a FIN exchange.	**ip inspect tcp finwait-time** *seconds*	5 seconds
The length of time a TCP session will still be managed after no activity (the TCP idle timeout).[1]	**ip inspect tcp idle-time** *seconds*	3600 seconds (1 hour)
The length of time a UDP session will still be managed after no activity (the UDP idle timeout).[1]	**ip inspect udp idle-time** *seconds*	30 seconds
The length of time a DNS name lookup session will still be managed after no activity.	**ip inspect dns-timeout** *seconds*	5 seconds
The number of existing half-open sessions that will cause the software to start deleting half-open sessions.[2]	**ip inspect max-incomplete high** *number*	500 existing half-open sessions

Timeout or Threshold Value to Change	Command	Default
The number of existing half-open sessions that will cause the software to stop deleting half-open sessions.[2]	**ip inspect max-incomplete low** *number*	400 existing half-open sessions
The rate of new unestablished sessions that will cause the software to start deleting half-open sessions.[2]	**ip inspect one-minute high** *number*	500 half-open sessions per minute
The rate of new unestablished sessions that will cause the software to stop deleting half-open sessions.[2]	**ip inspect one-minute low** *number*	400 half-open sessions per minute
The number of existing half-open TCP sessions with the same destination host address that will cause the software to start dropping half-open sessions to the same destination host address.[3]	**ip inspect tcp max-incomplete host** *number* **block-time** *seconds*	50 existing half-open TCP sessions; 0 seconds

1. The global TCP and UDP idle timeouts can be overridden for specified application-layer protocols' sessions as described in the **ip inspect name (global configuration)** command description, found in Chapter 24, "Context-Based Access Control Commands."
2. See the following section, "Half-Open Sessions," for more information.
3. Whenever the **max-incomplete host** threshold is exceeded, the software will drop half-open sessions differently depending on whether the **block-time** timeout is zero or a positive nonzero number. If the **block-time** timeout is zero, the software will delete the oldest existing half-open session for the host for every new connection request to the host and will let the SYN packet through. If the **block-time** timeout is greater than zero, the software will delete all existing half-open sessions for the host, and then block all new connection requests to the host. The software will continue to block all new connection requests until the **block-time** expires.

To return any threshold or timeout to the default value, use the **no** form of the commands in the preceding table.

Half-Open Sessions

An unusually high number of half-open sessions (either absolute or measured as the arrival rate) could indicate that a denial-of-service attack is occurring. For TCP, *half-open* means that the session has not reached the established state—the TCP three-way handshake has not yet been completed. For UDP, *half-open* means that the firewall has detected no return traffic.

CBAC measures both the total number of existing half-open sessions and the rate of session establishment attempts. Both TCP and UDP half-open sessions are counted in the total number and rate measurements. Measurements are made once per minute.

When the number of existing half-open sessions rises above a threshold (the **max-incomplete high** number), the software deletes half-open sessions as required to accommodate new connection requests. The software continues to delete half-open requests as necessary, until the number of existing half-open sessions drops below another threshold (the **max-incomplete low** number).

When the rate of new connection attempts rises above a threshold (the **one-minute high** number), the software deletes half-open sessions as required to accommodate new connection attempts. The software continues to delete half-open sessions as necessary, until the rate of new connection attempts drops below another threshold (the **one-minute low** number). The rate thresholds are measured as the number of new session connection attempts detected in the last one-minute sample period. (The rate is calculated as an exponentially decayed rate.)

Defining an Inspection Rule

After you configure global timeouts and thresholds, you must define an inspection rule. This rule specifies what IP traffic (which application-layer protocols) will be inspected by CBAC at an interface.

Normally, you define only one inspection rule. The only exception might occur if you want to enable CBAC in two directions as described earlier in the section "When and Where to Configure CBAC." For CBAC configured in both directions at a single firewall interface, you should configure two rules, one for each direction.

An inspection rule should specify each desired application-layer protocol as well as generic TCP or generic UDP if desired. The inspection rule consists of a series of statements each listing a protocol and specifying the same inspection rule name.

To define an inspection rule, follow the instructions in the following sections:

● Configuring Application-Layer Protocol Inspection

● Configuring Generic TCP and UDP Inspection

Configuring Application-Layer Protocol Inspection

NOTE If you want CBAC inspection to work with NetMeeting 2.0 traffic (an H.323 application-layer protocol), you must also configure inspection for TCP, as described later in the section "Configuring Generic TCP and UDP Inspection." This requirement exists because NetMeeting 2.0 uses an additional TCP channel not defined in the H.323 specification.

To configure CBAC inspection for an application-layer protocol, use one or both of the following global configuration commands:

Command	Purpose
ip inspect name *inspection-name protocol* [**timeout** *seconds*]	Configures CBAC inspection for an application-layer protocol (except for RPC and Java). Use one of the *protocol* keywords defined in Table 23-1.
	Repeats this command for each desired protocol. Use the same *inspection-name* to create a single inspection rule.
ip inspect name *inspection-name* **rpc program-number** *number* [**wait-time** *minutes*] [**timeout** *seconds*]	Enables CBAC inspection for the RPC application-layer protocol.
	You can specify multiple RPC program numbers by repeating this command for each program number.
	Use the same *inspection-name* to create a single inspection rule.

Refer to the description of the **ip inspect name (global configuration)** command in Chapter 24, "Context-Based Access Control Commands," for complete information about how the command works with each application-layer protocol.

To enable CBAC inspection for Java, see the following section, "Configuring Java Inspection."

Table 23-1 identifies application-protocol keywords.

Table 23-1   *Application-Protocol Keywords*

Application Protocol	*protocol* **Keyword**
CU-SeeMe	**cuseeme**
FTP	**ftp**
H.323	**h323**
UNIX r commands (rlogin, rexec, rsh)	**rcmd**
RealAudio	**realaudio**
SMTP	**smtp**
SQL*Net	**sqlnet**
StreamWorks	**streamworks**
TFTP	**tftp**
VDOLive	**vdolive**

Configuring Java Inspection

With Java, you must protect against the risk of users inadvertently downloading destructive applets into your network. To protect against this risk, you could require all users to disable Java in their browser. If this is not an agreeable solution, you can use CBAC to filter Java applets at the firewall, which allows users to download only applets residing within the firewall and trusted applets from outside the firewall.

Java applet filtering distinguishes between trusted and untrusted applets by relying on a list of external sites that you designate as "friendly." If an applet is from a friendly site, the firewall allows the applet through. If the applet is not from a friendly site, the applet will be blocked. (Alternatively, you could permit applets from all external sites except for those you specifically designate as hostile.)

To block all Java applets except for applets from friendly locations, use the following global configuration commands:

Step	Command	Purpose
1	**ip access-list standard** *name* **permit** ... **deny** ... (Use **permit** and **deny** statements as appropriate.) or **access-list** *access-list-number* {**deny** | **permit**} *source* [*source-wildcard*]	Creates a standard access list that permits only traffic from friendly sites, and denies traffic from hostile sites. If you want all internal users to be able to download friendly applets, use the **any** keyword for the destination as appropriate—but be careful to not misuse the **any** keyword to inadvertently allow all applets through.
2	**ip inspect name** *inspection-name* **http** [**java-list** *access-list*] [**timeout** *seconds*]	Blocks all Java applets except for applets from the friendly sites defined previously in the access list. Java blocking only works with standard access lists. Use the same *inspection-name* as when you specified other protocols to create a single inspection rule.

CAUTION   CBAC does not detect or block encapsulated Java applets. Therefore, Java applets that are wrapped or encapsulated, such as applets in .zip or .jar format, are *not* blocked at the firewall. CBAC also does not detect or block applets loaded from FTP, gopher, HTTP on a nonstandard port, and so forth.

Configuring Generic TCP and UDP Inspection

You can configure TCP and UDP inspection to permit TCP and UDP packets to enter the internal network through the firewall, even if the application-layer protocol is not configured to be inspected. However, TCP and UDP inspection do not recognize application-specific commands, and therefore might not permit all return packets for an application, particularly if the return packets have a different port number than the previous exiting packet.

Any application-layer protocol that is inspected will take precedence over the TCP or UDP packet inspection. For example, if inspection is configured for FTP, all control channel information will be recorded in the state table, and all FTP traffic will be permitted back through the firewall if the control channel information is valid for the state of the FTP session. The fact that TCP inspection is configured is irrelevant to the FTP state information.

With TCP and UDP inspection, packets entering the network must exactly match the corresponding packet that previously exited the network. The entering packets must have the same source/destination addresses and source/destination port numbers as the exiting packet (but reversed); otherwise, the entering packets will be blocked at the interface. Also, all TCP packets with a sequence number outside of the window are dropped.

With UDP inspection configured, replies will only be permitted back in through the firewall if they are received within a configurable time after the last request was sent out. (This time is configured with the **ip inspect udp idle-time** command.)

To configure CBAC inspection for TCP or UDP packets, use one or both of the following global configuration commands:

Command	Purpose
ip inspect name *inspection-name* **tcp** [**timeout** *seconds*]	Enables CBAC inspection for TCP packets.
	Use the same *inspection-name* as when you specified other protocols to create a single inspection rule.
ip inspect name *inspection-name* **udp** [**timeout** *seconds*]	Enables CBAC inspection for UDP packets.
	Use the same *inspection-name* as when you specified other protocols to create a single inspection rule.

Applying the Inspection Rule to an Interface

After you define an inspection rule, you apply this rule to an interface.

Normally, you apply only one inspection rule to one interface. The only exception might occur if you want to enable CBAC in two directions as described earlier in the section "When and Where to Configure CBAC." For CBAC configured in both directions at a single firewall interface, you should apply two rules, one for each direction.

If you are configuring CBAC on an external interface, apply the rule to outbound traffic.

If you are configuring CBAC on an internal interface, apply the rule to inbound traffic.

To apply an inspection rule to an interface, use the following interface configuration command:

Command	Purpose
ip inspect *inspection-name* {**in**	**out**}	Applies an inspection rule to an interface.

Displaying Configuration, Status, and Statistics for Context-Based Access Control

You can view certain CBAC information by using one or more of the following EXEC commands:

Command	Purpose
show ip inspect name *inspection-name*	Shows a particular configured inspection rule.
show ip inspect config	Shows the complete CBAC inspection configuration.
show ip inspect interfaces	Shows interface configuration with regards to applied inspection rules and access lists.
show ip inspect session [**detail**]	Shows existing sessions that are currently being tracked and inspected by CBAC.
show ip inspect all	Shows all CBAC configuration and all existing sessions that are currently being tracked and inspected by CBAC.

Debugging Context-Based Access Control

To assist in CBAC debugging, you can turn on audit trail messages that will be displayed on the console after each CBAC session closes.

To turn on audit trail messages, use the following global configuration command:

Command	Purpose
ip inspect audit trail	Turns on CBAC audit trail messages.

If required, you can also use the CBAC **debug** commands listed in this section. (Debugging can be turned off for each of the commands in this section by using the **no** form of the command. To disable all debugging, use the privileged EXEC commands **no debug all** or **undebug all**.)

The available **debug** commands are listed in the following categories:

- Generic Debug Commands
- Transport-Level Debug Commands
- Application-Protocol Debug Commands

Generic Debug Commands

You can use the following generic **debug** commands, entered in privileged EXEC mode:

Command	Purpose
debug ip inspect function-trace	Displays messages about software functions called by CBAC.
debug ip inspect object-creation	Displays messages about software objects being created by CBAC. Object creation corresponds to the beginning of CBAC-inspected sessions.
debug ip inspect object-deletion	Displays messages about software objects being deleted by CBAC. Object deletion corresponds to the closing of CBAC-inspected sessions.
debug ip inspect events	Displays messages about CBAC software events, including information about CBAC packet processing.
debug ip inspect timers	Displays messages about CBAC timer events such as when a CBAC idle timeout is reached.
debug ip inspect detail	Enables the detailed option, which can be used in combination with other options to get additional information.

Transport-Level Debug Commands

You can use the following transport-level **debug** commands, entered in privileged EXEC mode:

Command	Purpose
debug ip inspect tcp	Displays messages about CBAC-inspected TCP events, including details about TCP packets.
debug ip inspect udp	Displays messages about CBAC-inspected UDP events, including details about UDP packets.

Application-Protocol Debug Commands

You can use the following application protocol **debug** command, entered in privileged EXEC mode:

Command	Purpose
debug ip inspect *protocol*	Displays messages about CBAC-inspected protocol events, including details about the protocol's packets.
	Refer to Table 23-2 to determine the protocol keyword.

Table 23-2 identifies application protocol keywords for the **debug ip inspect** command.

Table 23-2   *Application Protocol Keywords for the **debug ip inspect** Command*

Application Protocol	*protocol* **keyword**
CU-SeeMe	**cuseeme**
FTP commands and responses	**ftp-cmd**
FTP tokens (enables tracing of the FTP tokens parsed)	**ftp-tokens**
H.323	**h323**
Java applets	**http**
UNIX r commands (rlogin, rexec, rsh)	**rcmd**
RealAudio	**realaudio**
RPC	**rpc**
SMTP	**smtp**
SQL*Net	**sqlnet**
StreamWorks	**streamworks**
TFTP	**tftp**
VDOLive	**vdolive**

Interpreting Syslog and Console Messages Generated by Context-Based Access Control

CBAC provides syslog messages, console alert messages, and audit trail messages. These messages are useful because they can alert you to network attacks and because they provide an audit trail that shows details about sessions inspected by CBAC. Although they are generally referred to as error messages, not all error messages indicate problems with your system.

The following types of error messages can be generated by CBAC:

- Denial-of-service attack detection error messages

- SMTP attack detection error messages

- Java blocking error messages

- FTP error messages

- Audit trail error message

Denial-of-Service Attack Detection Error Messages

CBAC detects and blocks denial-of-service attacks and notifies you when denial-of-service attacks occur. Error messages such as the following may indicate that denial-of-service attacks have occurred:

```
%FW-4-ALERT_ON: getting aggressive, count (550/500) current 1-min rate: 250
%FW-4-ALERT_OFF: calming down, count (0/400) current 1-min rate: 0
```

When %FW-4-ALERT_ON and %FW-4-ALERT_OFF error messages appear together, each "aggressive/calming" pair of messages indicates a separate attack. The above example shows one separate attack.

Error messages such as the following may indicate that a denial-of-service attack has occurred on a specific TCP host:

```
%FW-4-HOST_TCP_ALERT_ON: Max tcp half-open connections (50) exceeded for host
172.21.127.242.
%FW-4-BLOCK_HOST: Blocking new TCP connections to host 172.21.127.242 for 2 minutes (half-
open count 50 exceeded)
%FW-4-UNBLOCK_HOST: New TCP connections to host 172.21.127.242 no longer blocked
```

SMTP Attack Detection Error Messages

CBAC detects and blocks SMTP attacks (illegal SMTP commands) and notifies you when SMTP attacks occur. Error messages such as the following may indicate that an SMTP attack has occurred:

```
%FW-4-SMTP_INVALID_COMMAND: Invalid SMTP command from initiator (192.168.12.3:52419)
```

Java Blocking Error Messages

CBAC detects and selectively blocks Java applets and notifies you when a Java applet has been blocked. Error messages such as the following may indicate that a Java applet has been blocked:

```
%FW-4-HTTP_JAVA_BLOCK: JAVA applet is blocked from (172.21.127.218:80) to
(172.16.57.30:44673).
```

FTP Error Messages

CBAC detects and prevents certain FTP attacks and notifies you when this occurs. Error messages such as the following may appear when CBAC detects these FTP attacks:

```
%FW-3-FTP_PRIV_PORT: Privileged port 1000 used in PORT command  -- FTP client 10.0.0.1  FTP
server 10.1.0.1
           %FW-3-FTP_SESSION_NOT_AUTHENTICATED: Command issued before the session is
authenticated  -- FTP client 10.0.0.1
%FW-3-FTP_NON_MATCHING_IP_ADDR: Non-matching address 172.19.148.154 used in PORT
 command  -- FTP client 172.19.54.143  FTP server 172.16.127.242
```

Audit Trail Error Messages

CBAC provides audit trail messages to record details about inspected sessions. To determine which protocol was inspected, use the responder's port number. The port number follows the responder's address. The following are sample audit trail messages:

```
%FW-6-SESS_AUDIT_TRAIL: tcp session initiator (192.168.1.13:33192) sent 22 bytes --
responder (192.168.129.11:25) sent 208 bytes
%FW-6-SESS_AUDIT_TRAIL: http session initiator (172.16.57.30:44673) sent
1599 bytes -- responder (172.21.127.218:80) sent 93124 bytes
```

Turning Off CBAC

You can turn off CBAC, with the **no ip inspect** global configuration command.

NOTE   The **no ip inspect** command removes all CBAC configuration entries and resets all CBAC global timeouts and thresholds to the defaults. All existing sessions are deleted and their associated access lists removed.

In most situations, turning off CBAC has no negative security impact because CBAC creates permit access lists. Without CBAC configured, no permit access lists are maintained. Therefore, no derived traffic (returning traffic or traffic from the data channels) can go through the firewall. The exceptions are SMTP and Java blocking. With CBAC turned off, unacceptable SMTP commands or Java applets may go through the firewall.

CBAC Configuration Example

This sample configuration file shows a firewall configured with CBAC. The firewall is positioned between a protected field office's internal network and a WAN connection to the corporate headquarters. CBAC is configured on the firewall in order to protect the internal network from potential network threats coming from the WAN side.

The firewall has two interfaces configured:

* Ethernet 0 connects to the internal protected network

* Serial 0 connects to the WAN with Frame Relay

```
!---------------------------------------------------------------
! This first section contains some configuration that is not required for CBAC,
! but illustrates good security practices. Note that there are no services
! on the Ethernet side. E-mail is picked up via POP from a server on the corporate
! side.
!---------------------------------------------------------------
!
```

```
version 11.2
!
! The following three commands should appear in almost every config
!
service password-encryption
service udp-small-servers
no service tcp-small-servers
!
hostname fred-examplecorp-fr
!
boot system flash c1600-fw1600-l
enable secret 5 <elided>
!
username fred password <elided>
ip subnet-zero
no ip source-route
ip domain-name example.com
ip name-server 172.19.2.132
ip name-server 198.92.30.32
!
!
!----------------------------------------------------------------------
!The next section includes configuration required specifically for CBAC
!----------------------------------------------------------------------
!
!The following commands define the inspection rule "myfw", allowing
! the specified protocols to be inspected. Note that Java applets will be permitted
! according to access list 51, defined later in this configuration.
!
ip inspect name myfw cuseeme timeout 3600
ip inspect name myfw ftp timeout 3600
ip inspect name myfw http java-list 51 timeout 3600
ip inspect name myfw rcmd timeout 3600
ip inspect name myfw realaudio timeout 3600
ip inspect name myfw smtp timeout 3600
ip inspect name myfw tftp timeout 30
ip inspect name myfw udp timeout 15
ip inspect name myfw tcp timeout 3600
!
!The following interface configuration applies the "myfw" inspection rule to
! inbound traffic at Ethernet 0. Since this interface is on the internal network
! side of the firewall, traffic entering Ethernet 0 is actually exiting the
! internal network.
!Applying the inspection rule to this interface causes inbound traffic (which is
! exiting the network) to be inspected; return traffic will only be permitted back
! through the firewall if part of a session which began from within the network.
!Also note that access list 101 is applied to inbound traffic at Ethernet 0.
! Any traffic that passes the access list will be inspected by CBAC.
! (Traffic blocked by the access list will not be inspected.)
!
interface Ethernet0
 description ExampleCorp Ethernet chez fred
 ip address 172.19.139.1 255.255.255.248
 ip broadcast-address 172.19.131.7
```

```
 no ip directed-broadcast
 no ip proxy-arp
 ip inspect myfw in
 ip access-group 101 in
 no ip route-cache
 no cdp enable
!
interface Serial0
 description Frame Relay (Telco ID 22RTQQ062438-001) to ExampleCorp HQ
 no ip address
 ip broadcast-address 0.0.0.0
 encapsulation frame-relay IETF
 no ip route-cache
 no arp frame-relay
 bandwidth 56
 service-module 56k clock source line
 service-module 56k network-type dds
 frame-relay lmi-type ansi
!
!Note that the following interface configuration applies access list 111 to
! inbound traffic at the external serial interface. (Inbound traffic is
! entering the network.) When CBAC inspection occurs on traffic exiting the
! network, temporary openings will be added to access list 111 to allow returning
! traffic that is part of existing sessions.
!
interface Serial0.1 point-to-point
 ip unnumbered Ethernet0
 ip access-group 111 in
 no ip route-cache
 bandwidth 56
 no cdp enable
 frame-relay interface-dlci 16
!
ip classless
ip route 0.0.0.0 0.0.0.0 Serial0.1
!
!The following access list defines "friendly" and "hostile" sites for Java
! applet blocking. Because Java applet blocking is defined in the inspection
! rule "myfw" and references access list 51, applets will be actively denied
! if they are from any of the "deny" addresses and allowed only if they are from
! either of the two "permit" networks.
!
access-list 51 deny    172.19.1.203
access-list 51 deny    172.19.2.147
access-list 51 permit 172.18.0.0 0.1.255.255
access-list 51 permit 192.168.1.0 0.0.0.255
access-list 51 deny    any
!
!The following access list 101 is applied to interface Ethernet 0 above.
! This access list permits all traffic that should be CBAC inspected and also
! provides anti-spoofing. The access list is deliberately set up to deny unknown
! IP protocols, because no such unknown protocols will be in legitimate use.
!
access-list 101 permit tcp 172.19.139.0 0.0.0.7 any
access-list 101 permit udp 172.19.139.0 0.0.0.7 any
```

```
access-list 101 permit icmp 172.19.139.0 0.0.0.7 any
access-list 101 deny    ip any any
!
!The following access list 111 is applied to interface Serial 0.1 above.
! This access list filters traffic coming in from the external side. When
! CBAC inspection occurs, temporary openings will be added to the beginning of
! this access list to allow return traffic back into the internal network.
!This access list should restrict traffic that will be inspected by
! CBAC. (Remember that CBAC will open holes as necessary to permit returning traffic.)
!Comments precede each access list entry. These entries aren't all specifically related
! to CBAC, but are created to provide general good security.
!
! Anti-spoofing.
access-list 111 deny    ip 172.19.139.0 0.0.0.7 any
! Port 22 is SSH... encrypted, RSA-authenticated remote login. Can be used to get to
! field office host from ExampleCorp headquarters.
access-list 111 permit tcp any host 172.19.139.2 eq 22
! Sometimes EIGRP is run on the Frame Relay link. When you use an
! input access list, you have to explicitly allow even control traffic.
! This could be more restrictive, but there would have to be entries
! for the EIGRP multicast as well as for the office's own unicast address.
access-list 111 permit igrp any any
! These are the ICMP types actually used...
! administratively-prohibited is useful when you're trying to figure out why
! you can't reach something you think you should be able to reach.
access-list 111 permit icmp any 172.19.139.0 0.0.0.7 administratively-prohibited
! This allows network admins at headquarters to ping hosts at the field office:
access-list 111 permit icmp any 172.19.139.0 0.0.0.7 echo
! This allows the field office to do outgoing pings
access-list 111 permit icmp any 172.19.139.0 0.0.0.7 echo-reply
! Path MTU discovery requires too-big messages
access-list 111 permit icmp any 172.19.139.0 0.0.0.7 packet-too-big
! Outgoing traceroute requires time-exceeded messages to come back
access-list 111 permit icmp any 172.19.139.0 0.0.0.7 time-exceeded
! Incoming traceroute
access-list 111 permit icmp any 172.19.139.0 0.0.0.7 traceroute
! Permits all unreachables because if you are trying to debug
! things from the remote office, you want to see them. If nobody ever did
! any debugging from the network, it would be more appropriate to permit only
! port unreachables or no unreachables at all.
access-list 111 permit icmp any 172.19.139.0 0.0.0.7 unreachable
! These next two entries permit users on most ExampleCorp networks to telnet to
! a host in the field office. This is for remote administration by the network admins.
access-list 111 permit tcp 172.18.0.0 0.1.255.255 host 172.19.139.1 eq telnet
access-list 111 permit tcp 192.168.1.0 0.0.0.255 host 172.19.139.1 eq telnet
! Final deny for explicitness
access-list 111 deny    ip any any
!
no cdp run
snmp-server community <elided> RO
!
line con 0
 exec-timeout 0 0
 password <elided>
 login local
```

```
line vty 0
 exec-timeout 0 0
 password <elided>
 login local
 length 35
line vty 1
 exec-timeout 0 0
 password 7 <elided>
 login local
line vty 2
 exec-timeout 0 0
 password 7 <elided>
 login local
line vty 3
 exec-timeout 0 0
 password 7 <elided>
 login local
line vty 4
 exec-timeout 0 0
 password 7 <elided>
 login local
!
scheduler interval 500
end
```

## CHAPTER 24

Context-Based Access Control Commands

This chapter describes context-based access control (CBAC) commands. CBAC intelligently filters TCP and UDP packets based on application-layer protocol session information and can be used for intranets, extranets and internets. Without CBAC, traffic filtering is limited to access list implementations that examine packets at the network layer, or at most, the transport layer. CBAC inspects traffic that travels through the firewall to discover and manage state information for TCP and UDP sessions. This state information is used to create temporary openings in the firewall's access lists to allow return traffic and additional data connections for permissible sessions (sessions that originated from within the protected internal network).

You can search online at www.cisco.com to find complete descriptions of other commands used when configuring CBAC.

For configuration information, refer to Chapter 23, "Configuring Context-Based Access Control."

ip inspect audit trail

To turn on CBAC audit trail messages, which will be displayed on the console after each CBAC session closes, use the **ip inspect audit trail** global configuration command. Use the **no** form of this command to turn off CBAC audit trail messages.

> **ip inspect audit trail**
> **no ip inspect audit trail**

Syntax Description

This command has no arguments or keywords.

Default

Audit trail messages are not displayed.

Command Mode

Global configuration

Usage Guidelines

This command first appeared in Cisco IOS Release 11.2 P.

Example

The following example turns on CBAC audit trail messages:

```
ip inspect audit trail
```

Afterward, audit trail messages such as the following are displayed.

```
%FW-6-SESS_AUDIT_TRAIL: tcp session initiator (192.168.1.13:33192) sent 22 bytes --
responder (192.168.129.11:25) sent 208 bytes
%FW-6-SESS_AUDIT_TRAIL: ftp session initiator 192.168.1.13:33194) sent 336 bytes --
responder (192.168.129.11:21) sent 325 bytes
```

These messages are examples of audit trail messages. To determine which protocol was inspected, refer to the responder's port number. The port number follows the responder's IP address.

ip inspect dns-timeout

To specify the DNS idle timeout (the length of time a DNS name lookup session will still be managed after no activity), use the **ip inspect dns-timeout** global configuration command. Use the **no** form of this command to reset the timeout to the default of 5 seconds.

> **ip inspect dns-timeout** *seconds*
> **no ip inspect dns-timeout**

Syntax	Description
seconds	Specifies the length of time a DNS name lookup session will still be managed after no activity.

Default

5 seconds

Command Mode

Global configuration

Usage Guidelines

This command first appeared in Cisco IOS Release 11.2 P.

When the software detects a valid UDP packet for a new DNS name lookup session, if CBAC inspection is configured for UDP, the software establishes state information for the new DNS session.

If the software detects no packets for the DNS session for a time period defined by the DNS idle timeout, the software will not continue to manage state information for the session.

The DNS idle timeout applies to all DNS name lookup sessions inspected by CBAC.

The DNS idle timeout value overrides the global UDP timeout. The DNS idle timeout value also enters aggressive mode and overrides any timeouts specified for specific interfaces when you define a set of inspection rules with the **ip inspect name (global configuration)** command.

Examples

The following example sets the DNS idle timeout to 30 seconds:

```
ip inspect dns-timeout 30
```

The following example sets the DNS idle timeout back to the default (5 seconds):

```
no ip inspect dns-timeout
```

ip inspect (interface configuration)

To apply a set of inspection rules to an interface, use the **ip inspect** interface configuration command. Use the **no** form of this command to remove the set of rules from the interface.

> **ip inspect** *inspection-name* {**in** | **out**}
> **no ip inspect** *inspection-name* {**in** | **out**}

Syntax	Description
inspection-name	Identifies which set of inspection rules to apply.
in	Applies the inspection rules to inbound traffic.
out	Applies the inspection rules to outbound traffic.

Default

If no set of inspection rules is applies to an interface, no traffic will be inspected by CBAC.

Command Mode

Interface configuration

Usage Guidelines

This command first appeared in Cisco IOS Release 11.2 P.

Use this command to apply a set of inspection rules to an interface.

Typically, if the interface connects to the external network, you apply the inspection rules to outbound traffic; alternatively, if the interface connects to the internal network, you apply the inspection rules to inbound traffic.

If you apply the rules to outbound traffic, then return inbound packets will be permitted if they belong to a valid connection with existing state information. This connection must be initiated with an outbound packet.

If you apply the rules to inbound traffic, then return outbound packets will be permitted if they belong to a valid connection with existing state information. This connection must be initiated with an inbound packet.

Example

The following example applies a set of inspection rules named *outboundrules* to an external interface's outbound traffic. This causes inbound IP traffic to be permitted only if the traffic is part of an existing session, and to be denied if the traffic is not part of an existing session.

```
interface serial0
 ip inspect outboundrules out
```

Related Commands

You can search online at www.cisco.com to find documentation of related commands.

ip inspect name (global configuration)

ip inspect max-incomplete high

To define the number of existing half-open sessions that will cause the software to start deleting half-open sessions, use the **ip inspect max-incomplete high** global configuration command. Use the **no** form of this command to reset the threshold to the default of 500 half-open sessions.

> **ip inspect max-incomplete high** *number*
> **no ip inspect max-incomplete high**

Syntax   Description

number   Specifies the number of existing half-open sessions that will cause the software to start deleting half-open sessions.

Default
500 half-open sessions

Command Mode
Global configuration

Usage Guidelines
This command first appeared in Cisco IOS Release 11.2 P.

An unusually high number of half-open sessions (either absolute or measured as the arrival rate) could indicate that a denial-of-service attack is occurring. For TCP, *half-open* means that the session has not reached the established state. For UDP, *half-open* means that the firewall has detected traffic from one direction only.

CBAC measures both the total number of existing half-open sessions and the rate of session establishment attempts. Both TCP and UDP half-open sessions are counted in the total number and rate measurements. Measurements are made once a minute.

When the number of existing half-open sessions rises above a threshold (the **max-incomplete high** number), the software will delete half-open sessions as required to accommodate new connection requests. The software will continue to delete half-open requests as necessary, until the number of existing half-open sessions drops below another threshold (the **max-incomplete low** number).

The global value specified for this threshold applies to all TCP and UDP connections inspected by CBAC.

Example
The following example causes the software to start deleting half-open sessions when the number of existing half-open sessions rises above 900, and to stop deleting half-open sessions when the number drops below 800:

```
ip inspect max-incomplete high 900
ip inspect max-incomplete low 800
```

Related Commands
You can search online at www.cisco.com to find documentation of related commands.

ip inspect max-incomplete low
ip inspect one-minute high
ip inspect one-minute low
ip inspect tcp max-incomplete host

ip inspect max-incomplete low

To define the number of existing half-open sessions that will cause the software to stop deleting half-open sessions, use the **ip inspect max-incomplete low** global configuration command. Use the **no** form of this command to reset the threshold to the default of 400 half-open sessions.

> **ip inspect max-incomplete low** *number*
> **no ip inspect max-incomplete low**

Syntax   Description

number   Specifies the number of existing half-open sessions that will cause the software to stop deleting half-open sessions.

Default

400 half-open sessions

Command Mode

Global configuration

Usage Guidelines

This command first appeared in Cisco IOS Release 11.2 P.

An unusually large number of half-open sessions (either absolute or measured as the arrival rate) could indicate that a denial-of-service attack is occurring.

CBAC measures both the total number of existing half-open sessions and the rate of session establishment attempts. Both TCP and UDP half-open sessions are counted in the total number and rate measurements. Measurements are made once a minute.

When the number of existing half-open sessions rises above a threshold (the **max-incomplete high** number), the software will delete half-open sessions as required to accommodate new connection requests. The software will continue to delete half-open requests as necessary, until the number of existing half-open sessions drops below another threshold (the **max-incomplete low** number).

The global value specified for this threshold applies to all TCP and UDP connections inspected by CBAC.

Example

The following example causes the software to start deleting half-open sessions when the number of existing half-open sessions rises above 900, and to stop deleting half-open sessions when the number drops below 800:

```
ip inspect max-incomplete high 900
ip inspect max-incomplete low 800
```

Related Commands

You can search online at www.cisco.com to find documentation of related commands.

ip inspect max-incomplete high
ip inspect one-minute high
ip inspect one-minute low
ip inspect tcp max-incomplete host

ip inspect name (global configuration)

To define a set of inspection rules, use the **ip inspect name** global configuration command. Use the **no** form of this command to remove the inspection rule for a protocol or to remove the entire set of inspection rules.

> **ip inspect name** *inspection-name protocol* [**timeout** *seconds*]
> or
> **ip inspect name** *inspection-name* **http** [**java-list** *access-list*] [**timeout** *seconds*]
> (Java protocol only)
> or
> **ip inspect name** *inspection-name* **rpc program-number** *number*
> [**wait-time** *minutes*][**timeout** *seconds*] (RPC protocol only)

> **no ip inspect name** *inspection-name protocol* (removes the inspection rule for
> a protocol)
> **no ip inspect name** (removes the entire set of inspection rules)

Syntax	Description
inspection-name	Names the set of inspection rules. If you want to add a protocol to an existing set of rules, use the same *inspection-name* as the existing set of rules.
protocol	A protocol keyword listed in Table 24-1.

Syntax	Description
timeout seconds	(Optional) To override the global TCP or UDP idle timeouts for the specified protocol, specify the number of seconds for a different idle timeout.
	This timeout overrides the global TCP and UPD timeouts but will not override the global DNS timeout.
java-list *access-list*	(Optional) Specifies the access list (name or number) to use to determine friendly sites. This keyword is available only for the HTTP protocol, for Java applet blocking. Java blocking only works with standard access lists.
rpc program-number *number*	Specifies the program number to permit. This keyword is available only for the RPC protocol.
wait-time *minutes*	(Optional) Specifies the number of minutes to keep a small hole in the firewall to allow subsequent connections from the same source address and to the same destination address and port. The default wait-time is zero minutes. This keyword is available only for the RPC protocol.

Table 24-1 *Protocol Keywords*

Protocol	*protocol* **Keyword**
Transport-Layer Protocols	
TCP	**tcp**
UDP	**udp**
Application-Layer Protocols	
CU-SeeMe	**cuseeme**
FTP	**ftp**
Java (see the section "Java Inspection" later in this chapter)	**http**
H.323 (see the section "H.323 Inspection" later in this chapter)	**h323**
UNIX r commands (rlogin, rexec, rsh)	**rcmd**
RealAudio	**realaudio**
RPC (see the section "RPC Inspection" later in this chapter)	**rpc**
SMTP (see the section "SMTP Inspection" later in this chapter)	**smtp**

Table 24-1 *Protocol Keywords (Continued)*

Protocol	*protocol* **Keyword**
SQL*Net	**sqlnet**
StreamWorks	**streamworks**
TFTP	**tftp**
VDOLive	**vdolive**

Default

No inspection rules are defined until you define them using this command.

Command Mode

Global configuration

Usage Guidelines

This command first appeared in Cisco IOS Release 11.2 P.

To define a set of inspection rules, enter this command for each protocol that you want CBAC to inspect, using the same *inspection-name*. Give each set of inspection rules a unique *inspection-name*. Define either one or two sets of rules per interface—you can define one set to examine both inbound and outbound traffic; or you can define two sets: one for outbound traffic and one for inbound traffic.

To define a single set of inspection rules, configure inspection for all the desired application-layer protocols, and for TCP or UDP as desired. This combination of TCP, UDP, and application-layer protocols joins together to form a single set of inspection rules with a unique name.

In general, when inspection is configured for a protocol, return traffic entering the internal network will be permitted only if the packets are part of a valid, existing session for which state information is being maintained.

TCP and UDP Inspection

You can configure TCP and UDP inspection to permit TCP and UDP packets to enter the internal network through the firewall, even if the application-layer protocol is not configured to be inspected. However, TCP and UDP inspection do not recognize application-specific commands and therefore might not permit all return packets for an application, particularly if the return packets have a different port number than the previous exiting packet.

Any application-layer protocol that is inspected will take precedence over the TCP or UDP packet inspection. For example, if inspection is configured for FTP, all control channel information will be recorded in the state table, and all FTP traffic will be permitted back through the firewall if the control channel information is valid for the state of the FTP session. The fact that TCP inspection is configured is irrelevant.

With TCP and UDP inspection, packets entering the network must exactly match the corresponding packet that previously exited the network: The entering packets must have the same source/destination addresses and source/destination port numbers as the exiting packet (but reversed). Otherwise, the entering packets will be blocked at the interface. Also, all TCP packets with a sequence number outside of the window are dropped.

Application-Layer Protocol Inspection

In general, if you configure inspection for an application-layer protocol, packets for that protocol will be permitted to exit the firewall, and packets for that protocol will only be allowed back in through the firewall if they belong to a valid existing session. Each protocol packet is inspected to maintain information about the session state and to determine if that packet belongs to a valid existing session.

Java, H.323, RPC, and SMTP, and SQL*Net inspection are described in further detail in the next three sections.

Java Inspection

With Java, you must protect against the risk of users inadvertently downloading destructive applets into your network. To protect against this risk, you could require all users to disable Java in their browsers. If this is not an agreeable solution, you can use CBAC to filter Java applets at the firewall, which allows users to download only applets residing within the firewall and trusted applets from outside the firewall.

Java inspection enables Java applet filtering at the firewall. Java applet filtering distinguishes between trusted and untrusted applets by relying on a list of external sites that you designate as friendly. If an applet is from a friendly site, the firewall allows the applet through. If the applet is not from a friendly site, the applet will be blocked. Alternately, you could permit applets from all sites except for sites specifically designated as hostile.

NOTE   Before you configure Java inspection, you must configure a standard access list that defines friendly and hostile external sites. You configure this access list to permit traffic from friendly sites, and to deny traffic from hostile sites. If you do not configure an access list, but use a placeholder access list in the **ip inspect name** *inspection-name* **http** command, all Java applets will be blocked.

CAUTION	CBAC does not detect or block encapsulated Java applets. Therefore, Java applets that are wrapped or encapsulated, such as applets in .zip or .jar format, are *not* blocked at the firewall. CBAC also does not detect or block applets loaded via FTP, gopher, or HTTP on a nonstandard port.

H.323 Inspection

If you want CBAC inspection to work with NetMeeting 2.0 traffic (an H.323 application-layer protocol), you must also configure inspection for TCP, as described in Chapter 23, "Configuring Context-Based Access Control." This requirement exists because NetMeeting 2.0 uses an additional TCP channel not defined in the H.323 specification.

RPC Inspection

RPC inspection allows the specification of various program numbers. You can define multiple program numbers by creating multiple entries for RPC inspection, each with a different program number. If a program number is specified, all traffic for that program number will be permitted. If a program number is not specified, all traffic for that program number will be blocked. For example, if you created an RPC entry with the NFS program number, all NFS traffic will be allowed through the firewall.

SMTP Inspection

SMTP inspection causes SMTP commands to be inspected for illegal commands. Any packets with illegal commands are dropped, and the SMTP session will hang and eventually time out. An illegal command is any command other than the following legal commands:

- DATA
- EHLO
- EXPN
- HELO
- HELP
- MAIL
- NOOP
- QUIT
- RCPT
- RSET
- SAML

- SEND
- SOML
- VRFY

Use of the **timeout** Keyword

If you specify a timeout for any of the transport-layer or application-layer protocols, the timeout will override the global idle timeout for the interface that the set of inspection rules is applied to.

If the protocol is TCP or a TCP application-layer protocol, the timeout will override the global TCP idle timeout. If the protocol is UDP or a UDP application-layer protocol, the timeout will override the global UDP idle timeout.

If you do not specify a timeout for a protocol, the timeout value applied to a new session of that protocol will be taken from the corresponding TCP or UDP global timeout value valid at the time of session creation.

Example

The following example causes the software to inspect TCP sessions and UDP sessions, and to specifically allow CU-SeeMe, FTP, and RPC traffic back through the firewall for existing sessions only. For FTP traffic, the idle timeout is set to override the global TCP idle timeout. For RPC traffic, program numbers 100003, 100005, and 100021 are permitted.

```
ip inspect name myrules tcp
ip inspect name myrules udp
ip inspect name myrules cuseeme
ip inspect name myrules ftp timeout 120
ip inspect name myrules rpc program-number 100003
ip inspect name myrules rpc program-number 100005
ip inspect name myrules rpc program-number 100021
```

Related Commands

You can search online at www.cisco.com to find documentation of related commands.

ip inspect (interface configuration)

ip inspect one-minute high

To define the rate of new unestablished sessions that will cause the software to start deleting half-open sessions, use the **ip inspect one-minute high** global configuration command. Use the **no** form of this command to reset the threshold to the default of 500 half-open sessions.

> **ip inspect one-minute high** *number*
> **no ip inspect one-minute high**

Syntax	Description
number	Specifies the rate of new unestablished TCP sessions that will cause the software to start deleting half-open sessions.

Default

500 half-open sessions

Command Mode

Global configuration

Usage Guidelines

This command first appeared in Cisco IOS Release 11.2 P.

An unusually large number of half-open sessions (either absolute or measured as the arrival rate) could indicate that a denial-of-service attack is occurring.

CBAC measures both the total number of existing half-open sessions and the rate of session establishment attempts. Both TCP and UDP half-open sessions are included in the total number and rate measurements. Measurements are made once a minute.

When the rate of new connection attempts rises above a threshold (the **one-minute high** number), the software will delete half-open sessions as required to accommodate new connection attempts. The software will continue to delete half-open sessions as necessary, until the rate of new connection attempts drops below another threshold (the **one-minute low** number). The rate thresholds are measured as the number of new session connection attempts detected in the last 1-minute sample period. (The rate is calculated as an exponentially decayed rate.)

The global value specified for this threshold applies to all TCP and UDP connections inspected by CBAC.

Example

The following example causes the software to start deleting half-open sessions when more than 1000 session establishment attempts have been detected in the past minute and to stop deleting half-open sessions when fewer than 950 session establishment attempts have been detected in the past minute:

```
ip inspect one-minute high 1000
ip inspect one-minute low 950
```

Related Commands

You can search online at www.cisco.com to find documentation of related commands.

ip inspect one-minute low
ip inspect max-incomplete high
ip inspect max-incomplete low
ip inspect tcp max-incomplete host

ip inspect one-minute low

To define the rate of new unestablished TCP sessions that will cause the software to stop deleting half-open sessions, use the **ip inspect one-minute low** global configuration command. Use the **no** form of this command to reset the threshold to the default of 400 half-open sessions.

> **ip inspect one-minute low** *number*
> **no ip inspect one-minute low**

Syntax   Description

number   Specifies the rate of new unestablished TCP sessions that will cause the software to stop deleting half-open sessions.

Default
400 half-open sessions

Command Mode
Global configuration

Usage Guidelines
This command first appeared in Cisco IOS Release 11.2 P.

An unusually high number of half-open sessions (either absolute or measured as the arrival rate) could indicate that a denial-of-service attack is occurring.

CBAC measures both the total number of existing half-open sessions and the rate of session establishment attempts. Both TCP and UDP half-open sessions are included in the total number and rate measurements. Measurements are made once a minute.

When the rate of new connection attempts rises above a threshold (the **one-minute high** number), the software will delete half-open sessions as required to accommodate new connection attempts. The software will continue to delete half-open sessions as necessary, until the rate of new connection attempts drops below another threshold (the **one-minute low** number). The rate thresholds are measured as the number of new session connection attempts detected in the last 1-minute sample period. (The rate is calculated as an exponentially decayed rate.)

The global value specified for this threshold applies to all TCP and UDP connections inspected by CBAC.

Example

The following example causes the software to start deleting half-open sessions when more than 1000 session establishment attempts have been detected in the past minute and to stop deleting half-open sessions when fewer than 950 session establishment attempts have been detected in the past minute:

```
ip inspect one-minute high 1000
ip inspect one-minute low 950
```

Related Commands

You can search online at www.cisco.com to find documentation of related commands.

ip inspect one-minute high
ip inspect max-incomplete high
ip inspect max-incomplete low
ip inspect tcp max-incomplete host

ip inspect tcp finwait-time

To define how long a TCP session will still be managed after the firewall detects a FIN exchange, use the **ip inspect tcp finwait-time** global configuration command. Use the **no** form of this command to reset the timeout to the default of 5 seconds.

> **ip inspect tcp finwait-time** *seconds*
> **no ip inspect tcp finwait-time**

Syntax   Description

seconds	Specifies how long a TCP session will be managed after the firewall detects a FIN exchange.

Default

5 seconds

Command Mode
Global configuration

Usage Guidelines
This command first appeared in Cisco IOS Release 11.2 P.

When the software detects a valid TCP packet that is the first in a session, if CBAC inspection is configured for the packet's protocol, the software establishes state information for the new session.

Use this command to define how long TCP session state information will be maintained after the firewall detects a FIN exchange for the session. The FIN exchange occurs when the TCP session is ready to close.

The global value specified for this timeout applies to all TCP sessions inspected by CBAC.

The timeout set with this command is referred to as the *finwait* timeout.

NOTE   If the -n option is used with rsh, and the commands being executed do not produce output before the *finwait* timeout, the session will be dropped and no further output will be seen.

Examples
The following example changes the *finwait* timeout to 10 seconds:

```
ip inspect tcp finwait-time 10
```

The following example changes the *finwait* timeout back to the default (5 seconds):

```
no ip inspect tcp finwait-time
```

ip inspect tcp idle-time

To specify the TCP idle timeout (the length of time a TCP session will still be managed after no activity), use the **ip inspect tcp idle-time** global configuration command. Use the **no** form of this command to reset the timeout to the default of 3,600 seconds (1 hour).

> **ip inspect tcp idle-time** *seconds*
> **no ip inspect tcp idle-time**

Syntax   Description

seconds   Specifies the length of time a TCP session will still be managed after no activity.

Default

3600 seconds (1 hour)

Command Mode

Global configuration

Usage Guidelines

This command first appeared in Cisco IOS Release 11.2 P.

When the software detects a valid TCP packet that is the first in a session, if CBAC inspection is configured for the packet's protocol, the software establishes state information for the new session.

If the software detects no packets for the session for a time period defined by the TCP idle timeout, the software will not continue to manage state information for the session.

The global value specified for this timeout applies to all TCP sessions inspected by CBAC. This global value can be overridden for specific interfaces when you define a set of inspection rules with the **ip inspect name (global configuration)** command.

NOTE	This command does not affect any of the currently defined inspection rules that have explicitly defined timeouts. Sessions created based on these rules still inherit the explicitly defined timeout value. If you change the TCP idle timeout with this command, the new timeout will apply to any new inspection rules you define or to any existing inspection rules that do not have an explicitly defined timeout. That is, new sessions based on these rules (having no explicitly defined timeout) will inherit the global timeout value.

Examples

The following example sets the global TCP idle timeout to 1,800 seconds (30 minutes):

```
ip inspect tcp idle-time 1800
```

The following example sets the global TCP idle timeout back to the default of 3,600 seconds (one hour):

```
no ip inspect tcp idle-time
```

Part
III

Command Reference

ip inspect tcp max-incomplete host

To specify threshold and blocking time values for TCP host-specific denial-of-service detection and prevention, use the **ip inspect tcp max-incomplete host** global configuration command. Use the **no** form of this command to reset the threshold and blocking time to the default values.

> **ip inspect tcp max-incomplete host** *number* **block-time** *seconds*
> **no ip inspect tcp max-incomplete host**

Syntax   Description

number   Specifies how many half-open TCP sessions with the same host destination address can exist at a time before the software starts deleting half-open sessions to the host. Use a number from 1 to 250.

seconds   Specifies how long the software will continue to delete new connection requests to the host.

Default

50 half-open sessions and 0 seconds

Command Mode

Global configuration

Usage Guidelines

This command first appeared in Cisco IOS Release 11.2 P.

An unusually large number of half-open sessions with the same destination host address could indicate that a denial-of-service attack is being launched against the host.

Whenever the number of half-open sessions with the same destination host address rises above a threshold (the **max-incomplete host** number), the software deletes half-open sessions according to one of the following methods:

● If the **block-time** *seconds* timeout is 0 (the default), the software deletes the oldest existing half-open session for the host for every new connection request to the host. This ensures that the number of half-open sessions to a given host will never exceed the threshold.

● If the **block-time** *seconds* timeout is greater than 0, the software deletes all existing half-open sessions for the host, and then block all new connection requests to the host. The software continues to block all new connection requests until the **block-time** expires.

The software also sends syslog messages whenever the **max-incomplete host** number is exceeded, and when blocking of connection initiations to a host starts or ends.

The global values specified for the threshold and blocking time apply to all TCP connections inspected by CBAC.

Examples

The following example changes the **max-incomplete host** number to 40 half-open sessions, and changes the **block-time** timeout to 2 minutes (120 seconds):

```
ip inspect tcp max-incomplete host 40 block-time 120
```

The following example resets the defaults (50 half-open sessions and 0 seconds):

```
no ip inspect tcp max-incomplete host
```

Related Commands

You can search online at www.cisco.com to find documentation of related commands.

ip inspect max-incomplete high
ip inspect max-incomplete low
ip inspect one-minute high
ip inspect one-minute low

ip inspect tcp synwait-time

To define how long the software will wait for a TCP session to reach the established state before dropping the session, use the **ip inspect tcp synwait-time** global configuration command. Use the **no** form of this command to reset the timeout to the default of 30 seconds.

> **ip inspect tcp synwait-time** *seconds*
> **no ip inspect tcp synwait-time**

Syntax	Description
seconds	Specifies how long the software will wait for a TCP session to reach the established state before dropping the session.

Default

30 seconds

Command Mode

Global configuration

Usage Guidelines

This command first appeared in Cisco IOS Release 11.2 P.

Use this command to define how long software will wait for a TCP session to reach the established state before dropping the session. The session is considered to have reached the established state after the session's first SYN bit is detected.

The global value specified for this timeout applies to all TCP sessions inspected by CBAC.

Examples

The following example changes the *synwait* timeout to 20 seconds:

```
ip inspect tcp synwait-time 20
```

The following example changes the *synwait* timeout back to the default (30 seconds):

```
no ip inspect tcp synwait-time
```

ip inspect udp idle-time

To specify the UDP idle timeout (the length of time a UDP session will still be managed after no activity), use the **ip inspect udp idle-time** global configuration command. Use the **no** form of this command to reset the timeout to the default of 30 seconds.

> **ip inspect udp idle-time** *seconds*
> **no ip inspect udp idle-time**

Syntax	Description
seconds	Specifies the length of time a UDP session will still be managed after no activity.

Default

30 seconds

Command Mode

Global configuration

Usage Guidelines

This command first appeared in Cisco IOS Release 11.2 P.

When the software detects a valid UDP packet, if CBAC inspection is configured for the packet's protocol, the software establishes state information for a new UDP session. Because UDP is a connectionless service, there are no actual sessions, so the software approximates sessions by examining the information in the packet and determining if the packet is similar to other UDP packets (for example, similar source/destination addresses) and if the packet was detected soon after another similar UDP packet.

If the software detects no UDP packets for the UDP session for the a period of time defined by the UDP idle timeout, the software will not continue to manage state information for the session.

The global value specified for this timeout applies to all UDP sessions inspected by CBAC. This global value can be overridden for specific interfaces when you define a set of inspection rules with the **ip inspect name (global configuration)** command.

NOTE	This command does not affect any of the currently defined inspection rules that have explicitly defined timeouts. Sessions created based on these rules still inherit the explicitly defined timeout value. If you change the UDP idle timeout with this command, the new timeout will apply to any new inspection rules you define or to any existing inspection rules that do not have an explicitly defined timeout. That is, new sessions based on these rules (having no explicitly defined timeout) will inherit the global timeout value.

Examples

The following example sets the global UDP idle timeout to 120 seconds (2 minutes):

```
ip inspect udp idle-time 120
```

The following example sets the global UDP idle timeout back to the default (30 seconds):

```
no ip inspect udp idle-time
```

no ip inspect

To turn off CBAC completely at a firewall, use the **no ip inspect** global configuration command.

> **no ip inspect**

Syntax Description

This command has no arguments or keywords.

Command Mode

Global configuration

Usage Guidelines

This command first appeared in Cisco IOS Release 11.2 P.

Turn off CBAC with the **no ip inspect** global configuration command.

NOTE   The **no in inspect** command removes all CBAC configuration entries and resets all CBAC global timeouts and thresholds to the defaults. All existing sessions are deleted and their associated access lists removed.

Example

The following example turns off CBAC at a firewall:

```
no ip inspect
```

show ip inspect

To view CBAC configuration and session information, use the **show ip inspect** privileged EXEC command.

> **show ip inspect** {**name** *inspection-name* | **config** | **interfaces** | **session** [**detail**] | **all**}

Syntax	Description
name *inspection-name*	Shows the configured inspection rule with the name *inspection-name*.
config	Shows the complete CBAC inspection configuration.
interfaces	Shows interface configuration with respect to applied inspection rules and access lists.
session [**detail**]	Shows existing sessions that are currently being tracked and inspected by CBAC. The optional **detail** keyword causes additional details about these sessions to be shown.
all	Shows all CBAC configuration and all existing sessions that are currently being tracked and inspected by CBAC.

Command Mode

Privileged EXEC

Usage Guidelines

This command first appeared in Cisco IOS Release 11.2 P.

Sample Display

The following is sample output for **show ip inspect name myinspectionrule**, where the inspection rule *myinspectionrule* is configured:

```
Inspection Rule Configuration
 Inspection name myinspectionrule
    tcp timeout 3600
    udp timeout 30
    ftp timeout 3600
```

The output shows the protocols that should be inspected by CBAC and the corresponding idle timeouts for each protocol.

The following is sample output for **show ip inspect config**:

```
Session audit trail is disabled
one-minute (sampling period) thresholds are [400:500] connections
max-incomplete sessions thresholds are [400:500]
max-incomplete tcp connections per host is 50. Block-time 0 minute.
tcp synwait-time is 30 sec -- tcp finwait-time is 5 sec
tcp idle-time is 3600 sec -- udp idle-time is 30 sec
dns-timeout is 5 sec
Inspection Rule Configuration
 Inspection name myinspectionrule
    tcp timeout 3600
    udp timeout 30
    ftp timeout 3600
```

The output shows CBAC configuration, including global timeouts, thresholds, and inspection rules.

The following is sample output for **show ip inspect interfaces**:

```
Interface Configuration
 Interface Ethernet0
  Inbound inspection rule is myinspectionrule
    tcp timeout 3600
    udp timeout 30
    ftp timeout 3600
  Outgoing inspection rule is not set
  Inbound access list is not set
  Outgoing access list is not set
```

Part
III

Command Reference

The following is sample output for **show ip inspect sessions**:

```
Established Sessions
 Session 25A3318 (10.0.0.1:20)=>(10.1.0.1:46068) ftp-data SIS_OPEN
 Session 25A6E1C (10.1.0.1:46065)=>(10.0.0.1:21) ftp SIS_OPEN
```

The output shows the source and destination addresses and port numbers (separated by colons), and it indicates that the session is an FTP session.

The following is sample output for **show ip inspect sessions detail**:

```
Established Sessions
 Session 25A335C (40.0.0.1:20)=>(30.0.0.1:46069) ftp-data SIS_OPEN
   Created 00:00:07, Last heard 00:00:00
   Bytes sent (initiator:responder) [0:3416064] acl created 1
   Inbound access-list 111 applied to interface Ethernet1
 Session 25A6E1C (30.0.0.1:46065)=>(40.0.0.1:21) ftp SIS_OPEN
   Created 00:01:34, Last heard 00:00:07
   Bytes sent (initiator:responder) [196:616] acl created 1
   Inbound access-list 111 applied to interface Ethernet1
```

The output includes times, number of bytes sent, and which access list is applied.

The following is sample output for **show ip inspect all**:

```
Session audit trail is disabled
one-minute (sampling period) thresholds are [400:500] connections
max-incomplete sessions thresholds are [400:500]
max-incomplete tcp connections per host is 50. Block-time 0 minute.
tcp synwait-time is 30 sec -- tcp finwait-time is 5 sec
tcp idle-time is 3600 sec -- udp idle-time is 30 sec
dns-timeout is 5 sec
Inspection Rule Configuration
 Inspection name all
    tcp timeout 3600
    udp timeout 30
    ftp timeout 3600
Interface Configuration
 Interface Ethernet0
  Inbound inspection rule is all
    tcp timeout 3600
    udp timeout 30
    ftp timeout 3600
  Outgoing inspection rule is not set
  Inbound access list is not set
  Outgoing access list is not set
 Established Sessions
 Session 25A6E1C (30.0.0.1:46065)=>(40.0.0.1:21) ftp SIS_OPEN
 Session 25A34A0 (40.0.0.1:20)=>(30.0.0.1:46072) ftp-data SIS_OPEN
```

IP Security and Encryption

## CHAPTER 25

IP Security and Encryption Overview

This chapter briefly describes the following security features and how they relate to each other:

- Cisco Encryption Technology
- IPSec Network Security
- Internet Key Exchange Security Protocol
- Certification Authority Interoperability

Cisco Encryption Technology

Cisco Encryption Technology (CET) is a proprietary security solution introduced in Cisco IOS Release 11.2. It provides network data encryption at the IP packet level and implements the following standards:

- Digital Signature Standard (DSS)
- Diffie-Hellman (DH) public key algorithm
- Data Encryption Standard (DES)

For more information regarding CET, refer to Chapter 26, "Configuring Cisco Encryption Technology."

IPSec Network Security

IPSec is a framework of open standards developed by the Internet Engineering Task Force (IETF) that provides security for transmission of sensitive information over unprotected networks such as the Internet. It acts at the network level and implements the following standards:

- IPSec
- Internet Key Exchange (IKE)
- DES
- MD5 (HMAC variant)
- SHA (HMAC variant)
- Authentication Header (AH)
- Encapsulating Security Payload (ESP)

IPSec services are similar to those provided by CET. However, IPSec provides a more robust security solution and is standards based. IPSec also provides data authentication and anti-replay services in addition to data confidentiality services, whereas CET provides only data confidentiality services.

For more information about IPSec, refer to Chapter 28, "Configuring IPSec Network Security."

Comparison of IPSec to Cisco Encryption Technology

IPSec shares the same benefits as CET: Both technologies protect sensitive data that travels across unprotected networks, and, like CET, IPSec security services are provided at the network layer, so you do not have to configure individual workstations, PCs, or applications. This benefit can provide a great cost savings. Instead of providing the security services you do not need to deploy and coordinate security on a per-application, per-computer basis, you can simply change the network infrastructure to provide the needed security services.

IPSec also provides the following additional benefits not present in CET:

- Because IPSec is standards-based, Cisco devices are able to interoperate with other IPSec-compliant networking devices to provide the IPSec security services. IPSec-compliant devices could include both Cisco devices and non-Cisco devices such as PCs, servers, and other computing systems.

  Cisco and its partners, including Microsoft, are planning to offer IPSec across a wide range of platforms, including Cisco IOS software, the Cisco PIX Firewall, Windows 95, and Windows NT. Cisco is working closely with the IETF to ensure that IPSec is quickly standardized.

- A mobile user will be able to establish a secure connection back to his office. For example, the user can establish an IPSec tunnel with a corporate firewall—requesting authentication services—in order to gain access to the corporate network; all of the traffic between the user and the firewall will then be authenticated. The user can then establish an additional IPSec tunnel—requesting data privacy services—with an internal router or end system.

- IPSec provides support for the IKE protocol and for digital certificates. IKE provides negotiation services and key derivation services for IPSec. Digital certificates allow devices to be automatically authenticated to each other without the manual key exchanges required by Cisco Encryption Technology. For more information, see Chapter 32, "Configuring Internet Key Exchange Security Protocol."

  This support allows IPSec solutions to scale better than CET solutions, making IPSec preferable in many cases for use with medium-sized, large-sized, and growing networks, where secure connections between many devices are required.

These and other differences between IPSec and CET are described in the following sections.

Differences Between IPSec and Cisco Encryption Technology

Should you implement CET or IPSec network security in your network? The answer depends on your requirements.

If you require only Cisco router-to-Cisco router encryption, then you could run CET, which is a more mature, higher-speed solution.

If you require a standards-based solution that provides multivendor interoperability or remote client connections, then you should implement IPSec. Also, if you want to implement data authentication with or without privacy (encryption), then IPSec is the right choice.

If you want, you can configure both CET and IPSec simultaneously in your network, even simultaneously on the same device. A Cisco device can simultaneously have CET secure sessions and IPSec secure sessions, with multiple peers.

Table 25-1 compares CET and IPSec.

Table 25-1   *CET Versus IPSec*

Feature	Cisco Encryption Technology	IPSec
Availability	Cisco IOS Release 11.2 and later.	Cisco IOS Release 11.3(3)T and later.
Standards	Pre-IETF standards.	IETF standard.
Interoperability	Cisco router to Cisco router.	All IPSec compliant implementations.
Remote access solution	No.	Client encryption will be available.
Device authentication	Manual between each peer at installation.	IKE uses digital certificates as a type of "digital ID card" (when Certification Authority support is configured); also supports manually configured authentication shared secrets and manually configured public keys.
Certificate support	No.	X509.V3 support; will support public key infrastructure standard when the standard is completed.
Protected traffic	Selected IP traffic is encrypted, based on extended access lists you define.	Selected IP traffic is encrypted and/or authenticated, based on extended access lists; additionally, different traffic can be protected with different keys or different algorithms.
Hardware support	Encryption Service Adapter (ESA) for the Cisco 7200/7500.	Support planned for later.

Continues

Table 25-1 *CET Versus IPSec (Continued)*

Feature	Cisco Encryption Technology	IPSec
Packet expansion	None.	Tunnel mode adds a new IP and IPSec header to the packet; transport mode adds a new IPSec header.
Scope of encryption	IP and ULP headers remain in the clear.	In tunnel mode, both the IP and ULP headers are encrypted; in transport mode, IP headers remain in the clear but ULP headers are encrypted. (In tunnel mode, the inner IP header is also encrypted.)
Data authentication with or without encryption	Encryption only.	Can configure data authentication and encryption to both occur, or can use AH header to provide data authentication without encryption.
IKE support	No.	Yes.
Redundant topologies	Concurrent redundant CET peers not supported.	Concurrent redundant IPSec peers supported.

IPSec Performance Impacts

IPSec packet processing is slower than CET packet processing for these reasons:

- IPSec offers per-packet data authentication, an additional task not performed with CET.

- IPSec introduces packet expansion, which is more likely to require fragmentation/reassembly of IPSec packets.

IPSec Interoperability with Other Cisco IOS Software Features

You can use Cisco Encryption Technology and IPSec together; the two encryption technologies can coexist in your network. Each router may support concurrent encryption links using either IPSec or Cisco encryption technology. A single interface can even support the use of IPSec or CET for protecting different data flows.

Internet Key Exchange Security Protocol

IKE security protocol is a key management protocol standard that is used in conjunction with the IPSec standard. IPSec can be configured without IKE, but IKE enhances IPSec by providing additional features, flexibility, and ease of configuration for the IPSec standard.

For more information regarding IKE, refer to Chapter 32, "Configuring Internet Key Exchange Security Protocol."

Certification Authority Interoperability

Certification Authority (CA) interoperability is provided in support of the IPSec standard. It permits Cisco IOS devices and CAs to communicate so that your Cisco IOS device can obtain and use digital certificates from the CA. Although IPSec can be implemented in your network without the use of a CA, using a CA provides manageability and scalability for IPSec.

For more information regarding CA interoperability, refer to Chapter 30, "Configuring Certification Authority Interoperability."

## CHAPTER 26

Configuring Cisco Encryption Technology

This chapter describes how to configure your router for network data encryption using Cisco Encryption Technology (CET). This chapter includes the following sections:

- Why Encryption?
- Cisco's Implementation of Encryption
- Additional Sources of Information
- Prework: Before You Configure Encryption
- Configuring Encryption
- Configuring Encryption with GRE Tunnels
- Configuring Encryption with an ESA in a VIP2
- Configuring Encryption with an ESA in a Cisco 7200 Series Router
- Customizing Encryption (Configuring Options)
- Turning Off Encryption
- Testing and Troubleshooting Encryption
- Encryption Configuration Examples

NOTE   Whenever the term *encryption* is used in this chapter, it refers only to encryption of network data, not to other types of encryption.

For a complete description of the encryption commands in this chapter, refer to Chapter 27, "Cisco Encryption Technology Commands." To locate documentation of other commands that appear in this chapter, you can search online at www.cisco.com.

Why Encryption?

Data that traverses unsecured networks is open to many types of attacks. Data can be read, altered, or forged by anybody who has access to the route that your data takes. For example, a protocol analyzer can read packets and gain classified information. Or a hostile party can tamper with packets and cause damage by hindering, reducing, or preventing network communications within your organization.

Encryption provides a means to safeguard network data that travels from one Cisco router to another across unsecured networks. Encryption is particularly important if classified, confidential, or critical data is being sent.

Figure 26-1 illustrates the encryption of an IP packet as it travels across an unsecured network.

Figure 26-1 *IP Packet Encryption*

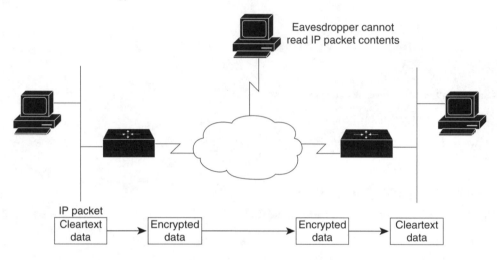

Cisco's Implementation of Encryption

The following sections answer these questions:

- What Gets Encrypted?
- Where Are Packets Encrypted and Decrypted in the Network?
- When Can Encrypted Packets Be Exchanged?
- How Does an Encrypting Router Identify Other Peer Encrypting Routers?
- What Standards Are Implemented in Cisco's Encryption?
- How Does Cisco's Encryption Work?

What Gets Encrypted?

Network data encryption is provided at the IP packet level; only IP packets can be encrypted. (If you wish to encrypt a network protocol other than IP, you must encapsulate the protocol within an IP packet.)

An IP packet is encrypted/decrypted only if the packet meets criteria you establish when you configure a router for encryption.

When encrypted, individual IP packets can be detected during transmission, but the IP packet contents (payload) cannot be read. Specifically, the IP header and upper-layer protocol headers (for example, TCP or UDP) are not encrypted, but all payload data within the TCP or UDP packet will be encrypted and, therefore, will not be readable during transmission.

Where Are Packets Encrypted and Decrypted in the Network?

The actual encryption and decryption of IP packets occur only at routers that you configure for CET. Such routers are considered to be *peer encrypting routers* (or simply *peer routers*). Intermediate hops do not participate in encryption/decryption.

Often, peer routers are situated at the edges of unsecured networks (such as the Internet), in order to provide secure communications between two secured networks that are physically separated. Clear-text (that is, not encrypted) traffic that enters a peer router from the secure network side is encrypted and forwarded across the unsecure network. When the encrypted traffic reaches the remote peer router, the router decrypts the traffic before forwarding it into the remote secure network.

Packets are encrypted at one peer router's outbound interface and decrypted at the other peer router's inbound interface.

When Can Encrypted Packets Be Exchanged?

Encrypted packets can be exchanged between peer routers only during encrypted sessions. When a peer router detects a packet that should be encrypted, an encrypted session must first be established. After an encrypted session is established, encrypted traffic can pass freely between peer routers. When the session expires, a new session must be established before encrypted traffic can continue to be sent.

How Does an Encrypting Router Identify Other Peer Encrypting Routers?

During the setup of every encrypted session, both participating peer routers attempt to authenticate each other. If either authentication fails, the encrypted session is not established, and no encrypted traffic passes. Peer authentication ensures that only known, trusted peer routers exchange encrypted traffic and prevents routers from being tricked into sending sensitive encrypted traffic to illegitimate or fraudulent destination routers.

What Standards Are Implemented in Cisco's Encryption?

To provide encryption services, Cisco implements the following standards: Digital Signature Standard (DSS), the Diffie-Hellman (DH) public key algorithm, and Data Encryption Standard (DES). DSS is used for peer router authentication. The DH algorithm and DES standard are used to initiate and conduct encrypted communication sessions between participating peer routers.

How Does Cisco's Encryption Work?

The following sections provide an overview of Cisco's encryption process:

● You Enable Peer Router Authentication with a DSS Key Exchange

● A Router Establishes an Encrypted Session with a Peer

● Peer Routers Encrypt and Decrypt Data During an Encrypted Session

You Enable Peer Router Authentication with a DSS Key Exchange

Peer router authentication occurs during the setup of each encrypted session. But before peer routers can authenticate each other, you must generate DSS keys (both public and private DSS keys) for each peer, and you must exchange (and verify) the DSS public keys with each peer (see Figure 26-2). You generate and exchange DSS keys only once per peer, and afterwards these DSS keys will be used each time an encrypted session occurs. (Generating and exchanging DSS keys are described later in the section "Configuring Encryption.")

Each peer router's DSS keys are unique: a unique DSS public key, and a unique DSS private key. DSS private keys are stored in a private portion of the router's NVRAM, which cannot be viewed with commands such as **more system:running-config** or **more nvram:startup-config**. If you have a router with an Encryption Service Adapter (ESA), DSS keys are stored in the tamper resistant memory of the ESA.

The DSS private key is not shared with any other device. However, the DSS public key is distributed to all other peer routers. You must cooperate with the peer router's administrator to exchange public keys between the two peer routers, and you and the other administrator must verbally verify to each other the public key of the other router. (The verbal verification is sometimes referred to as *voice authentication*.)

When an encrypted session is being established, each router uses the peer's DSS public key to authenticate the peer. The process of authenticating peers and establishing encrypted sessions is described next.

Figure 26-2 *Exchanging DSS Keys (Overview)*

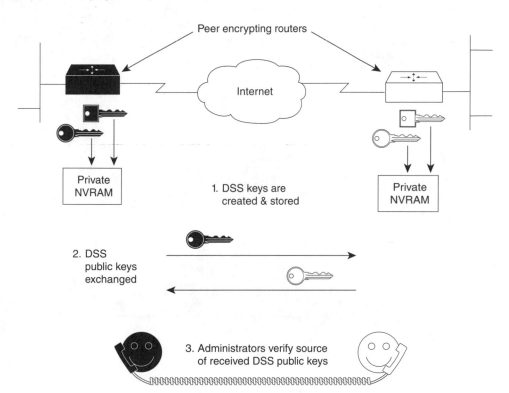

A Router Establishes an Encrypted Session with a Peer

An encrypted session must be established before a Cisco router can send encrypted data to a peer router. (See Figure 26-3.) An encrypted session is established whenever a router detects an IP packet that should be encrypted and no encrypted session already exists.

To establish a session, two peer routers exchange connection messages. These messages have two purposes. The first purpose is to authenticate each router to the other. Authentication is accomplished by attaching signatures to the connection messages: A *signature* is a character string that is created by each local router using its own DSS private key and verified by the remote router using the local router's DSS public key (previously exchanged). A signature is always unique to the sending router and cannot be forged by any other device. When a signature is verified, the router that sent the signature is authenticated.

The second purpose of the connection messages is to generate a temporary DES key (a *session key*), which is the key that will be used to actually encrypt data during the encrypted session. To generate the DES key, DH numbers must be exchanged in the connection messages. Then, the DH numbers are used to compute a common DES session key that is shared by both routers.

Figure 26-3 *Establishing an Encrypted Session*

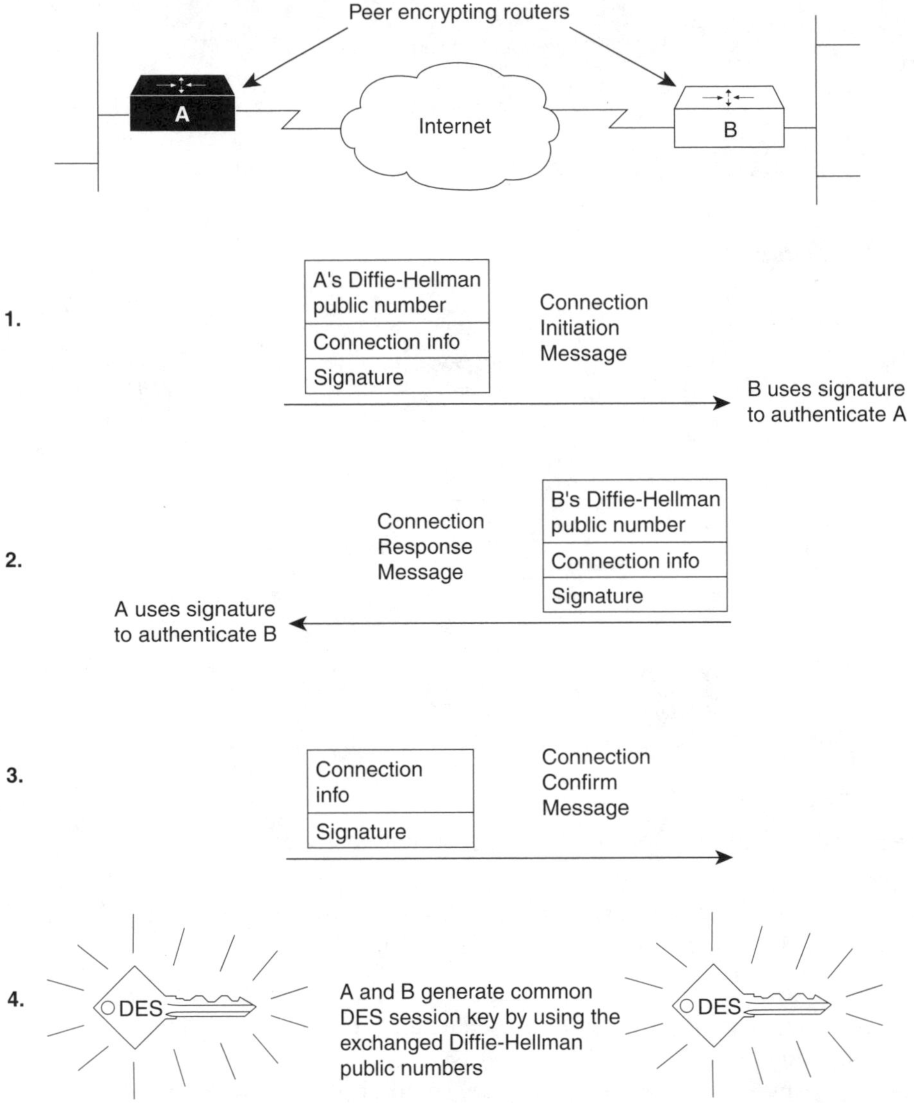

Peer Routers Encrypt and Decrypt Data During an Encrypted Session

After both peer routers are authenticated and the session key (a DES key) has been generated, data can be encrypted and transmitted. A DES encryption algorithm is used with the DES key to encrypt and decrypt IP packets during the encrypted session. (See Figure 26-4.)

An encrypted communication session will terminate when the session times out. When the session terminates, both the DH numbers and the DES key are discarded. When another encrypted session is required, new DH numbers and DES keys will be generated.

Figure 26-4 *Encrypting Data*

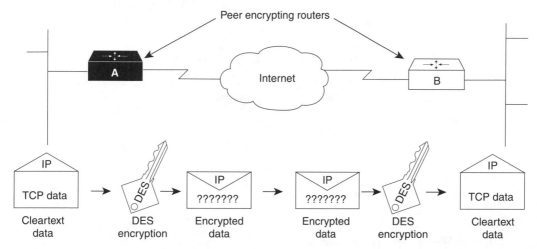

1. The DES key is used by routers A and B to encrypt outbound IP traffic and to decrypt inbound IP traffic.

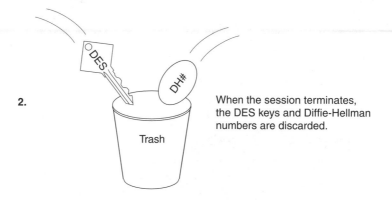

2. When the session terminates, the DES keys and Diffie-Hellman numbers are discarded.

Additional Sources of Information

The following material provides additional background information about network data encryption, including theory, standards, and legal requirements:

- *Applied Cryptography*, Bruce Schneier.

- *Network Security: Private Communication in a Public World*, Kaufman, Perlman, and Specinen.

- *Actually Useful Internet Security Techniques*, Larry J. Hughes, Jr.

- *FIPS140*, Federal Information Processing Standard.

- Defense Trade Regulations (Parts 120 to 126).

- *Information Security and Privacy in Network Environments*, Office of Technology Assessment.

Prework: Before You Configure Encryption

You should understand and follow the guidelines in this section before attempting to configure your system for CET. This section describes the following guidelines:

- Identifying Peer Routers

- Considering Your Network Topology

- Identifying Crypto Engines Within Each Peer Router

- Understanding Implementation Issues and Limitations

Identifying Peer Routers

You must identify all peer routers that will be participating in encryption. *Peer routers* are routers configured for encryption, between which all encrypted traffic is passed. These peers are usually routers within your administrative control that will be passing IP packets over an uncontrolled network (such as the Internet). Participating peer routers might also include routers not within your administrative control; however, this should only be the case if you share a trusted, cooperative relationship with the other router's administrator. This person should be known and trusted by both you and your organization.

Peer routers should be located within a network topology, according to the guidelines in the following sections.

Considering Your Network Topology

Take care in choosing a network topology between peer encrypting routers. Particularly, you should set up the network so that a stream of IP packets must use exactly one pair of encrypting routers at a time. Do not nest levels of encrypting routers. (That is, do not put encrypting routers in between two peer encrypting routers.)

Frequent route changes between pairs of peer encrypting routers, including for purposes of load balancing, will cause excessive numbers of connections to be set up and very few data packets to be delivered. Note that load balancing can still be used, but only if done transparently to the encrypting peer routers. That is, peer routers should not participate in the load balancing: Only devices in between the peer routers should provide load balancing.

A common network topology used for encryption is a hub-and-spokes arrangement between an enterprise router and branch routers. Also, Internet firewall routers are often designated as peer encrypting routers.

Identifying Crypto Engines Within Each Peer Router

Encryption is provided by a software service called a *crypto engine*. To perform encryption at a router, you must first configure the router's crypto engine to be an encrypting peer; then you can configure any interface governed by that crypto engine to perform encryption. (To configure a crypto engine, you must at a minimum generate and exchange DSS keys for that engine, as described in the section "Configuring Encryption" later in this chapter.)

Depending on your hardware configuration, different crypto engines govern different router interfaces. In some instances, you may even need to configure multiple crypto engines as peers within a single router, particularly if a router has multiple interfaces that you want to use for encryption, and those interfaces are governed by different crypto engines.

There are three types of crypto engines: the Cisco IOS crypto engine, the VIP2 crypto engine, and the ESA crypto engine.

If you have a Cisco 7200, RSP7000, or 7500 series router with one or more VIP2 boards (VIP2-40 or higher) or ESA cards, your router can have multiple crypto engines. All other routers have only one crypto engine, the Cisco IOS crypto engine.

When you configure a crypto engine on a Cisco 7200, RSP7000, or 7500 series router, you must identify which engine you are configuring by specifying the engine's chassis slot number when you enter the crypto commands.

NOTE   In Cisco 7500 and RSP7000-equipped Cisco 7000 systems, the ESA requires a VIP2-40 for operation and it must be installed in PA slot 1.

The three different crypto engines are described in the following sections.

The Cisco IOS Crypto Engine

Every router with Cisco IOS encryption software has a Cisco IOS crypto engine. For many Cisco routers, the Cisco IOS crypto engine is the only crypto engine available. The only exceptions are the Cisco 7200, RSP7000, and 7500 series routers, which can also have additional crypto engines as described in the next two sections.

If a router has no additional crypto engines, the Cisco IOS crypto engine governs all the router interfaces: You must configure the Cisco IOS crypto engine before you can configure any router interface for encryption.

The Cisco IOS crypto engine is identified by the chassis slot number of the Route Switch Processor (RSP). (For routers with no RSP, the Cisco IOS crypto engine is selected by default and does not need to be specifically identified during configuration.)

The VIP2 Crypto Engine (Cisco RSP7000 and 7500 Series Routers Only)

Cisco RSP7000 and 7500 series routers with a second-generation Versatile Interface Processor (VIP2; version VIP2-40 or greater) have two crypto engines: the Cisco IOS crypto engine and the VIP2 crypto engine.

The VIP2 crypto engine governs the adjoining VIP2 port interfaces. The Cisco IOS crypto engine governs all remaining router interfaces. (These rules assume there is no ESA installed in the VIP2. If the VIP2 has an installed ESA, the interfaces are governed differently, as explained in the next section.)

The VIP2 crypto engine is identified by the chassis slot number of the VIP2.

NOTE   In Cisco 7500 and RSP7000-equipped Cisco 7000 systems, the ESA requires a VIP2-40 for operation and it must be installed in PA slot 1.

The Encryption Service Adapter Crypto Engine (Cisco 7200, RSP7000, and 7500 Series Routers Only)

Cisco 7200, RSP7000, and 7500 series routers with an ESA have an ESA crypto engine.

Cisco 7200 Series Routers with an ESA

When a Cisco 7200 router has an active ESA, the ESA crypto engine—not the Cisco IOS crypto engine—governs all the router interfaces. (With an inactive ESA, the Cisco IOS crypto engine governs all the router interfaces. On the Cisco 7200, you can select which engine is active; only one engine is active at a time.)

The ESA plugs into the Cisco 7200 chassis, and the ESA crypto engine is identified by the ESA's chassis slot number.

Cisco RSP7000 and 7500 Series Routers with an ESA

The ESA and an adjoining port adapter plug into a VIP2 board. The ESA crypto engine—not the VIP2 crypto engine—governs the adjoining VIP2 port interfaces. The Cisco IOS crypto engine governs all remaining interfaces.

In a Cisco RSP7000 or 7500 series router, the ESA crypto engine is identified by the chassis slot number of the VIP2.

Understanding Implementation Issues and Limitations

The following sections describe issues and limitations related to encryption:

- Encapsulation

- Multicast of Encrypted Traffic

- IP Fragmentation

- Restrictions for Switching Types with the VIP2

- Number of Simultaneous Encrypted Sessions

- Performance Impacts

Encapsulation

You can use any type of encapsulation with IP encryption, except as follows: If you have a second-generation VIP2 with a serial interface, encryption will not work for traffic on the serial interface unless you use Point-to-Point Protocol (PPP), High-Level Data Link Control (HDLC) protocol, or Frame Relay protocol. For example, you cannot use encryption if you have X.25 or SMDS configured for the serial interface of a VIP2.

Table 26-1 shows port adapter support by platform.

Table 26-1 *Port Adapter Support*

Interface	Encapsulation	7200 Software	7200 ESA	7500/VIP Distribution Software	7500/VIP ESA
4E, 8E, 5EFL		Yes	Yes	Yes	Yes
FE		Yes	Yes	Yes	Yes
4R		Yes	Yes	Yes	Yes
FDDI		Yes	Yes	Yes	Yes
100VG		Yes	Yes	Yes	Yes

Continues

Table 26-1 *Port Adapter Support (Continued)*

Interface	Encapsulation	7200 Software	7200 ESA	7500/VIP Distribution Software	7500/VIP ESA
4T	PPP, HDLC, Frame Relay	No	No	Yes	No
4T+, 8T	PPP	Yes	Yes	Yes	Yes
	HDLC	Yes	Yes	Yes	Yes
	Frame Relay	Yes	Yes	Yes	Yes
	X.25	Yes	Yes	No	No
	SMDS	Yes	Yes	No	No
HSSI	PPP	Yes	Yes	Yes	Yes
	HDLC	Yes	Yes	Yes	Yes
	Frame Relay	Yes	Yes	Yes	Yes
	X.25	Yes	Yes	No	No
	SMDS	Yes	Yes	No	No
CT1, CE1	PPP	Yes	Yes	Yes	Yes
	HDLC	Yes	Yes	Yes	Yes
	Frame Relay	Yes	Yes	Yes	Yes
	X.25	Yes	Yes	No	No
	SMDS	Yes	Yes	No	No
PRI	HDLC	Yes	Yes	No	No
	PPP	Yes	Yes	No	No
BRI	HDLC	Yes	Yes	No	No
	PPP	Yes	Yes	No	No
ATM		Yes	Yes	Yes	No
CT3		No	No	Yes	No

Multicast of Encrypted Traffic

Encrypted multicast is not supported.

IP Fragmentation

IP fragmentation is supported with encryption for all platforms except the VIP2. If you configure encryption for VIP2 interfaces, all IP fragments will be dropped.

Restrictions for Switching Types with the VIP2

If you configure encryption for VIP2 interfaces on a Cisco RSP7000 or 7500 series router, you must use distributed switching (DSW) on the source and destination encrypting/decrypting interfaces.

This restriction means that any protocol that is not compatible with DSW, such as SMDS, cannot be used on VIP2 encrypting interfaces.

Number of Simultaneous Encrypted Sessions

Each encrypting router can set up encrypted sessions with many other routers, if these are peer encrypting routers. Encrypting routers can also set up multiple simultaneous encrypted sessions with multiple peer routers. Up to 299 concurrent encrypted sessions per router can be supported.

Performance Impacts

Because of the large amount of processing required for encryption, if you use encryption heavily, there will be performance impacts such as interface congestion or slowed CPU functioning. Using an ESA crypto engine rather than the Cisco IOS crypto engine can improve overall router performance because the Cisco IOS software will not be impacted by encryption processing.

Configuring Encryption

To pass encrypted traffic between two routers, you must configure encryption at both routers. This section describes the tasks required to configure encryption on one router: You must repeat these tasks for each peer encrypting router (routers that will participate in encryption).

To configure encryption on a router, complete the tasks described in the following sections:

● Generating DSS Public/Private Keys (required to configure a crypto engine)

● Exchanging DSS Public Keys (required to configure a crypto engine)

● Enabling DES Encryption Algorithms (required to configure the router)

● Defining Crypto Maps and Assigning Them to Interfaces (required to configure router interfaces)

● Backing Up Your Configuration

NOTE   There are additional steps required if you configure encryption with GRE tunnels or if you configure encryption with an ESA. These additional steps are described later in this chapter, in the sections "Configuring Encryption with GRE Tunnels," "Configuring Encryption with an ESA in a VIP2," and "Configuring Encryption with an ESA in a Cisco 7200 Series Router." Before you configure encryption, refer to these other sections as appropriate.

For examples of the configuration in this section, see the section "Encryption Configuration Examples" at the end of this chapter.

Generating DSS Public/Private Keys

You must generate DSS keys for each crypto engine you will use. If you will use more than one crypto engine, you must generate DSS keys separately for each engine. (These are the crypto engines you previously identified per the description in the earlier section "Identifying Crypto Engines Within Each Peer Router.")

The DSS key pair that you generate is used by peer routers to authenticate each other before each encrypted session. The same DSS key pair is used by a crypto engine with all its encrypted sessions (regardless of the peer encrypting router that it connects to).

Generate DSS keys for a crypto engine by using at least the first of the following commands in global configuration mode:

Command	Purpose
crypto key generate dss *key-name* [*slot*]	Generates DSS public and private keys.
show crypto key mypubkey dss [*slot*]	Views your DSS public key (private key not viewable).
copy system:running-config nvram:startup-config	Saves DSS keys to private NVRAM. (Complete this task only for Cisco IOS crypto engines.)

NOTE	You must use the **copy system:running-config nvram:startup-config** (previously **copy running-config startup-config**) command to save Cisco IOS crypto engine DSS keys to a private portion of NVRAM. DSS keys are *not* saved with your configuration when you perform a **copy system:running-config rcp:** or **copy system:running-config tftp:** command.

If you are generating keys for an ESA crypto engine, the following occurs during DSS key generation:

● You are prompted to enter a password.

— If you previously used the **crypto key zeroize dss** command to reset the ESA, you should create a new password for the ESA at this time.

— If you previously used the **crypto card clear-latch** command to reset the ESA, you should now use the password you assigned when you reset the ESA. If you do not remember the password, you must clear the ESA with the **crypto key zeroize dss** command; you can then generate keys and create a new password for the ESA.

● The DSS keys are automatically saved to the tamper resistant memory of the ESA.

Configuring encryption with an ESA is described later in the sections "Configuring Encryption with an ESA in a VIP2" and "Configuring Encryption with an ESA in a Cisco 7200 Series Router."

Exchanging DSS Public Keys

You must exchange DSS public keys with all participating peer routers. This allows peer routers to authenticate each other at the start of encrypted communication sessions.

If your network contains several peer encrypting routers, you need to exchange DSS keys multiple times (once for each peer router). If you ever add an encrypting peer router to your network topology, you will need to exchange DSS keys with the new router to enable encryption to occur with that new router.

NOTE   When you exchange DSS keys, you must call the administrator of the peer encrypting router. You need to be in voice contact with the other administrator during the key exchange in order to voice authenticate the source of exchanged DSS public keys.

You must exchange the DSS public keys of each crypto engine that you will use.

To successfully exchange DSS public keys, you must cooperate with a trusted administrator of the other peer router. You and the administrator of the peer router must complete the following steps in the order given (refer to Figure 26-5):

Step 1   Call the other administrator on the phone. Remain on the phone with this person until you complete all the steps in this list.

Step 2   You and the other administrator decide which of you will be called PASSIVE and which will be called ACTIVE.

Step 3   PASSIVE enables a DSS exchange connection by using the following command in global configuration mode:

Command	Purpose
crypto key exchange dss passive [*tcp-port*]	Enables a DSS exchange connection.

Step 4   ACTIVE initiates a DSS exchange connection and sends a DSS public key by using the following command in global configuration mode:

Command	Purpose
crypto key exchange dss *ip-address key-name* [*tcp-port*]	Initiates connection and sends a DSS public key.

The serial number and fingerprint of ACTIVE's DSS public key will display on both of your screens. The serial number and Fingerprint are numeric values generated from ACTIVE's DSS public key.

Step 5   You verbally verify that the serial number is the same on both your screens, and that the fingerprint is the same on both your screens.

Step 6   If the displayed serial numbers and Fingerprints match, PASSIVE should agree to accept ACTIVE's DSS key by typing **y** at the prompt.

Step 7   PASSIVE sends ACTIVE a DSS public key by pressing the Return key at the screen prompt and selecting a crypto engine at the next prompt.

Step 8   PASSIVE's DSS serial number and Fingerprint display on both of your screens.

Step 9   As before, you both verbally verify that the PASSIVE's DSS serial number and Fingerprint match on your two screens.

Step 10   ACTIVE agrees to accept PASSIVE's DSS public key.

Step 11   The exchange is complete, and you can end the phone call.

The previous steps (illustrated in Figure 26-5) must be accomplished between your router and a peer router for every peer router with which you will be conducting encrypted sessions.

Figure 26-5 *Exchanging DSS Public Keys*

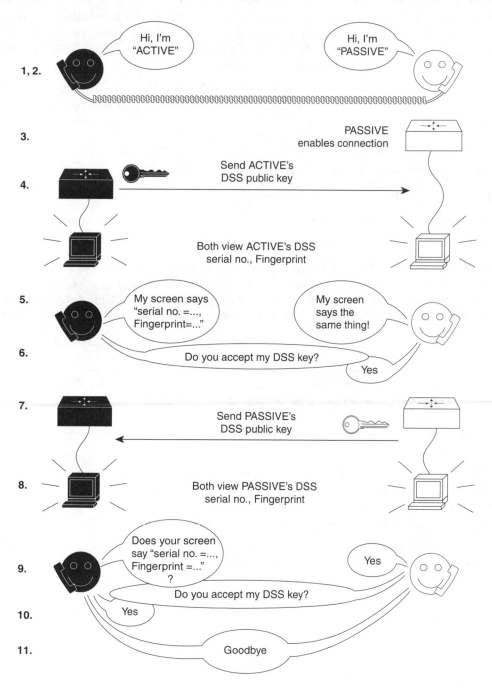

Enabling DES Encryption Algorithms

Cisco routers use DES encryption algorithms and DES keys to encrypt and decrypt data. You must globally enable all the DES encryption algorithms that your router will use during encrypted sessions. If a DES algorithm is not enabled globally, you will not be able to use it. (Enabling a DES algorithm once allows it to be used by all crypto engines of a router.)

To conduct an encrypted session with a peer router, you must enable at least one DES algorithm that the peer router also has enabled. You must configure the same DES algorithm on both peer routers for encryption to work.

CET supports the following four types of DES encryption algorithms:

● DES with 8-bit Cipher FeedBack (CFB)

● DES with 64-bit CFB

● 40-bit variation of DES with 8-bit CFB

● 40-bit variation of DES with 64-bit CFB

The 40-bit variations use a 40-bit DES key, which is easier for attackers to crack than basic DES, which uses a 56-bit DES key. However, some international applications might require you to use 40-bit DES because of export laws. Also, 8-bit CFB is more commonly used than 64-bit CFB, but requires more CPU time to process. Other conditions might also exist that require you to use one or another type of DES.

NOTE   If you are running an exportable image, you can only enable and use 40-bit variations of DES. You cannot enable or use the basic DES algorithms, which are not available with exportable images.

One DES algorithm is enabled for your router by default. If you do not plan to use the default DES algorithm, you may choose to disable it. If you are running a non-exportable image, the DES default algorithm will be basic DES with 64-bit CFB. If you are running an exportable image, the DES default algorithm will be the 40-bit variation of DES with 64-bit CFB.

If you do not know if your image is exportable or non-exportable, you can use the **show crypto cisco algorithms** command to determine which DES algorithms are currently enabled.

Globally enable one or more DES algorithms by using one or more of the following commands in global configuration mode:

Command	Purpose
**crypto cisco algorithm des [cfb-8	cfb-64]**	Enables DES with 8-bit or 64-bit CFB.
**crypto cisco algorithm 40-bit-des [cfb-8	cfb-64]**	Enables 40-bit DES with 8-bit or 64-bit CFB.
show crypto cisco algorithms	Views all enabled DES algorithms.

Defining Crypto Maps and Assigning Them to Interfaces

The purpose of this task is to tell your router which interfaces should encrypt/decrypt traffic, which IP packets to encrypt or decrypt at those interfaces, and which DES encryption algorithm to use when encrypting/decrypting the packets.

There are actually three steps required to complete this task:

Step 1   Set up encryption access list (to be used in the crypto map definition).

Step 2   Define crypto maps.

Step 3   Apply crypto maps to interfaces.

NOTE   You should select which interfaces to configure so that traffic is encrypted at the outbound interface of the local peer router and traffic is decrypted at the input interface of the remote peer.

Setting Up Encryption Access List

Encryption access lists are used in this step to define which IP packets will be encrypted and which IP packets will not be encrypted. Encryption access lists are defined using extended IP access lists. (Normally, IP access lists are used to filter traffic. Encryption access lists are *not* used to filter traffic but are used to specify which packets to encrypt or not encrypt.)

Set up encryption access lists for IP packet encryption by using either of the following commands in global configuration mode:

Command	Purpose
access-list *access-list-number* [**dynamic** *dynamic-name* [**timeout** *minutes*]] {**deny** | **permit**} *protocol source source-wildcard destination destination-wildcard* [**precedence** *precedence*] [**tos** *tos*] [**log**] or **ip access-list extended** *name* Follow with **permit** and **deny** statements as appropriate.	Specifies conditions to determine which IP packets will be encrypted. (Enable or disable encryption for traffic that matches these conditions.)[1]

1. You specify conditions using an IP access list designated by either a number or a name. The **access-list** command designates a numbered access list; the **ip access-list extended** command designates a named access list.

Using the **permit** keyword will cause the selected traffic that is passed between the specified source and destination addresses to be encrypted/decrypted by peer routers. Using the **deny** keyword prevents that traffic from being encrypted/decrypted by peer routers.

The encryption access list you define at the local router must have a mirror-image encryption access list defined at the remote router, so that traffic that is encrypted locally is decrypted at the remote peer.

The encryption access list you define will be applied to an interface as an outbound encryption access list after you define a crypto map and apply the crypto map to the interface. (These two tasks are described in the next sections.)

CAUTION   When you create encryption access lists, Cisco recommends *against* using the **any** keyword to specify source or destination addresses. Using the **any** keyword could cause extreme problems if a packet enters your router and is destined for a router that is not configured for encryption. This would cause your router to attempt to set up an encryption session with a nonencrypting router.

NOTE   If your encryption access lists define more than 100 distinct source addresses or more than 10 destination addresses for a given source address, you need to change certain defaults as described later, in the section "Changing Encryption Access List Limits."

NOTE	If you view your router's access lists by using a command such as **show ip access-lists**, *all* extended IP access lists will be shown in the command output. This includes extended IP access lists that are used for traffic filtering purposes as well as those that are used for encryption. The **show** command output does not differentiate between the two uses of the extended access lists.

About Crypto Maps

Crypto maps are used to specify which DES encryption algorithm(s) will be used in conjunction with each access list defined in the previous step. Crypto maps are also used to identify which peer routers will provide the remote end encryption services.

Crypto map entries with the same crypto map name (but different map sequence numbers) are grouped into a crypto map set. Later, you will apply these crypto map sets to interfaces; then, all IP traffic passing through the interface is evaluated against the applied crypto map set. If a crypto map entry sees outbound IP traffic that should be protected and the crypto map specifies the use of IKE, a security association is negotiated with the remote peer according to the parameters included in the crypto map entry; otherwise, if the crypto map entry specifies the use of manual security associations, a security association should have already been established via configuration. (If a dynamic crypto map entry sees outbound traffic that should be protected and no security association exists, the packet is dropped.)

The policy described in the crypto map entries is used during the negotiation of security associations. If the local router initiates the negotiation, it will use the policy specified in the static crypto map entries to create the offer to be sent to the specified IPSec peer. If the IPSec peer initiates the negotiation, the local router will check the policy from the static crypto map entries, as well as any referenced dynamic crypto map entries to decide whether to accept or reject the peer's request (offer).

If you create more than one crypto map entry for a given interface, use the *seq-num* of each map entry to rank the map entries: The lower the *seq-num*, the higher the priority. At the interface that has the crypto map set, traffic is evaluated against higher priority map entries first.

Defining Crypto Maps

You must define exactly one crypto map for each interface that will send encrypted data to a peer encrypting router. You can apply only one crypto map set to a single interface. Multiple interfaces can share the same crypto map set if you want to apply the same policy to multiple interfaces.

To define a crypto map, use the following commands. The first command is used in global configuration mode; the other commands are used in crypto map configuration mode:

Step	Command	Purpose
1	**crypto map** *map-name seq-num* [**cisco**]	Names the crypto map. (Executing this command causes you to enter the crypto map configuration mode.)
2	**set peer** *key-name*	Specifies the remote peer router.
3	**match address** [*access-list-number* | *name*]	Specifies at least one encryption access list.
4	**set algorithm des** [**cfb-8** | **cfb-64**] or **set algorithm 40-bit-des** [**cfb-8** | **cfb-64**]	Specifies at least one DES encryption algorithm. (This must be an algorithm you previously enabled.)

NOTE If you are running an exportable image, you can only specify 40-bit variations of DES. You cannot enable or use the basic DES algorithms, which are not available with exportable images.

To define an additional, different set of parameters for the same interface, repeat the steps in the previous task list, using the same *map-name* but use a different *seq-num* for the crypto map command. For more information about this, refer to the **crypto map** command description in Chapter 27, "Cisco Encryption Technology Commands."

Applying Crypto Maps to Interfaces

This step puts into effect the crypto maps just defined. You must apply exactly one crypto map set to each interface (physical or logical) that will encrypt outbound data and decrypt inbound data. This interface provides the encrypted connection to a peer encrypting router. An interface will not encrypt/decrypt data until you apply a crypto map to the interface.

To apply a crypto map to an interface, use the following command in interface configuration mode:

Command	Purpose
crypto map *map-name*	Applies a crypto map to an interface.

Backing Up Your Configuration

Cisco recommends that after you configure your router for encryption, you make a backup of your configuration. (Be careful to restrict unauthorized access of this backed-up configuration.)

Configuring Encryption with GRE Tunnels

When GRE tunnel endpoints are located at the peer encrypting routers, you can configure encryption so that all traffic through the GRE tunnel is encrypted.

Note that you cannot selectively encrypt GRE tunnel traffic: Either all the GRE tunnel traffic is encrypted or no GRE tunnel traffic is encrypted.

To configure encryption with GRE tunnels, perform the same basic tasks described previously in the section "Configuring Encryption." However, you also must follow the additional instructions described next (for two cases):

- Encrypting only GRE Tunnel Traffic

- Encrypting GRE Tunnel Traffic and Other Traffic

For examples of configuring encryption with a GRE tunnel, see the section "Examples of Configuring Encryption with GRE Tunnels" later in this chapter.

Encrypting only GRE Tunnel Traffic

To encrypt only traffic through the GRE tunnel, follow these two additional instructions:

- When you set up your encryption access list, the list should contain only one criteria statement. In this one statement, specify **gre** as the protocol, specify the tunnel source address as the source, and specify the tunnel destination address as the destination.

- Apply the crypto map to both the physical interface and to the tunnel interface. (Without GRE tunnels, you only have to apply the crypto map to the physical interface.)

  Remember to apply a crypto map to the physical interface and tunnel interface at both ends of the GRE tunnel.

Encrypting GRE Tunnel Traffic and Other Traffic

To encrypt both GRE tunnel traffic and other specified non-GRE tunnel traffic, follow these three additional instructions:

- Create two separate encryption access lists as follows:

  — The first encryption access list should contain only one criteria statement. In this one statement, specify **gre** as the protocol, specify the tunnel source address as the source, and specify the tunnel destination address as the destination.

  — In the second encryption access list, specify which non-GRE traffic should be encrypted. (For example, you could specify **tcp** as a protocol, and specify a subnet source/wildcard and a subnet destination/wildcard.)

- Create two separate crypto map sets as follows:

  — In the first crypto map set, specify a single crypto map that includes the first encryption access list, along with a DES algorithm and the remote peer.

  — In the second crypto map set, include at least two crypto map subdefinitions. The first subdefinition should exactly match the statements in the first crypto map. The second subdefinition should specify the second encryption access list, a DES algorithm, and the remote peer.

- Apply the first crypto map set to the tunnel interface, and apply the second crypto map set to the physical interface. (Without GRE tunnels, you have to apply only one crypto map to the physical interface.)

  Remember to apply a crypto map set to the physical interface and tunnel interface at both ends of the GRE tunnel.

Configuring Encryption with an ESA in a VIP2

To configure encryption with an ESA, there are additional instructions that you must follow in addition to the basic encryption configuration tasks described earlier in the chapter, in the section, "Configuring Encryption."

This section describes configuration for an ESA plugged into a VIP2 on a Cisco RSP7000 or 7500 series router.

To configure encryption with an ESA plugged into a VIP2, complete these tasks, in this order:

1 Reset the ESA.

2 Perform additional encryption configuration.

NOTE   In Cisco 7500 and RSP7000-equipped Cisco 7000 systems, the ESA requires a VIP2-40 for operation and it must be installed in PA slot 1. If you ever remove and reinstall the ESA or the VIP2, you must reset the ESA again.

For examples of ESA-specific configuration tasks, see the section "Examples of ESA-Specific Encryption Configuration Tasks" later in this chapter.

Resetting the ESA

If the ESA has never been used before, or if it has been removed and reinstalled, the ESA's "Tampered" LED is lit and it must be reset.

If you do not reset the ESA in a VIP2, the ESA crypto engine will not be used; instead, the VIP2 crypto engine will govern the adjoining VIP2 port interfaces (and the Cisco IOS crypto engine will govern the other router interfaces).

To reset an ESA, complete one of the following tasks:

- Reset an ESA that has never been used before (or was previously used and you know the ESA password), by using the following commands in global configuration mode:

Step	Command	Purpose
1	**crypto card clear-latch** *slot*	Resets the ESA by clearing the ESA hardware latch.
2	**password**	When prompted, creates a new password for the ESA or types the ESA password previously assigned.

- Reset an ESA that was previously used, but you do not know the ESA password, by using the following command in global configuration mode:

Command	Purpose
crypto key zeroize dss *slot*	Clears the ESA. (This deletes all DSS keys for the ESA.)

Performing Additional Encryption Configuration

If the router, VIP2, and ESA were all previously configured for encryption, you might not need to complete any additional configuration. However, you will need additional configuration in at least the following cases (see the section "Configuring Encryption" for descriptions of the tasks):

— If you have any concern that the old ESA keys are compromised, you should regenerate and exchange new DSS keys for the ESA. (Use the same ESA *key-name* previously assigned.)

— If the ESA was relocated and now governs different interfaces than before, either all peer routers must update their crypto maps to reflect the changed peers, or you must regenerate and exchange new DSS keys for the ESA, assigning the *key-name* that is currently in the peer routers' crypto maps.

— If you previously reset the ESA with the **crypto key zeroize dss** command because you did not know the ESA password, you must at a minimum generate and exchange DSS keys for the ESA crypto engine.

As always, remember to back up your configuration when you are done.

Configuring Encryption with an ESA in a Cisco 7200 Series Router

To configure encryption with an ESA, you must follow some special steps in addition to the basic encryption configuration tasks described previously in the section "Configuring Encryption."

This section describes configuration for an ESA plugged into a Cisco 7200 series router.

For examples of ESA-specific configuration tasks, see the section "Examples of ESA-Specific Encryption Configuration Tasks" later in this chapter.

Required Tasks

Complete the following tasks, in this order (see following sections for descriptions):

1　Resetting the ESA

2　Performing additional encryption configuration

3　Enabling the ESA

NOTE　　　If you ever remove and reinstall the ESA, you must reset the ESA again and re-enable the ESA.

Optional Tasks

You can optionally complete these additional tasks (see the following sections for descriptions):

● Select a crypto engine. (After encryption is configured, you might want to change which crypto engine to use—the Cisco IOS crypto engine or the ESA crypto engine.)

● Delete DSS keys. (If you ever remove or relocate the ESA or the Cisco 7200, you might want to delete DSS keys, to reduce any potential security risk.)

Resetting the ESA

If the ESA has never been used before, or if it has been removed and reinstalled, the ESA's "Tampered" LED is lit and it must be reset.

To reset an ESA in a Cisco 7200 series router, complete one of the following tasks:

● Reset an ESA that has never been used before by using the following commands in global configuration mode:

Step	Command	Purpose
1	**crypto card clear-latch** *slot*	Resets the ESA by clearing the ESA hardware latch.
2	**password**	When prompted, creates a new password for the ESA.

● Reset a previously used ESA that needs additional configuration (for example, the ESA's previous configuration was not complete or is uncertain; you know you want to generate new DSS keys for the ESA; or the router is not configured for encryption) by using the following commands in global configuration mode:

Step	Command	Purpose
1	**crypto card clear-latch** *slot*	Resets the ESA by clearing the ESA hardware latch.
2	**password**	When prompted, type the ESA password previously assigned.
3	**no**	If prompted to enable the ESA, type **no**.

● Reset a previously used ESA when encryption configuration is already complete and you are ready to start encrypting traffic with the ESA crypto engine by using the following commands in global configuration mode:

Step	Command	Purpose
1	**crypto card clear-latch** *slot*	Resets the ESA by clearing the ESA hardware latch.
2	**password**	When prompted, type the ESA password previously assigned.
3	**yes**	When prompted to enable the ESA, type **yes**.

NOTE   After you reset the ESA as just described, the ESA will automatically become active and begin encrypting traffic. For this case only, you do not need to complete any additional encryption configuration. (But as always, be sure to back up your configuration.)

- Reset a previously used ESA when you do not know the ESA password by using the following command in global configuration mode:

Command	Purpose
crypto key zeroize dss *slot*	Clears the ESA. (This deletes all DSS keys for the ESA.)

Performing Additional Encryption Configuration

After you reset the ESA in a Cisco 7200 series router, continue configuring encryption by following the instructions in one of the following bullets:

- If the router and ESA were never previously configured for encryption, complete all the tasks described earlier in the section "Configuring Encryption," and then enable the ESA as described in the next section, "Enabling the ESA."

- If the ESA was never previously configured for encryption, but the router is configured for encryption, complete only the following two tasks, which were described earlier, in the section "Configuring Encryption":

  — Generate DSS public/private keys (for the ESA crypto engine).

  — Exchange DSS public keys (for the ESA crypto engine).

  After you generate and exchange DSS keys for the ESA crypto engine, enable the ESA as described in the next section, "Enabling the ESA."

- If the router and ESA are both already configured for encryption, you might only need to enable the ESA, as described in the next section, "Enabling the ESA." However, in at least the following cases you will need additional configuration before you enable the ESA (see the section "Configuring Encryption" for descriptions of the tasks):

  — If the ESA has DSS keys generated but not exchanged with the peer routers, you must exchange the keys.

  — If you have any concern that the ESA's DSS keys are compromised, you should regenerate and exchange new DSS keys for the ESA, using the same *key-name* assigned to the router DSS keys.

  — If the ESA was relocated from a different router, regenerate and exchange DSS keys, using the same *key-name* assigned to the router DSS keys.

  — If you previously reset the ESA with the **crypto key zeroize dss** command because you did not know the ESA password, you must at a minimum generate and exchange DSS keys for the ESA crypto engine.

Enabling the ESA

Enable an ESA in a Cisco 7200 series router by using the following command in global configuration mode:

Command	Purpose
crypto card enable *slot*	Enables the ESA.

NOTE   If the Cisco IOS crypto engine is currently encrypting traffic when you enable the ESA, the session will be torn down, and a new session will be established using the ESA crypto engine. This could cause a momentary delay for encrypted traffic.

As always, remember to back up your configuration when you are done.

Selecting a Crypto Engine

This is an optional task.

After encryption is configured on a Cisco 7200 series router with an ESA, you might want to change which crypto engine to use—the Cisco IOS crypto engine or the ESA crypto engine. This section describes how to switch from one crypto engine to the other.

You should only select a crypto engine if the engine is fully configured for encryption.

If you boot the router with an operational ESA installed, the ESA will be the active crypto engine upon bootup, by default. Otherwise, the Cisco IOS crypto engine will be the default active crypto engine.

NOTE   If any encryption session is in progress when you switch from one crypto engine to the other, the session will be torn down, and a new session will be established using the newly selected crypto engine. This could cause a momentary delay for encrypted traffic.

Selecting the Cisco IOS Crypto Engine

If the ESA crypto engine is encrypting traffic, but you want to cause the Cisco IOS crypto engine to encrypt the traffic instead, you can switch to the Cisco IOS crypto engine without removing the ESA. (You might want to do this for testing purposes.)

CAUTION   Before you switch to the Cisco IOS crypto engine, be sure that the Cisco IOS crypto engine is configured with DSS keys generated and exchanged; otherwise, you will lose encryption capability when you switch engines.

Select the Cisco IOS crypto engine by using the following command in global configuration mode:

Command	Purpose
crypto card shutdown *slot*	Shuts down the ESA.

After you select the Cisco IOS crypto engine, the Cisco IOS crypto engine will be the active engine, governing the router interfaces. The Cisco IOS crypto engine will perform the encryption services, and the ESA will be inactive.

Selecting the ESA Crypto Engine

If the Cisco IOS crypto engine is encrypting traffic, but you want to cause an installed ESA crypto engine to encrypt the traffic instead, you can switch to the ESA crypto engine.

CAUTION   Before you switch to the ESA crypto engine, be sure that the ESA crypto engine is configured with DSS keys generated and exchanged; otherwise, you will lose encryption capability when you switch engines.

Select the ESA crypto engine by using the following command in global configuration mode:

Command	Purpose
crypto card enable *slot*	Enables the ESA.

After you select the ESA crypto engine, the ESA crypto engine will be the active engine, governing the router interfaces. The ESA crypto engine will perform encryption services for the router, and the Cisco IOS crypto engine will be inactive.

Deleting DSS Keys

This is an optional task.

If you ever remove or relocate the ESA or the Cisco 7200, the DSS keys ever become compromised, or if you want to turn encryption off at the router, you might want to delete DSS keys to reduce any potential security risk. This section describes how to delete a DSS key pair for an ESA or for a Cisco 7200 series router.

To delete DSS keys, use the following commands beginning in EXEC mode:

Step	Command	Purpose
1	**show crypto key mypubkey dss**	Views all existing sets of DSS keys (ESA and Cisco IOS keys).
2	**show crypto engine configuration**	Determines the current (active) crypto engine.
3	**crypto card enable** *slot* (switch to the Cisco IOS crypto engine) or **crypto card shutdown** *slot* (switch to the ESA crypto engine)	If the current engine is not the engine for which you want to delete keys, change engines. (When you delete keys, the software deletes keys for the current active engine.)
4	**show crypto engine configuration**	Verifies that the current crypto engine is the engine for which you want to delete keys.
5	**crypto key zeroize dss** (for the Cisco IOS crypto engine) or **crypto key zeroize dss** *slot* (for the ESA crypto engine)	Deletes the DSS keys for the current crypto engine.

After you delete DSS keys for a crypto engine, if you ever want to use that engine for encryption, you must regenerate and exchange new DSS keys for that engine. For the ESA crypto engine, you must also enable the ESA.

Customizing Encryption (Configuring Options)

This following sections describe options that you can configure to customize encryption on a router:

- Defining Time Duration of Encrypted Sessions
- Shortening Session Setup Times by Pregenerating DH Numbers
- Changing Encryption Access List Limits

Defining Time Duration of Encrypted Sessions

The default time duration of an encrypted session is 30 minutes. After the default time duration expires, an encrypted session must be renegotiated if encrypted communication is to continue. You can change this default to extend or shorten the time of encrypted sessions.

You might want to shorten session times if you believe that there is a risk of compromised session keys. You might want to extend session times if your system has trouble tolerating the interruptions caused when sessions are renegotiated.

Change the time duration of encrypted sessions by using at least the first of the following commands in global configuration mode:

Step	Command	Purpose
1	**crypto cisco key-timeout** *minutes*	Defines maximum time duration of encrypted sessions.
2	**show crypto cisco key-timeout**	Views defined time duration of encrypted sessions.

Shortening Session Setup Times by Pregenerating DH Numbers

DH numbers are generated in pairs during the setup of each encrypted session. (DH numbers are used during encrypted session setup to compute the DES session key.) Generating these numbers is a CPU-intensive activity, which can make session setup slow—especially for low-end routers. To speed up session setup time, you may choose to pregenerate DH numbers. It is usually necessary to pregenerate only one or two DH numbers.

Pregenerate DH numbers by using the following command in global configuration mode:

Command	Purpose
crypto cisco pregen-dh-pairs *count* [*slot*]	Pregenerates DH numbers.

Changing Encryption Access List Limits

When you configure encryption access lists, you configure source and destination pairs in criteria statements. Any traffic that matches the criteria is then encrypted.

By default, the maximum number of distinct sources (host or subnets) that you can define in an encryption access list is 100. Also, the maximum number of distinct destinations that you can define for any given source address is 10. For example, if you define six different source addresses, you can define up to 10 destination addresses for each of the six sources, for a total of 60 access list criteria statements.

Why Do These Limits Exist?

These limits exist because of the amount of memory that must be reserved for encryption connections. If there are more potential connections, there must be more memory preallocated.

When Should the Limits Be Changed?

For most situations, the defaults of 100 maximum sources and 10 maximum destinations per source are sufficient. Cisco recommends that you do not change the defaults unless you actually exceed the number of sources or destinations per source.

However, in some situations you might want to change one or both of these maximum values. For example, if more than 10 remote sites need to connect to one server behind your router, then you need more than 10 destination addresses (one for each remote site) to pair up with the server's source address in the local router's encryption access list. In this case, you need to change the default of 10 maximum destination addresses per source address.

When changing limits, you should consider the amount of memory that will be allocated. In general, if you increase one value, decrease the other value. This prevents your router from running out of memory because too much memory was preallocated.

How Much Memory Is Preallocated If the Limits Are Changed?

The amount of memory reserved for encrypted connections changes if you change the defaults.

For every additional source, the following additional bytes of memory will be allocated:

```
64 + (86 x the specified number of maximum destinations)
```

For every additional destination, the following additional bytes of memory will be allocated:

```
68 x the specified number of maximum sources
```

For example, if you specify 5 maximum sources, and 250 maximum destinations per source, the memory allocated for encryption connections is calculated as follows:

```
{5 x [64 + (68 x 250)]} + {250 x (68 x 5)} = 170320 bytes
```

How Are the Limits Changed?

Change the default limits by using one or both of the following commands in global configuration mode, then reboot the router for the changes to take effect:

Command	Purpose
crypto cisco entities *number*	Changes the maximum number of distinct sources (hosts or subnets) that you can define in the encryption access list statements.

Command	Purpose
crypto cisco connections *number*	Changes the maximum number of destinations (hosts or subnets) per source that you can define in the encryption access list statements.

NOTE   You must reboot the router for these changes to take effect.

For an example of changing these values, see the section "Example of Changing Encryption Access List Limits" later in this chapter.

Turning Off Encryption

You can turn off encryption for certain router interfaces, or you can turn off encryption completely for the entire router.

- To turn off encryption at all the interfaces governed by a single crypto engine, you can delete DSS keys for that engine. Deleting DSS keys is described in this section.

- To turn off encryption at certain random interfaces, you can remove the crypto maps from the interfaces with the **no crypto map (interface configuration)** command.

- To turn off encryption completely for a router, you can delete the DSS keys for all the router's crypto engines. Deleting DSS keys is described in this section.

Deleting DSS keys deconfigures encryption for the crypto engine and also reduces security risk by ensuring that the keys cannot be misused if you lose physical control over the router or ESA.

After you delete DSS keys for a crypto engine, you will not be able to perform encryption on the interfaces governed by that crypto engine.

CAUTION   DSS keys cannot be recovered after they have been deleted. Use this function only after careful consideration.

For all platforms other than Cisco 7200 series routers, to delete DSS public/private keys for a crypto engine, use the following command in global configuration mode:

Command	Purpose
crypto key zeroize dss [*slot*][1]	Deletes DSS keys for a crypto engine.

1. Only Cisco 7200 and 7500 series routers require the *slot* argument.

For a Cisco 7200 series router, to delete DSS public/private keys for a crypto engine, refer to the section "Deleting DSS Keys" earlier in this chapter.

Testing and Troubleshooting Encryption

This section discusses how to verify your configuration and the correct operation of encryption. This section also discusses diagnosing encryption problems.

You should complete all the required configuration tasks (as described earlier in this chapter) before trying to test or troubleshoot your encryption configuration.

This section includes the following topics:

- Testing the Encryption Configuration

- Diagnosing Connection Problems

- Diagnosing Other Miscellaneous Problems

- Using Debug Commands

Testing the Encryption Configuration

If you want to test the encryption setup between peer routers, you can attempt to manually establish a session using the IP address of a local host and a remote host which have been specified in an encryption access list. (The encryption access list must be specified in a crypto map definition, and that crypto map must be applied to an interface before this test will be successful.)

To test the encryption setup, use the following commands in privileged EXEC mode:

Step	Command	Purpose
1	**test crypto initiate-session** *src-ip-addr dst-ip-addr map-name seq-num*	Sets up a test encryption session.
2	**show crypto cisco connections**	Views the connection status.

An example at the end of this chapter explains how to interpret the **show crypto cisco connections** command output.

Diagnosing Connection Problems

If you need to verify the state of a connection, you can use the following commands in privileged EXEC mode:

Command	Purpose
show crypto cisco connections	Checks status of all encryption connections.
show crypto map	Checks status of a crypto map.
show crypto engine connections active	Checks that connection is established and that packets are being encrypted.

Diagnosing Other Miscellaneous Problems

When using encryption, you might encounter some of the problems described in the following sections:

- Dropped Packets
- Difficulty Establishing Telnet Sessions
- Invalid DSS Public/Private Keys
- ESA Crypto Engine Not Active
- Password Requested When You Generate DSS Keys
- Router Hanging

Dropped Packets

Packets are normally dropped while an encrypted session is being set up. If this poses a problem for your network, you should extend the length of encryption sessions as described previously in the section "Defining Time Duration of Encrypted Sessions." The longer the session time, the fewer the interruptions caused by session renegotiation.

Packets might also be dropped if you switch crypto engines in a Cisco 7200 series router with an ESA. If this is a problem, you should only switch crypto engines when encrypted traffic is light.

IP fragments are always dropped on VIP2 interfaces, because IP fragmentation is not supported with encryption on VIP2 interfaces.

Difficulty Establishing Telnet Sessions

Hosts might experience difficulty in establishing Telnet sessions if the session uses two encrypting peer routers to create the connection. This difficulty is more likely to occur if the peer routers are low-end routers such as Cisco 2500 series routers. Telnet sessions can fail to be established when a Telnet connection attempt times out before the encrypted session setup is complete.

If a Telnet session fails to establish, the host should wait a short time (a few seconds might be sufficient), and then attempt the Telnet connection again. After the short wait, the encrypted session setup should be complete, and the Telnet session can be established. Enabling pregeneration of DH numbers (described later in this chapter) might also help by speeding up encryption session connection setup times.

Invalid DSS Public/Private Keys

If NVRAM fails, or if your ESA is tampered with or replaced, DSS public/private keys will no longer be valid. If this happens, you will need to regenerate and re-exchange DSS keys. Generating and exchanging DSS keys are described earlier, in the section "Configuring Encryption."

ESA Crypto Engine Not Active

If an installed ESA is not active when you boot a router, the router displays a message similar to this message, indicating that the router switched over to the Cisco IOS crypto engine:

```
There are no keys on the ESA in slot 2- ESA not enabled

...switching to SW crypto engine
```

You can also determine whether the ESA crypto engine is active by using the **show crypto engine brief** command—look at the "crypto engine state" field in the output. If no crypto engine is active, the state field indicates "pending."

The ESA crypto engine will not be active if you removed and reinstalled the ESA, the ESA was tampered with, or encryption is not configured correctly for the ESA.

If the Cisco IOS crypto engine is active, but you want to use the ESA crypto engine instead, make sure that the ESA crypto engine is reset (**crypto card clear-latch** command), and for Cisco 7200 series routers, also make sure that the ESA crypto engine is enabled (**crypto card enable** command). You might also need to complete or verify additional configuration; refer to the instructions for configuring encryption with an ESA in the earlier sections "Configuring Encryption with an ESA in a VIP2" and "Configuring Encryption with an ESA in a Cisco 7200 Series Router."

To verify that the ESA has DSS keys, you can use the **show crypto card** command and look at the "DSS Key set" field in the output. If the field contains "Yes," the ESA has DSS keys generated and stored. In this case, you might only need to reset and re-enable the ESA to make it active.

Password Requested When You Generate DSS Keys

If you attempt to generate DSS keys for the Cisco IOS crypto engine on a Cisco 7200 series router with an installed ESA without DSS keys, the router might assume that you are trying to generate keys for the ESA and prompt for the ESA password:

- If you want to generate keys for the ESA, you must supply the ESA password. If you do not know the password, you must reset the ESA as described in the section "Configuring Encryption with an ESA in a Cisco 7200 Series Router" earlier in this chapter.

- If you want to generate keys for the Cisco IOS crypto engine, not the ESA crypto engine, you must select the Cisco IOS crypto engine to make it the active engine.

  Select the Cisco IOS crypto engine by using the following command in global configuration mode:

Command	Purpose
crypto card shutdown *slot*	Shuts down the ESA.

- When the Cisco IOS crypto engine is active, you can generate keys for the router, and you will not be prompted for a password.

Router Hanging

If you remove a configured ESA from a VIP2, you must reboot the router. If you do not, the router might hang when it tries to access the absent ESA.

Using Debug Commands

Debug commands are also available to assist in problem solving.

Encryption Configuration Examples

The following sections provide examples of configuring and testing your router for CET:

- Example of Generating DSS Public/Private Keys

- Example of Exchanging DSS Public Keys

- Example of Enabling DES Encryption Algorithms

- Examples of Setting Up Encryption Access Lists, Defining Crypto Maps, and Applying Crypto Maps to Interfaces

- Example of Changing Encryption Access List Limits

- Examples of Configuring Encryption with GRE Tunnels

- Examples of ESA-Specific Encryption Configuration Tasks

- Examples of Deleting DSS Keys

- Example of Testing the Encryption Connection

Example of Generating DSS Public/Private Keys

The following example illustrates two encrypting peer routers (named Apricot and Banana) generating their respective DSS public/private keys. Apricot is a Cisco 2500 series router. Banana is a Cisco 7500 series router with an RSP in chassis slot 4 and an ESA/VIP2 in chassis slot 2.

Apricot

```
Apricot(config)# crypto key generate dss Apricot
Generating DSS keys .... [OK]
Apricot(config)#
```

Banana

```
Banana(config)# crypto key generate dss BananaIOS 4
Generating DSS keys .... [OK]
Banana(config)# crypto key generate dss BananaESA 2
% Initialize the crypto card password. You will need
    this password in order to generate new signature
    keys or clear the crypto card extraction latch.

Password: <passwd>

Re-enter password: <passwd>

Generating DSS keys .... [OK]
Banana(config)#
```

The password entered in this example is a new password that you create when you generate DSS keys for an ESA crypto engine for the first time. If you ever generate DSS keys a second time for the same ESA crypto engine, you must use the same password to complete the key regeneration.

Example of Exchanging DSS Public Keys

The following is an example of a DSS public key exchange between two peer encrypting routers (Apricot and Banana). Apricot is a Cisco 2500 series router, and Banana is a Cisco 7500 series router with an ESA. In this example, Apricot sends its Cisco IOS DSS public key, and Banana sends its ESA DSS public key. DSS keys have already been generated as shown in the previous example.

Before any commands are entered, one administrator must call the other administrator. After the phone call is established, the two administrators decide which router is PASSIVE and which is ACTIVE (an arbitrary choice). In this example, router Apricot is ACTIVE and router Banana is PASSIVE. To start, PASSIVE enables a connection as follows:

Banana (PASSIVE)

```
Banana(config)# crypto key exchange dss passive
Enter escape character to abort if connection does not complete.
Wait for connection from peer[confirm]<Return>
Waiting ....
```

PASSIVE must wait while ACTIVE initiates the connection and sends a DSS public key.

Apricot (ACTIVE)

```
Apricot(config)# crypto key exchange dss 192.168.114.68 Apricot
Public key for Apricot:
    Serial Number 01461300
    Fingerprint   0F1D 373F 2FC1 872C D5D7

Wait for peer to send a key[confirm]<Return>
Waiting ....
```

After ACTIVE sends a DSS public key, the key's serial number and Fingerprint display on both terminals, as shown previously and as follows:

Banana (PASSIVE)

```
Public key for Apricot:
    Serial Number 01461300
    Fingerprint   0F1D 373F 2FC1 872C D5D7
Add this public key to the configuration? [yes/no]: y
```

Now the two administrators both must verbally verify that their two screens show the same serial number and Fingerprint. If they do, PASSIVE will accept the DSS key as shown previously by typing **y** and continue by sending ACTIVE a DSS public key:

```
Send peer a key in return[confirm]<Return>
Which one?

BananaIOS? [yes]: n
BananaESA? [yes]: <Return>
Public key for BananaESA:
    Serial Number 01579312
    Fingerprint   BF1F 9EAC B17E F2A1 BA77

Banana(config)#
```

Both administrators observe Banana's serial number and Fingerprint on their screens. Again, they verbally verify that the two screens show the same numbers.

Apricot (ACTIVE):

```
Public key for BananaESA:
    Serial Number 01579312
    Fingerprint   BF1F 9EAC B17E F2A1 BA77

Add this public key to the configuration? [yes/no]: y
Apricot(config)#
```

ACTIVE accepts Apricot's DSS public key. Both administrators hang up the phone and the key exchange is complete.

Figure 26-6 shows complete screens of the two routers. The steps are numbered on the figure to show the sequence of the entire exchange.

Figure 26-6 *DSS Public Key Exchange (Numbers Indicate Sequence of Events)*

```
     Banana (config) # crypto key exchange dss passive
     Enter escape character to abort if connection does not complete.
2.   Wait for connection from peer [confirm]<Return>
     Waiting ....
     Public key for Apricot:
4b.     Serial Number 01461300
        Fingerprint   0F1D 373F 2FC1 872C D5D7

5b.  Add this public key to the configuration? [yes/no]: y
     Send peer a key in return[confirm]<Return>
     Which one?
6.   BananaIOS? [yes]: n
     BananaESA? [yes]: <Return>
     Public key for BananaESA:
7a.     Serial Number 01579312
        Fingerprint   BF1F 9EAC B17E F2A1 BA77

8c.  Banana(config)#
```

```
3.   Apricot(config)# crypto key exchange dss 192.168.114.68 Apricot
     Public key for Apricot:
4a.     Serial Number 01461300
        Fingerprint 0F1D 373F 2FC1 872C D5D7

5c.  Wait for peer to send a key[confirm]<Return>
     Waiting ...
     Public key for BananaESA:
7b.     Serial Number 01579312
        Fingerprint BF1F 9EAC B17E F2A1 BA77

8b.  Add this public key to the configuration? [yes/no]: y
     Apricot(config)#
```

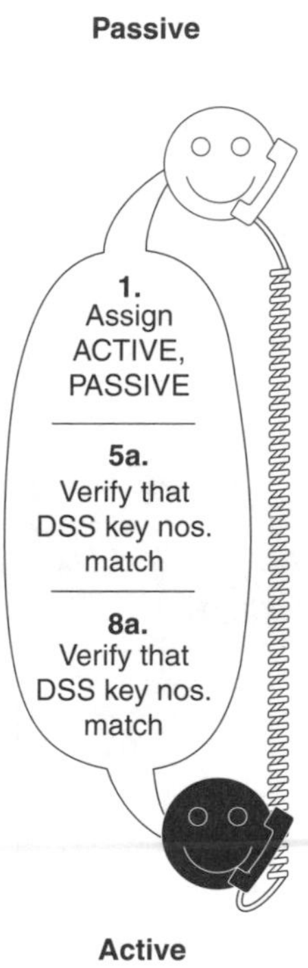

Passive

1.
Assign
ACTIVE,
PASSIVE

5a.
Verify that
DSS key nos.
match

8a.
Verify that
DSS key nos.
match

Active

Example of Enabling DES Encryption Algorithms

In this example, a router (Apricot) globally enables two DES algorithms: the basic DES algorithm with 8-bit Cipher FeedBack (CFB) and the 40-bit DES algorithm with 8-bit CFB. Another router (Banana) globally enables three DES algorithms: the basic DES algorithm with 8-bit CFB, the basic DES algorithm with 64-bit CFB, and the 40-bit DES algorithm with 8-bit CFB.

The following commands are entered from the global configuration mode.

Apricot

```
crypto cisco algorithm des cfb-8
crypto cisco algorithm 40-bit-des cfb-8
```

Banana

```
crypto cisco algorithm des cfb-8
crypto cisco algorithm des cfb-64
crypto cisco algorithm 40-bit-des cfb-8
```

Examples of Setting Up Encryption Access Lists, Defining Crypto Maps, and Applying Crypto Maps to Interfaces

The following two examples show how to set up interfaces for encrypted transmission. Participating routers will be configured as encrypting peers for IP packet encryption.

Example 1

In the first example, a team of researchers at a remote site communicates with a research coordinator at headquarters. Company-confidential information is exchanged by IP traffic that consists only of TCP data. Figure 26-7 shows the network topology.

Figure 26-7 *Example 1 Network Topology*

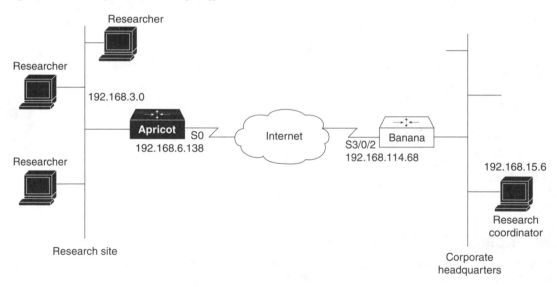

Apricot is a Cisco 2500 series router, and Banana is a Cisco 7500 series router with an ESA/VIP2 in chassis slot 3.

Apricot

```
Apricot(config)# access-list 101 permit tcp 192.168.3.0 0.0.0.15 host 192.168.15.6
Apricot(config)# crypto map Research 10
Apricot(config-crypto-map)# set peer BananaESA
Apricot(config-crypto-map)# set algorithm des cfb-8
Apricot(config-crypto-map)# match address 101
Apricot(config-crypto-map)# exit
Apricot(config)# interface s0
Apricot(config-if)# crypto map Research
Apricot(config-if)# exit
Apricot(config)#
```

Banana

```
Banana(config)# access-list 110 permit tcp host 192.168.15.6 192.168.3.0 0.0.0.15
Banana(config)# crypto map Rsrch 10
Banana(config-crypto-map)# set peer Apricot
Banana(config-crypto-map)# set algorithm des cfb-8
Banana(config-crypto-map)# set algorithm des cfb-64
Banana(config-crypto-map)# match address 110
Banana(config-crypto-map)# exit
Banana(config)# interface s3/0/2
Banana(config-if)# crypto map Rsrch
Banana(config-if)# exit
Banana(config)#
```

Because Banana set two DES algorithms for crypto map Rsrch, Banana could use either algorithm with traffic on the S3/0/2 interface. However, because Apricot only set one DES algorithm (CFB-8 DES) for the crypto map Research, that is the only DES algorithm that will be used for all encrypted traffic between Apricot and Banana.

Example 2

In the second example, employees at two branch offices and at headquarters must communicate sensitive information. A mix of TCP and UDP traffic is transmitted by IP packets. Figure 26-8 shows the network topology used in this example.

Figure 26-8 *Example 2 Network Topology*

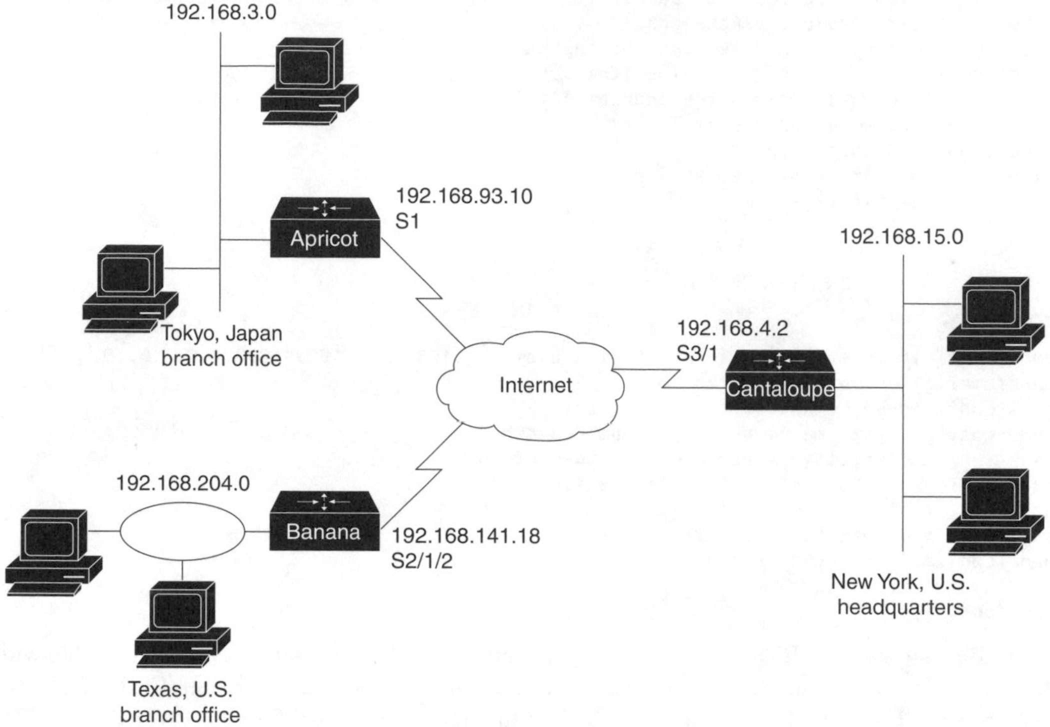

Apricot is a Cisco 2500 series router and connects to the Internet through interface S1. Both Banana and Cantaloupe are Cisco 7500 series routers with ESA cards. Banana connects to the Internet using the ESA-governed VIP2 interface S2/1/2. Cantaloupe is already using every VIP2 interface (governed by the ESA card) to connect to several offsite financial services, so it must connect to the Internet using a serial interface (S3/1) in slot 3. (Cantaloupe's interface S3/1 is governed by the Cisco IOS crypto engine.)

Apricot will be using one interface to communicate with both Banana and Cantaloupe. Because only one crypto map can be applied to this interface, Apricot creates a crypto map that has two distinct definition sets by using two different *seq-num* values with the same *map-name*. By using *seq-num* values of 10 and 20, Apricot creates a single crypto map set named "TXandNY" that contains a subset of definitions for encrypted sessions with Banana and a second distinct subset for definitions for encrypted sessions with Cantaloupe.

Banana and Cantaloupe each also use a single interface to communicate with the other two routers, and therefore will use the same strategy as Apricot does for creating crypto map sets.

In this example, Apricot has generated DSS keys with the *key-name* Apricot.TokyoBranch, Banana has generated DSS keys with the *key-name* BananaESA.TXbranch, and Cantaloupe has generated DSS keys with the *key-name* CantaloupeIOS.NY. Also, each router has exchanged DSS public keys with the other two routers, and each router has enabled each DES algorithm that is specified in the crypto maps.

Apricot

```
Apricot(config)# access-list 105 permit tcp 192.168.3.0 0.0.0.15 192.168.204.0 0.0.0.255
Apricot(config)# access-list 105 permit udp 192.168.3.0 0.0.0.15 192.168.204.0 0.0.0.255
Apricot(config)# access-list 106 permit tcp 192.168.3.0 0.0.0.15 192.168.15.0 0.0.0.255
Apricot(config)# access-list 106 permit udp 192.168.3.0 0.0.0.15 192.168.15.0 0.0.0.255
Apricot(config)# crypto map TXandNY 10
Apricot(config-crypto-map)# set peer BananaESA.TXbranch
Apricot(config-crypto-map)# set algorithm 40-bit-des cfb-8
Apricot(config-crypto-map)# match address 105
Apricot(config-crypto-map)# exit
Apricot(config)# crypto map TXandNY 20
Apricot(config-crypto-map)# set peer CantaloupeIOS.NY
Apricot(config-crypto-map)# set algorithm 40-bit-des cfb-64
Apricot(config-crypto-map)# match address 106
Apricot(config-crypto-map)# exit
Apricot(config)# interface s1
Apricot(config-if)# crypto map TXandNY
Apricot(config-if)# exit
Apricot(config)#
```

Banana

```
Banana(config)# access-list 110 permit tcp 192.168.204.0 0.0.0.255 192.168.3.0 0.0.0.15
Banana(config)# access-list 110 permit udp 192.168.204.0 0.0.0.255 192.168.3.0 0.0.0.15
Banana(config)# access-list 120 permit tcp 192.168.204.0 0.0.0.255 192.168.15.0 0.0.0.255
Banana(config)# access-list 120 permit udp 192.168.204.0 0.0.0.255 192.168.15.0 0.0.0.255
Banana(config)# crypto map USA 10
Banana(config-crypto-map)# set peer Apricot.TokyoBranch
Banana(config-crypto-map)# set algorithm 40-bit-des cfb-8
Banana(config-crypto-map)# match address 110
Banana(config-crypto-map)# exit
Banana(config)# crypto map USA 20
Banana(config-crypto-map)# set peer CantaloupeIOS.NY
Banana(config-crypto-map)# set algorithm des cfb-64
Banana(config-crypto-map)# match address 120
Banana(config-crypto-map)# exit
Banana(config)# interface s2/1/2
Banana(config-if)# crypto map USA
Banana(config-if)# exit
Banana(config)#
```

Cantaloupe

```
Cantaloupe(config)# access-list 101 permit tcp 192.168.15.0 0.0.0.255 192.168.3.0 0.0.0.15
Cantaloupe(config)# access-list 101 permit udp 192.168.15.0 0.0.0.255 192.168.3.0 0.0.0.15
Cantaloupe(config)# access-list 102 permit tcp 192.168.15.0 0.0.0.255 192.168.204.0
0.0.0.255
Cantaloupe(config)# access-list 102 permit udp 192.168.15.0 0.0.0.255 192.168.204.0
0.0.0.255
Cantaloupe(config)# crypto map satellites 10
Cantaloupe(config-crypto-map)# set peer Apricot.TokyoBranch
Cantaloupe(config-crypto-map)# set algorithm 40-bit-des cfb-64
```

```
Cantaloupe(config-crypto-map)# match address 101
Cantaloupe(config-crypto-map)# exit
Cantaloupe(config)# crypto map satellites 20
Cantaloupe(config-crypto-map)# set peer BananaESA.TXbranch
Cantaloupe(config-crypto-map)# set algorithm des cfb-64
Cantaloupe(config-crypto-map)# match address 102
Cantaloupe(config-crypto-map)# exit
Cantaloupe(config)# interface s3/1
Cantaloupe(config-if)# crypto map satellites
Cantaloupe(config-if)# exit
Cantaloupe(config)#
```

The previous configurations will result in DES encryption algorithms being applied to encrypted IP traffic, as shown in Figure 26-9.

Figure 26-9 *Example 2 DES Encryption Algorithms*

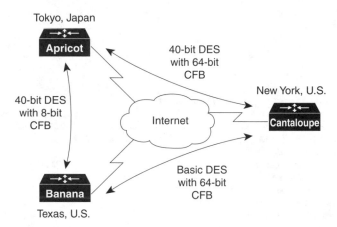

Example of Changing Encryption Access List Limits

In this example, there are 50 remote sites connecting to a single server. The connections between the server and each site need to be encrypted. The server is located behind the local router named Apricot. Each of the remote sites connects through its own router.

Because of the large number of destination addresses that must be paired with the same source address in the local encryption access list, the default limits are changed.

```
Apricot(config)# crypto cisco connections 60
%Please reboot for the new connection size to take effect

Apricot(config)# crypto cisco entities 5
%Please reboot for the new table size to take effect
```

Even though there is only 1 server, and only 50 remote sites, this example defines 5 sources and 60 destinations. This allows room for future growth of the encryption access list. If another source or destination is added later, the limits will not have to be increased and the router rebooted again, which is a disruptive process.

Examples of Configuring Encryption with GRE Tunnels

There are two example configurations for encryption with GRE tunnels:

- Example of Encrypting Only GRE Tunnel Traffic
- Example of Encrypting Both GRE Tunnel Traffic and Other Non-GRE Traffic

Example of Encrypting Only GRE Tunnel Traffic

This configuration causes all traffic through the GRE tunnel to be encrypted. No other traffic at the interface will be encrypted. The GRE tunnel is from router Apricot to router Banana. (Only partial configuration files are shown for each router.)

Apricot

```
crypto map BananaMap 10
 set algorithm 40-bit-des
 set peer Banana
 match address 101
!
interface Tunnel0
 no ip address
 ipx network 923FA800
 tunnel source 10.1.1.2
 tunnel destination 10.1.1.1
 crypto map BananaMap
!
interface Serial0
 ip address 10.1.1.2 255.255.255.0
 crypto map BananaMap
!
access-list 101 permit gre host 10.1.1.2 host 10.1.1.1
```

Banana

```
crypto map ApricotMap 10
 set algorithm 40-bit-des
 set peer Apricot
 match address 102
!
interface Tunnel0
 no ip address
 ipx network 923FA800
 tunnel source 10.1.1.1
 tunnel destination 10.1.1.2
 crypto map ApricotMap
!
```

```
interface Serial0
 ip address 10.1.1.1 255.255.255.0
 clockrate 2000000
 no cdp enable
 crypto map ApricotMap
!
access-list 102 permit gre host 10.1.1.1 host 10.1.1.2
```

Example of Encrypting Both GRE Tunnel Traffic and Other Non-GRE Traffic

This configuration encrypts all GRE tunnel traffic, and it also encrypts TCP traffic between two hosts with the IP addresses 172.16.25.3 and 192.168.3.5. The GRE tunnel is from router Apricot to router Banana. (Only partial configuration files are shown for each router.)

Apricot

```
crypto map BananaMapTunnel 10
 set algorithm 40-bit-des
 set peer Banana
 match address 101
!
crypto map BananaMapSerial 10
 set algorithm 40-bit-des
 set peer Banana
 match address 101
crypto map BananaMapSerial 20
 set algorithm 40-bit-des
 set peer Banana
 match address 110
!
interface Tunnel0
 no ip address
 ipx network 923FA800
 tunnel source 10.1.1.2
 tunnel destination 10.1.1.1
 crypto map BananaMapTunnel
!
interface Serial0
 ip address 10.1.1.2 255.255.255.0
 crypto map BananaMapSerial
!
access-list 101 permit gre host 10.1.1.2 host 10.1.1.1
access-list 110 permit tcp host 172.16.25.3 host 192.168.3.5
```

Banana

```
crypto map ApricotMapTunnel 10
 set algorithm 40-bit-des
 set peer Apricot
 match address 102
!
```

```
crypto map ApricotMapSerial 10
 set algorithm 40-bit-des
 set peer Apricot
 match address 102
crypto map ApricotMapSerial 20
 set algorithm 40-bit-des
 set peer Apricot
 match address 112
!
interface Tunnel0
 no ip address
 ipx network 923FA800
 tunnel source 10.1.1.1
 tunnel destination 10.1.1.2
 crypto map ApricotMapTunnel
!
interface Serial0
 ip address 10.1.1.1 255.255.255.0
 clockrate 2000000
 no cdp enable
 crypto map ApricotMapSerial
!
access-list 102 permit gre host 10.1.1.1 host 10.1.1.2
access-list 112 permit tcp host 192.168.3.5 host 172.16.25.3
```

Examples of ESA-Specific Encryption Configuration Tasks

This section includes examples of the following:

● Examples of Resetting an ESA

● Example of Enabling an ESA (Cisco 7200 Series Routers Only)

● Examples of Selecting a Different Crypto Engine (Cisco 7200 Series Routers Only)

Examples of Resetting an ESA

The following example resets an ESA on a Cisco 7500 series router. The ESA is in a VIP2 that is in slot 4 of the router chassis.

```
Banana(config)# crypto card clear-latch 4
% Enter the crypto card password.
Password: <passwd>
Banana(config)#
```

The following example resets an ESA without DSS keys, for a Cisco 7200 series router. The ESA is in the router chassis slot 2.

```
Apricot(config)# crypto card clear-latch 2
% Enter the crypto card password.
Password: <passwd>
ESA in slot 2 not enabled.
```

```
[OK]
Apricot(config)#
```

The following example resets an ESA with DSS keys for a Cisco 7200 series router; the ESA was previously in use on the same router, but was removed and reinstalled. No changes to the encryption configuration are desired by the administrator. The ESA is in the router chassis slot 2.

```
Apricot(config)# crypto card clear-latch 2
% Enter the crypto card password.
Password: <passwd>
Keys were found for this ESA- enable ESA now? [yes/no]: yes
...switching to HW crypto engine
[OK]
Apricot(config)#
```

The following example resets an ESA with DSS keys, for a Cisco 7200 series router; the ESA was previously used in a different router and requires new DSS keys to be generated and exchanged before the ESA can become operational. The ESA is in the router chassis slot 2.

```
Apricot(config)# crypto card clear-latch 2
% Enter the crypto card password.
Password: <passwd>
Keys were found for this ESA- enable ESA now? [yes/no]: no
ESA in slot 2 not enabled.
[OK]
Apricot(config)#
```

Example of Enabling an ESA (Cisco 7200 Series Routers Only)

The following example enables an ESA in the router chassis slot 2:

```
Apricot(config)# crypto card enable 2
...switching to HW crypto engine
Apricot(config)#
```

Examples of Selecting a Different Crypto Engine (Cisco 7200 Series Routers Only)

Select a different crypto engine only if the new engine is fully configured for encryption.

The following example switches from the Cisco IOS crypto engine to the ESA crypto engine. The ESA crypto engine is in the router chassis slot 4.

```
Apricot(config)# crypto card enable 4
...switching to HW crypto engine
Apricot(config)#
```

The following example switches from the ESA crypto engine to the Cisco IOS crypto engine. The ESA crypto engine is in the router chassis slot 4.

```
Apricot(config)# crypto card shutdown 4
...switching to SW crypto engine
Apricot(config)#
```

Examples of Deleting DSS Keys

This section includes an example for a Cisco 7500 series router and an example for a Cisco 7200 series router with an installed ESA.

Example for a Cisco 7500 Series Router

The following example deletes all the DSS keys on a Cisco 7500 series router. The RSP is in chassis slot 3 and a VIP2 is in chassis slot 4. Deleting all the DSS keys turns off encryption completely for the router. The Cisco IOS crypto engine keys are deleted first, then the VIP2 crypto engine keys.

```
Apricot(config)# crypto key zeroize dss 3
Warning! Zeroize will remove your DSS signature keys.
Do you want to continue? [yes/no]: y
Keys to be removed are named Apricot.IOS.
Do you really want to remove these keys? [yes/no]: y
[OK]
Apricot(config)# crypto key zeroize dss 4
Warning! Zeroize will remove your DSS signature keys.
Do you want to continue? [yes/no]: y
Keys to be removed are named Apricot.VIP.
Do you really want to remove these keys? [yes/no]: y
[OK]
Apricot(config)#
```

Example for a Cisco 7200 Series Router

The following example deletes DSS keys only for an ESA, in chassis slot 2 of a Cisco 7200 series router. The Cisco IOS crypto engine DSS keys are not deleted in this example.

1 View existing DSS keys:

```
Apricot# show crypto key mypubkey dss
crypto key pubkey-chain dss Apricot.IOS 01709642
BDD99A6E EEE53D30 BC0BFAE6 948C40FB 713510CB 32104137 91B06C8D C2D5B422
D9C154CA 00CDE99B 425DB9FD FE3162F1 1E5866AF CF66DD33 677259FF E5C24812
quit
crypto key pubkey-chain dss Apricot.ESA 01234567
866AFCF6 E99B425D FDFE3162 BC0BFAE6 13791B06 713510CB 4CA00CDE 0BC0BFAE
3791B06C 154C0CDE F11E5866 AE6948C4 DD336772 3F66DF33 355459FF 2350912D
quit

Apricot#
```

This output shows that DSS keys exist for both the Cisco IOS crypto engine and for the ESA crypto engine.

2 Determine the active crypto engine:

```
Apricot# show crypto engine configuration
engine name:      Apricot.IOS
engine type:      software
```

```
serial number:        01709642
platform:             rsp crypto engine

Encryption Process Info:
input queue top:    44
input queue bot:    44
input queue count:  0

Apricot#
```

The output shows that the Cisco IOS crypto engine is the active engine.

3 To delete DSS keys for the ESA crypto engine, change to the ESA crypto engine:

```
Apricot# config terminal
Enter configuration commands, one per line.  End with Ctrl-Z.
Apricot(config)# crypto card enable 2
...switching to HW crypto engine
Apricot(config)#
```

4 Verify that the ESA crypto engine is the active engine:

```
Apricot(config)# exit
Apricot# show crypto engine configuration
engine name:          Apricot.ESA
engine type:          hardware
serial number:        01234567
platform:             esa crypto engine

Encryption Process Info:
input queue top:    0
input queue bot:    0
input queue count:  0

Apricot#
```

The output shows that the ESA crypto engine is now the active engine.

5 Delete the ESA DSS keys:

```
Apricot# config terminal
Enter configuration commands, one per line.  End with Ctrl-Z.
Apricot(config)# crypto key zeroize dss 2
Warning! Zeroize will remove your DSS signature keys.
Do you want to continue? [yes/no]: y
Keys to be removed are named Apricot.ESA.
Do you really want to remove these keys? [yes/no]: y
[OK]

Apricot(config)#
```

6 View existing DSS keys:

```
Apricot(config)# exit
Apricot# show crypto key mypubkey dss
```

```
crypto key pubkey-chain dss Apricot.IOS 01709642
BDD99A6E EEE53D30 BC0BFAE6 948C40FB 713510CB 32104137 91B06C8D C2D5B422
D9C154CA 00CDE99B 425DB9FD FE3162F1 1E5866AF CF66DD33 677259FF E5C24812
quit

Apricot#
```

The output shows that the ESA crypto engine keys have been deleted.

7   Determine the active crypto engine:

```
Apricot# show crypto engine configuration
engine name:      Apricot.IOS
engine type:      software
serial number:    01709642
platform:         rsp crypto engine

Encryption Process Info:
input queue top:   0
input queue bot:   0
input queue count: 0

Apricot#
```

The output shows that the system has defaulted back to the Cisco IOS crypto engine as the active engine.

Example of Testing the Encryption Connection

The following example sets up and verifies a test encryption session.

Assume the same network topology and configuration as in the previous example and shown in Figure 26-8.

In this example, router Apricot sets up a test encryption session with router Banana and then views the connection status to verify a successful encrypted session connection.

1   Router Apricot sets up a test encryption connection with router Banana:

```
Apricot# test crypto initiate-session 192.168.3.12 192.168.204.110 BananaESA.TXbranch 10
Sending CIM to: 192.168.204.110 from: 192.168.3.12.
Connection id: -1
```

Notice that the Connection id value is −1. A negative value indicates that the connection is being set up.

2   Router Apricot issues the **show crypto cisco connections** command:

```
Apricot# show crypto cisco connections
Pending Connection Table
PE              UPE             Timestamp           Conn_id
192.168.3.10    192.168.204.100 Mar 01 1993 00:01:09  -1
```

```
Connection Table
PE              UPE             Conn_id New_id  Alg     Time
192.168.3.10    192.168.204.100 -1      1       0       Not Set
                flags:PEND_CONN
```

Look in the Pending Connection Table for an entry with a Conn_id value equal to the previously shown Connection id value—in this case, look for an entry with a Conn_id value of –1. If this is the first time an encrypted connection has been attempted, there will only be one entry (as shown).

Note the PE and UPE addresses for this entry.

3　Now, look in the Connection Table for an entry with the same PE and UPE addresses. In this case, there is only one entry in both tables, so finding the right Connection Table entry is easy.

4　At the Connection Table entry, note the Conn_id and New_id values. In this case, Conn_id equals –1 (as in the Pending Connection Table), and New_id equals 1. The New_id value of 1 will be assigned to the test connection when setup is complete. (Positive numbers are assigned to established, active connections.)

5　Apricot waits a few seconds for the test connection to establish and then reissues the **show crypto cisco connections** command:

```
Apricot# show crypto cisco connections
Connection Table
PE              UPE             Conn_id New_id  Alg     Time
192.168.3.10    192.168.204.100 1       0       0       Mar 01 1993 00:02:00
                flags:TIME_KEYS
```

Again, look for the Connection Table entry with the same PE and UPE addresses as shown before. In this entry, notice that the Conn_id value has changed to 1. This indicates that the test connection has been successfully established, because the Conn_id value has changed to match the New_id value of Step 4. Also, New_id has been reset to 0 at this point, indicating that there are no new connections currently being set up.

In the command output of Step 5, there is no longer a Pending Connection Table being displayed, which indicates that there are currently no pending connections. This is also a good clue that the test connection was successfully established.

The **show crypto cisco connections** command is explained in greater detail in Chapter 27, "Cisco Encryption Technology Commands." There you can find a description of how connection IDs are assigned during and following connection setup.

Cisco Encryption Technology Commands

This chapter describes Cisco Encryption Technology (CET) commands. Cisco provides network data encryption as a means to safeguard network data that travels from one Cisco router to another across unsecured networks.

You can search online at www.cisco.com to find complete descriptions of other commands used when configuring CET. For configuration information, refer to Chapter 26, "Configuring Cisco Encryption Technology."

access-list (encryption)

To define an encryption access list by number, use the extended IP **access-list** global configuration command. Use the **no** form of this command to remove a numbered encryption access list.

> **access-list** *access-list-number* [**dynamic** *dynamic-name* [**timeout** *minutes*]]
> {**deny** | **permit**} *protocol source source-wildcard destination*
> *destination-wildcard* [**precedence** *precedence*] [**tos** *tos*] [**log**]
> **no access-list** *access-list-number*

For Internet Control Message Protocol (ICMP), you can also use the following syntax:

> **access-list** *access-list-number* [**dynamic** *dynamic-name* [**timeout** *minutes*]]
> {**deny** | **permit**} **icmp** *source source-wildcard destination*
> *destination-wildcard* [*icmp-type* [*icmp-code*] | *icmp-message*]
> [**precedence** *precedence*] [**tos** *tos*] [**log**]

For Internet Group Management Protocol (IGMP), you can also use the following syntax:

> **access-list** *access-list-number* [**dynamic** *dynamic-name* [**timeout** *minutes*]]
> {**deny** | **permit**} **igmp** *source source-wildcard destination*
> *destination-wildcard* [**igmp-type**] [**precedence** *precedence*] [**tos** *tos*]
> [**log**]

For TCP, you can also use the following syntax:

> **access-list** *access-list-number* [**dynamic** *dynamic-name* [**timeout** *minutes*]]
> {**deny** | **permit**} **tcp** *source source-wildcard* [*operator port* [*port*]]
> *destination destination-wildcard* [*operator port* [*port*]] [**established**]
> [**precedence** *precedence*] [**tos** *tos*] [**log**]

For User Datagram Protocol (UDP), you can also use the following syntax:

> **access-list** *access-list-number* [**dynamic** *dynamic-name* [**timeout** *minutes*]]
> {**deny** | **permit**} **udp** *source source-wildcard* [*operator port* [*port*]]
> *destination destination-wildcard* [*operator port* [*port*]] [**precedence**
> *precedence*] [**tos** *tos*] [**log**]

Syntax	Description
access-list-number	Number of an encryption access list. This is a decimal number from 100 to 199.
dynamic *dynamic-name*	(Optional) Identifies this encryption access list as a dynamic encryption access list. For more information on lock-and-key access, see Chapter 17, "Configuring Lock-and-Key Security (Dynamic Access Lists)."
timeout *minutes*	(Optional) Specifies the absolute length of time (in minutes) that a temporary access list entry can remain in a dynamic access list. The default is an infinite length of time and allows an entry to remain permanently. For more information on lock-and-key access, see Chapter 17, "Configuring Lock-and-Key Security (Dynamic Access Lists)."
deny	Does not encrypt/decrypt IP traffic if the conditions are matched.
permit	Encrypts/decrypts IP traffic if the conditions are matched.
protocol	Name or number of an IP protocol. It can be one of the keywords **eigrp**, **gre**, **icmp**, **igmp**, **igrp**, **ip**, **ipinip**, **nos**, **ospf**, **tcp**, or **udp**, or an integer in the range 0 to 255 representing an IP protocol number. To match any Internet protocol, including ICMP, TCP, and UDP, use the keyword **ip**. Some protocols allow further qualifiers, as described in text that follows.
source	Number of the network or host from which the packet is being sent. There are three other ways to specify the source: • Use a 32-bit quantity in four-part dotted-decimal format. • Use the keyword **any** as an abbreviation for a *source* and *source-wildcard* of 0.0.0.0 255.255.255.255. This keyword is normally *not* recommended. • Use **host** *source* as an abbreviation for a *source* and *source-wildcard* of *source* 0.0.0.0.

Syntax	Description
source-wildcard	Wildcard bits (mask) to be applied to source. There are three other ways to specify the source wildcard:
	• Use a 32-bit quantity in four-part dotted-decimal format. Place ones in the bit positions you want to ignore.
	• Use the keyword **any** as an abbreviation for a *source* and *source-wildcard* of 0.0.0.0 255.255.255.255. This keyword is normally *not* recommended.
	• Use **host** *source* as an abbreviation for a *source* and *source-wildcard* of *source* 0.0.0.0.
destination	Number of the network or host to which the packet is being sent. There are three other ways to specify the destination:
	• Use a 32-bit quantity in four-part dotted-decimal format.
	• Use the keyword **any** as an abbreviation for the *destination* and *destination-wildcard* of 0.0.0.0 255.255.255.255. This keyword is normally *not* recommended.
	• Use **host** *destination* as an abbreviation for a *destination* and *destination-wildcard* of *destination* 0.0.0.0.
destination-wildcard	Wildcard bits to be applied to the destination. There are three other ways to specify the destination wildcard:
	• Use a 32-bit quantity in four-part dotted-decimal format. Place ones in the bit positions you want to ignore.
	• Use the keyword **any** as an abbreviation for a *destination* and *destination-wildcard* of 0.0.0.0 255.255.255.255. This keyword is normally *not* recommended.
	• Use **host** *destination* as an abbreviation for a *destination* and *destination-wildcard* of *destination* 0.0.0.0.
precedence *precedence*	(Optional) Packets can be matched for encryption by precedence level, as specified by a number from 0 to 7 or by name.
tos *tos*	(Optional) Packets can be matched for encryption by type of service level, as specified by a number from 0 to 15 or by name.
icmp-type	(Optional) ICMP packets can be matched for encryption by ICMP message type. The type is a number from 0 to 255.

Syntax	Description
icmp-code	(Optional) ICMP packets that are matched for encryption by ICMP message type can also be matched by the ICMP message code. The code is a number from 0 to 255.
icmp-message	(Optional) ICMP packets can be matched for encryption by an ICMP message type name or ICMP message type and code name.
igmp-type	(Optional) IGMP packets can be matched for encryption by IGMP message type or message name. A message type is a number from 0 to 15.
operator	(Optional) Compares source or destination ports. Possible operands include **lt** (less than), **gt** (greater than), **eq** (equal), **neq** (not equal), and **range** (inclusive range).
	If the operator is positioned after the *source* and *source-wildcard*, it must match the source port.
	If the operator is positioned after the *destination* and *destination-wildcard*, it must match the destination port.
	The **range** operator requires two port numbers. All other operators require one port number.
port	(Optional) The decimal number or name of a TCP or UDP port. A port number is a number from 0 to 65,535.
	TCP port names can be used only when filtering TCP.
	UDP port names can be used only when filtering UDP.
established	(Optional) For the TCP protocol only: Indicates an established connection. A match occurs if the TCP datagram has the ACK or RST bits set. The nonmatching case is that of the initial TCP datagram to form a connection.
log	(Optional) Causes an informational logging message about the packet that matches the entry to be sent to the console. (The level of messages logged to the console is controlled by the **logging console** command.)
	The message includes the access list number, whether the packet was encrypted/decrypted or not; the protocol, whether it was TCP, UDP, ICMP, or a number; and, if appropriate, the source and destination addresses and source and destination port numbers. The message is generated for the first packet that matches, and then at 5-minute intervals, including the number of packets encrypted/decrypted or not in the prior 5-minute interval.

Default

No numbered encryption access lists are defined, and therefore no traffic will be encrypted/decrypted. After being defined, all encryption access lists contain an implicit "deny" ("do not encrypt/decrypt") statement at the end of the list.

Command Mode

Global configuration

Usage Guidelines

This command first appeared in Cisco IOS Release 11.2.

Use encryption access lists to control which packets on an interface are encrypted/decrypted and which are transmitted as plain text (unencrypted).

When a packet is examined for an encryption access list match, encryption access list statements are checked in the order that the statements were created. After a packet matches the conditions in a statement, no more statements are checked. This means that you need to consider carefully the order in which you enter the statements.

To use the encryption access list, you must first specify the access list in a crypto map and then apply the crypto map to an interface, using the **crypto map (global configuration)** and **crypto map (interface configuration)** commands.

Fragmented IP packets, other than the initial fragment, are immediately accepted by any extended IP access list. Extended access lists used to control virtual terminal line access or restrict contents of routing updates must not match the TCP source port, the type of service value, or the packet's precedence.

NOTE	After an access list is created initially, any subsequent additions (possibly entered from the terminal) are placed at the end of the list. You cannot selectively add or remove access list command lines from a specific access list.

CAUTION	When creating encryption access lists, Cisco does *not* recommend using the **any** keyword to specify source or destination addresses. Using the **any** keyword with a **permit** statement could cause extreme problems if a packet enters your router and is destined for a router that is not configured for encryption. This would cause your router to attempt to set up an encryption session with a nonencrypting router.
	If you incorrectly use the **any** keyword with a **deny** statement, you might inadvertently prevent all packets from being encrypted, which could present a security risk.

NOTE	If you view your router's access lists by using a command such as **show ip access-lists**, *all* extended IP access lists are shown in the command output. This includes extended IP access lists that are used for traffic filtering purposes as well as those that are used for encryption. The **show** command output does not differentiate between the two uses of the extended access lists.

The following is a list of precedence names:

- **critical**
- **flash**
- **flash-override**
- **immediate**
- **internet**
- **network**
- **priority**
- **routine**

The following is a list of type of service (TOS) names:

- **max-reliability**
- **max-throughput**
- **min-delay**

- **min-monetary-cost**
- **normal**

The following is a list of ICMP message type names and code names:

- **administratively-prohibited**
- **alternate-address**
- **conversion-error**
- **dod-host-prohibited**
- **dod-net-prohibited**
- **echo**
- **echo-reply**
- **general-parameter-problem**
- **host-isolated**
- **host-precedence-unreachable**
- **host-redirect**
- **host-tos-redirect**
- **host-tos-unreachable**
- **host-unknown**
- **host-unreachable**
- **information-reply**
- **information-request**
- **mask-reply**
- **mask-request**
- **mobile-redirect**
- **net-redirect**
- **net-tos-redirect**
- **net-tos-unreachable**

Part
IV

Command Reference

- **net-unreachable**
- **network-unknown**
- **no-room-for-option**
- **option-missing**
- **packet-too-big**
- **parameter-problem**
- **port-unreachable**
- **precedence-unreachable**
- **protocol-unreachable**
- **reassembly-timeout**
- **redirect**
- **router-advertisement**
- **router-solicitation**
- **source-quench**
- **source-route-failed**
- **time-exceeded**
- **timestamp-reply**
- **timestamp-request**
- **traceroute**
- **ttl-exceeded**
- **unreachable**

The following is a list of IGMP message names:

- **dvmrp**
- **host-query**
- **host-report**

- **pim**
- **trace**

The following is a list of TCP port names that can be used instead of port numbers. Refer to the current Assigned Numbers RFC to find a reference to these protocols. Port numbers corresponding to these protocols can also be found by typing a **?** in the place of a port number.

- **bgp**
- **chargen**
- **daytime**
- **discard**
- **domain**
- **echo**
- **finger**
- **ftp**
- **ftp-data**
- **gopher**
- **hostname**
- **irc**
- **klogin**
- **kshell**
- **lpd**
- **nntp**
- **pop2**
- **pop3**
- **smtp**
- **sunrpc**
- **syslog**

- **tacacs-ds**

- **talk**

- **telnet**

- **time**

- **uucp**

- **whois**

- **www**

The following is a list of UDP port names that can be used instead of port numbers. Refer to the current Assigned Numbers RFC to find a reference to these protocols. Port numbers corresponding to these protocols can also be found by typing a **?** in the place of a port number.

- **biff**

- **bootpc**

- **bootps**

- **discard**

- **dns**

- **dnsix**

- **echo**

- **mobile-ip**

- **nameserver**

- **netbios-dgm**

- **netbios-ns**

- **ntp**

- **rip**

- **snmp**

- **snmptrap**

- **sunrpc**

- **syslog**

- **tacacs-ds**
- **talk**
- **tftp**
- **time**
- **who**
- **xdmcp**

Example

The following example creates a numbered encryption access list that specifies a Class C subnet for the source and a Class C subnet for the destination of IP packets. When the router uses this encryption access list, all TCP traffic that is exchanged between the source and destination subnets is encrypted.

```
Router1(config)# access-list 101 permit tcp 172.21.3.0 0.0.0.255 172.22.2.0 0.0.0.255
```

This encryption access list will be applied to an interface as an outbound encryption access list after the router administrator defines a crypto map and applies the crypto map to the interface.

Related Commands

You can search online at www.cisco.com to find documentation of related commands.

access-list (extended) (used for traffic filtering purposes)
crypto map (global configuration)
crypto map (interface configuration)
ip access-list extended (encryption)
show ip access-lists

clear crypto connection

To terminate an encrypted session in progress, use the **clear crypto connection** global configuration command.

> **clear crypto connection** *connection-id* [*slot* | **rsm** | **vip**]

Syntax	Description
connection-id	Identifies the encrypted session to terminate.
slot	(Optional) Identifies the crypto engine. This argument is available only on Cisco 7200, RSP7000, and 7500 series routers.
	If no slot is specified, the Cisco IOS crypto engine is selected.
	Use the chassis slot number of the crypto engine location. For the Cisco IOS crypto engine, this is the chassis slot number of the Route Switch Processor (RSP). For the Versatile Interface Processor (VIP2) crypto engine, this is the chassis slot number of the VIP2. For the ESA crypto engine, this is the chassis slot number of the ESA (Cisco 7200) or of the VIP2 (Cisco RSP7000 and 7500).
rsm	(Optional) This keyword is only available on the Cisco Catalyst 5000 series switch. It identifies the Route Switch Module (RSM) on the Cisco Catalyst 5000 series switch.
vip	(Optional) This keyword is only available on the Cisco Catalyst 5000 series switch. It identifies the VIP2 on the Cisco Catalyst 5000 series switch.

Command Mode

Global configuration

Usage Guidelines

This command first appeared in Cisco IOS Release 11.2. The *slot* argument and **rsm** and **vip** keywords were added in Cisco IOS Release 12.0.

Use this command to terminate an encrypted session currently in progress. Encrypted sessions normally terminate when the session times out. Use the **show crypto cisco connections** command to learn the connection-id value.

Example

The following example clears a pending encrypted session. (You could also clear an established encrypted session in the same way.)

```
Router1# show crypto cisco connections
Pending Connection Table
PE              UPE             Timestamp           Conn_id
192.168.3.10    192.168.204.100 Mar 01 1993 00:01:09  -1
```

```
Connection Table
PE              UPE             Conn_id New_id  Alg     Time        Slot
192.168.3.10    192.168.204.100 -1      1       0       Not Set     4
                flags:PEND_CONN

Router1# clear crypto connection -1
Router1# show crypto cisco connections
Connection Table
PE              UPE             Conn_id New_id  Alg     Time
192.168.3.10    192.168.204.100 0       0       0       Mar 01 1993 00:02:00
                flags:BAD_CONN

Router1#
```

First, the **show crypto cisco connections** command is issued to learn the connection-id for the pending connection (-1). This value is then used to specify which connection to clear.

Notice that after the connection is cleared, the Pending Connection Table containing the connection entry (connection-id of -1) has disappeared from the **show crypto cisco connections** output. Also, the connection table no longer shows a -1 Conn_id.

Related Commands

You can search online at www.cisco.com to find documentation of related commands.

show crypto cisco connections

crypto algorithm 40-bit-des

The **crypto cisco algorithm 40-bit-des** command replaces this command. Refer to the description of the **crypto cisco algorithm 40-bit-des** command for more information.

crypto algorithm des

The **crypto cisco algorithm des** command replaces this command. Refer to the description of the **crypto cisco algorithm des** command for more information.

crypto card

To enable (select) either the ESA crypto engine or the Cisco IOS crypto engine in Cisco 7200 series routers, use the **crypto card** global configuration command.

crypto card {**enable** | **shutdown**} *slot*

Syntax	Description
enable	Selects the ESA crypto engine by enabling the ESA.
shutdown	Selects the Cisco IOS crypto engine by shutting down the ESA.
slot	The ESA chassis slot number.

Default

The Cisco IOS crypto engine is the selected (active) crypto engine.

Command Mode

Global configuration

Usage Guidelines

This command first appeared in Cisco IOS Release 11.2 P.

This command only applies to Cisco 7200 series routers with an installed ESA.

Until the ESA is enabled, the Cisco IOS crypto engine functions as the crypto engine.

If you want to select the ESA crypto engine with this command, all other encryption configuration must already have been completed for the ESA.

If you select a crypto engine (either the ESA or the Cisco IOS crypto engine) that has not been completely configured for encryption, the router is not able to encrypt any traffic. Any existing encryption sessions abruptly terminate. Therefore, you must complete all encryption configuration for before you enable a crypto engine with this command.

NOTE   If any encryption session is in progress when you switch from one crypto engine to the other, the session is torn down, and a new session is established using the newly selected crypto engine. This could cause a momentary delay for encrypted traffic.

Examples

The following example enables an ESA in the router chassis slot 2:

```
Router1(config)# crypto card enable 2
...switching to HW crypto engine
Router1(config)#
```

The following example switches from the Cisco IOS crypto engine to the ESA crypto engine. The ESA crypto engine is in the router chassis slot 4.

```
Router1(config)# crypto card enable 4
...switching to HW crypto engine
Router1(config)#
```

The following example switches from the ESA crypto engine to the Cisco IOS crypto engine. The ESA crypto engine is in the router chassis slot 4.

```
Router1(config)# crypto card shutdown 4
...switching to SW crypto engine
Router1(config)
```

crypto card clear-latch

To reset an Encryption Service Adapter (ESA), use the **crypto card clear-latch** global configuration command. This command resets the ESA by clearing a hardware extraction latch that is set when an ESA is removed and reinstalled in the chassis.

crypto card clear-latch {*slot* | **vip**}

Syntax	Description
slot	Identifies the ESA to reset. This argument is available only on Cisco 7200, RSP7000, and 7500 series routers.
	On a Cisco 7200 series router, this is the ESA chassis slot number. On a Cisco RSP7000 or 7500 series router, this is the chassis slot number of the ESA's second-generation VIP2.
vip	This keyword is only available on the Cisco Catalyst 5000 series switch. Identifies the VIP2 on the Cisco Catalyst 5000 series switch.

Default

The ESA latch is not cleared.

Command Mode

Global configuration

Usage Guidelines

This command first appeared in Cisco IOS Release 11.2. The **vip** keyword was added in Cisco IOS Release 12.0.

If an ESA is installed for the first time, or removed and reinstalled, the ESA will not function unless you reset it by using this command. Before the ESA is reset, the hardware extraction latch is set and the "Tampered" LED is on.

To complete this command, you must enter the ESA password. If the ESA does not have a password, you must create one at this time. (The ESA might not have a password if it has never been used, or if the **crypto key zeroize dss** command was previously issued for the ESA.)

If you have forgotten a previously assigned password, you have to use the **crypto key zeroize dss** command instead of the **crypto card clear-latch** command to reset the ESA. After issuing the **crypto key zeroize dss** command, you must regenerate and re-exchange DSS keys. When you regenerate DSS keys, you are prompted to create a new password.

Example

The following example resets an ESA card. The ESA card is housed in a VIP2 that is in slot 1.

```
Router1(config)# crypto card clear-latch 1
% Enter the crypto card password.
Password: <passwd>
Router1(config)#
```

The following example resets an ESA card housed in a VIP2 on a Cisco Catalyst 5000 series switch:

```
Router1(config)# crypto card clear-latch vip
% Enter the crypto card password.
Password: <passwd>
Router1(config)#
```

Related Commands

You can search online at www.cisco.com to find documentation of related commands.

crypto key generate dss
crypto key zeroize dss

crypto cisco algorithm 40-bit-des

To enable 40-bit Data Encryption Standard (DES) algorithm types globally, use the **crypto cisco algorithm 40-bit-des** global configuration command. Use the **no** form of this command to disable a 40-bit DES algorithm type globally.

crypto cisco algorithm 40-bit-des [cfb-8 | cfb-64]
no crypto cisco algorithm 40-bit-des [cfb-8 | cfb-64]

Syntax	Description
cfb-8	(Optional) Selects the 8-bit Cipher FeedBack (CFB) mode of the 40-bit DES algorithm. If no CFB mode is specified when you issue the command, 64-bit CFB mode is the default.
cfb-64	(Optional) Selects the 64-bit CFB mode of the 40-bit DES algorithm. If no CFB mode is specified when you issue the command, 64-bit CFB mode is the default.

Default

One DES algorithm is enabled by default, even if you never issue this command. If you are running a nonexportable image, the basic DES algorithm with 8-bit CFB is enabled by default. (The basic DES algorithm uses a 56-bit DES key.) If you are running an exportable image, the 40-bit DES algorithm with 8-bit CFB is enabled by default.

If you do not know whether your image is exportable or nonexportable, you can perform the **show crypto cisco algorithms** command to determine which DES algorithms are currently enabled.

Command Mode

Global configuration

Usage Guidelines

This command first appeared in Cisco IOS Release 11.2.

Use this command to enable a 40-bit DES algorithm type. Enabling a DES algorithm type once allows it to be used by all crypto engines of a router.

You must enable all DES algorithms that will be used to communicate with any other peer encrypting router. If you do not enable a DES algorithm, you will not be able to use that algorithm, even if you try to assign the algorithm to a crypto map at a later time.

If your router tries to set up an encrypted communication session with a peer router, and the two routers do not have the same DES algorithm enabled at both ends, the encrypted session fails. If at least one common DES algorithm is enabled at both ends, the encrypted session proceeds.

The 40-bit DES uses a 40-bit DES key, which is easier for attackers to crack than basic DES, which uses a 56-bit DES key. However, some international applications might require you to use 40-bit DES, because of export laws.

NOTE	If you are running an exportable image, you can only enable and use 40-bit variations of DES. You cannot enable or use the basic DES algorithms, which are not available with exportable images.

The 8-bit CFB is more commonly used than 64-bit CFB, but requires more CPU processing time. If you do not specify 8-bit or 64-bit CFB, 64-bit CFB is selected by default.

Example

The following example enables 40-bit DES with 8-bit CFB and 40-bit DES with 64-bit CFB:

```
crypto cisco algorithm 40-bit-des cfb-8
crypto cisco algorithm 40-bit-des cfb-64
```

Related Commands

You can search online at www.cisco.com to find documentation of related commands.

crypto cisco algorithm des
show crypto cisco algorithms

crypto cisco algorithm des

To enable DES algorithm types that use a 56-bit DES key globally, use the **crypto cisco algorithm des** global configuration command. Use the **no** form of this command to disable a DES algorithm type globally.

> **crypto cisco algorithm des [cfb-8 | cfb-64]**
> **no crypto cisco algorithm des [cfb-8 | cfb-64]**

Syntax   Description

Syntax	Description
cfb-8	(Optional) Selects the 8-bit CFB mode of the basic DES algorithm. If no CFB mode is specified when you issue the command, 64-bit CFB mode is the default.
cfb-64	(Optional) Selects the 64-bit CFB mode of the basic DES algorithm. If no CFB mode is specified when you issue the command, 64-bit CFB mode is the default.

Default

One DES algorithm is enabled by default, even if you never issue this command. If you are running a nonexportable image, the basic DES algorithm with 8-bit CFB is enabled by default. (The basic DES algorithm uses a 56-bit DES key.) If you are running an exportable image, the 40-bit DES algorithm with 8-bit CFB is enabled by default.

If you do not know whether your image is exportable or nonexportable, you can perform the **show crypto cisco algorithms** command to determine which DES algorithms are currently enabled.

Command Mode

Global configuration

Usage Guidelines

This command first appeared in Cisco IOS Release 11.2.

Use this command to enable a DES algorithm type that uses a 56-bit DES key. Enabling a DES algorithm type once allows it to be used by all crypto engines of a router.

You must enable all DES algorithms that will be used to communicate with any other peer encrypting router. If you do not enable a DES algorithm, you will not be able to use that algorithm, even if you try to assign the algorithm to a crypto map at a later time.

If your router tries to set up an encrypted communication session with a peer router, and the two routers do not have the same DES algorithm enabled at both ends, the encrypted session fails. If at least one common DES algorithm is enabled at both ends, the encrypted session proceeds.

NOTE   If you are running an exportable image, you can only enable and use 40-bit variations of DES. You cannot enable or use the basic DES algorithms, which are not available with exportable images.

The 8-bit CFB is more commonly used than 64-bit CFB, but requires more CPU processing time. If you do not specify 8-bit or 64-bit CFB, 64-bit CFB is selected by default.

Example

The following example enables DES with 8-bit CFB and DES with 64-bit CFB:

```
crypto cisco algorithm des cfb-8
crypto cisco algorithm des cfb-64
```

Related Commands

You can search online at www.cisco.com to find documentation of related commands.

crypto cisco algorithm 40-bit-des
show crypto cisco algorithms

crypto cisco connections

To change the maximum number of destinations (hosts or subnets) per source that you can define in encryption access list statements, use the **crypto cisco connections** global configuration command. Use the **no** form of the command to restore the default.

> **crypto cisco connections** *number*
> **no crypto cisco connections** [*number*]

Syntax   Description

number   Specifies the maximum number of destinations per source. Use a value from 3 to 500.

This argument is not required when using the **no** form of the command.

Default

A maximum of 10 destinations can be paired with each source specified in encryption access list criteria statements.

Command Mode

Global configuration

Usage Guidelines

This command first appeared in Cisco IOS Release 11.3.

When you configure encryption access lists, you configure source and destination pairs in criteria statements. Any traffic that matches the criteria is then encrypted.

By default, the maximum number of distinct sources (host or subnets) that you can define in your encryption access lists is 100. Also, the maximum number of distinct destinations that you can define for any given source address is 10. For example, if you define six different source addresses, you can define up to 10 destination addresses for each of the six sources, for a total of 60 access list criteria statements.

Use this command if you need to specify more than 10 destinations for a particular source (host or subnet) in encryption access list statements.

For most situations, the defaults of 100 maximum sources and 10 maximum destinations per source are sufficient. Cisco recommends that you do not change the defaults unless you actually exceed the number of sources or destinations per source.

NOTE   You must reboot the router before this command takes effect.

Memory Impact

The amount of memory reserved for encrypted connections changes if you change the defaults with this command.

When using this command, you should consider the amount of memory that will be allocated. In general, use the **crypto cisco entities** and **crypto cisco connections** commands together: If you increase one value, decrease the other value. This prevents your router from running out of memory because too much memory was preallocated.

For every additional source specified with the **crypto cisco entities** command, the following additional bytes of memory are allocated:

```
64 + (68 x the specified number of maximum destinations)
```

For every additional destination specified with the **crypto cisco connections**, the following additional bytes of memory are allocated:

```
68 x the specified number of maximum sources
```

For example, if you specify five maximum sources, and 250 maximum destinations per source, the memory allocated for encryption connections is calculated as follows:

```
{5 x [64 + (68 x 250)]} + {250 x (68 x 5)} = 170320 bytes
```

Example

In this example, there are 50 remote sites connecting to a single server. The connections between the server and each site need to be encrypted. The server is located behind the local router named Router1. Each of the remote sites connects through its own router.

Because of the large number of destination addresses that must be paired with the same source address in the local encryption access list, the default limits are changed:

```
Router1(config)# crypto cisco connections 60
%Please reboot for the new connection size to take effect

Router1(config)# crypto cisco entities 5
%Please reboot for the new table size to take effect
```

Part
IV

Command Reference

Note that the maximum number of sources is reduced to balance the increase in maximum destinations per source. This prevents too much memory from being preallocated to encryption connections.

Also note that even though there is only one server and only 50 remote sites, this example defines five sources and 60 destinations. This allows room for future growth of the encryption access list. If another source or destination is added later, the limits do not have to be increased and the router rebooted again, which is a disruptive process.

Related Commands

You can search online at www.cisco.com to find documentation of related commands.

crypto cisco entities

crypto cisco entities

To change the maximum number of sources (hosts or subnets) that you can define in encryption access list statements, use the **crypto cisco entities** global configuration command. Use the **no** form of the command to restore the default.

> **crypto cisco entities** *number*
> **no crypto cisco entities** [*number*]

Syntax	Description
number	Specifies the maximum number of sources. Use a value from 3 to 500.
	This argument is not required when using the **no** form of the command.

Default

A maximum of 100 sources can be specified in encryption access list criteria statements.

Command Mode

Global configuration

Usage Guidelines

This command first appeared in Cisco IOS Release 11.3.

When you configure encryption access lists, you configure source and destination pairs in criteria statements. Any traffic that matches the criteria is then encrypted.

By default, the maximum number of distinct sources (host or subnets) that you can define in your encryption access lists is 100. Also, the maximum number of distinct destinations that you can define for any given source address is 10. For example, if you define six different source addresses, you can define up to 10 destination addresses for each of the six sources, for a total of 60 access list criteria statements.

Use this command if you need to specify more than 100 sources (host or subnet) in encryption access list statements.

 For most situations, the defaults of 100 maximum sources and 10 maximum destinations per source are sufficient. Cisco recommends that you do not change the defaults unless you actually exceed the number of sources or destinations per source.

NOTE   You must reboot the router before this command takes effect.

Memory Impact

The amount of memory reserved for encrypted connections changes if you change the defaults with this command.

When using this command, you should consider the amount of memory that will be allocated. In general, use the **crypto cisco entities** and **crypto cisco connections** commands together: If you increase one value, decrease the other value. This prevents your router from running out of memory because too much memory was preallocated.

For every additional source specified with the **crypto cisco entities** command, the following additional bytes of memory are allocated:

```
64 + (68 x the specified number of maximum destinations)
```

For every additional destination specified with the **crypto cisco connections**, the following additional bytes of memory are allocated

```
68 x the specified number of maximum sources
```

For example, if you specify five maximum sources, and 250 maximum destinations per source, the memory allocated for encryption connections is calculated as follows:

```
{5 x [64 + (68 x 250)]} + {250 x (68 x 5)} = 170320 bytes
```

Example

In this example, there are 50 remote sites connecting to a single server. The connections between the server and each site need to be encrypted. The server is located behind the local router named Router1. Each of the remote sites connects through its own router.

Because of the large number of destination addresses that must be paired with the same source address in the local encryption access list, the default limits are changed.

```
Router1(config)# crypto cisco connections 60
%Please reboot for the new connection size to take effect

Router1(config)# crypto cisco entities 5
%Please reboot for the new table size to take effect
```

Note that the maximum number of sources is reduced to balance the increase in maximum destinations per source. This prevents too much memory from being preallocated to encryption connections.

Also note that even though there is only one server and only 50 remote sites, this example defines five sources and 60 destinations. This allows room for future growth of the encryption access list. If another source or destination is added later, the limits do not have to be increased and the router rebooted again, which is a disruptive process.

Related Commands

You can search online at www.cisco.com to find documentation of related commands.

crypto cisco connections

crypto cisco key-timeout

To specify the duration of encrypted sessions, use the **crypto cisco key-timeout** global configuration command. Use the **no** form to restore the duration of encrypted sessions to the default of 30 minutes.

> **crypto cisco key-timeout** *minutes*
> **no crypto cisco key-timeout** *minutes*

Syntax	Description
minutes	Specifies the duration of encrypted sessions. Can be from 1 to 1440 minutes (24 hours) in 1-minute increments. Specified by an integer from 1 to 1440.
	When the **no** form of the command is used, this argument is optional. Any value supplied for the argument is ignored by the router.

Default

Encrypted sessions time out in 30 minutes.

Command Mode

Global configuration

Usage Guidelines

This command first appeared in Cisco IOS Release 11.2.

After an encrypted communication session is established, it is valid for a specific length of time. After this length of time, the session times out. A new session must be negotiated, and a new DES (session) key must be generated for encrypted communication to continue. Use this command to change the time that an encrypted communication session lasts before it expires (times out).

Examples

The following example sets encrypted session timeouts to 2 hours:

```
crypto cisco key-timeout 120
```

The following example shows one way to restore the default session time of 30 minutes:

```
no crypto cisco key-timeout
```

The following example shows another way to restore the default session time of 30 minutes:

```
crypto cisco key-timeout 30
```

Related Commands

You can search online at www.cisco.com to find documentation of related commands.

show crypto cisco key-timeout

crypto cisco pregen-dh-pairs

To enable pregeneration of Diffie-Hellman (DH) public numbers, use the **crypto cisco pregen-dh-pairs** global configuration command. Use the **no** form to disable pregeneration of DH public numbers for all crypto engines.

> **crypto cisco pregen-dh-pairs** *count* [*slot* | **rsm** | **vip**]
> **no crypto cisco pregen-dh-pairs**

Syntax	Description
count	Specifies how many DH public numbers to pregenerate and hold in reserve. Specified by an integer from 0 to 10.
slot	(Optional) Identifies the crypto engine. This argument is available only on Cisco 7200, RSP7000, and 7500 series routers.
	If no slot is specified, the Cisco IOS crypto engine is selected.
	Use the chassis slot number of the crypto engine location. For the Cisco IOS crypto engine, this is the chassis slot number of the RSP. For the VIP2 crypto engine, this is the chassis slot number of the VIP2. For the ESA crypto engine, this is the chassis slot number of the ESA (Cisco 7200) or of the VIP2 (Cisco RSP7000 and 7500).
rsm	(Optional) This keyword is only available on the Cisco Catalyst 5000 series switch. Identifies the RSM on the Cisco Catalyst 5000 series switch.
vip	(Optional) This keyword is only available on the Cisco Catalyst 5000 series switch. Identifies the VIP2 on the Cisco Catalyst 5000 series switch.

Default

DH number pairs are generated only when needed, during encrypted session setup.

Command Mode

Global configuration

Usage Guidelines

This command first appeared in Cisco IOS Release 11.2. The **rsm** and **vip** keywords were added in Cisco IOS Release 12.0.

Each encrypted session uses a unique pair of DH numbers. Every time a new session is set up, new DH number pairs must be generated. When the session completes, these numbers are discarded. Generating new DH number pairs is a CPU-intensive activity, which can make session setup slow—especially for low-end routers.

To speed up session setup, you can choose to have a specified amount of DH number pairs pregenerated and held in reserve. Then, when an encrypted communication session is being set up, a DH number pair is provided from that reserve. After a DH number pair is used, the reserve is automatically replenished with a new DH number pair, so there should always be a DH number pair ready for use.

It is usually not necessary to have more than one or two DH number pairs pregenerated, unless your router will be setting up multiple encrypted sessions so frequently that a pregenerated reserve of one or two DH number pairs will be depleted too quickly.

If you have a Cisco 7200, RSP7000, or 7500 series router or Cisco Catalyst 5000 series switch, you can perform this command for each crypto engine in service.

Setting the number of pregenerated pairs to be zero disables pregeneration but allows you to use the pairs already in reserve. Using the **no** form of the command disables pregeneration for *all* crypto engines of your router and deletes any DH number pairs currently in reserve. If you have a Cisco 7200, RSP7000, or 7500 series router or Cisco Catalyst 5000 series switch and wish to discontinue pregenerating DH numbers for only one crypto engine, set the *count* argument to 0, and specify the crypto engine with the *slot* argument.

Examples

The following example turns on pregeneration of DH public number pairs for a Cisco 2500 series router. Two DH number pairs will be held in constant reserve.

```
crypto cisco pregen-dh-pairs 2
```

The following example turns on pregeneration of DH public numbers for the ESA crypto engine of a VIP2 card in slot 3 of a Cisco 7500 series router. One DH number pair will be held in constant reserve.

```
crypto cisco pregen-dh-pairs 1 3
```

The following example turns on pregeneration of DH public numbers for a VIP on a Cisco Catalyst 5000 series switch:

```
crypto cisco pregen-dh-pairs 1 vip
```

Related Commands

You can search online at www.cisco.com to find documentation of related commands.

show crypto cisco pregen-dh-pairs

crypto clear-latch

The **crypto card clear-latch** command replaces this command. Refer to the description of the **crypto card clear-latch** command for more information.

crypto esa

The **crypto card** command replaces this command. Refer to the description of the **crypto card** command for more information.

crypto gen-signature-keys

The **crypto key generate dss** command replaces this command. Refer to the description of the **crypto key generate dss** command for more information.

crypto key-exchange

The **crypto key exchange dss** command replaces this command. Refer to the description of the **crypto key exchange dss** command for more information.

crypto key exchange dss

To exchange Digital Signature Standard (DSS) public keys, the administrator of the peer encrypting router that is designated ACTIVE must use the **crypto key exchange dss** global configuration command.

> **crypto key exchange dss** *ip-address key-name* [*tcp-port*]

Syntax	Description
ip-address	The IP address of the peer router (designated PASSIVE) participating with you in the key exchange.
key-name	Identifies the crypto engine—either the Cisco IOS crypto engine, a second-generation VIP2 crypto engine, or an ESA crypto engine. This name must match the key-name argument assigned when you generated DSS keys using the **crypto key generate dss** command.
tcp-port	(Optional) Cisco IOS software uses the unassigned[1] TCP port number of 1964 to designate a key exchange. You may use this optional keyword to select a different number to designate a key exchange if your system already uses the port number 1964 for a different purpose. If this keyword is used, you must use the same value as the PASSIVE router's *tcp-port* value.

1. 1964 is a TCP port number that has not been preassigned by the Internetworking Engineering Task Force (IETF).

Default
No DSS keys are exchanged.

Command Mode
Global configuration

Usage Guidelines
This command first appeared in Cisco IOS Release 11.2.

Peer encrypting routers must exchange DSS public keys before any encrypted communication can occur.

If you have a Cisco 7200, RSP7000, or 7500 series router, you need to exchange DSS public keys for each crypto engine you plan to use.

To exchange DSS public keys, the two router administrators must call each other on the phone and verbally assign one router to the PASSIVE role and the other router to the ACTIVE role.

The PASSIVE administrator uses the **crypto key exchange dss passive** command to start the DSS key exchange. Then the ACTIVE administrator uses the **crypto key exchange dss** command to send the first DSS public key. During the key exchange sequence, the two administrators must remain on the phone to verify the receipt of DSS keys. To verify the receipt of DSS keys, the administrators should compare screens to match DSS key serial numbers and fingerprints. Screen prompts guide both administrators through the exchange.

Example
The following example shows a DSS key exchange sequence from the point of view of a router named Router2. Router2 is designated ACTIVE. The other router is named Router1. Router1 is designated PASSIVE and has previously generated DSS keys with the *key-name* Router1. Router2 has previously generated DSS keys with the *key-name* Router2ESA:

```
Router2(config)# crypto key exchange dss 172.21.114.68 Router2ESA
Public key for Router2ESA:
    Serial Number 01461300
    Fingerprint   0F1D 373F 2FC1 872C D5D7

Wait for peer to send a key[confirm]<Return>
Waiting ....
Public key for Router1:
    Serial Number 01579312
    Fingerprint   BF1F 9EAC B17E F2A1 BA77

Add this public key to the configuration? [yes/no]: y
Router2(config)#
```

Related Commands

You can search online at www.cisco.com to find documentation of related commands.

crypto key exchange dss passive
crypto key pubkey-chain dss
show crypto key mypubkey dss
show crypto key pubkey-chain dss

crypto key exchange dss passive

To enable an exchange of DSS public keys, the administrator of the peer encrypting router that is designated PASSIVE must use the **crypto key exchange dss passive** global configuration command.

> **crypto key exchange dss passive** [*tcp-port*]

Syntax	Description
tcp-port	(Optional) Cisco IOS software uses the unassigned[1] TCP port number of 1964 to designate a key exchange. You may use this optional keyword to select a different number to designate a key exchange if your system already uses the port number 1964 for a different purpose. If this keyword is used, you must use the same value as the ACTIVE router's *tcp-port* value.

1. 1964 is a TCP port number that has not been preassigned by the IETF.

Default

No DSS keys are exchanged.

Command Mode

Global configuration

Usage Guidelines

This command first appeared in Cisco IOS Release 11.2.

Peer encrypting routers must exchange DSS public keys before any encrypted communication can occur.

To exchange DSS public keys, the two router administrators must call each other on the phone and verbally assign one router to the PASSIVE role and the other router to the ACTIVE role.

Then the PASSIVE administrator should use the **crypto key exchange dss passive** command to start the DSS key exchange. During the key exchange sequence, the two administrators must remain on the phone to verify the receipt of DSS keys. To verify the receipt of DSS keys, the administrators should compare screens to match DSS key serial numbers and fingerprints. Screen prompts guide both administrators through the exchange.

Example

The following example shows a DSS key exchange sequence from the point of view of a router named Router1. Router1 is designated PASSIVE and has previously generated DSS keys with the *key-name* Router1. The other router is named Router2 and has previously generated DSS keys with the *key-name* Router2ESA:

```
Router1(config)# crypto key exchange dss passive
Enter escape character to abort if connection does not complete.
Wait for connection from peer[confirm]<Return>
Waiting ....
Public key for Router2ESA:
   Serial Number 01461300
   Fingerprint  0F1D 373F 2FC1 872C D5D7
Add this public key to the configuration? [yes/no]: y
Send peer a key in return[confirm]<Return>
Which one?

Router1? [yes]: <Return>
Public key for Router1:
   Serial Number 01579312
   Fingerprint  BF1F 9EAC B17E F2A1 BA77

Router1(config)#
```

Related Commands

You can search online at www.cisco.com to find documentation of related commands.

crypto key exchange dss
crypto key pubkey-chain dss
show crypto key mypubkey dss
show crypto key pubkey-chain dss

crypto key-exchange passive

The **crypto key exchange dss passive** command replaces this command. Refer to the description of the **crypto key exchange dss passive** command for more information.

Part
IV

Command Reference

crypto key generate dss

To generate a DSS public/private key pair, use the **crypto key generate dss** global configuration command.

crypto key generate dss *key-name* [*slot* | **rsm** | **vip**]

Syntax	Description
key-name	A name you assign to the crypto engine. This names either the Cisco IOS software crypto engine, a second-generation VIP2 crypto engine, or an ESA crypto engine. Any character string is valid. Using a fully qualified domain name might make it easier to identify public keys.
slot	(Optional) Identifies the crypto engine. This argument is available only on Cisco 7200, RSP7000, and 7500 series routers.
	If no slot is specified, the Cisco IOS crypto engine is selected.
	Use the chassis slot number of the crypto engine location. For the Cisco IOS crypto engine, this is the chassis slot number of the RSP. For the VIP2 crypto engine, this is the chassis slot number of the VIP2. For the ESA crypto engine, this is the chassis slot number of the ESA (Cisco 7200) or of the VIP2 (Cisco RSP7000 and 7500).
rsm	(Optional) This keyword is only available on the Cisco Catalyst 5000 series switch. Identifies the RSM on the Cisco Catalyst 5000 series switch.
vip	(Optional) This keyword is only available on the Cisco Catalyst 5000 series switch. Identifies the VIP2 on the Cisco Catalyst 5000 series switch.

Default

No DSS public/private keys are defined.

Command Mode

Global configuration

Usage Guidelines

This command first appeared in Cisco IOS Release 11.2. The **rsm** and **vip** keywords were added in Cisco IOS Release 12.0.

Use this command to generate a DSS public/private key pair. This is the first configuration task required to set up a router for network data encryption.

If you have a Cisco 7200, RSP7000, or 7500 series router, use the *slot* argument. If you have a Cisco Catalyst 5000 series switch, use the **rsm** or **vip** keyword. You must perform this command once for each crypto engine you plan to use.

NOTE   DSS keys of the Cisco IOS crypto engine are saved to a private portion of NVRAM when you perform a **copy system:running-config nvram:startup-config** (previously **copy running-config startup-config**) command. DSS keys are *not* saved with your configuration when you perform a **copy sytem:running-config rcp:** or **copy system:running-config tftp:** command.

If you are using a Cisco 7200, RSP7000, or 7500 series router or a Cisco Catalyst 5000 series switch with an ESA, DSS keys generated for the ESA crypto engine are automatically saved to tamper-resistant memory of the ESA during the DSS key generation process.

NOTE   If NVRAM fails, or if your ESA is tampered with or replaced, DSS public/private keys will no longer be valid. If this happens, you need to regenerate and re-exchange DSS keys.

The ESA Password

If you are using a Cisco 7200, RSP7000, or 7500 series router or a Cisco Catalyst 5000 series switch with an ESA, you are prompted to enter a password when you generate DSS keys for the ESA crypto engine.

If you previously reset the ESA with the **crypto key zeroize dss** command, you must create a new password at this time.

If you previously reset the ESA with the **crypto card clear-latch** command, you created a password at that time; use that same password now. If you have forgotten the password, the only workaround is to first use the **crypto key zeroize dss** command and then regenerate DSS keys.

If you need to regenerate DSS keys for the ESA, you are required to enter the same ESA password to complete the DSS key regeneration.

Examples

The following example generates a DSS public/private key pair for the first time on a Cisco 2500 series router:

```
Router1(config)# crypto key generate dss Router1
Generating DSS keys .... [OK]
Router1(config)#
```

The following example generates DSS public/private key pairs for a Cisco 7500 series router with an RSP in slot 4 and a VIP2 (with an ESA) in slot 3. The ESA was previously reset with the **crypto key zeroize dss** command. Notice that when DSS keys are generated for the ESA, you must type a newly created password:

```
Router1(config)# crypto key generate dss Router1RSP 4
Generating DSS keys .... [OK]
Router1(config)# crypto key generate dss Router1ESA 3
% Initialize the crypto card password. You will need
    this password in order to generate new signature
    keys or clear the crypto card extraction latch.

Password: <passwd>

Re-enter password: <passwd>

Generating DSS keys .... [OK]
Router1(config)#
```

In the previous example, the ESA crypto engine provides encryption services for the VIP2 interfaces, and the Cisco IOS crypto engine (located in the RSP) provides encryption services for all other designated ports.

The next example shows DSS keys being generated a second time for the same ESA crypto engine shown in the previous example (DSS keys already exist for this crypto engine). Notice that the password used in the previous example must be entered in this example to complete the DSS key regeneration.

```
Router1(config)# crypto key generate dss Router1ESA 3
% Generating new DSS keys will require re-exchanging
    public keys with peers who already have the public key
    named Router1ESA!
Generate new DSS keys? [yes/no]: y
% Enter the crypto card password.
Password: <passwd>
Generating DSS keys .... [OK]
```

Related Commands

You can search online at www.cisco.com to find documentation of related commands.

show crypto key mypubkey dss

crypto key pubkey-chain dss

To specify the DSS public key of a peer encrypting router manually, use the **crypto key pubkey-chain dss** global configuration command. Use the **no** form of this command to delete the DSS public key of a peer encrypting router.

> **crypto key pubkey-chain dss**
>   **named-key** <*key-name*> [**special-usage**]
>   **serial-number** [**special-usage**]
>   **key-string**
>   <*hex*> <*hex*> <*hex*> ...
>   <*hex*> <*hex*> <*hex*> ...
>   **quit**
> **no crypto key pubkey-chain dss** *key-name* [*serial-number*]

Syntax	Description
key-name	Identifies the crypto engine of the peer encrypting router. If the device is a Cisco router, the name should be a fully qualified domain name.
special-usage	If the special-usage parameter is not specified, the key is considered a general-purpose key.
serial-number	The serial number of the peer encrypting router's public DSS key.
	When the **no** form of the command is used, this argument is optional. Any value supplied for the argument is ignored by the router.
hex	The DSS public key of the peer encrypting router, in hexadecimal format.
quit	When you are done entering the public key, type **quit** to exit the hex input mode.

Default

No peer encrypting router DSS keys are known.

Command Mode

Global configuration

Performing this command invokes the hex input mode. To complete the command, you must return to the global configuration mode by typing **quit** at the config-pubkey prompt.

Usage Guidelines

This command first appeared in Cisco IOS Release 11.2.

Use this command to specify DSS public keys of peer encrypting routers instead of using the **crypto key exchange dss passive** and **crypto key exchange dss** commands. The administrator of the peer router can provide the exact values for the *key-name*, *serial-number,* and *hex-key-data* command arguments. The administrator of the peer router can discover these values by performing the **show crypto key mypubkey dss** command at the peer router.

Example

The following example specifies the DSS public key of a peer encrypting router:

```
Router1(config)# crypto key pubkey-chain dss
Router1(config-pubkey)# named-key router.domain.com
Router1(config-pubkey)# serial-number 03259625
Router1(config-pubkey)# key-string 8F1440B9 4C860989 8791A12B 69746E27 307ACACB
62915B02 0261B58F 1F7ABB10 90CE70A9 08F86652 16B52064 37C857D4 7066DAA3 7FC33212
445275EE 542DCD06
Router1(config-pubkey)# quit
Router1(config)# exit
Router1#
%SYS-5-CONFIG_I: Configured from console by console
Router1# show crypto key pubkey-chain dss name router.domain.com
Key name: router.domain.com
Serial number: 03259625
Usage: Signature Key
Source: Manually entered
Data:
8F1440B9 4C860989 8791A12B 69746E27 307ACACB 62915B02 0261B58F 1F7ABB10
90CE70A9 08F86652 16B52064 37C857D4 7066DAA3 7FC33212 445275EE 542DCD06
Router1#
```

Related Commands

You can search online at www.cisco.com to find documentation of related commands.

crypto key exchange dss
crypto key exchange dss passive
show crypto key mypubkey dss
show crypto key pubkey-chain dss

crypto key-timeout

The **crypto cisco key-timeout** command replaces this command. Refer to the description of the **crypto cisco key-timeout** command for more information.

crypto key zeroize dss

To delete the DSS public/private key pair of a crypto engine, use the **crypto key zeroize dss** global configuration command.

crypto key zeroize dss [*slot* | **rsm** | **vip**]

CAUTION   DSS keys cannot be recovered after they have been removed. Use this command only after careful consideration.

Syntax

Syntax	Description
slot	(Optional) Identifies the crypto engine. This argument is available only on Cisco 7200, RSP7000, and 7500 series routers.
	If no slot is specified, the Cisco IOS crypto engine is selected.
	Use the chassis slot number of the crypto engine location. For the Cisco IOS crypto engine, this is the chassis slot number of the RSP. For the VIP2 crypto engine, this is the chassis slot number of the VIP2. For the ESA crypto engine, this is the chassis slot number of the ESA (Cisco 7200) or of the VIP2 (Cisco RSP7000 and 7500).
rsm	(Optional) This keyword is only available on the Cisco Catalyst 5000 series switch. It identifies the RSM on the Cisco Catalyst 5000 series switch.
vip	(Optional) This keyword is only available on the Cisco Catalyst 5000 series switch. It identifies the VIP2 on the Cisco Catalyst 5000 series switch.

Default

DSS public/private keys remain valid indefinitely.

Command Mode

Global configuration

Usage Guidelines

This command first appeared in Cisco IOS Release 11.2. The **rsm** and **vip** keywords were added in Cisco IOS Release 12.0.

If you choose to stop using encryption on a router, completely or for a specific crypto engine, you may delete the public/private DSS key pair(s) for your router's crypto engine(s). However, after you delete them, you cannot use that crypto engine for any encrypted sessions with peer routers, unless you regenerate and re-exchange new DSS keys. If only one crypto engine is configured at your router, issuing this command prevents you from performing any encryption at the router.

CAUTION   If you use this command on a Cisco 7200 series router, the currently active crypto engine's DSS keys are deleted. Be certain that the engine for which you want to delete keys is the engine that is currently selected. You can use the **show crypto engine configuration** command to verify the current crypto engine. If the current crypto engine is not the engine for which you want to delete DSS keys, you must select the correct crypto engine using the **crypto esa** command.

This command can be used if you lose the password required to complete the **crypto card clear-latch** or **crypto key generate dss** commands. After using the **crypto key zeroize dss** command, you need to regenerate and re-exchange new DSS keys. You are prompted to supply a new password when you regenerate new DSS keys with the **crypto key generate dss** command.

Examples

The following example deletes the DSS public/private key of a router named Router1, which is a Cisco 7500 series router with an RSP in slot 4:

```
Router1(config)# crypto key zeroize dss 4
Warning! Zeroize will remove your DSS signature keys.
Do you want to continue? [yes/no]: y
Keys to be removed are named Router1IOS.
Do you really want to remove these keys? [yes/no]: y
[OK]
Router1(config)#
```

The following example deletes the DSS public/private key on the RSM of a Cisco Catalyst 5000 series switch:

```
Router1(config)# crypto key zeroize dss rsm
Warning! Zeroize will remove your DSS signature keys.
Do you want to continue? [yes/no]: y
Keys to be removed are named Router1IOS.
Do you really want to remove these keys? [yes/no]: y
[OK]
Router1(config)#
```

Related Commands

You can search online at www.cisco.com to find documentation of related commands.

crypto key generate dss

crypto map (global configuration)

To create or modify a crypto map entry and enter the crypto map configuration mode, use the **crypto map** global configuration command. Use the **no** form of this command to delete a crypto map entry or set.

> **crypto map** *map-name seq-num* [**cisco**]
> **no crypto map** *map-name* [*seq-num*]

NOTE   Issue the **crypto map** *map-name seq-num* command without a keyword to modify an existing crypto map entry.

Syntax	Description
cisco	(Default value) Indicates that CET will be used instead of IPSec for protecting the traffic specified by this newly specified crypto map entry. If you use this keyword, none of the IPSec-specific crypto map configuration commands are available. Instead, the CET-specific commands are available.
map-name	The name you assign to the crypto map set.
seq-num	The number you assign to the crypto map entry. See additional explanation for using this argument in the "Usage Guidelines" section.

Default

No crypto maps exist.

Command Mode

Global configuration.

Performing this command invokes the crypto map configuration command mode.

Usage Guidelines

This command first appeared in Cisco IOS Release 11.2. The **cisco** keyword was added in Cisco IOS Release 11.3 T.

This command is also documented in Chapter 29, "IPSec Network Security Commands," where it has slightly different functionality.

Use this command either to create a new crypto map definition or to modify an existing crypto map definition. Crypto maps link together definitions of encryption access lists, peer routers, and DES algorithms. A crypto map must later be applied to an interface for the definitions to take effect; this is done using the **crypto map (interface configuration)** command.

When you issue the **crypto map (global configuration)** command, the router invokes the crypto map configuration command mode. While in this mode, you specify the crypto map definitions. Crypto map configuration command mode commands are used to create these definitions.

A crypto map definition must have three parts. First, you specify which remote peer encrypting router (crypto engine) will provide the far-end encryption services (the remote encryption end-point). This is accomplished by using the **set peer** command. Next, you specify which encryption access list(s) will participate in encryption services with the peer router. This is accomplished using the **match address** command. Finally, you specify which DES algorithm(s) to apply to the encrypted packets in the access list. This is accomplished using either the **set algorithm 40-bit-des** command or the **set algorithm des** command.

Because only one crypto map can be applied to a given interface, the *seq-num* argument provides a way to create several distinct definition sets that coexist within a single crypto map. Figure 27-1 illustrates the sequence number concept.

Having multiple distinct definition sets is useful if one router port will provide the encryption interface to more than one peer router.

Figure 27-1 *Crypto Map with Subdefinitions*

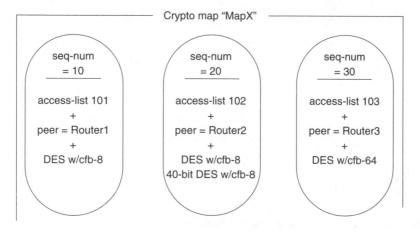

Multiple Crypto Maps Entries with the Same *map-name* Form a Crypto Map Set

A *crypto map set* is a collection of crypto map entries each with a different *seq-num* but the same *map-name*. Therefore, for a given interface, you could have certain traffic forwarded to one IPSec peer with specified security applied to that traffic and other traffic forwarded to the same or a different IPSec peer with different IPSec security applied. To accomplish this you would create two crypto maps, each with the same *map-name*, but each with a different *seq-num*. A crypto map set can include a combination of CET and IPSec crypto map entries.

The *seq-num* Argument

The number you assign to the *seq-num* argument should not be arbitrary. This number is used to rank multiple crypto map entries within a crypto map set. Within a crypto map set, a crypto map entry with a lower *seq-num* is evaluated before a map entry with a higher *seq-num*; that is, the map entry with the lower number has a higher priority.

For example, imagine there is a crypto map set that contains three crypto map entries: mymap 10, mymap 20, and mymap 30. The crypto map set named mymap is applied to interface Serial 0. When traffic passes through the Serial 0 interface, the traffic is evaluated first for mymap 10. If the traffic matches a **permit** entry in the extended access list in mymap 10, the traffic is processed according to the information defined in mymap 10 (including establishing IPSec security associations or CET connections when necessary). If the traffic does not match the mymap 10 access list, the traffic is evaluated for mymap 20, and then mymap 30, until the traffic matches a **permit** entry in a map entry. If the traffic does not match a **permit** entry in any crypto map entry, it is forwarded without any CET (or IPSec) security.

Example

The following example creates a crypto map and defines the map parameters:

```
Router1(config)# crypto map Research 10
Router1(config-crypto-map)# set peer Router2ESA.HQ
Router1(config-crypto-map)# set algorithm des cfb-8
Router1(config-crypto-map)# match address 101
Router1(config-crypto-map)# exit
Router1(config)#
```

Related Commands

You can search online at www.cisco.com to find documentation of related commands.

crypto map (interface configuration)
match address
set algorithm 40-bit-des
set algorithm des

set peer
show crypto map
show crypto mypubkey

crypto map (interface configuration)

To apply a previously defined crypto map to an interface, use the **crypto map** interface configuration command. Use the **no** form of the command to eliminate the crypto map from the interface.

> **crypto map** *map-name*
> **no crypto map** [*map-name*]

Syntax   Description

map-name   The name that identifies the crypto map. This is the name assigned when the crypto map was created.

When the **no** form of the command is used, this argument is optional. Any value supplied for the argument is ignored.

Default

No crypto maps are assigned to interfaces.

Command Mode

Interface configuration

Usage Guidelines

This command first appeared in Cisco IOS Release 11.2.

This command is also documented in Chapter 29, "IPSec Network Security Commands."

Use this command to assign a crypto map set to an interface. You must assign a crypto map set to an interface before that interface can provide CET or IPSec services. Only one crypto map set can be assigned to an interface. If multiple crypto map entries have the same *map-name* but a different *seq-num*, they are considered to be part of the same set and are all applied to the interface. The crypto map entry with the lowest *seq-num* is considered the highest priority and is evaluated first.

Example

The following example assigns crypto map set mymap to the S0 interface. When traffic passes through S0, the traffic is evaluated against all the crypto map entries in the mymap set. When outbound traffic matches an access list in one of the mymap crypto map entries, a security association (if IPsec) or CET connection (if CET) is established per that crypto map entry's configuration (if no security association or connection already exists).

```
interface S0
 crypto map mymap
```

Related Commands

You can search online at www.cisco.com to find documentation of related commands.

crypto map (global configuration)
show crypto map

crypto pregen-dh-pairs

The **crypto cisco pregen-dh-pairs** command replaces this command. Refer to the description of the **crypto cisco pregen-dh-pairs** command for more information.

crypto public-key

The **crypto key pubkey-chain dss** command replaces this command. Refer to the description of the **crypto key pubkey-chain dss** command for more information.

crypto sdu connections

The **crypto cisco connections** command replaces this command. Refer to the description of the **crypto cisco connections** command for more information.

crypto sdu entities

The **crypto cisco entities** command replaces this command. Refer to the description of the **crypto cisco entities** command for more information.

crypto zeroize

The **crypto key zeroize dss** command replaces this command. Refer to the description of the **crypto key zeroize dss** command for more information.

deny

To set conditions for a named encryption access list, use the **deny** access-list configuration command. The **deny** command prevents IP traffic from being encrypted/decrypted if the conditions are matched. Use the **no** form of this command to remove a deny condition from an encryption access list.

> **deny** *source* [*source-wildcard*]
> **no deny** *source* [*source-wildcard*]

> **deny** *protocol source source-wildcard destination destination-wildcard* [**precedence** *precedence*] [**tos** *tos*] [**log**]

> **no deny** *protocol source source-wildcard destination destination-wildcard* [**precedence** *precedence*] [**tos** *tos*] [**log**]

For ICMP, you can also use the following syntax:

> **deny icmp** *source source-wildcard destination destination-wildcard* [*icmp-type* [*icmp-code*] | *icmp-message*] [**precedence** *precedence*] [**tos** *tos*] [**log**]

For IGMP, you can also use the following syntax:

> **deny igmp** *source source-wildcard destination destination-wildcard* [*igmp-type*] [**precedence** *precedence*] [**tos** *tos*] [**log**]

For TCP, you can also use the following syntax:

> **deny tcp** *source source-wildcard* [*operator port* [*port*]] *destination destination-wildcard* [*operator port* [*port*]] [**established**] [**precedence** *precedence*] [**tos** *tos*] [**log**]

For UDP, you can also use the following syntax:

> **deny udp** *source source-wildcard* [*operator port* [*port*]] *destination destination-wildcard* [*operator port* [*port*]] [**precedence** *precedence*] [**tos** *tos*] [**log**]

Syntax	Description
source	Number of the network or host from which the packet is being sent. There are two ways to specify the source: • Use a 32-bit quantity in four-part, dotted-decimal format. • Use the keyword **any** as an abbreviation for a *source* and *source-wildcard* of 0.0.0.0 255.255.255.255. This keyword is normally *not* recommended.
source-wildcard	(Optional) Wildcard bits to be applied to the *source*. There are two ways to specify the source wildcard: • Use a 32-bit quantity in four-part, dotted-decimal format. Place ones in the bit positions you want to ignore. • Use the keyword **any** as an abbreviation for a *source* and *source-wildcard* of 0.0.0.0 255.255.255.255. This keyword is normally *not* recommended.
protocol	Name or number of an IP protocol. It can be one of the keywords **eigrp**, **gre**, **icmp**, **igmp**, **igrp**, **ip**, **ipinip**, **nos**, **ospf**, **tcp**, or **udp**, or an integer in the range 0 through 255 representing an IP protocol number. To match any Internet protocol (including ICMP, TCP, and UDP), use the keyword **ip**. Some protocols allow further qualifiers described later.
source	Number of the network or host from which the packet is being sent. There are three ways to specify the source: • Use a 32-bit quantity in four-part, dotted-decimal format. • Use the keyword **any** as an abbreviation for a *source* and *source-wildcard* of 0.0.0.0 255.255.255.255. This keyword is normally *not* recommended. • Use **host** *source* as an abbreviation for a *source* and *source-wildcard* of *source* 0.0.0.0.
source-wildcard	Wildcard bits to be applied to source. There are three ways to specify the source wildcard: • Use a 32-bit quantity in four-part, dotted-decimal format. Place ones in the bit positions you want to ignore. • Use the keyword **any** as an abbreviation for a *source* and *source-wildcard* of 0.0.0.0 255.255.255.255. This keyword is normally *not* recommended. • Use **host** *source* as an abbreviation for a *source* and *source-wildcard* of *source* 0.0.0.0.

Syntax	Description
destination	Number of the network or host to which the packet is being sent. There are three ways to specify the destination:
	• Use a 32-bit quantity in four-part, dotted-decimal format.
	• Use the keyword **any** as an abbreviation for the *destination* and *destination-wildcard* of 0.0.0.0 255.255.255.255. This keyword is normally *not* recommended.
	• Use **host** *destination* as an abbreviation for a *destination* and *destination-wildcard* of *destination* 0.0.0.0.
destination-wildcard	Wildcard bits to be applied to the destination. There are three ways to specify the destination wildcard:
	• Use a 32-bit quantity in four-part, dotted-decimal format. Place ones in the bit positions you want to ignore.
	• Use the keyword **any** as an abbreviation for a *destination* and *destination-wildcard* of 0.0.0.0 255.255.255.255. This keyword is normally *not* recommended. (See the section "Usage Guidelines.")
	• Use **host** *destination* as an abbreviation for a *destination* and *destination-wildcard* of *destination* 0.0.0.0.
precedence *precedence*	(Optional) Packets can be matched for encryption by precedence level, as specified by a number from 0 to 7 or by name as listed in the section "Usage Guidelines" section of the **access-list (encryption)** command.
tos *tos*	(Optional) Packets can be matched for encryption by type of service level, as specified by a number from 0 to 15 or by name as listed in the "Usage Guidelines" section of the **access-list (encryption)** command.
icmp-type	(Optional) ICMP packets can be matched for encryption by ICMP message type. The type is a number from 0 to 255.
icmp-code	(Optional) ICMP packets which are matched for encryption by ICMP message type can also be matched by the ICMP message code. The code is a number from 0 to 255.
icmp-message	(Optional) ICMP packets can be matched for encryption by an ICMP message type name or ICMP message type and code name. The possible names are found in the "Usage Guidelines" section of the **access-list (encryption)** command.
igmp-type	(Optional) IGMP packets can be matched for encryption by IGMP message type or message name. A message type is a number from 0 to 15. IGMP message names are listed in the "Usage Guidelines" section of the **access-list (encryption)** command.

Syntax	Description
operator	(Optional) Compares source or destination ports. Possible operands include **lt** (less than), **gt** (greater than), **eq** (equal), **neq** (not equal), and **range** (inclusive range).
	If the operator is positioned after the *source* and *source-wildcard*, it must match the source port.
	If the operator is positioned after the *destination* and *destination-wildcard*, it must match the destination port.
	The **range** operator requires two port numbers. All other operators require one port number.
port	(Optional) The decimal number or name of a TCP or UDP port. A port number is a number from 0 to 65,535. TCP and UDP port names are listed in the "Usage Guidelines" section of the **access-list (encryption)** command. TCP port names can only be used when filtering TCP. UDP port names can only be used when filtering UDP.
established	(Optional) For the TCP protocol only: Indicates an established connection. A match occurs if the TCP datagram has the ACK or RST bits set. The nonmatching case is that of the initial TCP datagram to form a connection.
log	(Optional) Causes an informational logging message about the packet that matches the entry to be sent to the console. (The level of messages logged to the console is controlled by the **logging console** command.)
	The message includes the access list number, whether the packet was permitted or denied; the protocol, whether it was TCP, UDP, ICMP or a number; and, if appropriate, the source and destination addresses and source and destination port numbers. The message is generated for the first packet that matches, and then at 5-minute intervals, including the number of packets permitted or denied in the prior 5-minute interval.

Default

There is no specific condition under which a packet is prevented from being encrypted/decrypted. However, if a packet does not match any **deny** or **permit** command statements, the packet will not be encrypted/decrypted. (See the "Usage Guidelines" section that follows for more information about matching encryption access list conditions.)

Command Mode

Access-list configuration

Usage Guidelines

This command first appeared in Cisco IOS Release 11.2.

Use this command to specify conditions under which a packet will not be encrypted/decrypted. Use this command after you use the **ip access-list extended (encryption)** command.

After a named encryption access list is fully specified using the **permit** and **deny** commands, the encryption access list must be specified in a crypto map, and the crypto map must be applied to an interface. After this is accomplished, packets will be either encrypted/decrypted or not encrypted/decrypted at the router depending on the conditions defined within the **permit** and **deny** commands.

If a packet matches the conditions in any **deny** command, the packet will not be encrypted/decrypted. Also, if a packet does not match any conditions in either a **deny** or a **permit** command, the packet will not be encrypted/decrypted. This occurs because all encryption access lists contain an implicit "deny" ("do not encrypt/decrypt") statement at the end of the list.

CAUTION   When creating encryption access lists, Cisco does *not* recommend using the **any** keyword to specify source or destination addresses for **permit** or **deny** commands. Using the **any** keyword with a **permit** command could cause extreme problems if a packet enters your router and is destined for a router that is not configured for encryption. This would cause your router to attempt to set up an encryption session with a nonencrypting router.

If you incorrectly use the **any** keyword with a **deny** command, you might inadvertently prevent all packets from being encrypted, which could present a security risk.

Examples

Example 1: An Inappropriately Configured Access List

This first example shows a named encryption access list configured in an inappropriate way. After this list is applied to an interface using a crypto map, no UDP traffic will be encrypted. This occurs even though there are **permit** commands.

```
ip access-list extended Router1cryptomap10
 deny UDP any any
 permit UDP 192.168.33.145  0.0.0.15  172.31.0.0  0.0.255.255
 permit UDP 192.168.33.145  0.0.0.15  10.0.0.0  0.255.255.255
```

Example 2: Another Inappropriately Configured Access List

The second example shows another inappropriate configuration for an encryption access list. This example causes the router to encrypt all UDP traffic leaving the interface, including traffic to routers not configured for encryption. When this happens, the router attempts to set up an encryption session with a non-encrypting router.

```
ip access-list extended Router1cryptomap10
 permit UDP 192.168.33.145  0.0.0.15  172.31.0.0  0.0.255.255
 permit UDP 192.168.33.145  0.0.0.15  10.0.0.0  0.255.255.255
 permit UDP any any
```

Example 3: A Correctly Configured Access List

The third example encrypts/decrypts only traffic that matches the source and destination addresses defined in the two permit statements. All other traffic is not encrypted/decrypted.

```
ip access-list extended Router1cryptomap10
 permit UDP 192.168.33.145  0.0.0.15  172.31.0.0  0.0.255.255
 permit UDP 192.168.33.145  0.0.0.15  10.0.0.0  0.255.255.255
```

Related Commands

You can search online at www.cisco.com to find documentation of related commands.

access-list (encryption)
ip access-list extended (encryption)
permit
show ip access-list

ip access-list extended (encryption)

To define an encryption access list by name, use the **ip access-list extended** global configuration command. Use the **no** form of this command to remove a named encryption access list.

> **ip access-list extended** *name*
> **no ip access-list extended** *name*

Syntax   Description

name   Name of the encryption access list. Names cannot contain a space or quotation mark and must begin with an alphabetic character to prevent ambiguity with numbered access lists.

Default

There is no named encryption access list.

Command Mode

Global configuration

This command invokes the access-list configuration command mode.

Usage Guidelines

This command first appeared in Cisco IOS Release 11.2.

Use this command to configure a named IP access list (as opposed to a numbered IP access list). This command takes you into access list configuration mode. From this mode you use the **deny** and **permit** commands to define the conditions for which traffic will be encrypted/decrypted or not encrypted/decrypted.

To use the encryption access list, you must first specify the access list in a crypto map definition, and then apply the crypto map to an interface.

Examples

Example 1: An Inappropriately Configured Access List

The first example shows a named encryption access list configured in an inappropriate way. After this list is applied to an interface using a crypto map, no UDP traffic will be encrypted. This occurs even though there are **permit** commands.

```
ip access-list extended Router1cryptomap10
 deny UDP any any
 permit UDP 192.168.33.145  0.0.0.15  172.31.0.0  0.0.255.255
 permit UDP 192.168.33.145  0.0.0.15  10.0.0.0  0.255.255.255
```

Example 2: Another Inappropriately Configured Access List

The second example shows another inappropriate configuration for an encryption access list. This example causes the router to encrypt all UDP traffic leaving the interface, including traffic to routers not configured for encryption. When this happens, the router attempts to set up an encryption session with a non-encrypting router.

```
ip access-list extended Router1cryptomap10
 permit UDP 192.168.33.145  0.0.0.15  172.31.0.0  0.0.255.255
 permit UDP 192.168.33.145  0.0.0.15  10.0.0.0  0.255.255.255
 permit UDP any any
```

Example 3: A Correctly Configured Access List

The third example encrypts/decrypts only traffic that matches the source and destination addresses defined in the two permit statements. All other traffic is not encrypted/decrypted.

```
ip access-list extended Router1cryptomap10
 permit UDP 192.168.33.145  0.0.0.15  172.31.0.0  0.0.255.255
 permit UDP 192.168.33.145  0.0.0.15  10.0.0.0  0.255.255.255
```

Related Commands

You can search online at www.cisco.com to find documentation of related commands.

access-list (encryption)
crypto map (global configuration)
crypto map (interface configuration)
deny
ip access-list (used for traffic filtering purposes)
permit
show ip access-list

match address

To specify an extended access list for a crypto map entry, use the **match address** crypto map configuration command. Use the **no** form of this command to remove the extended access list from a crypto map entry.

> **match address** [*access-list-id* | *name*]
> **no match address** [*access-list-id* | *name*]

Syntax	Description
access-list-id	(Optional) Identifies the extended access list by its name or number. This value should match the *access-list-number* or *name* argument of the extended access list being matched.
name	(Optional) Identifies the named encryption access list. This name should match the *name* argument of the named encryption access list being matched.

Default

No access lists are matched to the crypto map entry.

Command Mode

Crypto map configuration

Usage Guidelines

This command first appeared in Cisco IOS Release 11.2.

This command is also documented in Chapter 29, "IPSec Network Security Commands."

This command is required for all static crypto map entries. If you are defining a dynamic crypto map entry (with the **crypto dynamic-map** command), this command is not required but is strongly recommended.

Use this command to assign an extended access list to a crypto map entry. You also need to define this access list using the **access-list** or **ip access-list extended** commands.

The extended access list specified with this command will be used by IPSec (or CET, depending on the setting of the crypto map entry) to determine which traffic should be protected by crypto and which traffic does not need crypto protection. (Traffic that is permitted by the access list will be protected. Traffic that is denied by the access list will not be protected in the context of the corresponding crypto map entry.)

NOTE   The crypto access list is *not* used to determine whether to permit or deny traffic through the interface. An access list applied directly to the interface makes that determination.

The crypto access list specified by this command is used when evaluating both inbound and outbound traffic. Outbound traffic is evaluated against the crypto access lists specified by the interface's crypto map entries to determine whether it should be protected by crypto and if so (if traffic matches a **permit** entry), which crypto policy applies. (If necessary, in the case of static IPSec crypto maps, new security associations are established using the data flow identity as specified in the **permit** entry; in the case of CET, new connections are established; in the case of dynamic crypto map entries, if no SA exists, the packet is dropped.) After passing the regular access lists at the interface, inbound traffic is evaluated against the crypto access lists specified by the entries of the interface's crypto map set to determine if it should be protected by crypto and, if so, which crypto policy applies. (In the case of IPSec, unprotected traffic is discarded because it should have been protected by IPSec; in the case of CET, the traffic is decrypted even though it was never encrypted.)

In the case of IPSec, the access list is also used to identify the flow for which the IPSec security associations are established. In the outbound case, the **permit** entry is used as the data flow identity (in general), while in the inbound case the data flow identity specified by the peer must be permitted by the crypto access list.

Example

The following example creates a crypto map and defines an encryption access list for the map:

```
Router1(config)# crypto map Research 10
Router1(config-crypto-map)# match address 101
```

Related Commands

You can search online at www.cisco.com to find documentation of related commands.

access-list (encryption)
crypto map (global configuration)
ip access-list extended (encryption)
show crypto map

permit

To set conditions for a named encryption access list, use the **permit** access-list configuration command. The **permit** command causes IP traffic to be encrypted/decrypted if the conditions are matched. Use the **no** form of this command to remove a permit condition from an encryption access list.

> **permit** *source* [*source-wildcard*]
> **no permit** *source* [*source-wildcard*]

> **permit** *protocol source source-wildcard destination destination-wildcard* [**precedence** *precedence*] [**tos** *tos*] [**log**]
> **no permit** *protocol source source-wildcard destination destination-wildcard* [**precedence** *precedence*] [**tos** *tos*] [**log**]

For ICMP, you can also use the following syntax:

> **permit icmp** *source source-wildcard destination destination-wildcard* [*icmp-type* [*icmp-code*] | *icmp-message*] [**precedence** *precedence*] [**tos** *tos*] [**log**]

For IGMP, you can also use the following syntax:

> **permit igmp** *source source-wildcard destination destination-wildcard* [*igmp-type*] [**precedence** *precedence*] [**tos** *tos*] [**log**]

For TCP, you can also use the following syntax:

> **permit tcp** *source source-wildcard* [*operator port* [*port*]] *destination destination-wildcard* [*operator port* [*port*]] [**established**] [**precedence** *precedence*] [**tos** *tos*] [**log**]

For UDP, you can also use the following syntax:

> **permit udp** *source source-wildcard* [*operator port* [*port*]] *destination destination-wildcard*
> [*operator port* [*port*]] [**precedence** *precedence*] [**tos** *tos*] [**log**]

Syntax   Description

source   Number of the network or host from which the packet is being sent. There are two ways to specify the source:

- Use a 32-bit quantity in four-part, dotted-decimal format.

- Use the keyword **any** as an abbreviation for a *source* and *source-wildcard* of 0.0.0.0 255.255.255.255. This keyword is normally *not* recommended.

source-wildcard   (Optional) Wildcard bits to be applied to the *source*. There are two ways to specify the source wildcard:

- Use a 32-bit quantity in four-part, dotted-decimal format. Place ones in the bit positions you want to ignore.

- Use the keyword **any** as an abbreviation for a *source* and *source-wildcard* of 0.0.0.0 255.255.255.255. This keyword is normally *not* recommended.

protocol   Name or number of an IP protocol. It can be one of the keywords **eigrp**, **gre**, **icmp**, **igmp**, **igrp**, **ip**, **ipinip**, **nos**, **ospf**, **tcp**, or **udp**, or an integer in the range 0 through 255 representing an IP protocol number. To match any Internet protocol (including ICMP, TCP, and UDP), use the keyword **ip**. Some protocols allow further qualifiers described later.

source   Number of the network or host from which the packet is being sent. There are three ways to specify the source:

- Use a 32-bit quantity in four-part, dotted-decimal format.

- Use the keyword **any** as an abbreviation for a *source* and *source-wildcard* of 0.0.0.0 255.255.255.255. This keyword is normally *not* recommended.

- Use **host** *source* as an abbreviation for a *source* and *source-wildcard* of *source* 0.0.0.0.

Syntax	Description
source-wildcard	Wildcard bits to be applied to source. There are three ways to specify the source wildcard:
	• Use a 32-bit quantity in four-part, dotted-decimal format. Place ones in the bit positions you want to ignore.
	• Use the keyword **any** as an abbreviation for a *source* and *source-wildcard* of 0.0.0.0 255.255.255.255. This keyword is normally *not* recommended.
	• Use **host** *source* as an abbreviation for a *source* and *source-wildcard* of *source* 0.0.0.0.
destination	Number of the network or host to which the packet is being sent. There are three ways to specify the destination:
	• Use a 32-bit quantity in four-part, dotted-decimal format.
	• Use the keyword **any** as an abbreviation for the *destination* and *destination-wildcard* of 0.0.0.0 255.255.255.255. This keyword is normally *not* recommended.
	• Use **host** *destination* as an abbreviation for a *destination* and *destination-wildcard* of *destination* 0.0.0.0.
destination-wildcard	Wildcard bits to be applied to the destination. There are three ways to specify the destination wildcard:
	• Use a 32-bit quantity in four-part, dotted-decimal format. Place ones in the bit positions you want to ignore.
	• Use the keyword **any** as an abbreviation for a *destination* and *destination-wildcard* of 0.0.0.0 255.255.255.255. This keyword is normally *not* recommended.
	• Use **host** *destination* as an abbreviation for a *destination* and *destination-wildcard* of *destination* 0.0.0.0.
precedence *precedence*	(Optional) Packets can be matched for encryption by precedence level, as specified by a number from 0 to 7 or by name as listed in the section "Usage Guidelines" section of the **access-list (encryption)** command.
tos *tos*	(Optional) Packets can be matched for encryption by type of service level, as specified by a number from 0 to 15 or by name as listed in the "Usage Guidelines" section of the **access-list (encryption)** command.
icmp-type	(Optional) ICMP packets can be matched for encryption by ICMP message type. The type is a number from 0 to 255.

Part
IV

Command Reference

Syntax	Description
icmp-code	(Optional) ICMP packets that are matched for encryption by ICMP message type can also be matched by the ICMP message code. The code is a number from 0 to 255.
icmp-message	(Optional) ICMP packets can be matched for encryption by an ICMP message type name or ICMP message type and code name. The possible names are found in the "Usage Guidelines" section of the **access-list (extended)** command.
igmp-type	(Optional) IGMP packets can be matched for encryption by IGMP message type or message name. A message type is a number from 0 to 15. IGMP message names are listed in the "Usage Guidelines" section of the **access-list (extended)** command.
operator	(Optional) Compares source or destination ports. Possible operands include **lt** (less than), **gt** (greater than), **eq** (equal), **neq** (not equal), and **range** (inclusive range).
	If the operator is positioned after the *source* and *source-wildcard*, it must match the source port.
	If the operator is positioned after the *destination* and *destination-wildcard*, it must match the destination port.
	The **range** operator requires two port numbers. All other operators require one port number.
port	(Optional) The decimal number or name of a TCP or UDP port. A port number is a number from 0 to 65,535. TCP and UDP port names are listed in the "Usage Guidelines" section of the **access-list (extended)** command. TCP port names can only be used when filtering TCP. UDP port names can only be used when filtering UDP.
established	(Optional) For the TCP protocol only: Indicates an established connection. A match occurs if the TCP datagram has the ACK or RST bits set. The nonmatching case is that of the initial TCP datagram to form a connection.

Syntax	Description
log	(Optional) Causes an informational logging message about the packet that matches the entry to be sent to the console. (The level of messages logged to the console is controlled by the **logging console** command.)
	The message includes the access list number, whether the packet was permitted or denied; the protocol, whether it was TCP, UDP, ICMP or a number; and, if appropriate, the source and destination addresses and source and destination port numbers. The message is generated for the first packet that matches and then at 5-minute intervals, including the number of packets permitted or denied in the prior 5-minute interval.

Default

There is no specific condition under which a packet is caused to be encrypted/decrypted. However, if a packet does not match any **deny** or **permit** command statements, the packet will not be encrypted/decrypted. (See the "Usage Guidelines" section for more information about matching encryption access list conditions.)

Command Mode

Access list configuration

Usage Guidelines

This command first appeared in Cisco IOS Release 11.2.

Use this command following the **ip access-list extended (encryption)** command to specify conditions under which a packet will be encrypted/decrypted.

After a named encryption access list is fully specified using **permit** and **deny** commands, the encryption access list must be specified in a crypto map, and the crypto map must be applied to an interface. After this is accomplished, packets will be either encrypted/decrypted or not encrypted/decrypted at the router depending on the conditions defined within the **permit** and **deny** commands.

If a packet matches the conditions in any **permit** command, the packet will be encrypted/decrypted. If a packet does not match any conditions in either a **deny** or a **permit** command, the packet will not be encrypted/decrypted. This occurs because all encryption access lists contain an implicit "deny" ("do not encrypt/decrypt") statement at the end of the list.

> **CAUTION**   When creating encryption access lists, Cisco does *not* recommend using the **any** keyword to specify source or destination addresses for **permit** or **deny** commands. Using the **any** keyword with a **permit** command could cause extreme problems if a packet enters your router and is destined for a router that is not configured for encryption. This would cause your router to attempt to set up an encryption session with a nonencrypting router.
>
> If you incorrectly use the **any** keyword with a **deny** command, you might inadvertently prevent all packets from being encrypted, which could present a security risk.

Examples

Example 1: An Inappropriately Configured Access List

The first example shows a named encryption access list configured in an inappropriate way. After this list is applied to an interface using a crypto map, no UDP traffic will be encrypted. This occurs even though there are **permit** commands.

```
ip access-list extended Router1cryptomap10
 deny UDP any any
 permit UDP 192.168.33.145  0.0.0.15  172.31.0.0  0.0.255.255
 permit UDP 192.168.33.145  0.0.0.15  10.0.0.0  0.255.255.255
```

Example 2: Another Inappropriately Configured Access List

The second example shows another inappropriate configuration for an encryption access list. This example causes the router to encrypt all UDP traffic leaving the interface, including traffic to routers not configured for encryption. When this happens, the router attempts to set up an encryption session with a non-encrypting router.

```
ip access-list extended Router1cryptomap10
 permit UDP 192.168.33.145  0.0.0.15  172.31.0.0  0.0.255.255
 permit UDP 192.168.33.145  0.0.0.15  10.0.0.0  0.255.255.255
 permit UDP any any
```

Example 3: A Correctly Configured Access List

The third example encrypts/decrypts only traffic that matches the source and destination addresses defined in the two permit statements. All other traffic is not encrypted/decrypted.

```
ip access-list extended Router1cryptomap10
 permit UDP 192.168.33.145  0.0.0.15  172.31.0.0  0.0.255.255
 permit UDP 192.168.33.145  0.0.0.15  10.0.0.0  0.255.255.255
```

Related Commands

You can search online at www.cisco.com to find documentation of related commands.

access-list (encryption)
deny
ip access-list extended (encryption)
show ip access-list

set algorithm 40-bit-des

To specify a 40-bit DES algorithm type within a crypto map definition, use the **set algorithm 40-bit-des** crypto map configuration command. Use the **no** form of this command to disable a 40-bit DES algorithm type within a crypto map definition.

> **set algorithm 40-bit-des [cfb-8 | cfb-64]**
> **no set algorithm 40-bit-des [cfb-8 | cfb-64]**

Syntax	Description
cfb-8	(Optional) Selects the 8-bit CFB mode of the 40-bit DES algorithm. If no CFB mode is specified when the command is issued, 64-bit CFB mode is the default.
cfb-64	(Optional) Selects the 64-bit CFB mode of the 40-bit DES algorithm. If no CFB mode is specified when the command is issued, 64-bit CFB mode is the default.

Default

If no DES algorithm is specified within a crypto map, all globally enabled DES algorithms will be matched to the map by default. Refer to the **crypto cisco algorithm 40-bit-des** or **crypto cisco algorithm des** command descriptions to learn about globally enabling DES algorithms.

Command Mode

Crypto map configuration

Usage Guidelines

This command first appeared in Cisco IOS Release 11.2.

Use this command to specify 40-bit DES algorithm types for a given crypto map definition. The 40-bit DES algorithms use a 40-bit DES key. The DES algorithms specified within a crypto map definition will be used to encrypt/decrypt all traffic at an interface when the crypto map is applied to the interface.

NOTE   If you are running an exportable image, you can only use 40-bit variations of DES. You cannot enable or use the basic DES algorithms, which are not available with exportable images.

Example

The following example defines a 40-bit DES algorithm type for a crypto map:

```
Router1(config)# crypto map Research 10
Router1(config-crypto-map)# set algorithm 40-bit-des cfb-8
```

Related Commands

You can search online at www.cisco.com to find documentation of related commands.

crypto map (global configuration)
set algorithm des
show crypto map
show crypto mypubkey

set algorithm des

To enable basic DES algorithm types within a crypto map definition, use the **set algorithm des** crypto map configuration command. Use the **no** form of this command to disable a basic DES algorithm type within a crypto map definition.

> **set algorithm des [cfb-8 | cfb-64]**
> **no set algorithm des [cfb-8 | cfb-64]**

Syntax	Description
cfb-8	(Optional) Selects the 8-bit CFB mode of the basic DES algorithm. If no CFB mode is specified when the command is issued, 64-bit CFB mode is the default.
cfb-64	(Optional) Selects the 64-bit CFB mode of the basic DES algorithm. If no CFB mode is specified when the command is issued, 64-bit CFB mode is the default.

Default

If no DES algorithm is specified within a crypto map, all globally enabled DES algorithms are matched to the map by default. Refer to the **crypto cisco algorithm 40-bit-des** or **crypto cisco algorithm des** commands descriptions to learn about globally enabling DES algorithms.

Command Mode

Crypto map configuration

Usage Guidelines

This command first appeared in Cisco IOS Release 11.2.

Use this command to specify basic DES algorithm types for a given crypto map definition. Basic DES algorithms use a 56-bit DES key. The DES algorithms specified within a crypto map definition will be used to encrypt/decrypt all traffic at an interface when the crypto map is applied to the interface.

NOTE	If you are running an exportable image, you can only use 40-bit variations of DES. You cannot enable or use the basic DES algorithms, which are not available with exportable images.

Example

The following example defines a DES algorithm type for a crypto map:

```
Router1(config)# crypto map Research 10
Router1(config-crypto-map)# set algorithm des cfb-8
```

Related Commands

You can search online at www.cisco.com to find documentation of related commands.

crypto map (global configuration)
set algorithm 40-bit-des
show crypto map
show crypto mypubkey

set peer

To specify a peer encrypting router within a crypto map definition, use the **set peer** crypto map configuration command. Use the **no** form of this command to eliminate a peer encrypting router from a crypto map definition.

> **set peer** *key-name*
> **no set peer** *key-name*

Syntax	Description
key-name	Identifies the crypto engine of the peer encrypting router.

Default

No peer is defined by default.

Command Mode

Crypto map configuration

Usage Guidelines

This command first appeared in Cisco IOS Release 11.2.

This command is also documented in Chapter 29, "IPSec Network Security Commands," where it has slightly different functionality.

Use this command to specify a peer encrypting router as the remote encryption route endpoint for a given crypto map definition.

Example

The following example creates a crypto map and defines a peer router for the map:

```
Router1(config)# crypto map Research 10
Router1(config-crypto-map)# set peer Router2ESA.HQ
```

Related Commands

You can search online at www.cisco.com to find documentation of related commands.

crypto map (global configuration)
show crypto map
show crypto mypubkey

show crypto algorithms

The **show crypto cisco algorithms** command replaces this command. Refer to the description of the **show crypto cisco algorithms** command for more information.

show crypto card

To view the operational status of an ESA, use the **show crypto card** privileged EXEC command. This command is available only on Cisco 7200, RSP7000, or 7500 series routers with an installed ESA.

> **show crypto card** [*slot* | **vip**]

Syntax	Description
slot	(Optional) This argument is available only on Cisco 7200, RSP7000, and 7500 series routers.
	Identifies the ESA to show. Use the chassis slot number of the VIP2 containing the ESA.
vip	(Optional) This keyword is only available on the Cisco Catalyst 5000 series switch. It identifies the VIP2 on the Cisco Catalyst 5000 series switch.

Command Mode

Privileged EXEC

Usage Guidelines

This command first appeared in Cisco IOS Release 11.2. The **vip** keyword was added in Cisco IOS Release 12.0.

Sample Display

The following is sample output from the **show crypto card** command:

```
Router1# show crypto card 1
Crypto card in slot: 1

Tampered:        No
Xtracted:        No
Password set:    Yes
DSS Key set:     Yes
FW version:      5049702
```

The following is sample output from the **show crypto card** command for the VIP2 on a Cisco Catalyst 5000 series switch:

```
Router1# show crypto card vip
Crypto card in slot: vip

Tampered:        No
Xtracted:        No
Password set:    Yes
DSS Key set:     Yes
FW version:      5049702
```

Table 27-1 explains each field.

Table 27-1 *show crypto card Field Descriptions*

Field	Description
Tampered	Yes indicates that someone attempted to physically remove the tamper shield cover from the ESA card. Such an action causes the ESA card to clear its memory, which is similar to issuing the **crypto key zeroize dss** command for the ESA.
Xtracted	Yes indicates that the ESA card has been extracted (removed) from the router.
Password set	Yes indicates that the ESA card password has already been set. This password is set with the **crypto card clear-latch** or **crypto key generate dss** command and is required for subsequent issues of the **crypto card clear-latch** and **crypto key generate dss** commands.
DSS Key set	Yes indicates that DSS keys are generated and ready for use. DSS keys are generated using the **crypto key generate dss** command.
FW version	Version number of the firmware running on the ESA card.

show crypto cisco algorithms

To view which DES algorithm types are globally enabled for your router, use the **show crypto cisco algorithms** privileged EXEC command. This displays all basic DES and 40-bit DES algorithm types globally enabled.

> **show crypto cisco algorithms**

Syntax Description

This command has no arguments or keywords.

Command Mode

Privileged EXEC

Usage Guidelines

This command first appeared in Cisco IOS Release 11.2.

Sample Display

The following is sample output from the **show crypto cisco algorithms** command:

```
Router1# show crypto cisco algorithms
  des cfb-8
```

Related Commands

You can search online at www.cisco.com to find documentation of related commands.

crypto cisco algorithm 40-bit-des
crypto cisco algorithm des

show crypto cisco connections

To view current and pending encrypted session connections, use the **show crypto cisco connections** privileged EXEC command.

show crypto cisco connections

Syntax Description

This command has no arguments or keywords.

Command Mode

Privileged EXEC

Usage Guidelines

This command first appeared in Cisco IOS Release 11.2.

Sample Display

The following is sample output from the **show crypto cisco connections** command:

```
Router1# show crypto cisco connections
Pending Connection Table
PE                UPE             Timestamp             Conn_id
172.21.115.22     172.21.115.18   Mar 01 1993 00:01:09  -1

Connection Table
PE                UPE             Conn_id New_id  Alg         Time
172.21.115.22     172.21.115.18   -1      1       DES_56_CFB64  Not Set
                  flags:PEND_CONN
```

Table 27-2 explains each field.

Table 27-2 *show crypto cisco connections Field Descriptions*

Field	Description
PE	Protected Entity. This shows a representative source IP address as specified in the crypto map's encryption access list. This IP address can be any host that matches a source in the encryption access list being used in the connection.
UPE	Unprotected Entity. This shows a representative destination IP address as specified in the crypto map's encryption access list. This IP address can be any host that matches a destination in the encryption access list that is being used in the connection.
Timestamp	Identifies the time when the connection was initiated.
Conn_id	A number used to identify and track the connection. This can be a positive integer value from 1 to 299 or any negative integer value. Each connection is assigned a negative connection-id when the connection is pending (being set up). When the connection is established, a positive connection-id is assigned to the connection.
New_id	Lists the connection-id number that will be assigned to a connection, after the connection is set up. The New_id value is a positive number from 0 to 299.
	If the New_id value is 0, there is no pending connection.
	If the New_id value is a positive integer, a connection is pending.
	As soon as the pending connection has been established, the New_id value will be transferred to the Conn_id for the established connection, and New_id will be reset to 0.
Alg	Identifies the DES encryption algorithm used for the current connection.
	DES_56_CFB8 = basic DES (56-bit) with 8-bit CFB
	DES_56_CFB64 = basic DES (56-bit) with 64-bit CFB
	DES_40_CFB8 = 40-bit DES with 8-bit CFB
	DEC_40_CFB64 = 40-bit DES with 64-bit CFB
	Unknown = no connection
Time	Identifies the time when the connection was initiated.
flags	PEND_CONN = identifies the table entry as a pending connection
	XCHG_KEYS = the connection has timed out; for encrypted communication to occur again, the router must first exchange DH numbers and generate a new session (DES) key
	TIME_KEYS = the encrypted communication session is currently in progress (a session key is currently installed, and the session is counting down to timeout)
	BAD_CONN = no existing or pending connection exists for this table entry
	UNK_STATUS = invalid status (error)

show crypto cisco key-timeout

To view the current setting for the duration of encrypted sessions, use the **show crypto cisco key-timeout** privileged EXEC command.

show crypto cisco key-timeout

Syntax Description

This command has no arguments or keywords.

Command Mode

Privileged EXEC

Usage Guidelines

This command first appeared in Cisco IOS Release 11.2.

Sample Display

The following is sample output from the **show crypto cisco key-timeout** command:

```
Router1# show crypto cisco key-timeout
Session keys will be re-negotiated every 120 minutes.
```

Related Commands

You can search online at www.cisco.com to find documentation of related commands.

crypto cisco key-timeout

show crypto cisco pregen-dh-pairs

To view the number of DH number pairs currently generated, use the **show crypto cisco pregen-dh-pairs** privileged EXEC command.

show crypto cisco pregen-dh-pairs [*slot* | **rsm** | **vip**]

Syntax	Description
slot	(Optional) Identifies the crypto engine. This argument is available only on Cisco 7200, RSP7000, and 7500 series routers.
	If no slot is specified, the Cisco IOS crypto engine is selected.
	Use the chassis slot number of the crypto engine location. For the Cisco IOS crypto engine, this is the chassis slot number of the RSP. For the VIP2 crypto engine, this is the chassis slot number of the VIP2. For the ESA crypto engine, this is the chassis slot number of the ESA (Cisco 7200) or of the VIP2 (Cisco RSP7000 and 7500).
rsm	(Optional) This keyword is only available on the Cisco Catalyst 5000 series switch. It identifies the RSM on the Cisco Catalyst 5000 series switch.
vip	(Optional) This keyword is only available on the Cisco Catalyst 5000 series switch. It identifies the VIP2 on the Cisco Catalyst 5000 series switch.

Command Mode

Privileged EXEC

Usage Guidelines

This command first appeared in Cisco IOS Release 11.2. The **rsm** and **vip** keywords were added in Cisco IOS Release 12.0.

Sample Display

The following is sample output from the **show crypto cisco pregen-dh-pairs** command:

```
Router1# show crypto cisco pregen-dh-pairs

Number of pregenerated DH pairs: 1
```

The number 1 shown in the output indicates that there is one DH number pair ready and available for the next encrypted connection.

The following is sample output from the **show crypto cisco pregen-dh-pairs** command for a Cisco Catalyst 5000 series switch:

```
Router1# show crypto cisco pregen-dh-pairs rsm

Number of pregenerated DH pairs for slot rsm: 1
```

The following is sample output from the **show crypto cisco pregen-dh-pairs** command (using the *slot* argument) for a Cisco 7500 series router:

```
Router1# show crypto cisco pregen-dh-pairs 2

Number of pregenerated DH pairs for slot 2: 1
```

If you do not enter a slot number on a Cisco 7500 series router, the default, which is the slot number of the RSP, is used.

Related Commands

You can search online at www.cisco.com to find documentation of related commands.

crypto cisco pregen-dh-pairs

show crypto connections

The **show crypto cisco connections** command replaces this command. Refer to the description of the **show crypto cisco connections** command for more information.

show crypto engine brief

To view all crypto engines within a Cisco 7200, RSP7000, or 7500 series router, use the **show crypto engine brief** privileged EXEC command.

> **show crypto engine brief**

Syntax Description

This command has no arguments or keywords.

Command Mode

Privileged EXEC

Usage Guidelines

This command first appeared in Cisco IOS Release 11.2.

This command is only available on Cisco 7200, RSP7000, and 7500 series routers.

Sample Display

The following is sample output from the **show crypto engine brief** command. In this example, the router has two crypto engines: a Cisco IOS crypto engine and an ESA crypto engine. Both crypto engines have DSS keys generated.

```
Router1# show crypto engine brief
crypto engine name:    Router1ESA
crypto engine type:    ESA
crypto engine state:   dss key generated
crypto firmware version:  5049702
crypto engine in slot: 1

crypto engine name:    Router1IOS
crypto engine type:    software
crypto engine state:   dss key generated
crypto lib version:    2.0.0
crypto engine in slot: 4
```

Table 27-3 explains each field.

Table 27-3 *show crypto engine brief Field Descriptions*

Field	Description
crypto engine name	Name of the crypto engine as assigned with the *key-name* argument in the **crypto key generate dss** command.
crypto engine type	If software is listed, the crypto engine resides in either the RSP (the Cisco IOS crypto engine) or in a second-generation VIP2.
	If crypto card or ESA is listed, the crypto engine is associated with an ESA.
crypto engine state	The state installed indicates that a crypto engine is located in the given slot, but is not configured for encryption.
	The state dss key generated indicates that the crypto engine found in that slot has DSS keys already generated.
	In a Cisco 7200 series router, the state installed (ESA pending) indicates that the ESA crypto engine will be replaced with the Cisco IOS crypto engine as soon as it becomes available.
crypto firmware version	Version number of the crypto firmware running on the ESA.
crypto lib version	Version number of the crypto library running on the router.

Table 27-3   *show crypto engine brief Field Descriptions (Continued)*

Field	Description
crypto engine in slot	Chassis slot number of the crypto engine. For the Cisco IOS crypto engine, this is the chassis slot number of the RSP. For the VIP2 crypto engine, this is the chassis slot number of the VIP2. For the ESA crypto engine, this is the chassis slot number of the ESA (Cisco 7200) or of the VIP2 (Cisco RSP7000 and 7500).

Related Commands

You can search online at www.cisco.com to find documentation of related commands.

show crypto engine configuration

show crypto engine configuration

To view the Cisco IOS crypto engine of your router, use the **show crypto engine configuration** privileged EXEC command.

> **show crypto engine configuration**

Syntax Description

This command has no arguments or keywords.

Command Mode

Privileged EXEC

Usage Guidelines

This command first appeared in Cisco IOS Release 11.2.

Sample Display

The following is sample output from the **show crypto engine configuration** command for a Cisco 2500 series router:

```
Router1# show crypto engine configuration
engine name:       Router1
engine type:       software
serial number:     01709642
platform:          rp crypto engine
```

```
Encryption Process Info:
input queue top:    75
input queue bot:    75
input queue count:  0
```

The following is sample output from the **show crypto engine configuration** command for a Cisco 7500 series router:

```
Router2# show crypto engine configuration
engine name:       Router2IOS
engine type:       software
serial number:     02863239
platform:          rsp crypto engine

Encryption Process Info:
input queue top:    44
input queue bot:    44
input queue count:  0
```

Table 27-4 explains each field.

Table 27-4   *show crypto engine configuration* *Field Descriptions*

Field	Description
engine name	Name of the crypto engine as assigned with the *key-name* argument in the **crypto key generate dss** command.
engine type	Should always display software.
serial number	Serial number of the RP or RSP.
platform	If the router is a Cisco RSP7000 or 7500 series router, this field displays rsp crypto engine. If the router is a Cisco 7200 series router, this field displays rp crypto engine.
input queue top (Encryption Process Info)	The queue location of the (inbound) packet next in line to be processed (decrypted). This packet will come off the top of the circular queue next. (This field is useful for debugging purposes.)
input queue bot (Encryption Process Info)	The queue location of the (inbound) packet last in line to be processed (decrypted). The packet is the most recently received and queued at the bottom of the circular queue. (This field is useful for debugging purposes.)
input queue count (Encryption Process Info)	The total number of packets currently in the circular queue. These are inbound packets waiting for processing. (This field is useful for debugging purposes.)

Related Commands

You can search online at www.cisco.com to find documentation of related commands.

show crypto engine brief

show crypto engine connections active

To view the current active encrypted session connections for all crypto engines, use the **show crypto engine connections active** privileged EXEC command.

show crypto engine connections active [*slot* | **rsm** | **vip**]

Syntax	Description
slot	(Optional) Identifies the crypto engine. This argument is available only on Cisco 7200, RSP7000, and 7500 series routers.
If no slot is specified, the Cisco IOS crypto engine is selected.
Use the chassis slot number of the crypto engine location. For the Cisco IOS crypto engine, this is the chassis slot number of the RSP. For the VIP2 crypto engine, this is the chassis slot number of the VIP2. For the ESA crypto engine, this is the chassis slot number of the ESA (Cisco 7200) or of the VIP2 (Cisco RSP7000 and 7500).
rsm	(Optional) This keyword is only available on the Cisco Catalyst 5000 series switch. It identifies the RSM on the Cisco Catalyst 5000 series switch.
vip	(Optional) This keyword is only available on the Cisco Catalyst 5000 series switch. It identifies the VIP2 on the Cisco Catalyst 5000 series switch.

Command Mode

Privileged EXEC

Usage Guidelines

This command first appeared in Cisco IOS Release 11.2. The **rsm** and **vip** keywords were added in Cisco IOS Release 12.0.

Sample Display

The following is sample output from the **show crypto engine connections active** command:

```
Router1# show crypto engine connections active
Connection Interface  IP-Address     State Algorithm     Encrypt  Decrypt
2          Ethernet0  172.21.114.9   set   DES_56_CFB64 41       32
3          Ethernet1  172.29.13.2    set   DES_56_CFB64 110      65
4          Serial0    172.17.42.1    set   DES_56_CFB64 36       27
```

The following is sample output from the **show crypto engine connections active** command on a Cisco 7500 series router, where the VIP is in slot 4:

```
Router1# show crypto engine connections active 4
Connection Interface  IP-Address     State Algorithm     Encrypt  Decrypt
2          Ethernet0  172.21.114.9   set   DES_56_CFB64 41       32
3          Ethernet1  172.29.13.2    set   DES_56_CFB64 110      65
4          Serial0    172.17.42.1    set   DES_56_CFB64 36       27
```

If you do not enter a slot number on a Cisco 7500 series router, the default is the slot number of the RSP.

The following is sample output from the **show crypto engine connections active** command on a Cisco Catalyst 5000 series switch:

```
Router1# show crypto engine connections active vip
Connection Interface  IP-Address     State Algorithm     Encrypt  Decrypt
2          Ethernet0  172.21.114.9   set   DES_56_CFB64 41       32
3          Ethernet1  172.29.13.2    set   DES_56_CFB64 110      65
4          Serial0    172.17.42.1    set   DES_56_CFB64 36       27
```

If you do not enter a keyword on a Cisco Catalyst 5000 series switch, the default is **rsm**.

Table 27-5 explains each field.

Table 27-5 *show crypto engine connections active Field Descriptions*

Field	Description
Connection	Identifies the connection by its number. Each active encrypted session connection is identified by a positive number from 1 to 299. These connection numbers correspond to the table entry numbers.
Interface	Identifies the interface involved in the encrypted session connection. This displays only the actual interface, not a subinterface (even if a subinterface is defined and used for the connection).
IP-Address	Identifies the IP address of the interface.
	Note that if a subinterface is used for the connection, this field displays unassigned.
State	The state set indicates an active connection.
Algorithm	Identifies the DES algorithm used to encrypt/decrypt packets at the interface.

Table 27-5 *show crypto engine connections active Field Descriptions (Continued)*

Field	Description
Encrypt	Shows the total number of encrypted outbound IP packets.
Decrypt	Shows the total number of decrypted inbound IP packets.

Related Commands

You can search online at www.cisco.com to find documentation of related commands.

show crypto engine connections dropped-packets

show crypto engine connections dropped-packets

To view information about packets dropped during encrypted sessions for all router crypto engines, use the **show crypto engine connections dropped-packets** privileged EXEC command.

show crypto engine connections dropped-packets

Syntax Description

This command has no arguments or keywords.

Command Mode

Privileged EXEC

Usage Guidelines

This command first appeared in Cisco IOS Release 11.2.

Sample Display

The following is sample output from the **show crypto engine connections dropped-packets** command:

```
Router1# show crypto engine connections dropped-packets
Interface     IP-Address     Drop Count
Ethernet0/0   172.21.114.165 4
```

The Drop Count number indicates the total number of dropped packets for the lifetime of the crypto engine.

Related Commands

You can search online at www.cisco.com to find documentation of related commands.

show crypto engine connections active

show crypto key mypubkey dss

To view DSS public keys (for all your router crypto engines) in hexadecimal form, use the **show crypto key mypubkey dss** EXEC command.

show crypto key mypubkey dss

Syntax Description

This command has no arguments or keywords.

Command Mode

EXEC

Usage Guidelines

This command first appeared in Cisco IOS Release 11.2.

Sample Display

The following is sample output from the **show crypto key mypubkey dss** command for a Cisco 2500 series router with a crypto engine called Router1.branch:

```
Router1# show crypto key mypubkey dss
Key name: Router1
Serial number: 05706421
Usage: Signature Key
Key Data:
8F1440B9 4C860989 8791A12B 69746E27 307ACACB 62915B02 0261B58F 1F7ABB10
90CE70A9 08F86652 16B52064 37C857D4 7066DAA3 7FC33212 445275EE 542DCD06
```

Related Commands

You can search online at www.cisco.com to find documentation of related commands.

show crypto key pubkey-chain dss

show crypto key pubkey-chain dss

To view peer router DSS public keys known to your router, use the **show crypto key pubkey-chain dss** EXEC command.

show crypto key pubkey-chain dss [**name** *key-name* | **serial** *serial-number*]

Syntax	Description
name	The name assigned when the DSS public key was created with the **crypto key pubkey-chain dss** command.
serial-number	The serial number of the encrypting router's public DSS key.

Command Mode

EXEC

Usage Guidelines

This command first appeared in Cisco IOS Release 11.2.

Sample Display

The following is sample output from the **show crypto key pubkey-chain dss** command:

```
Router1# show crypto key pubkey-chain dss
Codes: M - Manually configured
Code Usage     Serial Number    Name
M  Signing     03259625         router1
```

The following is sample output from the **show crypto key pubkey-chain dss** command using the *name* keyword:

```
Router1# show crypto key pubkey-chain dss name router1
Key name: router1
Serial number: 03259625
Usage: Signature Key
Source: Manually entered
Data:
8F1440B9 4C860989 8791A12B 69746E27 307ACACB 62915B02 0261B58F 1F7ABB10
90CE70A9 08F86652 16B52064 37C857D4 7066DAA3 7FC33212 445275EE 542DCD06
```

The following is sample output from the **show crypto key pubkey-chain dss** command using the *serial-number* keyword:

```
Router1# show crypto key pubkey-chain dss serial 03259625
Key name: router1
Serial number: 03259625
Usage: Signature Key
```

```
Source: Manually entered
Data:
8F1440B9 4C860989 8791A12B 69746E27 307ACACB 62915B02 0261B58F 1F7ABB10
90CE70A9 08F86652 16B52064 37C857D4 7066DAA3 7FC33212 445275EE 542DCD06
```

Related Commands

You can search online at www.cisco.com to find documentation of related commands.

crypto key exchange dss
crypto key generate dss
show crypto key pubkey-chain dss

show crypto key-timeout

The **show crypto cisco key-timeout** command replaces this command. Refer to the description of the **show crypto cisco key-timeout** command for more information.

show crypto map

To view the crypto map configuration, use the **show crypto map** privileged EXEC command.

show crypto map [**interface** *interface* | **tag** *map-name*]

Syntax	Description
interface *interface*	(Optional) Shows only the crypto map set applied to the specified interface.
tag *map-name*	(Optional) Shows only the crypto map set with the specified *map-name*.

Default

If no keywords are used, all crypto maps configured at the router are displayed.

Command Mode

Privileged EXEC

Usage Guidelines

This command first appeared in Cisco IOS Release 11.2.

This command is also documented in Chapter 29, "IPSec Network Security Commands," where it has slightly different functionality.

Sample Display

The following is sample output from the **show crypto map** command performed at a Cisco 2500 series router:

```
Router1# show crypto map

Crypto Map "Canada" 10
        Connection Id = UNSET     (2 established,    0 failed)
        Crypto Engine = Router1IOS (2)
        Algorithm = 40-bit-des cfb-64
        Peer = Router2
        PE = 172.21.114.9
        UPE = 192.168.23.116
        Extended IP access list 101
                access-list 101 permit ip host 10.0.0.1 host 192.168.15.0
                access-list 101 permit ip host 172.21.114.9 host 192.168.23.116
```

The following is sample output from the **show crypto map** command performed at a Cisco 7500 series router. Two crypto maps are shown: a crypto map named ResearchSite with subdefinitions 10 and 20, and another crypto map named HQ.

```
Router2# show crypto map

Crypto Map "ResearchSite" 10
        Connection Id = 6         (6 established,    0 failed)
        Crypto Engine = Router2IOS (4)
        Algorithm = 40-bit-des cfb-64
        Peer = Router1
        PE = 192.168.15.0
        UPE = 10.0.0.1
        Extended IP access list 102
                access-list 102 permit ip host 192.168.15.0 host 10.0.0.1
Crypto Map "ResearchSite" 20
        Connection Id = UNSET     (0 established,    0 failed)
        Crypto Engine = Router2IOS (4)
        Algorithm = 56-bit-des cfb-64
        Peer = Router3
        PE = 192.168.129.33
        UPE = 172.21.114.165
        Extended IP access list 103
                access-list 103 permit ip host 192.168.129.33 host 172.21.114.165
Crypto Map "HQ" 10
        Connection Id = UNSET     (3 established,    0 failed)
        Crypto Engine = Router2ESA (2)
        Algorithm = 56-bit-des cfb-64
        Peer = Eggplant
        PE = 192.168.129.10
        UPE = 10.1.2.3
        Extended IP access list 104
                access-list 104 permit ip host 192.168.129.10 host 10.1.2.3
```

The command output separately lists each crypto map subdefinition.

If more than one subdefinition exists for a crypto map, each subdefinition is listed separately by sequence number (per the *seq-num* argument of the **crypto map (global configuration)** command). The sequence number is shown following the crypto map name.

Table 27-6 explains each field.

Table 27-6 *show crypto map Field Descriptions*

Field	Description
Connection Id	Identifies the connection by its number. Each active encrypted session connection is identified by a positive number from 1 to 299. The value UNSET indicates that no connection currently exists and is using the crypto map.
established	Indicates the total number of encrypted connections that have been successfully established using the crypto map.
failed	Indicates the total number of attempted encrypted connections that failed to be established while using the crypto map. *Continues*
Crypto Engine	Lists the name of the governing crypto engine, followed by the crypto engine slot number in parentheses. The slot number could be either the RSP slot number, indicating a Cisco IOS crypto engine, a second-generation VIP2 slot number, indicating a VIP2 or an ESA crypto engine, or (Cisco 7200 only) an ESA slot number, indicating an ESA crypto engine. (Not displayed on routers other than Cisco 7200, RSP7000, or 7500 series routers.)
Algorithm	Indicates the type of DES encryption algorithm used by the crypto map.
Peer	Indicates the name of the crypto map of the remote peer encrypting router.
PE	Protected Entity. This shows a representative source IP address as specified in the crypto map's encryption access list. This IP address can be any host that matches a source in the encryption access list that is being used in the connection.

Table 27-6 *show crypto map* Field Descriptions (Continued)

Field	Description
UPE	Unprotected Entity. This shows a representative destination IP address as specified in the crypto map's encryption access list. This IP address can be any host that matches a destination in the encryption access list that is being used in the connection.
Extended IP access list	Lists the access list associated with the crypto map. If no access list is associated, the message "No matching address list set" is displayed.

Related Commands

You can search online at www.cisco.com to find documentation of related commands.

crypto map (global configuration)
crypto map (interface configuration)

show crypto mypubkey

The **show crypto key mypubkey dss** command replaces this command. Refer to the description of the **show crypto key mypubkey dss** command for more information.

show crypto pregen-dh-pairs

The **show crypto cisco pregen-dh-pairs** command replaces this command. Refer to the description of the **show crypto cisco pregen-dh-pairs** command for more information.

show crypto pubkey

The **show crypto key pubkey-chain dss** command replaces this command. Refer to the description of the **show crypto key pubkey-chain dss** command for more information.

show crypto pubkey name

The **show crypto key pubkey-chain dss** command replaces this command. Refer to the description of the **show crypto key pubkey-chain dss** command for more information.

show crypto pubkey serial

The **show crypto key pubkey-chain dss** command replaces this command. Refer to the description of the **show crypto key pubkey-chain dss** command for more information.

test crypto initiate-session

To set up a test encryption session, use the **test crypto initiate-session** privileged EXEC command.

test crypto initiate-session *src-ip-addr dst-ip-addr map-name seq-num*

Syntax	Description
src-ip-addr	IP address of source host. Should be included in an encryption access list definition as a valid IP address source address.
dst-ip-addr	IP address of destination host. Should be included in an encryption access list definition as a valid IP address destination address.
map-name	Names the crypto map to be used.
seq-num	Names the crypto map sequence number.

Command Mode

Privileged EXEC

Usage Guidelines

This command first appeared in Cisco IOS Release 11.2.

Use this command to set up a test encryption session. This command can be used after you have completed all the essential encryption configuration tasks for your router. After issuing this command, use the **show crypto cisco connections** command to verify the status of the connection just created.

Example

The following example sets up and verifies a test encryption session.

Router1 sets up a test encryption session with Router2 and then views the connection status to verify a successful encrypted session connection.

> **Step 1** Router1 sets up a test encryption connection with Router2:

```
Router1# test crypto initiate-session 192.168.3.12 192.168.204.110
Router2ESA.TXbranch 10
Sending CIM to: 192.168.204.110 from: 192.168.3.12.
Connection id: -1
```

> Notice the connection-id value is -1. A negative value indicates that the connection is being set up. (CIM stands for connection initiation message.)

Step 2 Router1 issues the **show crypto cisco connections** command:

```
Router1# show crypto cisco connections
Pending Connection Table
PE                UPE               Timestamp           Conn_id
192.168.3.10      192.168.204.100 Mar 01 1993 00:01:09  -1

Connection Table
PE                UPE               Conn_id New_id  Alg    Time
192.168.3.10      192.168.204.100 -1       1       0      Not Set
                  flags:PEND_CONN
```

> Look in the pending connection table for an entry with a Conn_id value equal to the previously shown connection-id value—in this case, look for an entry with a Conn_id value of -1. If this is the first time an encrypted connection has been attempted, there is only one entry (as shown).
>
> Note the PE and UPE addresses for this entry.

Step 3 Now, look in the connection table for an entry with the same PE and UPE addresses. In this case, there is only one entry in both tables, so finding the right connection table entry is easy.

Step 4 At the connection table entry, note the Conn_id and New_id values. In this case, Conn_id equals -1, and New_id equals 1. The New_id value of 1 is assigned to the test connection when setup is complete. (Positive numbers are assigned to established, active connections.)

Step 5 Router1 waits a moment for the test connection to set up and then reissues the **show crypto cisco connections** command:

```
Router1# show crypto cisco connections
Connection Table
PE                UPE               Conn_id New_id  Alg    Time
192.168.3.10      192.168.204.100 1       0       10     Mar 01 1993 00:02:00
                  flags:TIME_KEYS
```

> Again, look for the connection table entry with the same PE and UPE addresses as shown before. In this entry, notice that the Conn_id value has changed to 1. This indicates that the test connection has been successfully established, because the Conn_id value has changed to match the New_id value of Step 4. Also, New_id has been reset to 0 at this point, indicating that there are no new connections currently being set up.
>
> In the command output of Step 5, there is no longer a pending connection table being displayed, which indicates that there are currently no pending connections. This is also indicates that the test connection was successfully established.

The **show crypto cisco connections** command is explained in greater detail earlier in this chapter, including a description of how connection-ids are assigned during and following connection setup.

Related Commands

You can search online at www.cisco.com to find documentation of related commands.

show crypto cisco connections

## CHAPTER 28

Configuring IPSec Network Security

This chapter describes how to configure IPSec, which is a framework of open standards developed by the Internet Engineering Task Force (IETF). IPSec provides security for transmission of sensitive information over unprotected networks such as the Internet. IPSec acts at the network layer, protecting and authenticating IP packets between participating IPSec devices (that is, *peers*), such as Cisco routers.

IPSec provides the following network security services. These services are optional. In general, local security policy will dictate the use of one or more of these services:

● Data Confidentiality—The IPSec sender can encrypt packets before transmitting them across a network.

● Data Integrity—The IPSec receiver can authenticate packets sent by the IPSec sender to ensure that the data has not been altered during transmission.

● Data Origin Authentication—The IPSec receiver can authenticate the source of the IPSec packets sent. This service is dependent on the data integrity service.

● Anti-Replay—The IPSec receiver can detect and reject replayed packets.

NOTE   The term *data authentication* is generally used to mean data integrity and data origin authentication. In this chapter it also includes anti-replay services, unless otherwise specified.

With IPSec, data can be transmitted across a public network without fear of observation, modification, or spoofing. This enables applications such as virtual private networks (VPNs), including intranets, extranets, and remote user access.

For a complete description of the IPSec Network Security commands used in this chapter, refer to Chapter 29, "IPSec Network Security Commands." To locate documentation of other commands that appear in this chapter, you can search online at www.cisco.com.

IPSec Overview

IPSec services are similar to those provided by Cisco Encryption Technology (CET), a proprietary security solution introduced in Cisco IOS Software Release 11.2. (The IPSec standard was not yet available at Release 11.2.) However, IPSec provides a more robust security solution and is standards based. IPSec also provides data authentication and anti-replay services in addition to data confidentiality services, while CET provides only data confidentiality services.

For information comparing IPSec and CET, refer to Chapter 25, "IP Security and Encryption Overview."

Supported Standards

Cisco implements the following standards with this feature:

- **IPSec**—IP Security Protocol. IPSec is a framework of open standards that provides data confidentiality, data integrity, and data authentication between participating peers. IPSec provides these security services at the IP layer; it uses IKE to handle negotiation of protocols and algorithms based on local policy, and to generate the encryption and authentication keys to be used by IPSec. IPSec can be used to protect one or more data flows between a pair of hosts, a pair of security gateways, or a security gateway and a host.

  IPSec is documented in a series of Internet Drafts, all available at www.ietf.org/html.charters/ipsec-charter.html (as of the first publication of this document). The overall IPSec implementation is per the latest version of the "Security Architecture for the Internet Protocol" Internet Draft (draft-ietf-arch-sec-xx.txt). An earlier version of IPSec is described in RFCs 1825 through 1829. While Internet Drafts supersede these RFCs, Cisco IOS IPSec implements RFC 1828 (IP Authentication using Keyed MD5) and RFC 1829 (ESP DES-CBC Transform) for backwards compatibility.

- **Internet Key Exchange (IKE)**—A hybrid protocol that implements Oakley and SKEME key exchanges inside the ISAKMP framework. Although IKE can be used with other protocols, its initial implementation is with the IPSec protocol. IKE provides authentication of the IPSec peers, negotiates IPSec security associations, and establishes IPSec keys.

  For more information on IKE, see Chapter 32, "Configuring Internet Key Exchange Security Protocol."

The component technologies implemented for IPSec include the following:

- **DES**—The Data Encryption Standard (DES) is used to encrypt packet data. Cisco IOS implements the mandatory 56-bit DES-CBC with Explicit IV. Cipher Block Chaining (CBC) requires an initialization vector (IV) to start encryption. The IV is explicitly given in the IPSec packet. For backward compatibility, Cisco IOS IPSec also implements the RFC 1829 version of ESP DES-CBC.

- **MD5 (HMAC variant)**—Message Digest 5 (MD5) is a hash algorithm. HMAC is a keyed hash variant used to authenticate data.

- **SHA (HMAC variant)**—Secure Hash Algorithm (SHA) is a hash algorithm. HMAC is a keyed hash variant used to authenticate data.

IPSec as implemented in Cisco IOS software supports the following additional standards:

- **AH**—Authentication Header. A security protocol that provides data authentication and optional anti-replay services. AH is embedded in the data to be protected (a full IP datagram).

   Both the older RFC 1828 AH and the updated AH protocol are implemented. The updated AH protocol is per the latest version of the "IP Authentication Header" Internet Draft (draft-ietf-ipsec-auth-header-xx.txt).

   RFC 1828 specifies the Keyed MD5 authentication algorithm; it does not provide anti-replay services. The updated AH protocol allows for the use of various authentication algorithms; Cisco IOS has implemented the mandatory MD5 and SHA (HMAC variants) authentication algorithms. The updated AH protocol provides anti-replay services.

- **ESP**—Encapsulating Security Payload. A security protocol that provides data privacy services and optional data authentication, as well as anti-replay services. ESP encapsulates the data to be protected.

   Both the older RFC 1829 ESP and the updated ESP protocol are implemented. The updated ESP protocol is per the latest version of the "IP Encapsulating Security Payload" Internet Draft (draft-ietf-ipsec-esp-v2-xx.txt).

   RFC 1829 specifies DES-CBC as the encryption algorithm; it does not provide data authentication or anti-replay services. The updated ESP protocol allows for the use of various cipher algorithms and (optionally) various authentication algorithms. Cisco IOS implements the mandatory 56-bit DES-CBC with Explicit IV as the encryption algorithm, and MD5 or SHA (HMAC variants) as the authentication algorithms. The updated ESP protocol provides anti-replay services.

List of Terms

anti-replay—A security service where the receiver can reject old or duplicate packets in order to protect itself against replay attacks. IPSec provides this optional service by use of a sequence number combined with the use of data authentication. Cisco IOS IPSec provides this service whenever it provides the data authentication service, except in the following cases:

- RFC 1828 does not provide support for this service.

- The service is not available for manually established security associations (that is, security associations established by configuration and not by IKE).

data authentication—Includes two concepts:

- Data integrity (verifying that data has not been altered).

- Data origin authentication (verifying that the data was actually sent by the claimed sender).

Data authentication can refer either to integrity alone or to both of these concepts (although data origin authentication is dependent upon data integrity).

data confidentiality—A security service where the protected data cannot be observed.

data flow—A grouping of traffic, identified by a combination of source address/mask, destination address/mask, IP next protocol field, and source and destination ports, where the protocol and port fields can have the values of **any**. In effect, all traffic matching a specific combination of these values is logically grouped together into a data flow. A data flow can represent a single TCP connection between two hosts, or it can represent all of the traffic between two subnets. IPSec protection is applied to data flows.

peer—In the context of this chapter, a router or another device that participates in IPSec.

perfect forward secrecy (PFS)—A cryptographic characteristic associated with a derived shared secret value. With PFS, if one key is compromised, previous and subsequent keys are not compromised, because subsequent keys are not derived from previous keys.

security association—An IPSec security association (SA) is a description of how two or more entities will use security services in the context of a particular security protocol (AH or ESP) to communicate securely on behalf of a particular data flow. It includes such things as the transform and the shared secret keys to be used for protecting the traffic.

The IPSec security association is established either by IKE or by manual user configuration. Security associations are unidirectional and are unique per security protocol. So when security associations are established for IPSec, the security associations (for each protocol) for both directions are established at the same time.

When using IKE to establish the security associations for the data flow, the security associations are established when needed and expire after a period of time (or volume of traffic). If the security associations are manually established, they are established as soon as the necessary configuration is completed and do not expire.

security parameter index (SPI)—This is a number that, together with a destination IP address and security protocol, uniquely identifies a particular security association. When using IKE to establish the security associations, the SPI for each security association is a pseudo-randomly derived number. Without IKE, the SPI is manually specified for each security association.

transform—A transform lists a security protocol (AH or ESP) with its corresponding algorithms. For example, one transform is the AH protocol with the HMAC-MD5 authentication algorithm; another transform is the ESP protocol with the 56-bit DES encryption algorithm and the HMAC-SHA authentication algorithm.

tunnel—In the context of this chapter, a secure communication path between two peers, such as two routers. It does not refer to using IPSec in tunnel mode.

IPSec Interoperability with Other Cisco IOS Software Features

You can use CET and IPSec together; the two encryption technologies can coexist in your network. Each router may support concurrent encryption links using either IPSec or Cisco Encryption Technology. A single interface can even support the use of IPSec or CET for protecting different data flows.

Supported Hardware, Switching Paths, and Encapsulation

IPSec has certain restrictions for hardware, switching paths, and encapsulation methods as follows.

Supported Hardware

IPSec is not supported on VIP2 interfaces (VIP2-40 or above) or the Encryption Service Adapter (ESA) card. There is currently no hardware accelerator for IPSec.

Supported Switching Paths

IPSec works with both process switching and fast switching. IPSec does not work with optimum or flow switching.

Supported Encapsulation

IPSec works with the following serial encapsulations: High-Level Data-Links Control (HDLC), Point-to-Point Protocol (PPP), and Frame Relay.

IPSec also works with the GRE and IPinIP Layer 3, L2F, and L2TP tunneling protocols; however, multipoint tunnels are not supported. Other Layer 3 tunneling protocols (DLSw, SRB, etc.) are currently not supported for use with IPSec.

Since the IPSec Working Group has not yet addressed the issue of group key distribution, IPSec currently cannot be used to protect group traffic (such as broadcast or multicast traffic).

Restrictions

At this time, IPSec can be applied to unicast IP datagrams only. Because the IPSec Working Group has not yet addressed the issue of group key distribution, IPSec does not currently work with multicasts or broadcast IP datagrams.

If you use network address translation (NAT), you should configure static NAT translations so that IPSec will work properly. In general, NAT translation should occur before the router performs IPSec encapsulation; in other words, IPSec should be working with global addresses.

Overview of How IPSec Works

In simple terms, IPSec provides secure *tunnels* between two peers, such as two routers. You define which packets are considered sensitive and should be sent through these secure tunnels, and you define the parameters that should be used to protect these sensitive packets by specifying characteristics of these tunnels. Then, when the IPSec peer sees such a sensitive packet, it sets up the appropriate secure tunnel and sends the packet through the tunnel to the remote peer.

NOTE	The use of the term *tunnel* in this chapter does not refer to using IPSec in tunnel mode.

More accurately, these *tunnels* are sets of security associations that are established between two IPSec peers. The security associations define which protocols and algorithms should be applied to sensitive packets and also specify the keying material to be used by the two peers. Security associations are unidirectional and are established per security protocol (AH or ESP).

With IPSec, you define what traffic should be protected between two IPSec peers by configuring access lists and applying these access lists to interfaces by way of crypto map sets. Therefore, traffic may be selected based on source and destination address, and optionally Layer 4 protocol, and port. (Similar to CET, the access lists used for IPSec are used only to determine which traffic should be protected by IPSec, not which traffic should be blocked or permitted through the interface. Separate access lists define blocking and permitting at the interface.

A crypto map set can contain multiple entries, each with a different access list. The crypto map entries are searched in order—the router attempts to match the packet to the access list specified in that entry.

When a packet matches a **permit** entry in a particular access list, and the corresponding crypto map entry is tagged as **cisco**, then CET is triggered, and connections are established if necessary. If the crypto map entry is tagged as **ipsec-isakmp**, IPSec is triggered. If no security association exists that IPSec can use to protect this traffic to the peer, IPSec uses IKE to negotiate with the remote peer to set up the necessary IPSec security associations on behalf of the data flow. The negotiation uses information specified in the crypto map entry as well as the data flow information from the specific access list entry. (The behavior is different for dynamic crypto map entries. Refer to the section "Creating Dynamic Crypto Maps.")

If the crypto map entry is tagged as **ipsec-manual**, IPSec is triggered. If no security association exists that IPSec can use to protect this traffic to the peer, the traffic is dropped. In this case, the security associations are installed via the configuration, without the intervention of IKE. If the security associations did not exist, IPSec did not have all of the necessary pieces configured.

Once established, the set of security associations (outbound, to the peer) is then applied to the triggering packet as well as to subsequent applicable packets as those packets exit the router. *Applicable packets* are packets that match the same access list criteria that the original packet matched. For example, all applicable packets could be encrypted before being forwarded to the remote peer. The corresponding inbound security associations are used when processing the incoming traffic from that peer.

If IKE is used to establish the security associations, the security associations will have lifetimes so that they will periodically expire and require renegotiation. (This provides an additional level of security.)

Multiple IPSec tunnels can exist between two peers to secure different data streams, with each tunnel using a separate set of security associations. For example, some data streams might be authenticated only, whereas other data streams must both be encrypted and authenticated.

Access lists associated with IPSec crypto map entries also represent which traffic the router requires to be protected by IPSec. Inbound traffic is processed against the crypto map entries—if an unprotected packet matches a **permit** entry in a particular access list associated with an IPSec crypto map entry, that packet is dropped because it was not sent as an IPSec-protected packet.

Crypto map entries also include transform sets. A transform set is an acceptable combination of security protocols, algorithms and other settings to apply to IPSec protected traffic. During the IPSec security association negotiation, the peers agree to use a particular transform set when protecting a particular data flow.

Nesting of IPSec Traffic to Multiple Peers

You can nest IPSec traffic to a series of IPSec peers. For example, in order for traffic to traverse multiple firewalls (and these firewalls have a policy of not letting through traffic that they themselves have not authenticated), the router needs to establish IPSec tunnels with each firewall in turn. The nearest firewall becomes the outermost IPSec peer.

In the example shown in Figure 28-1, Router A encapsulates the traffic destined for Router C in IPSec (Router C is the IPSec peer). However, before Router A can send this traffic, it must first re-encapsulate this traffic in IPSec in order to send it to Router B (Router B is the outermost IPSec peer).

Figure 28-1 *Nesting Example of IPSec Peers*

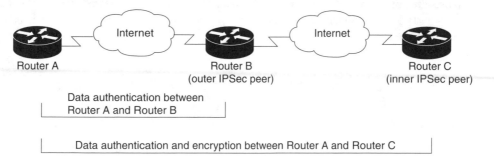

It is possible for the traffic between the outer peers to have one kind of protection (such as data authentication) and for traffic between the inner peers to have different protection (such as both data authentication and encryption).

Prerequisites

You need to configure IKE as described in Chapter 32, "Configuring Internet Key Exchange Security Protocol."

Even if you decide to not use IKE, you still need to disable it as described in Chapter 32, "Configuring Internet Key Exchange Security Protocol."

IPSec Configuration Task List

After you have completed IKE configuration, configure IPSec. To configure IPSec, complete the tasks in the following sections at each participating IPSec peer.

● Ensuring That Access Lists Are Compatible with IPSec

● Setting Global Lifetimes for IPSec Security Associations

● Creating Crypto Access Lists

● Defining Transform Sets

● Creating Crypto Map Entries

● Applying Crypto Map Sets to Interfaces

● Monitoring and Maintaining IPSec

For IPSec configuration examples, refer to the "IPSec Configuration Example" section at the end of this chapter.

Ensuring That Access Lists Are Compatible with IPSec

IKE uses UDP port 500. The IPSec ESP and AH protocols use protocol numbers 50 and 51. Ensure that your access lists are configured so that protocols 50 and 51 and UDP port 500 traffic are not blocked at interfaces used by IPSec. In some cases you might need to add a statement to your access lists to explicitly permit this traffic.

Setting Global Lifetimes for IPSec Security Associations

You can change the global lifetime values that are used when negotiating new IPSec security associations. (These global lifetime values can be overridden for a particular crypto map entry).

These lifetimes only apply to security associations established via IKE. Manually established security associations do not expire.

There are two lifetimes: a timed lifetime and a traffic-volume lifetime. A security association expires after the first of these lifetimes is reached. The default lifetimes are 3600 seconds (1 hour) and 4,608,000 kilobytes (10 megabytes per second for 1 hour).

If you change a global lifetime, the new lifetime value will not be applied to currently existing security associations, but will be used in the negotiation of subsequently established security associations. If you wish to use the new values immediately, you can clear all or part of the security association database. Refer to the **clear crypto sa** command for more details.

IPSec security associations use one or more shared secret keys. These keys and their security associations time out together.

To change a global lifetime for IPSec security associations, use one or more of the following commands in global configuration mode:

Command	Purpose
crypto ipsec security-association lifetime seconds *seconds*	Changes the global timed lifetime for IPSec SAs. This command causes the security association to time out after the specified number of seconds have passed.
crypto ipsec security-association lifetime kilobytes *kilobytes*	Changes the global traffic-volume lifetime for IPSec SAs. This command causes the security association to time out after the specified amount of traffic (in kilobytes) have passed through the IPSec tunnel using the security association.
clear crypto sa or **clear crypto sa peer** {*ip-address* | *peer-name*} or **clear crypto sa map** *map-name* or **clear crypto sa entry** *destination-address protocol spi*	(Optional) Clears existing security associations. This causes any existing security associations to expire immediately; future security associations will use the new lifetimes. Otherwise, any existing security associations will expire according to the previously configured lifetimes. **Note** Using the **clear crypto sa** command without parameters will clear out the full SA database, which will clear out active security sessions. You may also specify the **peer**, **map**, or **entry** keywords to clear out only a subset of the SA database. For more information, see the **clear crypto sa** command.

How These Lifetimes Work

Assuming that the particular crypto map entry does not have lifetime values configured, when the router requests new security associations it will specify its global lifetime values in the request to the peer; it will use this value as the lifetime of the new security associations. When the router receives a negotiation request from the peer, it will use the smaller of either the lifetime value proposed by the peer or the locally configured lifetime value as the lifetime of the new security associations.

The security association (and corresponding keys) expires according to whichever comes sooner: the number of seconds has passed (specified by the **seconds** keyword) or the amount of traffic in kilobytes is passed (specified by the **kilobytes** keyword). Security associations that are established manually (via a crypto map entry marked as **ipsec-manual**) have an infinite lifetime.

A new security association is negotiated *before* the lifetime threshold of the existing security association is reached, to ensure that a new security association is ready for use when the old one expires. The new security association is negotiated either 30 seconds before the **seconds** lifetime expires or when the volume of traffic through the tunnel reaches 256 kilobytes less than the **kilobytes** lifetime (whichever comes first).

If no traffic has passed through the tunnel during the entire life of the security association, a new security association is not negotiated when the lifetime expires. Instead, a new security association is negotiated only when IPSec sees another packet that should be protected.

Creating Crypto Access Lists

Crypto access lists are used to define which IP traffic will be protected by crypto and which traffic will not be protected by crypto. (These access lists are *not* the same as regular access lists, which determine what traffic to forward or block at an interface.) For example, access lists can be created to protect all IP traffic between Subnet A and Subnet Y or Telnet traffic between Host A and Host B.

The access lists themselves are not specific to IPSec—they are no different from what is used for CET. It is the crypto map entry referencing the specific access list that defines whether IPSec or CET processing is applied to the traffic matching a **permit** in the access list.

Crypto access lists associated with IPSec crypto map entries have four primary functions:

- Select outbound traffic to be protected by IPSec (permit = protect).

- Indicate the data flow to be protected by the new security associations (specified by a single **permit** entry) when initiating negotiations for IPSec security associations.

- Process inbound traffic in order to filter out and discard traffic that should have been protected by IPSec.

- Determine whether to accept requests for IPSec security associations on behalf of the requested data flows when processing IKE negotiation from the IPSec peer. (Negotiation is only done for **ipsec-isakmp** crypto map entries.) In order to be accepted, if the peer initiates the IPSec negotiation, it must specify a data flow that is permitted by a crypto access list associated with an **ipsec-isakmp** crypto map entry.

If you want certain traffic to receive one combination of IPSec protection (for example, authentication only) and other traffic to receive a different combination of IPSec protection (for example, both authentication and encryption), you need to create two different crypto access lists to define the two different types of traffic. These different access lists are then used in different crypto map entries which specify different IPSec policies.

Later, you will associate the crypto access lists to particular interfaces when you configure and apply crypto map sets to the interfaces (following instructions in the sections "Creating Crypto Map Entries" and "Applying Crypto Map Sets to Interfaces").

To create crypto access lists, use the following command in global configuration mode:

Command	Purpose
access-list *access-list-number* {**deny** | **permit**} *protocol source source-wildcard destination destination-wildcard* [**precedence** *precedence*] [**tos** *tos*] [**log**] or **ip access-list extended** *name* Follow with **permit** and **deny** statements as appropriate.	Specifies conditions to determine which IP packets will be protected.[1] (Enable or disable crypto for traffic that matches these conditions.) Cisco recommends that you configure mirror image crypto access lists for use by IPSec and that you avoid using the **any** keyword, as described in the sections "Defining Mirror Image Crypto Access Lists at each IPSec Peer" and "Using the any Keyword in Crypto Access Lists." Also see the "Crypto Access List Tips" section.

1. You specify conditions using an IP access list designated by either a number or a name. The **access-list** command designates a numbered extended access list; the **ip access-list extended** command designates a named access list.

Crypto Access List Tips

Using the **permit** keyword causes all IP traffic that matches the specified conditions to be protected by crypto through the policy described by the corresponding crypto map entry. Using the **deny** keyword prevents traffic from being protected by crypto in the context of that particular crypto map entry. (In other words, it does not allow the policy as specified in this crypto map entry to be applied to this traffic.) If this traffic is denied in all the crypto map entries for that interface, then the traffic is not protected by crypto (either CET or IPSec).

The crypto access list you define will be applied to an interface after you define the corresponding crypto map entry and apply the crypto map set to the interface. Different access lists must be used in different entries of the same crypto map set. (These two tasks are described in following sections.) However, both inbound and outbound traffic will be evaluated against the same outbound IPSec access list. Therefore, the access list's criteria is applied in the forward direction to traffic exiting your router and the reverse direction to traffic entering your router. In Figure 28-2, IPSec protection is applied to traffic between Host 10.0.0.1 and Host 20.0.0.2 as the data exits Router A's S0 interface enroute to Host 20.0.0.2. For traffic from Host 10.0.0.1 to Host 20.0.0.2, the access list entry on Router A is evaluated as follows:

```
source = host 10.0.0.1
dest = host 20.0.0.2
```

For traffic from Host 20.0.0.2 to Host 10.0.0.1, that same access list entry on Router A is evaluated as follows:

```
source = host 20.0.0.2
dest = host 10.0.0.1
```

Figure 28-2 *How Crypto Access Lists Are Applied for Processing IPSec*

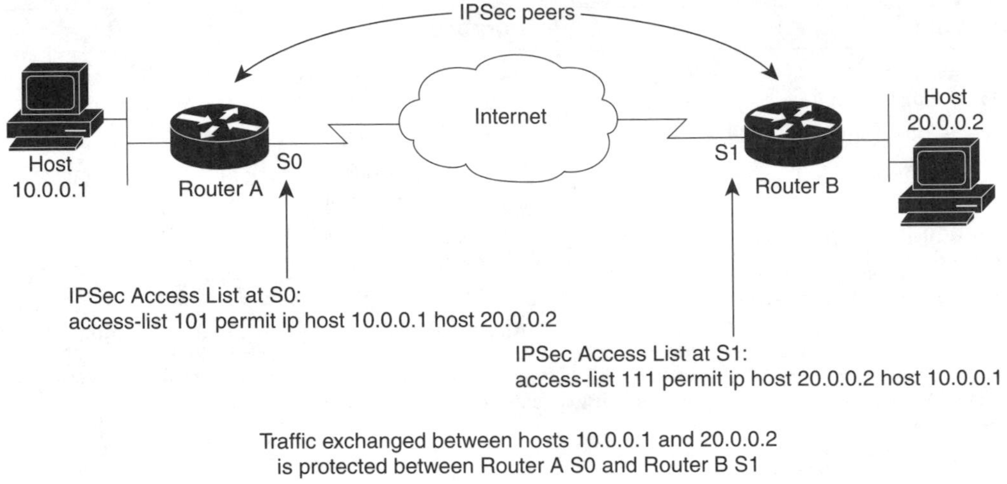

If you configure multiple statements for a given crypto access that which is used for IPSec, in general the first **permit** statement that is matched will be the statement used to determine the scope of the IPSec security association. That is, the IPSec security association will be set up to protect traffic that meets the criteria of the matched statement only. Later, if traffic matches a different **permit** statement of the crypto access list, a new, separate IPSec security association will be negotiated to protect traffic matching the newly matched access list statement.

NOTE   Access lists for crypto map entries tagged as **ipsec-manual** are restricted to a single **permit** entry, and subsequent entries are ignored. In other words, the security associations established by that particular crypto map entry are only for a single data flow. To be able to support multiple manually established security associations for different kinds of traffic, define multiple crypto access lists, and then apply each one to a separate **ipsec-manual** crypto map entry. Each access list should include one **permit** statement defining what traffic to protect.

Any unprotected inbound traffic that matches a **permit** entry in the crypto access list for a crypto map entry flagged as IPSec will be dropped, since this traffic was expected to be protected by IPSec.

NOTE	If you view your router's access lists by using a command such as **show ip access-lists**, *all* extended IP access lists will be shown in the command output. This includes extended IP access lists that are used for traffic filtering purposes as well as those that are used for crypto. The **show** command output does not differentiate between the different uses of the extended access lists.

See Chapter 29, "IPSec Network Security Commands," for complete details about the extended IP access list commands used to create IPSec access lists.

Defining Mirror Image Crypto Access Lists at each IPSec Peer

Cisco recommends that for every crypto access list specified for a static crypto map entry that you define at the local peer, you define a mirror image crypto access list at the remote peer. This ensures that traffic that has IPSec protection applied locally can be processed correctly at the remote peer. (The crypto map entries themselves must also support common transforms and must refer to the other system as a peer.)

Figure 28-3 shows some sample scenarios when you have mirror image access lists and when you do not have mirror image access lists.

Figure 28-3   *Mirror Image Versus Non-Mirror Image Crypto Access Lists (for IPSec)*

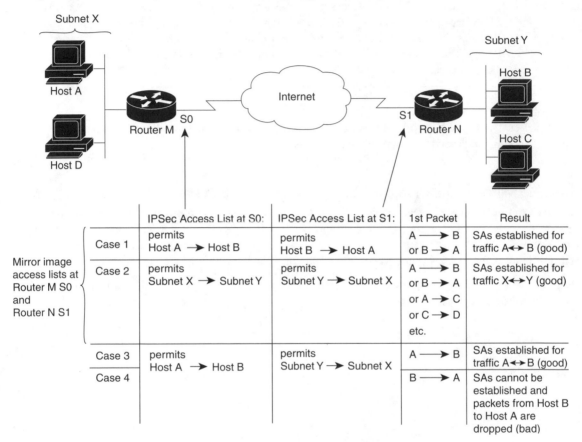

As Figure 28-3 indicates, IPSec SAs can be established as expected whenever the two peers' crypto access lists are mirror images of each other. However, an IPSec SA can be established only some of the time when the access lists are not mirror images of each other. This can happen in the case where an entry in one peer's access list is a subset of an entry in the other peer's access list, such as shown in Cases 3 and 4 of Figure 28-3. IPSec SA establishment is critical to IPSec—without SAs, IPSec does not work, causing any packets matching the crypto access list criteria to be silently dropped instead of being forwarded with IPSec security.

In Figure 28-3, an SA cannot be established in Case 4. This is because SAs are always requested according to the crypto access lists at the initiating packet's end. In Case 4, Router B requests that all traffic between Subnet X and Subnet Y be protected, but this is a superset of the specific flows permitted by the crypto access list at Router A so the request is therefore not permitted. Case 3 works because Router A's request is a subset of the specific flows permitted by the crypto access list at Router B.

Because of the complexities introduced when crypto access lists are not configured as mirror images at peer IPSec devices, Cisco strongly encourages you to use mirror image crypto access lists.

Using the **any** Keyword in Crypto Access Lists

When you create crypto access lists, using the **any** keyword could cause problems. Cisco discourages the use of the **any** keyword to specify source or destination addresses.

The **any** keyword in a **permit** statement is discouraged when you have multicast traffic flowing through the IPSec interface; the **any** keyword can cause multicast traffic to fail. (This is true for both CET and IPSEC.)

The **permit any any** statement is strongly discouraged, as this will cause all outbound traffic to be protected (and all protected traffic sent to the peer specified in the corresponding crypto map entry) and will require protection for all inbound traffic. Then, all inbound packets that lack IPSec protection will be silently dropped, including packets for routing protocols, NTP, echo, echo response, etc. The difference here between CET and IPSec is that CET would attempt to decrypt and then forward the (now garbage) data, while IPSec would simply drop any packets that did not have IPSec protection.

You need to be sure you define which packets to protect. If you *must* use the **any** keyword in a **permit** statement, you must preface that statement with a series of **deny** statements to filter out any traffic (that would otherwise fall within that **permit** statement) that you do not want to be protected.

Defining Transform Sets

A transform set represents a certain combination of security protocols and algorithms. During the IPSec security association negotiation, the peers agree to use a particular transform set for protecting a particular data flow.

You can specify multiple transform sets, and then specify one or more of these transform sets in a crypto map entry. The transform set defined in the crypto map entry will be used in the IPSec security association negotiation to protect the data flows specified by that crypto map entry's access list.

During IPSec security association negotiations with IKE, the peers search for a transform set that is the same at both peers. When such a transform set is found, it is selected and applied to the protected traffic as part of both peers' IPSec security associations.

With manually established security associations, there is no negotiation with the peer, so both sides must specify the same transform set.

If you change a transform set definition, the change is only applied to crypto map entries that reference the transform set. The change is not applied to existing security associations, but is used in subsequent negotiations to establish new security associations. If you want the new settings to take effect sooner, you can clear all or part of the security association database by using the **clear crypto sa** command.

To define a transform set, use the following commands starting in global configuration mode:

Step	Command	Purpose
1	**crypto ipsec transform-set** *transform-set-name transform1* [*transform2* [*transform3*]]	Defines a transform set. There are complex rules defining which entries you can use for the transform arguments. These rules are explained in the command description for the **crypto ipsec transform-set** command, and Table 28-1 provides a list of allowed transform combinations. This command puts you into the crypto transform configuration mode.
2	**initialization-vector size [4 | 8]**	(Optional) If you specified the esp-rfc1829 transform in the transform set, you can change the initialization vector size to be used with the esp-rfc1829 transform.
3	**mode [tunnel | transport]**	(Optional) Changes the mode associated with the transform set. The mode setting is only applicable to traffic whose source and destination addresses are the IPSec peer addresses; it is ignored for all other traffic. (All other traffic is in tunnel mode only.)
4	**exit**	Exit the crypto transform configuration mode.
5	**clear crypto sa** or **clear crypto sa peer** {*ip-address* | *peer-name*} or **clear crypto sa map** *map-name* or **clear crypto sa entry** *destination-address protocol spi*	This step clears existing IPSec security associations so that any changes to a transform set will take effect on subsequently established security associations. (Manually established SAs are re-established immediately.) **Note** Using the **clear crypto sa** command without parameters will clear out the full SA database, which will clear out active security sessions. You may also specify the **peer**, **map**, or **entry** keywords to clear out only a subset of the SA database. For more information, see the **clear crypto sa** command.

Table 28-1 shows allowed transform combinations.

Table 28-1   *Allowed Transform Combinations*

AH Transform *pick up to one*		ESP Encryption Transform *pick up to one*		ESP Authentication Transform *Pick up to one, only if you also selected the esp-des transform (not esp-rfc1829)*	
Transform	**Description**	**Transform**	**Description**	**Transform**	**Description**
ah-md5- hmac	AH with the MD5 (HMAC variant) authentication algorithm	**esp-des**	ESP with the 56-bit DES encryption algorithm	**esp-md5- hmac**	ESP with the MD5 (HMAC variant) authentication algorithm
ah-sha- hmac	AH with the SHA (HMAC variant) authentication algorithm	**esp- rfc1829**	older version of the ESP protocol (per RFC 1829); does not allow an accompanying ESP authentication transform	**esp-sha- hmac**	ESP with the SHA (HMAC variant) authentication algorithm
ah-rfc1828	older version of the AH protocol (per RFC 1828)				

Creating Crypto Map Entries

To create crypto map entries, follow the guidelines and tasks described in these sections:

● About Crypto Maps

● Load Sharing

● How Many Crypto Maps Should You Create?

● Creating Crypto Map Entries for Establishing Manual Security Associations

● Creating Crypto Map Entries that Use IKE to Establish Security Associations

● Creating Dynamic Crypto Maps

About Crypto Maps

Crypto maps, used with CET, are now expanded to also specify IPSec policy.

Crypto map entries created for IPSec pull together the various parts used to set up IPSec security associations, including the following:

- Which traffic should be protected by IPSec (per a crypto access list)

- The granularity of the flow to be protected by a set of security associations

- Where IPSec-protected traffic should be sent (who the remote IPSec peer is)

- The local address to be used for the IPSec traffic (See the "Applying Crypto Map Sets to Interfaces" section for more details.)

- What IPSec security should be applied to this traffic (selecting from a list of one or more transform sets)

- Whether security associations are manually established or are established via IKE

- Other parameters that might be necessary to define an IPSec security association

Crypto map entries with the same crypto map name (but different map sequence numbers) are grouped into a crypto map set. Later, you will apply these crypto map sets to interfaces; then, all IP traffic passing through the interface is evaluated against the applied crypto map set. If a crypto map entry sees outbound IP traffic that should be protected and the crypto map specifies the use of IKE, a security association is negotiated with the remote peer according to the parameters included in the crypto map entry; otherwise, if the crypto map entry specifies the use of manual security associations, a security association should have already been established via configuration. (If a dynamic crypto map entry sees outbound traffic that should be protected and no security association exists, the packet is dropped.)

The policy described in the crypto map entries is used during the negotiation of security associations. If the local router initiates the negotiation, it will use the policy specified in the static crypto map entries to create the offer to be sent to the specified IPSec peer. If the IPSec peer initiates the negotiation, the local router will check the policy from the static crypto map entries, as well as any referenced dynamic crypto map entries to decide whether to accept or reject the peer's request (offer).

For IPSec to succeed between two IPSec peers, both peers' crypto map entries must contain compatible configuration statements.

When two peers try to establish a security association, they must each have at least one crypto map entry that is compatible with one of the other peer's crypto map entries. For two crypto map entries to be compatible, they must at least meet the following criteria:

- The crypto map entries must contain compatible crypto access lists (for example, mirror image access lists). In the case where the responding peer is using dynamic crypto maps, the entries in the local crypto access list must be permitted by the peer's crypto access list.

- The crypto map entries must each identify the other peer (unless the responding peer is using dynamic crypto maps).

- The crypto map entries must have at least one transform set in common.

Load Sharing

You can define multiple remote peers by using crypto maps to allow for load sharing. If one peer fails, there will still be a protected path. The peer that packets are actually sent to is determined by the last peer that the router heard from (received either traffic or a negotiation request from) for a given data flow. If the attempt fails with the first peer, IKE tries the next peer on the crypto map list.

If you are not sure how to configure each crypto map parameter to guarantee compatibility with other peers, you might consider configuring dynamic crypto maps, as described in the section "Creating Dynamic Crypto Maps." Dynamic crypto maps are useful when the establishment of the IPSec tunnels is initiated by the remote peer (such as in the case of an IPSec router fronting a server). They are not useful if the establishment of the IPSec tunnels is locally initiated, because the dynamic crypto maps are policy templates, not complete statements of policy. (Although the access lists in any referenced dynamic crypto map entry are used for crypto packet filtering.)

How Many Crypto Maps Should You Create?

You can apply only one crypto map set to a single interface. The crypto map set can include a combination of CET, IPSec/IKE, and IPSec/manual entries. Multiple interfaces can share the same crypto map set if you want to apply the same policy to multiple interfaces.

If you create more than one crypto map entry for a given interface, use the *seq-num* of each map entry to rank the map entries: The lower the *seq-num*, the higher the priority. At the interface that has the crypto map set, traffic is evaluated against higher priority map entries first.

You must create multiple crypto map entries for a given interface if any of the following conditions exist:

- If different data flows are to be handled by separate IPSec peers.

- If you want to apply different IPSec security to different types of traffic (to the same or separate IPSec peers); for example, if you want traffic between one set of subnets to be authenticated and traffic between another set of subnets to be both authenticated and encrypted. In this case the different types of traffic should have been defined in two separate access lists, and you must create a separate crypto map entry for each crypto access list.

- If you are not using IKE to establish a particular set of security associations and want to specify multiple access list entries, you must create separate access lists (one per **permit** entry) and specify a separate crypto map entry for each access list.

Creating Crypto Map Entries for Establishing Manual Security Associations

The use of manual security associations is a result of a prior arrangement between the users of the local router and the IPSec peer. The two parties may wish to begin with manual security associations, and then move to using security associations established via IKE, or the remote party's system may not support IKE. If IKE is not used for establishing the security associations, there is no negotiation of security associations, so the configuration information in both systems must be the same in order for traffic to be processed successfully by IPSec.

The local router can simultaneously support manual and IKE-established security associations, even within a single crypto map set. There is very little reason to disable IKE on the local router (unless the router only supports manual security associations, which is unlikely).

To create crypto map entries to establish manual SAs (that is, when IKE is not used to establish the SAs), use the following commands starting in global configuration mode:

Step	Command	Purpose
1	**crypto map** *map-name seq-num* **ipsec-manual**	Specifies the crypto map entry to create (or modify).
		This command puts you into the crypto map configuration mode.
2	**match address** *access-list-id*	Names an IPSec access list. This access list determines which traffic should be protected by IPSec and which traffic should not be protected by IPSec security in the context of this crypto map entry. (The access list can specify only one **permit** entry when IKE is not used.)
3	**set peer** {*hostname* | *ip-address*}	Specifies the remote IPSec peer. This is the peer to which IPSec protected traffic should be forwarded.
		(Only one peer can be specified when IKE is not used.)
4	**set transform-set** *transform-set-name*	Specifies which transform set should be used.
		This must be the same transform set that is specified in the remote peer's corresponding crypto map entry.
		(Only one transform set can be specified when IKE is not used.)
5	**set session-key inbound ah** *spi hex-key-data* and **set session-key outbound ah** *spi hex-key-data*	If the specified transform set includes the AH protocol, sets the AH Security Parameter Indexes (SPIs) and keys to apply to inbound and outbound protected traffic.
		(This manually specifies the AH security association to be used with protected traffic.)

Step	Command	Purpose
6	**set session-key inbound esp** *spi* **cipher** *hex-key-data* [**authenticator** *hex-key-data*] and **set session-key outbound esp** *spi* **cipher** *hex-key-data* [**authenticator** *hex-key-data*]	If the specified transform set includes the ESP protocol, sets the ESP SPIs and keys to apply to inbound and outbound protected traffic. If the transform set includes an ESP cipher algorithm, specify the cipher keys. If the transform set includes an ESP authenticator algorithm, specify the authenticator keys. (This manually specifies the ESP security association to be used with protected traffic.)
7	**exit**	Exits crypto-map configuration mode and return to global configuration mode.

Repeat these steps to create additional crypto map entries as required.

Creating Crypto Map Entries that Use IKE to Establish Security Associations

When IKE is used to establish security associations, the IPSec peers can negotiate the settings they will use for the new security associations. This means that you can specify lists (such as lists of acceptable transforms) within the crypto map entry.

To create crypto map entries that will use IKE to establish the security associations, use the following commands starting in global configuration mode:

Step	Command	Purpose
1	**crypto map** *map-name seq-num* **ipsec-isakmp**	Names the crypto map entry to create (or modify). This command puts you into the crypto map configuration mode.
2	**match address** *access-list-id*	Names an extended access list. This access list determines which traffic should be protected by IPSec and which traffic should not be protected by IPSec security in the context of this crypto map entry.
3	**set peer** {*hostname* | *ip-address*}	Specifies a remote IPSec peer. This is the peer to which IPSec protected traffic can be forwarded. Repeat for multiple remote peers.
4	**set transform-set** *transform-set-name1* [*transform-set-name2...transform-set-name6*]	Specifies which transform sets are allowed for this crypto map entry. List multiple transform sets in order of priority (highest priority first).

Step	Command	Purpose
5	**set security-association lifetime seconds** *seconds* and/or **set security-association lifetime kilobytes** *kilobytes*	(Optional) If you want the security associations for this crypto map entry to be negotiated using different IPSec security association lifetimes than the global lifetimes, specify a security association lifetime for the crypto map entry.
6	**set security-association level per-host**	(Optional) Specifies that separate security associations should be established for each source/destination host pair. Without this command, a single IPSec tunnel could carry traffic for multiple source hosts and multiple destination hosts. With this command, when the router requests new security associations it will establish one set for traffic between Host A and Host B and a separate set for traffic between Host A and Host C. Use this command with care, as multiple streams between given subnets can rapidly consume resources.
7	**set pfs [group1	group2]**	(Optional) Specifies that IPSec should ask for perfect forward secrecy when requesting new security associations for this crypto map entry or should demand PFS in requests received from the IPSec peer.
8	**exit**	Exits crypto-map configuration mode and return to global configuration mode.

Repeat these steps to create additional crypto map entries as required.

Creating Dynamic Crypto Maps

Dynamic crypto maps (this requires IKE) can ease IPSec configuration and are recommended for use with networks where the peers are not always predetermined. An example of this is mobile users, who obtain dynamically assigned IP addresses. First, the mobile clients need to authenticate themselves to the local router's IKE by something other than an IP address, such as a fully qualified domain name. Once authenticated, the security association request can be processed against a dynamic crypto map which is set up to accept requests (matching the specified local policy) from previously unknown peers.

To configure dynamic crypto maps, follow these instructions:

● Understanding Dynamic Crypto Maps

● Creating a Dynamic Crypto Map Set

● Adding the Dynamic Crypto Map Set into a Regular (Static) Crypto Map Set

Understanding Dynamic Crypto Maps

Dynamic crypto maps are only available for use by IKE.

A dynamic crypto map entry is essentially a crypto map entry without all the parameters configured. It acts as a policy template where the missing parameters are later dynamically configured (as the result of an IPSec negotiation) to match a remote peer's requirements. This allows remote peers to exchange IPSec traffic with the router even if the router does not have a crypto map entry specifically configured to meet all of the remote peer's requirements.

Dynamic crypto maps are not used by the router to initiate new IPSec security associations with remote peers. Dynamic crypto maps are used when a remote peer tries to initiate an IPSec security association with the router. Dynamic crypto maps are also used in evaluating traffic.

A dynamic crypto map set is included by reference as part of a crypto map set. Any crypto map entries that reference dynamic crypto map sets should be the lowest-priority crypto map entries in the crypto map set (that is, have the highest sequence numbers) so that the other crypto map entries are evaluated first; that way, the dynamic crypto map set is examined only when the other (static) map entries are not successfully matched.

If the router accepts the peer's request, at the point that it installs the new IPSec security associations it also installs a temporary crypto map entry. This entry is filled in with the results of the negotiation. At this point, the router performs normal processing using this temporary crypto map entry as a normal entry, even requesting new security associations if the current ones are expiring (based upon the policy specified in the temporary crypto map entry). When the flow expires (that is, all of the corresponding security associations expire), the temporary crypto map entry is then removed.

For both static and dynamic crypto maps, if unprotected inbound traffic matches a **permit** statement in an access list, and the corresponding crypto map entry is tagged as IPSec. Then the traffic is dropped because it is not IPSec protected. (This is because the security policy as specified by the crypto map entry states that this traffic must be IPSec protected.)

For static crypto map entries, if outbound traffic matches a **permit** statement in an access list and the corresponding SA is not yet established, the router initiates new SAs with the remote peer. In the case of dynamic crypto map entries, if no SA existed, the traffic would simply be dropped (because dynamic crypto maps are not used for initiating new SAs).

NOTE	Be careful when using the **any** keyword in **permit** entries in dynamic crypto maps. If it is possible for the traffic covered by such a **permit** entry to include multicast or broadcast traffic, the access list should include **deny** entries for the appropriate address range. Access lists should also include **deny** entries for network and subnet broadcast traffic, and for any other traffic that should not be IPSec protected.

Creating a Dynamic Crypto Map Set

Dynamic crypto map entries, like regular static crypto map entries, are grouped into sets. A set is a group of dynamic crypto map entries all with the same *dynamic-map-name* but each with a different *dynamic-seq-num*.

To create a dynamic crypto map entry, use the following commands, starting in global configuration mode:

Step	Command	Purpose
1	**crypto dynamic-map** *dynamic-map-name dynamic-seq-num*	Creates a dynamic crypto map entry.
2	**set transform-set** *transform-set-name1* [*transform-set-name2...transform-set-name6*]	Specifies which transform sets are allowed for the crypto map entry. List multiple transform sets in order of priority (highest priority first).
		This is the only configuration statement required in dynamic crypto map entries.
3	**match address** *access-list-id*	(Optional) Names an extended access list. This access list determines which traffic should be protected by IPSec and which traffic should not be protected by IPSec.
		If this is configured, the data flow identity proposed by the IPSec peer must fall within a **permit** statement for this crypto access list.
		If this is not configured, the router will accept any data flow identity proposed by the IPSec peer. However, if this is configured but the specified access list does not exist or is empty, the router drops all packets. This is similar to static crypto maps because they also require that an access list be specified.
		Care must be taken if the **any** keyword is used in the access list, since the access list is used for packet filtering as well as for negotiation.

Step	Command	Purpose
4	**set peer** {*hostname* | *ip-address*}	(Optional) Specifies a remote IPSec peer. Repeat for multiple remote peers.
		This is rarely configured in dynamic crypto map entries. Dynamic crypto map entries are often used for unknown remote peers.
5	**set security-association lifetime seconds** *seconds* and/or **set security-association lifetime kilobytes** *kilobytes*	(Optional) If you want the security associations for this crypto map to be negotiated using shorter IPSec security association lifetimes than the globally specified lifetimes, specifies a key lifetime for the crypto map entry.
6	**set pfs** [group1 | group2]	(Optional) Specifies that IPSec should ask for perfect forward secrecy when requesting new security associations for this crypto map entry or should demand perfect forward secrecy in requests received from the IPSec peer.
7	**exit**	Exits crypto map configuration mode and returns to global configuration mode.

Dynamic crypto map entries specify crypto access lists that limit traffic for which IPSec security associations can be established. A dynamic crypto map entry that does not specify an access list will be ignored during traffic filtering. A dynamic crypto map entry with an empty access list causes traffic to be dropped. If there is only one dynamic crypto map entry in the crypto map set, it must specify acceptable transform sets.

Adding the Dynamic Crypto Map Set into a Regular (Static) Crypto Map Set

You can add one or more dynamic crypto map sets into a crypto map set via crypto map entries that reference the dynamic crypto map sets. You should set the crypto map entries referencing dynamic maps to be the lowest priority entries in a crypto map set (that is, have the highest sequence numbers).

To add a dynamic crypto map set into a crypto map set, use the following command in global configuration mode:

Command	Purpose
crypto map *map-name seq-num* **ipsec-isakmp dynamic** *dynamic-map-name*	Adds a dynamic crypto map set to a static crypto map set.

Applying Crypto Map Sets to Interfaces

You need to apply a crypto map set to each interface through which IPSec or CET traffic will flow. Applying the crypto map set to an interface instructs the router to evaluate all the interface's traffic against the crypto map set and to use the specified policy during connection or security association negotiation on behalf of traffic to be protected by crypto (either CET or IPSec).

To apply a crypto map set to an interface, use the following command in interface configuration mode:

Command	Purpose
crypto map *map-name*	Applies a crypto map set to an interface.

For redundancy, you could apply the same crypto map set to more than one interface. The default behavior is as follows:

● Each interface will have its own piece of the security association database.

● The IP address of the local interface will be used as the local address for IPSec traffic originating from or destined to that interface.

If you apply the same crypto map set to multiple interfaces for redundancy purposes, you need to specify an identifying interface. This has the following effects:

● The per-interface portion of the IPSec security association database will be established one time and shared for traffic through all the interfaces that share the same crypto map.

● The IP address of the identifying interface will be used as the local address for IPSec traffic originating from or destined to those interfaces sharing the same crypto map set.

One suggestion is to use a loopback interface as the identifying interface.

To specify redundant interfaces and name an identifying interface, use the following command in global configuration mode:

Command	Purpose
crypto map *map-name* **local-address** *interface-id*	Permits redundant interfaces to share the same crypto map, using the same local identity.

Monitoring and Maintaining IPSec

Certain configuration changes only take effect when negotiating subsequent security associations. If you want the new settings to take effect immediately, you must clear the existing security associations so that they will be re-established with the changed configuration. For manually established security associations, you must clear and reinitialize the security associations, or the changes will never take effect. If the router is actively processing IPSec traffic, it is desirable to clear only the portion of the security association database that would be affected by the configuration changes (that is, clear only the security associations established by a given crypto map set). Clearing the full security association database should be reserved for large-scale changes or when the router is processing very little other IPSec traffic.

To clear (and reinitialize) IPSec security associations, use one of the following commands in global configuration mode:

Command	Purpose
clear crypto sa	Clears IPSec security associations.
or	**Note** Using the **clear crypto sa** command without
clear crypto sa peer {*ip-address*	*peer-name*}	parameters will clear out the full SA database, which will clear out active security sessions. You may also
or	specify the **peer**, **map**, or **entry** keywords to clear
clear crypto sa map *map-name*	out only a subset of the SA database. For more information, see the **clear crypto sa** command.
or	
clear crypto sa entry *destination-address protocol spi*	

To view information about your IPSec configuration, use one or more of the following commands in EXEC mode:

Command	Purpose
show crypto ipsec transform-set	Views your transform set configuration.
show crypto map [**interface** *interface*	**tag** *map-name*]	Views your crypto map configuration.
show crypto ipsec sa [**map** *map-name*	**address**	**identity**] [**detail**]	Views information about IPSec security associations.
show crypto dynamic-map [**tag** *map-name*]	Views information about dynamic crypto maps.
show crypto ipsec security-association lifetime	Views global security association lifetime values.

IPSec Configuration Example

The following is an example of a minimal IPSec configuration where the security associations will be established via IKE. For more information about IKE, see Chapter 32, "Configuring Internet Key Exchange Security Protocol."

An IPSec access list defines which traffic to protect:

```
access-list 101 permit ip 10.0.0.0 0.0.0.255 10.2.2.0 0.0.0.255
```

A transform set defines how the traffic will be protected:

```
crypto ipsec transform-set myset esp-des esp-sha
```

A crypto map joins together the IPSec access list and transform set and specifies where the protected traffic is sent (the remote IPSec peer):

```
crypto map toRemoteSite 10 ipsec-isakmp
 match address 101
 set transform-set myset
 set peer 10.2.2.5
```

The crypto map is applied to an interface:

```
interface Serial0
 ip address 10.0.0.2
 crypto map toRemoteSite
```

NOTE   In this example, IKE must be enabled.

## CHAPTER 29

IPSec Network Security Commands

This chapter describes IPSec network security commands. IPSec provides security for transmission of sensitive information over unprotected networks such as the Internet. IPSec services are similar to those provided by Cisco Encryption Technology (CET), a proprietary security solution introduced in Cisco IOS Software Release 11.2. However, IPSec provides a more robust security solution and is standards based. IPSec also provides data authentication and anti-replay services in addition to data confidentiality services, whereas CET provides only data confidentiality services.

You can search online at www.cisco.com to find complete descriptions of other commands used when configuring IPSec.

For configuration information, refer to Chapter 28, "Configuring IPSec Network Security."

clear crypto sa

To delete IPSec security associations, use the **clear crypto sa** global configuration command.

> **clear crypto sa**
> **clear crypto sa peer** {*ip-address* | *peer-name*}
> **clear crypto sa map** *map-name*
> **clear crypto sa entry** *destination-address protocol spi*
> **clear crypto sa counters**

Syntax	Description
ip-address	Specifies a remote peer's IP address.
peer-name	Specifies a remote peer's name as the fully qualified domain name, for example *remotepeer.domain.com*.
map-name	Specifies the name of a crypto map set.
destination-address	Specifies the IP address of your peer or the remote peer.
protocol	Specifies either the Encapsulation Security Protocol (ESP) or Authentication Header (AH) protocol.
spi	Specifies an SPI (found by displaying the security association database).

Default

If the **peer**, **map**, **entry**, or **counters** keywords are not used, all IPSec security associations are deleted.

Command Mode

Global configuration

Usage Guidelines

This command first appeared in Cisco IOS Release 11.3 T.

This command clears (deletes) IPSec security associations.

If the security associations were established via IKE, they are deleted, and future IPSec traffic requires new security associations to be negotiated. (When IKE is used, the IPSec security associations are established only when needed.)

If the security associations are manually established, the security associations are deleted and reinstalled. (When IKE is not used, the IPSec security associations are created as soon as the configuration is completed.)

If the **peer**, **map**, **entry**, or **counters** keywords are not used, all IPSec security associations are deleted.

The **peer** keyword deletes any IPSec security associations for the specified peer.

The **map** keyword deletes any IPSec security associations for the named crypto map set.

The **entry** keyword deletes the IPSec security association with the specified address, protocol, and SPI.

If any of the above commands cause a particular security association to be deleted, all the "sibling" security associations—those that were established during the same IKE negotiation—are deleted as well.

The **counters** keyword clears the traffic counters maintained for each security association; it does not clear the security associations themselves.

If you make configuration changes that affect security associations, these changes will not apply to existing security associations but to negotiations for subsequent security associations. You can use the **clear crypto sa** command to restart all security associations so that they will use the most current configuration settings. In the case of manually established security associations, if you make changes that affect security associations, you must use the **clear crypto sa** command before the changes take effect.

If the router is processing active IPSec traffic, it is suggested that you only clear the portion of the security association database that is affected by the changes, to avoid causing active IPSec traffic to temporarily fail.

Note that this command only clears IPSec security associations; to clear IKE state, use the **clear crypto isakmp** command.

Examples

The following example clears (and reinitializes, if appropriate) all IPSec security associations at the router:

```
clear crypto sa
```

The following example clears (and reinitializes, if appropriate) the inbound and outbound IPSec security associations established, along with the security association established for address 10.0.0.1 using the AH protocol with the SPI of 256:

```
clear crypto sa entry 10.0.0.1 AH 256
```

Related Commands

You can search online at www.cisco.com to find documentation of related commands.

clear crypto isakmp

crypto dynamic-map

To create a dynamic crypto map entry and enter the crypto map configuration command mode, use the **crypto dynamic-map** global configuration command. Use the **no** form of this command to delete a dynamic crypto map set or entry.

> **crypto dynamic-map** *dynamic-map-name dynamic-seq-num*
> **no crypto dynamic-map** *dynamic-map-name* [*dynamic-seq-num*]

Syntax	Description
dynamic-map-name	Specifies the name of the dynamic crypto map set.
dynamic-seq-num	Specifies the number of the dynamic crypto map entry.

Default

No dynamic crypto maps exist.

Command Mode

Global configuration. Using this command puts you into crypto map configuration mode.

Part
IV

Command Reference

Usage Guidelines

This command first appeared in Cisco IOS Release 11.3 T.

Use dynamic crypto maps to create policy templates that can be used when processing negotiation requests for new security associations from a remote IPSec peer, even if you do not know all the crypto map parameters required to communicate with the remote peer (such as the peer's IP address). For example, if you do not know about all the IPSec remote peers in your network, a dynamic crypto map allows you to accept requests for new security associations from previously unknown peers. (However, these requests are not processed until the IKE authentication has been completed successfully.)

When a router receives a negotiation request via IKE from another IPSec peer, the request is examined to determine whether it matches a crypto map entry. If the negotiation does not match any explicit crypto map entry, it is rejected unless the crypto map set includes a reference to a dynamic crypto map.

The dynamic crypto map is a policy template; it accepts wildcard parameters for any parameters not explicitly stated in the dynamic crypto map entry. This allows you to set up IPSec security associations with a previously unknown IPSec peer. (The peer still must specify matching values for the nonwildcard IPSec security association negotiation parameters.)

If the router accepts the peer's request, at the point that it installs the new IPSec security associations, it also installs a temporary crypto map entry. This entry is filled in with the results of the negotiation. At this point, the router performs normal processing, using this temporary crypto map entry as a normal entry, even requesting new security associations if the current ones are expiring (based on the policy specified in the temporary crypto map entry). When the flow expires (that is, all the corresponding security associations expire), the temporary crypto map entry is removed.

Dynamic crypto map sets are not used for initiating IPSec security associations. However, they are used for determining whether or not traffic should be protected.

The only configuration required in a dynamic crypto map is the **set transform-set** command. All other configuration is optional.

Dynamic crypto map entries, like regular static crypto map entries, are grouped into sets. After you define a dynamic crypto map set (which commonly contains only one map entry) using this command, you include the dynamic crypto map set in an entry of the parent crypto map set by using the **crypto map (global configuration)** command. The parent crypto map set is then applied to an interface.

You should make crypto map entries referencing dynamic maps the lowest-priority map entries, so that negotiations for security associations will try to match the static crypto map entries first. Only after the negotiation request does not match any of the static map entries do you want it to be evaluated against the dynamic map.

To make a dynamic crypto map the lowest-priority map entry, give the map entry referencing the dynamic crypto map the highest *seq-num* of all the map entries in a crypto map set.

For both static and dynamic crypto maps, if unprotected inbound traffic matches a **permit** statement in an access list, and the corresponding crypto map entry is tagged as IPSec, then the traffic is dropped because it is not IPSec protected. (This is because the security policy as specified by the crypto map entry states that this traffic must be IPSec protected.)

For static crypto map entries, if outbound traffic matches a **permit** statement in an access list and the corresponding security association (SA) is not yet established, the router will initiate new SAs with the remote peer. In the case of dynamic crypto map entries, if no SA existed, the traffic would simply be dropped (since dynamic crypto maps are not used for initiating new SAs).

NOTE   Use care when using the **any** keyword in **permit** entries in dynamic crypto maps. If it is possible for the traffic covered by such a **permit** entry to include multicast or broadcast traffic, the access list should include **deny** entries for the appropriate address range. Access lists should also include **deny** entries for network and subnet broadcast traffic and for any other traffic that should not be IPSec protected.

Example

The following example configures an IPSec crypto map set:

```
crypto map mymap 10 ipsec-isakmp
 match address 101
 set transform-set my_t_set1
 set peer 10.0.0.1
 set peer 10.0.0.2
crypto map mymap 20 ipsec-isakmp
 match address 102
 set transform-set my_t_set1 my_t_set2
 set peer 10.0.0.3
crypto map mymap 30 ipsec-isakmp dynamic mydynamicmap
!
crypto dynamic-map mydynamicmap 10
 match address 103
 set transform-set my_t_set1 my_t_set2 my_t_set3
```

Crypto map entry *mymap 30* references the dynamic crypto map set *mydynamicmap*, which can be used to process inbound security association negotiation requests that do not match the *mymap 10* and *mymap 20*. In this case, if the peer specifies a transform set that matches one of the transform sets specified in *mydynamicmap*, for a flow permitted by the access list 103, IPSec accepts the request and sets up security associations with the remote peer without previously knowing about the remote peer. If accepted, the resulting security associations (and temporary crypto map entry) are established according to the settings specified by the remote peer.

The access list associated with *mydynamicmap 10* is also used as a filter. Inbound packets that match a **permit** statement in this list are dropped for not being IPSec protected. (The same is true for access lists associated with static crypto maps entries.) Outbound packets that match a **permit** statement without an existing corresponding IPSec SA are also dropped.

Part
IV

Command Reference

Related Commands

You can search online at www.cisco.com to find documentation of related commands.

crypto map (global configuration)
crypto map (interface configuration)
crypto map local-address
match address
set peer
set pfs
set security-association lifetime
set transform-set
show crypto dynamic-map
show crypto map

crypto ipsec security-association lifetime

To change global lifetime values used when negotiating IPSec security associations, use the **crypto ipsec security-association lifetime** global configuration command. To reset a lifetime to the default value, use the **no** form of the command.

> **crypto ipsec security-association lifetime** {**seconds** *seconds* | **kilobytes** *kilobytes*}
> **no crypto ipsec security-association lifetime** {**seconds** | **kilobytes**}

Syntax	Description
seconds *seconds*	Specifies the number of seconds a security association will live before expiring. The default is 3600 seconds (1 hour).
kilobytes *kilobytes*	Specifies the volume of traffic (in kilobytes) that can pass between IPSec peers using a given security association before that security association expires. The default is 4,608,000 kilobytes.

Default

3600 seconds (1 hour) and 4,608,000 kilobytes (10 megabytes per second for 1 hour)

Command Mode

Global configuration

Usage Guidelines

This command first appeared in Cisco IOS Release 11.3 T.

IPSec security associations use shared secret keys. These keys and their security associations time out together.

Assuming that the particular crypto map entry does not have lifetime values configured when the router requests new security associations during security association negotiation, it will specify its global lifetime value in the request to the peer; it will use this value as the lifetime of the new security associations. When the router receives a negotiation request from the peer, it will use the smaller of the lifetime values proposed by the peer or the locally configured lifetime value as the lifetime of the new security associations.

There are two lifetimes: a *timed lifetime* and a *traffic-volume lifetime*. The security association expires after the first of these lifetimes is reached.

If you change a global lifetime, the change is only applied when the crypto map entry does not have a lifetime value specified. The change will not be applied to existing security associations, but will be used in subsequent negotiations to establish new security associations. If you want the new settings to take effect sooner, you can clear all or part of the security association database by using the **clear crypto sa** command. Refer to the **clear crypto sa** command for more detail.

To change the global timed lifetime, use the **crypto ipsec security-association lifetime seconds** form of the command. The timed lifetime causes the security association to time out after the specified number of seconds have passed.

To change the global traffic-volume lifetime, use the **crypto ipsec security-association lifetime kilobytes** form of the command. The traffic-volume lifetime causes the security association to time out after the specified amount of traffic (in kilobytes) has been protected by the security associations' key.

Shorter lifetimes can make it harder to mount a successful key recovery attack because the attacker has less data encrypted under the same key to work with. However, shorter lifetimes require more CPU processing time for establishing new security associations.

The lifetime values are ignored for manually established security associations (security associations installed using an **ipsec-manual** crypto map entry).

How These Lifetimes Work

The security association (and corresponding keys) expires according to which event occurs sooner: either after the number of seconds has passed (specified by the **seconds** keyword) or after the amount of traffic in kilobytes has passed (specified by the **kilobytes** keyword).

A new SA is negotiated *before* the lifetime threshold of the existing security association is reached to ensure that a new security association is ready for use when the old one expires. The new security association is negotiated either 30 seconds before the **seconds** lifetime expires or when the volume of traffic through the tunnel reaches 256 kilobytes less than the **kilobytes** lifetime (whichever occurs first).

If no traffic has passed through the tunnel during the entire life of the security association, a new security association is not negotiated when the lifetime expires. Instead, a new security association will be negotiated only when IPSec sees another packet that should be protected.

Example

This example shortens both lifetimes, because the administrator feels there is a higher risk that the keys could be compromised. The timed lifetime is shortened to 2700 seconds (45 minutes), and the traffic-volume lifetime is shortened to 2,304,000 kilobytes (10 megabytes per second for 1/2 hour).

```
crypto ipsec security-association lifetime seconds 2700
crypto ipsec security-association lifetime kilobytes 2304000
```

Related Commands

You can search online at www.cisco.com to find documentation of related commands.

set security-association lifetime
show crypto ipsec security-association lifetime

crypto ipsec transform-set

To define a transform set—an acceptable combination of security protocols and algorithms— use the **crypto ipsec transform-set** global configuration command. To delete a transform set, use the **no** form of the command.

> **crypto ipsec transform-set** *transform-set-name transform1*
> [*transform2* [*transform3*]]
> **no crypto ipsec transform-set** *transform-set-name*

Syntax

Syntax	Description
transform-set-name	Specifies the name of the transform set to create (or modify).
transform1 *transform2* *transform3*	Specifies up to three transforms. These transforms define the IPSec security protocol(s) and algorithm(s). Accepted transform values are described in the "Usage Guidelines" section.

Default

None

Command Mode

Global configuration. This command invokes the crypto transform configuration mode.

Usage Guidelines

This command first appeared in Cisco IOS Release 11.3 T.

A transform set is an acceptable combination of security protocols, algorithms and other settings to apply to IPSec protected traffic. During the IPSec security association negotiation, the peers agree to use a particular transform set when protecting a particular data flow.

You can configure multiple transform sets and then specify one or more of these transform sets in a crypto map entry. The transform set defined in the crypto map entry is used in the IPSec security association negotiation to protect the data flows specified by that crypto map entry's access list. During the negotiation, the peers search for a transform set that is the same at both peers. When such a transform set is found, it is selected and will be applied to the protected traffic as part of both peer's IPSec security associations.

When IKE is not used to establish security associations, a single transform set must be used. The transform set is not negotiated.

Before a transform set can be included in a crypto map entry, it must be defined using this command.

A transform set specifies one or two IPSec security protocols (either ESP or AH or both) and specifies which algorithms to use with the selected security protocol. The ESP and AH IPSec security protocols are described in the section "IPSec Protocols: Encapsulation Security Protocol and Authentication Header."

To define a transform set, you specify one to three transforms—each transform represents an IPSec security protocol (ESP or AH) plus the algorithm you want to use. When the particular transform set is used during negotiations for IPSec security associations, the entire transform set (the combination of protocols, algorithms, and other settings) must match a transform set at the remote peer.

In a transform set you could specify the AH protocol, ESP, or both. If you specify an ESP in a transform set, you can specify just an ESP encryption transform or both an ESP encryption transform and an ESP authentication transform.

Acceptable combinations of transforms are shown in Table 29-1.

.

Table 29-1   *Selecting Transforms for a Transform Set: Allowed Transform Combinations*

AH Transform *Pick up to one*		**ESP Encryption Transform** *Pick up to one*		**ESP Authentication Transform** *Pick up to one, only if you also selected the esp-des transform (not esp-rfc1829)*	
Transform	**Description**	**Transform**	**Description**	**Transform**	**Description**
ah-md5-hmac	AH with the MD5 (HMAC variant) authentication algorithm	**esp-des**	ESP with the 56-bit DES encryption algorithm	**esp-md5-hmac**	ESP with the MD5 (HMAC variant) authentication algorithm
ah-sha-hmac	AH with the SHA (HMAC variant) authentication algorithm	**esp-rfc1829**	Older version of the ESP protocol (per RFC 1829); does not allow an accompanying ESP authentication transform	**esp-sha-hmac**	ESP with the SHA (HMAC variant) authentication algorithm
ah-rfc1828	Older version of the AH protocol (per RFC 1828)				

The following are examples of acceptable transform combinations:

● **ah-md5-hmac**

● **esp-des**

● **esp-des** and **esp-md5-hmac**

● **ah-sha-hmac** and **esp-des** and **esp-sha-hmac**

● **ah-rfc1828** and **esp-rfc1829**

The parser prevents you from entering invalid combinations; for example, when you specify an AH transform, the parser will not allow you to specify another AH transform for the current transform set.

IPSec Protocols: Encapsulation Security Protocol and Authentication Header

Both the ESP and AH protocols implement security services for IPSec.

ESP provides packet encryption and optional data authentication and anti-replay services. The older IPSec version of ESP, per RFC 1829, provides only encryption services.

AH provides data authentication and anti-replay services. The older IPSec version of AH, per RFC 1828, provides only data authentication services.

ESP encapsulates the protected data—either a full IP datagram (or only the payload)—with an ESP header and an ESP trailer. AH is embedded in the protected data; it inserts an AH header immediately after the outer IP header and before the inner IP datagram or payload. Traffic that originates and terminates at the IPSec peers can be sent in either tunnel or transport mode; all other traffic is sent in tunnel mode. Tunnel mode encapsulates and protects a full IP datagram, while transport mode encapsulates/protects the payload of an IP datagram. For more information about modes, see the **mode** command description.

Selecting Appropriate Transforms

If the router will be establishing IPSec secure tunnels with a device that supports only the older IPSec transforms (ah-rfc1828 and esp-rfc1829), then you must specify these older transforms. Because RFC 1829 ESP does not provide authentication, you should probably always include the ah-rfc1828 transform in a transform set that has esp-rfc1829. For interoperability with a peer that supports only the older IPSec transforms, recommended transform combinations are as follows:

● **ah-rfc1828**

● **ah-rfc1828** and **esp-rfc1829**

If the peer supports the newer IPSec transforms, your choices are more complex. The following tips may help you select transforms that are appropriate for your situation:

● If you want to provide data confidentiality, include an ESP encryption transform.

● If you want to ensure data authentication for the outer IP header as well as the data, include an AH transform. (Some consider the benefits of outer IP header data integrity to be debatable.)

● If you use an ESP encryption transform, also consider including an ESP authentication transform or an AH transform to provide authentication services for the transform set.

● If you want data authentication (either using ESP or AH) you can choose from the MD5 or SHA (HMAC keyed hash variants) authentication algorithms. The SHA algorithm is generally considered stronger than MD5, but is slower.

● Note that some transforms might not be supported by the IPSec peer.

Suggested transform combinations:

● **esp-des** and **esp-sha-hmac**

● **ah-sha-hmac** and **esp-des** and **esp-sha-hmac**

The Crypto Transform Configuration Mode

After you issue the **crypto ipsec transform-set** command, you are put into the crypto transform configuration mode. While in this mode, you can change the initialization vector length for the esp-rfc1829 transform, or you can change the mode to tunnel or transport. (These are optional changes.) After you have made either of these changes, type **exit** to return to global configuration mode. For more information about these optional changes, see the **initialization-vector size** and **mode** command descriptions.)

Changing Existing Transforms

If one or more transforms are specified in the **crypto ipsec transform-set** command for an existing transform set, the specified transforms will replace the existing transforms for that transform set.

If you change a transform set definition, the change is only applied to crypto map entries that reference the transform set. The change will not be applied to existing security associations, but will be used in subsequent negotiations to establish new security associations. If you want the new settings to take effect sooner, you can clear all or part of the security association database by using the **clear crypto sa** command.

Example

This example defines two transform sets. The first transform set is used with an IPSec peer that supports the newer ESP and AH protocols. The second transform set is used with an IPSec peer that only supports the older transforms.

```
crypto ipsec transform-set newer esp-des esp-sha-hmac
crypto ipsec transform-set older ah-rfc-1828 esp-rfc1829
```

Related Commands

You can search online at www.cisco.com to find documentation of related commands.

initialization-vector size
mode
set transform-set
show crypto ipsec transform-set

crypto map (global configuration)

To create or modify a crypto map entry and enter the crypto map configuration mode, use the **crypto map** global configuration command. Use the **no** form of this command to delete a crypto map entry or set.

> **crypto map** *map-name seq-num* [**cisco**]
> **crypto map** *map-name seq-num* **ipsec-manual**
> **crypto map** *map-name seq-num* **ipsec-isakmp** [**dynamic** *dynamic-map-name*]
> **no crypto map** *map-name* [*seq-num*]

NOTE   Issue the **crypto map** *map-name seq-num* command without a keyword to modify an existing crypto map entry. However, if the *seq-num* specified does not already exist, you will create a CET crypto map, which is the default.

Syntax

Syntax	Description
cisco	(Default value) Indicates that CET will be used instead of IPSec for protecting the traffic specified by this newly specified crypto map entry. If you use this keyword, none of the IPSec-specific crypto map configuration commands will be available. Instead, the CET-specific commands will be available.
map-name	The name you assign to the crypto map set.
seq-num	The number you assign to the crypto map entry. See additional explanation for using this argument in the "Usage Guidelines" section.
ipsec-manual	Indicates that IKE will not be used to establish the IPSec security associations for protecting the traffic specified by this crypto map entry.
ipsec-isakmp	Indicates that IKE will be used to establish the IPSec security associations for protecting the traffic specified by this crypto map entry.
dynamic	(Optional) Specifies that this crypto map entry is to reference a pre-existing dynamic crypto map. Dynamic crypto maps are policy templates used in processing negotiation requests from a peer IPSec device. If you use this keyword, none of the crypto map configuration commands will be available.
dynamic-map-name	(Optional) Specifies the name of the dynamic crypto map set that should be used as the policy template.

Default

No crypto maps exist.

Part
IV

Command Reference

Command Mode

Global configuration. Using this command puts you into crypto map configuration mode, unless you use the **dynamic** keyword.

Usage Guidelines

This command first appeared in Cisco IOS Release 11.2. The **cisco**, **ipsec-manual**, **ipsec-isakmp**, and **dynamic** keywords were added in Cisco IOS Release 11.3 T. The *dynamic-map-name* argument was also added in Cisco IOS Release 11.3 T.

This command is also documented in Chapter 27, "Cisco Encryption Technology Commands," where it has slightly different functionality.

Use this command to create a new crypto map entry or to modify an existing crypto map entry.

After a crypto map entry has been created, you cannot change the parameters specified at the global configuration level, because these parameters determine which of the configuration commands are valid at the crypto map level. For example, once a map entry has been created as **ipsec-isakmp**, you cannot change it to **ipsec-manual** or **cisco**; you must delete and re-enter the map entry.

After you define crypto map entries, you can assign the crypto map set to interfaces using the **crypto map (interface configuration)** command.

What Crypto Maps Are For

Crypto maps provide two functions: filtering/classifying traffic to be protected and defining the policy to be applied to that traffic. The first use affects the flow of traffic on an interface; the second affects the negotiation performed (via IKE) on behalf of that traffic.

IPSec crypto maps link together definitions of the following:

- What traffic should be protected

- Which IPSec peer(s) the protected traffic can be forwarded to—these are the peers with which a security association can be established

- Which transform sets are acceptable for use with the protected traffic

- How keys and security associations should be used/managed (or what the keys are, if IKE is not used)

Multiple Crypto Maps Entries with the Same *map-name* Form a Crypto Map Set

A crypto map set is a collection of crypto map entries, each with a different *seq-num* but the same *map-name*. Therefore, for a given interface, you could have certain traffic forwarded to one IPSec peer with specified security applied to that traffic and other traffic forwarded to the same or a different IPSec peer with different IPSec security applied. To accomplish this you would create two crypto maps, each with the same *map-name*, but each with a different *seq-num*. A crypto map set can include a combination of CET and IPSec crypto map entries.

The *seq-num* Argument

The number you assign to the *seq-num* argument should not be arbitrary. This number is used to rank multiple crypto map entries within a crypto map set. Within a crypto map set, a crypto map entry with a lower *seq-num* is evaluated before a map entry with a higher *seq-num*; that is, the map entry with the lower number has a higher priority.

For example, imagine that there is a crypto map set that contains three crypto map entries: *mymap 10*, *mymap 20*, and *mymap 30*. The crypto map set named mymap is applied to interface Serial 0. When traffic passes through the Serial 0 interface, the traffic is evaluated first for *mymap 10*. If the traffic matches a **permit** entry in the extended access list in *mymap 10*, the traffic will be processed according to the information defined in *mymap 10* (including establishing IPSec security associations or CET connections when necessary). If the traffic does not match the *mymap 10* access list, the traffic will be evaluated for *mymap 20* and then *mymap 30*, until the traffic matches a **permit** entry in a map entry. (If the traffic does not match a **permit** entry in any crypto map entry, it will be forwarded without any IPSec [or CET] security.)

Dynamic Crypto Maps

Refer to the "Usage Guidelines" section of the **crypto dynamic-map** command for a discussion on dynamic crypto maps.

You should make crypto map entries that reference dynamic map sets the lowest-priority map entries so that inbound security association negotiations requests will try to match the static maps first. Only after the request does not match any of the static maps do you want it to be evaluated against the dynamic map set.

To make a crypto map entry referencing a dynamic crypto map set the lowest-priority map entry, give the map entry the highest *seq-num* of all the map entries in a crypto map set.

Create dynamic crypto map entries using the **crypto dynamic-map** command. After you create a dynamic crypto map set, add the dynamic crypto map set to a static crypto map set with the **crypto map (global configuration)** command using the **dynamic** keyword.

Examples

The following example shows the minimum required crypto map configuration when IKE will be used to establish the security associations:

```
crypto map mymap 10 ipsec-isakmp
 match address 101
 set transform-set my_t_set1
 set peer 10.0.0.1
```

The following example shows the minimum required crypto map configuration when the security associations are manually established:

```
crypto transform-set someset ah-md5-hmac esp-des
crypto map mymap 10 ipsec-manual
 match address 102
 set transform-set someset
 set peer 10.0.0.5
 set session-key inbound ah 256 9876543210987654987654321098765
 set session-key outbound ah 256 fedcbafedcbafedcfedcbafedcbafedc
 set session-key inbound esp 256 cipher 0123456789012345
 set session-key outbound esp 256 cipher abcdefabcdefabcd
```

The following example configures an IPSec crypto map set that includes a reference to a dynamic crypto map set.

```
crypto map mymap 10 ipsec-isakmp
 match address 101
 set transform-set my_t_set1
 set peer 10.0.0.1
 set peer 10.0.0.2
crypto map mymap 20 ipsec-isakmp
 match address 102
 set transform-set my_t_set1 my_t_set2
 set peer 10.0.0.3
crypto map mymap 30 ipsec-isakmp dynamic mydynamicmap
!
crypto dynamic-map mydynamicmap 10
 match address 103
 set transform-set my_t_set1 my_t_set2 my_t_set3
```

Crypto map *mymap 10* allows security associations to be established between the router and either (or both) of two remote IPSec peers for traffic matching access list 101. Crypto map *mymap 20* allows either of two transform sets to be negotiated with the remote peer for traffic matching access list 102.

Crypto map entry *mymap 30* references the dynamic crypto map set *mydynamicmap*, which can be used to process inbound security association negotiation requests that do not match the *mymap 10* or *mymap 20* entries. In this case, if the peer specifies a transform set that matches one of the transform sets specified in *mydynamicmap*, for a flow permitted by the access list 103, IPSec will accept the request and set up security associations with the remote peer without previously knowing about the remote peer. If accepted, the resulting security associations (and temporary crypto map entry) are established according to the settings specified by the remote peer.

The access list associated with *mydynamicmap 10* is also used as a filter. Inbound packets that match a **permit** statement in this list are dropped for not being IPSec protected. (The same is true for access lists associated with static crypto maps entries.) Outbound packets that match a **permit** statement without an existing corresponding IPSec SA are also dropped.

Related Commands

You can search online at www.cisco.com to find documentation of related commands.

crypto dynamic-map
crypto map (interface configuration)
crypto map local-address
match address
set peer
set pfs
set security-association level per-host
set security-association lifetime
set session-key
set transform-set
show crypto map

crypto map (interface configuration)

To apply a previously defined crypto map set to an interface, use the **crypto map** interface configuration command. Use the **no** form of the command to remove the crypto map set from the interface.

> **crypto map** *map-name*
> **no crypto map** [*map-name*]

Syntax   Description

map-name	The name that identifies the crypto map set. This is the name assigned when the crypto map was created.
	When the **no** form of the command is used, this argument is optional. Any value supplied for the argument is ignored.

Default

No crypto maps are assigned to interfaces.

Command Mode

Interface configuration

Part
IV

Command Reference

Usage Guidelines

This command first appeared in Cisco IOS Release 11.2.

This command is also documented in Chapter 27, "Cisco Encryption Technology Commands."

Use this command to assign a crypto map set to an interface. You must assign a crypto map set to an interface before that interface can provide IPSec or CET services. Only one crypto map set can be assigned to an interface. If multiple crypto map entries have the same *map-name* but a different *seq-num*, they are considered to be part of the same set and will all be applied to the interface. The crypto map entry with the lowest *seq-num* is considered the highest priority and will be evaluated first. A single crypto map set can contain a combination of **cisco**, **ipsec-isakmp**, and **ipsec-manual** crypto map entries.

Example

The following example assigns crypto map set *mymap* to the S0 interface. When traffic passes through S0, the traffic will be evaluated against all the crypto map entries in the *mymap* set. When outbound traffic matches an access list in one of the *mymap* crypto map entries, a security association (if IPsec) or CET connection (if CET) will be established per that crypto map entry's configuration (if no security association or connection already exists).

```
interface S0
 crypto map mymap
```

Related Commands

You can search online at www.cisco.com to find documentation of related commands.

crypto map (global configuration)
crypto map local-address
show crypto map

crypto map local-address

To specify and name an identifying interface to be used by the crypto map for IPSec traffic, use the **crypto map local-address** global configuration command. Use the **no** form of the command to remove this command from the configuration.

> **crypto map** *map-name* **local-address** *interface-id*
> **no crypto map** *map-name* **local-address**

Syntax	Description
map-name	The name that identifies the crypto map set. This is the name assigned when the crypto map was created.
interface-id	Specifies the identifying interface that should be used by the router to identify itself to remote peers.
	If IKE is enabled and you are using a certification authority (CA) to obtain certificates, this should be the interface with the address specified in the CA certificates.

Default

None.

Command Mode

Global configuration

Usage Guidelines

This command first appeared in Cisco IOS Release 11.3 T.

If you apply the same crypto map to two interfaces and do not use this command, two separate security associations (with different local IP addresses) could be established to the same peer for similar traffic. If you are using the second interface as redundant to the first interface, it could be preferable to have a single security association (with a single local IP address) created for traffic sharing the two interfaces. Having a single security association decreases overhead and makes administration simpler.

This command allows a peer to establish a single security association (and use a single local IP address) that is shared by the two redundant interfaces.

If applying the same crypto map set to more than one interface, the default behavior is as follows:

● Each interface will have its own security association database.

● The IP address of the local interface will be used as the local address for IPSec traffic originating from/destined to that interface.

However, if you use a local address for that crypto map set, it has multiple effects:

● Only one IPSec security association database will be established and shared for traffic through both interfaces.

● The IP address of the specified interface will be used as the local address for IPSec (and IKE) traffic originating from or destined to that interface.

One suggestion is to use a loopback interface as the referenced local address interface, because the loopback interface never goes down.

Example

The following example assigns crypto map set *mymap* to the S0 interface and to the S1 interface. When traffic passes through either S0 or S1, the traffic will be evaluated against the all the crypto maps in the *mymap* set. When traffic through either interface matches an access list in one of the *mymap* crypto maps, a security association will be established. This same security association will then apply to both S0 and S1 traffic that matches the originally matched IPSec access list. The local address that IPSec will use on both interfaces will be the IP address of interface loopback0:

```
interface S0
 crypto map mymap

interface S1
 crypto map mymap

crypto map mymap local-address loopback0
```

Related Commands

You can search online at www.cisco.com to find documentation of related commands.

crypto map (interface configuration)

initialization-vector size

To change the length of the initialization vector for the esp-rfc1829 transform, use the **initialization-vector size** crypto transform configuration command. To reset the initialization vector length to the default value, use the **no** form of the command.

> **initialization-vector size [4 | 8]**
> **no initialization-vector size**

Syntax   Description

4 | 8   (Optional) Specifies the length of the initialization vector: either 4 bytes or 8 bytes. If neither **4** nor **8** is specified, the default length of 8 is assigned.

Default

8 bytes

Command Mode

Crypto transform configuration

Usage Guidelines

This command first appeared in Cisco IOS Release 11.3 T.

Use this command to change the initialization vector (IV) length for the **esp-rfc1829** transform.

During negotiation, the IV length must match the IV length in the remote peer's transform set. Otherwise, the transform sets will not be considered a match.

After you define a transform set, you are put into the crypto transform configuration mode. While in this mode, you can change the **esp-rfc1829** initialization vector length to either 4 bytes or 8 bytes. This change only applies to the transform set just defined. (This command is only available when the transform set includes the **esp-rfc1829** transform.)

If you do not change the IV length when you first define the transform set, but later decide you want to change the IV length for the transform set, you must re-enter the transform set (specifying the transform name without the transform list), and then change the IV length.

If you use this command to change the IV length, the change will only affect the negotiation of subsequent IPSec security associations via crypto map entries that specify this transform set. If you want to use the new settings sooner, you can clear all or part of the security association database. Refer to the **clear crypto sa** command for more details.

Example

This example defines a transform set and changes the IV length to 4 bytes:

```
MyPeerRouter(config)# crypto ipsec transform-set older ah-rfc-1828 esp-rfc1829
MyPeerRouter(cfg-crypto-trans)# initialization-vector size 4
MyPeerRouter(cfg-crypto-trans)# exit
MyPeerRouter(config)#
```

Related Commands

You can search online at www.cisco.com to find documentation of related commands.

crypto ipsec transform-set
mode

match address

To specify an extended access list for a crypto map entry, use the **match address** crypto map configuration command. Use the **no** form of this command to remove the extended access list from a crypto map entry.

> **match address** [*access-list-id* | *name*]
> **no match address** [*access-list-id* | *name*]

Syntax   Description

access-list-id   (Optional) Identifies the extended access list by its name or number. This value should match the *access-list-number* or *name* argument of the extended access list being matched.

name   (Optional) Identifies the named encryption access list. This name should match the *name* argument of the named encryption access list being matched.

Default

No access lists are matched to the crypto map entry.

Command Mode

Crypto map configuration

Usage Guidelines

This command first appeared in Cisco IOS Release 11.2.

This command is also documented in Chapter 27, "Cisco Encryption Technology Commands."

This command is required for all static crypto map entries. If you are defining a dynamic crypto map entry (with the **crypto dynamic-map** command), this command is not required but is strongly recommended.

Use this command to assign an extended access list to a crypto map entry. You also need to define this access list using the **access-list** or **ip access-list extended** commands.

The extended access list specified with this command will be used by IPSec (or CET, depending on the setting of the crypto map entry) to determine which traffic should be protected by crypto and which traffic does not need crypto protection. (Traffic that is permitted by the access list will be protected. Traffic that is denied by the access list will not be protected in the context of the corresponding crypto map entry.)

Note that the crypto access list is *not* used to determine whether to permit or deny traffic through the interface. An access list applied directly to the interface makes that determination.

The crypto access list specified by this command is used when evaluating both inbound and outbound traffic. Outbound traffic is evaluated against the crypto access lists specified by the interface's crypto map entries to determine if it should be protected by crypto and, if so, (if traffic matches a **permit** entry) which crypto policy applies. (If necessary, in the case of static IPSec crypto maps, new security associations are established using the data flow identity as specified in the **permit** entry; in the case of CET, new connections are established; in the case of dynamic crypto map entries, if no SA exists, the packet is dropped.) After passing the regular access lists at the interface, inbound traffic is evaluated against the crypto access lists specified by the entries of the interface's crypto map set to determine whether it should be protected by crypto and, if so, which crypto policy applies. (In the case of IPSec, unprotected traffic is discarded because it should have been protected by IPSec; in the case of CET, the traffic is decrypted even though it was never encrypted.)

In the case of IPSec, the access list is also used to identify the flow for which the IPSec security associations are established. In the outbound case, the **permit** entry is used as the data flow identity (in general), while in the inbound case the data flow identity specified by the peer must be permitted by the crypto access list.

Example

The following example shows the minimum required crypto map configuration when IKE will be used to establish the security associations. (This example is for a static crypto map.)

```
crypto map mymap 10 ipsec-isakmp
 match address 101
 set transform-set my_t_set1
 set peer 10.0.0.1
```

Related Commands

You can search online at www.cisco.com to find documentation of related commands.

crypto dynamic-map
crypto map (global configuration)
crypto map (interface configuration)
crypto map local-address
set peer
set pfs
set security-association level per-host
set security-association lifetime
set session-key
set transform-set
show crypto map

Part
IV

Command Reference

mode

To change the mode for a transform set, use the **mode** crypto transform configuration command. To reset the mode to the default value of tunnel mode, use the **no** form of the command.

> **mode** [**tunnel** | **transport**]
> **no mode**

Syntax   Description

tunnel | (Optional) Specifies the mode for a transform set: either tunnel or transport
transport   mode. If neither **tunnel** nor **transport** is specified, the default (tunnel mode) is assigned.

Default

Tunnel mode

Command Mode

Crypto transform configuration

Usage Guidelines

This command first appeared in Cisco IOS Release 11.3 T.

Use this command to change the mode specified for the transform. This setting is only used when the traffic to be protected has the same IP addresses as the IPSec peers (this traffic can be encapsulated either in tunnel or transport mode). This setting is ignored for all other traffic (all other traffic is encapsulated in tunnel mode).

If the traffic to be protected has the same IP address as the IPSec peers and transport mode is specified, during negotiation the router will request transport mode but will accept either transport or tunnel mode. If tunnel mode is specified, the router will request tunnel mode and will accept only tunnel mode.

After you define a transform set, you are put into the crypto transform configuration mode. While in this mode, you can change the mode to either tunnel or transport. This change applies only to the transform set just defined.

If you do not change the mode when you first define the transform set, but later decide you want to change the mode for the transform set, you must re-enter the transform set (specifying the transform name and all its transforms) and then change the mode.

If you use this command to change the mode, the change will only affect the negotiation of subsequent IPSec security associations via crypto map entries which specify this transform set. (If you want the new settings to take effect sooner, you can clear all or part of the security association database.) Refer to the **clear crypto sa** command for more details.

Tunnel Mode

With tunnel mode, the entire original IP packet is protected (encrypted, authenticated, or both) and is encapsulated by the IPSec headers and trailers (an ESP header and trailer, an AH header, or both). Then, a new IP header is prefixed to the packet, specifying the IPSec endpoints as the source and destination.

Tunnel mode can be used with any IP traffic. Tunnel mode must be used if IPSec is protecting traffic from hosts behind the IPSec peers. For example, tunnel mode is used with virtual private networks (VPNs) where hosts on one protected network send packets to hosts on a different protected network via a pair of IPSec peers. With VPNs, the IPSec peers tunnel the protected traffic between the peers while the hosts on their protected networks are the session endpoints.

Transport Mode

With transport mode, only the payload (data) of the original IP packet is protected (encrypted, authenticated, or both). The payload is encapsulated by the IPSec headers and trailers (an ESP header and trailer, an AH header, or both). The original IP headers remain intact and are not protected by IPSec.

Use transport mode only when the IP traffic to be protected has IPSec peers as both the source and destination. For example, you could use transport mode to protect router management traffic. Specifying transport mode allows the router to negotiate with the remote peer whether to use transport or tunnel mode.

Example

This example defines a transform set and changes the mode to transport mode. The mode value only applies to IP traffic with the source and destination addresses at the local and remote IPSec peers:

```
MyPeerRouter(config)# crypto ipsec transform-set newer esp-des esp-sha-hmac
MyPeerRouter(cfg-crypto-trans)# mode transport
MyPeerRouter(cfg-crypto-trans)# exit
MyPeerRouter(config)#
```

Related Commands

You can search online at www.cisco.com to find documentation of related commands.

crypto ipsec transform-set
initialization-vector size

Part
IV

Command Reference

set peer

To specify an IPSec peer in a crypto map entry, use the **set peer** crypto map configuration command. Use the **no** form of this command to remove an IPSec peer from a crypto map entry.

> **set peer** {*hostname* | *ip-address*}
> **no set peer** {*hostname* | *ip-address*}

Syntax   Description

hostname   Specifies the IPSec peer by its host name. This is the peer's host name concatenated with its domain name (for example, myhost.domain.com).

ip-address   Specifies the IPSec peer by its IP address.

Default

No peer is defined by default.

Command Mode

Crypto map configuration

Usage Guidelines

This command first appeared in Cisco IOS Release 11.2.

This command is also documented in Chapter 27, "Cisco Encryption Technology Commands," where it has slightly different functionality.

Use this command to specify an IPSec peer for a crypto map.

This command is required for all static crypto maps. If you are defining a dynamic crypto map (with the **crypto dynamic-map** command), this command is not required, and in most cases is not used (because, in general, the peer is unknown).

For **ipsec-isakmp** crypto map entries, you can specify multiple peers by repeating this command. The peer that packets are actually sent to is determined by the last peer that the router heard from (received either traffic or a negotiation request from) for a given data flow. If the attempt fails with the first peer, IKE tries the next peer on the crypto map list.

For **ipsec-manual** crypto entries, you can specify only one IPSec peer per crypto map. If you want to change the peer, you must first delete the old peer and then specify the new peer.

You can specify the remote IPSec peer by its host name only if the host name is mapped to the peer's IP address in a DNS server or if you manually map the host name to the IP address with the **ip host** command.

Example

The following example shows a crypto map configuration when IKE will be used to establish the security associations. In this example, a security association could be set up to either the IPSec peer at 10.0.0.1 or the peer at 10.0.0.2:

```
crypto map mymap 10 ipsec-isakmp
 match address 101
 set transform-set my_t_set1
 set peer 10.0.0.1
 set peer 10.0.0.2
```

Related Commands

You can search online at www.cisco.com to find documentation of related commands.

crypto dynamic-map
crypto map (global configuration)
crypto map (interface configuration)
crypto map local-address
match address
set pfs
set security-association level per-host
set security-association lifetime
set session-key
set transform-set
show crypto map

set pfs

To specify that IPSec should ask for perfect forward secrecy (PFS) when requesting new security associations for this crypto map entry or that IPSec requires PFS when receiving requests for new security associations, use the **set pfs** crypto map configuration command. To specify that IPSec should not request PFS, use the **no** form of the command.

> **set pfs [group1 | group2]**
> **no set pfs**

Syntax	Description
group1	Specifies that IPSec should use the 768-bit Diffie-Hellman prime modulus group when performing the new Diffie-Hellman exchange.
group2	Specifies that IPSec should use the 1024-bit Diffie-Hellman prime modulus group when performing the new Diffie-Hellman exchange.

Default

By default, PFS is not requested. If no group is specified with this command, **group1** is used as the default.

Command Mode

Crypto map configuration

Usage Guidelines

This command first appeared in Cisco IOS Release 11.3 T.

This command is only available for **ipsec-isakmp** crypto map entries and dynamic crypto map entries.

During negotiation, this command causes IPSec to request PFS when requesting new security associations for the crypto map entry. The default (**group1**) is sent if the **set pfs** statement does not specify a group. If the peer initiates the negotiation and the local configuration specifies PFS, the remote peer must perform a PFS exchange or the negotiation will fail. If the local configuration does not specify a group, a default of **group1** will be assumed, and an offer of either **group1** or **group2** will be accepted. If the local configuration specifies **group2**, that group *must* be part of the peer's offer or the negotiation will fail. If the local configuration does not specify PFS it will accept any offer of PFS from the peer.

PFS adds another level of security because if one key is ever cracked by an attacker then only the data sent with that key will be compromised. Without PFS, data sent with other keys could be also compromised.

With PFS, every time a new security association is negotiated, a new Diffie-Hellman exchange occurs. (This exchange requires additional processing time.)

The 1024-bit Diffie-Hellman prime modulus group, **group2**, provides more security than **group1**, but requires more processing time than **group1**.

Example

This example specifies that PFS should be used whenever a new security association is negotiated for the crypto map *mymap 10*:

```
crypto map mymap 10 ipsec-isakmp
 set pfs group2
```

Related Commands

You can search online at www.cisco.com to find documentation of related commands.

crypto dynamic-map
crypto map (global configuration)
crypto map (interface configuration)
crypto map local-address
match address
set peer
set security-association level per-host
set security-association lifetime
set transform-set
show crypto map

set security-association level per-host

To specify that separate IPSec security associations should be requested for each source/destination host pair, use the **set security-association level per-host** crypto map configuration command. Use the **no** form of this command to specify that one security association should be requested for each crypto map access list **permit** entry.

> **set security-association level per-host**
> **no set security-association level per-host**

Syntax Description

This command has no arguments or keywords.

Default

For a given crypto map, all traffic between two IPSec peers matching a single crypto map access list **permit** entry will share the same security association.

Command Mode

Crypto map configuration

Usage Guidelines

This command first appeared in Cisco IOS Release 11.3 T.

This command is only available for **ipsec-isakmp** crypto map entries and is not supported for dynamic crypto map entries.

When you use this command to specify that a separate security association should be used for each source/destination host pair.

Normally, within a given crypto map, IPSec will attempt to request security associations at the granularity specified by the access list entry. For example, if the access list entry specifies permit ip between Subnet A and Subnet B, IPSec will attempt to request security associations between Subnet A and Subnet B (for any IP protocol), and unless finer-grained security associations are established (by a peer request), all IPSec-protected traffic between these two subnets would use the same security association.

This command causes IPSec to request separate security associations for each source/destination host pair. In this case, each host pairing (where one host was in Subnet A and the other host was in Subnet B) would cause IPSec to request a separate security association.

With this command, one security association would be requested to protect traffic between Host A and Host B, and a different security association would be requested to protect traffic between Host A and Host C.

The access list entry can specify local and remote subnets, or it can specify a host-and-subnet combination. If the access list entry specifies protocols and ports, these values are applied when establishing the unique security associations.

Use this command with care, as multiple streams between given subnets can rapidly consume system resources.

Example

With an access list entry of **permit ip 1.1.1.0 0.0.0.255 2.2.2.0 0.0.0.255** and a per-host level:

- A packet from 1.1.1.1 to 2.2.2.1 will initiate a security association request that looks like it originated via **permit ip host 1.1.1.1 host 2.2.2.1**.

- A packet from 1.1.1.1 to 2.2.2.2 will initiate a security association request that looks like it originated via **permit ip host 1.1.1.1 host 2.2.2.2**.

- A packet from 1.1.1.2 to 2.2.2.1 will initiate a security association request that looks like it originated via **permit ip host 1.1.1.2 host 2.2.2.1.**

Without the per-host level, any of the above packets initiate a single security association request originated via **permit ip 1.1.1.0 0.0.0.255 2.2.2.0 0.0.0.255**.

Related Commands

You can search online at www.cisco.com to find documentation of related commands.

crypto dynamic-map
crypto map (global configuration)
crypto map (interface configuration)
crypto map local-address
match address

set peer
set pfs
set security-association lifetime
set transform-set
show crypto map

set security-association lifetime

To override (for a particular crypto map entry) the global lifetime value, which is used when negotiating IPSec security associations, use the **set security-association lifetime** crypto map configuration command. To reset a crypto map entry's lifetime value to the global value, use the **no** form of the command.

set security-association lifetime {**seconds** *seconds* | **kilobytes** *kilobytes*}
no set security-association lifetime {**seconds** | **kilobytes**}

Syntax	Description
seconds *seconds*	Specifies the number of seconds a security association will live before expiring.
kilobytes *kilobytes*	Specifies the volume of traffic (in kilobytes) that can pass between IPSec peers using a given security association before that security association expires.

Default

The crypto map's security associations are negotiated according to the global lifetimes.

Command Mode

Crypto map configuration

Usage Guidelines

This command first appeared in Cisco IOS Release 11.3 T.

This command is only available for **ipsec-isakmp** crypto map entries and dynamic crypto map entries.

IPSec security associations use shared secret keys. These keys and their security associations time out together.

Assuming that the particular crypto map entry has lifetime values configured, when the router requests new security associations during security association negotiation, it specifies its crypto map lifetime value in the request to the peer; it uses this value as the lifetime of the new security associations. When the router receives a negotiation request from the peer, it uses the smaller of the lifetime value proposed by the peer or the locally configured lifetime value as the lifetime of the new security associations.

There are two lifetimes: a *timed lifetime* and a *traffic-volume lifetime*. The session keys/security association expires after the first of these lifetimes is reached.

If you change a lifetime, the change will not be applied to existing security associations, but will be used in subsequent negotiations to establish security associations for data flows supported by this crypto map entry. If you want the new settings to take effect sooner, you can clear all or part of the security association database by using the **clear crypto sa** command. Refer to the **clear crypto sa** command for more detail.

To change the timed lifetime, use the **set security-association lifetime seconds** form of the command. The timed lifetime causes the keys and security association to time out after the specified number of seconds have passed.

To change the traffic-volume lifetime, use the **set security-association lifetime kilobytes** form of the command. The traffic-volume lifetime causes the key and security association to time out after the specified amount of traffic (in kilobytes) has been protected by the security association's key.

Shorter lifetimes can make it harder to mount a successful key recovery attack, since the attacker has less data encrypted under the same key to work with. However, shorter lifetimes require more CPU processing time.

The lifetime values are ignored for manually established security associations (security associations installed via an **ipsec-manual** crypto map entry).

How These Lifetimes Work

Assuming that the particular crypto map entry does not have lifetime values configured, when the router requests new security associations it specifies its global lifetime values in the request to the peer; it uses this value as the lifetime of the new security associations. When the router receives a negotiation request from the peer, it uses the smaller of either the lifetime value proposed by the peer or the locally configured lifetime value as the lifetime of the new security associations.

The security association (and corresponding keys) expires according to which event occurs sooner: either after the **seconds** timeout or after the **kilobytes** amount of traffic is passed.

A new security association is negotiated *before* the lifetime threshold of the existing security association is reached to ensure that a new security association is ready for use when the old one expires. The new security association is negotiated either 30 seconds before the **seconds** lifetime expires or when the volume of traffic through the tunnel reaches 256 kilobytes less than the **kilobytes** lifetime (whichever occurs first).

If no traffic has passed through the tunnel during the entire life of the security association, a new security association is not negotiated when the lifetime expires. Instead, a new security association will be negotiated only when IPSec sees another packet that should be protected.

Example

This example shortens the timed lifetime for a particular crypto map entry, because there is a higher risk that the keys could be compromised for security associations belonging to the crypto map entry. The traffic-volume lifetime is not changed because there is not a high volume of traffic anticipated for these security associations. The timed lifetime is shortened to 2700 seconds (45 minutes).

```
crypto map mymap 10 ipsec-isakmp
 set security-association lifetime seconds 2700
```

Related Commands

You can search online at www.cisco.com to find documentation of related commands.

crypto dynamic-map
crypto ipsec security-association lifetime
crypto map (global configuration)
crypto map (interface configuration)
crypto map local-address
match address
set peer
set pfs
set security-association level per-host
set transform-set
show crypto map

set session-key

To manually specify the IPSec session keys within a crypto map entry, use the **set session-key** crypto map configuration command. Use the **no** form of this command to remove IPSec session keys from a crypto map entry. This command is only available for **ipsec-manual** crypto map entries.

> **set session-key** {**inbound** | **outbound**} **ah** *spi hex-key-string*
> **set session-key** {**inbound** | **outbound**} **esp** *spi* **cipher** *hex-key-string*
> [**authenticator** *hex-key-string*]
> **no set session-key** {**inbound** | **outbound**} **ah**
> **no set session-key** {**inbound** | **outbound**} **esp**

Syntax	Description
inbound	Sets the inbound IPSec session key. (You must set both inbound and outbound keys.)
outbound	Sets the outbound IPSec session key. (You must set both inbound and outbound keys.)
ah	Sets the IPSec session key for the AH protocol. Use when the crypto map entry's transform set includes an AH transform.
esp	Sets the IPSec session key for the ESP protocol. Use when the crypto map entry's transform set includes an ESP transform.
spi	Specifies the security parameter index (SPI), a number that is used to uniquely identify a security association. The SPI is an arbitrary number you assign in the range of 256 to 4,294,967,295 (FFFF FFFF).
	You can assign the same SPI to both directions and both protocols. However, not all peers have the same flexibility in SPI assignment. For a given destination address/protocol combination, unique SPI values must be used. The destination address is that of the router if inbound, the peer if outbound.
hex-key-string	Specifies the session key; enter in hexadecimal format.
	This is an arbitrary hexadecimal string of 8, 16, or 20 bytes.
	If the crypto map's transform set includes a DES algorithm, specify at least 8 bytes per key.
	If the crypto map's transform set includes an MD5 algorithm, specify at least 16 bytes per key.
	If the crypto map's transform set includes an SHA algorithm, specify 20 bytes per key.
	Keys longer than the above sizes are simply truncated.
cipher	Indicates that the key string is to be used with the ESP encryption transform.
authenticator	(Optional) Indicates that the key string is to be used with the ESP authentication transform. This argument is required only when the crypto map entry's transform set includes an ESP authentication transform.

Default

No session keys are defined by default.

Command Mode

Crypto map configuration

Usage Guidelines

This command first appeared in Cisco IOS Release 11.3 T.

Use this command to define IPSec keys for security associations via **ipsec-manual** crypto map entries. (In the case of **ipsec-isakmp** crypto map entries, the security associations with their corresponding keys are automatically established via the IKE negotiation.)

If the crypto map's transform set includes an AH protocol, you must define IPSec keys for AH for both inbound and outbound traffic. If the crypto map's transform set includes an ESP encryption protocol, you must define IPSec keys for ESP encryption for both inbound and outbound traffic. If your transform set includes an ESP authentication protocol, you must define IPSec keys for ESP authentication for inbound and outbound traffic.

When you define multiple IPSec session keys within a single crypto map, you can assign the same SPI number to all the keys. The SPI is used to identify the security association used with the crypto map. However, not all peers have the same flexibility in SPI assignment. You should coordinate SPI assignment with your peer's operator, making certain that the same SPI is not used more than once for the same destination address/protocol combination.

Security associations established via this command do not expire (unlike security associations established via IKE).

Session keys at one peer must match the session keys at the remote peer.

If you change a session key, the security association using the key will be deleted and reinitialized.

Examples

The following example shows a crypto map entry for manually established security associations. The transform set *t_set* includes only an AH protocol.

```
crypto ipsec transform-set t_set ah-sha-hmac

crypto map mymap 20 ipsec-manual
 match address 102
 set transform-set t_set
 set peer 10.0.0.21
 set session-key inbound ah 300 1111111111111111111111111111111111111111
 set session-key outbound ah 300 2222222222222222222222222222222222222222
```

The following example shows a crypto map entry for manually established security associations. The transform set *someset* includes both an AH and an ESP protocol, so session keys are configured for both AH and ESP for both inbound and outbound traffic. The transform set includes both encryption and authentication ESP transforms, so session keys are created for both using the **cipher** and **authenticator** keywords.

```
crypto ipsec transform-set someset ah-sha-hmac esp-des esp-sha-hmac

crypto map mymap 10 ipsec-manual
 match address 101
 set transform-set someset
 set peer 10.0.0.1
 set session-key inbound ah 300 9876543210987654321098765432109876543210
 set session-key outbound ah 300 fedcbafedcbafedcbafedcbafedcbafedcbafedc
 set session-key inbound esp 300 cipher 0123456789012345
  authenticator 0000111122223333444455556666777788889999
 set session-key outbound esp 300 cipher abcdefabcdefabcd
  authenticator 9999888877776666555544443333222211110000
```

Related Commands

You can search online at www.cisco.com to find documentation of related commands.

crypto map (global configuration)
crypto map (interface configuration)
crypto map local-address
match address
set peer
set transform-set
show crypto map

set transform-set

To specify which transform sets can be used with the crypto map entry, use the **set transform-set** crypto map configuration command. Use the **no** form of this command to remove all transform sets from a crypto map entry.

> **set transform-set** *transform-set-name1* [*transform-set-name2...transform-set-name6*]
> **no set transform-set**

Syntax	Description
transform-set-name	Name of the transform set.
	For an **ipsec-manual** crypto map entry, you can specify only one transform set.
	For an **ipsec-isakmp** or dynamic crypto map entry, you can specify up to six transform sets.

Default

No transform sets are included by default.

Command Mode

Crypto map configuration

Usage Guidelines

This command first appeared in Cisco IOS Release 11.3 T.

This command is required for all static and dynamic crypto map entries.

Use this command to specify which transform sets to include in a crypto map entry.

For an **ipsec-isakmp** crypto map entry, you can list multiple transform sets with this command. List the higher-priority transform sets first.

If the local router initiates the negotiation, the transform sets are presented to the peer in the order specified in the crypto map entry. If the peer initiates the negotiation, the local router accepts the first transform set that matches one of the transform sets specified in the crypto map entry.

The first matching transform set that is found at both peers is used for the security association. If no match is found, IPSec will not establish a security association. The traffic will be dropped because there is no security association to protect the traffic.

For an **ipsec-manual** crypto map entry, you can specify only one transform set. If the transform set does not match the transform set at the remote peer's crypto map, the two peers will fail to correctly communicate because the peers are using different rules to process the traffic.

If you want to change the list of transform sets, respecify the new list of transform sets to replace the old list. This change is only applied to crypto map entries that reference this transform set. The change will not be applied to existing security associations, but will be used in subsequent negotiations to establish new security associations. If you want the new settings to take effect sooner, you can clear all or part of the security association database by using the **clear crypto sa** command.

Any transform sets included in a crypto map must previously have been defined using the **crypto ipsec transform-set** command.

Example

The following example defines two transform sets and specifies that they can both be used within a crypto map entry. (This example applies only when IKE is used to establish security associations. With crypto maps used for manually established security associations, only one transform set can be included in a given crypto map entry.)

```
crypto ipsec transform-set my_t_set1 esp-des esp-sha-hmac
crypto ipsec transform-set my_t_set2 ah-sha-hmac esp-des esp-sha-hmac

crypto map mymap 10 ipsec-isakmp
 match address 101
 set transform-set my_t_set1 my_t_set2
 set peer 10.0.0.1
 set peer 10.0.0.2
```

In this example, when traffic matches access list 101 the security association can use either transform set *my_t_set1* (first priority) or *my_t_set2* (second priority), depending on which transform set matches the remote peer's transform sets.

Related Commands

You can search online at www.cisco.com to find documentation of related commands.

crypto dynamic-map
crypto map (global configuration)
crypto map (interface configuration)
crypto map local-address
match address
set peer
set pfs
set security-association level per-host
set security-association lifetime
set session-key
show crypto map

show crypto ipsec sa

To view the settings used by current security associations, use the **show crypto ipsec sa** EXEC command.

show crypto ipsec sa [**map** *map-name* | **address** | **identity**] [**detail**]

Syntax	Description
map *map-name*	(Optional) Shows any existing security associations created for the crypto map set named *map-name*.
address	(Optional) Shows the all existing security associations, sorted by the destination address (either the local address or the address of the IPSec remote peer) and then by protocol (AH or ESP).
identity	(Optional) Shows only the flow information. It does not show the security association information.

Syntax	Description
detail	(Optional) Shows detailed error counters. (The default is the high-level send/receive error counters.)

Default

If no keyword is used, all security associations are displayed. They are sorted first by interface, and then by traffic flow (for example, source/destination address, mask, protocol, port). Within a flow, the SAs are listed by protocol (ESP/AH) and direction (inbound/outbound).

Command Mode

EXEC

Usage Guidelines

This command first appeared in Cisco IOS Release 11.3 T.

Sample Display

The following is a sample output for the **show crypto ipsec sa** command:

```
Router#show crypto ipsec sa

interface: Ethernet0
    Crypto map tag: router-alice, local addr. 172.21.114.123

   local  ident (addr/mask/prot/port): (172.21.114.123/255.255.255.255/0/0)
   remote ident (addr/mask/prot/port): (172.21.114.67/255.255.255.255/0/0)
   current_peer: 172.21.114.67
     PERMIT, flags={origin_is_acl,}
    #pkts encaps: 10, #pkts encrypt: 10, #pkts digest 10
    #pkts decaps: 10, #pkts decrypt: 10, #pkts verify 10
    #send errors 10, #recv errors 0

     local crypto endpt.: 172.21.114.123, remote crypto endpt.: 172.21.114.67
     path mtu 1500, media mtu 1500
     current outbound spi: 20890A6F

     inbound esp sas:
      spi: 0x257A1039(628756537)
        transform: esp-des esp-md5-hmac ,
        in use settings ={Tunnel, }
        slot: 0, conn id: 26, crypto map: router-alice
        sa timing: remaining key lifetime (k/sec): (4607999/90)
        IV size: 8 bytes
        replay detection support: Y
```

```
    inbound ah sas:

    outbound esp sas:
     spi: 0x20890A6F(545852015)
       transform: esp-des esp-md5-hmac ,
       in use settings ={Tunnel, }
       slot: 0, conn id: 27, crypto map: router-alice
       sa timing: remaining key lifetime (k/sec): (4607999/90)
       IV size: 8 bytes
       replay detection support: Y

    outbound ah sas:

interface: Tunnel0
    Crypto map tag: router-alice, local addr. 172.21.114.123

   local  ident (addr/mask/prot/port): (172.21.114.123/255.255.255.255/0/0)
   remote ident (addr/mask/prot/port): (172.21.114.67/255.255.255.255/0/0)
   current_peer: 172.21.114.67
     PERMIT, flags={origin_is_acl,}
   #pkts encaps: 10, #pkts encrypt: 10, #pkts digest 10
   #pkts decaps: 10, #pkts decrypt: 10, #pkts verify 10
   #send errors 10, #recv errors 0

    local crypto endpt.: 172.21.114.123, remote crypto endpt.: 172.21.114.67
    path mtu 1500, media mtu 1500
    current outbound spi: 20890A6F

    inbound esp sas:
     spi: 0x257A1039(628756537)
       transform: esp-des esp-md5-hmac ,
       in use settings ={Tunnel, }
       slot: 0, conn id: 26, crypto map: router-alice
       sa timing: remaining key lifetime (k/sec): (4607999/90)
       IV size: 8 bytes
       replay detection support: Y

    inbound ah sas:

    outbound esp sas:
     spi: 0x20890A6F(545852015)
       transform: esp-des esp-md5-hmac ,
       in use settings ={Tunnel, }
       slot: 0, conn id: 27, crypto map: router-alice
       sa timing: remaining key lifetime (k/sec): (4607999/90)
       IV size: 8 bytes
       replay detection support: Y

    outbound ah sas:
```

show crypto ipsec security-association lifetime

To view the security-association lifetime value configured for a particular crypto map entry, use the **show crypto ipsec security-association lifetime** EXEC command.

show crypto ipsec security-association lifetime

Syntax Description

This command has no arguments or keywords.

Default

None.

Command Mode

EXEC

Usage Guidelines

This command first appeared in Cisco IOS Release 11.3 T.

Sample Display

The following is a sample output for the **show crypto ipsec security-association lifetime** command:

```
router#show crypto ipsec security-association lifetime
Security-association lifetime: 4608000 kilobytes/120 seconds
```

The following configuration was in effect when the above **show crypto ipsec security-association lifetime** command was issued:

```
crypto ipsec security-association lifetime seconds 120
```

show crypto ipsec transform-set

To view the configured transform sets, use the **show crypto ipsec transform-set** EXEC command.

show crypto ipsec transform-set [**tag** *transform-set-name*]

Syntax	Description
tag *transform-set-name*	(Optional) Shows only the transform sets with the specified *transform-set-name*.

Default
If no keyword is used, all transform sets configured at the router will be displayed.

Command Mode
EXEC

Usage Guidelines
This command first appeared in Cisco IOS Release 11.3 T.

Sample Display
The following is a sample output for the **show crypto ipsec transform-set** command:

```
Router#show crypto ipsec transform-set
Transform set combined-des-sha: { esp-des esp-sha-hmac  }
   will negotiate = { Tunnel,  },

Transform set combined-des-md5: { esp-des esp-md5-hmac  }
   will negotiate = { Tunnel,  },

Transform set t1: { esp-des esp-md5-hmac  }
   will negotiate = { Tunnel,  },

Transform set t100: { ah-sha-hmac  }
   will negotiate = { Transport,  },

Transform set t2: { ah-sha-hmac  }
   will negotiate = { Tunnel,  },
   { esp-des  }
   will negotiate = { Tunnel,  },
```

The following configuration was in effect when the above **show crypto ipsec transform-set** command was issued:

```
crypto ipsec transform-set combined-des-sha esp-des esp-sha-hmac
crypto ipsec transform-set combined-des-md5 esp-des esp-md5-hmac
crypto ipsec transform-set t1 esp-des esp-md5-hmac
crypto ipsec transform-set t100 ah-sha-hmac
 mode transport
crypto ipsec transform-set t2 ah-sha-hmac esp-des
```

show crypto dynamic-map
To view a dynamic crypto map set, use the **show crypto dynamic-map** EXEC command.

> **show crypto dynamic-map** [**tag** *map-name*]

Syntax

tag *map-name*

Description

(Optional) Shows only the crypto dynamic map set with the specified *map-name*.

Default

If no keywords are used, all dynamic crypto maps configured at the router will be displayed.

Command Mode

EXEC

Usage Guidelines

This command first appeared in Cisco IOS Release 11.3 T.

Sample Display

The following is sample output for the **show crypto dynamic-map** command:

```
Router#show crypto dynamic-map
Crypto Map Template"dyn1" 10
        Extended IP access list 152
            access-list 152 permit ip
                source: addr = 172.21.114.67/0.0.0.0
                dest:   addr = 0.0.0.0/255.255.255.255
        Current peer: 0.0.0.0
        Security association lifetime: 4608000 kilobytes/120 seconds
        PFS (Y/N): N
        Transform sets={ tauth, t1, }
```

The following partial configuration was in effect when the above **show crypto dynamic-map** command was issued:

```
crypto ipsec security-association lifetime seconds 120
!
crypto ipsec transform-set t1 esp-des esp-md5-hmac
crypto ipsec transform-set tauth ah-sha-hmac
!
crypto dynamic-map dyn1 10
 set transform-set tauth t1
 match address 152
crypto map to-router local-address Ethernet0
crypto map to-router 10 ipsec-isakmp
 set peer 172.21.114.123
 set transform-set tauth t1
 match address 150
crypto map to-router 20 ipsec-isakmp dynamic dyn1
!
```

```
access-list 150 permit ip host 172.21.114.67 host 172.21.114.123
access-list 150 permit ip host 15.15.15.1 host 172.21.114.123
access-list 150 permit ip host 15.15.15.1 host 8.8.8.1
access-list 152 permit ip host 172.21.114.67 any
```

show crypto map

To view the crypto map configuration, use the **show crypto map** EXEC command.

show crypto map [**interface** *interface* | **tag** *map-name*]

Syntax	Description
interface *interface*	(Optional) Shows only the crypto map set applied to the specified interface.
tag *map-name*	(Optional) Shows only the crypto map set with the specified *map-name*.

Default

If no keywords are used, all crypto maps configured at the router are displayed.

Command Mode

EXEC

Usage Guidelines

This command first appeared in Cisco IOS Release 11.2.

This command is also documented in Chapter 27, "Cisco Encryption Technology Commands," where it has slightly different functionality.

Sample Display

The following is sample output for the **show crypto map** command:

```
Router#show crypto map
Crypto Map: "router-alice" idb: Ethernet0 local address: 172.21.114.123

Crypto Map "router-alice" 10 ipsec-isakmp
        Peer = 172.21.114.67
        Extended IP access list 141
            access-list 141 permit ip
                source: addr = 172.21.114.123/0.0.0.0
                dest:   addr = 172.21.114.67/0.0.0.0
        Current peer: 172.21.114.67
        Security-association lifetime: 4608000 kilobytes/120 seconds
```

```
      PFS (Y/N): N
      Transform sets={ t1, }
```

The following configuration was in effect when the above **show crypto map** command was issued:

```
crypto map router-alice local-address Ethernet0
crypto map router-alice 10 ipsec-isakmp
 set peer 172.21.114.67
 set transform-set t1
 match address 141
```

The following is sample output for the **show crypto map** command when manually established security associations are used:

```
Router#show crypto map
Crypto Map "multi-peer" 20 ipsec-manual
        Peer = 172.21.114.67
        Extended IP access list 120
            access-list 120 permit ip
                source: addr = 1.1.1.1/0.0.0.0
                dest:   addr = 1.1.1.2/0.0.0.0
        Current peer: 172.21.114.67
        Transform sets={ t2, }
        Inbound esp spi: 0,
         cipher key: ,
         auth_key: ,
        Inbound ah spi: 256,
            key: 010203040506070809010203040506070809010203040506070809,
        Outbound esp spi: 0
         cipher key: ,
         auth key: ,
        Outbound ah spi: 256,
            key: 010203040506070809010203040506070809010203040506070809,
```

The following configuration was in effect when the above **show crypto map** command was issued:

```
crypto map multi-peer 20 ipsec-manual
 set peer 172.21.114.67
 set session-key inbound ah 256
010203040506070809010203040506070809010203040506070809
 set session-key outbound ah 256
010203040506070809010203040506070809010203040506070809
 set transform-set t2
 match address 120
```

Table 29-2 explains each field.

Table 29-2 *show crypto map Field Descriptions*

Field	Description
Peer	Indicates the IP address(es) of the remote IPSec peer(s).
Extended IP access list	Lists the access list associated with the crypto map. If no access list is associated, the message "No matching address list set" is displayed.

Continues

Table 29-2 *show crypto map Field Descriptions (Continued)*

Field	Description
Current Peer	Indicates the current IPSec peer.
Security-association lifetime	Indicates the lifetime of the security association.
PFS	Indicates whether IPSec will negotiate perfect forward secrecy when establishing new SAs for this crypto map.
Transform sets	Indicates the name(s) of the transform set(s) that can be used with the crypto map.
Inbound	Indicates the setting for the inbound IPSec session key(s).
Outbound	Indicates the setting for the outbound IPSec session key(s).

## CHAPTER 30

Configuring Certification Authority Interoperability

This chapter describes how to configure certification authority (CA) interoperability, which is provided in support of the IP Security (IPSec) standard. CA interoperability permits Cisco IOS devices and CAs to communicate so that your Cisco IOS device can obtain and use digital certificates from the CA. Although IPSec can be implemented in your network without the use of a CA, using a CA provides manageability and scalability for IPSec.

For background and configuration information for IPSec, see Chapter 28, "Configuring IPSec Network Security."

For a complete description of the commands used in this chapter, refer to Chapter 31, "Certification Authority Interoperability Commands." To locate documentation of other commands that appear in this chapter, you can search online at www.cisco.com.

CA Interoperability Overview

Without CA interoperability, Cisco IOS devices could not use CAs when deploying IPSec. CAs provide a manageable, scalable solution for IPSec networks. For details, see the section "Overview of Certificate Authorities."

Supported Standards

Cisco supports the following standards with this feature:

- **IPSec**—IPSec is a framework of open standards that provides data confidentiality, data integrity, and data authentication between participating peers. IPSec provides these security services at the IP layer; it uses IKE to handle negotiation of protocols and algorithms based on local policy, and to generate the encryption and authentication keys to be used by IPSec. IPSec can be used to protect one or more data flows between a pair of hosts, between a pair of security gateways, or between a security gateway and a host.

  For more information on IPSec, see Chapter 28, "Configuring IPSec Network Security."

- **Internet Key Exchange (IKE)**—IKE is a hybrid protocol that implements Oakley and Skeme key exchanges inside the ISAKMP framework. Although IKE can be used with other protocols, its initial implementation is with the IPSec protocol. IKE provides authentication of the IPSec peers, negotiates IPSec keys, and negotiates IPSec security associations.

  For more information on IKE, see Chapter 32, "Configuring Internet Key Exchange Security Protocol."

- **Public-Key Cryptography Standard #7 (PKCS #7)**—PKCS #7 is a standard from RSA Data Security, Inc., which is used to encrypt and sign certificate enrollment messages.

- **Public-Key Cryptography Standard #10 (PKCS #10)**—PKCS #10 is a standard syntax from RSA Data Security, Inc., for certificate requests.

- **RSA keys**—RSA is the public key cryptographic system developed by Ron Rivest, Adi Shamir, and Leonard Adleman. RSA keys come in pairs: one public key and one private key.

- **X.509v3 certificates**—X.509v3 certificate support allows the IPSec-protected network to scale by providing the equivalent of a digital ID card to each device. When two devices wish to communicate, they exchange digital certificates to prove their identity (thus removing the need to manually exchange public keys with each peer or to manually specify a shared key at each peer). These certificates are obtained from a CA. X.509 is part of the X.500 standard by the ITU.

Restrictions

This feature is useful and should be configured only when you also configure both IPSec and IKE in your network.

Prerequisites

You need to have a CA available to your network before you configure this interoperability feature. The CA must support Cisco's PKI protocol, the Certificate Enrollment Protocol (CEP).

Overview of Certificate Authorities

This section provides background information about CAs, including the following:

- Purpose of CAs

- Implementing IPSec Without CAs

- Implementing IPSec With CAs

- How CA Certificates Are Used by IPSec Devices

- About Registration Authorities

Purpose of CAs

CAs are responsible for managing certificate requests and issuing certificates to participating IPSec network devices. These services provide centralized key management for the participating devices.

CAs simplify the administration of IPSec network devices. You can use a CA with a network containing multiple IPSec-compliant devices such as routers.

Digital signatures, enabled by public key cryptography, provide a means to digitally authenticate devices and individual users. In public key cryptography, such as the RSA encryption system, each user has a key pair containing both a public and a private key. The keys act as complements, and anything encrypted with one of the keys can be decrypted with the other. A signature is formed when data is encrypted with a user's private key. The receiver verifies the signature by decrypting the message with the sender's public key. The fact that the message could be decrypted using the sender's public key indicates that the holder of the private key, the sender, must have created the message. This process relies on the receiver having a copy of the sender's public key and knowing with a high degree of certainty that it really does belong to the sender and not to someone pretending to be the sender.

Digital certificates provide this link. A digital certificate contains information to identify a user or device, such as the name, serial number, company, department, or IP address. It also contains a copy of the entity's public key. The certificate is itself signed by a CA and a third party that is explicitly trusted by the receiver to validate identities and to create digital certificates.

In order to validate the CA's signature, the receiver must first know the CA's public key. Normally this is handled out-of-band or through an operation done at installation. For instance, most Web browsers are configured with the public keys of several CAs by default. IKE, a key component of IPSec, can use digital signatures to scalably authenticate peer devices before setting up security associations.

Without digital signatures, you must manually exchange public keys or secrets between each pair of devices that use IPSec to protect communications between them. Without certificates, every new device added to the network requires a configuration change on every other device it securely communicates with. However, by using digital certificates, each device is enrolled with a certificate authority. When two devices wish to communicate, they exchange certificates and digitally sign data to authenticate each other. When a new device is added to the network, you simply enroll that device with a CA, and none of the other devices need modification. When the new device attempts an IPSec connection, certificates are automatically exchanged and the device can be authenticated.

Implementing IPSec Without CAs

Without a CA, if you want to enable IPSec services (such as encryption) between two Cisco routers, you must first ensure that each router has the other router's key (such as an RSA public key or a shared key). This requires that you manually perform one of the following:

- At each router, enter the other router's RSA public key.

- At each router, specify a shared key to be used between the routers.

In Figure 30-1, each router uses the other router's key to authenticate the identity of the other router; this authentication always occurs whenever IPSec traffic is exchanged between the two routers.

If you have multiple Cisco routers in a mesh topology and wish to exchange IPSec traffic passing between all those routers, you must first configure shared keys or RSA public keys between all those routers.

Figure 30-1 *Without a CA: Key Configuration Between Two Routers*

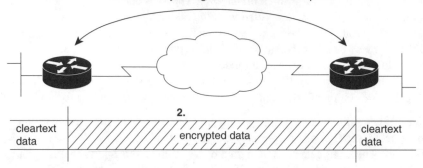

1. Manual key configuration at both IPSec peers

Figure 30-2 *Without a CA: Six Two-Part Key Configurations Required for Four IPSec Routers*

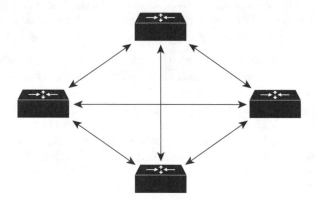

Every time a new router is added to the IPSec network, you must configure keys between the new router and each of the existing routers. (In Figure 30-2, four additional 2-part key configurations would be required to add a single encrypting router to the network).

Consequently, the more devices there are that require IPSec services, the more involved the key administration becomes. Obviously, this approach does not scale well for larger, more complex encrypting networks.

Implementing IPSec With CAs

With a CA, you do not need to configure keys between all the encrypting routers. Instead, you individually enroll each participating router with the CA, requesting a certificate for the router. When this has been accomplished, each participating router can dynamically authenticate all the other participating routers. This is illustrated in Figure 30-3.

Figure 30-3 *With a CA: Each Router Individually Makes Requests of the CA at Installation*

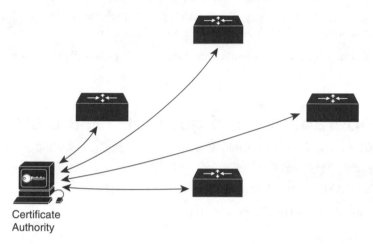

Certificate
Authority

To add a new IPSec router to the network, you only need to configure that new router to request a certificate from the CA, instead of making multiple key configurations with all the other existing IPSec routers.

How CA Certificates Are Used by IPSec Devices

When two IPSec routers want to exchange IPSec-protected traffic passing between them, they must first authenticate each other; otherwise, IPSec protection cannot occur. The authentication is done with IKE.

Without a CA, a router authenticates itself to the remote router using either RSA encrypted nonces or pre-shared keys. Both methods require that keys must have been previously configured between the two routers.

With a CA, a router authenticates itself to the remote router by sending a certificate to the remote router and performing some public key cryptography. Each router must send its own unique certificate which was issued and validated by the CA. This process works because each router's certificate encapsulates the router's public key, each certificate is authenticated by the CA, and all participating routers recognize the CA as an authenticating authority. This is called IKE with an RSA signature.

Your router can continue sending its own certificate for multiple IPSec sessions and to multiple IPSec peers, until the certificate expires. When its certificate expires, the router administrator must obtain a new one from the CA.

CAs can also revoke certificates for devices that will no longer participate in IPSec. Revoked certificates are not recognized as valid by other IPSec devices. Revoked certificates are listed in a certificate revocation list (CRL), which each peer may check before accepting another peer's certificate.

About Registration Authorities

Some CAs have a registration authority (RA) as part of their implementation. An RA is essentially a server that acts as a proxy for the CA so that CA functions can continue when the CA is offline.

Some of the configuration tasks described in this document differ slightly depending on whether your CA supports an RA.

CA Interoperability Configuration Task Lists

To enable your Cisco device to interoperate with a CA, complete the tasks in the following sections. Some of the tasks are optional; the remaining are required:

- Managing NVRAM Memory Usage (Optional)
- Configuring the Router's Host Name and IP Domain Name
- Generating an RSA Key Pair
- Declaring a CA
- Authenticating the CA
- Requesting Your Own Certificate(s)
- Saving Your Configuration
- Monitoring and Maintaining Certification Authority Interoperability (Optional)

For CA interoperability configuration examples, refer to the "CA Interoperability Configuration Examples" section at the end of this chapter.

Managing NVRAM Memory Usage (Optional)

Certificates and CRLs are used by your router when a CA is used. Normally certain of these certificates and all CRLs are stored locally in the router's NVRAM, and each certificate and CRL uses a moderate amount of memory.

- What certificates are normally stored at your router?
    - Your router's certificate
    - The CA's certificate
    - Two RA certificates (only if the CA supports an RA)
- What CRLs are normally stored at your router?
    - If your CA does not support an RA, only one CRL is stored at your router.
    - If your CA supports an RA, multiple CRLs can be stored at your router.

In some cases, storing these certificates and CRLs locally does not present a problem. However, in other cases, memory might become an issue—particularly if your CA supports an RA and a large number of CRLs end up being stored on your router.

To save NVRAM space, you can specify that certificates and CRLs should not be stored locally, but should be retrieved from the CA when needed. This will save NVRAM space but could result in a slight performance impact.

To specify that certificates and CRLs should not be stored locally on your router, but should be retrieved when required, turn on query mode by using the following command in global configuration mode:

Command	Purpose
crypto ca certificate query	Turns on query mode, which causes certificates and CRLs to not be stored locally.

NOTE   Query mode may affect availability if the CA is down.

If you do not turn on query mode at this time, but later decide that you should, you can turn on query mode at that time even if certificates and CRLs have already been stored on your router. In this case, when you turn on query mode, the stored certificates and CRLs will be deleted from the router after you save your configuration. (If you copy your configuration to a TFTP site prior to turning on query mode, you will save any stored certificates and CRLs at the TFTP site.)

If you turn on query mode now, you can turn off query mode later if you wish. If you turn off query mode later, you could also perform the **copy system:running-config nvram:startup-config** command at that time to save all current certificates and CRLs to NVRAM (otherwise, they could be lost during a reboot and would need to be retrieved the next time they were needed by your router).

Configuring the Router's Host Name and IP Domain Name

You must configure the router's host name and IP domain name if this has not already been done. This is required because the router assigns a fully qualified domain name (FQDN) to the keys and certificates used by IPSec, and the FQDN is based on the host name and IP domain name you assign to the router. For example, a certificate is named *router20.domain.com* based on a router host name of router20 and a router IP domain name of *domain.com*.

To configure the router's host name and IP domain name, use the following commands in global configuration mode:

Step	Command	Purpose
1	**hostname** *name*	Configures the router's host name.
2	**ip domain-name** *name*	Configures the router's IP domain name.

Generating an RSA Key Pair

RSA key pairs are used to sign and encrypt IKE key management messages and are required before you can obtain a certificate for your router.

To generate an RSA key pair, use the following command in global configuration mode:

Command	Purpose
crypto key generate rsa [usage-keys]	Generates an RSA key pair.
	Use the **usage-keys** keyword to specify special-usage keys instead of general-purpose keys. See the command description for an explanation of special-usage versus general-purpose keys.

Declaring a CA

You should declare one CA to be used by your router. To declare a CA, use the following commands, starting in global configuration mode:

Step	Command	Purpose
1	**crypto ca identity** *name*	Declares a CA. The name should be the CA's domain name.
		This command puts you into the ca-identity configuration mode.
2	**enrollment url** *url*	Specifies the URL of the CA. (The URL should include any nonstandard cgi-bin script location.)
3	**enrollment mode ra**	If your CA system provides an RA, specifies RA mode.
4	**query url** *url*	If your CA system provides an RA and supports the LDAP protocol, specifies the location of the LDAP server.

Step	Command	Purpose
5	**enrollment retry-period** *minutes*	(Optional) Specifies a retry period.
		After requesting a certificate, the router waits to receive a certificate from the CA. If the router does not receive a certificate within a period of time (the retry period), the router sends another certificate request.
		You can change the retry period from the default of 1 minute.
6	**enrollment retry-count** *count*	(Optional) Specifies how many times the router will continue to send unsuccessful certificate requests before giving up.
		By default, the router will never give up trying.
7	**crl optional**	(Optional) Specifies that other peers' certificates can still be accepted by your router even if the appropriate CRL is not accessible to your router.
8	**exit**	Exits ca-identity configuration mode.

The trade-off between security and availability is determined by the **query url** and **crl optional** commands, as shown in Table 30-1.

Table 30-1 *Security and CA Availability*

	Query - Yes	Query - No
CRL Optional - Yes	Sessions will go through even if the CA is not available, but the certificate might have been revoked.	Sessions will go through even if the CA is not available, but the certificate might have been revoked.
CRL Optional - No	Certificates will not be accepted if the CA is not available.	Sessions will go through and will be verified against the CRL stored locally.

Authenticating the CA

The router needs to authenticate the CA. It does this by obtaining the CA's self-signed certificate, which contains the CA's public key. Because the CA's certificate is self-signed (the CA signs its own certificate), the CA's public key should be manually authenticated by contacting the CA administrator to compare the CA certificate's fingerprint when you perform this step.

To get the CA's public key, use the following command in global configuration mode:

Command	Purpose
crypto ca authenticate *name*	Gets the CA's public key. Use the same *name* that you used when declaring the CA with the **crypto ca identity** command.

Requesting Your Own Certificate(s)

You need to obtain a signed certificate from the CA for each of your router's RSA key pairs. If you generated general-purpose RSA keys, your router only has one RSA key pair and needs only one certificate. If you previously generated special-usage RSA keys, your router has two RSA key pairs and needs two certificates.

To request signed certificates from the CA, use the following command in global configuration mode:

Command	Purpose
crypto ca enroll *name*	Requests certificates for all your RSA key pairs.
	This command causes your router to request as many certificates as there are RSA key pairs, so you only need to perform this command once, even if you have special-usage RSA key pairs.
	Note: This command requires you to create a challenge password that is not saved with the configuration. This password is required in the event that your certificate needs to be revoked, so remember this password.

NOTE If your router reboots after you issued the **crypto ca enroll** command but before you received the certificate(s), you must reissue the command and notify the CA administrator.

Saving Your Configuration

Always remember to save your work when you make configuration changes.

Use the **copy system:running-config nvram:startup-config** command to save your configuration. This command includes saving RSA keys to private NVRAM. RSA keys are *not* saved with your configuration when you perform a **copy system:running-config rcp:** or **copy system:running-config tftp:** command.

Monitoring and Maintaining Certification Authority Interoperability (Optional)

The following tasks are optional, depending on your particular requirements:

- Requesting a CRL
- Deleting Your Router's RSA Keys
- Deleting a Peer's Public Keys
- Deleting Certificates from the Configuration
- Viewing Keys and Certificates

Requesting a CRL

You can request a CRL only if your CA does not support an RA. The following description and task applies only when the CA does not support an RA.

When your router receives a certificate from a peer, the router downloads a CRL from the CA. The router then checks the CRL to make sure the certificate the peer sent has not been revoked. (If the certificate appears on the CRL, the router will not accept the certificate and will not authenticate the peer.)

A CRL can be reused with subsequent certificates until the CRL expires if query mode is off. If your router receives a peer's certificate after the applicable CRL has expired, the router will download the new CRL.

If your router has a CRL that has not yet expired, but you suspect that the CRL's contents are out of date, you can request that the latest CRL be immediately downloaded to replace the old CRL.

To request immediate download of the latest CRL, use the following command in global configuration mode:

Command	Purpose
crypto ca crl request *name*	Requests an updated CRL.
	This command replaces the currently stored CRL at your router with the newest version of the CRL.

Deleting Your Router's RSA Keys

There might be circumstances where you want to delete your router's RSA keys. For example, if you believe the RSA keys are compromised in some way and should no longer be used, you should delete the keys.

To delete all your router's RSA keys, use the following command in global configuration mode:

Command	Purpose
crypto key zeroize rsa	Deletes all your router's RSA keys.

After you delete a router's RSA keys, you should also complete these two additional tasks:

- Ask the CA administrator to revoke your router's certificates at the CA; you must supply the challenge password you created when you originally obtained the router's certificates with the **crypto ca enroll** command.

- Manually remove the router's certificates from the router configuration as described in the section, "Deleting Certificates from the Configuration."

Deleting a Peer's Public Keys

There might be circumstances where you would want to delete another peer's RSA public keys from your router's configuration. For example, if you no longer trust the integrity of a peer's public key, you should delete the key.

To delete a peer's RSA public key, use the following commands, starting in global configuration mode:

Step	Command	Purpose
1	**crypto key pubkey-chain rsa**	Enters public key configuration mode.
2	**no named-key** *key-name* [**encryption** | **signature**] or **no addressed-key** *key-address* [**encryption** | **signature**]	Deletes a remote peer's RSA public key. Specifies the peer's FQDN or the remote peer's IP address.
3	**exit**	Returns to global configuration mode.

Deleting Certificates from the Configuration

If the need arises, you can delete certificates that are saved at your router. Your router saves its own certificate(s), the CA's certificate, and any RA certificates (unless you put the router into query mode per the "Managing NVRAM Memory Usage (Optional)" section).

To delete your router's certificate or RA certificates from your router's configuration, use the following commands in global configuration mode:

Step	Command	Purpose
1	**show crypto ca certificates**	Views the certificates stored on your router; note (or copy) the serial number of the certificate you wish to delete.
2	**crypto ca certificate chain** *name*	Enters certificate chain configuration mode.
3	**no certificate** *certificate-serial-number*	Deletes the certificate.

To delete the CA's certificate, you must remove the entire CA identity, which also removes all certificates associated with the CA—your router's certificate, the CA certificate, and any RA certificates.

To remove a CA identity, use the following command in global configuration mode:

Command	Purpose
no crypto ca identity *name*	Deletes all identity information and certificates associated with the CA.

Viewing Keys and Certificates

To view keys and certificates, use the following commands in EXEC mode:

Step	Command	Purpose
1	**show crypto key mypubkey rsa**	Views your router's RSA public keys.
2	**show crypto key pubkey-chain rsa**	Views a list of all the RSA public keys stored on your router. These include the public keys of peers that have sent your router their certificates during peer authentication for IPSec.
3	**show crypto key pubkey-chain rsa** [**name** *key-name* | **address** *key-address*]	Views details of a particular RSA public key stored on your router.
4	**show crypto ca certificates**	Views information about your certificate, the CA's certificate, and any RA certificates.

What to Do Next

After you are done configuring this feature, you should configure IKE and IPSec. IKE configuration is described in Chapter 32, "Configuring Internet Key Exchange Security Protocol." IPSec configuration is described in Chapter 28, "Configuring IPSec Network Security."

CA Interoperability Configuration Examples

The following configuration is for a router named *myrouter*. In this example IPSec is configured and the IKE protocol and CA interoperability are configured in support of IPSec.

In this example, general-purpose RSA keys were generated, but you will notice that the keys are not saved or displayed in the configuration.

Comments are included within the configuration to explain various commands.

```
!
version 11.3
no service password-encryption
service udp-small-servers
service tcp-small-servers
!
! CA interoperability requires you to configure your router's hostname:
hostname myrouter
!
enable secret 5 <removed>
enable password <removed>
!
! CA interoperability requires you to configure your router's IP domain name:
ip domain-name domain.com
ip name-server 172.29.2.132
ip name-server 192.168.30.32
!
! The following configures a transform set (part of IPSec configuration):
crypto ipsec transform-set my-transformset esp-des esp-sha-hmac
!
! The following declares the CA. (In this example, the CA does not support an RA.)
crypto ca identity domain.com
 enrollment url http://ca_server
!
! The following shows the certificates and CRLs stored at the router, including
!   the CA certificate (shown first), the router's certificate (shown next)
!   and a CRL (shown last).
crypto ca certificate chain domain.com
! The following is the CA certificate
!   received via the 'crypto ca authenticate' command:
 certificate ca 3051DF7169BEE31B821DFE4B3A338E5F
  30820182 3082012C A0030201 02021030 51DF7169 BEE31B82 1DFE4B3A 338E5F30
  0D06092A 864886F7 0D010104 05003042 31163014 06035504 0A130D43 6973636F
  20537973 74656D73 3110300E 06035504 0B130744 65767465 73743116 30140603
  55040313 0D434953 434F4341 2D554C54 5241301E 170D3937 31323032 30313036
  32385A17 0D393831 32303230 31303632 385A3042 31163014 06035504 0A130D43
```

```
    6973636F 20537973 74656D73 3110300E 06035504 0B130744 65767465 73743116
    30140603 55040313 0D434953 434F4341 2D554C54 5241305C 300D0609 2A864886
    F70D0101 01050003 4B003048 024100C1 B69D7BF6 34E4EE28 A84E0DC6 FCA4DEA8
    04D89E50 C5EBE862 39D51890 D0D4B732 678BDBF2 80801430 E5E56E7C C126E2DD
    DBE9695A DF8E5BA7 E67BAE87 29375302 03010001 300D0609 2A864886 F70D0101
    04050003 410035AA 82B5A406 32489413 A7FF9A9A E349E5B4 74615E05 058BA3CE
    7C5F00B4 019552A5 E892D2A3 86763A1F 2852297F C68EECE1 F41E9A7B 2F38D02A
    B1D2F817 3F7B
    quit
! The following is the router's certificate
!   received via the 'crypto ca enroll' command:
certificate 7D28D4659D22C49134B3D1A0C2C9C8FC
    308201A6 30820150 A0030201 0202107D 28D4659D 22C49134 B3D1A0C2 C9C8FC30
    0D06092A 864886F7 0D010104 05003042 31163014 06035504 0A130D43 6973636F
    20537973 74656D73 3110300E 06035504 0B130744 65767465 73743116 30140603
    55040313 0D434953 434F4341 2D554C54 5241301E 170D3938 30343234 30303030
    30305A17 0D393930 34323432 33353935 395A302F 311D301B 06092A86 4886F70D
    01090216 0E73636F 742E6369 73636F2E 636F6D31 0E300C06 03550405 13053137
    41464230 5C300D06 092A8648 86F70D01 01010500 034B0030 48024100 A207ED75
    DE8A9BC4 980958B7 28ADF562 1371D043 1FC93C24 8E9F8384 4D1A2407 60CBD7EC
    B15BD782 A687CA49 883369BE B35A4219 8FE742B0 91CF76EE 07EC9E69 02030100
    01A33530 33300B06 03551D0F 04040302 05A03019 0603551D 11041230 10820E73
    636F742E 63697363 6F2E636F 6D300906 03551D13 04023000 300D0609 2A864886
    F70D0101 04050003 410085F8 A5AFA907 B38731A5 0195D921 D8C45EFD B6082C28
    04A88CEC E9EC6927 F24874E4 30C4D7E2 2686E0B5 77F197E4 F82A8BA2 1E03944D
    286B661F 0305DF5F 3CE7
    quit
! The following is a CRL received by the router (via the router's own action):
crl
    3081C530 71300D06 092A8648 86F70D01 01020500 30423116 30140603 55040A13
    0D436973 636F2053 79737465 6D733110 300E0603 55040B13 07446576 74657374
    31163014 06035504 03130D43 4953434F 43412D55 4C545241 170D3938 30333233
    32333232 31305A17 0D393930 34323230 30303030 305A300D 06092A86 4886F70D
    01010205 00034100 7AA83057 AC5E5C65 B9812549 37F11B7B 5CA4CAED 830B3955
    A4DDD268 F567E29A E4B34691 C2162BD1 0540D7E6 5D6650D1 81DBBF1D 788F1DAC
    BBF761B2 81FCC0F1
    quit
!
! The following is an IPSec crypto map (part of IPSec configuration):
crypto map map-to-remotesite 10 ipsec-isakmp
 set peer 172.21.114.196
 set transform-set my-transformset
 match address 124
!
!
interface Loopback0
 ip address 10.0.0.1 255.0.0.0
!
interface Tunnel0
 ip address 10.0.0.2 255.0.0.0
 ip mtu 1490
 no ip route-cache
 no ip mroute-cache
 tunnel source 10.10.0.1
 tunnel destination 172.21.115.119
!
```

```
interface FastEthernet0/0
 ip address 172.21.115.118 255.255.255.240
 no ip mroute-cache
 loopback
 no keepalive
 shutdown
 media-type MII
 full-duplex
!
! The IPSec crypto map is applied to interface Ethernet1/0:
interface Ethernet1/0
 ip address 172.21.114.197 255.255.255.0
 bandwidth 128
 no keepalive
 no fair-queue
 no cdp enable
 crypto map map-to-remotesite
!
crypto isakmp policy 15
 encryption des
 hash md5
 authentication rsa-sig
 group 2
 lifetime 5000
crypto isakmp policy 20
 authentication pre-share
 lifetime 10000
crypto isakmp key 1234567890 address 171.69.224.33
```

## CHAPTER 31

Certification Authority Interoperability Commands

This chapter describes certification authority (CA) interoperability commands. CA interoperability is provided in support of the IP Security (IPSec) standard. CA interoperability permits Cisco IOS devices and CAs to communicate so that a Cisco IOS device can obtain and use digital certificates from the CA. Although IPSec can be implemented in your network without the use of a CA, using a CA provides manageability and scalability for IPSec.

Without CA interoperability, Cisco IOS devices could not use CAs when deploying IPSec. CAs provide a manageable, scalable solution for IPSec networks.

You can search online at www.cisco.com to find complete descriptions of other commands used when configuring CA interoperability.

For configuration information, refer to Chapter 30, "Configuring Certification Authority Interoperability."

certificate

To manually add certificates, use the **certificate** certificate chain configuration command. Use the **no** form of this command to delete your router's certificate or any RA certificates stored on your router.

> **certificate** *certificate-serial-number*
> **no certificate** *certificate-serial-number*

Syntax

Description

certificate-serial-number

Specifies the serial number of the certificate to add or delete.

Default

There are no defaults for this command.

Command Mode

Certificate chain configuration (config-cert-chain)

Usage Guidelines

This command first appeared in Cisco IOS Release 11.3 T.

You could use this command to manually specify a certificate. However, this command is rarely used in this manner. Instead, this command is usually used only to delete certificates.

Example

The following example deletes the router's certificate. In this example, the router had a general-purpose RSA key pair with one corresponding certificate. The **show** command is used in this example to determine the serial number of the certificate to be deleted.

```
myrouter# show crypto ca certificates

Certificate
  Subject Name
    Name: myrouter.companyx.com
    IP Address: 10.0.0.1
  Status: Available
  Certificate Serial Number: 0123456789ABCDEF0123456789ABCDEF
  Key Usage: General Purpose

CA Certificate
  Status: Available
  Certificate Serial Number: 3051DF7123BEE31B8341DFE4B3A338E5F
  Key Usage: Not Set

myrouter# configure terminal
myrouter(config)# crypto ca certificate chain myca
myrouter(config-cert-chain)# no certificate 0123456789ABCDEF0123456789ABCDEF
% Are you sure you want to remove the certificate [yes/no]? yes
% Be sure to ask the CA administrator to revoke this certificate.
myrouter(config-cert-chain)# exit
myrouter(config)#
```

Related Commands

You can search online at www.cisco.com to find documentation of related commands.

crypto ca certificate chain

crl optional

To allow other peers' certificates to still be accepted by your router even if the appropriate certificate revocation list (CRL) is not accessible to your router, use the **crl optional** ca-identity configuration command. Use the **no** form of the command to return to the default behavior in which CRL checking is mandatory before your router can accept a certificate.

> **crl optional**
> **no crl optional**

Syntax Description

There are no arguments or keywords with this command.

Default

The router must have and check the appropriate CRL before accepting another IPSec peer's certificate.

Command Mode

ca-identity configuration

Usage Guidelines

This command first appeared in Cisco IOS Release 11.3 T.

When your router receives a certificate from a peer, it will download a CRL from either the CA or a CRL distribution point as designated in the peer's certificate. Your router then checks the CRL to make sure the certificate the peer sent has not been revoked. (If the certificate appears on the CRL, your router will not accept the certificate and will not authenticate the peer.)

With CA systems that support registration authorities (RAs), multiple CRLs exist and the peer's certificate will indicate which CRL applies and should be downloaded by your router.

If your router does not have the applicable CRL and is unable to obtain one, your router will reject the peer's certificate—unless you include the **crl optional** command in your configuration. If you use the **crl optional** command, your router will still try to obtain a CRL, but if it cannot obtain a CRL, it can accept the peer's certificate anyway.

When your router receives additional certificates from peers, your router will continue to attempt to download the appropriate CRL, even if it was previously unsuccessful and even if the **crl optional** command is enabled. The **crl optional** command only specifies that when the router cannot obtain the CRL, the router is not forced to reject a peer's certificate outright.

Example

The following example declares a CA and permits your router to accept certificates when CRLs are not obtainable. This example also specifies a nonstandard retry period and retry count.

```
crypto ca identity myca
 enrollment url http://ca_server
 enrollment retry-period 20
 enrollment retry-count 100
 crl optional
```

Related Commands

You can search online at www.cisco.com to find documentation of related commands.

crypto ca identity

crypto ca authenticate

To authenticate the CA (by getting the CA's certificate), use the **crypto ca authenticate** global configuration command.

> **crypto ca authenticate** *name*

Syntax	Description
name	Specifies the name of the CA. This is the same name used when the CA was declared with the **crypto ca identity** command.

Default

There are no defaults for this command.

Command Mode

Global configuration

Usage Guidelines

This command first appeared in Cisco IOS Release 11.3 T.

This command is required when you initially configure CA support at your router.

This command authenticates the CA to your router by obtaining the CA's self-signed certificate, which contains the CA's public key. Because the CA signs its own certificate, you should manually authenticate the CA's public key by contacting the CA administrator when you perform this command.

If you are using RA mode (using the **enrollment mode ra** command) when you issue the **crypto ca authenticate** command, then RA signing and encryption certificates will be returned from the CA as well as the CA certificate.

This command is not saved to the router configuration. However, the public keys embedded in the received CA (and RA) certificates are saved to the configuration as part of the RSA public key record (called the *RSA public key chain*).

If the CA does not respond by a timeout period after this command is issued, the terminal control will be returned so that it will not be tied up. If this happens, you must re-enter the command.

Example

In this example, the router requests the CA's certificate. The CA sends its certificate, and the router prompts the administrator to verify the CA's certificate by checking the CA certificate's fingerprint. The CA administrator can also view the CA certificate's fingerprint, so you should compare what the CA administrator sees to what the router displays on the screen. If the fingerprint on the router's screen matches the fingerprint viewed by the CA administrator, you should accept the certificate as valid.

```
myrouter# crypto ca authenticate myca
Certificate has the following attributes:
Fingerprint: 0123 4567 89AB CDEF 0123
Do you accept this certificate? [yes/no] y
myrouter#
```

Related Commands

You can search online at www.cisco.com to find documentation of related commands.

crypto ca identity
show crypto ca certificates

crypto ca certificate chain

To enter the certificate chain configuration mode, use the **crypto ca certificate chain** global configuration command. (You need to be in certificate chain configuration mode to delete certificates.)

> **crypto ca certificate chain** *name*

Syntax	Description
name	Specifies the name of the CA. Use the same name as when you declared the CA using the **crypto ca identity** command.

Default

There are no defaults for this command.

Command Mode

Global configuration.

Usage Guidelines

This command first appeared in Cisco IOS Release 11.3 T.

This command puts you into certificate chain configuration mode. When you are in certificate chain configuration mode, you can delete certificates using the **certificate** command.

Example

The following example deletes the router's certificate. In this example, the router had a general-purpose RSA key pair with one corresponding certificate. The **show** command is used to determine the serial number of the certificate to be deleted.

```
myrouter# show crypto ca certificates

Certificate
  Subject Name
    Name: myrouter.companyx.com
    IP Address: 10.0.0.1
  Status: Available
  Certificate Serial Number: 0123456789ABCDEF0123456789ABCDEF
  Key Usage: General Purpose

CA Certificate
  Status: Available
  Certificate Serial Number: 3051DF7123BEE31B8341DFE4B3A338E5F
  Key Usage: Not Set

myrouter# configure terminal
myrouter(config)# crypto ca certificate chain myca
myrouter(config-cert-chain)# no certificate 0123456789ABCDEF0123456789ABCDEF
% Are you sure you want to remove the certificate [yes/no]? yes
% Be sure to ask the CA administrator to revoke this certificate.
myrouter(config-cert-chain)# exit
myrouter(config)#
```

Related Commands

You can search online at www.cisco.com to find documentation of related commands.

certificate

crypto ca certificate query

To specify that certificates and CRLs should not be stored locally but retrieved from the CA when needed, use the **crypto ca certificate query** global configuration command. This command puts the router into query mode. Use the **no** form of this command to cause certificates and CRLs to be stored locally (the default).

> **crypto ca certificate query**
> **no crypto ca certificate query**

Syntax Description

This command has no arguments or keywords.

Default

Certificates and CRLs are stored locally in the router's NVRAM.

Command Mode

Global configuration

Usage Guidelines

This command first appeared in Cisco IOS Release 11.3 T.

Normally, certain certificates and CRLs are stored locally in the router's NVRAM, and each certificate and CRL uses a moderate amount of memory.

To save NVRAM space, you can use this command to put the router into query mode, which prevents certificates and CRLs from being stored locally; instead, they are retrieved from the CA when needed. This saves NVRAM space but could result in a slight performance impact.

Examples

This example prevents certificates and CRLs from being stored locally on the router; instead, they are retrieved from the CA when needed:

```
crypto ca certificate query
```

crypto ca crl request

To request that a new CRL be obtained immediately from the CA, use the **crypto ca crl request** global configuration command. Use this command only when your CA does not support an RA.

> **crypto ca crl request** *name*.

Syntax	Description
name	Specifies the name of the CA. This is the same name used when the CA was declared with the **crypto ca identity** command.

Part
IV

Command Reference

Default

Normally, the router requests a new CRL only after the existing one expires.

Command Mode

Global configuration

Usage Guidelines

This command first appeared in Cisco IOS Release 11.3 T.

Use this command only if your CA does not support an RA.

A CRL lists all the network's devices' certificates that have been revoked. Revoked certificates will not be honored by your router; therefore, any IPSec device with a revoked certificate cannot exchange IPSec traffic with your router.

The first time your router receives a certificate from a peer, it will download a CRL from the CA. Your router then checks the CRL to make sure the peer's certificate has not been revoked. (If the certificate appears on the CRL, it will not accept the certificate and will not authenticate the peer.)

A CRL can be reused with subsequent certificates until the CRL expires. If your router receives a peer's certificate after the applicable CRL has expired, it will download the new CRL.

If your router has a CRL that has not yet expired, but you suspect that the CRL's contents are out of date, use the **crypto ca crl request** command to request that the latest CRL be immediately downloaded to replace the old CRL.

This command is not saved to the configuration.

Example

The following example immediately downloads the latest CRL to your router:

```
crypto ca crl request
```

crypto ca enroll

To obtain your router's certificate(s) from the CA, use the **crypto ca enroll** global configuration command. Use the **no** form of this command to delete a current enrollment request.

> **crypto ca enroll** *name*
> **no crypto ca enroll** *name*

Syntax   Description

name   Specifies the name of the CA. Use the same name as when you declared the CA
                using the **crypto ca identity** command.

Default

There are no defaults for this command.

Command Mode

Global configuration

Usage Guidelines

This command first appeared in Cisco IOS Release 11.3 T.

This command requests certificates from the CA for all of your router's RSA key pairs. This task is also known as *enrolling* with the CA. (Technically, enrolling and obtaining certificates are two separate events, but they both occur when this command is issued.)

Your router needs a signed certificate from the CA for each of your router's RSA key pairs; if you previously generated general-purpose keys, this command will obtain the one certificate corresponding to the one general-purpose RSA key pair. If you previously generated special-usage keys, this command will obtain two certificates corresponding to each of the special-usage RSA key pairs.

If you already have a certificate for your keys, you will be unable to complete this command; instead, you will be prompted to remove the existing certificate first. (You can remove existing certificates with the **no certificate** command.)

The **crypto ca enroll** command is not saved in the router configuration.

NOTE	If your router reboots after you issue the **crypto ca enroll** command but before you receive the certificate(s), you must reissue the command.

Responding to Prompts

When you issue the **crypto ca enroll** command, you are prompted a number of times.

First, you are prompted to create a challenge password. This password can be up to 80 characters in length and is necessary in the event that you need to revoke your router's certificate(s). When you ask the CA administrator to revoke your certificate, you must supply this challenge password as a protection against fraudulent or mistaken revocation requests.

NOTE	This password is not stored anywhere, so you need to remember this password.

If you lose the password, the CA administrator may still be able to revoke the router's certificate, but will require further manual authentication of the router administrator identity.

You are also prompted to indicate whether your router's serial number should be included in the obtained certificate. The serial number is not used by IPSec or IKE, but may be used by the CA to either authenticate certificates or to later associate a certificate with a particular router. (Note that the serial number stored is the serial number of the internal board, not the one on the enclosure.) Ask your CA administrator if serial numbers should be included. If you are in doubt, include the serial number.

Normally, you would not include the IP address because the IP address binds the certificate more tightly to a specific entity. Also, if the router is moved, you would need to issue a new certificate. Finally, a router has multiple IP addresses, any of which might be used with IPSec.

If you indicate that the IP address should be included, you will then be prompted to specify the interface of the IP address. This interface should correspond to the interface to which you apply your crypto map set. If you apply crypto map sets to more than one interface, specify the interface that you name in the **crypto map local-address** command.

Example

In this example, a router with a general-purpose RSA key pair requests a certificate from the CA. When the router displays the certificate fingerprint, the administrator verifies this number by calling the CA administrator, who checks the number. If fingerprint is correct, the router administrator accepts the certificate.

There can be a delay between when the router administrator sends the request and when the certificate is actually received by the router. The amount of delay depends on the CA method of operation:

```
myrouter(config)# crypto ca enroll myca
%
% Start certificate enrollment ..
% Create a challenge password. You will need to verbally provide this
    password to the CA Administrator in order to revoke your certificate.
    For security reasons your password will not be saved in the configuration.
    Please make a note of it.

Password: <mypassword>
Re-enter password: <mypassword>

% The subject name in the certificate will be: myrouter.companyx.com
% Include the router serial number in the subject name? [yes/no]: yes
% The serial number in the certificate will be: 03433678
% Include an IP address in the subject name [yes/no]? yes
Interface: ethernet0/0
Request certificate from CA [yes/no]? yes
% Certificate request sent to Certificate Authority
% The certificate request fingerprint will be displayed.
% The 'show crypto ca certificate' command will also show the fingerprint.

myrouter(config)#
```

Some time later, the router receives the certificate from the CA and displays this confirmation message:

```
myrouter(config)#    Fingerprint: 01234567 89ABCDEF FEDCBA98 75543210

%CRYPTO-6-CERTRET: Certificate received from Certificate Authority

myrouter(config)#
```

If necessary, the router administrator can verify the displayed fingerprint with the CA administrator.

If there is a problem with the certificate request and the certificate is not granted, the following message is displayed on the console instead:

```
%CRYPTO-6-CERTREJ: Certificate enrollment request was rejected by Certificate Authority
```

The subject name in the certificate is automatically assigned to be the same as the RSA key pair's name. In the above example, the RSA key pair is named *myrouter.domain.com*. (The router assigned this name.)

Requesting certificates for a router with special-usage keys would be the same as the previous example, except that two certificates would have been returned by the CA. When the router received the two certificates, the router would have displayed the same confirmation message:

```
%CRYPTO-6-CERTRET: Certificate received from Certificate Authority
```

Related Commands

You can search online at www.cisco.com to find documentation of related commands.

show crypto ca certificates

crypto ca identity

To declare the CA your router should use, use the **crypto ca identity** global configuration command. Use the **no** form of this command to delete all identity information and certificates associated with the CA.

> **crypto ca identity** *name*
> **no crypto ca identity** *name*

Syntax   Description

name   Creates a name for the CA. (If you previously declared the CA and just want to update its characteristics, specify the name you previously created.) The CA might require a particular name, such as its domain name.

Default

Your router does not know about any CA until you declare one with this command.

Command Mode

Global configuration

Usage Guidelines

This command first appeared in Cisco IOS Release 11.3 T.

Use this command to declare a CA. Using this command puts you into the ca-identity configuration mode, where you can specify characteristics for the CA with the following commands:

- **enrollment url** (Specify the URL of the CA—always required.)

- **enrollment mode ra** (Specify RA mode, required only if your CA system provides an RA).

- **query url** (Specify the URL of the LDAP server; required only if your CA supports an RA and the LDAP protocol.)

- **enrollment retry-period** (Specify a period of time the router should wait between sending certificate request retries—optional.)

- **enrollment retry-count** (Specify how many certificate request retries your router will send before giving up—optional.)

- **crl optional** (Specify that your router can still accept other peers' certificates if the CRL is not accessible—optional.)

Examples

The following example declares a CA and identifies characteristics of the CA. In this example, the name *myca* is created for the CA, which is located at http://ca_server.

The CA does not use an RA or LDAP, and the CA's scripts are stored in the default location. This is the minimum possible configuration required to declare a CA.

```
crypto ca identity myca
 enrollment url http://ca_server
```

The following example declares a CA when the CA uses an RA. The CA's scripts are stored in the default location, and the CA uses the Certificate Enrollment Protocol (CEP) instead of LDAP. This is the minimum possible configuration required to declare a CA that uses an RA.

```
crypto ca identity myca_with_ra
 enrollment url http://ca_server
 enrollment mode ra
 query url ldap://serverx
```

The following example declares a CA that uses an RA and a nonstandard cgi-bin script location. This example also specifies a non-standard retry period and retry count and permits the router to accept certificates when CRLs are not obtainable.

```
crypto ca identity myca_with_ra
 enrollment url http://companyx_ca/cgi-bin/somewhere/scripts.exe
 enrollment mode ra
 query url ldap://serverx
 enrollment retry-period 20
 enrollment retry-count 100
 crl optional
```

In the previous example, if the router does not receive a certificate from the CA within 20 minutes of sending a certificate request, the router re-sends the certificate request. The router keeps sending a certificate request every 20 minutes until a certificate is received or until 100 requests have been sent.

If the CA cgi-bin script location is not /cgi-bin/pkiclient.exe at the CA (the default CA cgi-bin script location), you need to also include the nonstandard script location in the URL, in the form of http://CA_name/script_location where script_location is the full path to the CA scripts.

Related Commands

You can search online at www.cisco.com to find documentation of related commands.

enrollment url
enrollment mode ra
query url
enrollment retry-period
enrollment retry-count
crl optional

crypto key generate rsa

To generate RSA key pairs, use the **crypto key generate rsa** global configuration command.

> **crypto key generate rsa** [**usage-keys**]

Syntax	Description
usage-keys	(Optional) Specifies that two special-usage key pairs should be generated instead of one general-purpose key pair.

Default

RSA key pairs do not exist. If the **usage-keys** keyword is not used, general-purpose keys will be generated.

Command Mode

Global configuration

Usage Guidelines

This command first appeared in Cisco IOS Release 11.3 T.

Use this command to generate RSA key pairs for your Cisco device (such as a router).

RSA keys are generated in pairs—one public RSA key and one private RSA key.

If your router already has RSA keys when you issue this command, you will be warned and prompted to replace the existing keys with new keys.

NOTE	Before issuing this command, make sure your router has a hostname and an IP domain name configured (with the **hostname** and **ip domain-name** commands). You will be unable to complete the **crypto key generate rsa** command without a hostname and IP domain name.

This command is not saved in the router configuration; however, the keys generated by this command are saved in the private configuration in NVRAM (which is never displayed to the user or backed up to another device).

There are two mutually exclusive styles of RSA key pairs: special-usage keys and general-purpose keys. When you generate RSA key pairs, you will be prompted to select whether to generate special-usage keys or general-purpose keys.

Special-Usage Keys

If you generate special-usage keys, two pairs of RSA keys will be generated. One pair will be used with any IKE policy that specifies RSA signatures as the authentication method, and the other pair used with any IKE policy that specifies RSA encrypted nonces as the authentication method. (You configure RSA signatures or RSA encrypted nonces in your IKE policies as described in Chapter 32, "Configuring Internet Key Exchange Security Protocol.")

A CA is used only with IKE policies specifying RSA signatures, not with IKE policies specifying RSA encrypted nonces. (However, you could specify more than one IKE policy and have RSA signatures specified in one policy and RSA encrypted nonces in another policy.)

If you plan to have both types of RSA authentication methods in your IKE policies, you might prefer to generate special-usage keys. With special-usage keys, each key is not unnecessarily exposed. (Without special-usage keys, one key is used for both purposes, increasing that key's exposure.)

General-Purpose Keys

If you generate general-purpose keys, only one pair of RSA keys will be generated. This pair will be used with IKE policies specifying either RSA signatures or RSA encrypted nonces. Therefore, a general-purpose key pair might get used more frequently than a special-usage key pair.

Modulus Length

When you generate RSA keys, you will be prompted to enter a modulus length. A longer modulus could offer stronger security, but takes longer to generate (see Table 31-1 for sample times) and takes longer to use. Below 512 is normally not recommended. (In certain situations, the shorter modulus may not function properly with IKE, so Cisco recommends using a minimum modulus of 1024.)

Table 31-1 *Sample Times Required to Generate RSA Keys*

	Modulus Length			
Router	**360 bits**	**512 bits**	**1024 bits**	**2048 bits**
Cisco 2500	11 seconds	20 seconds	4 minutes, 38 seconds	Longer than 1 hour
Cisco 4700	Less than 1 second	1 second	4 seconds	50 seconds

Examples

This example generates special-usage RSA keys:

```
myrouter(config)# crypto key generate rsa usage-keys
The name for the keys will be: myrouter.companyx.com

Choose the size of the key modulus in the range of 360 to 2048 for your Signature Keys.
Choosing a key modulus greater than 512 may take a few minutes.
How many bits in the modulus[512]? <return>
Generating RSA keys.... [OK].

Choose the size of the key modulus in the range of 360 to 2048 for your Encryption Keys.
Choosing a key modulus greater than 512 may take a few minutes.
How many bits in the modulus[512]? <return>
Generating RSA keys.... [OK].

myrouter(config)#
```

This example generates general-purpose RSA keys:

```
myrouter(config)# crypto key generate rsa
The name for the keys will be: myrouter.companyx.com

Choose the size of the key modulus in the range of 360 to 2048 for your General Purpose Keys.
Choosing a key modulus greater than 512 may take a few minutes.
How many bits in the modulus[512]? <return>
Generating RSA keys.... [OK].

myrouter(config)#
```

NOTE You cannot generate both special-usage and general-purpose keys; you can only generate one or the other.

Related Commands

You can search online at www.cisco.com to find documentation of related commands.

show crypto key mypubkey rsa

crypto key zeroize rsa

To delete all of your router's RSA keys, use the **crypto key zeroize rsa** global configuration command.

> **crypto key zeroize rsa**

Syntax Description

There are no arguments or keywords for this command.

Default

There are no defaults for this command.

Command Mode

Global configuration.

Usage Guidelines

This command first appeared in Cisco IOS Release 11.3 T.

This command deletes all RSA keys that were previously generated by your router. If you issue this command, you must also perform two additional tasks:

- Ask the CA administrator to revoke your router's certificates at the CA; you must supply the challenge password you created when you originally obtained the router's certificates with the **crypto ca enroll** command.

- Manually remove the router's certificates from the configuration using the **certificate** command.

NOTE   This command cannot be undone (after you save your configuration), and after RSA keys have been deleted you cannot use certificates or the CA or participate in certificate exchanges with other IPSec peers unless you reconfigure CA interoperability by regenerating RSA keys, getting the CA's certificate, and requesting your own certificate again.

This command is not saved to the configuration.

Example

This example deletes the general-purpose RSA key pair that was previously generated for the router. After deleting the RSA key pair, the administrator contacts the CA administrator and requests that the router's certificate be revoked. The administrator then deletes the router's certificate from the configuration.

```
crypto key zeroize rsa
crypto ca certificate chain
 no certificate
```

Related Commands

You can search online at www.cisco.com to find documentation of related commands.

crypto ca certificate chain
certificate

enrollment mode ra

To turn on RA mode, use the **enrollment mode ra** ca-identity configuration command. Use the **no** form of the command to turn off RA mode.

enrollment mode ra
no enrollment mode ra

Syntax Description

This command has no arguments or keywords.

Default

RA mode is turned off.

Command Mode

ca-identity configuration

Usage Guidelines

This command first appeared in Cisco IOS Release 11.3 T.

This command is required if your CA system provides an RA. This command provides compatibility with RA systems.

Example

The following is an example of the minimum configuration required to declare a CA when the CA provides an RA:

```
crypto ca identity myca
 enrollment url http://ca_server
 enrollment mode ra
 query url ldap://serverx
```

Related Commands

You can search online at www.cisco.com to find documentation of related commands.

crypto ca identity

enrollment retry-count

To specify how many times a router will resend a certificate request, use the **enrollment retry-count** ca-identity configuration command. Use the **no** form of the command to reset the retry count to the default of 0, which indicates an infinite number of retries.

> **enrollment retry-count** *number*
> **no enrollment retry-count**

Syntax	Description
number	Specifies how many times the router will resend a certificate request when the router does not receive a certificate from the CA from the previous request.
	Specifies from 1 to 100 retries.

Default

The router will send the CA another certificate request until a valid certificate is received (no limit to the number of retries).

Command Mode

ca-identity configuration

Usage Guidelines

This command first appeared in Cisco IOS Release 11.3 T.

After requesting a certificate, the router waits to receive a certificate from the CA. If the router does not receive a certificate within a period of time (the retry period) the router sends another certificate request. The router continues to send requests until it receives a valid certificate, until the CA returns an enrollment error, or until the configured number of retries (the retry count) is exceeded. By default, the router keeps sending requests forever, but you can change this to a finite number with this command.

A retry count of 0 indicates that there is no limit to the number of times the router should resend the certificate request. By default, the retry count is 0.

Examples

This example declares a CA, changes the retry period to 10 minutes, and changes the retry count to 60 retries. The router will resend the certificate request every 10 minutes until the router receives the certificate or until approximately 10 hours pass since the original request was sent, whichever occurs first. (10 minutes x 60 tries = 600 minutes = 10 hours.)

```
crypto ca identity myca
 enrollment url http://ca_server
 enrollment retry-period 10
 enrollment retry-count 60
```

Related Commands

You can search online at www.cisco.com to find documentation of related commands.

crypto ca identity
enrollment retry-period

enrollment retry-period

To specify the wait period between certificate request retries, use the **enrollment retry-period** ca-identity configuration command. Use the **no** form of the command to reset the retry period to the default of 1 minute.

> **enrollment retry-period** *minutes*
> **no enrollment retry-period**

Syntax	Description
minutes	Specifies the number of minutes the router waits before resending a certificate request to the CA when the router does not receive a certificate from the CA by the previous request.
	Specifies from 1 to 60 minutes. By default, the router retries every 1 minute.

Default

The router will send the CA another certificate request every 1 minute until a valid certificate is received.

Command Mode

ca-identity configuration

Usage Guidelines

This command first appeared in Cisco IOS Release 11.3 T.

After requesting a certificate, the router waits to receive a certificate from the CA. If the router does not receive a certificate within a period of time (the retry period), the router will send another certificate request. The router will continue to send requests until it receives a valid certificate, until the CA returns an enrollment error or until the configured number of retries is exceeded. (By default, the router will keep sending requests forever, but you can change this to a finite number of permitted retries with the **enrollment retry-count** command.)

Use the **enrollment retry-period** command to change the retry period from the default of 1 minute between retries.

Example

This example declares a CA and changes the retry period to 5 minutes:

```
crypto ca identity myca
 enrollment url http://ca_server
 enrollment retry-period 5
```

Related Commands

You can search online at www.cisco.com to find documentation of related commands.

crypto ca identity
enrollment retry-count

enrollment url

To specify the CA location by naming the CA's URL, use the **enrollment url** ca-identity configuration command. Use the **no** form of this command to remove the CA's URL from the configuration.

> **enrollment url** *url*
> **no enrollment url** *url*

Syntax   Description

url   Specifies the URL of the CA where your router should send certificate requests, for example, http://ca_server.

This URL must be in the form of http://CA_name where CA_name is the CA's host DNS name or IP address.

If the CA cgi-bin script location is not /cgi-bin/pkiclient.exe at the CA (the default CA cgi-bin script location) you need to also include the non-standard script location in the URL, in the form of http://CA_name/script_location where script_location is the full path to the CA scripts.

Default

Your router does not know the CA URL until you specify it with this command.

Command Mode

ca-identity configuration

Usage Guidelines

This command first appeared in Cisco IOS Release 11.3 T.

Use this command to specify the CA's URL. This command is required when you declare a CA with the **crypto ca identity** command.

The URL must include the CA script location if the CA scripts are not loaded into the default cgi-script location. The CA administrator should be able to tell you where the CA scripts are located.

To change a CA's URL, repeat the **enrollment url** command to overwrite the older URL.

Example

The following is an example of the absolute minimum configuration required to declare a CA:

```
crypto ca identity myca
 enrollment url http://ca_server
```

Related Commands

You can search online at www.cisco.com to find documentation of related commands.

crypto ca identity

query url

To specify LDAP protocol support, use the **query url** ca-identity configuration command. Use the **no** form of this command to remove the query URL from the configuration and specify the default query protocol, CEP.

> **query url** *url*
> **no query url** *url*

Syntax   Description

url   Specifies the URL of the LDAP server; for example, ldap://another_server.

                This URL must be in the form of ldap://server_name where server_name is the host DNS name or IP address of the LDAP server.

Default

The router uses CEP.

Command Mode

ca-identity configuration

Usage Guidelines

This command first appeared in Cisco IOS Release 11.3 T.

This command is required if the CA supports an RA and LDAP; LDAP is a query protocol used when the router retrieves certificates and CRLs. The CA administrator should be able to tell you whether the CA supports LDAP or CEP; if the CA supports the LDAP protocol, the CA administrator can tell you the LDAP location where certificates and CRLs should be retrieved.

To change the query URL, repeat the **query url** command to overwrite the older URL.

This command is only valid if you also use the **enrollment mode ra** command.

Example

The following is an example of a configuration required to declare a CA when the CA supports LDAP:

```
crypto ca identity myca
 enrollment url http://ca_server
 enrollment mode ra
 query url ldap://bobs_server
```

Related Commands

You can search online at www.cisco.com to find documentation of related commands.

crypto ca identity

show crypto ca certificates

To view information about your certificate, the CA's certificate, and any RA certificates, use the **show crypto ca certificates** EXEC command.

> **show crypto ca certificates**

Syntax Description

This command has no arguments or keywords.

Command Mode

EXEC

Usage Guidelines

This command first appeared in Cisco IOS Release 11.3 T.

This command shows information about the following certificates:

● Your certificate, if you have requested one from the CA (see the **crypto ca enroll** command)

● The CA's certificate, if you have received the CA's certificate (see the **crypto ca authenticate** command)

● RA certificates, if you have received RA certificates (see the **crypto ca authenticate** command)

Sample Display

The following is sample output from the **show crypto ca certificates** command after you authenticated the CA by requesting the CA's certificate and public key with the **crypto ca authenticate** command:

```
CA Certificate
  Status: Available
  Certificate Serial Number: 3051DF7123BEE31B8341DFE4B3A338E5F
  Key Usage: Not Set
```

The CA certificate might show Key Usage as Not Set.

The following is sample output from the **show crypto ca certificates** command, and shows the router's certificate and the CA's certificate. In this example, a single, general-purpose RSA key pair was previously generated and a certificate was requested but not received for that key pair:

```
Certificate
  Subject Name
    Name: myrouter.companyx.com
    IP Address: 10.0.0.1
    Serial Number: 04806682
  Status: Pending
  Key Usage: General Purpose
    Fingerprint: 428125BD A3419600 3F6C7831 6CD8FA95 00000000

CA Certificate
  Status: Available
  Certificate Serial Number: 3051DF7123BEE31B8341DFE4B3A338E5F
  Key Usage: Not Set
```

Note that in the previous sample, the router's certificate Status shows Pending. After the router receives its certificate from the CA, the Status field changes to Available in the **show** output.

The following is sample output from the **show crypto ca certificates** command, and shows two router's certificates and the CA's certificate. In this example, special-usage RSA key pairs were previously generated, and a certificate was requested and received for each key pair:

```
Certificate
  Subject Name
    Name: myrouter.companyx.com
    IP Address: 10.0.0.1
```

```
  Status: Available
  Certificate Serial Number: 428125BDA34196003F6C78316CD8FA95
  Key Usage: Signature

Certificate
  Subject Name
    Name: myrouter.companyx.com
    IP Address: 10.0.0.1
  Status: Available
  Certificate Serial Number: AB352356AFCD0395E333CCFD7CD33897
  Key Usage: Encryption

CA Certificate
  Status: Available
  Certificate Serial Number: 3051DF7123BEE31B8341DFE4B3A338E5F
  Key Usage: Not Set
```

The following is sample output from the **show crypto ca certificates** command when the CA supports an RA. In this example, the CA and RA certificates were previously requested with the **crypto ca authenticate** command:

```
CA Certificate
  Status: Available
  Certificate Serial Number: 3051DF7123BEE31B8341DFE4B3A338E5F
  Key Usage: Not Set

RA Signature Certificate
  Status: Available
  Certificate Serial Number: 34BCF8A0
  Key Usage: Signature

RA KeyEncipher Certificate
  Status: Available
  Certificate Serial Number: 34BCF89F
  Key Usage: Encryption
```

Related Commands

You can search online at www.cisco.com to find documentation of related commands.

crypto ca enroll
crypto ca authenticate

Configuring Internet Key Exchange Security Protocol

This chapter describes how to configure the Internet Key Exchange (IKE) protocol. IKE is a key management protocol standard that is used in conjunction with the IPSec standard. IPSec is an IP security feature that provides robust authentication and encryption of IP packets.

IPSec can be configured without IKE, but IKE enhances IPSec by providing additional features, flexibility, and ease of configuration for the IPSec standard.

IKE is a hybrid protocol which implements the Oakley key exchange and Skeme key exchange inside the Internet Security Association and Key Management Protocol (ISAKMP) framework. (ISAKMP, Oakley, and Skeme are security protocols implemented by IKE.)

For a complete description of the IKE commands used in this chapter, refer to Chapter 33, "Internet Key Exchange Security Protocol Commands." To locate documentation of other commands that appear in this chapter, you can search online at www.cisco.com.

IKE Overview

IKE automatically negotiates IPSec security associations (SAs) and enables IPSec secure communications without costly manual preconfiguration.

Specifically, IKE provides these benefits:

- It eliminates the need to manually specify all the IPSec security parameters in the crypto maps at both peers.

- It allows you to specify a lifetime for the IPSec security association.

- It allows encryption keys to change during IPSec sessions.

- It allows IPSec to provide anti-replay services.

- It permits certification authority (CA) support for a manageable, scalable IPSec implementation.

- It allows dynamic authentication of peers.

Supported Standards

Cisco implements the following standards:

- **IPSec**—IPSec is a framework of open standards that provides data confidentiality, data integrity, and data authentication between participating peers. IPSec provides these security services at the IP layer; it uses IKE to handle negotiation of protocols and algorithms based on local policy, and to generate the encryption and authentication keys to be used by IPSec. IPSec can be used to protect one or more data flows between a pair of hosts, between a pair of security gateways, or between a security gateway and a host.

  For more information on IPSec, see Chapter 28, "Configuring IPSec Network Security."

- **IKE**—This hybrid protocol that implements Oakley and Skeme key exchanges inside the ISAKMP framework can be used with other protocols, but its initial implementation is with the IPSec protocol. IKE provides authentication of the IPSec peers, negotiates IPSec keys, and negotiates IPSec security associations.

  IKE is implemented per the latest version of the Internet Draft "The Internet Key Exchange" (draft-ietf-ipsec-isakmp-oakley-xx.txt).

- **ISAKMP**—This protocol framework which defines payload formats, the mechanics of implementing a key exchange protocol, and the negotiation of a security association.

  ISAKMP is implemented per the latest version of the Internet Draft "Internet Security Association and Key Management Protocol (ISAKMP)" (draft-ietf-ipsec-isakmp-xx.txt).

- **Oakley**—A key exchange protocol that defines how to derive authenticated keying material.

- **Skeme**—A key exchange protocol that defines how to derive authenticated keying material, with rapid key refreshment.

The component technologies implemented for use by IKE include the following:

- **DES**—The Data Encryption Standard (DES) is used to encrypt packet data. IKE implements the 56-bit DES-CBC with Explicit IV standard.

  Cipher Block Chaining (CBC) requires an initialization vector (IV) to start encryption. The IV is explicitly given in the IPSec packet.

- **Diffie-Hellman**—A public-key cryptography protocol which allows two parties to establish a shared secret over an unsecure communications channel. Diffie-Hellman is used within IKE to establish session keys. 768-bit and 1024-bit Diffie-Hellman groups are supported.

- **MD5 (HMAC variant)**—MD5 (Message Digest 5) is a hash algorithm used to authenticate packet data. HMAC is a variant which provides an additional level of hashing.

- **SHA (HMAC variant)**—SHA (Secure Hash Algorithm) is a hash algorithm used to authenticate packet data. HMAC is a variant which provides an additional level of hashing.

- **RSA signatures** and **RSA encrypted nonces**—RSA is the public key cryptographic system developed by Ron Rivest, Adi Shamir, and Leonard Adleman. RSA signatures provides non-repudiation while RSA encrypted nonces provide repudiation.

IKE interoperates with the following standard:

- **X.509v3 certificates**—Used with the IKE protocol when authentication requires public keys. This certificate support allows the protected network to scale by providing the equivalent of a digital ID card to each device. When two devices wish to communicate, they exchange digital certificates to prove their identity (thus removing the need to manually exchange public keys with each peer or to manually specify a shared key at each peer).

List of Terms

anti-replay—A security service in which the receiver can reject old or duplicate packets in order to protect itself against replay attacks. IPSec provides optional anti-replay services by use of a sequence number combined with the use of authentication.

data authentication—Includes two concepts:

- Data integrity (verify that data has not been altered).

- Data origin authentication (verify that the data was actually sent by the claimed sender).

Data authentication can refer either to integrity alone or to both of these concepts (although data origin authentication is dependent upon data integrity).

peer—In the context of this chapter, a router or other device that participates in IPSec and IKE.

perfect forward secrecy (PFS)—A cryptographic characteristic associated with a derived shared secret value. With PFS, if one key is compromised, previous and subsequent keys are not also compromised because subsequent keys are not derived from previous keys.

repudiation—A quality that prevents a third party from being able to prove that a communication between two other parties ever took place. This is a desirable quality if you do not want your communications to be traceable. **Nonrepudiation** is the opposite quality—a third party can prove that a communication between two other parties took place. Nonrepudiation is desirable if you want to be able to trace your communications and prove that they occurred.

security association—An SA describes how two or more entities will utilize security services to communicate securely. For example, an IPSec SA defines the encryption algorithm (if used), the authentication algorithm, and the shared session key to be used during the IPSec connection.

Both IPSec and IKE require and use SAs to identify the parameters of their connections. IKE can negotiate and establish its own SA. The IPSec SA is established either by IKE or by manual user configuration.

IKE Configuration Task List

To configure IKE, perform the tasks in the following sections. The tasks in the first three sections are required; the remaining may be optional, depending on what parameters are configured.

- Enabling or Disabling IKE

- Ensuring That Access Lists Are Compatible with IKE

- Creating IKE Policies

- Manually Configuring RSA Keys (Optional, depending on IKE parameters)

- Configuring Pre-Shared Keys (Optional, depending on IKE parameters)

- Clearing IKE Connections (Optional)

- Troubleshooting IKE (Optional)

For IKE configuration examples, refer to the "IKE Configuration Example" section at the end of this chapter.

Enabling or Disabling IKE

IKE is enabled by default. IKE does not have to be enabled for individual interfaces, but is enabled globally for all interfaces at the router.

If you do not want IKE to be used with your IPSec implementation, you can disable it at all IPSec peers.

If you disable IKE, you will have to make these concessions at the peers:

- You must manually specify all the IPSec security associations in the crypto maps at all peers. (Crypto map configuration is described in Chapter 28, "Configuring IPSec Network Security.")

- The peers' IPSec security associations will never time out for a given IPSec session.

- During IPSec sessions between the peers, the encryption keys will never change.

- Anti-replay services will not be available between the peers.

- CA support cannot be used.

To disable or enable IKE, use one of the following commands in global configuration mode:

Command	Purpose
no crypto isakmp enable	Disables IKE.
crypto isakmp enable	Enables IKE.

If you disable IKE, you can skip the rest of the tasks in this chapter and go directly to IPSec configuration as described in Chapter 28, "Configuring IPSec Network Security."

Ensuring That Access Lists Are Compatible with IKE

IKE negotiation uses UDP on port 500. Ensure that your access lists are configured so that UDP port 500 traffic is not blocked at interfaces used by IKE and IPSec. In some cases you might need to add a statement to your access lists to explicitly permit UDP port 500 traffic.

Creating IKE Policies

You must create IKE policies at each peer. An IKE policy defines a combination of security parameters to be used during the IKE negotiation.

To create an IKE policy, follow the guidelines in these sections:

- Why Do You Need to Create These Policies?
- What Parameters Do You Define in a Policy?
- How Do IKE Peers Agree on a Matching Policy?
- Which Value Should You Select for Each Parameter?
- Creating Policies
- Additional Configuration Required for IKE Policies

Why Do You Need to Create These Policies?

IKE negotiations must be protected, so each IKE negotiation begins by each peer agreeing on a common (shared) IKE policy. This policy states which security parameters will be used to protect subsequent IKE negotiations.

After the two peers agree on a policy, the security parameters of the policy are identified by a security association established at each peer, and these security associations apply to all subsequent IKE traffic during the negotiation.

You can create multiple, prioritized policies at each peer to ensure that at least one policy will match a remote peer's policy.

What Parameters Do You Define in a Policy?

There are five parameters to define in each IKE policy:

Parameter	Accepted Values	Keyword	Default Value
Encryption algorithm	56-bit DES-CBC	**des**	56-bit DES-CBC
Hash algorithm	SHA-1 (HMAC variant)	**sha**	SHA-1
	MD5 (HMAC variant)	**md5**	

Parameter	Accepted Values	Keyword	Default Value
Authentication method	RSA signatures	**rsa-sig**	RSA signatures
	RSA encrypted nonces	**rsa-encr**	
	Pre-shared keys	**pre-share**	
Diffie-Hellman group identifier	768-bit Diffie-Hellman or	1	768-bit Diffie-Hellman
	1024-bit Diffie-Hellman	2	
Security association's lifetime[1]	Can specify any number of seconds	-	86,400 seconds (one day)

1. For information about this lifetime and how it is used, see the command description for the **lifetime (IKE policy)** command.

These parameters apply to the IKE negotiations when the IKE security association is established.

How Do IKE Peers Agree on a Matching Policy?

When the IKE negotiation begins, IKE looks for an IKE policy that is the same on both peers. The peer that initiates the negotiation will send all its policies to the remote peer, and the remote peer will try to find a match. The remote peer looks for a match by comparing its own highest-priority policy against the other peer's received policies. The remote peer checks each of its policies in order of its priority (highest priority first) until a match is found.

A match is made when both policies from the two peers contain the same encryption, hash, authentication, and Diffie-Hellman parameter values, and when the remote peer's policy specifies a lifetime less than or equal to the lifetime in the policy being compared. (If the lifetimes are not identical, the shorter lifetime—from the remote peer's policy—will be used.)

If no acceptable match is found, IKE refuses negotiation and IPSec will not be established.

If a match is found, IKE will complete negotiation, and IPSec security associations will be created.

NOTE   Depending on which authentication method is specified in a policy, additional configuration might be required (as described in the section, "Additional Configuration Required for IKE Policies"). If a peer's policy does not have the required companion configuration, the peer will not submit the policy when attempting to find a matching policy with the remote peer.

Which Value Should You Select for Each Parameter?

You can select certain values for each parameter, per the IKE standard. But why chose one value over another?

If you are interoperating with a device that supports only one of the values for a parameter, your choice is limited to the other device's supported value. Aside from this, there is often a trade-off between security and performance, and many of these parameter values represent such a trade-off. You should evaluate the level of your network's security risks and your tolerance for these risks. Then the following tips might help you select which value to specify for each parameter:

- The encryption algorithm currently has only one option: 56-bit DES-CBC.

- The hash algorithm has two options: SHA-1 and MD5.

  MD5 has a smaller digest and is considered to be slightly faster than SHA-1. There has been a demonstrated successful (but extremely difficult) attack against MD5; however, the HMAC variant used by IKE prevents this attack.

- The authentication method has three options:

  — RSA signatures provides nonrepudiation for the IKE negotiation (you can prove to a third party after the fact that you did indeed have an IKE negotiation with the remote peer).

    RSA signatures requires use of a CA. Using a CA can dramatically improve the manageability and scalability of your IPSec network.

  — RSA encrypted nonces provides repudiation for the IKE negotiation (you cannot prove to a third party that you had an IKE negotiation with the remote peer). This is used to prevent a third party from knowing about your activity over the network.

    RSA encrypted nonces require that peers possess each other's public keys but do not use a CA. Instead, there are two ways for peers to get each others' public keys:

    1) During configuration you manually configure RSA keys (as described in the section "Manually Configuring RSA Keys") or

    2) If your local peer has previously used RSA signatures during a successful IKE negotiation with a remote peer, your local peer already possesses the remote peer's public key. (The peers' public keys are exchanged during the RSA-signatures-based IKE negotiations.)

  — Pre-shared keys are clumsy to use if your secured network is large, and do not scale well with a growing network. However, they do not require use of a CA, as do RSA signatures, and might be easier to set up in a small network with fewer than 10 nodes.

- The Diffie-Hellman group identifier has two options: 768-bit or 1024-bit Diffie-Hellman.

  1024-bit Diffie-Hellman is harder to crack, but requires more CPU time to execute.

● The security association's lifetime can be set to any value.

As a general rule, the shorter the lifetime (up to a point), the more secure your IKE negotiations will be. However, with longer lifetimes, future IPSec security associations can be set up more quickly. For more information about this parameter and how it is used, see the command description for the **lifetime (IKE policy)** command.

Creating Policies

You can create multiple IKE policies, each with a different combination of parameter values. For each policy that you create, you assign a unique priority (1 through 10,000, with 1 being the highest priority).

You can configure multiple policies on each peer—but at least one of these policies must contain exactly the same encryption, hash, authentication, and Diffie-Hellman parameter values as one of the policies on the remote peer. (The lifetime parameter does not necessarily have to be the same; see details in the section "How Do IKE Peers Agree on a Matching Policy?")

If you do not configure any policies, your router will use the default policy, which is always set to the lowest priority and contains each parameter's default value.

To configure a policy, use the following commands, starting in global configuration mode:

Step	Command	Purpose
1	**crypto isakmp policy** *priority*	Identifies the policy to create. (Each policy is uniquely identified by the priority number you assign.)
		(This command puts you into config-isakmp command mode.)
2	**encryption des**	Specifies the encryption algorithm.
3	**hash** {**sha** | **md5**}	Specifies the hash algorithm.
4	**authentication** {**rsa-sig** | **rsa-encr** | **pre-share**}	Specifies the authentication method.
5	**group** {**1** | **2**}	Specifies the Diffie-Hellman group identifier.
6	**lifetime** *seconds*	Specifies the security association's lifetime.
7	**exit**	Exits config-isakmp command mode.
8	**show crypto isakmp policy**	(Optional) Views all existing IKE policies.
		(Use this command in EXEC mode.)

If you do not specify a value for a parameter, the default value is assigned.

NOTE	The default policy and the default values for configured policies do not show up in the configuration when you issue a **show running** command. Instead, to see the default policy and any default values within configured policies, use the **show crypto isakmp policy** command.

Additional Configuration Required for IKE Policies

Depending on which authentication method you specify in your IKE policies, you need to do certain additional configuration before IKE and IPSec can successfully use the IKE policies.

Each authentication method requires additional companion configuration, as follows:

- RSA signatures method—If you specify RSA signatures as the authentication method in a policy, you must configure the peers to obtain certificates from a CA. (And, of course, the CA must be properly configured to issue the certificates.) Configure this certificate support as described in Chapter 30, "Configuring Certification Authority Interoperability."

  The certificates are used by each peer to securely exchange public keys. (RSA signatures requires that each peer has the remote peer's public signature key.) When both peers have valid certificates, they will automatically exchange public keys with each other as part of any IKE negotiation in which RSA signatures are used.

- RSA encrypted nonces method—If you specify RSA encrypted nonces as the authentication method in a policy, you need to ensure that each peer has the other peers' public keys.

  Unlike RSA signatures, the RSA encrypted nonces method does not use certificates to exchange public keys. Instead, you ensure that each peer has the others' public keys as follows:

  — Either manually configure RSA keys as described in the section "Manually Configuring RSA Keys" or

  — Ensure that an IKE exchange using RSA signatures has already occurred between the peers. (The peers' public keys are exchanged during the RSA-signatures-based IKE negotiations.)

    To make this happen, specify two policies: a higher-priority policy with RSA encrypted nonces and a lower-priority policy with RSA signatures. When IKE negotiations occur, RSA signatures will be used the first time because the peers do not yet have each others' public keys. Then, future IKE negotiations will be able to use RSA encrypted nonces because the public keys will have been exchanged.

    Of course, this alternative requires that you have Certification Authority support configured.

● Pre-shared keys authentication method—If you specify pre-shared keys as the authentication method in a policy, you must configure these pre-shared keys as described in the section, "Configuring Pre-Shared Keys."

If RSA encryption is configured and signature mode is negotiated, the peer will request both signature and encryption keys. Basically, the router will request as many keys as the configuration will support. If RSA encryption is not configured, it will just request a signature key.

Manually Configuring RSA Keys

Manually configure RSA keys when you specify RSA encrypted nonces as the authentication method in an IKE policy and you are not using a CA.

To manually configure RSA keys, perform the tasks in the following sections at each IPSec peer that uses RSA encrypted nonces in an IKE policy:

● Generating RSA Keys

● Setting ISAKMP Identity

● Specifying All the Other Peers' RSA Public Keys

Generating RSA Keys

To generate RSA keys, use the following commands starting in global configuration mode:

Step	Command	Purpose
1	**crypto key generate rsa** [*usage-keys*]	Generates RSA keys.
2	**show crypto key mypubkey rsa**	Views the generated RSA public key (in EXEC mode).

Remember to repeat these tasks at each peer (without CA support) that uses RSA encrypted nonces in an IKE policy.

Setting ISAKMP Identity

You should set the ISAKMP identity for each peer that uses pre-shared keys in an IKE policy.

When two peers use IKE to establish IPSec security associations, each peer sends its identity to the remote peer. Each peer sends either its host name or its IP address, depending on how you have the router's ISAKMP identity set.

By default, a peer's ISAKMP identity is the peer's IP address. If appropriate, you could change the identity to be the peer's host name instead. As a general rule, set all peers' identities the same way—either all peers should use their IP address, or all peers should use their host name. If some peers use their host name and some peers use their IP address to identify themselves to each other, IKE negotiations could fail if a remote peer's identity is not recognized and a DNS lookup is unable to resolve the identity.

To set a peer's ISAKMP identity, use the following commands in global configuration mode:

Step	Command	Purpose
1	**crypto isakmp identity** {**address** | **hostname**}	**At the local peer**: Specifies the peer's ISAKMP identity by IP address or by host name.[1]
2	**ip host** *hostname address1* [*address2...address8*]	**At all remote peers**: If the local peer's ISAKMP identity was specified using a host name, maps the peer's host name to its IP address(es) at all the remote peers. (This step might be unnecessary if the host name/address is already mapped in a DNS server.)

1. See the **crypto isakmp identity** command description for guidelines for when to use the IP address versus the host name.

Remember to repeat these tasks at each peer that uses pre-shared keys in an IKE policy.

Specifying All the Other Peers' RSA Public Keys

At each peer, specify all the other peers' RSA public keys by using the following commands starting in global configuration mode:

Step	Command	Purpose
1	**crypto key pubkey-chain rsa**	Enters public key configuration mode.
2	**named-key** *key-name* [**encryption** | **signature**] or **addressed-key** *key-address* [**encryption** | **signature**]	Indicates which remote peer's RSA public key you are going to specify. If the remote peer uses its host name as its ISAKMP identity, use the **named-key** command and specify the remote peer's fully qualified domain name (such as *somerouter.domain.com*) as the *key-name*. If the remote peer uses its IP address as its ISAKMP identity, use the **addressed-key** command and specify the remote peer's IP address as the *key-address*.
3	**address** *ip-address*	If you used a fully qualified domain name to name the remote peer in step 2 (using the **named-key** command), you can optionally specify the remote peer's IP address.
4	**key-string** *key-string* **quit**	Specifies the remote peer's RSA public key. This is the key viewed by the remote peer's administrator previously when he generated his router's RSA keys.

Step	Command	Purpose
5		Repeat steps 2 through 4 to specify the RSA public keys of all the other IPSec peers that use RSA encrypted nonces in an IKE policy.
6	**exit**	Returns to global configuration mode.

Remember to repeat these tasks at each peer that uses RSA encrypted nonces in an IKE policy.

To view RSA public keys while or after you configure them, use the following command in EXEC mode:

Command	Purpose
show crypto key pubkey-chain rsa {**name** *key-name* | **address** *key-address*}	Views a list of all the RSA public keys stored on your router or views details of a particular RSA public key stored on your router.

Configuring Pre-Shared Keys

To configure pre-shared keys, perform these tasks at each peer that uses pre-shared keys in an IKE policy:

- First, set each peer's ISAKMP identity. Each peer's identity should be set to either its host name or by its IP address. By default, a peer's identity is set to its IP address. Setting ISAKMP identities is described previously in this chapter in the section "Setting ISAKMP Identity."

- Next, specify the shared keys at each peer. Note that a given pre-shared key is shared between two peers. At a given peer you could specify the same key to share with multiple remote peers; however, a more secure approach is to specify different keys to share between different pairs of peers.

To specify pre-shared keys at a peer, use the following commands in global configuration mode;

Step	Command	Purpose
1	**crypto isakmp key** *keystring* **address** *peer-address* or **crypto isakmp key** *keystring* **hostname** *peer-hostname*	**At the local peer**: Specifies the shared key to be used with a particular remote peer. If the remote peer specified their ISAKMP identity with an address, use the **address** keyword in this step; otherwise use the **hostname** keyword in this step.

Step	Command	Purpose
2	**crypto isakmp key** *keystring* **address** *peer-address* or **crypto isakmp key** *keystring* **hostname** *peer-hostname*	**At the remote peer**: Specifies the shared key to be used with the local peer. This is the same key you just specified at the local peer. If the local peer specified their ISAKMP identity with an address, use the **address** keyword in this step; otherwise, use the **hostname** keyword in this step.
3		Repeat the previous two steps for each remote peer.

Remember to repeat these tasks at each peer that uses pre-shared keys in an IKE policy.

Clearing IKE Connections

If you want, you can clear existing IKE connections.

To clear IKE connections, use the following commands in EXEC mode:

Step	Command	Purpose
1	**show crypto isakmp sa**	Views existing IKE connections; notes the connection identifiers for connections you wish to clear.
2	**clear crypto isakmp** [*connection-id*]	Clears IKE connections.

Troubleshooting IKE

To assist in IKE troubleshooting, use the following commands in EXEC mode:

Command	Purpose
show crypto isakmp policy	Views the parameters for each configured IKE policy.
show crypto isakmp sa	Views all current IKE security associations.
debug crypto isakmp	Displays **debug** messages about IKE events.

What to Do Next

After IKE configuration is complete, you can configure IPSec. IPSec configuration is described in Chapter 28, "Configuring IPSec Network Security."

IKE Configuration Example

This example creates two IKE policies, with policy 15 as the highest priority, policy 20 as the next priority, and the existing default priority as the lowest priority. it also creates a pre-shared key to be used with policy 20 with the remote peer whose IP address is 192.168.224.33.

```
crypto isakmp policy 15
 encryption des
 hash md5
 authentication rsa-sig
 group 2
 lifetime 5000
crypto isakmp policy 20
 authentication pre-share
 lifetime 10000
crypto isakmp key 1234567890 address 192.168.224.33
```

In the above example, the **encryption des** of policy 15 would not appear in the written configuration because this is the default value for the encryption algorithm parameter.

If the **show crypto isakmp policy** command is issued with this configuration, the output would be as follows:

```
Protection suite priority 15
          encryption algorithm:DES - Data Encryption Standard (56 bit keys)
          hash algorithm:Message Digest 5
          authentication method:Rivest-Shamir-Adleman Signature
          Diffie-Hellman group:#2 (1024 bit)
          lifetime:5000 seconds, no volume limit
Protection suite priority 20
          encryption algorithm:DES - Data Encryption Standard (56 bit keys)
          hash algorithm:Secure Hash Standard
          authentication method:Pre-Shared Key
          Diffie-Hellman group:#1 (768 bit)
          lifetime:10000 seconds, no volume limit
Default protection suite
          encryption algorithm:DES - Data Encryption Standard (56 bit keys)
          hash algorithm:Secure Hash Standard
          authentication method:Rivest-Shamir-Adleman Signature
          Diffie-Hellman group:#1 (768 bit)
          lifetime:86400 seconds, no volume limit
```

Note that although the output shows *no volume limit* for the lifetimes, you can currently only configure a time lifetime (such as 86,400 seconds); volume limit lifetimes are not configurable.

## CHAPTER 33

Internet Key Exchange Security Protocol Commands

This chapter describes Internet Key Exchange Security Protocol (IKE) commands.

IKE is a key management protocol standard that is used in conjunction with the IPSec standard. IPSec is an IP security feature that provides robust authentication and encryption of IP packets.

IPSec can be configured without IKE, but IKE enhances IPSec by providing additional features, flexibility, and ease of configuration for the IPSec standard.

IKE is a hybrid protocol that implements the Oakley key exchange and Skeme key exchange inside the Internet Security Association and Key Management Protocol (ISAKMP) framework. (ISAKMP, Oakley, and Skeme are security protocols implemented by IKE.)

You can search online at www.cisco.com to find complete descriptions of other commands used when configuring IKE.

For configuration information, refer to Chapter 32, "Configuring Internet Key Exchange Security Protocol."

address

To specify the IP address of the remote peer's RSA public key you will manually configure, use the **address** public key configuration command. This command should only be used when the router has a single interface that processes IPSec.

> **address** *ip-address*

Syntax	Description
ip-address	Specifies the IP address of the remote peer.

Default

This command has no defaults.

Command Mode

Public key configuration

Usage Guidelines

This command first appeared in Cisco IOS Release 11.3 T.

Use this command in conjunction with the **named-key** command to specify which IPSec peer's RSA public key you will manually configure next.

Example

This example manually specifies the RSA public keys of an IPSec peer:

```
myrouter(config)# crypto key pubkey-chain rsa
myrouter(config-pubkey-chain)# named-key otherpeer.domain.com
myrouter(config-pubkey-key)# address 10.5.5.1
myrouter(config-pubkey-key)# key-string
myrouter(config-pubkey)# 005C300D 06092A86 4886F70D 01010105
myrouter(config-pubkey)# 00034B00 30480241 00C5E23B 55D6AB22
myrouter(config-pubkey)# 04AEF1BA A54028A6 9ACC01C5 129D99E4
myrouter(config-pubkey)# 64CAB820 847EDAD9 DF0B4E4C 73A05DD2
myrouter(config-pubkey)# BD62A8A9 FA603DD2 E2A8A6F8 98F76E28
myrouter(config-pubkey)# D58AD221 B583D7A4 71020301 0001
myrouter(config-pubkey)# quit
myrouter(config-pubkey-key)# exit
myrouter(config-pubkey-chain)# exit
myrouter(config)#
```

Related Commands

You can search online at www.cisco.com to find documentation of related commands.

addressed-key
crypto key pubkey-chain rsa
key-string
show crypto key pubkey-chain rsa

addressed-key

To specify which peer's RSA public key you will manually configure, use the **addressed-key** public key chain configuration command.

> **addressed-key** *key-address* [**encryption** | **signature**]

Syntax	Description
key-address	Specifies the IP address of the remote peer's RSA keys.
encryption	(Optional) Indicates that the RSA public key to be specified will be an encryption special-usage key.
signature	(Optional) Indicates that the RSA public key to be specified will be a signature special-usage key.

Default

If neither the **encryption** nor **signature** keywords are used, general-purpose keys will be specified.

Command Mode

Public key chain configuration. This command invokes public key configuration mode.

Usage Guidelines

This command first appeared in Cisco IOS Release 11.3 T.

Use this command or the **named-key** command to specify which IPSec peer's RSA public key you will manually configure next.

Follow this command with the **key-string** command to specify the key.

If the IPSec remote peer generated general-purpose RSA keys, do not use the **encryption** or **signature** keywords.

If the IPSec remote peer generated special-usage keys, you must manually specify both keys: Perform this command and the **key-string** command twice and use the **encryption** and **signature** keywords, respectively.

Example

This example manually specifies the RSA public keys of two IPSec peers. The peer at 10.5.5.1 uses general-purpose keys, and the other peer uses special-usage keys.

```
myrouter(config)# crypto key pubkey-chain rsa
myrouter(config-pubkey-chain)# named-key otherpeer.domain.com
myrouter(config-pubkey-key)# address 10.5.5.1
myrouter(config-pubkey-key)# key-string
myrouter(config-pubkey)# 005C300D 06092A86 4886F70D 01010105
myrouter(config-pubkey)# 00034B00 30480241 00C5E23B 55D6AB22
myrouter(config-pubkey)# 04AEF1BA A54028A6 9ACC01C5 129D99E4
myrouter(config-pubkey)# 64CAB820 847EDAD9 DF0B4E4C 73A05DD2
myrouter(config-pubkey)# BD62A8A9 FA603DD2 E2A8A6F8 98F76E28
myrouter(config-pubkey)# D58AD221 B583D7A4 71020301 0001
myrouter(config-pubkey)# quit
myrouter(config-pubkey-key)# exit
myrouter(config-pubkey-chain)# addressed-key 10.1.1.2 encryption
myrouter(config-pubkey-key)# key-string
myrouter(config-pubkey)# 00302017 4A7D385B 1234EF29 335FC973
myrouter(config-pubkey)# 2DD50A37 C4F4B0FD 9DADE748 429618D5
myrouter(config-pubkey)# 18242BA3 2EDFBDD3 4296142A DDF7D3D8
myrouter(config-pubkey)# 08407685 2F2190A0 0B43F1BD 9A8A26DB
myrouter(config-pubkey)# 07953829 791FCDE9 A98420F0 6A82045B
myrouter(config-pubkey)# 90288A26 DBC64468 7789F76E EE21
myrouter(config-pubkey)# quit
```

Part IV

Command Reference

```
myrouter(config-pubkey-key)# exit
myrouter(config-pubkey-chain)# addressed-key 10.1.1.2 signature
myrouter(config-pubkey-key)# key-string
myrouter(config-pubkey)# 0738BC7A 2BC3E9F0 679B00FE 53987BCC
myrouter(config-pubkey)# 01030201 42DD06AF E228D24C 458AD228
myrouter(config-pubkey)# 58BB5DDD F4836401 2A2D7163 219F882E
myrouter(config-pubkey)# 64CE69D4 B583748A 241BED0F 6E7F2F16
myrouter(config-pubkey)# 0DE0986E DF02031F 4B0B0912 F68200C4
myrouter(config-pubkey)# C625C389 0BFF3321 A2598935 C1B1
myrouter(config-pubkey)# quit
myrouter(config-pubkey-key)# exit
myrouter(config-pubkey-chain)# exit
myrouter(config)#
```

Related Commands

You can search online at www.cisco.com to find documentation of related commands.

crypto key pubkey-chain rsa
key-string
named-key
show crypto key pubkey-chain rsa

authentication (IKE policy)

To specify the authentication method within an IKE policy, use the **authentication (IKE policy)** ISAKMP policy configuration command. IKE policies define a set of parameters to be used during IKE negotiation. Use the **no** form of this command to reset the authentication method to the default value.

> **authentication {rsa-sig | rsa-encr | pre-share}**
> **no authentication**

Syntax	Description
rsa-sig	Specifies RSA signatures as the authentication method.
rsa-encr	Specifies RSA encrypted nonces as the authentication method.
pre-share	Specifies pre-shared keys as the authentication method.

Default

RSA signatures

Command Mode

ISAKMP policy configuration (config-isakmp)

Usage Guidelines

This command first appeared in Cisco IOS Release 11.3 T.

Use this command to specify the authentication method to be used in an IKE policy.

If you specify RSA signatures, you must configure your peer routers to obtain certificates from a certification authority (CA).

If you specify RSA encrypted nonces, you must ensure that each peer has the other peer's RSA public keys. (See the **crypto key pubkey-chain rsa**, **addressed-key**, **named-key**, **address**, and **key-string** commands.)

If you specify pre-shared keys, you must also separately configure these pre-shared keys. (See the **crypto isakmp identity** and **crypto isakmp key** commands.)

Example

This example configures an IKE policy with pre-shared keys as the authentication method (all other parameters are set to the defaults):

```
MyPeerRouter(config)# crypto isakmp policy 15
MyPeerRouter(config-isakmp)# authentication pre-share
MyPeerRouter(config-isakmp)# exit
MyPeerRouter(config)#
```

Related Commands

You can search online at www.cisco.com to find documentation of related commands.

crypto isakmp key
crypto isakmp policy
crypto key generate rsa
encryption (IKE policy)
group (IKE policy)
hash (IKE policy)
lifetime (IKE policy)
show crypto isakmp policy

clear crypto isakmp

To clear active IKE connections, use the **clear crypto isakmp** global configuration command.

> **clear crypto isakmp** [*connection-id*]

Syntax   Description

connection-id   (Optional) Specifies which connection to clear. If this argument is not used, all
               existing connections will be cleared.

Default

If the *connection-id* argument is not used, all existing IKE connections will be cleared when this
command is issued.

Command Mode

Global configuration

Usage Guidelines

This command first appeared in Cisco IOS Release 11.3 T.

Use this command to clear active IKE connections.

Example

This example clears an IKE connection between two peers connected by interfaces 172.21.114.123 and
172.21.114.67:

```
MyPeerRouter# show crypto isakmp sa
    dst           src           state        conn-id   slot
172.21.114.123 172.21.114.67  QM_IDLE          1        0
155.0.0.2      155.0.0.1      QM_IDLE          8        0

MyPeerRouter# configure terminal
Enter configuration commands, one per line.  End with CTRL-Z.
MyPeerRouter(config)# clear crypto isakmp 1
MyPeerRouter(config)# exit
MyPeerRouter# show crypto isakmp sa
    dst           src           state        conn-id   slot
155.0.0.2      155.0.0.1      QM_IDLE          8        0

MyPeerRouter#
```

Related Commands

You can search online at www.cisco.com to find documentation of related commands.

show crypto isakmp sa

crypto isakmp enable

To globally enable IKE at your peer router, use the **crypto isakmp enable** global configuration command. Use the **no** form of this command to disable IKE at the peer.

> **crypto isakmp enable**
> **no crypto isakmp enable**

Syntax Description

This command has no arguments or keywords.

Default

IKE is enabled.

Command Mode

Global configuration

Usage Guidelines

This command first appeared in Cisco IOS Release 11.3 T.

IKE is enabled by default. IKE does not have to be enabled for individual interfaces, but is enabled globally for all interfaces at the router.

If you do not want IKE to be used in your IPSec implementation, you can disable IKE at all your IPSec peers. If you disable IKE at one peer you must disable it at all your IPSec peers.

If you disable IKE, you will have to make these concessions at the peers:

- You must manually specify all the IPSec security associations (SAs) in the crypto maps at the peers. (Crypto map configuration is described in Chapter 28, "Configuring IPSec Network Security.")

- The peers' IPSec SAs will never time out for a given IPSec session.

- During IPSec sessions between the peers, the encryption keys will never change.

- Anti-replay services will not be available between the peers.

- CA support cannot be used.

Example

This example disables IKE at one peer. (The same command should be issued at all remote peers.)

```
no crypto isakmp enable
```

crypto isakmp identity

To define the identity the router uses when participating in the IKE protocol, use the **crypto isakmp identity** global configuration command. Set an ISAKMP identity whenever you specify pre-shared keys. Use the **no** form of this command to reset the ISAKMP identity to the default value (address).

> **crypto isakmp identity** {**address** | **hostname**}
> **no crypto isakmp identity**

Syntax	Description
address	Sets the ISAKMP identity to the IP address of the interface that is used to communicate to the remote peer during IKE negotiations.
hostname	Sets the ISAKMP identity to the host name concatenated with the domain name (for example, myhost.domain.com).

Default

The IP address is used for the ISAKMP identity.

Command Mode

Global configuration

Usage Guidelines

This command first appeared in Cisco IOS Release 11.3 T.

Use this command to specify an ISAKMP identity either by IP address or by host name.

The **address** keyword is typically used when there is only one interface (and therefore only one IP address) that will be used by the peer for IKE negotiations, and the IP address is known.

The **hostname** keyword should be used if there is more than one interface on the peer that might be used for IKE negotiations or if the interface's IP address is unknown (such as with dynamically assigned IP addresses).

As a general rule, you should set all peers' identities in the same way, either by IP address or by host name.

Examples

The following example uses pre-shared keys at two peers and sets both their ISAKMP identities to IP address.

At the local peer (at 10.0.0.1) the ISAKMP identity is set and the pre-shared key is specified:

```
crypto isakmp identity address
crypto isakmp key sharedkeystring address 192.168.1.33
```

At the remote peer (at 192.168.1.33) the ISAKMP identity is set and the same pre-shared key is specified:

```
crypto isakmp identity address
crypto isakmp key sharedkeystring address 10.0.0.1
```

NOTE   In the preceding example if the **crypto isakmp identity** command had not been performed, the ISAKMP identities would have still been set to IP address, the default identity.

The following example uses pre-shared keys at two peers and sets both their ISAKMP identities to hostname.

At the local peer the ISAKMP identity is set and the pre-shared key is specified:

```
crypto isakmp identity hostname
crypto isakmp key sharedkeystring hostname RemoteRouter.domain.com
ip host RemoteRouter.domain.com 192.168.0.1
```

At the remote peer the ISAKMP identity is set and the same pre-shared key is specified:

```
crypto isakmp identity hostname
crypto isakmp key sharedkeystring hostname LocalRouter.domain.com
ip host LocalRouter.domain.com 10.0.0.1 10.0.0.2
```

In the above example, host names are used for the peers' identities because the local peer has two interfaces that might be used during an IKE negotiation.

In the above example the IP addresses are also mapped to the host names; this mapping is not necessary if the routers' host names are already mapped in DNS.

Related Commands

You can search online at www.cisco.com to find documentation of related commands.

authentication (IKE policy)
crypto isakmp key

crypto isakmp key

To configure a pre-shared authentication key, use the **crypto isakmp key** global configuration command. You must configure this key whenever you specify pre-shared keys in an IKE policy. Use the **no** form of this command to delete a pre-shared authentication key.

> **crypto isakmp key** *keystring* **address** *peer-address*
> **crypto isakmp key** *keystring* **hostname** *peer-hostname*
> **no crypto isakmp key** *keystring* **address** *peer-address*
> **no crypto isakmp key** *keystring* **hostname** *peer-hostname*

Syntax	Description
keystring	Specifies the pre-shared key. Use any combination of alphanumeric characters up to 128 bytes. This pre-shared key must be identical at both peers.
peer-address	Specifies the IP address of the remote peer.
hostname	Specifies the host name of the remote peer. This is the peer's host name concatenated with its domain name (for example, myhost.domain.com).

Default

There is no default pre-shared authentication key.

Command Mode

Global configuration

Usage Guidelines

This command first appeared in Cisco IOS Release 11.3 T.

Use this command to configure pre-shared authentication keys. You must perform this command at both peers.

If an IKE policy includes pre-shared keys as the authentication method, these pre-shared keys must be configured at both peers; otherwise, the policy cannot be used (the policy will not be submitted for matching by the IKE process). The **crypto isakmp key** command is the second task required to configure the pre-shared keys at the peers. (The first task is accomplished with the **crypto isakmp identity** command.)

Use the **address** keyword if the remote peer ISAKMP identity was set with its IP address.

Use the **hostname** keyword if the remote ISAKMP identity was set with its host name.

With the **hostname** keyword, you might also need to map the remote peer's host name to all IP addresses of the remote peer interfaces that could be used during the IKE negotiation. (This is done with the **ip host** command.) You need to map the host name to IP address unless this mapping is already done in a DNS server.

Example

The remote peer RemoteRouter specifies an ISAKMP identity by address:

```
crypto isakmp identity address
```

The local peer LocalRouter also specifies an ISAKMP identity, but by host name:

```
crypto isakmp identity hostname
```

Now, the pre-shared key must be specified at each peer.

The local peer specifies the pre-shared key and designates the remote peer by its IP address:

```
crypto isakmp key sharedkeystring address 192.168.1.33
```

The remote peer specifies the same pre-shared key and designates the local peer by its host name:

```
crypto isakmp key sharedkeystring hostname LocalRouter.domain.com
```

The remote peer also maps multiple IP addresses to the same host name for the local peer because the local peer has two interfaces which both might be used during an IKE negotiation with the local peer. These two interfaces' IP addresses (10.0.0.1 and 10.0.0.2) are both mapped to the remote peer's host name:

```
ip host LocalRouter.domain.com 10.0.0.1 10.0.0.2
```

(This mapping would not have been necessary if *LocalRouter.domain.com* was already mapped in DNS.)

In this example, a remote peer specifies its ISAKMP identity by address, and the local peer specifies its ISAKMP identity by host name. Depending on the circumstances in your network, both peers could specify their ISAKMP identity by address or both by host name.

Related Commands

You can search online at www.cisco.com to find documentation of related commands.

authentication (IKE policy)
crypto isakmp identity
ip host

crypto isakmp policy

To define an IKE policy, use the **crypto isakmp policy** global configuration command. IKE policies define a set of parameters to be used during the IKE negotiation. Use the **no** form of this command to delete an IKE policy.

> **crypto isakmp policy** *priority*
> **no crypto isakmp policy**

Syntax	Description
priority	Uniquely identifies the IKE policy and assigns a priority to the policy. Use an integer from 1 to 10,000, with 1 being the highest priority and 10,000 the lowest.

Default

There is a default policy, which is always the lowest priority. This default policy contains default values for the encryption, hash, authentication, Diffie-Hellman group, and lifetime parameters. (The parameter defaults are listed in the "Usage Guidelines" section.)

When you create an IKE policy, if you do not specify a value for a particular parameter, the default for that parameter will be used.

Command Mode

Global configuration

Usage Guidelines

This command first appeared in Cisco IOS Release 11.3 T.

Use this command to specify the parameters to be used during an IKE negotiation. (These parameters are used to create the IKE SA.)

This command invokes the ISAKMP policy configuration (config-isakmp) command mode. While in the ISAKMP policy configuration command mode, the following commands are available to specify the parameters in the policy:

- **encryption (IKE policy)**; default = 56-bit DES-CBC

- **hash (IKE policy)**; default = SHA-1

- **authentication (IKE policy)**; default = RSA signatures

- **group (IKE policy)**; default = 768-bit Diffie-Hellman

- **lifetime (IKE policy)**; default = 86,400 seconds (one day)

If you do not specify one of these commands for a policy, the default value will be used for that parameter.

To exit the config-isakmp command mode, type **exit**.

You can configure multiple IKE policies on each peer participating in IPSec. When the IKE negotiation begins, it tries to find a common policy configured on both peers, starting with the highest-priority policies as specified on the remote peer.

Example

The following example configures two policies for the peer:

```
crypto isakmp policy 15
 hash md5
 authentication rsa-sig
 group 2
 lifetime 5000
crypto isakmp policy 20
 authentication pre-share
 lifetime 10000
```

The above configuration results in the following policies:

```
MyPeerRouter# show crypto isakmp policy

Protection suite priority 15
encryption algorithm:DES - Data Encryption Standard (56 bit keys)
hash algorithm:Message Digest 5
authentication method:Rivest-Shamir-Adleman Signature
Diffie-Hellman Group:#2 (1024 bit)
lifetime:   5000 seconds, no volume limit
Protection suite priority 20
encryption algorithm:DES - Data Encryption Standard (56 bit keys)
hash algorithm:Secure Hash Standard
authentication method:Pre-Shared Key
Diffie-Hellman Group:#1 (768 bit)
lifetime:   10000 seconds, no volume limit
Default protection suite
encryption algorithm:DES - Data Encryption Standard (56 bit keys)
hash algorithm:Secure Hash Standard
authentication method:Rivest-Shamir-Adleman Signature
Diffie-Hellman Group:#1 (768 bit)
lifetime:   86400 seconds, no volume limit
```

Related Commands

You can search online at www.cisco.com to find documentation of related commands.

authentication (IKE policy)
encryption (IKE policy)
group (IKE policy)
hash (IKE policy)
lifetime (IKE policy)
show crypto isakmp policy

crypto key generate rsa

To generate RSA key pairs, use the **crypto key generate rsa** global configuration command.

crypto key generate rsa [**usage-keys**]

Syntax	Description
usage-keys	(Optional) Specifies that two RSA special-usage key pairs (that is, one encryption pair and one signature pair) should be generated instead of one general-purpose key pair.

Default

RSA key pairs do not exist. If the **usage-keys** keyword is not used, general-purpose keys will be generated.

Command Mode

Global configuration

Usage Guidelines

This command first appeared in Cisco IOS Release 11.3 T.

Use this command to generate RSA key pairs for your Cisco device (such as a router).

RSA keys are generated in pairs—one public RSA key and one private RSA key.

If your router already has RSA keys when you issue this command, you will be warned and prompted to replace the existing keys with new keys.

NOTE	Before issuing this command, make sure your router has a host name and IP domain name configured (with the **hostname** and **ip domain-name** commands). You will be unable to complete the **crypto key generate rsa** command without a host name and IP domain name.

This command is not saved in the router configuration; however, the keys generated by this command are saved in the private configuration in NVRAM (which is never displayed to the user or backed up to another device).

There are two mutually exclusive types of RSA key pairs: special-usage keys and general-purpose keys. When you generate RSA key pairs, you can indicate whether to generate special-usage keys or general-purpose keys.

Special-Usage Keys

If you generate special-usage keys, two pairs of RSA keys will be generated. One pair will be used with any IKE policy that specifies RSA signatures as the authentication method and the other pair used with any IKE policy that specifies RSA encrypted nonces as the authentication method.

If you plan to have both types of RSA authentication methods in your IKE policies, you might prefer to generate special-usage keys. With special-usage keys, each key is not unnecessarily exposed. (Without special-usage keys, one key is used for both authentication methods, increasing that key's exposure.)

General-Purpose Keys

If you generate general-purpose keys, only one pair of RSA keys will be generated. This pair will be used with IKE policies specifying either RSA signatures or RSA encrypted nonces. Therefore, a general-purpose key pair might get used more frequently than a special-usage key pair.

Modulus Length

When you generate RSA keys, you will be prompted to enter a modulus length. A longer modulus could offer stronger security, but takes longer to generate (see Table 33-1 for sample times) and takes longer to use. Below 512 is normally not recommended. (In certain situations, the shorter modulus may not function properly with IKE, so Cisco recommends using a minimum modulus of 1024.)

Table 33-1 *Sample Times Required to Generate RSA Keys*

Router	Modulus Length			
	360 bits	**512 bits**	**1024 bits**	**2048 bits**
Cisco 2500	11 seconds	20 seconds	4 minutes, 38 seconds	Longer than 1 hour
Cisco 4700	Less than 1 second	1 second	4 seconds	50 seconds

Examples

The following example generates special-usage RSA keys:

```
myrouter(config)# crypto key generate rsa usage-keys
The name for the keys will be: myrouter.domain.com

Choose the size of the key modulus in the range of 360 to 2048 for your Signature Keys.
Choosing a key modulus greater than 512 may take a few minutes.
How many bits in the modulus[512]? <return>
Generating RSA keys.... [OK].

Choose the size of the key modulus in the range of 360 to 2048 for your Encryption Keys.
Choosing a key modulus greater than 512 may take a few minutes.
How many bits in the modulus[512]? <return>
Generating RSA keys.... [OK].

myrouter(config)#
```

The following example generates general-purpose RSA keys:

```
myrouter(config)# crypto key generate rsa
The name for the keys will be: myrouter.domain.com

Choose the size of the key modulus in the range of 360 to 2048 for your General Purpose Keys.
Choosing a key modulus greater than 512 may take a few minutes.
How many bits in the modulus[512]? <return>
Generating RSA keys.... [OK].

myrouter(config)#
```

NOTE   You cannot generate both special-usage and general-purpose keys; you can only generate one or the other.

Related Commands

You can search online at www.cisco.com to find documentation of related commands.

show crypto key mypubkey rsa

crypto key pubkey-chain rsa

To enter public key configuration mode (so you can manually specify other devices' RSA public keys), use the **crypto key pubkey-chain rsa** global configuration command.

> **crypto key pubkey-chain rsa**

Syntax Description

This command has no arguments or keywords.

Default

This command has no defaults.

Command Mode

Global configuration. This command invokes public key chain configuration mode.

Usage Guidelines

This command first appeared in Cisco IOS Release 11.3 T.

Use this command to enter public key chain configuration mode. Use this command when you need to manually specify other IPSec peers' RSA public keys. You need to specify other peers' keys when you configure RSA encrypted nonces as the authentication method in an IKE policy at your peer router.

Example

This example manually specifies the RSA public keys of two other IPSec peers. The remote peers use their IP address as their identity.

```
myrouter(config)# crypto key pubkey-chain rsa
myrouter(config-pubkey-chain)# addressed-key 10.5.5.1
myrouter(config-pubkey-key)# key-string
myrouter(config-pubkey)# 00302017 4A7D385B 1234EF29 335FC973
myrouter(config-pubkey)# 2DD50A37 C4F4B0FD 9DADE748 429618D5
myrouter(config-pubkey)# 18242BA3 2EDFBDD3 4296142A DDF7D3D8
myrouter(config-pubkey)# 08407685 2F2190A0 0B43F1BD 9A8A26DB
myrouter(config-pubkey)# 07953829 791FCDE9 A98420F0 6A82045B
myrouter(config-pubkey)# 90288A26 DBC64468 7789F76E EE21
myrouter(config-pubkey)# quit
myrouter(config-pubkey-key)# exit
myrouter(config-pubkey-chain)# addressed-key 10.1.1.2
myrouter(config-pubkey-key)# key-string
myrouter(config-pubkey)# 0738BC7A 2BC3E9F0 679B00FE 53987BCC
myrouter(config-pubkey)# 01030201 42DD06AF E228D24C 458AD228
```

```
myrouter(config-pubkey)# 58BB5DDD F4836401 2A2D7163 219F882E
myrouter(config-pubkey)# 64CE69D4 B583748A 241BED0F 6E7F2F16
myrouter(config-pubkey)# 0DE0986E DF02031F 4B0B0912 F68200C4
myrouter(config-pubkey)# C625C389 0BFF3321 A2598935 C1B1
myrouter(config-pubkey)# quit
myrouter(config-pubkey-key)# exit
myrouter(config-pubkey-chain)# exit
myrouter(config)#
```

Related Commands

You can search online at www.cisco.com to find documentation of related commands.

address
addressed-key
key-string
named-key
show crypto key pubkey-chain rsa

encryption (IKE policy)

To specify the encryption algorithm within an IKE policy, use the **encryption (IKE policy)** ISAKMP policy configuration command. IKE policies define a set of parameters to be used during IKE negotiation. Use the **no** form of this command to reset the encryption algorithm to the default value.

encryption des
no encryption

Syntax	Description
des	Specifies 56-bit DES-CBC as the encryption algorithm.

Default

The 56-bit DES-CBC encryption algorithm.

Command Mode

ISAKMP policy configuration (config-isakmp)

Usage Guidelines

This command first appeared in Cisco IOS Release 11.3 T.

Use this command to specify the encryption algorithm to be used in an IKE policy.

Example

This example configures an IKE policy with the 56-bit DES encryption algorithm (all other parameters are set to the defaults):

```
MyPeerRouter(config)# crypto isakmp policy 15
MyPeerRouter(config-isakmp)# encryption des
MyPeerRouter(config-isakmp)# exit
MyPeerRouter(config)#
```

Related Commands

You can search online at www.cisco.com to find documentation of related commands.

authentication (IKE policy)
crypto isakmp policy
group (IKE policy)
hash (IKE policy)
lifetime (IKE policy)
show crypto isakmp policy

group (IKE policy)

To specify the Diffie-Hellman group identifier within an IKE policy, use the **group (IKE policy)** ISAKMP policy configuration command. IKE policies define a set of parameters to be used during IKE negotiation. Use the **no** form of this command to reset the Diffie-Hellman group identifier to the default value.

group {1 | 2}
no group

Syntax	Description
1	Specifies the 768-bit Diffie-Hellman group.
2	Specifies the 1024-bit Diffie-Hellman group.

Default

768-bit Diffie-Hellman (group 1)

Command Mode

ISAKMP policy configuration (config-isakmp)

Usage Guidelines

This command first appeared in Cisco IOS Release 11.3 T.

Use this command to specify the Diffie-Hellman group to be used in an IKE policy.

Example

This example configures an IKE policy with the 1024-bit Diffie-Hellman group (all other parameters are set to the defaults):

```
MyPeerRouter(config)# crypto isakmp policy 15
MyPeerRouter(config-isakmp)# group 2
MyPeerRouter(config-isakmp)# exit
MyPeerRouter(config)#
```

Related Commands

You can search online at www.cisco.com to find documentation of related commands.

authentication (IKE policy)
crypto isakmp policy
encryption (IKE policy)
hash (IKE policy)
lifetime (IKE policy)
show crypto isakmp policy

hash (IKE policy)

To specify the hash algorithm within an IKE policy, use the **hash (IKE policy)** ISAKMP policy configuration command. IKE policies define a set of parameters to be used during IKE negotiation. Use the **no** form of this command to reset the hash algorithm to the default SHA-1 hash algorithm.

> **hash {sha | md5}**
> **no hash**

Syntax	Description
sha	Specifies SHA-1 (HMAC variant) as the hash algorithm.
md5	Specifies MD5 (HMAC variant) as the hash algorithm.

Default

The SHA-1 hash algorithm.

Command Mode

ISAKMP policy configuration (config-isakmp)

Usage Guidelines

This command first appeared in Cisco IOS Release 11.3 T.

Use this command to specify the hash algorithm to be used in an IKE policy.

Example

This example configures an IKE policy with the MD5 hash algorithm (all other parameters are set to the defaults):

```
MyPeerRouter(config)# crypto isakmp policy 15
MyPeerRouter(config-isakmp)# hash md5
MyPeerRouter(config-isakmp)# exit
MyPeerRouter(config)#
```

Related Commands

You can search online at www.cisco.com to find documentation of related commands.

authentication (IKE policy)
crypto isakmp policy
encryption (IKE policy)
group (IKE policy)
lifetime (IKE policy)
show crypto isakmp policy

key-string

To manually specify a remote peer's RSA public key, use the **key-string** public key configuration command.

> **key-string**
> *key-string*

Syntax   Description

key-string   Enter the key in hexadecimal format. While entering the key data, you can press the Return key to continue entering data.

Default

This command has no defaults.

Command Mode

Public key configuration

Usage Guidelines

This command first appeared in Cisco IOS Release 11.3 T.

Use this command to manually specify the RSA public key of an IPSec peer. Before using this command you must identify the remote peer using either the **addressed-key** or **named-key** command.

If possible, to avoid mistakes, you should cut and paste the key data (instead of attempting to type in the data).

Example

This example manually specifies the RSA public keys of an IPSec peer:

```
myrouter(config)# crypto key pubkey-chain rsa
myrouter(config-pubkey-chain)# named-key otherpeer.domain.com
myrouter(config-pubkey-key)# address 10.5.5.1
myrouter(config-pubkey-key)# key-string
myrouter(config-pubkey)# 005C300D 06092A86 4886F70D 01010105
myrouter(config-pubkey)# 00034B00 30480241 00C5E23B 55D6AB22
myrouter(config-pubkey)# 04AEF1BA A54028A6 9ACC01C5 129D99E4
myrouter(config-pubkey)# 64CAB820 847EDAD9 DF0B4E4C 73A05DD2
myrouter(config-pubkey)# BD62A8A9 FA603DD2 E2A8A6F8 98F76E28
myrouter(config-pubkey)# D58AD221 B583D7A4 71020301 0001
myrouter(config-pubkey)# quit
myrouter(config-pubkey-key)# exit
myrouter(config-pubkey-chain)# exit
myrouter(config)#
```

Related Commands

You can search online at www.cisco.com to find documentation of related commands.

addressed-key
crypto key pubkey-chain rsa
named-key
show crypto key pubkey-chain rsa

lifetime (IKE policy)

To specify the lifetime of an IKE SA, use the **lifetime (IKE policy)** ISAKMP policy configuration command. Use the **no** form of this command to reset the SA lifetime to the default value.

> **lifetime** *seconds*
> **no lifetime**

Syntax	Description
seconds	Specifies how many seconds each SA should exist before expiring. Use an integer from 60 to 86,400 seconds.

Default

86,400 seconds (1 day)

Command Mode

ISAKMP policy configuration (config-isakmp)

Usage Guidelines

This command first appeared in Cisco IOS Release 11.3 T.

Use this command to specify how long an IKE SA exists before expiring.

When IKE begins negotiations, the first thing it does is agree on the security parameters for its own session. The agreed-on parameters are then referenced by an SA at each peer. The SA is retained by each peer until the SA's lifetime expires. Before an SA expires, it can be reused by subsequent IKE negotiations, which can save time when setting up new IPSec SAs. New SAs are negotiated before current SAs expire.

So, to save setup time for IPSec, configure a longer IKE SA lifetime. However, the shorter the lifetime (up to a point), the more secure the IKE negotiation is likely to be.

Note that when your local peer initiates an IKE negotiation between itself and a remote peer, an IKE policy can be selected only if the lifetime of the remote peer's policy is shorter than or equal to the lifetime of the local peer's policy. Then, if the lifetimes are not equal, the shorter lifetime will be selected. To restate this behavior: If the two peer's policies' lifetimes are not the same, the initiating peer's lifetime must be longer and the responding peer's lifetime must be shorter, and the shorter lifetime will be used.

Example

This example configures an IKE policy with a security association lifetime of 600 seconds (10 minutes), and all other parameters are set to the defaults:

```
MyPeerRouter(config)# crypto isakmp policy 15
MyPeerRouter(config-isakmp)# lifetime 600
MyPeerRouter(config-isakmp)# exit
MyPeerRouter(config)#
```

Related Commands

You can search online at www.cisco.com to find documentation of related commands.

authentication (IKE policy)
crypto isakmp policy
encryption (IKE policy)
group (IKE policy)
hash (IKE policy)
show crypto isakmp policy

named-key

To specify which peer's RSA public key you will manually configure, use the **named-key** public key chain configuration command. This command should only be used when the router has a single interface that processes IPSec.

> **named-key** *key-name* [**encryption** | **signature**]

Syntax	Description
key-name	Specifies the name of the remote peer's RSA keys. This is always the fully qualified domain name of the remote peer; for example, *router.domain.com*.
encryption	(Optional) Indicates that the RSA public key to be specified will be an encryption special-usage key.
signature	(Optional) Indicates that the RSA public key to be specified will be a signature special-usage key.

Default

If neither the **encryption** nor **signature** keywords are used, general-purpose keys will be specified.

Command Mode

Public key chain configuration. This command invokes public key configuration mode.

Usage Guidelines

This command first appeared in Cisco IOS Release 11.3 T.

Use this command or the **addressed-key** command to specify which IPSec peer's RSA public key you will manually configure next.

Follow this command with the **key-string** command to specify the key.

If you use the **named-key** command you also need to use the **address** public key configuration command to specify the IP address of the peer.

If the IPSec remote peer generated general-purpose RSA keys, do not use the **encryption** or **signature** keywords.

If the IPSec remote peer generated special-usage keys, you must manually specify both keys: Perform this command and the **key-string** command twice and use the **encryption** and **signature** keywords, respectively.

Example

This example manually specifies the RSA public keys of two IPSec peers. The peer at 10.5.5.1 uses general-purpose keys, and the other peer uses special-usage keys.

```
myrouter(config)# crypto key pubkey-chain rsa
myrouter(config-pubkey-chain)# named-key otherpeer.domain.com
myrouter(config-pubkey-key)# address 10.5.5.1
myrouter(config-pubkey-key)# key-string
myrouter(config-pubkey)# 005C300D 06092A86 4886F70D 01010105
myrouter(config-pubkey)# 00034B00 30480241 00C5E23B 55D6AB22
myrouter(config-pubkey)# 04AEF1BA A54028A6 9ACC01C5 129D99E4
myrouter(config-pubkey)# 64CAB820 847EDAD9 DF0B4E4C 73A05DD2
myrouter(config-pubkey)# BD62A8A9 FA603DD2 E2A8A6F8 98F76E28
myrouter(config-pubkey)# D58AD221 B583D7A4 71020301 0001
myrouter(config-pubkey)# quit
myrouter(config-pubkey-key)# exit
myrouter(config-pubkey-chain)# addressed-key 10.1.1.2 encryption
myrouter(config-pubkey-key)# key-string
myrouter(config-pubkey)# 00302017 4A7D385B 1234EF29 335FC973
myrouter(config-pubkey)# 2DD50A37 C4F4B0FD 9DADE748 429618D5
myrouter(config-pubkey)# 18242BA3 2EDFBDD3 4296142A DDF7D3D8
myrouter(config-pubkey)# 08407685 2F2190A0 0B43F1BD 9A8A26DB
myrouter(config-pubkey)# 07953829 791FCDE9 A98420F0 6A82045B
myrouter(config-pubkey)# 90288A26 DBC64468 7789F76E EE21
myrouter(config-pubkey)# quit
myrouter(config-pubkey-key)# exit
myrouter(config-pubkey-chain)# addressed-key 10.1.1.2 signature
```

Part
IV

Command Reference

```
myrouter(config-pubkey-key)# key-string
myrouter(config-pubkey)# 0738BC7A 2BC3E9F0 679B00FE 098533AB
myrouter(config-pubkey)# 01030201 42DD06AF E228D24C 458AD228
myrouter(config-pubkey)# 58BB5DDD F4836401 2A2D7163 219F882E
myrouter(config-pubkey)# 64CE69D4 B583748A 241BED0F 6E7F2F16
myrouter(config-pubkey)# 0DE0986E DF02031F 4B0B0912 F68200C4
myrouter(config-pubkey)# C625C389 0BFF3321 A2598935 C1B1
myrouter(config-pubkey)# quit
myrouter(config-pubkey-key)# exit
myrouter(config-pubkey-chain)# exit
myrouter(config)#
```

Related Commands

You can search online at www.cisco.com to find documentation of related commands.

address
addressed-key
crypto key pubkey-chain rsa
key-string
show crypto key pubkey-chain rsa

show crypto isakmp policy

To view the parameters for each IKE policy, use the **show crypto isakmp policy** EXEC command.

show crypto isakmp policy

Syntax Description

This command has no arguments or keywords.

Command Mode

EXEC

Usage Guidelines

This command first appeared in Cisco IOS Release 11.3 T.

Sample Display

The following is sample output from the **show crypto isakmp policy** command, after two IKE policies have been configured (with priorities 15 and 20, respectively):

```
MyPeerRouter# show crypto isakmp policy

Protection suite priority 15
          encryption algorithm:DES - Data Encryption Standard (56 bit keys)
          hash algorithm:Message Digest 5
          authentication method:Rivest-Shamir-Adleman Signature
          Diffie-Hellman Group:#2 (1024 bit)
          lifetime:5000 seconds, no volume limit
Protection suite priority 20
          encryption algorithm:DES - Data Encryption Standard (56 bit keys)
          hash algorithm:Secure Hash Standard
          authentication method:Pre-Shared Key
          Diffie-Hellman Group:#1 (768 bit)
          lifetime:10000 seconds, no volume limit
Default protection suite
          encryption algorithm:DES - Data Encryption Standard (56 bit keys)
          hash algorithm:Secure Hash Standard
          authentication method:Rivest-Shamir-Adleman Signature
          Diffie-Hellman Group:#1 (768 bit)
          lifetime:86400 seconds, no volume limit
```

NOTE   Although the output shows *no volume limit* for the lifetimes, you can currently only configure a time lifetime (such as 86,400 seconds); volume limit lifetimes are not configurable.

Related Commands

You can search online at www.cisco.com to find documentation of related commands.

authentication (IKE policy)
crypto isakmp policy
encryption (IKE policy)
group (IKE policy)
hash (IKE policy)
lifetime (IKE policy)

show crypto isakmp sa

To view all current IKE SAs at a peer, use the **show crypto isakmp sa** EXEC command.

show crypto isakmp sa

Syntax Description

This command has no arguments or keywords.

Command Mode

EXEC

Usage Guidelines

This command first appeared in Cisco IOS Release 11.3 T.

Sample Display

The following is sample output from the **show crypto isakmp sa** command, after IKE negotiations have successfully completed between two peers:

```
MyPeerRouter# show crypto isakmp sa
     dst            src         state      conn-id   slot
172.21.114.123 172.21.114.67  QM_IDLE         1       0
155.0.0.2      155.0.0.1      QM_IDLE         8       0
```

Table 33-2 through Table 33-4 show the various states that may be displayed in the output of the **show crypto isakmp sa** command. When an ISAKMP SA exists, it will most likely be in its quiescent state (OAK_QM_IDLE). For long exchanges, some of the OAK_MM_xxx states may be observed.

Table 33-2   *States in Main Mode Exchange*

State	Explanation
OAK_MM_NO_STATE	The ISAKMP SA has been created, but nothing else has happened yet. It is "larval" at this stage—there is no state.
OAK_MM_SA_SETUP	The peers have agreed on parameters for the ISAKMP SA.
OAK_MM_KEY_EXCH	The peers have exchanged Diffie-Hellman public keys and have generated a shared secret. The ISAKMP SA remains unauthenticated.
OAK_MM_KEY_AUTH	The ISAKMP SA has been authenticated. If the router initiated this exchange, this state transitions immediately to OAK_QM_IDLE and a quick mode exchange begins.

Table 33-3 *States in Aggressive Mode Exchange*

State	Explanation
OAK_AG_NO_STATE	The ISAKMP SA has been created but nothing else has happened yet. It is "larval" at this stage—there is no state.
OAK_AG_INIT_EXCH	The peers have done the first exchange in aggressive mode but the SA is not authenticated.
OAK_AG_AUTH	The ISAKMP SA has been authenticated. If the router initiated this exchange, this state transitions immediately to OAK_QM_IDLE and a quick mode exchange begins.

Table 33-4 *States in Quick Mode Exchange*

State	Explanation
OAK_QM_IDLE	The ISAKMP SA is idle. It remains authenticated with its peer and may be used for subsequent quick mode exchanges. It is in a quiescent state.

Related Commands

You can search online at www.cisco.com to find documentation of related commands.

crypto isakmp policy
lifetime (IKE policy)

show crypto key mypubkey rsa

To view your router's RSA public key(s), use the **show crypto key mypubkey rsa** EXEC command.

> **show crypto key mypubkey rsa**

Syntax Description

There are no arguments or keywords with this command.

Command Mode

EXEC

Usage Guidelines

This command first appeared in Cisco IOS Release 11.3 T.

Part
IV

Command Reference

This command displays your router's RSA public key(s).

Sample Display

The following is sample output from the **show crypto key mypubkey rsa** command. Special-usage RSA keys were previously generated for this router using the **crypto key generate rsa** command:

```
% Key pair was generated at: 06:07:49 UTC Jan 13 1996
Key name: myrouter.domain.com
 Usage: Signature Key
 Key Data:
  005C300D 06092A86 4886F70D 01010105 00034B00 30480241 00C5E23B 55D6AB22
  04AEF1BA A54028A6 9ACC01C5 129D99E4 64CAB820 847EDAD9 DF0B4E4C 73A05DD2
  BD62A8A9 FA603DD2 E2A8A6F8 98F76E28 D58AD221 B583D7A4 71020301 0001

% Key pair was generated at: 06:07:50 UTC Jan 13 1996
Key name: myrouter.domain.com
 Usage: Encryption Key
 Key Data:
  00302017 4A7D385B 1234EF29 335FC973 2DD50A37 C4F4B0FD 9DADE748 429618D5
  18242BA3 2EDFBDD3 4296142A DDF7D3D8 08407685 2F2190A0 0B43F1BD 9A8A26DB
  07953829 791FCDE9 A98420F0 6A82045B 90288A26 DBC64468 7789F76E EE21
```

Related Commands

You can search online at www.cisco.com to find documentation of related commands.

crypto key generate rsa

show crypto key pubkey-chain rsa

To view peers' RSA public keys stored on your router, use the **show crypto key pubkey-chain rsa** EXEC command.

> **show crypto key pubkey-chain rsa** [**name** *key-name* | **address** *key-address*]

Syntax	Description
name *key-name*	(Optional) Specifies the name of a particular public key to view.
address *key-address*	(Optional) Specifies the address of a particular public key to view.

Default

If no keywords are used, this command displays a list of all RSA public keys stored on your router.

Command Mode

EXEC

Usage Guidelines

This command first appeared in Cisco IOS Release 11.3 T.

This command shows RSA public keys stored on your router. This includes peers' RSA public keys manually configured at your router and keys received by your router via other means (such as by a certificate, if CA support is configured).

If a router reboots, any public key derived by certificates will be lost. This is because the router will ask for certificates again, at which time the public key will be derived again.

Use the **name** or **address** keywords to display details about a particular RSA public key stored on your router.

Sample Display

The following is sample output from the **show crypto key pubkey-chain rsa** command:

```
Codes: M - Manually Configured, C - Extracted from certificate

Code   Usage        IP-address      Name
M      Signature    10.0.0.1        myrouter.domain.com
M      Encryption   10.0.0.1        myrouter.domain.com
C      Signature    172.16.0.1      routerA.domain.com
C      Encryption   172.16.0.1      routerA.domain.com
C      General      192.168.10.3    routerB.domain1.com
```

This sample shows manually configured special-usage RSA public keys for the peer *somerouter*. This sample also shows three keys obtained from peers' certificates: special-usage keys for peer *routerA* and a general-purpose key for peer *routerB*.

Certificate support is used in the above example; if certificate support was not in use, none of the peers' keys would show C in the code column, but would all have to be manually configured.

The following is sample output when you issue the command **show crypto key pubkey rsa name somerouter.domain.com**:

```
Key name: somerouter.domain.com
Key address: 10.0.0.1
 Usage: Signature Key
 Source: Manual
 Data:
  305C300D 06092A86 4886F70D 01010105 00034B00 30480241 00C5E23B 55D6AB22
  04AEF1BA A54028A6 9ACC01C5 129D99E4 64CAB820 847EDAD9 DF0B4E4C 73A05DD2
  BD62A8A9 FA603DD2 E2A8A6F8 98F76E28 D58AD221 B583D7A4 71020301 0001

Key name: somerouter.domain.com
```

```
Key address: 10.0.0.1
 Usage: Encryption Key
 Source: Manual
 Data:
  00302017 4A7D385B 1234EF29 335FC973 2DD50A37 C4F4B0FD 9DADE748 429618D5
  18242BA3 2EDFBDD3 4296142A DDF7D3D8 08407685 2F2190A0 0B43F1BD 9A8A26DB
  07953829 791FCDE9 A98420F0 6A82045B 90288A26 DBC64468 7789F76E EE21
```

NOTE	The Source field in the above example indicates *Manual*, meaning that the keys were manually configured on the router, not received in the peer's certificate.

The following is sample output when you issue the command **show crypto key pubkey rsa address 192.168.10.3**:

```
Key name: routerB.domain.com
Key address: 192.168.10.3
 Usage: General Purpose Key
 Source: Certificate
 Data:
  0738BC7A 2BC3E9F0 679B00FE 53987BCC 01030201 42DD06AF E228D24C 458AD228
  58BB5DDD F4836401 2A2D7163 219F882E 64CE69D4 B583748A 241BED0F 6E7F2F16
  0DE0986E DF02031F 4B0B0912 F68200C4 C625C389 0BFF3321 A2598935 C1B1
```

NOTE	The Source field in the above example indicates *Certificate*, meaning that the keys were received by the router by way of the other router's certificate.

PART V

Other Security Features

## CHAPTER 34

Configuring Passwords and Privileges

Using passwords and assigning privilege levels is a simple way of providing terminal access control in your network.

This chapter describes the following topics and tasks:

- Protecting Access to Privileged EXEC Commands

- Encrypting Passwords

- Configuring Multiple Privilege Levels

- Recovering a Lost Enable Password

- Recovering a Lost Line Password

- Configuring Identification Support

- Passwords and Privileges Configuration Examples

For a complete description of the commands used in this chapter, refer to Chapter 35, "Passwords and Privileges Commands." To locate documentation of other commands that appear in this chapter, you can search online at www.cisco.com.

Protecting Access to Privileged EXEC Commands

The following tasks provide a way to control access to the system configuration file and privileged EXEC (enable) commands:

- Setting or Changing a Static Enable Password

- Protecting Passwords with enable password and enable secret

- Setting or Changing a Line Password

- Setting TACACS Password Protection for Privileged EXEC Mode

Setting or Changing a Static Enable Password

To set or change a static password that controls access to privileged EXEC (enable) mode, use the following command in global configuration mode:

Command	Purpose
enable password *password*	Establishes a new password or changes an existing password for the privileged command level.

For examples of how to define enable passwords for different privilege levels, see the "Multiple Levels of Privileges Examples" section at the end of this chapter.

Protecting Passwords with enable password and enable secret

To provide an additional layer of security, particularly for passwords that cross the network or are stored on a TFTP server, you can use either the **enable password** or **enable secret** commands. Both commands accomplish the same thing; that is, they allow you to establish an encrypted password that users must enter to access enable mode (the default), or any privilege level you specify.

Cisco recommends that you use the **enable secret** command because it uses an improved encryption algorithm. Use the **enable password** command only if you boot an older image of the Cisco IOS software or if you boot older boot ROMs that do not recognize the **enable secret** command.

If you configure the **enable secret** command, it takes precedence over the **enable password** command. The two commands cannot be in effect simultaneously.

To configure the router to require an enable password, use either of the following commands in global configuration mode:

Command	Purpose
enable password [**level** *level*] {*password* | *encryption-type encrypted-password*} or **enable secret** [**level** *level*] {*password* | *encryption-type encrypted-password*}	Establishes a password for a privilege command mode. Specifies a secret password, saved using a nonreversible encryption method. (If enable password and enable secret are both set, users must enter the enable secret password.)

Use either of these commands with the **level** option to define a password for a specific privilege level. After you specify the level and set a password, give the password only to users who need to have access at this level. Use the **privilege level** configuration command to specify commands accessible at various levels.

If you have the **service password-encryption** command enabled, the password you enter is encrypted. When you display it with the **more system:running-config** command, it is displayed in encrypted form.

If you specify an encryption type, you must provide an encrypted password—an encrypted password you copy from another router configuration.

NOTE   You cannot recover a lost encrypted password. You must clear NVRAM and set a new password. See the sections "Recovering a Lost Enable Password" or "Recovering a Lost Line Password" in this chapter if you have lost or forgotten your password.

Setting or Changing a Line Password

To set or change a password on a line, use the following command in global configuration mode:

Command	Purpose
password *password*	Establishes a new password or changes an existing password for the privileged command level.

Setting TACACS Password Protection for Privileged EXEC Mode

You can set the TACACS protocol to determine whether a user can access privileged EXEC (enable) mode. To do so, use the following command in global configuration mode:

Command	Purpose
enable use-tacacs	Sets the TACACS-style user ID and password-checking mechanism at the privileged EXEC level.

When you set TACACS password protection at the privileged EXEC mode, the **enable** EXEC command prompts for both a new username and a password. This information is then passed to the TACACS server for authentication. If you are using the extended TACACS, it also passes any existing UNIX user identification code to the TACACS server.

CAUTION   If you use the **enable use-tacacs** command, you must also specify **tacacs-server authenticate enable**, or you will be locked out of the privileged EXEC (enable) mode.

NOTE	When used without extended TACACS, the **enable use-tacacs** command allows anyone with a valid username and password to access the privileged EXEC mode, creating a potential security problem. This occurs because the TACACS query resulting from entering the **enable** command is indistinguishable from an attempt to log in without extended TACACS.

Encrypting Passwords

Because protocol analyzers can examine packets (and read passwords), you can increase access security by configuring the Cisco IOS software to encrypt passwords. Encryption prevents the password from being readable in the configuration file.

To configure the Cisco IOS software to encrypt passwords, use the following command in global configuration mode:

Command	Purpose
service password-encryption	Encrypts a password.

The actual encryption process occurs when the current configuration is written or when a password is configured. Password encryption is applied to all passwords, including authentication key passwords, the privileged command password, console and virtual terminal line access passwords, and BGP neighbor passwords. The **service password-encryption** command is primarily useful for keeping unauthorized individuals from viewing your password in your configuration file.

CAUTION	The **service password-encryption** command does not provide a high level of network security. If you use this command, you should also take additional network security measures.

Although you cannot recover a lost encrypted password (that is, you cannot get the original password back), you can recover from a lost encrypted password. See the sections "Recovering a Lost Enable Password" or "Recovering a Lost Line Password" in this chapter if you have lost or forgotten your password.

Configuring Multiple Privilege Levels

By default, the Cisco IOS software has two modes of password security: user mode (EXEC) and privilege mode (enable). You can configure up to 16 hierarchical levels of commands for each mode. By configuring multiple passwords, you can allow different sets of users to have access to specified commands.

For example, if you want the **configure** command to be available to a more restricted set of users than the **clear line** command, you can assign level 2 security to the **clear line** command and distribute the level 2 password fairly widely, and assign level 3 security to the **configure** command and distribute the password to level 3 commands to fewer users.

The following tasks describe how to configure additional levels of security:

● Setting the Privilege Level for a Command

● Changing the Default Privilege Level for Lines

● Displaying Current Privilege Levels

● Logging In to a Privilege Level

Setting the Privilege Level for a Command

To set the privilege level for a command, use the following commands in global configuration mode:

Step	Command	Purpose
1	**privilege** *mode* **level** *level command*	Sets the privilege level for a command.
2	**enable password level** *level* [*encryption-type*] *password*	Specifies the enable password for a privilege level.

Changing the Default Privilege Level for Lines

To change the default privilege level for a given line or a group of lines, use the following command in line configuration mode:

Command	Purpose
privilege level *level*	Specifies a default privilege level for a line.

Displaying Current Privilege Levels

To display the current privilege level you can access based on the password you used, use the following command in EXEC mode:

Command	Purpose
show privilege	Displays your current privilege level.

Logging In to a Privilege Level

To log in to a router at a specified privilege level, use the following command in EXEC mode:

Command	Purpose
enable *level*	Logs in to a specified privilege level.

To exit to a specified privilege level, use the following command in EXEC mode:

Command	Purpose
disable *level*	Exits to a specified privilege level.

Recovering a Lost Enable Password

You can restore access to enable mode on a router when the password is lost by using one of the three procedures described in this section. The procedure you use depends on your router platform.

You can perform password recovery on most of the platforms without changing hardware jumpers, but all platforms require the configuration to be reloaded. Password recovery can be done only from the console port on the router. Table 34-1 shows which password recovery procedure to use with each router platform.

Table 34-1 *Platform-Specific Password Recovery Procedures*

Password Recovery Procedure	Router Platform
Password Recovery Procedure 1	Cisco 2000 series
	Cisco 2500 series
	Cisco 3000 series
	Cisco 4000 series with 680x0 Motorola CPU
	Cisco 7000 series running Cisco IOS Release 10.0 or later in ROMs installed on the RP card
	IGS series running Cisco Release IOS 9.1 or later in ROMs

Table 34-1 *Platform-Specific Password Recovery Procedures (Continued)*

Password Recovery Procedure	Router Platform
Password Recovery Procedure 2	Cisco 1003
	Cisco 1600 series
	Cisco 3600 series
	Cisco 4500 series
	Cisco 7200 series
	Cisco 7500 series
	IDT Orion-based routers
	AS5200 and AS5300 platforms

Password Recovery Process

Both password recovery procedures involve the following basic steps:

Step 1   Configure the router to boot up without reading the configuration memory (NVRAM). This is sometimes called the test system mode.

Step 2   Reboot the system.

Step 3   Access enable mode (which can be done without a password if you are in test system mode).

Step 4   View or change the password, or erase the configuration.

Step 5   Reconfigure the router to boot up and read the NVRAM as it normally does.

Step 6   Reboot the system.

NOTE   Some password recovery requires that a terminal issue a Break signal; you must be familiar with how your terminal or PC terminal emulator issues this signal. For example, in ProComm, the keys Alt-B by default generate the Break signal, and in a Windows terminal you press Break or Ctrl-Break. A Windows terminal also allows you to define a function key as a Break signal. To do so, select function keys from the Terminal window and define one as Break by entering the characters **^$B** (**Shift-6**, **Shift-4**, and uppercase **B**).

Password Recovery Procedure 1

Use this procedure to recover lost passwords on the following Cisco routers:

● Cisco 2000 series

● Cisco 2500 series

- Cisco 3000 series

- Cisco 4000 series with 680x0 Motorola CPU

- Cisco 7000 series running Cisco IOS Release 10.0 or later in ROMs installed on the RP card. The router can be booting Cisco IOS Release 10.0 software in Flash memory, but it also needs the actual ROMs on the processor card.

- IGS Series running Cisco IOS Release 9.1 or later in ROMs

To recover a password using Procedure 1, perform the following steps:

Step 1   Attach a terminal or PC with terminal emulation software to the console port of the router.

Step 2   Enter the **show version** command and record the setting of the configuration register. It is usually 0x2102 or 0x102.

The configuration register value is on the last line of the display. Note whether the configuration register is set to enable Break or disable Break.

The factory-default configuration register value is 0x2102. Notice that the third digit from the left in this value is 1, which disables Break. If the third digit is *not* 1, Break is enabled.

Step 3   Turn off the router, and then turn it on.

Step 4   Press the **Break** key on the terminal within 60 seconds of turning on the router.

The rommon> prompt with no router name appears. If it does not appear, the terminal is not sending the correct Break signal. In that case, check the terminal or terminal emulation setup.

Step 5   Enter **o/r0x42** at the rommon> prompt to boot from Flash memory or **o/r0x41** to boot from the boot ROMs.

NOTE   The first character is the letter o, not the numeral zero. If you have Flash memory and it is intact, 0x42 is the best setting. Use 0x41 only if the Flash memory is erased or not installed. If you use 0x41, you can only view or erase the configuration. You cannot change the password.

Step 6   At the rommon> prompt, enter the initialize command to initialize the router.

This causes the router to reboot but ignore its saved configuration and use the image in Flash memory instead. The system configuration display appears.

NOTE	If you normally use the **boot network** command, or if you have multiple images in Flash memory and you boot a non-default image, the image in Flash might be different.

Step 7   Enter **no** in response to the System Configuration Dialog prompts until the following message appears:

```
Press RETURN to get started!
```

Step 8   Press **Return**.

The Router> prompt appears.

Step 9   Enter the **enable** command.

The Router# prompt appears.

Step 10   Choose one of the following options:

● To view the password, if it is not encrypted, enter the **more nvram:startup-config** command.

● To change the password (if it is encrypted, for example), enter the following commands:

```
Router # configure memory
Router # configure terminal
Router(config)# enable secret 1234abcd
Router(config)# ctrl-z
Router # write memory
```

NOTE	The **enable secret** command provides increased security by storing the enable secret password using a non-reversible cryptographic function; however, you cannot recover a lost password that has been encrypted.

Step 11   Enter the **configure terminal** command at the EXEC prompt to enter configuration mode.

Step 12   Enter the **config-register** command and whatever value you recorded in Step 2.

Step 13   Press **Ctrl-Z** to quit from the configuration editor.

Step 14   Enter the **reload** command at the privileged EXEC prompt and issue the **write memory** command to save the configuration.

Password Recovery Procedure 2

Use this procedure to recover lost passwords on the following Cisco routers:

- Cisco 1003

- Cisco 1600 series

- Cisco 3600 series

- Cisco 4500 series

- Cisco 7200 series

- Cisco 7500 series

- IDT Orion-Based Routers

- AS5200 and AS5300 platforms

To recover a password using Procedure 2, perform the following steps:

Step 1   Attach a terminal or PC with terminal emulation software to the console port of the router.

Step 2   Enter the **show version** command and record the setting of the configuration register. It is usually 0x2102 or 0x102.

The configuration register value is on the last line of the display. Note whether the configuration register is set to enable Break or disable Break.

The factory-default configuration register value is 0x2102. Notice that the third digit from the left in this value is 1, which disables Break. If the third digit is *not* 1, Break is enabled.

Step 3   Turn off the router, then turn it on.

Step 4   Press the **Break** key on the terminal within 60 seconds of turning on the router.

The rommon> prompt appears. If it does not appear, the terminal is not sending the correct Break signal. In that case, check the terminal or terminal emulation setup.

Step 5   Enter the **confreg** command at the rommon> prompt.

The following prompt appears:

```
Do you wish to change configuration[y/n]?
```

Step 6   Enter **yes** and press **Return**.

Step 7   Enter **no** to subsequent questions until the following prompt appears:

```
ignore system config info[y/n]?
```

Step 8   Enter **yes**.

Step 9   Enter **no** to subsequent questions until the following prompt appears:

```
change boot characteristics[y/n]?
```

Step 10   Enter **yes**.

The following prompt appears:

```
enter to boot:
```

Step 11   At this prompt, either enter **2** and press **Return** if Flash memory or, if Flash memory is erased, enter **1**. If Flash memory is erased, the Cisco 4500 must be returned to Cisco for service. If you enter **1**, you can only view or erase the configuration. You cannot change the password.

A configuration summary is displayed and the following prompt appears:

```
Do you wish to change configuration[y/n]?
```

Step 12   Answer **no** and press **Return**.

The following prompt appears:

```
rommon>
```

Step 13   Enter the **reload** command at the privileged EXEC prompt or, for Cisco 4500 series and Cisco 7500 series routers, power cycle the router.

Step 14   As the router boots, enter **no** to all the setup questions until the following prompt appears:

```
Router>
```

Step 15   Enter the **enable** command to enter enable mode.

The `Router#` prompt appears.

Step 16   Choose one of the following options:

● To view the password, if it is not encrypted, enter the **more nvram:startup-config** command.

● To change the password (if it is encrypted, for example), enter the following commands:

```
Router # configure memory
Router # configure terminal
Router(config)# enable secret 1234abcd
Router(config)# ctrl-z
Router # write memory
```

NOTE   The **enable secret** command provides increased security by storing the enable secret password using a nonreversible cryptographic function; however, you cannot recover a lost password that has been encrypted.

Step 17   Enter the **configure terminal** command at the prompt.

Step 18   Enter the **config-register** command and whatever value you recorded in Step 2.

Step 19   Press **Ctrl-Z** to quit from the configuration editor.

Step 20   Enter the **reload** command at the prompt and issue the **write memory** command to save the configuration.

Recovering a Lost Line Password

If your router has the nonvolatile memory option, you can accidentally lock yourself out of enable mode if you enable password checking on the console terminal line and then forget the line password. To recover a lost line password, perform the following steps:

Step 1   Force the router into factory diagnostic mode.

See the hardware installation and maintenance publication for your product for specific information about setting the processor configuration register to factory diagnostic mode. Table 34-2 summarizes the hardware or software settings required by various products to set factory diagnostic mode.

Step 2   Enter **Yes** when asked if you want to set the manufacturers' addresses.

The following prompt appears:

```
TEST-SYSTEM >
```

Step 3   Issue the **enable** command to enter enable mode:

```
TEST-SYSTEM > enable
```

Step 4   Enter the **more nvram:startup-config** command to review the system configuration and find the password. Do not change anything in the factory diagnostic mode.

```
TEST-SYSTEM # more nvram:startup-config
```

Step 5   To resume normal operation, restart the router or reset the configuration register.

Step 6   Log in to the router with the password that was shown in the configuration file.

NOTE   All debugging capabilities are turned on during diagnostic mode.

See the hardware installation and maintenance publication for your product for specific information about configuring the processor configuration register for factory diagnostic mode. Table 34-2 summarizes the hardware or software settings required by the various products to set factory diagnostic mode.

Table 34-2   *Factory Diagnostic Mode Settings for the Configuration Register*

Platform	Setting
Modular products	Set jumper in bit 15 of the processor configuration register, then restart; remove the jumper when finished.
Cisco AS5100 Cisco AS5200 Cisco AS5300 Cisco 1600 series Cisco 2500 series Cisco 3000 series Cisco 3600 series Cisco 4000 series Cisco 4500 series Cisco 7000 series Cisco 7200 series Cisco 7500 series	Use the **config-register** command to set the processor configuration register to 0x8000, then **initialize** and **boot** the system. Use the **reload** command to restart and set the processor configuration register to 0x2102 when finished.

Configuring Identification Support

Identification support allows you to query a Transmission Control Protocol (TCP) port for identification. This feature enables an unsecure protocol, described in RFC 1413, to report the identity of a client initiating a TCP connection and a host responding to the connection. With identification support, you can connect a TCP port on a host, issue a simple text string to request information, and receive a simple text-string reply.

To configure identification support, use the following command in global configuration mode:

Command	Purpose
ip identd	Enables identification support.

Passwords and Privileges Configuration Examples

This section describes multiple privilege level and username authentication examples and contains the following sections:

- Multiple Levels of Privileges Examples
- Username Examples

Multiple Levels of Privileges Examples

This section provides examples of using multiple privilege levels to specify who can access different sets of commands.

Allow Users to Clear Lines Examples

If you want to allow users to clear lines, you can do either of the following:

- Change the privilege level for the **clear** and **clear line** commands to 1, or ordinary user level, as follows. This allows any user to clear lines.

      ```
      privilege exec level 1 clear line
      ```

- Change the privilege level for the **clear** and **clear line** commands to level 2. To do so, use the **privilege level** global configuration command to specify privilege level 2. Then define an enable password for privilege level 2 and tell only those users who need to know what the password is.

      ```
      enable password level 2 pswd2
      privilege exec level 2 clear line
      ```

Define an Enable Password for System Operators Examples

In the following example, you define an enable password for privilege level 10 for system operators and make **clear** and **debug** commands available to anyone with that privilege level enabled:

```
enable password level 10 pswd10
privilege exec level 10 clear line
privilege exec level 10 debug ppp chap
privilege exec level 10 debug ppp error
privilege exec level 10 debug ppp negotiation
```

The following example lowers the privilege level of the **more system:running-config** command and most configuration commands to operator level so that the configuration can be viewed by an operator. It leaves the privilege level of the **configure** command at 15. Individual configuration commands are displayed in the **more system:running-config** output only if the privilege level for a command has been lowered to 10. Users are allowed to see only those commands that have a privilege level less than or equal to their current privilege level.

```
enable password level 15 pswd15
privilege exec level 15 configure
enable password level 10 pswd10
privilege exec level 10 more system:running-config
```

Disable a Privilege Level Example

In the following example, the **show ip route** command is set to privilege level 15. To keep all **show ip** and **show** commands from also being set to privilege level 15, these commands are specified to be privilege level 1.

```
privilege exec level 15 show ip route
privilege exec level 1 show ip
privilege exec level 1 show
```

Username Examples

The following sample configuration sets up secret passwords on Routers A, B, and C, to enable the three routers to connect to each other.

To authenticate connections between Routers A and B, enter the following commands:

On Router A:

```
username B password a-b_secret
```

On Router B:

```
username A password a-b_secret
```

To authenticate connections between Routers A and C, enter the following commands:

On Router A:

```
username C password a-c_secret
```

On Router C:

```
username A password a-c_secret
```

To authenticate connections between Routers B and C, enter the following commands:

On Router B:

```
username C password b-c_secret
```

On Router C:

```
username B password b-c_secret
```

For example, suppose you enter the following command:

```
username bill password westward
```

The system displays this command as follows:

```
username bill password 7 21398211
```

The encrypted version of the password is 21398211. The password was encrypted by the Cisco-defined encryption algorithm, as indicated by the 7.

However, if you enter the following command, the system determines that the password is already encrypted and performs no encryption. Instead, it displays the command exactly as you entered it:

```
username bill password 7 21398211
username bill password 7 21398211
```

## CHAPTER 35

Passwords and Privileges Commands

This chapter describes the commands used to establish password protection and configure privilege levels. Password protection lets you restrict access to a network or a network device. Privilege levels let you define what commands users can issue after they have logged in to a network device.

For information on how to establish password protection or configure privilege levels, refer to Chapter 34, "Configuring Passwords and Privileges." For configuration examples using the commands in this chapter, refer to the "Passwords and Privileges Configuration Examples" section at the end of Chapter 34, "Configuring Passwords and Privileges."

enable

To log on to the router at a specified level, use the **enable** EXEC command.

> **enable** [*level*]

Syntax	Description
level	(Optional) Defines the privilege level that a user logs in to on the router.

Default
Level 15

Command Mode
EXEC

Usage Guidelines
This command first appeared in Cisco IOS Release 10.0.

NOTE The **enable** command is associated with privilege level 0. If you configure authentication, authorization, and accounting (AAA) authorization for a privilege level greater than 0, this command will not be included in the privilege level command set.

Example

In the following example, the user is logging on to privilege level 5 on a router:

```
enable 5
```

Related Commands

You can search online at www.cisco.com to find documentation of related commands.

disable
privilege level (global)
privilege level (line)

enable password

To set a local password to control access to various privilege levels, use the **enable password** global configuration command. Use the **no** form of this command to remove the password requirement.

> **enable password** [**level** *level*] {*password* | [*encryption-type*] *encrypted-password*}
> **no enable password** [**level** *level*]

Syntax

Syntax	Description
level *level*	(Optional) Level for which the password applies. You can specify up to 16 privilege levels by using the numbers 0 through 15. Level 1 is normal EXEC-mode user privileges. If this argument is not specified in the command or the **no** form of the command, the privilege level defaults to 15 (traditional enable privileges).
password	Password users type to enter enable mode.
encryption-type	(Optional) Cisco-proprietary algorithm used to encrypt the password. Currently the only encryption type available is 7. If you specify *encryption-type*, the next argument you supply must be an encrypted password (a password already encrypted by a Cisco router).
encrypted-password	Encrypted password you enter, copied from another router configuration.

Default

No password is defined. The default is level 15.

Command Mode

Global configuration

Usage Guidelines

This command first appeared in Cisco IOS Release 10.0.

Use this command with the **level** option to define a password for a specific privilege level. After you specify the level and the password, give the password to the users who need to access this level. Use the **privilege level (global)** configuration command to specify commands accessible at various levels.

You will not ordinarily enter an encryption type. Typically, you enter an encryption type only if you copy and paste into this command a password that has already been encrypted by a Cisco router.

CAUTION   If you specify an encryption type and then enter a clear text password, you will not be able to re-enter enable mode. You cannot recover a lost password that has been encrypted by any method.

If the **service password-encryption** command is set, the encrypted form of the password you create with the **enable password** command is displayed when a **more nvram:startup-config** command is entered.

You can enable or disable password encryption with the **service password-encryption** command.

An enable password is defined as follows:

- Must contain from 1 to 25 uppercase and lowercase alphanumeric characters.

- Must not have a number as the first character.

- Can have leading spaces, but they are ignored. However, intermediate and trailing spaces are recognized.

- Can contain the question mark (**?**) character if you precede the question mark with the key combination **Ctrl-V** when you create the password; for example, to create the password *abc?123*, do the following:

    — Enter **abc**.

    — Type **Ctrl-V**.

    — Enter **?123**.

When the system prompts you to enter the enable password, you need not precede the question mark with the **Ctrl-V**; you can simply enter **abc?123** at the password prompt.

Examples

The following example enables the password *pswd2* for privilege level 2:

```
enable password level 2 pswd2
```

The following example sets the encrypted password *1i5Rkls3LoyxzS8t9*, which has been copied from a router configuration file, for privilege level 2 using encryption type 7:

```
enable password level 2 7 $1$i5Rkls3LoyxzS8t9
```

Related Commands

You can search online at www.cisco.com to find documentation of related commands.

disable
enable
enable secret
privilege level (global)
service password-encryption
show privilege
more nvram:startup-config

enable secret

To specify an additional layer of security over the **enable password** command, use the **enable secret** global configuration command. Use the **no** form of this command to turn off the enable secret function.

> **enable secret** [**level** *level*] {*password* | [*encryption-type*] *encrypted-password*}
> **no enable secret** [**level** *level*]

Syntax	Description
level *level*	(Optional) Level for which the password applies. You can specify up to sixteen privilege levels, using numbers 0 through 15. Level 1 is normal EXEC-mode user privileges. If this argument is not specified in the command or in the **no** form of the command, the privilege level defaults to 15 (traditional enable privileges). The same holds true for the **no** form of the command.
password	Password for users to enter enable mode. This password should be different from the password created with the **enable password** command.

Syntax	Description
encryption-type	(Optional) Cisco-proprietary algorithm used to encrypt the password. Currently, the only encryption type available for this command is 5. If you specify *encryption-type*, the next argument you supply must be an encrypted password (a password encrypted by a Cisco router).
encrypted-password	Encrypted password you enter, copied from another router configuration.

Default

No password is defined. The default level is 15.

Command Mode

Global configuration

Usage Guidelines

This command first appeared in Cisco IOS Release 11.0.

Use this command to provide an additional layer of security over the enable password. The **enable secret** command provides better security by storing the enable secret password using a non-reversible cryptographic function. The added layer of security encryption provides is useful in environments where the password crosses the network or is stored on a TFTP server.

You will not ordinarily enter an encryption type. Typically you enter an encryption type only if you paste into this command an encrypted password that you copied from a router configuration file.

CAUTION	If you specify an encryption-type and then enter a clear text password, you will not be able to re-enter enable mode. You cannot recover a lost password that has been encrypted by any method.

If you use the same password for the **enable password** and **enable secret** commands, you receive an error message warning that this practice is not recommended, but the password will be accepted. By using the same password, however, you undermine the additional security the **enable secret** command provides.

NOTE   After you set a password using the **enable secret** command, a password set using the **enable password** command works only if the **enable secret** is disabled or an older version of Cisco IOS software is being used, such as when running an older rxboot image. Additionally, you cannot recover a lost password that has been encrypted by any method.

If **service password-encryption** is set, the encrypted form of the password you create here is displayed when a **more nvram:startup-config** command is entered.

You can enable or disable password encryption with the **service password-encryption** command.

An enable password is defined as follows:

● Must contain from 1 to 25 uppercase and lowercase alphanumeric characters

● Must not have a number as the first character

● Can have leading spaces, but they are ignored. However, intermediate and trailing spaces are recognized.

● Can contain the question mark (?) character if you precede the question mark with the key combination **Ctrl-V** when you create the password; for example, to create the password *abc?123,* do the following:

— Enter **abc**.

— Type **Ctrl-V**.

— Enter **?123**.

When the system prompts you to enter the enable password, you need not precede the question mark with the **Ctrl-V**; you can simply enter **abc?123** at the password prompt.

Examples

The following example specifies the **enable secret** password *gobbledegook*:

```
enable secret gobbledegook
```

After specifying an **enable secret** password, users must enter this password to gain access. Any passwords set through the **enable** password will no longer work.

```
Password: gobbledegook
```

The following example enables the encrypted password *1FaD0$Xyti5Rkls3LoyxzS8*, which has been copied from a router configuration file, for privilege level 2 using encryption type 5:

```
enable password level 2 5 $1$FaD0$Xyti5Rkls3LoyxzS8
```

Related Commands

You can search online at www.cisco.com to find documentation of related commands.

enable
enable password

ip identd

To enable identification support, use the **ip identd** global configuration command. Use the **no** form of this command to disable identification support.

> **ip identd**
> **no ip identd**

Syntax Description

This command has no arguments or keywords.

Default

Identification support is not enabled.

Command Mode

Global configuration

Usage Guidelines

This command first appeared in Cisco IOS Release 11.1.

The **ip identd** command returns accurate information about the host TCP port; however, no attempt is made to protect against unauthorized queries.

Example

The following example enables identification support:

```
ip identd
```

password

To specify a password on a line, use the **password** line configuration command. Use the **no** form of this command to remove the password.

> **password** *password*
> **no password**

Syntax   Description

password   Character string that specifies the line password. The first character cannot be a number. The string can contain any alphanumeric characters, including spaces, up to 80 characters. You cannot specify the *password* in the format *number-space-anything*. The space after the number causes problems. For example, *hello 21* is a legal password, but *21 hello* is not. The password checking is case sensitive. For example, the password *Secret* is different than the password *secret*.

Default

No password is specified.

Command Mode

Line configuration

Usage Guidelines

This command first appeared in Cisco IOS Release 10.0.

When an EXEC process is started on a line with password protection, the EXEC prompts for the password. If the user enters the correct password, the EXEC prints its normal privileged prompt. The user can try three times to enter a password before the EXEC exits and returns the terminal to the idle state.

Example

The following example removes the password from virtual terminal lines 1 to 4:

```
line vty 1 4
 no password
```

Related Commands

You can search online at www.cisco.com to find documentation of related commands.

enable password

privilege level (global)

To set the privilege level for a command, use the **privilege level** global configuration command. Use the **no** form of this command to revert to default privileges for a given command.

> **privilege** *mode* **level** *level command*
> **no privilege** *mode* **level** *level command*

Syntax	Description
mode	Configuration mode. See Table 35-1 for a list of options for this argument.
level	Privilege level associated with the specified command. You can specify up to 16 privilege levels, using numbers 0 through 15.
command	Command to which privilege level is associated.

Table 35-1 shows the acceptable options for the mode argument in the **privilege level** command.

Table 35-1 *Mode Argument Options*

Argument Options	Mode
configuration	Global configuration
controller	Controller configuration
exec	EXEC
hub	Hub configuration
interface	Interface configuration
ipx-router	IPX router configuration
line	Line configuration
map-class	Map class configuration
map-list	Map list configuration
route-map	Route map configuration
router	Router configuration

Defaults

Level 15 is the level of access permitted by the **enable** password.

Level 1 is normal EXEC-mode user privileges.

Command Mode

Global configuration

Usage Guidelines

This command first appeared in Cisco IOS Release 10.3.

The password for a privilege level defined using the **privilege level** global configuration command is configured using the **enable password** command.

Level 0 can be used to specify a more limited subset of commands for specific users or lines. For example, you can allow user *guest* to use only the **show users** and **exit** commands.

NOTE   There are five commands associated with privilege level 0: **disable**, **enable**, **exit**, **help**, and **logout**. If you configure AAA authorization for a privilege level greater than 0, these five commands will not be included.

When you set a command to a privilege level, all commands whose syntax is a subset of that command are also set to that level. For example, if you set the **show ip route** command to level 15, the **show** commands and **show ip** commands are automatically set to privilege level 15—unless you set them individually to different levels.

Example

The commands in the following example set the **configure** command to privilege level 14 and establish *SecretPswd14* as the password users must enter to use level 14 commands:

```
privilege exec level 14 configure
enable secret level 14 SecretPswd14
```

Related Commands

You can search online at www.cisco.com to find documentation of related commands.

enable password
enable secret
privilege level (line)

privilege level (line)

To set the default privilege level for a line, use the **privilege level** line configuration command. Use the **no** form of this command to restore the default user privilege level to the line.

> **privilege level** *level*
> **no privilege level**

Syntax	Description
level	Privilege level associated with the specified line.

Defaults

Level 15 is the level of access permitted by the enable password.

Level 1 is normal EXEC-mode user privileges.

Command Mode

Line configuration

Usage Guidelines

This command first appeared in Cisco IOS Release 10.3.

Users can override the privilege level you set using this command by logging in to the line and enabling a different privilege level. They can lower the privilege level by using the **disable** command. If users know the password to a higher privilege level, they can use that password to enable the higher privilege level.

You can use level 0 to specify a subset of commands for specific users or lines. For example, you can allow user *guest* to use only the **show users** and **exit** commands.

You might specify a high level of privilege for your console line to restrict line usage.

Examples

The commands in the following example configure the auxiliary line for privilege level 5. Anyone using the auxiliary line has privilege level 5 by default.

```
line aux 0
 privilege level 5
```

The command in the following example sets all **show ip** commands, which includes all **show** commands, to privilege level 7:

```
 privilege exec level 7 show ip route
```

This is equivalent to the following command:

```
 privilege exec level 7 show
```

The commands in the following example set **show ip route** to level 7 and the **show** and **show ip** commands to level 1:

```
 privilege exec level 7 show ip route
 privilege exec level 1 show ip
```

Related Commands

You can search online at www.cisco.com to find documentation of related commands.

enable password
privilege level (line)

service password-encryption

To encrypt passwords, use the **service password-encryption** global configuration command. Use the **no** form of this command to restore the default.

> **service password-encryption**
> **no service password-encryption**

Syntax Description

This command has no arguments or keywords.

Default

No encryption

Part
V

Command Reference

Command Mode
Global configuration

Usage Guidelines
This command first appeared in Cisco IOS Release 10.0.

The actual encryption process occurs when the current configuration is written or when a password is configured. Password encryption is applied to all passwords, including username passwords, authentication key passwords, the privileged command password, console and virtual terminal line access passwords, and BGP neighbor passwords. This command is primarily useful for keeping unauthorized individuals from viewing your password in your configuration file.

When password encryption is enabled, the encrypted form of the passwords is displayed when a **more system:running-config** command is entered.

CAUTION	This command does not provide a high level of network security. If you use this command, you should also take additional network security measures.

NOTE	You cannot recover a lost encrypted password. You must clear NVRAM and set a new password.

Example
The following example causes password encryption to take place:

```
service password-encryption
```

Related Commands
You can search online at www.cisco.com to find documentation of related commands.

enable password
key-string
neighbor password

show privilege

To display your current level of privilege, use the **show privilege** EXEC command.

> **show privilege**

Syntax Description

This command has no arguments or keywords.

Command Mode

EXEC

Usage Guidelines

This command first appeared in Cisco IOS Release 10.3.

Sample Display

The following is sample output from the **show privilege** command; the current privilege level is 15:

```
Router# show privilege
Current privilege level is 15
```

Related Commands

You can search online at www.cisco.com to find documentation of related commands.

enable password
enable secret

username

To establish a username-based authentication system, use the **username** global configuration command.

> **username** *name* {**nopassword** | **password** *password* [*encryption-type*
> *encrypted-password*]}
> **username** *name* **password** *secret*
> **username** *name* [**access-class** *number*]
> **username** *name* [**autocommand** *command*]
> **username** *name* [**callback-dialstring** *telephone-number*]
> **username** *name* [**callback-rotary** *rotary-group-number*]

username *name* [**callback-line** [**tty**] *line-number* [*ending-line-number*]]
username *name* [**nocallback-verify**]
username *name* [**noescape**] [**nohangup**]
username *name* [**privilege** *level*]

Syntax	Description
name	Host name, server name, user ID, or command name. The *name* argument can be only one word. White spaces and quotation marks are not allowed.
nopassword	No password is required for this user to log in. This is usually most useful in combination with the **autocommand** keyword.
password	Specifies a possibly encrypted password for this username.
password	Password a user enters.
encryption-type	(Optional) Single-digit number that defines whether the text immediately following is encrypted, and, if so, what type of encryption is used. Currently defined encryption types are 0, which means that the text immediately following is not encrypted, and 7, which means that the text is encrypted using a Cisco-defined encryption algorithm.
encrypted-password	Encrypted password a user enters.
password	(Optional) Password to access the name argument. A password must be from 1 to 25 characters, can contain embedded spaces, and must be the last option specified in the **username** command.
secret	For CHAP authentication, specifies the secret for the local router or the remote device. The secret is encrypted when it is stored on the local router. The secret can consist of any string of up to 11 ASCII characters. There is no limit to the number of username and password combinations that can be specified, allowing any number of remote devices to be authenticated.
access-class	(Optional) Specifies an outgoing access list that overrides the access list specified in the **access-class** line configuration command. It is used for the duration of the user's session.
number	Access list number.
autocommand	(Optional) Causes the specified command to be issued automatically after the user logs in. When the command is complete, the session is terminated. Because the command can be any length and contain embedded spaces, commands using the **autocommand** keyword must be the last option on the line.
command	The command string. Because the command can be any length and contain embedded spaces, commands using the **autocommand** keyword must be the last option on the line.

Syntax	Description
callback-dialstring	(Optional) For asynchronous callback only, permits you to specify a telephone number to pass to the DCE device.
telephone-number	For asynchronous callback only, telephone number to pass to the DCE device.
callback-rotary	(Optional) For asynchronous callback only, permits you to specify a rotary group number. The next available line in the rotary group is selected.
rotary-group-number	For asynchronous callback only, integer between 1 and 100 that identifies the group of lines on which you want to enable a specific username for callback.
callback-line	(Optional) For asynchronous callback only, specific line on which you enable a specific username for callback.
tty	(Optional) For asynchronous callback only, standard asynchronous line.
line-number	For asynchronous callback only, relative number of the terminal line (or the first line in a contiguous group) on which you want to enable a specific username for callback. Numbering begins with zero.
ending-line-number	(Optional) Relative number of the last line in a contiguous group on which you want to enable a specific username for callback. If you omit the keyword (such as **tty**), then *line-number* and *ending-line-number* are absolute rather than relative line numbers.
nocallback-verify	(Optional) Authentication not required for EXEC callback on the specified line.
noescape	(Optional) Prevents a user from using an escape character on the host to which that user is connected.
nohangup	(Optional) Prevents the security server from disconnecting the user after an automatic command (set up with the **autocommand** keyword) has completed. Instead, the user gets another login prompt.
privilege	(Optional) Sets the privilege level for the user.
level	(Optional) Number between 0 and 15 that specifies the privilege level for the user.

Default

No username-based authentication system is established.

Command Mode

Global configuration

Usage Guidelines

The following commands first appeared in Cisco IOS Release 10.0:

username *name* {**nopassword** | **password** *password* [*encryption-type encrypted-password*]}

username *name* **password** *secret*

username *name* [**access-class** *number*]

username *name* [**autocommand** *command*]

username *name* [**noescape**] [**nohangup**]

username *name* [privilege *level*]

The following commands first appeared in Cisco IOS Release 11.1:

username *name* [**callback-dialstring** *telephone-number*]

username *name* [**callback-rotary** *rotary-group-number*]

username *name* [**callback-line** [**tty**] *line-number* [*ending-line-number*]]

username *name* [**nocallback-verify**]

The **username** command provides username and/or password authentication for login purposes only. (Note that it does not provide username and/or password authentication for enable mode when the **enable use-tacacs** command is also configured.)

Multiple **username** commands can be used to specify options for a single user.

Add a **username** entry for each remote system that the local router communicates with and requires authentication from. The remote device must have a **username** entry for the local router. This entry must have the same password as the local router's entry for that remote device.

This command can be useful for defining usernames that get special treatment. For example, you can use this command to define an *info* username that does not require a password, but connects the user to a general-purpose information service.

The **username** command is required as part of the configuration for the Challenge Handshake Authentication Protocol (CHAP). Add a **username** entry or each remote system from which the local router requires authentication.

NOTE   To enable the local router to respond to remote CHAP challenges, one **username** *name* entry must be the same as the **hostname** *name* entry that has already been assigned to your router.

If there is no *secret* specified and the **debug serial-interface** command is enabled, an error is displayed when a link is established and the CHAP challenge is not implemented. CHAP debugging information is available using the **debug serial-interface** and **debug serial-packet** commands.

Examples

To implement a service similar to the UNIX **who** command, which can be entered at the login prompt and lists the current users of the router, the **username** command takes the following form:

```
username who nopassword nohangup autocommand show users
```

To implement an information service that does not require a password to be used, the command takes the following form:

```
username info nopassword noescape autocommand telnet nic.ddn.mil
```

To implement an ID that works even if the TACACS servers all break, the command takes the following form:

```
username superuser password superpassword
```

The following example configuration enables CHAP on interface serial 0. It also defines a password for the local server named server_l, and a remote server named server_r.

```
hostname server_l
interface serial 0
 encapsulation ppp
 ppp authentication chap
 username server_l password oursystem
 username server_r password theirsystem
```

When you look at your configuration file, the passwords will be encrypted and the display will look similar to the following:

```
hostname server_l
interface serial 0
 encapsulation ppp
 ppp authentication chap
 username server_l password 7 1514040356
 username server_r password 7 121F0A18
```

Related Commands

You can search online at www.cisco.com to find documentation of related commands.

arap callback
callback-forced-wait
debug callback
ppp callback

## CHAPTER 36

Neighbor Router Authentication: Overview and Guidelines

You can prevent your router from receiving fraudulent route updates by configuring neighbor router authentication.

This chapter describes neighbor router authentication as part of a total security plan. It also describes what neighbor router authentication is, how it works, and why you should use it to increase your overall network security.

This chapter refers to neighbor router authentication as *neighbor authentication*. Neighbor router authentication is also sometimes called *route authentication*.

This chapter describes the following topics:

- Benefits of Neighbor Authentication
- Protocols That Use Neighbor Authentication
- When to Configure Neighbor Authentication
- How Neighbor Authentication Works
- Key Management (Key Chains)

Benefits of Neighbor Authentication

When configured, neighbor authentication occurs whenever routing updates are exchanged between neighbor routers. This authentication ensures that a router receives reliable routing information from a trusted source.

Without neighbor authentication, unauthorized or deliberately malicious routing updates could compromise the security of your network traffic. A security compromise could occur if an unfriendly party diverts or analyzes your network traffic. For example, an unauthorized router could send a fictitious routing update to convince your router to send traffic to an incorrect destination. This diverted traffic could be analyzed to learn confidential information of your organization, or merely used to disrupt your organization's ability to effectively communicate using the network.

Neighbor authentication prevents any such fraudulent route updates from being received by your router.

Protocols That Use Neighbor Authentication

Neighbor authentication can be configured for the following routing protocols:

- Border Gateway Protocol (BGP)

- DRP Server Agent

- Intermediate System-to-Intermediate System (IS-IS)

- IP Enhanced Interior Gateway Routing Protocol (IGRP)

- Open Shortest Path First (OSPF)

- Routing Information Protocol (RIP) version 2

When to Configure Neighbor Authentication

You should configure any router for neighbor authentication if that router meets all of these conditions:

- The router uses any of the routing protocols previously mentioned.

- It is conceivable that the router might receive a false route update.

- If the router were to receive a false route update, your network might be compromised.

- If you configure a router for neighbor authentication, you also need to configure the neighbor router for neighbor authentication.

How Neighbor Authentication Works

When neighbor authentication has been configured on a router, the router authenticates the source of each routing update packet that it receives. This is accomplished by the exchange of an authenticating key (sometimes referred to as a password) that is known to both the sending and the receiving router.

There are two types of neighbor authentication used: plain text authentication and Message Digest Algorithm Version 5 (MD5) authentication. Both forms work in the same way, with the exception that MD5 sends a message digest instead of the authenticating key itself. The message digest is created using the key and a message, but the key itself is not sent, preventing it from being read while it is being transmitted. Plain text authentication sends the authenticating key itself over the wire.

NOTE   Note that plain text authentication is not recommended for use as part of your security strategy. Its primary use is to avoid accidental changes to the routing infrastructure. Using MD5 authentication, however, is a recommended security practice.

CAUTION   As with all keys, passwords, and other security secrets, it is imperative that you closely guard authenticating keys used in neighbor authentication. The security benefits of this feature are reliant on your keeping all authenticating keys confident. Also, when performing router management tasks via Simple Network Management Protocol (SNMP), do not ignore the risk associated with sending keys using non-encrypted SNMP.

Plain Text Authentication

Each participating neighbor router must share an authenticating key. This key is specified at each router during configuration. Multiple keys can be specified with some protocols; each key must then be identified by a key number.

In general, when a routing update is sent, the following authentication sequence occurs:

Step 1   A router sends a routing update with a key and the corresponding key number to the neighbor router. In protocols that can have only one key, the key number is always zero.

Step 2   The receiving (neighbor) router checks the received key against the same key stored in its own memory.

Step 3   If the two keys match, the receiving router accepts the routing update packet. If the two keys did not match, the routing update packet is rejected.

These protocols use plain text authentication:

- DRP Server Agent
- IS-IS
- OSPF
- RIP version 2

MD5 Authentication

MD5 authentication works similarly to plain text authentication, except that the key is never sent over the wire. Instead, the router uses the MD5 algorithm to produce a message digest of the key (also called a *hash*). The message digest is then sent instead of the key itself. This ensures that nobody can eavesdrop on the line and learn keys during transmission.

These protocols use MD5 authentication:

- OSPF
- RIP version 2
- BGP
- IP Enhanced IGRP

Key Management (Key Chains)

You can configure key chains for these routing protocols:

- RIP version 2

- IP Enhanced IGRP

- DRP Server Agent

These routing protocols both offer the additional function of managing keys by using key chains. When you configure a key chain, you specify a series of keys with lifetimes, and the Cisco IOS software rotates through each of these keys. This decreases the likelihood that keys will be compromised.

Each key definition within the key chain must specify a time interval for which that key will be activated (that is, its lifetime). Then, during a given key's lifetime, routing update packets are sent with this activated key. Keys cannot be used during time periods for which they are not activated. Therefore, it is recommended that for a given key chain, key activation times overlap to avoid any period of time for which no key is activated. If a time period occurs during which no key is activated, neighbor authentication cannot occur and therefore routing updates will fail.

Multiple key chains can be specified.

Note that the router needs to know the time to be able to rotate through keys in synchronization with the other participating routers, so that all routers are using the same key at the same moment.

## CHAPTER 37

Configuring IP Security Options

Cisco provides IP Security Option (IPSO) support, as described in RFC 1108. Cisco's implementation is only minimally compliant with RFC 1108 because the Cisco IOS software only accepts and generates a 4-byte IPSO.

IPSO is generally used to comply with the U.S. Government's Department of Defense security policy.

For a complete description of IPSO commands, refer to Chapter 38, "IP Security Options Commands." To locate documentation of other commands that appear in this chapter, you can search online at www.cisco.com.

This chapter describes how to configure IPSO for both the basic and extended security options described in RFC 1108. This chapter also describes how to configure auditing for IPSO. This chapter includes the following sections:

- Configuring Basic IP Security Options
- Configuring Extended IP Security Options
- Configuring the DNSIX Audit Trail Facility
- IPSO Configuration Examples

Configuring Basic IP Security Options

Cisco's basic IPSO support provides the following features:

- Defines security level on a per-interface basis
- Defines single-level or multilevel interfaces
- Provides a label for incoming packets
- Strips labels on a per-interface basis
- Reorders options to put any basic security options first

To configure basic IPSO, complete the tasks in the following sections:

- Enabling IPSO and Setting the Security Classifications
- Specifying How IP Security Options Are Processed

Enabling IPSO and Setting the Security Classifications

To enable IPSO and set security classifications on an interface, use either of the following commands in interface configuration mode:

Command	Purpose
ip security dedicated *level authority* [*authority...*]	Sets an interface to the requested IPSO classification and authorities.
ip security multilevel *level1* [*authority1...*] **to** *level2 authority2* [*authority2...*]	Sets an interface to the requested IPSO range of classifications and authorities.

Use the **no ip security** command to reset an interface to its default state.

Specifying How IP Security Options Are Processed

To specify how IP security options are processed, use any of the following optional commands in interface configuration mode:

Command	Purpose
ip security ignore-authorities	Enables an interface to ignore the authorities field of all incoming packets.
ip security implicit-labelling [*level authority* [*authority...*]]	Classifies packets that have no IPSO with an implicit security label.
ip security extended-allowed	Accepts packets on an interface that has an extended security option present.
ip security add	Ensures that all packets leaving the router on an interface contain a basic security option.
ip security strip	Removes any basic security option that might be present on a packet leaving the router through an interface.
ip security first	Prioritizes security options on a packet.
ip security reserved-allowed	Treats as valid any packets that have Reserved1 through Reserved4 security levels.

Default Values for Command Keywords

In order to fully comply with IPSO, the default values for the minor keywords have become complex. Default value usages include the following:

- The default for all the minor keywords is *off,* with the exception of **implicit-labelling** and **add.**

- The default value of **implicit-labelling** is *on* if the interface is Unclassified Genser; otherwise, it is *off.*

- The default value for **add** is *on* if the interface is not Unclassified Genser; otherwise, it is *off.*

Table 37-1 provides a list of all default values.

Table 37-1 *Default Security Keyword Values*

Interface Type	Level	Authority	Implicit Labeling	Add IPSO
None	None	None	On	Off
Dedicated	Unclassified	Genser	On	Off
Dedicated	Any	Any	Off	On
Multilevel	Any	Any	Off	On

The default value for any interface is Dedicated, Unclassified Genser. Note that this indicates implicit labeling. This might seem unusual, but it makes the system entirely transparent to packets without options. This is the setting generated when you specify the **no ip security** interface configuration command.

Configuring Extended IP Security Options

Cisco's extended IPSO support is compliant with the Department of Defense Intelligence Information System Network Security for Information Exchange (DNSIX) specification documents. Extended IPSO functionality can unconditionally accept or reject Internet traffic that contains extended security options by comparing those options to configured allowable values. This support allows DNSIX networks to use additional security information to achieve a higher level of security than is achievable with basic IPSO.

Cisco also supports a subset of the security features defined in the DNSIX version 2.1 specification. Specifically, Cisco supports DNSIX definitions of the following:

- How extended IPSO is processed
- Audit trail facility

There are two kinds of extended IPSO fields defined by the DNSIX 2.1 specification and supported by Cisco's implementation of extended IPSO—Network-Level Extended Security Option (NLESO) and Auxiliary Extended Security Option (AESO) fields.

NLESO processing requires that security options be checked against configured allowable information, source, and compartment bit values, and requires that the router be capable of inserting extended security options in the IP header.

AESO is similar to NLESO, except that its contents are not checked and are assumed to be valid if its source is listed in the AESO table.

To configure extended IPSO, complete the tasks in the following sections:

- Configuring Global Default Settings

- Attaching ESOs to an Interface

- Attaching AESOs to an Interface

DNSIX version 2.1 causes slow-switching code.

Configuring Global Default Settings

To configure global default setting for extended IPSO, including AESOs, use the following command in global configuration mode:

Command	Purpose
ip security eso-info *source compartment-size default-bit*	Configures systemwide default settings.

Attaching ESOs to an Interface

To specify the minimum and maximum sensitivity levels for an interface, use the following commands in interface configuration mode:

Command	Purpose
ip security eso-min *source compartment-bits*	Sets the minimum sensitivity level for an interface.
ip security eso-max *source compartment-bits*	Sets the maximum sensitivity level for an interface.

Attaching AESOs to an Interface

To specify the extended IPSO sources that are to be treated as AESO sources, use the following command in interface configuration mode:

Command	Purpose
ip security aeso *source compartment-bits*	Specifies AESO sources.

Configuring the DNSIX Audit Trail Facility

The audit trail facility is a UDP-based protocol that generates an audit trail of IPSO security violations. This facility allows the system to report security failures on incoming and outgoing packets. The audit trail facility sends DNSIX audit trail messages when a datagram is rejected because of IPSO security violations. This feature allows you to configure organization-specific security information.

The DNSIX audit trail facility consists of two protocols:

- DNSIX Message Deliver Protocol (DMDP) provides a basic message-delivery mechanism for all DNSIX elements.

- Network Audit Trail Protocol provides a buffered logging facility for applications to use to generate auditing information. This information is then passed on to DMDP.

To configure the DNSIX auditing facility, complete the tasks in the following sections:

- Enabling the DNSIX Audit Trail Facility
- Specifying Hosts to Receive Audit Trail Messages
- Specifying Transmission Parameters

Enabling the DNSIX Audit Trail Facility

To enable the DNSIX audit trail facility, use the following command in global configuration mode:

Command	Purpose
dnsix-nat source *ip-address*	Starts the audit writing module.

Specifying Hosts to Receive Audit Trail Messages

To define and change primary and secondary addresses of the host to receive audit messages, use the following commands in global configuration mode:

Step	Command	Purpose
1	**dnsix-nat primary** *ip-address*	Specifies the primary address for the audit trail.
2	**dnsix-nat secondary** *ip-address*	Specifies the secondary address for the audit trail.
3	**dnsix-nat authorized-redirection** *ip-address*	Specifies the address of a collection center that is authorized to change primary and secondary addresses. Specified hosts are authorized to change the destination of audit messages.

Specifying Transmission Parameters

To specify transmission parameters, use the following commands in global configuration mode:

Step	Command	Purpose
1	**dnsix-nat transmit-count** *count*	Specifies the number of records in a packet before it is sent to a collection center.
2	**dnsix-dmdp retries** *count*	Specifies the number of transmit retries for DMDP.

IPSO Configuration Examples

There are three IPSO examples in this section:

- Example 1
- Example 2
- Example 3

Example 1

In this example, three Ethernet interfaces are presented. These interfaces are running at security levels of Confidential Genser, Secret Genser, and Confidential to Secret Genser, as shown in Figure 37-1.

Figure 37-1 *IPSO Security Levels*

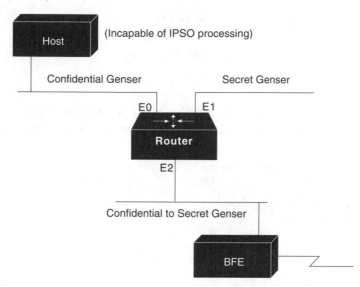

The following commands set up interfaces for the configuration in Figure 37-1:

```
interface ethernet 0
 ip security dedicated confidential genser
interface ethernet 1
 ip security dedicated secret genser
interface ethernet 2
 ip security multilevel confidential genser to secret genser
```

It is possible for the setup to be much more complex.

Example 2

In the following example, devices on Ethernet 0 cannot generate a security option, and so must accept packets without a security option. These hosts do not understand security options; therefore, never place one on such interfaces. Furthermore, hosts on the other two networks are using the extended security option to communicate information, so you must allow these to pass through the system. Finally, a host (a Blacker front end) on Ethernet 2 requires the security option to be the first option present, and this condition also must be specified. The new configuration follows:

```
interface ethernet 0
 ip security dedicated confidential genser
 ip security implicit-labelling
 ip security strip
interface ethernet 1
 ip security dedicated secret genser
 ip security extended-allowed
```

```
!
interface ethernet 2
 ip security multilevel confidential genser to secret genser
 ip security extended-allowed
 ip security first
```

Example 3

This example configures a Cisco router with HP-UX CMW DNSIX hosts. The following commands should be configured on each LAN interface of the router in order for two DNSIX hosts to communicate:

```
ip security multilevel unclassified nsa to top secret nsa
ip security extended allowed
```

DNSIX hosts do not need to know the router's IP addresses, and DNSIX hosts do not need to set up M6RHDB entries for the routers.

## CHAPTER 38

IP Security Options Commands

This chapter describes IP Security Options (IPSO) commands. IPSO is generally used to comply with the U.S. Government's Department of Defense security policy.

You can search online at www.cisco.com to find complete descriptions of other commands used when configuring IPSO.

For IPSO configuration information, refer to Chapter 37, "Configuring IP Security Options."

dnsix-dmdp retries

To set the retransmit count used by the Department of Defense Intelligence Information System Network Security for Information Exchange (DNSIX) Message Delivery Protocol (DMDP), use the **dnsix-dmdp retries** global configuration command. Use the **no** form of this command to restore the default number of retries.

> **dnsix-dmdp retries** *count*
> **no dnsix-dmdp retries** *count*

Syntax	Description
count	Number of times DMDP will retransmit a message. It can be an integer from 0 to 200. The default is four retries, or until acknowledged.

Default

Retransmits messages up to four times, or until acknowledged.

Command Mode

Global configuration

Usage Guidelines

This command first appeared in Cisco IOS Release 10.0.

Example

The following example sets the number of times DMDP will attempt to retransmit a message to 150:

```
dnsix-dmdp retries 150
```

Related Commands

You can search online at www.cisco.com to find documentation of related commands.

dnsix-nat authorized-redirection
dnsix-nat primary
dnsix-nat secondary
dnsix-nat source
dnsix-nat transmit-count

dnsix-nat authorized-redirection

To specify the address of a collection center that is authorized to change the primary and secondary addresses of the host to receive audit messages, use the **dnsix-nat authorized-redirection** global configuration command. Use the **no** form of this command to delete an address.

> **dnsix-nat authorized-redirection** *ip-address*
> **no dnsix-nat authorized-redirection** *ip-address*

Syntax   Description

ip-address   IP address of the host from which redirection requests are permitted.

Default

An empty list of addresses

Command Mode

Global configuration

Usage Guidelines

This command first appeared in Cisco IOS Release 10.0.

Use multiple **dnsix-nat authorized-redirection** commands to specify a set of hosts that are authorized to change the destination for audit messages. Redirection requests are checked against the configured list, and if the address is not authorized, the request is rejected and an audit message is generated. If no address is specified, no redirection messages are accepted.

Example

The following example specifies that the address of the collection center that is authorized to change the primary and secondary addresses is 192.168.1.1:

```
dnsix-nat authorization-redirection 192.168.1.1.
```

dnsix-nat primary

To specify the IP address of the host to which DNSIX audit messages are sent, use the **dnsix-nat primary** global configuration command. Use the **no** form of this command to delete an entry.

> **dnsix-nat primary** *ip-address*
> **no dnsix-nat primary** *ip-address*

Syntax   Description

ip-address   IP address for the primary collection center.

Default

Messages are not sent.

Command Mode

Global configuration

Usage Guidelines

This command first appeared in Cisco IOS Release 10.0.

An IP address must be configured before audit messages can be sent.

Example

The following example configures an IP address as the address of the host to which DNSIX audit messages are sent:

```
dnsix-nat primary 172.1.1.1
```

dnsix-nat secondary

To specify an alternate IP address for the host to which DNSIX audit messages are sent, use the **dnsix-nat secondary** global configuration command. Use the **no** form of this command to delete an entry.

> **dnsix-nat secondary** *ip-address*
> **no dnsix-nat secondary** *ip-address*

Syntax

Syntax	Description
ip-address	IP address for the secondary collection center.

Default

No alternate IP address is known.

Command Mode

Global configuration

Usage Guidelines

This command first appeared in Cisco IOS Release 10.0.

When the primary collection center is unreachable, audit messages are sent to the secondary collection center instead.

Example

The following example configures an IP address as the address of an alternate host to which DNSIX audit messages are sent:

```
dnsix-nat secondary 192.168.1.1
```

dnsix-nat source

To start the audit-writing module and to define the audit trail source address, use the **dnsix-nat source** global configuration command. Use the **no** form of this command to disable the DNSIX audit trail writing module.

> **dnsix-nat source** *ip-address*
> **no dnsix-nat source** *ip-address*

Syntax	Description
ip-address	Source IP address for DNSIX audit messages.

Default
Disabled

Command Mode
Global configuration

Usage Guidelines
This command first appeared in Cisco IOS Release 10.0.

You must issue the **dnsix-nat source** command before any of the other **dnsix-nat** commands. The configured IP address is used as the source IP address for DMDP protocol packets sent to any of the collection centers.

Example
The following example enables the audit trail writing module and specifies that the source IP address for any generated audit messages should be the same as the primary IP address of Ethernet interface 0:

```
dnsix-nat source 192.168.2.5
interface ethernet 0
 ip address 192.168.2.5 255.255.255.0
```

dnsix-nat transmit-count

To have the audit writing module collect multiple audit messages in the buffer before sending the messages to a collection center, use the **dnsix-nat transmit-count** global configuration command. Use the **no** form of this command to revert to the default audit message count.

> **dnsix-nat transmit-count** *count*
> **no dnsix-nat transmit-count** *count*

Syntax	Description
count	Number of audit messages to buffer before transmitting to the server. It can be an integer from 1 to 200.

Default

One message is sent at a time.

Command Mode

Global configuration

Usage Guidelines

This command first appeared in Cisco IOS Release 10.0.

An audit message is sent as soon as the message is generated by the IP packet-processing code. The audit writing module can, instead, buffer up to several audit messages before transmitting to a collection center.

Example

The following example configures the system to buffer five audit messages before transmitting them to a collection center:

```
dnsix-nat transmit-count 5
```

ip security add

To add a basic security option to all outgoing packets, use the **ip security add** interface configuration command. Use the **no** form of this command to disable the adding of a basic security option to all outgoing packets.

> **ip security add**
> **no ip security add**

Syntax Description

This command has no arguments or keywords.

Default

Disabled, when the security level of the interface is Unclassified Genser (or Unconfigured). Otherwise, the default is enabled.

Command Mode

Interface configuration

Usage Guidelines

This command first appeared in Cisco IOS Release 10.0.

If an outgoing packet does not have a security option present, this interface configuration command adds one as the first IP option. The security label added to the option field is the label that was computed for this packet when it first entered the router. Because this action is performed after all the security tests have been passed, this label will either be the same or will fall within the range of the interface.

Example

The following example adds a basic security option to each packet leaving Ethernet interface 0:

```
interface ethernet 0
 ip security add
```

Related Commands

You can search online at www.cisco.com to find documentation of related commands.

ip security dedicated
ip security extended-allowed
ip security first
ip security ignore-authorities
ip security implicit-labelling
ip security multilevel
ip security reserved-allowed
ip security strip

ip security aeso

To attach Auxiliary Extended Security Options (AESOs) to an interface, use the **ip security aeso** interface configuration command. Use the **no** form of this command to disable AESO on an interface.

> **ip security aeso** *source compartment-bits*
> **no ip security aeso** *source compartment-bits*

Syntax	Description
source	Extended Security Option (ESO) source. This can be an integer from 0 to 255.
compartment-bits	Compartment bits in hexadecimal.

Default
Disabled

Command Mode
Interface configuration

Usage Guidelines
This command first appeared in Cisco IOS Release 10.0.

Compartment bits are specified only if this AESO is to be inserted in a packet. On every incoming packet at this level on this interface, these AESOs should be present.

Beyond being recognized, no further processing of AESO information is performed. AESO contents are not checked and are assumed to be valid if the source is listed in the configurable AESO table.

Configuring any per-interface extended IPSO information automatically enables **ip security extended-allowed** (disabled by default).

Example
The following example defines the extended security option source as 5 and sets the compartments bits to 5:

```
interface ethernet 0
 ip security aeso 5 5
```

Related Commands
You can search online at www.cisco.com to find documentation of related commands.

ip security eso-info
ip security eso-max
ip security eso-min
ip security extended-allowed

ip security dedicated

To set the level of classification and authority on the interface, use the **ip security dedicated** interface configuration command. Use the **no** form of this command to reset the interface to the default classification and authorities.

> **ip security dedicated** *level authority* [*authority...*]
> **no ip security dedicated** *level authority* [*authority...*]

Syntax

Syntax	Description
level	Degree of sensitivity of information. The level keywords are listed in Table 38-1.
authority	Organization that defines the set of security levels that will be used in a network. The authority keywords are listed in Table 38-2.

Default

Disabled

Command Mode

Interface configuration

Usage Guidelines

This command first appeared in Cisco IOS Release 10.0.

All traffic entering the system on this interface must have a security option that exactly matches this label. Any traffic leaving via this interface will have this label attached to it.

The following definitions apply to the descriptions of the IPSO in this section:

- **Level**—The degree of sensitivity of information. For example, data marked TOPSECRET is more sensitive than data marked SECRET. The level keywords and their corresponding bit patterns are shown in Table 38-1.

Table 38-1 *IPSO Level Keywords and Bit Patterns*

Level Keyword	Bit Pattern
Reserved4	0000 0001
TopSecret	0011 1101
Secret	0101 1010
Confidential	1001 0110
Reserved3	0110 0110
Reserved2	1100 1100
Unclassified	1010 1011
Reserved1	1111 0001

- **Authority**—An organization that defines the set of security levels that will be used in a network. For example, the Genser authority consists of level names defined by the U.S. Defense Communications Agency (DCA). The authority keywords and their corresponding bit patterns are shown in Table 38-2.

Table 38-2 *IPSO Authority Keywords and Bit Patterns*

Authority Keyword	Bit Pattern
Genser	1000 0000
Siop-Esi	0100 0000
DIA	0010 0000
NSA	0001 0000
DOE	0000 1000

- **Label**—A combination of a security level and an authority or authorities.

Example

The following example sets a confidential level with Genser authority:

```
ip security dedicated confidential Genser
```

Related Commands

You can search online at www.cisco.com to find documentation of related commands.

ip security add
ip security extended-allowed
ip security first
ip security ignore-authorities
ip security implicit-labelling
ip security multilevel
ip security reserved-allowed
ip security strip

ip security eso-info

To configure systemwide defaults for extended IPSO information, use the **ip security eso-info** global configuration command. Use the **no** form of this command to return to the default settings.

ip security eso-info *source compartment-size default-bit*
no ip security eso-info *source compartment-size default-bit*

Syntax

Syntax	Description
source	Hexadecimal or decimal value representing the extended IPSO source. This is an integer from 0 to 255.
compartment-size	Maximum number of bytes of compartment information allowed for a particular extended IPSO source. This is an integer from 1 to 16.
default-bit	Default bit value for any unsent compartment bits.

Default

Disabled

Command mode

Global configuration

Usage Guidelines

This command first appeared in Cisco IOS Release 10.0.

This command configures ESO information, including AESO. Transmitted compartment info is padded to the size specified by the *compartment-size* argument.

Example

The following example sets systemwide defaults for source, compartment size, and the default bit value:

```
ip security eso-info 100 5 1
```

Related Commands

You can search online at www.cisco.com to find documentation of related commands.

ip security eso-max
ip security eso-min

ip security eso-max

To specify the maximum sensitivity level for an interface, use the **ip security eso-max** interface configuration command. Use the **no** form of this command to return to the default.

> **ip security eso-max** *source compartment-bits*
> **no ip security eso-max** *source compartment-bits*

Syntax

Description

| *source* | ESO source. This is an integer from 1 to 255. |
| *compartment-bits* | Compartment bits in hexadecimal. |

Default

Disabled

Command Mode

Interface configuration

Usage Guidelines

This command first appeared in Cisco IOS Release 10.0.

The command is used to specify the maximum sensitivity level for a particular interface. Before the per-interface compartment information for a particular Network-Level Extended Security Option (NLESO) source can be configured, the **ip security eso-info** global configuration command must be used to specify the default information.

On every incoming packet on the interface, these extended security options should be present at the minimum level and should match the configured compartment bits. Every outgoing packet must have these ESOs.

On every packet transmitted or received on this interface, any NLESO sources present in the IP header should be bounded by the minimum sensitivity level and bounded by the maximum sensitivity level configured for the interface.

When transmitting locally generated traffic out this interface, or adding security information (with the **ip security add** command), the maximum compartment bit information can be used to construct the NLESO sources placed in the IP header.

A maximum of 16 NLESO sources can be configured per interface. Due to IP header length restrictions, a maximum of 9 of these NLESO sources appear in the IP header of a packet.

Example

In the following example, the specified ESO source is 240 and the compartment bits are specified as 500:

```
interface ethernet 0
 ip security eso-max 240 500
```

Related Commands

You can search online at www.cisco.com to find documentation of related commands.

ip security eso-info
ip security eso-min

ip security eso-min

To configure the minimum sensitivity for an interface, use the **ip security eso-min** interface configuration command. Use the **no** form of this command to return to the default.

> **ip security eso-min** *source compartment-bits*
> **no ip security eso-min** *source compartment-bits*

Syntax	Description
source	ESO source. This is an integer from 1 to 255.
compartment-bits	Compartment bits in hexadecimal.

Default

Disabled

Command Mode

Interface configuration

Usage Guidelines

This command first appeared in Cisco IOS Release 10.0.

The command is used to specify the minimum sensitivity level for a particular interface. Before the per-interface compartment information for a particular NLESO source can be configured, the **ip security eso-info** global configuration command must be used to specify the default information.

On every incoming packet on this interface, these extended security options should be present at the minimum level and should match the configured compartment bits. Every outgoing packet must have these ESOs.

On every packet transmitted or received on this interface, any NLESO sources present in the IP header should be bounded by the minimum sensitivity level and bounded by the maximum sensitivity level configured for the interface.

When transmitting locally generated traffic out this interface or adding security information (with the **ip security add** command), the maximum compartment bit information can be used to construct the NLESO sources placed in the IP header.

A maximum of 16 NLESO sources can be configured per interface. Due to IP header length restrictions, a maximum of 9 of these NLESO sources appear in the IP header of a packet.

Example

In the following example, the specified ESO source is 5 and the compartment bits are specified as 5:

```
interface ethernet 0
 ip security eso-min 5 5
```

Related Commands

You can search online at www.cisco.com to find documentation of related commands.

ip security eso-info
ip security eso-max

ip security extended-allowed

To accept packets on an interface that has an extended security option present, use the **ip security extended-allowed** interface configuration command. Use the **no** form of this command to restore the default.

> **ip security extended-allowed**
> **no ip security extended-allowed**

Syntax Description

This command has no arguments or keywords.

Default

Disabled

Command Mode

Interface configuration

Usage Guidelines

This command first appeared in Cisco IOS Release 10.0.

Packets containing extended security options are rejected.

Example

The following example allows interface Ethernet 0 to accept packets that have an extended security option present:

```
interface ethernet 0
 ip security extended-allowed
```

Related Commands

You can search online at www.cisco.com to find documentation of related commands.

ip security add
ip security dedicated
ip security first
ip security ignore-authorities
ip security implicit-labelling
ip security multilevel
ip security reserved-allowed
ip security strip

ip security first

To prioritize the presence of security options on a packet, use the **ip security first** interface configuration command. Use the **no** form of this command to not move packets that include security options to the front of the options field.

> **ip security first**
> **no ip security first**

Syntax Description

This command has no arguments or keywords.

Default

Disabled

Command Mode

Interface configuration

Usage Guidelines

This command first appeared in Cisco IOS Release 10.0.

If a basic security option is present on an outgoing packet, but it is not the first IP option, then the packet is moved to the front of the options field when this interface configuration command is used.

Example

The following example ensures that if a basic security option is present in the options field of a packet exiting interface Ethernet 0, the packet is moved to the front of the options field:

```
interface ethernet 0
 ip security first
```

Related Commands

You can search online at www.cisco.com to find documentation of related commands.

ip security add
ip security dedicated
ip security extended-allowed
ip security ignore-authorities
ip security implicit-labelling
ip security multilevel
ip security reserved-allowed
ip security strip

ip security ignore-authorities

To have the Cisco IOS software ignore the authorities field of all incoming packets, use the **ip security ignore-authorities** interface configuration command. Use the **no** form of this command to disable this function.

> **ip security ignore-authorities**
> **no ip security ignore-authorities**

Syntax Description

This command has no arguments or keywords.

Default

Disabled

Command Mode

Interface configuration

Usage Guidelines

This command first appeared in Cisco IOS Release 10.0.

When the packet's authority field is ignored, the value used in place of this field is the authority value declared for the specified interface. The **ip security ignore-authorities** can only be configured on interfaces with dedicated security levels.

Example

The following example causes interface Ethernet 0 to ignore the authorities field on all incoming packets:

```
interface ethernet 0
 ip security ignore-authorities
```

Related Commands

You can search online at www.cisco.com to find documentation of related commands.

ip security add
ip security dedicated
ip security extended-allowed
ip security first
ip security implicit-labelling
ip security multilevel
ip security reserved-allowed
ip security strip

ip security implicit-labelling

To force the Cisco IOS software to accept packets on the interface, even if they do not include a security option, use the **ip security implicit-labelling** interface configuration command. Use the **no** form of this command to require security options.

> **ip security implicit-labelling** [*level authority* [*authority...*]]
> **no ip security implicit-labelling** [*level authority* [*authority...*]]

Syntax   Description

level   (Optional) Degree of sensitivity of information. If your interface has multilevel security set, you must specify this argument. (See the *level* keywords listed in Table 38-1 in the **ip security dedicated** command section.)

authority   (Optional) Organization that defines the set of security levels that will be used in a nctwork. If your interface has multilevel security set, you must specify this argument. You can specify more than one. (See the *authority* keywords listed in Table 38-2 in the **ip security dedicated** command section.)

Default

Enabled, when the security level of the interface is Unclassified Genser (or Unconfigured). Otherwise, the default is disabled.

Command Mode

Interface configuration

Usage Guidelines

This command first appeared in Cisco IOS Release 10.0.

If your interface has multilevel security set, you must use the expanded form of the command (with the optional arguments, as noted in brackets) because the arguments are used to specify the precise level and authority to use when labeling the packet. If your interface has dedicated security set, the additional arguments are ignored.

Example

In the following example, an interface is set for security and will accept unlabeled packets:

```
ip security dedicated confidential genser
ip security implicit-labelling
```

Related Commands

You can search online at www.cisco.com to find documentation of related commands.

ip security add
ip security dedicated
ip security extended-allowed
ip security first
ip security ignore-authorities
ip security multilevel
ip security reserved-allowed
ip security strip

ip security multilevel

To set the range of classifications and authorities on an interface, use the **ip security multilevel** interface configuration command. Use the **no** form of this command to remove security classifications and authorities.

ip security multilevel *level1* [*authority1*...] **to** *level2 authority2* [*authority2*...]
no ip security multilevel

Syntax	Description
level1	Degree of sensitivity of information. The classification level of incoming packets must be equal to or greater than this value for processing to occur. (See the *level* keywords found in Table 38-1 in the **ip security dedicated** command section.)
authority1	(Optional) Organization that defines the set of security levels that will be used in a network. The authority bits must be a superset of this value. (See the *authority* keywords listed in Table 38-2 in the **ip security dedicated** command section.)
to	Separates the range of classifications and authorities.
level2	Degree of sensitivity of information. The classification level of incoming packets must be equal to or less than this value for processing to occur. (See the *level* keywords found in Table 38-1 in the **ip security dedicated** command section.)
authority2	Organization that defines the set of security levels that will be used in a network. The authority bits must be a proper subset of this value. (See the *authority* keywords listed in Table 38-2 in the **ip security dedicated** command section.)

Default
Disabled

Command Mode
Interface configuration

Usage Guidelines
This command first appeared in Cisco IOS Release 10.0.

All traffic entering or leaving the system must have a security option that falls within this range. Being within range requires that the following two conditions be met:

- The classification level must be greater than or equal to *level1* and less than or equal to *level2*.

- The authority bits must be a superset of *authority1* and a proper subset of *authority2*. That is, *authority1* specifies those authority bits that are required on a packet, and *authority2* specifies the required bits plus any optional authorities that also can be included. If the *authority1* field is the empty set, then a packet is required to specify any one or more of the authority bits in *authority2*.

Example
The following example specifies levels Unclassified to Secret and NSA authority:

```
ip security multilevel unclassified to secret nsa
```

Related Commands
You can search online at www.cisco.com to find documentation of related commands.

ip security add
ip security dedicated
ip security extended-allowed
ip security first
ip security ignore-authorities
ip security implicit-labelling
ip security reserved-allowed
ip security strip

ip security reserved-allowed

To treat as valid any packets that have Reserved1 through Reserved4 security levels, use the **ip security reserved-allowed** interface configuration command. Use the **no** form of this command to not allow packets that have security levels of Reserved3 and Reserved2.

> **ip security reserved-allowed**
> **no ip security reserved-allowed**

Syntax Description

This command has no arguments or keywords.

Default

Disabled

Command Mode

Interface configuration

Usage Guidelines

This command first appeared in Cisco IOS Release 10.3.

When you set multilevel security on an interface, and indicate, for example, that the highest range allowed is Confidential and the lowest is Unclassified, the Cisco IOS software neither allows nor operates on packets that have security levels of Reserved3 and Reserved2 because they are undefined.

If you use the IPSO to block transmission out of unclassified interfaces, and you use one of the Reserved security levels, you *must* enable this feature to preserve network security.

Example

The following example allows a security level of Reserved through Ethernet interface 0:

```
interface ethernet 0
 ip security reserved-allowed
```

Related Commands

You can search online at www.cisco.com to find documentation of related commands.

ip security add
ip security dedicated
ip security extended-allowed
ip security first
ip security ignore-authorities
ip security implicit-labelling
ip security multilevel
ip security strip

ip security strip

To remove any basic security option on outgoing packets on an interface, use the **ip security strip** interface configuration command. Use the **no** form of this command to restore security options.

> **ip security strip**
> **no ip security strip**

Syntax Description

This command has no arguments or keywords.

Default

Disabled

Command Mode

Interface configuration

Usage Guidelines

This command first appeared in Cisco IOS Release 10.0.

The removal procedure is performed after all security tests in the router have been passed. This command is not allowed for multilevel interfaces.

Example

The following example removes any basic security options on outgoing packets on Ethernet interface 0:

```
interface ethernet 0
 ip security strip
```

Related Commands

You can search online at www.cisco.com to find documentation of related commands.

ip security add
ip security dedicated
ip security extended-allowed
ip security first
ip security ignore-authorities
ip security implicit-labelling
ip security multilevel
ip security reserved-allowed

show dnsix

To display state information and the current configuration of the DNSIX audit writing module, use the **show dnsix** privileged EXEC command.

> **show dnsix**

Syntax Description

This command has no arguments or keywords.

Command Mode

Privileged EXEC

Usage Guidelines

This command first appeared in Cisco IOS Release 10.0.

Sample Display

The following is sample output from the **show dnsix** command:

```
Router# show dnsix

Audit Trail Enabled with Source 192.168.2.5
          State: PRIMARY
          Connected to 192.168.2.4
          Primary 192.168.2.4
          Transmit Count 1
          DMDP retries 4
          Authorization Redirection List:
              192.168.2.4
          Record count: 0
          Packet Count: 0
          Redirect Rcv: 0
```

PART VI

Appendixes

RADIUS Attributes

Remote Authentication Dial-In User Service (RADIUS) attributes are used to define specific authentication, authorization, and accounting (AAA) elements in a user profile, which is stored on the RADIUS daemon. This appendix lists the RADIUS attributes currently supported.

This appendix is divided into two sections:

● Supported RADIUS Attributes

● Comprehensive List of RADIUS Attributes

The first section lists the Cisco IOS releases in which supported Internet Engineering Task Force (IETF) RADIUS and vendor-proprietary RADIUS are implemented. The second section provides a comprehensive list and description of both IETF RADIUS and vendor-proprietary RADIUS attributes.

Supported RADIUS Attributes

Table A-1 lists and describes Cisco-supported IETF RADIUS attributes and the Cisco IOS release in which they are implemented. In cases where the attribute has a security server-specific format, the format is specified.

NOTE Attributes implemented in special (AA) or early development (T) releases will be added to the next mainline image.

Table A-1 *Supported RADIUS (IETF) Attributes*

Number	Attribute	11.1	11.2	11.3	11.3 AA	11.3T	12.0
1	User-Name	yes	yes	yes	yes	yes	yes
2	User-Password	yes	yes	yes	yes	yes	yes
3	CHAP-Password	yes	yes	yes	yes	yes	yes
4	NAS-IP Address	yes	yes	yes	yes	yes	yes
5	NAS-Port	yes	yes	yes	yes	yes	yes
6	Service-Type	yes	yes	yes	yes	yes	yes
7	Framed-Protocol	yes	yes	yes	yes	yes	yes
8	Framed-IP-Address	yes	yes	yes	yes	yes	yes

Continues

Table A-1 *Supported RADIUS (IETF) Attributes (Continued)*

Number	Attribute	11.1	11.2	11.3	11.3 AA	11.3T	12.0
9	Framed-IP-Netmask	yes	yes	yes	yes	yes	yes
10	Framed-Routing	yes	yes	yes	yes	yes	yes
11	Filter-Id	yes	yes	yes	yes	yes	yes
12	Framed-MTU	yes	yes	yes	yes	yes	yes
13	Framed-Compression	yes	yes	yes	yes	yes	yes
14	Login-IP-Host	yes	yes	yes	yes	yes	yes
15	Login-Service	yes	yes	yes	yes	yes	yes
16	Login-TCP-Port	yes	yes	yes	yes	yes	yes
18	Reply-Message	yes	yes	yes	yes	yes	yes
19	Callback-Number	no	no	no	no	no	no
20	Callback-ID	no	no	no	no	no	no
22	Framed-Route	yes	yes	yes	yes	yes	yes
23	Framed-IPX-Network	no	no	no	no	no	no
24	State	yes	yes	yes	yes	yes	yes
25	Class	yes	yes	yes	yes	yes	yes
26	Vendor-Specific	yes	yes	yes	yes	yes	yes
27	Session-Timeout	yes	yes	yes	yes	yes	yes
28	Idle-Timeout	yes	yes	yes	yes	yes	yes
29	Termination-Action	no	no	no	no	no	no
30	Called-Station-Id	yes	yes	yes	yes	yes	yes
31	Calling-Station-Id	yes	yes	yes	yes	yes	yes
32	NAS-Identifier	no	no	no	no	no	no
33	Proxy-State	no	no	no	no	no	no
34	Login-LAT-Service	yes	yes	yes	yes	yes	yes
35	Login-LAT-Node	no	no	no	no	no	no
36	Login-LAT-Group	no	no	no	no	no	no
37	Framed-AppleTalk-Link	no	no	no	no	no	no
38	Framed-AppleTalk-Network	no	no	no	no	no	no
39	Framed-AppleTalk-Zone	no	no	no	no	no	no
40	Acct-Status-Type	yes	yes	yes	yes	yes	yes

Table A-1 *Supported RADIUS (IETF) Attributes (Continued)*

Number	Attribute	11.1	11.2	11.3	11.3 AA	11.3T	12.0
41	Acct-Delay-Time	yes	yes	yes	yes	yes	yes
42	Acct-Input-Octets	yes	yes	yes	yes	yes	yes
43	Acct-Output-Octets	yes	yes	yes	yes	yes	yes
44	Acct-Session-Id	yes	yes	yes	yes	yes	yes
45	Acct-Authentic	yes	yes	yes	yes	yes	yes
46	Acct-Session-Time	yes	yes	yes	yes	yes	yes
47	Acct-Input-Packets	yes	yes	yes	yes	yes	yes
48	Acct-Output-Packets	yes	yes	yes	yes	yes	yes
49	Acct-Terminate-Cause	yes	yes	yes	yes	yes	yes
50	Acct-Multi-Session-Id[1]	no	no	no	no	no	no
51	Acct-Link-Count[2]	no	no	no	no	no	no
60	CHAP-Challenge	no	no	no	no	no	no
61	NAS-Port-Type	yes	yes	yes	yes	yes	yes
62	Port-Limit	yes	yes	yes	yes	yes	yes
63	Login-LAT-Port	no	no	no	no	no	no
200	IETF-Token-Immediate	no	no	no	no	no	no

1.Only stop records containing multisession IDs because start records are issued before any multilink processing takes place.
2.Only stop records containing link counts because start records are issued before any multilink processing takes place.

Table A-2 lists and describes Cisco-supported vendor-proprietary RADIUS attributes and the Cisco IOS release in which they are implemented. In cases where the attribute has a security server-specific format, the format is specified.

NOTE	Attributes implemented in special (AA) or early development (T) releases will be added to the next mainline image.

Table A-2   *Supported Vendor-Proprietary RADIUS Attributes*

Number	Vendor-Proprietary Attribute	11.1	11.2	11.3	11.3AA	11.3T	12.0
17	Change-Password	no	no	yes	yes	yes	yes
21	Password-Expiration	no	no	yes	yes	yes	yes
64	Tunnel-Type	no	no	no	no	no	no
65	Tunnel-Medium-Type	no	no	no	no	no	no
66	Tunnel-Client-Endpoint	no	no	no	no	no	no
67	Tunnel-Server-Endpoint	no	no	no	no	no	no
68	Tunnel-ID	no	no	no	no	no	no
108	My-Endpoint-Disc-Alias	no	no	no	no	no	no
109	My-Name-Alias	no	no	no	no	no	no
110	Remote-FW	no	no	no	no	no	no
111	Multicast-GLeave-Delay	no	no	no	no	no	no
112	CBCP-Enable	no	no	no	no	no	no
113	CBCP-Mode	no	no	no	no	no	no
114	CBCP-Delay	no	no	no	no	no	no
115	CBCP-Trunk-Group	no	no	no	no	no	no
116	AppleTalk-Route	no	no	no	no	no	no
117	AppleTalk-Peer-Mode	no	no	no	no	no	no
118	Route-AppleTalk	no	no	no	no	no	no
119	FCP-Parameter	no	no	no	no	no	no
120	Modem-PortNo	no	no	no	no	no	no
121	Modem-SlotNo	no	no	no	no	no	no
122	Modem-ShelfNo	no	no	no	no	no	no
123	Call-Attempt-Limit	no	no	no	no	no	no
124	Call-Block-Duration	no	no	no	no	no	no
125	Maximum-Call-Duration	no	no	no	no	no	no
126	Router-Preference	no	no	no	no	no	no
127	Tunneling-Protocol	no	no	no	no	no	no
128	Shared-Profile-Enable	no	no	no	no	no	no

Table A-2   *Supported Vendor-Proprietary RADIUS Attributes (Continued)*

Number	Vendor-Proprietary Attribute	11.1	11.2	11.3	11.3AA	11.3T	12.0
129	Primary-Home-Agent	no	no	no	no	no	no
130	Secondary-Home-Agent	no	no	no	no	no	no
131	Dialout-Allowed	no	no	no	no	no	no
133	BACP-Enable	no	no	no	no	no	no
134	DHCP-Maximum-Leases	no	no	no	no	no	no
135	Primary-DNS-Server	no	no	no	no	yes	yes
136	Secondary-DNS-Server	no	no	no	no	yes	yes
137	Client-Assign-DNS	no	no	no	no	no	no
138	User-Acct-Type	no	no	no	no	no	no
139	User-Acct-Host	no	no	no	no	no	no
140	User-Acct-Port	no	no	no	no	no	no
141	User-Acct-Key	no	no	no	no	no	no
142	User-Acct-Base	no	no	no	no	no	no
143	User-Acct-Time	no	no	no	no	no	no
144	Assign-Ip-Client	no	no	no	no	no	no
145	Assign-IP-Server	no	no	no	no	no	no
146	Assign-IP-Global-Pool	no	no	no	no	no	no
147	DHCP-Reply	no	no	no	no	no	no
148	DHCP-Pool-Number	no	no	no	no	no	no
149	Expect-Callback	no	no	no	no	no	no
150	Event-Type	no	no	no	no	no	no
151	Session-Svr-Key	no	no	no	no	no	no
152	Multicast-Rate-Limit	no	no	no	no	no	no
153	IF-Netmask	no	no	no	no	no	no
154	Remote-Addr	no	no	no	no	no	no
155	Multicast-Client	no	no	no	no	no	no
156	FR-Circuit-Name	no	no	no	no	no	no
157	FR-LinkUp	no	no	no	no	no	no
158	FR-Nailed-Grp	no	no	no	no	no	no

Continues

Table A-2 *Supported Vendor-Proprietary RADIUS Attributes (Continued)*

Number	Vendor-Proprietary Attribute	11.1	11.2	11.3	11.3AA	11.3T	12.0
159	FR-Type	no	no	no	no	no	no
160	FR-Link-Mgt	no	no	no	no	no	no
161	FR-N391	no	no	no	no	no	no
162	FR-DCE-N392	no	no	no	no	no	no
163	FR-DTE-N392	no	no	no	no	no	no
164	FR-DCE-N393	no	no	no	no	no	no
165	FR-DTE-N393	no	no	no	no	no	no
166	FR-T391	no	no	no	no	no	no
167	FR-T392	no	no	no	no	no	no
168	Bridge-Address	no	no	no	no	no	no
169	TS-Idle-Limit	no	no	no	no	no	no
170	TS-Idle-Mode	no	no	no	no	no	no
171	DBA-Monitor	no	no	no	no	no	no
172	Base-Channel-Count	no	no	no	no	no	no
173	Minimum-Channels	no	no	no	no	no	no
174	IPX-Route	no	no	no	no	no	no
175	FT1-Caller	no	no	no	no	no	no
176	Backup	no	no	no	no	no	no
177	Call-Type	no	no	no	no	no	no
178	Group	no	no	no	no	no	no
179	FR-DLCI	no	no	no	no	no	no
180	FR-Profile-Name	no	no	no	no	no	no
181	Ara-PW	no	no	no	no	no	no
182	IPX-Node-Addr	no	no	no	no	no	no
183	Home-Agent-IP-Addr	no	no	no	no	no	no
184	Home-Agent-Password	no	no	no	no	no	no
185	Home-Network-Name	no	no	no	no	no	no
186	Home-Agent-UDP-Port	no	no	no	no	no	no
187	Multilink-ID	no	no	no	no	yes	yes

Table A-2 *Supported Vendor-Proprietary RADIUS Attributes (Continued)*

Number	Vendor-Proprietary Attribute	11.1	11.2	11.3	11.3AA	11.3T	12.0
188	Num-In-Multilink	no	no	no	no	yes	yes
189	First-Dest	no	no	no	no	no	no
190	Pre-Input-Octets	no	no	no	no	yes	yes
191	Pre-Output-Octets	no	no	no	no	yes	yes
192	Pre-Input-Packets	no	no	no	no	yes	yes
193	Pre-Output-Packets	no	no	no	no	yes	yes
194	Maximum-Time	no	no	yes	yes	yes	yes
195	Disconnect-Cause	no	no	yes	yes	yes	yes
196	Connect-Progress	no	no	no	no	no	no
197	Data-Rate	no	no	no	no	yes	yes
198	PreSession-Time	no	no	no	no	yes	yes
199	Token-Idle	no	no	no	no	no	no
201	Require-Auth	no	no	no	no	no	no
202	Number-Sessions	no	no	no	no	no	no
203	Authen-Alias	no	no	no	no	no	no
204	Token-Expiry	no	no	no	no	no	no
205	Menu-Selector	no	no	no	no	no	no
206	Menu-Item	no	no	no	no	no	no
207	PW-Warntime	no	no	no	no	no	no
208	PW-Lifetime	no	no	yes	yes	yes	yes
209	IP-Direct	no	no	yes	yes	yes	yes
210	PPP-VJ-Slot-Comp	no	no	yes	yes	yes	yes
211	PPP-VJ-1172	no	no	no	no	no	no
212	PPP-Async-Map	no	no	no	no	no	no
213	Third-Prompt	no	no	no	no	no	no
214	Send-Secret	no	no	no	no	no	no
215	Receive-Secret	no	no	no	no	no	no
216	IPX-Peer-Mode	no	no	no	no	no	no
217	IP-Pool-Definition	no	no	yes	yes	yes	yes

Continues

Table A-2   *Supported Vendor-Proprietary RADIUS Attributes (Continued)*

Number	Vendor-Proprietary Attribute	11.1	11.2	11.3	11.3AA	11.3T	12.0
218	Assign-IP-Pool	no	no	yes	yes	yes	yes
219	FR-Direct	no	no	no	no	no	no
220	FR-Direct-Profile	no	no	no	no	no	no
221	FR-Direct-DLCI	no	no	no	no	no	no
222	Handle-IPX	no	no	no	no	no	no
223	Netware-Timeout	no	no	no	no	no	no
224	IPX-Alias	no	no	no	no	no	no
225	Metric	no	no	no	no	no	no
226	PRI-Number-Type	no	no	no	no	no	no
227	Dial-Number	no	no	no	no	no	no
228	Route-IP	no	no	yes	yes	yes	yes
229	Route-IPX	no	no	no	no	no	no
230	Bridge	no	no	no	no	no	no
231	Send-Auth	no	no	no	no	no	no
232	Send-Passwd	no	no	no	no	no	no
233	Link-Compression	no	no	yes	yes	yes	yes
234	Target-Util	no	no	yes	yes	yes	yes
235	Maximum-Channels	no	no	yes	yes	yes	yes
236	Inc-Channel-Count	no	no	no	no	no	no
237	Dec-Channel-Count	no	no	no	no	no	no
238	Seconds-of-History	no	no	no	no	no	no
239	History-Weigh-Type	no	no	no	no	no	no
240	Add-Seconds	no	no	no	no	no	no
241	Remove-Seconds	no	no	no	no	no	no
242	Data-Filter	no	no	yes	yes	yes	yes
243	Call-Filter	no	no	yes	yes	yes	yes
244	Idle-Limit	no	no	yes	yes	yes	yes
245	Preempt-Limit	no	no	no	no	no	no
246	Callback	no	no	no	no	no	no

Table A-2 *Supported Vendor-Proprietary RADIUS Attributes (Continued)*

Number	Vendor-Proprietary Attribute	11.1	11.2	11.3	11.3AA	11.3T	12.0
247	Data-Svc	no	no	no	no	no	no
248	Force-56	no	no	no	no	no	no
249	Billing Number	no	no	no	no	no	no
250	Call-By-Call	no	no	no	no	no	no
251	Transit-Number	no	no	no	no	no	no
252	Host-Info	no	no	no	no	no	no
253	PPP-Address	no	no	no	no	no	no
254	MPP-Idle-Percent	no	no	no	no	no	no
255	Xmit-Rate	no	no	no	no	no	no

For more information about Cisco's implementation of RADIUS, refer to Chapter 8, "Configuring RADIUS."

Comprehensive List of RADIUS Attributes

The following pages provide a comprehensive listing and description of known RADIUS attributes:

Table A-3 lists and describes IETF RADIUS attributes. In cases where the attribute has a security server-specific format, the format is specified.

Table A-3 *RADIUS (IETF) Attributes*

Number	Attribute	Description
1	User-Name	Indicates the name of the user being authenticated.
2	User-Password	Indicates the user's password or the user's input following an Access-Challenge. Passwords longer than 16 characters are encrypted using the IETF Draft #2 (or later) specifications.
3	CHAP-Password	Indicates the response value provided by a PPP Challenge-Handshake Authentication Protocol (CHAP) user in response to an Access-Challenge.
4	NAS-IP Address	Specifies the IP address of the network access server that is requesting authentication.

Continues

Table A-3 *RADIUS (IETF) Attributes (Continued)*

Number	Attribute	Description
5	NAS-Port	Indicates the physical port number of the network access server that is authenticating the user. The NAS-Port value (32 bits) consists of one or two 16-bit values (depending on the setting of the **radius-server extended-portnames** command). Each 16-bit number should be viewed as a 5-digit decimal integer for interpretation as follows: • For asynchronous terminal lines, async network interfaces, and virtual async interfaces, the value is **00ttt**, where **ttt** is the line number or async interface unit number. • For ordinary synchronous network interface, the value is **10xxx**. • For channels on a primary rate ISDN interface, the value is **2ppcc**. • For channels on a basic rate ISDN interface, the value is **3bb0c**. • For other types of interfaces, the value is **6nnss**.
6	Service-Type	Indicates the type of service requested or the type of service to be provided: • In a request: Framed for known PPP or SLIP connection. Administrative-user for **enable** command. • In response: Login—Make a connection. Framed—Start SLIP or PPP. Administrative User—Start an EXEC or **enable ok**. Exec User—Start an EXEC session. Service type is indicated by a particular numeric value as follows: • 1: Login • 2: Framed • 3: Callback-Login • 4: Callback-Framed • 5: Outbound • 6: Administrative • 7: NAS-Prompt • 8: Authenticate Only • 9: Callback-NAS-Prompt

Table A-3 *RADIUS (IETF) Attributes (Continued)*

Number	Attribute	Description
7	Framed-Protocol	Indicates the framing to be used for framed access.
		Framing is indicated by a numeric value as follows:
		• 1: PPP
		• 2: SLIP
		• 3: ARA
		• 4: Gandalf-proprietary single-link/multilink protocol
		• 5: Xylogics-proprietary IPX/SLIP
8	Framed-IP-Address	Indicates the IP address to be configured for the user.
9	Framed-IP-Netmask	Indicates the IP netmask to be configured for the user when the user is a router to a network. This attribute value results in a static route being added for Framed-IP-Address with the mask specified.
10	Framed-Routing	Indicates the routing method for the user when the user is a router to a network. Only None and Send and Listen values are supported for this attribute.
		Routing method is indicated by a numeric value as follows:
		• 0: None
		• 1: Send routing packets
		• 2: Listen for routing packets
		• 3: Send routing packets and listen for routing packets
11	Filter-Id	Indicates the name of the filter list for the user and is formatted as follows: %d, %d.in, or %d.out. This attribute is associated with the most recent service-type command. For login and EXEC, use %d or %d.out as the line access list value from 0 to 199. For Framed service, use %d or %d.out as interface output access list, and %d.in for input access list. The numbers are self-encoding to the protocol to which they refer.
12	Framed-MTU	Indicates the maximum transmission unit (MTU) that can be configured for the user when the MTU is not negotiated by PPP or some other means.

Continues

Table A-3   *RADIUS (IETF) Attributes (Continued)*

Number	Attribute	Description
13	Framed-Compression	Indicates a compression protocol used for the link. This attribute results in /compress being added to the PPP or SLIP autocommand generated during EXEC authorization. Not currently implemented for non-EXEC authorization. Compression protocol is indicated by a numeric value as follows: • 0: None • 1: VJ-TCP/IP header compression • 2: IPX header compression
14	Login-IP-Host	Indicates the host to which the user will connect when the Login-Service attribute is included.
15	Login-Service	Indicates the service that should be used to connect the user to the login host. Service is indicated by a numeric value as follows: • 0: Telnet • 1: Rlogin • 2: TCP-Clear • 3: PortMaster • 4: LAT
16	Login-TCP-Port	Defines the TCP port with which the user is to be connected when the Login-Service attribute is also present.
18	Reply-Message	Indicates text that might be displayed to the user.
19	Callback-Number	Defines a dialing string to be used for callback.
20	Callback-ID	Defines the name (consisting of one or more octets) of a place to be called, to be interpreted by the network access server.
22	Framed-Route	Provides routing information to be configured for the user on this network access server. The RADIUS RFC format (net/bits [router [metric]]) and the old style dotted mask (net mask [router [metric]]) are supported. If the router field is omitted or 0, the peer IP address is used. Metrics are currently ignored.
23	Framed-IPX-Network	Defines the IPX network number configured for the user.
24	State	Allows state information to be maintained between the network access server and the RADIUS server. This attribute is applicable only to CHAP challenges.

Table A-3 *RADIUS (IETF) Attributes (Continued)*

Number	Attribute	Description
25	Class	(Accounting) Arbitrary value that the network access server includes in all accounting packets for this user if supplied by the RADIUS server.

26	Vendor-Specific	Allows vendors to support their own extended attributes not suitable for general use. The Cisco RADIUS implementation supports one vendor-specific option using the format recommended in the specification. Cisco's vendor-ID is 9, and the supported option has vendor-type 1, which is named cisco-avpair. The value is a string of the format
		
		`protocol : attribute sep value`
		
		protocol is a value of the Cisco *protocol* attribute for a particular type of authorization. *attribute* and *value* are an appropriate AV pair defined in the Cisco TACACS+ specification, and *sep* is = for mandatory attributes and * for optional attributes. This allows the full set of features available for TACACS+ authorization to also be used for RADIUS. For example:
		
		`cisco-avpair= "ip:addr-pool=first"`
		`cisco-avpair= "shell:priv-lvl=15"`
		
		The first example causes Cisco's multiple named ip address pools feature to be activated during IP authorization (during PPP's IPCP address assignment). The second example causes a user logging in from a network access server to have immediate access to EXEC commands.
		
		Table A-4 provides a complete list of supported TACACS+ AV pairs that can be used with IETF Attribute 26.
		
		Cisco has added two new vendor-specific RADIUS attributes (IETF Attribute 26) to enable RADIUS to support MS-CHAP:
		
		• Vendor ID Number: 311 (Microsoft)
		Vendor Type Number: 11
		Attribute: MSCHAP-Challenge
		Description: Contains the challenge sent by a network access server to an MS-CHAP user. It can be used in both Access-Request and Access-Challenge packets.
		
		• Vendor ID Number 311: (Microsoft)
		Vendor Type Number: 11
		Attribute: MSCHAP-Response
		Description: Contains the response value provided by a PPP MS-CHAP user in response to the challenge. It is only used in Access-Request packets. This attribute is identical to the PPP CHAP Identifier.

Continues

Table A-3 *RADIUS (IETF) Attributes (Continued)*

Number	Attribute	Description
27	Session-Timeout	Sets the maximum number of seconds of service to be provided to the user before the session terminates. This attribute value becomes the per-user absolute timeout. This attribute is not valid for PPP sessions.
28	Idle-Timeout	Sets the maximum number of consecutive seconds of idle connection allowed to the user before the session terminates. This attribute value becomes the per-user session-timeout. This attribute is not valid for PPP sessions.
29	Termination-Action	Termination is indicated by a numeric value as follows: • 0: Default • 1: RADIUS request
30	Called-Station-Id	(Accounting) Allows the network access server to send the telephone number the user called as part of the Access-Request packet (using Dialed Number Identification [DNIS] or similar technology). This attribute is only supported on ISDN, and modem calls on the Cisco AS5200 if used with PRI.
31	Calling-Station-Id	(Accounting) Allows the network access server to send the telephone number the call came from as part of the Access-Request packet (using Automatic Number Identification or similar technology). This attribute has the same value as remote-addr from TACACS+. This attribute is only supported on ISDN, and modem calls on the Cisco AS5200 if used with PRI.
32	NAS-Identifier	String identifying the network access server originating the Access-Request.
33	Proxy-State	Attribute that can be sent by a proxy server to another server when forwarding Access-Requests; this must be returned unmodified in the Access-Accept, Access-Reject or Access-Challenge and removed by the proxy server before sending the response to the network access server.
34	Login-LAT-Service	Indicates the system with which the user is to be connected by LAT. This attribute is only available in the EXEC mode.
35	Login-LAT-Node	Indicates the node with which the user is to be automatically connected by LAT.
36	Login-LAT-Group	Identifies the LAT group codes that this user is authorized to use.
37	Framed-AppleTalk-Link	Indicates the AppleTalk network number that should be used for serial links to the user, which is another AppleTalk router.
38	Framed-AppleTalk-Network	Indicates the AppleTalk network number that the network access server uses to allocate an AppleTalk node for the user.

Table A-3 *RADIUS (IETF) Attributes (Continued)*

Number	Attribute	Description
39	Framed-AppleTalk-Zone	Indicates the AppleTalk Default Zone to be used for this user.
40	Acct-Status-Type	(Accounting) Indicates whether this Accounting-Request marks the beginning of the user service (start) or the end (stop).
41	Acct-Delay-Time	(Accounting) Indicates how many seconds the client has been trying to send a particular record.
42	Acct-Input-Octets	(Accounting) Indicates how many octets have been received from the port over the course of this service being provided.
43	Acct-Output-Octets	(Accounting) Indicates how many octets have been sent to the port in the course of delivering this service.
44	Acct-Session-Id	(Accounting) A unique accounting identifier that makes it easy to match start and stop records in a log file. Acct-Session ID numbers restart at 1 each time the router is power cycled or the software is reloaded.
45	Acct-Authentic	(Accounting) Indicates how the user was authenticated, whether by RADIUS, the network access server itself, or another remote authentication protocol. This attribute is set to radius for users authenticated by RADIUS; remote for TACACS+ and Kerberos; or local for local, enable, line, and if-needed methods. For all other methods, the attribute is omitted.
46	Acct-Session-Time	(Accounting) Indicates how long (in seconds) the user has received service.
47	Acct-Input-Packets	(Accounting) Indicates how many packets have been received from the port over the course of this service being provided to a framed user.
48	Acct-Output-Packets	(Accounting) Indicates how many packets have been sent to the port in the course of delivering this service to a framed user.

Continues

Table A-3 *RADIUS (IETF) Attributes (Continued)*

Number	Attribute	Description
49	Acct-Terminate-Cause	(Accounting) Reports details on why the connection was terminated. Termination causes are indicated by a numeric value as follows: • 1: User request • 2: Lost carrier • 3: Lost service • 4: Idle timeout • 5: Session-timeout • 6: Admin reset • 7: Admin reboot • 8: Port error • 9: NAS error • 10: NAS request • 11: NAS reboot • 12: Port unneeded • 13: Port pre-empted • 14: Port suspended • 15: Service unavailable • 16: Callback • 17: User error • 18: Host request
50	Acct-Multi-Session-Id[1]	(Accounting) A unique accounting identifier used to link multiple related sessions in a log file. Each linked session in a multilink session has a unique Acct-Session-Id value, but shares the same Acct-Multi-Session-Id.
51	Acct-Link-Count[2]	(Accounting) Indicates the number of links known in a given multilink session at the time an accounting record is generated. The network access server can include this attribute in any accounting request that might have multiple links.
60	CHAP-Challenge	Contains the CHAP challenge sent by the network access server to a PPP CHAP user.

Table A-3 *RADIUS (IETF) Attributes (Continued)*

Number	Attribute	Description
61	NAS-Port-Type	Indicates the type of physical port the network access server is using to authenticate the user.
		Physical ports are indicated by a numeric value as follows:
		• 0: Asynchronous
		• 1: Synchronous
		• 2: ISDN-Synchronous
		• 3: ISDN-Asynchronous (V.120)
		• 4: ISDN- Asynchronous (V.110)
		• 5: Virtual
62	Port-Limit	Sets the maximum number of ports to be provided to the user by the network access server.
63	Login-LAT-Port	Defines the port with which the user is to be connected by LAT.
200	IETF-Token-Immediate	Determines how RADIUS treats passwords received from login users when their file entry specifies a hand-held security card server.
		The value for this attribute is indicated by a numeric value as follows:
		• 0: No, meaning that the password is ignored.
		• 1: Yes, meaning that the password is used for authentication.

1.Only stop records containing multi-session IDs because start records are issued before any multilink processing takes place.
2.Only stop records containing link counts because start records are issued before any multilink processing takes place.

Table A-4 lists the supported TACACS+ AV pairs and their meanings for the Vendor-Specific (26) attribute. For more information about TACACS+ AV pairs, refer to Appendix B, "TACACS+ Attribute-Value Pairs."

Table A-4 *Supported TACACS+ AV Pairs*

Attribute	Description
service=x	The primary service. Specifying a service attribute indicates that this is a request for authorization or accounting of that service. Current values are **slip**, **ppp**, **arap**, **shell**, **tty-daemon**, **connection**, and **system**. This attribute must always be included.
protocol=x	A protocol that is a subset of a service. An example would be any PPP NCP. Currently known values are **lcp**, **ip**, **ipx**, **atalk**, **vines**, **lat**, **xremote**, **tn3270**, **telnet**, **rlogin**, **pad**, **vpdn**, **osicp**, **deccp**, **ccp**, **cdp**, **bridging**, **xns**, **nbf**, **bap**, **multilink**, and **unknown**.

Continues

Table A-4   *Supported TACACS+ AV Pairs (Continued)*

Attribute	Description
cmd=x	A shell (EXEC) command. This indicates the command name for a shell command that is to be run. This attribute must be specified if service equals shell. A NULL value indicates that the shell itself is being referred to.
cmd-arg=x	An argument to a shell (EXEC) command. This indicates an argument for the shell command that is to be run. Multiple cmd-arg attributes can be specified, and they are order-dependent.
acl=x	ASCII number representing a connection access list. Used only when service=shell.
inacl=x	ASCII identifier for an interface input access list. Used with service=ppp and protocol=ip. Per-user access lists do not currently work with ISDN interfaces.
inacl#<n>	ASCII access list identifier for an input access list to be installed and applied to an interface for the duration of the current connection. Used with service=ppp and protocol=ip, and service=ppp and protocol =ipx. Per-user access lists do not currently work with ISDN interfaces.
outacl=x	ASCII identifier for an interface output access list. Used with service=ppp and protocol=ip, and service service=ppp and protocol=ipx. Contains an IP output access list for SLIP or PPP/IP (for example, outacl=4). The access list itself must be preconfigured on the router. Per-user access lists do not currently work with ISDN interfaces.
outacl#<n>	ASCII access list identifier for an interface output access list to be installed and applied to an interface for the duration of the current condition. Used with service=ppp and protocol=ip, and service=ppp and protocol=ipx. Per-user access lists do not currently work with ISDN interfaces.
zonelist=x	A numeric zonelist value. Used with service=arap. Specifies an AppleTalk zonelist for ARA (for example, zonelist=5).
addr=x	A network address. Used with service=slip, service=ppp, and protocol=ip. Contains the IP address that the remote host should use when connecting via SLIP or PPP/IP. For example, addr=10.2.3.4.

addr-pool=x	Specifies the name of a local pool from which to get the address of the remote host. Used with service=ppp and protocol=ip.
	
	Note that **addr-pool** works in conjunction with local pooling. It specifies the name of a local pool (which must be preconfigured on the network access server). Use the **ip-local pool** command to declare local pools. For example:
	
	`ip address-pool local`
	
	`ip local pool boo 10.0.0.1 10.0.0.10`
	
	`ip local pool moo 10.0.0.1 10.0.0.20`
	
	You can then use TACACS+ to return addr-pool=boo or addr-pool=moo to indicate the address pool from which you want to get this remote node's address.

Table A-4 *Supported TACACS+ AV Pairs (Continued)*

Attribute	Description
routing=x	Specifies whether routing information is to be propagated to and accepted from this interface. Used with service=slip, service=ppp, and protocol=ip. Equivalent in function to the /routing flag in SLIP and PPP commands. Can either be true or false (for example, routing=true).
route	Specifies a route to be applied to an interface. Used with service=slip, service=ppp, and protocol=ip.
	During network authorization, the route attribute can be used to specify a per-user static route, to be installed by TACACS+ as follows:
	`route="dst_address mask [gateway]"`
	This indicates a temporary static route that is to be applied. *dst_address*, *mask*, and *gateway* are expected to be in the usual dotted-decimal notation, with the same meanings as in the familiar **ip route** configuration command on a network access server.
	If *gateway* is omitted, the peer's address is the gateway. The route is expunged when the connection terminates.
route#<n>	Like the route AV pair, this specifies a route to be applied to an interface, but these routes are numbered, allowing multiple routes to be applied. Used with service=ppp and protocol=ip, and service=ppp and protocol=ipx.
timeout=x	The number of minutes before an EXEC or ARA session disconnects (for example, timeout=60). A value of zero indicates no timeout. Used with service=arap.
idletime=x	Sets a value, in minutes, after which an idle session is terminated. Does not work for PPP. A value of zero indicates no timeout.
autocmd=x	Specifies an autocommand to be executed at EXEC startup (for example, autocmd=telnet muruga.com). Used only with service=shell.
noescape=x	Prevents user from using an escape character. Used with service=shell. Can be either true or false (for example, noescape=true).
nohangup=x	Used with service=shell. Specifies the nohangup option, which means that after an EXEC shell is terminated, the user is presented with another login (username) prompt. Can be either true or false (for example, nohangup=false).
priv-lvl=x	Privilege level to be assigned for the EXEC. Used with service=shell. Privilege levels range from 0 to 15, with 15 being the highest.
callback-dialstring	Sets the telephone number for a callback (for example: callback-dialstring=408-555-1212). Value is NULL, or a dial-string. A NULL value indicates that the service might choose to get the dialstring through other means. Used with service=arap, service=slip, service=ppp, service=shell. Not valid for ISDN.
callback-line	The number of a TTY line to use for callback (for example: callback-line=4). Used with service=arap, service=slip, service=ppp, service=shell. Not valid for ISDN.

Continues

Table A-4 *Supported TACACS+ AV Pairs (Continued)*

Attribute	Description
callback-rotary	The number of a rotary group (between 0 and 100 inclusive) to use for callback (for example: callback-rotary=34). Used with service=arap, service=slip, service=ppp, service=shell. Not valid for ISDN.
nocallback-verify	Indicates that no callback verification is required. The only valid value for this parameter is 1 (for example, nocallback-verify=1). Used with service=arap, service=slip, service=ppp, service=shell. There is no authentication on callback. Not valid for ISDN.
tunnel-id	Specifies the username that will be used to authenticate the tunnel over which the individual user MID will be projected. This is analogous to the *remote name* in the **vpdn outgoing** command. Used with service=ppp and protocol=vpdn.
ip-addresses	Space-separated list of possible IP addresses that can be used for the end-point of a tunnel. Used with service=ppp and protocol=vpdn.
nas-password	Specifies the password for the network access server during the L2F tunnel authentication. Used with service=ppp and protocol=vpdn.
gw-password	Specifies the password for the home gateway during the L2F tunnel authentication. Used with service=ppp and protocol=vpdn.
rte-ftr-in#<n>	Specifies an input access list definition to be installed and applied to routing updates on the current interface for the duration of the current connection. Used with service=ppp and protocol=ip, and with service=ppp and protocol=ipx.
rte-ftr-out#<n>	Specifies an output access list definition to be installed and applied to routing updates on the current interface for the duration of the current connection. Used with service=ppp and protocol=ip, and with service=ppp and protocol=ipx.
sap#<n>	Specifies static Service Advertising Protocol (SAP) entries to be installed for the duration of a connection. Used with service=ppp and protocol=ipx.
sap-fltr-in#<n>	Specifies an input SAP filter access list definition to be installed and applied on the current interface for the duration of the current connection. Used with service=ppp and protocol=ipx.
sap-fltr-out#<n>	Specifies an output SAP filter access list definition to be installed and applied on the current interface for the duration of the current connection. Used with service=ppp and protocol=ipx.
pool-def#<n>	Defines IP address pools on the network access server. Used with service=ppp and protocol=ip.
pool-timeout=	Defines (in conjunction with pool-def) IP address pools on the network access server. During IPCP address negotiation, if an IP pool name is specified for a user (see the addr-pool attribute), a check is made to see whether the named pool is defined on the network access server. If it is, the pool is consulted for an IP address.
source-ip=x	Used as the source IP address of all VPDN packets generated as part of a VPDN tunnel. This is equivalent to the Cisco **vpdn outgoing** global configuration command.

Table A-4   *Supported TACACS+ AV Pairs (Continued)*

Attribute	Description
max-links=\<n>	Restricts the number of links that a user can have in a multilink bundle. Used with service=ppp and protocol=multilink. The range for \<n> is from 1 to 255.
load-threshold=\<n>	Sets the load threshold at which additional links are either added to or deleted from the multilink bundle. If the load goes above the specified value, additional links are added. If the load goes below the specified value, links are deleted. Used with service=ppp and protocol=multilink. The range for \<n> is from 1 to 255.
interface-config=	Specifies user-specific AAA interface configuration information with virtual profiles. The information that follows the equal sign (=) can be any Cisco IOS interface configuration command.
ppp-vj-slot-compression	Instructs the Cisco router not to use slot compression when sending Van Jacobsen-compressed packets over a PPP link.
link-compression=	Defines whether to turn on or turn off stac compression over a PPP link. Link compression is defined as a numeric value as follows: • 0: None • 1: Stac • 2: Stac-Draft-9 • 3: MS-Stac
old-prompts	Allows providers to make the prompts in TACACS+ appear identical to those of earlier systems (TACACS and Extended TACACS). This allows administrators to upgrade from TACACS/Extended TACACS to TACACS+ transparently to users.
dns-servers=	Identifies a DNS server (primary or secondary) that can be requested by Microsoft PPP clients from the network access server during IPCP negotiation. To be used with service=ppp and protocol=ip. The IP address identifying each DNS server is entered in dotted decimal format.
wins-servers=	Identifies a Windows NT server that can be requested by Microsoft PPP clients from the network access server during IPCP negotiation. To be used with service=ppp and protocol=ip. The IP address identifying each Windows NT server is entered in dotted decimal format.

Table A-5 lists the supported TACACS+ accounting AV pairs and their meanings for the Vendor-Specific (26) attribute. For more information about TACACS+ AV pairs, refer to Appendix B, "TACACS+ Attribute-Value Pairs."

Table A-5   *Supported TACACS+ Accounting AV Pairs*

Attribute	Description
service	The service the user used.
port	The port the user was logged in to.
task_id	Start and stop records for the same event must have matching (unique) task_id numbers.
start_time	The time the action started (in seconds since the epoch, 12:00 a.m. Jan 1 1970). The clock must be configured to receive this information.
stop_time	The time the action stopped (in seconds since the epoch). The clock must be configured to receive this information.
elapsed_time	The elapsed time in seconds for the action. Useful when the device does not keep real time.
timezone	The time zone abbreviation for all timestamps included in this packet.
priv_level	The privilege level associated with the action.
cmd	The command the user executed.
protocol	The protocol associated with the action.
bytes_in	The number of input bytes transferred during this connection.
bytes_out	The number of output bytes transferred during this connection.
paks_in	The number of input packets transferred during this connection.
paks_out	The number of output packets transferred during this connection.
event	Information included in the accounting packet that describes a state change in the router. Events described are accounting starting and accounting stopping.
reason	Information included in the accounting packet that describes the event that caused a system change. Events described are system reload, system shutdown, or when accounting is reconfigured (turned on or off).
mlp-sess-id	Reports the identification number of the multilink bundle when the session closes. This attribute applies to sessions that are part of a multilink bundle. This attribute is sent in authentication-response packets.
mlp-links-max	Gives the count of links which are known to have been in a given multilink session at the time the accounting record is generated.
disc-cause	Specifies the reason a connection was taken off-line. The Disconnect-Cause attribute is sent in accounting-stop records. This attribute also causes stop records to be generated without first generating start records if disconnection occurs before authentication is performed. Refer to Table A-7 for a list of Disconnect-Cause values and their meanings.
disc-cause-ext	Extends the disc-cause attribute to support vendor-specific reasons that a connection was taken off-line.
pre-bytes-in	Records the number of input bytes before authentication. This attribute is sent in accounting-stop records.

Table A-5 *Supported TACACS+ Accounting AV Pairs (Continued)*

Attribute	Description
pre-bytes-out	Records the number of output bytes before authentication. This attribute is sent in accounting-stop records.
pre-paks-in	Records the number of input packets before authentication. This attribute is sent in accounting-stop records.
pre-paks-out	Records the number of output packets before authentication. The Pre-Output-Packets attribute is sent in accounting-stop records.
pre-session-time	Specifies the length of time, in seconds, from when a call first connects to when it completes authentication.
data-rate	Specifies the average number of bits per second over the course of the connection's lifetime. This attribute is sent in accounting-stop records.
xmit-rate	Reports the transmit speed negotiated by the two modems.

Although an IETF draft standard for RADIUS specifies a method for communicating vendor-proprietary information between the network access server and the RADIUS server, some vendors have extended the RADIUS attribute set in a unique way. Table A-6 lists the known vendor-proprietary RADIUS attributes:

Table A-6 *Vendor-Proprietary RADIUS Attributes*

Number	Vendor-Proprietary Attribute	Description
17	Change-Password	Specifies a request to change a user's password.
21	Password-Expiration	Specifies an expiration date for a user's password in the user's file entry.
64	Tunnel-Type	(Ascend 5) No description available.
65	Tunnel-Medium-Type	(Ascend 5) No description available.
66	Tunnel-Client-Endpoint	(Ascend 5) No description available.
67	Tunnel-Server-Endpoint	(Ascend 5) No description available.
68	Tunnel-ID	(Ascend 5) No description available.
108	My-Endpoint-Disc-Alias	(Ascend 5) No description available.
109	My-Name-Alias	(Ascend 5) No description available.
110	Remote-FW	(Ascend 5) No description available.
111	Multicast-GLeave-Delay	(Ascend 5) No description available.
112	CBCP-Enable	(Ascend 5) No description available.
113	CBCP-Mode	(Ascend 5) No description available.

Continues

Table A-6 *Vendor-Proprietary RADIUS Attributes (Continued)*

Number	Vendor-Proprietary Attribute	Description
114	CBCP-Delay	(Ascend 5) No description available.
115	CBCP-Trunk-Group	(Ascend 5) No description available.
116	Appletalk-Route	(Ascend 5) No description available.
117	Appletalk-Peer-Mode	(Ascend 5) No description available.
118	Route-Appletalk	(Ascend 5) No description available.
119	FCP-Parameter	(Ascend 5) No description available.
120	Modem-PortNo	(Ascend 5) No description available.
121	Modem-SlotNo	(Ascend 5) No description available.
122	Modem-ShelfNo	(Ascend 5) No description available.
123	Call-Attempt-Limit	(Ascend 5) No description available.
124	Call-Block-Duration	(Ascend 5) No description available.
125	Maximum-Call-Duration	(Ascend 5) No description available.
126	Router-Preference	(Ascend 5) No description available.
127	Tunneling-Protocol	(Ascend 5) No description available.
128	Shared-Profile-Enable	(Ascend 5) No description available.
129	Primary-Home-Agent	(Ascend 5) No description available.
130	Secondary-Home-Agent	(Ascend 5) No description available.
131	Dialout-Allowed	(Ascend 5) No description available.
133	BACP-Enable	(Ascend 5) No description available.
134	DHCP-Maximum-Leases	(Ascend 5) No description available.
135	Primary-DNS-Server	Identifies a primary DNS server that can be requested by Microsoft PPP clients from the network access server during IPCP negotiation.
136	Secondary-DNS-Server	Identifies a secondary DNS server that can be requested by Microsoft PPP clients from the network access server during IPCP negotiation.
137	Client-Assign-DNS	No description available.
138	User-Acct-Type	No description available.
139	User-Acct-Host	No description available.
140	User-Acct-Port	No description available.
141	User-Acct-Key	No description available.

Table A-6 *Vendor-Proprietary RADIUS Attributes (Continued)*

Number	Vendor-Proprietary Attribute	Description
142	User-Acct-Base	No description available.
143	User-Acct-Time	No description available.
144	Assign-Ip-Client	No description available.
145	Assign-IP-Server	No description available.
146	Assign-IP-Global-Pool	No description available.
147	DHCP-Reply	No description available.
148	DHCP-Pool-Number	No description available.
149	Expect-Callback	No description available.
150	Event-Type	No description available.
151	Session-Svr-Key	No description available.
152	Multicast-Rate-Limit	No description available.
153	IF-Netmask	No description available.
154	Remote-Addr	No description available.
155	Multicast-Client	No description available.
156	FR-Circuit-Name	No description available.
157	FR-LinkUp	No description available.
158	FR-Nailed-Grp	No description available.
159	FR-Type	No description available.
160	FR-Link-Mgt	No description available.
161	FR-N391	No description available.
162	FR-DCE-N392	No description available.
163	FR-DTE-N392	No description available.
164	FR-DCE-N393	No description available.
165	FR-DTE-N393	No description available.
166	FR-T391	No description available.
167	FR-T392	No description available.
168	Bridge-Address	No description available.
169	TS-Idle-Limit	No description available.
170	TS-Idle-Mode	No description available.
171	DBA-Monitor	No description available.

Continues

Table A-6 *Vendor-Proprietary RADIUS Attributes (Continued)*

Number	Vendor-Proprietary Attribute	Description
172	Base-Channel-Count	No description available.
173	Minimum-Channels	No description available.
174	IPX-Route	No description available.
175	FT1-Caller	No description available.
176	Backup	No description available.
177	Call-Type	No description available.
178	Group	No description available.
179	FR-DLCI	No description available.
180	FR-Profile-Name	No description available.
181	Ara-PW	No description available.
182	IPX-Node-Addr	No description available.
183	Home-Agent-IP-Addr	Indicates the home agent's IP address (in dotted decimal format) when using Ascend Tunnel Management Protocol (ATMP).
184	Home-Agent-Password	With ATMP, specifies the password that the foreign agent uses to authenticate itself.
185	Home-Network-Name	With ATMP, indicates the name of the connection profile to which the home agent sends all packets.
186	Home-Agent-UDP-Port	Indicates the UDP port number the foreign agent uses to send ATMP messages to the home agent.
187	Multilink-ID	Reports the identification number of the multilink bundle when the session closes. This attribute applies to sessions that are part of a multilink bundle. The Multilink-ID attribute is sent in authentication-response packets.
188	Num-In-Multilink	Reports the number of sessions remaining in a multilink bundle when the session reported in an accounting-stop packet closes. This attribute applies to sessions that are part of a multilink bundle. The Num-In-Multilink attribute is sent in authentication-response packets and in some accounting-request packets.
189	First-Dest	Records the destination IP address of the first packet received after authentication.

Table A-6 *Vendor-Proprietary RADIUS Attributes (Continued)*

Number	Vendor-Proprietary Attribute	Description
190	Pre-Input-Octets	Records the number of input octets before authentication. The Pre-Input-Octets attribute is sent in accounting-stop records.
191	Pre-Output-Octets	Records the number of output octets before authentication. The Pre-Output-Octets attribute is sent in accounting-stop records.
192	Pre-Input-Packets	Records the number of input packets before authentication. The Pre-Input-Packets attribute is sent in accounting-stop records.
193	Pre-Output-Packets	Records the number of output packets before authentication. The Pre-Output-Packets attribute is sent in accounting-stop records.
194	Maximum-Time	Specifies the maximum length of time (in seconds) allowed for any session. After the session reaches the time limit, its connection is dropped.
195	Disconnect-Cause	Specifies the reason a connection was taken offline. The Disconnect-Cause attribute is sent in accounting-stop records. This attribute also causes stop records to be generated without first generating start records if disconnection occurs before authentication is performed. Refer to Table A-7 for a list of Disconnect-Cause values and their meanings.
196	Connect-Progress	Indicates the connection state before the connection is disconnected.
197	Data-Rate	Specifies the average number of bits per second over the course of the connection's lifetime. The Data-Rate attribute is sent in accounting-stop records.
198	PreSession-Time	Specifies the length of time, in seconds, from when a call first connects to when it completes authentication. The PreSession-Time attribute is sent in accounting-stop records.
199	Token-Idle	Indicates the maximum amount of time (in minutes) a cached token can remain alive between authentications.
201	Require-Auth	Defines whether additional authentication is required for class that has been CLID authenticated.

Continues

Table A-6 *Vendor-Proprietary RADIUS Attributes (Continued)*

Number	Vendor-Proprietary Attribute	Description
202	Number-Sessions	Specifies the number of active sessions (per class) reported to the RADIUS accounting server.
203	Authen-Alias	Defines the RADIUS server's login name during PPP authentication.
204	Token-Expiry	Defines the lifetime of a cached token.
205	Menu-Selector	Defines a string to be used to cue a user to input data.
206	Menu-Item	Specifies a single menu item for a user profile. Up to 20 menu items can be assigned per profile.
207	PW-Warntime	(Ascend 5) No description available.
208	PW-Lifetime	Enables you to specify on a per-user basis the number of days that a password is valid.
209	IP-Direct	Specifies in a user's file entry the IP address to which the Cisco router redirects packets from the user. When you include this attribute in a user's file entry, the Cisco router bypasses all internal routing and bridging tables and sends all packets received on this connection's WAN interface to the specified IP address.
210	PPP-VJ-Slot-Comp	Instructs the Cisco router not to use slot compression when sending VJ-compressed packets over a PPP link.
211	PPP-VJ-1172	Instructs PPP to use the 0x0037 value for VJ compression.
212	PPP-Async-Map	Gives the Cisco router the asynchronous control character map for the PPP session. The specified control characters are passed through the PPP link as data and used by applications running over the link.
213	Third-Prompt	Defines a third prompt (after username and password) for additional user input.
214	Send-Secret	Enables an encrypted password to be used in place of a regular password in outdial profiles.
215	Receive-Secret	Enables an encrypted password to be verified by the RADIUS server.
216	IPX-Peer-Mode	(Ascend 5) No description available.

Table A-6 *Vendor-Proprietary RADIUS Attributes (Continued)*

Number	Vendor-Proprietary Attribute	Description
217	IP-Pool-Definition	Defines a pool of addresses using the following format: X a.b.c Z; where X is the pool index number, a.b.c is the pool's starting IP address, and Z is the number of IP addresses in the pool. For example, 3 10.0.0.1 5 allocates 10.0.0.1 through 10.0.0.5 for dynamic assignment.
218	Assign-IP-Pool	Tells the router to assign the user and IP address from the IP pool.
219	FR-Direct	Defines whether the connection profile operates in Frame Relay redirect mode.
220	FR-Direct-Profile	Defines the name of the Frame Relay profile carrying this connection to the Frame Relay switch.
221	FR-Direct-DLCI	Indicates the DLCI carrying this connection to the Frame Relay switch.
222	Handle-IPX	Indicates how NCP watchdog requests will be handled.
223	Netware-Timeout	Defines, in minutes, how long the RADIUS server responds to NCP watchdog packets.
224	IPX-Alias	Allows you to define an alias for IPX routers requiring numbered interfaces.
225	Metric	No description available.
226	PRI-Number-Type	No description available.
227	Dial-Number	No description available.
228	Route-IP	Indicates whether IP routing is allowed for the user's file entry.
229	Route-IPX	Allows you to enable IPX routing.
230	Bridge	No description available.
231	Send-Auth	Defines the protocol to use (PAP or CHAP) for username-password authentication following CLID authentication.
232	Send-Passwd	No description available.

Continues

Table A-6 *Vendor-Proprietary RADIUS Attributes (Continued)*

Number	Vendor-Proprietary Attribute	Description
233	Link-Compression	Defines whether to turn on or turn off stac compression over a PPP link. Link compression is defined as a numeric value as follows: • 0: None • 1: Stac • 2: Stac-Draft-9 • 3: MS-Stac
234	Target-Util	Specifies the load-threshold percentage value for bringing up an additional channel when PPP multilink is defined.
235	Maximum-Channels	Specifies allowed/allocatable maximum number of channels.
236	Inc-Channel-Count	No description available.
237	Dec-Channel-Count	No description available.
238	Seconds-of-History	No description available.
239	History-Weigh-Type	No description available.
240	Add-Seconds	No description available.
241	Remove-Seconds	No description available.
242	Data-Filter	Defines per-user IP data filters. These filters are retrieved only when a call is placed using a RADIUS outgoing profile or answered using a RADIUS incoming profile. Filter entries are applied on a first-match basis; therefore, the order in which filter entries are entered is important.
243	Call-Filter	Defines per-user IP data filters. On a Cisco router, this attribute is identical to the Data-Filter attribute.
244	Idle-Limit	Specifies the maximum time (in seconds) that any session can be idle. When the session reaches the idle time limit, its connection is dropped.
245	Preempt-Limit	No description available.
246	Callback	Allows you to enable or disable callback.
247	Data-Svc	No description available.
248	Force-56	No description available.
249	Billing Number	No description available.

Table A-6   *Vendor-Proprietary RADIUS Attributes (Continued)*

Number	Vendor-Proprietary Attribute	Description
250	Call-By-Call	No description available.
251	Transit-Number	No description available.
252	Host-Info	No description available.
253	PPP-Address	Indicates the IP address reported to the calling unit during PPP IPCP negotiations.
254	MPP-Idle-Percent	No description available.
255	Xmit-Rate	(Ascend 5) No description available.

Table A-7 lists the values and their meanings for the Disconnect-Cause (195) attribute.

Table A-7   *Disconnect-Cause Attribute Values*

Value	Description
Unknown (2)	Reason unknown.
CLID-Authentication-Failure (4)	Failure to authenticate calling-party number.
No-Carrier (10)	No carrier detected. This value applies to modem connections.
Lost-Carrier (11)	Loss of carrier. This value applies to modem connections.
No-Detected-Result-Codes (12)	Failure to detect modem result codes. This value applies to modem connections.
User-Ends-Session (20)	User terminates a session. This value applies to EXEC sessions.
Idle-Timeout (21)	Timeout waiting for user input. This value applies to all session types.
Exit-Telnet-Session (22)	Disconnect due to exiting Telnet session. This value applies to EXEC sessions.
No-Remote-IP-Addr (23)	Could not switch to SLIP/PPP; the remote end has no IP address. This value applies to EXEC sessions.
Exit-Raw-TCP (24)	Disconnect due to exiting raw TCP. This value applies to EXEC sessions.
Password-Fail (25)	Bad passwords. This value applies to EXEC sessions.
Raw-TCP-Disabled (26)	Raw TCP disabled. This value applies to EXEC sessions.
Control-C-Detected (27)	Control-C detected. This value applies to EXEC sessions.
EXEC-Process-Destroyed (28)	EXEC process destroyed. This value applies to EXEC sessions.
Timeout-PPP-LCP (40)	PPP LCP negotiation timed out. This value applies to PPP sessions.
Failed-PPP-LCP-Negotiation (41)	PPP LCP negotiation failed. This value applies to PPP sessions.

Continues

Table A-7   *Disconnect-Cause Attribute Values (Continued)*

Value	Description
Failed-PPP-PAP-Auth-Fail (42)	PPP PAP authentication failed. This value applies to PPP sessions.
Failed-PPP-CHAP-Auth (43)	PPP CHAP authentication failed. This value applies to PPP sessions.
Failed-PPP-Remote-Auth (44)	PPP remote authentication failed. This value applies to PPP sessions.
PPP-Remote-Terminate (45)	PPP received a terminate request from remote end. This value applies to PPP sessions.
PPP-Closed-Event (46)	Upper layer requested that the session be closed. This value applies to PPP sessions.
Session-Timeout (100)	Session timed out. This value applies to all session types.
Session-Failed-Security (101)	Session failed for security reasons. This value applies to all session types.
Session-End-Callback (102)	Session terminated due to callback. This value applies to all session types.
Invalid-Protocol (120)	Call refused because the detected protocol is disabled. This value applies to all session types.

TACACS+ Attribute-Value Pairs

Terminal Access Controller Access Control System Plus (TACACS+) attribute-value (AV) pairs are used to define specific authentication, authorization, and accounting elements in a user profile, which is stored on the TACACS+ daemon. This appendix lists the TACACS+ AV pairs currently supported.

TACACS+ AV Pairs

Table B-1 lists the supported TACACS+ AV pairs and specifies the Cisco IOS release in which they are implemented.

Table B-1   *Supported TACACS+ AV Pairs*

Attribute	Description	11.0	11.1	11.2	11.3	12.0
acl=x	ASCII number representing a connection access list. Used only when service=shell.	yes	yes	yes	yes	yes
addr-pool=x	Specifies the name of a local pool from which to get the address of the remote host. Used with service=ppp and protocol=ip.	yes	yes	yes	yes	yes
	Note that **addr-pool** works in conjunction with local pooling. It specifies the name of a local pool (which must be preconfigured on the network access server). Use the **ip-local pool** command to declare local pools. For example:					
	`ip address-pool local`					
	`ip local pool boo 10.0.0.1 10.0.0.10`					
	`ip local pool moo 10.0.0.1 10.0.0.20`					

Continues

Table B-1 *Supported TACACS+ AV Pairs (Continued)*

Attribute	Description	11.0	11.1	11.2	11.3	12.0
	You can then use TACACS+ to return addr-pool=boo or addr-pool=moo to indicate the address pool from which you want to get this remote node's address.					
addr=x	A network address. Used with service=slip, service=ppp, and protocol=ip. Contains the IP address that the remote host should use when connecting via SLIP or PPP/IP. For example, addr=10.2.3.4.	yes	yes	yes	yes	yes
autocmd=x	Specifies an autocommand to be executed at EXEC startup (for example, autocmd=telnet domain.com). Used only with service=shell.	yes	yes	yes	yes	yes
callback-dialstring	Sets the telephone number for a callback (for example: callback-dialstring=408-555-1212). Value is NULL, or a dial-string. A NULL value indicates that the service might choose to get the dialstring through other means. Used with service=arap, service=slip, service=ppp, service=shell. Not valid for ISDN.	no	yes	yes	yes	yes
callback-line	The number of a TTY line to use for callback (for example: callback-line=4). Used with service=arap, service=slip, service=ppp, service=shell. Not valid for ISDN.	no	yes	yes	yes	yes

Table B-1 *Supported TACACS+ AV Pairs (Continued)*

Attribute	Description	11.0	11.1	11.2	11.3	12.0
callback-rotary	The number of a rotary group (between 0 and 100 inclusive) to use for callback (for example: callback-rotary=34). Used with service=arap, service=slip, service=ppp, service=shell. Not valid for ISDN.	no	yes	yes	yes	yes
cmd-arg=x	An argument to a shell (EXEC) command. This indicates an argument for the shell command that is to be run. Multiple cmd-arg attributes can be specified, and they are order dependent.	yes	yes	yes	yes	yes
cmd=x	A shell (EXEC) command. This indicates the command name for a shell command that is to be run. This attribute must be specified if service equals "shell." A NULL value indicates that the shell itself is being referred to.	yes	yes	yes	yes	yes
dns-servers=	Identifies a DNS server (primary or secondary) that can be requested by Microsoft PPP clients from the network access server during IPCP negotiation. To be used with service=ppp and protocol=ip. The IP address identifying each DNS server is entered in dotted-decimal format.	no	no	no	yes	yes
gw-password	Specifies the password for the home gateway during the L2F tunnel authentication. Used with service=ppp and protocol=vpdn.	no	no	yes	yes	yes

Continues

Table B-1 *Supported TACACS+ AV Pairs (Continued)*

Attribute	Description	11.0	11.1	11.2	11.3	12.0
idletime=x	Sets a value, in minutes, after which an idle session is terminated. Does not work for PPP. A value of zero indicates no timeout.	no	yes	yes	yes	yes
inacl#<n>	ASCII access list identifier for an input access list to be installed and applied to an interface for the duration of the current connection. Used with service=ppp and protocol=ip, and service service=ppp and protocol =ipx. Per-user access lists do not currently work with ISDN interfaces.	no	no	no	yes	yes
inacl=x	ASCII identifier for an interface input access list. Used with service=ppp and protocol=ip. Per-user access lists do not currently work with ISDN interfaces.	yes	yes	yes	yes	yes
interface-config=	Specifies user-specific AAA interface configuration information with virtual profiles. The information that follows the equal sign (=) can be any Cisco IOS interface configuration command.	no	no	no	yes	yes
ip-addresses	Space-separated list of possible IP addresses that can be used for the end-point of a tunnel. Used with service=ppp and protocol=vpdn.	no	no	yes	yes	yes

Table B-1 *Supported TACACS+ AV Pairs (Continued)*

Attribute	Description	11.0	11.1	11.2	11.3	12.0
link-compression=	Defines whether to turn on or turn off "stac" compression over a PPP link. Link compression is defined as a numeric value as follows: • 0: None • 1: Stac • 2: Stac-Draft-9 • 3: MS-Stac	no	no	no	yes	yes
load-threshold=\<n\>	Sets the load threshold for the caller at which additional links are either added to or deleted from the multilink bundle. If the load goes above the specified value, additional links are added. If the load goes below the specified value, links are deleted. Used with service=ppp and protocol=multilink. The range for \<n\> is from 1 to 255.	no	no	no	yes	yes
max-links=\<n\>	Restricts the number of links that a user can have in a multilink bundle. Used with service=ppp and protocol=multilink. The range for \<n\> is from 1 to 255.	no	no	no	yes	yes
nas-password	Specifies the password for the network access server during the L2F tunnel authentication. Used with service=ppp and protocol=vpdn.	no	no	yes	yes	yes

Continues

Table B-1   *Supported TACACS+ AV Pairs (Continued)*

Attribute	Description	11.0	11.1	11.2	11.3	12.0
nocallback-verify	Indicates that no callback verification is required. The only valid value for this parameter is 1 (for example, nocallback-verify=1). Used with service=arap, service=slip, service=ppp, service=shell. There is no authentication on callback. Not valid for ISDN.	no	yes	yes	yes	yes
noescape=x	Prevents user from using an escape character. Used with service=shell. Can be either true or false (for example, noescape=true).	yes	yes	yes	yes	yes
nohangup=x	Used with service=shell. Specifies the nohangup option, which means that after an EXEC shell is terminated, the user is presented with another login (username) prompt. Can be either true or false (for example, nohangup=false).	yes	yes	yes	yes	yes
old-prompts	Allows providers to make the prompts in TACACS+ appear identical to those of earlier systems (TACACS and extended TACACS). This allows administrators to upgrade from TACACS or extended TACACS to TACACS+ transparently to users.	yes	yes	yes	yes	yes

Table B-1 *Supported TACACS+ AV Pairs (Continued)*

Attribute	Description	11.0	11.1	11.2	11.3	12.0
outacl#<n>	ASCII access list identifier for an interface output access list to be installed and applied to an interface for the duration of the current condition. Used with service=ppp and protocol=ip, and service service=ppp and protocol=ipx. Per-user access lists do not currently work with ISDN interfaces.	no	no	no	yes	yes
outacl=x	ASCII identifier for an interface output access list. Used with service=ppp and protocol=ip, and service service=ppp and protocol=ipx. Contains an IP output access list for SLIP or PPP/IP (for example, outacl=4). The access list itself must be preconfigured on the router. Per-user access lists do not currently work with ISDN interfaces.	yes (PPP/IP only)	yes	yes	yes	yes
pool-def#<n>	Defines IP address pools on the network access server. Used with service=ppp and protocol=ip.	no	no	no	yes	yes
pool-timeout=	Defines (in conjunction with pool-def) IP address pools on the network access server. During IPCP address negotiation, if an IP pool name is specified for a user (see the addr-pool attribute), a check is made to see whether the named pool is defined on the network access server. If it is, the pool is consulted for an IP address.	no	no	yes	yes	yes

Continues

Table B-1 *Supported TACACS+ AV Pairs (Continued)*

Attribute	Description	11.0	11.1	11.2	11.3	12.0
ppp-vj-slot-compression	Instructs the Cisco router not to use slot compression when sending VJ-compressed packets over a PPP link.	no	no	no	yes	yes
priv-lvl=x	Privilege level to be assigned for the EXEC. Used with service=shell. Privilege levels range from 0 to 15, with 15 being the highest.	yes	yes	yes	yes	yes
protocol=x	A protocol that is a subset of a service. An example would be any PPP NCP. Currently known values are **lcp**, **ip**, **ipx**, **atalk**, **vines**, **lat**, **xremote**, **tn3270**, **telnet**, **rlogin**, **pad**, **vpdn**, **osicp**, **deccp**, **ccp**, **cdp**, **bridging**, **xns**, **nbf**, **bap**, **multilink**, and **unknown**.	yes	yes	yes	yes	yes
route	Specifies a route to be applied to an interface. Used with service=slip, service=ppp, and protocol=ip. During network authorization, the route attribute can be used to specify a per-user static route, to be installed by TACACS+ as follows: `route="`*`dst_address mask [gateway]`*`"`	no	yes	yes	yes	yes

Table B-1 *Supported TACACS+ AV Pairs (Continued)*

Attribute	Description	11.0	11.1	11.2	11.3	12.0
	This indicates a temporary static route that is to be applied. *dst_address*, *mask*, and *gateway* are expected to be in the usual dotted-decimal notation, with the same meanings as in the familiar **ip route** configuration command on a network access server. If *gateway* is omitted, the peer's address is the gateway. The route is expunged when the connection terminates.					
route#<n>	Like the route AV pair, this specifies a route to be applied to an interface, but these routes are numbered, allowing multiple routes to be applied. Used with service=ppp and protocol=ip, and service=ppp and protocol=ipx.	no	no	no	yes	yes
routing=x	Specifies whether routing information is to be propagated to and accepted from this interface. Used with service=slip, service=ppp, and protocol=ip. Equivalent in function to the /routing flag in SLIP and PPP commands. Can either be true or false (for example, routing=true).	yes	yes	yes	yes	yes
rte-ftr-in#<n>	Specifies an input access list definition to be installed and applied to routing updates on the current interface for the duration of the current connection. Used with service=ppp and protocol=ip, and with service=ppp and protocol=ipx.	no	no	no	yes	yes

Continues

Table B-1   *Supported TACACS+ AV Pairs (Continued)*

Attribute	Description	11.0	11.1	11.2	11.3	12.0
rte-ftr-out#<n>	Specifies an output access list definition to be installed and applied to routing updates on the current interface for the duration of the current connection. Used with service=ppp and protocol=ip, and with service=ppp and protocol=ipx.	no	no	no	yes	yes
sap#<n>	Specifies static Service Advertising Protocol (SAP) entries to be installed for the duration of a connection. Used with service=ppp and protocol=ipx.	no	no	no	yes	yes
sap-fltr-in#<n>	Specifies an input SAP filter access list definition to be installed and applied on the current interface for the duration of the current connection. Used with service=ppp and protocol=ipx.	no	no	no	yes	yes
sap-fltr-out#<n>	Specifies an output SAP filter access list definition to be installed and applied on the current interface for the duration of the current connection. Used with service=ppp and protocol=ipx.	no	no	no	yes	yes
service=x	The primary service. Specifying a service attribute indicates that this is a request for authorization or accounting of that service. Current values are **slip**, **ppp**, **arap**, **shell**, **tty-daemon**, **connection**, and **system**. This attribute must always be included.	yes	yes	yes	yes	yes

Table B-1 *Supported TACACS+ AV Pairs (Continued)*

Attribute	Description	11.0	11.1	11.2	11.3	12.0
source-ip=x	Used as the source IP address of all VPDN packets generated as part of a VPDN tunnel. This is equivalent to the Cisco **vpdn outgoing** global configuration command.	no	no	yes	yes	yes
timeout=x	The number of minutes before an EXEC or ARA session disconnects (for example, timeout=60). A value of zero indicates no timeout. Used with service=arap.	yes	yes	yes	yes	yes
tunnel-id	Specifies the username that will be used to authenticate the tunnel over which the individual user MID will be projected. This is analogous to the *remote name* in the **vpdn outgoing** command. Used with service=ppp and protocol=vpdn.	no	no	yes	yes	yes
wins-servers=	Identifies a Windows NT server that can be requested by Microsoft PPP clients from the network access server during IPCP negotiation. To be used with service=ppp and protocol=ip. The IP address identifying each Windows NT server is entered in dotted-decimal format.	no	no	no	yes	yes
zonelist=x	A numeric zonelist value. Used with service=arap. Specifies an AppleTalk zonelist for ARA (for example, zonelist=5).	yes	yes	yes	yes	yes

For more information about configuring TACACS+, refer to Chapter 10, "Configuring TACACS+." For more information about configuring TACACS+ authentication, refer to Chapter 4, "Configuring Authorization."

TACACS+ Accounting AV Pairs

Table B-2 lists the supported TACACS+ accounting AV pairs and the Cisco IOS releases in which they are implemented.

Table B-2   *Supported TACACS+ Accounting AV Pairs*

Attribute	Description	11.0	11.1	11.2	11.3	12.0
bytes_in	The number of input bytes transferred during this connection.	yes	yes	yes	yes	yes
bytes_out	The number of output bytes transferred during this connection.	yes	yes	yes	yes	yes
cmd	The command the user executed.	yes	yes	yes	yes	yes
data-rate --This AV pair has been renamed. See nas-rx-speed.						
disc-cause	Specifies the reason a connection was taken off-line. The Disconnect-Cause attribute is sent in accounting-stop records. This attribute also causes stop records to be generated without first generating start records if disconnection occurs before authentication is performed. Refer to Table B-3 for a list of Disconnect-Cause values and their meanings.	no	no	no	yes	yes
disc-cause-ext	Extends the disc-cause attribute to support vendor-specific reasons that a connection was taken offline.	no	no	no	yes	yes
elapsed_time	The elapsed time in seconds for the action. Useful when the device does not keep real time.	yes	yes	yes	yes	yes

Table B-2 *Supported TACACS+ Accounting AV Pairs (Continued)*

Attribute	Description	11.0	11.1	11.2	11.3	12.0
event	Information included in the accounting packet that describes a state change in the router. Events described are accounting starting and accounting stopping.	yes	yes	yes	yes	yes
mlp-links-max	Gives the count of links that are known to have been in a given multilink session at the time the accounting record is generated.	no	no	no	yes	yes
mlp-sess-id	Reports the identification number of the multilink bundle when the session closes. This attribute applies to sessions that are part of a multilink bundle. This attribute is sent in authentication-response packets.	no	no	no	yes	yes
nas-rx-speed	Specifies the average number of bits per second over the course of the connection's lifetime. This attribute is sent in accounting-stop records.	no	no	no	yes	yes
nas-tx-speed	Reports the transmit speed negotiated by the two modems.	no	no	no	yes	yes
paks_in	The number of input packets transferred during this connection.	yes	yes	yes	yes	yes
paks_out	The number of output packets transferred during this connection.	yes	yes	yes	yes	yes
port	The port the user was logged in to.	yes	yes	yes	yes	yes
pre-bytes-in	Records the number of input bytes before authentication. This attribute is sent in accounting-stop records.	no	no	no	yes	yes

Continues

Table B-2 *Supported TACACS+ Accounting AV Pairs (Continued)*

Attribute	Description	11.0	11.1	11.2	11.3	12.0
pre-bytes-out	Records the number of output bytes before authentication. This attribute is sent in accounting-stop records.	no	no	no	yes	yes
pre-paks-in	Records the number of input packets before authentication. This attribute is sent in accounting-stop records.	no	no	no	yes	yes
pre-paks-out	Records the number of output packets before authentication. The Pre-Output-Packets attribute is sent in accounting-stop records.	no	no	no	yes	yes
pre-session-time	Specifies the length of time, in seconds, from when a call first connects to when it completes authentication.	no	no	no	yes	yes
priv_level	The privilege level associated with the action.	yes	yes	yes	yes	yes
protocol	The protocol associated with the action.	yes	yes	yes	yes	yes
reason	Information included in the accounting packet that describes the event that caused a system change. Events described are system reload, system shutdown, or when accounting is reconfigured (turned on or off).	yes	yes	yes	yes	yes
service	The service the user used.	yes	yes	yes	yes	yes
start_time	The time the action started (in seconds since the epoch, 12:00 a.m. Jan 1 1970). The clock must be configured to receive this information.	yes	yes	yes	yes	yes
stop_time	The time the action stopped (in seconds since the epoch). The clock must be configured to receive this information.	yes	yes	yes	yes	yes

Table B-2 *Supported TACACS+ Accounting AV Pairs (Continued)*

Attribute	Description	11.0	11.1	11.2	11.3	12.0
task_id	Start and stop records for the same event must have matching (unique) task_id numbers.	yes	yes	yes	yes	yes
timezone	The time zone abbreviation for all timestamps included in this packet.	yes	yes	yes	yes	yes

xmit-rate--This AV pair has been renamed. See nas-tx-speed.

Table B-3 lists the values and their meanings for the Disconnect-Cause (disc-cause) attribute.

Table B-3 *Disc-Cause Attribute Values*

Value	Description
CLID-Authentication-Failure (4)	Failure to authenticate calling-party number.
Control-C-Detected (27)	Control-C detected. This value applies to EXEC sessions.
EXEC-Process-Destroyed (28)	EXEC process destroyed. This value applies to EXEC sessions.
Exit-Raw-TCP (24)	Disconnect due to exiting raw TCP. This value applies to EXEC sessions.
Exit-Telnet-Session (22)	Disconnect due to exiting Telnet session. This value applies to EXEC sessions.
Failed-PPP-CHAP-Auth (43)	PPP CHAP authentication failed. This value applies to PPP sessions.
Failed-PPP-LCP-Negotiation (41)	PPP LCP negotiation failed. This value applies to PPP sessions.
Failed-PPP-PAP-Auth-Fail (42)	PPP PAP authentication failed. This value applies to PPP sessions.
Failed-PPP-Remote-Auth (44)	PPP remote authentication failed. This value applies to PPP sessions.
Idle-Timeout (21)	Timeout waiting for user input. This value applies to all session types.
Invalid-Protocol (120)	Call refused because the detected protocol is disabled. This value applies to all session types.
Lost-Carrier (11)	Loss of carrier. This value applies to modem connections.
No-Carrier (10)	No carrier detected. This value applies to modem connections.
No-Detected-Result-Codes (12)	Failure to detect modem result codes. This value applies to modem connections.
No-Remote-IP-Addr (23)	Could not switch to SLIP/PPP; the remote end has no IP address. This value applies to EXEC sessions.
Password-Fail (25)	Bad passwords. This value applies to EXEC sessions.

Continues

Table B-3   *Disc-Cause Attribute Values (Continued)*

Value	Description
PPP-Closed-Event (46)	Upper layer requested that the session be closed. This value applies to PPP sessions.
PPP-Remote-Terminate (45)	PPP received a Terminate Request from remote end. This value applies to PPP sessions.
Raw-TCP-Disabled (26)	Raw TCP disabled. This value applies to EXEC sessions.
Session-End-Callback (102)	Session terminated due to callback. This value applies to session types.
Session-Failed-Security (101)	Session failed for security reasons. This value applies to session types.
Session-Timeout (100)	Session timed out. This value applies to all session types.
Timeout-PPP-LCP (40)	PPP LCP negotiation timed out. This value applies to PPP sessions.
Unknown (2)	Reason unknown.
User-Ends-Session (20)	User terminates a session. This value applies to EXEC sessions.

For more information about configuring TACACS+, refer to Chapter 10, "Configuring TACACS+." For more information about configuring TACACS+ accounting, refer to Chapter 6, "Configuring Accounting."

INDEX

Symbols

A

E

F

J-K

M

N

O

Q-R

S

T

W-Z

CCIE Professional Development

Cisco LAN Switching

Kennedy Clark, CCIE; Kevin Hamilton, CCIE

1-57870-094-9 • AVAILABLE NOW

This volume provides an in-depth analysis of Cisco LAN switching technologies, architectures, and deployments, including unique coverage of Catalyst network design essentials. Network designs and configuration examples are incorporated throughout to demonstrate the principles and enable easy translation of the material into practice in production networks.

Advanced IP Network Design

Alvaro Retana, CCIE; Don Slice, CCIE; and Russ White, CCIE

1-57870-097-3 • AVAILABLE NOW

Network engineers and managers can use these case studies, which highlight various network design goals, to explore issues including protocol choice, network stability, and growth. This book also includes theoretical discussion on advanced design topics.

Large-Scale IP Network Solutions

Khalid Raza, CCIE; and Mark Turner

1-57870-084-1 • AVAILABLE NOW

Network engineers can find solutions as their IP networks grow in size and complexity. Examine all the major IP protocols in-depth and learn about scalability, migration planning, network management, and security for large-scale networks.

Routing TCP/IP, Volume I

Jeff Doyle, CCIE

1-57870-041-8 • AVAILABLE NOW

This book takes the reader from a basic understanding of routers and routing protocols through a detailed examination of each of the IP interior routing protocols. Learn techniques for designing networks that maximize the efficiency of the protocol being used. Exercises and review questions provide core study for the CCIE Routing and Switching exam.

Cisco Press   **www.ciscopress.com**

Cisco Career Certifications

Cisco CCNA Exam #640-507 Certification Guide

Wendell Odom, CCIE

0-7357-0971-8 • AVAILABLE NOW

Although it's only the first step in Cisco Career Certification, the Cisco Certified Network Associate (CCNA) exam is a difficult test. Your first attempt at becoming Cisco certified requires a lot of study and confidence in your networking knowledge. When you're ready to test your skills, complete your knowledge of the exam topics, and prepare for exam day, you need the preparation tools found in *Cisco CCNA Exam #640-507 Certification Guide* from Cisco Press.

CCDA Exam Certification Guide

Anthony Bruno, CCIE & Jacqueline Kim

0-7357-0074-5 • AVAILABLE NOW

CCDA Exam Certification Guide is a comprehensive study tool for DCN Exam #640-441. Written by a CCIE and a CCDA, and reviewed by Cisco technical experts, *CCDA Exam Certification Guide* will help you understand and master the exam objectives. In this solid review on the design areas of the DCN exam, you'll learn to design a network that meets a customer's requirements for perfomance, security, capacity, and scalability.

Interconnecting Cisco Network Devices

Edited by Steve McQuerry

1-57870-111-2 • AVAILABLE NOW

Based on the Cisco course taught worldwide, *Interconnecting Cisco Network Devices* teaches you how to configure Cisco switches and routers in multi-protocol internetworks. ICND is the primary course recommended by Cisco Systems for CCNA #640-507 preparation. If you are pursuing CCNA certification, this book is an excellent starting point for your study.

Designing Cisco Networks

Edited by Diane Teare

1-57870-105-8 • AVAILABLE NOW

Based on the Cisco Systems instructor-led and self-study course available worldwide, *Designing Cisco Networks* will help you understand how to analyze and solve existing network problems while building a framework that supports the functionality, performance, and scalability required from any given environment. Self-assessment through exercises and chapter-ending tests starts you down the path for attaining your CCDA certification.

Cisco Press Solutions

Enhanced IP Services for Cisco Networks
Donald C. Lee, CCIE
1-57870-106-6 • **AVAILABLE NOW**

This is a guide to improving your network's capabilities by understanding
the new enabling and advanced Cisco IOS services that build more scalable,
intelligent, and secure networks. Learn the technical details necessary to deploy
Quality of Service, VPN technologies, IPsec, the IOS firewall and IOS Intrusion
Detection. These services will allow you to extend the network to new frontiers
securely, protect your network from attacks, and increase the sophistication of
network services.

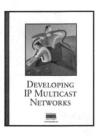

Developing IP Multicast Networks, Volume I
Beau Williamson, CCIE
1-57870-077-9 • **AVAILABLE NOW**

This book provides a solid foundation of IP multicast concepts and explains
how to design and deploy the networks that will support appplications such as
audio and video conferencing, distance-learning, and data replication. Includes
an in-depth discussion of the PIM protocol used in Cisco routers and detailed
coverage of the rules that control the creation and maintenance of Cisco mroute
state entries.

Designing Network Security
Merike Kaeo
1-57870-043-4 • **AVAILABLE NOW**

Designing Network Security is a practical guide designed to help you
understand the fundamentals of securing your corporate infrastructure. This
book takes a comprehensive look at underlying security technologies, the
process of creating a security policy, and the practical requirements necessary to
implement a corporate security policy.

Cisco Press

www.ciscopress.com

Cisco Press

c i s c o p r e s s . c o m

Committed to being your long-term learning resource while you grow as a Cisco Networking Professional

Help Cisco Press **stay connected** to the issues and challenges you face on a daily basis by registering your product and filling out our brief survey. Complete and mail this form, or better yet ...

Register online and enter to win a FREE book!

Jump to **www.ciscopress.com/register** and register your product online. Each complete entry will be eligible for our monthly drawing to win a FREE book of the winner's choice from the Cisco Press library.

May we contact you via e-mail with information about **new releases, special promotions**, and **customer benefits**?

❐ Yes   ❐ No

E-mail address _____

Name _____

Address _____

City _____ State/Province _____

Country _____ Zip/Post code _____

Where did you buy this product?

❐ Bookstore   ❐ Computer store/Electronics store   ❐ Direct from Cisco Systems
❐ Online retailer   ❐ Direct from Cisco Press   ❐ Office supply store
❐ Mail order   ❐ Class/Seminar   ❐ Discount store
❐ Other_____

When did you buy this product? _____ Month _____ Year

What price did you pay for this product?

❐ Full retail price   ❐ Discounted price   ❐ Gift

Was this purchase reimbursed as a company expense?

❐ Yes   ❐ No

How did you learn about this product?

❐ Friend   ❐ Store personnel   ❐ In-store ad   ❐ cisco.com
❐ Cisco Press catalog   ❐ Postcard in the mail   ❐ Saw it on the shelf   ❐ ciscopress.com
❐ Other catalog   ❐ Magazine ad   ❐ Article or review
❐ School   ❐ Professional organization   ❐ Used other products
❐ Other_____

What will this product be used for?

❐ Business use   ❐ School/Education
❐ Certification training   ❐ Professional development/Career growth
❐ Other_____

How many years have you been employed in a computer-related industry?

❐ less than 2 years   ❐ 2–5 years   ❐ more than 5 years

Have you purchased a Cisco Press product before?

❐ Yes   ❐ No

How many computer technology books do you own?

❑ 1   ❑ 2–7   ❑ more than 7

Which best describes your job function? (check all that apply)

❑ Corporate Management   ❑ Systems Engineering   ❑ IS Management   ❑ Cisco Networking
❑ Network Design   ❑ Network Support   ❑ Webmaster   Academy Program
❑ Marketing/Sales   ❑ Consultant   ❑ Student   Instuctor
❑ Professor/Teacher   ❑ Other _____

Do you hold any computer certifications? (check all that apply)

❑ MCSE   ❑ CCNA   ❑ CCDA
❑ CCNP   ❑ CCDP   ❑ CCIE   ❑ Other _____

Are you currently pursuing a certification? (check all that apply)

❑ MCSE   ❑ CCNA   ❑ CCDA
❑ CCNP   ❑ CCDP   ❑ CCIE   ❑ Other _____

On what topics would you like to see more coverage?

_____

_____

Do you have any additional comments or suggestions?

_____

_____

Thank you for completing this survey and registration. Please fold here, seal, and mail to Cisco Press.

Cisco IOS 12.0 Network Security   1-57870-160-0